For Gail

NIGHT DRIVE

TRAVELS WITH MY BROTHER

A Memoir by Garnet Rogers

All images (unless otherwise noted): Garnet Rogers archives
Cover design: Ball Media
Interior design: Ball Media
Back cover photograph: John R. Templeton

Printed and bound in Canada
by Ball Media, Brantford, ON, Canada

Published by Tickle Shore Publishing

ISBN 978-0-9950742-0-0 (paperback)

CONTENTS

Foreword   9
Acknowledgements   14
Chapter 1 "There are no career moves in Folk Music." Utah Phillips. 16
Chapter 2 In the Beginning   27
Chapter 3 Bullying   42
Chapter 4 Nova Scotia   47
Chapter 5 Radio   51
Chapter 6 Bob Dylan   59
Chapter 7 The Predators   62
Chapter 8 High School   68
Chapter 9 Port Dover   73
Chapter 10 Rubbers   76
Chapter 11 Bill Powell   81
Chapter 12 Jackie Washington   88
Chapter 13 Trent University   92
Chapter 14 Stan and Nigel   96
Chapter 15 Moving to London   103
Chapter 16 Cedar Lake   111
Chapter 17 Brampton   134
Chapter 18 Montreal   144
Chapter 19 Noel Harrison   148
Chapter 20 The Stampeders   155
Chapter 21 Secret Agent Man   158
Chapter 22 Jimmy Leaves the Band   167
Chapter 23 Feelings   172
Chapter 24 David Woodhead Joins   177
Chapter 25 Labrador City   183
Chapter 26 Recording Fogarty's Cove   198
Chapter 27 The Trapper's Festival   218
Chapter 28 Fogarty's Cove Music   227
Chapter 29 First US Tour   230
Chapter 30 Mariposa 1977   247
Chapter 31 Owen Sound   258
Chapter 32 Ye Olde Chestrnut Inn   264

Chapter 33 Turnaround   270
Chapter 34 Kingston: David Alan Eadie Joins The Band   282
Chapter 35 The Dixie Flyers   295
Chapter 36 Chicago   298
Chapter 37 The Burro   305
Chapter 38 Photo Sessions   311
Chapter 39 Ryan's Fancy   313
Chapter 40 The Winnipeg Folk Festival   324
Chapter 41 Between the Breaks Live   335
Chapter 42 March Break   352
Chapter 43 The Atlantic Folk Festival   370
Chapter 44 The Kindness Of Strangers   382
Chapter 45 Road Food   387
Chapter 46 10 Pound Fiddle   393
Chapter 47 New Jersey   402
Chapter 48 New London   407
Chapter 49 The Folkway   412
Chapter 50 Ottawa   420
Chapter 51 Jasper   432
Chapter 52 Firing Ronald   445
Chapter 53 The Philly Folk Festival   454
Chapter 54 Return to John and Peter's Place   469
Chapter 55 The Calgary Folk Club   472
Chapter 56 Canada Day on Parliament Hill   478
Chapter 57 Ann Arbor / Pete Seeger   484
Chapter 58 Peter Bellamy   489
Chapter 59 Bermuda   496
Chapter 60 Birth of a Nathan   504
Chapter 61 Night Run From Vancouver   508
Chapter 62 The Vancouver Folk Festival   514
Chapter 63 Silly Wizard   529
Chapter 64 My Big Mouth   536
Chapter 65 Northwest Passage   539
Chapter 66 A Prairie Home Companion   560
Chapter 67 Winter Tour 1980   564
Chapter 68 Klag   575
Chapter 69 The Gathering Of The Clans   588
Chapter 70 Jim Morison   593
Chapter 71 Jim Fleming   600
Chapter 72 Fast Forward   610
Chapter 73 At Last I'm Ready For Christmas   616
Chapter 74 The Iron Horse   619
Chapter 75 Speeding   624

Chapter 76 Dad's Western Tour   633
Chapter 77 By Any Other Name   640
Chapter 78 Madison Wisconsin   645
Chapter 79 Home in Halifax   649
Chapter 80 Calgary Folk Festival 1982   653
Chapter 81 I Leave the Band   660
Chapter 82 The Great Lakes Project   666
Chapter 83 Last Tour / The East Coast   678
Chapter 84 On to Texas   692
Chapter 85 Night Drive   717

FOREWORD

"You should write this stuff down."

People have been saying that to me for years now.
Always, after I've ingested too much coffee, or booze or sugar, and have
launched into some lurid and horrible and unlikely story about life on
the road with Stan.
Stories that mostly revolved around just how foolish and misguided
and delusional we were, trying to make a living playing "folk music" in
the 70's and 80's.
Clapped out cars, bad drugs, and weird drifters. Venal club owners,
managers who would rather lie than draw breath, and well-meaning
agents who couldn't tie their own shoes.
What the hell were we thinking?
We weren't, mostly.
Bad food, and horrible vermin infested motel rooms.
Booze, booze and more booze.
Screaming fights, band firings, and band resignations.
Drunken maudlin rapprochements in parking lots behind some tiny
coffeehouse as the terrified staff cowered inside.
Walking back into a gig with bloodied knuckles after taking some
unruly audience member outside and giving him a stern talking-to
about why we didn't play "The Wild Rover"...ever...and there was
simply no point in yelling for it every couple of minutes.
Meaningless gigs in the middle of nowhere, where the only reward was
that we had simply delivered what we had contracted to do, and the
fact that we were neither paid nor listened to was beside the point.
We'd done our part.

There were police chases and arrests.
Some, for minor stuff like drunk driving without a license on a stolen
motorcycle. The cop was pretty good about me smacking into the
cruiser, all things being equal. He was inclined to see it as merely
youthful high spirits.
Those were the days.

And there was the more serious stuff, like the night in Jasper Alberta, where Stan sat in a jail cell, waiting to be charged with attempted murder.

It's all true.

At the Astoria Hotel they will still show you the repaired place in the wall beside the stage, where the mic stand Stan was wielding just missed the guy's head, and it swung around and exploded like a cruise missile through the wall into the manager's office.
And then there is the really scary stuff.
The stuff that can go bad and get you killed.
Tire jack handle fights with bike gangs in festival parking lots.
Sudden snow storms on the highway north of Lake Superior at 3 in the morning, with black rock on one side, black water on the other, and black ice on the road beneath your wheels.
And then there's the utterly terrifying.
Earnest under aged college girls in fluffy sweaters, who turn up at the coffeehouse after the show wanting you to read their god-awful poetry.
As the song goes, "It's a damned tough life."

There was terrible bad luck, like the van motor exploding into fragments after the gig at 40 below, and there being no money in the kitty to replace it. And there was extraordinarily good luck, like having the OPP turn up with a search warrant one morning when there was about 30 pounds of nicely cleaned and bagged pot ready for sale in plain view on the table behind me, and they decided not to come in, because the person they were looking for wasn't there. And given that I was inviting them in for coffee and to use the phone, it was obvious that I was too stupid to be of any danger to the public.
In my defense, I had simply forgotten all about the dope that Stan and Jimmy and I had spent the night sorting. Anybody could have made the same mistake.

I saw all of it, and the stories became a repertoire of party pieces for me, told to whatever long-suffering person was in the room with me at the time.

"You should write this stuff down."
Right.
Whether it was said out of a desire to have me preserve it as some sort of sick history, or merely (and more likely) in an effort to get me to shut the hell up, I don't know.

What I do know is that over the years immediately following Stan's death, there arose a cottage industry surrounding his music, and a closely managed version of what was supposed to have been his life. It turns out it is easier to market a carefully crafted and maintained legend than a real person.

It was frustrating to watch from the sidelines.

As time went by, the brother I had grown up with, and the complex and kind and frustrating man I knew and loved, and with whom I worked for nearly 10 years had been made into another person entirely, a caricature, and a man I never knew.

And all trace of the part I had played in the music, and the part our parents had played in supporting and financing the whole operation had been erased.

So, I did begin to write the stories down, starting one night in Grande Prairie, Alberta, sitting backstage waiting for the sound crew to return from dinner.

It was a way to relax, and Stan as always, had been on my mind that day.

If one travels for a living, over the years the journey is less about getting from point A to point B, and more like a long badly edited film of old memories being shown in one's mind.

I can be sitting at a stop light in some small town drumming my fingers on the wheel, thinking of nothing in particular, and look around and realize, hey, we played a show here.

There's the old Odd Fellows Hall where we had to carry all the gear up two flights of rickety and highly conductive iron fire escape in a thunderstorm, as the lightning cracked all around us, and the rain pissed down in sheets.

There's the rat hole motel we racked up in, three to a room, with an extra mattress on the floor, and the sound of shouting and gun fire and sirens down the street.

There's the old chrome diner where we got the big Greek salads, thinking we'd eat something healthy for a change.

And there's the spot at the side of the road where we barfed up the big Greek salads.

The anchovies were off, I expect, and the three of us blew lunch, one after the other, in perfect sequence like a naval barrage.

There's where we had the big fight before the show, and everyone got fired and / or quit.

There's the bar parking lot where we patched things up and had a big manly cry and hug.

Any band can tell you similar stories.

This is just the story I remember in the way that I remember it, a series of nonlinear snap shots, with only the merest attempt to put it into some sort of chronological order.

And it's all true.

Mostly.

If something gets enlarged or embroidered upon it's all in service of the truth, if that makes any sense at all.

It's one thing to casually mention that yes, those two upwardly nubile poetry-writing college girls turned up after our show at the Yellow Door Coffee House with their toothbrushes and their notebooks full of bad scribble, and that we virtuously shooed them away. It's another thing to try to describe the sheer horror and paralyzing fear as you cower under the window sill with the lights out, listening to them trying and failing to get their car out of the snow bank on a steep Montreal street at 2 a.m. and then hear them banging on the door downstairs, pleading to be let back in.

Being in a band is a bit like running away to join a low rent circus, or a badly organized pirate ship.

The band develops its own language and rules and strictly controlled and ritualized behaviour.

Any outsider is viewed with suspicion and hostility if they attempt to breach the inner wall.

Within the band, loyalties shift and morph, and hostility develops.

Even something as simple as the way another chews his food is an excuse for a fight and a death grudge that can last for years, and a different person at any given time becomes the butt of all the jokes that day or week.

As a result, even a few months on the road will turn the closest and most well intentioned of friends into a small band of ragged savages, and the jokes are no longer funny. And your glasses are permanently broken, and you've lost control of the conch shell. And your former friends are now advancing towards you with sharpened sticks.

As a result some of the behaviour in this story will be inexplicable by any decent person's standards.

All I can say is we got away with it mostly, because the first rule was to always have the other guy's back when outsiders were present, even if you had plans to kill him later.

There are a few people in this story who get slagged pretty badly.

Keep in mind that it's my opinion being expressed.

Sometimes the chemistry is wrong between two people and it never gets sorted.

Sometimes events conspire and turn people who might ordinarily be friends into bitter rivals.

And sometimes they are just assholes.

In any case, these people have their own side of the story, as well as loving families and good friends, who will no doubt be outraged by whatever I've written.

That's okay.

This isn't a history. It's a memoir.

Histories have to be impartial and scrupulously precise.

Memoirs, not so much.

That being said, this is the truth, near as I can make it.

Whether the stories work on the printed page, as opposed to being told to whatever unlucky soul happens to be in the room with me is up to the reader.

I keep thinking of Utah Philips, whom I also loved, and miss daily.

He said, "Punctuation is no substitute for timing."

In any case, I've done it.

I've written this stuff down.

Maybe now I can shut the hell up.

Canso, Nova Scotia

ACKNOWLEDGEMENTS

I'm inevitably going to miss someone here, but here goes...

Gail, first and foremost, for her steadfast love and endless patience, not just during this project, but over (as of this writing,) 35 years of marriage. A marriage that neither of us had looked for or foreseen before we met, but for me inevitable the moment I met her, if I could just figure out some way of tricking her into it. For her support and encouragement as well, listening patiently while I read aloud whatever I'd written that day to see if it made any sense, and gently correcting me when it didn't.

My parents, Al and Valerie Rogers, for the obvious reason that they spawned us, but more importantly for the love, support, and encouragement they gave us over the years. I can say absolutely that the albums that Stan and I made would not have existed had they not opened their wallets to finance them, and their home to sell and distribute them. They both passed just as I was starting this project in earnest, and I am torn between regret that they will never know the real story about what life on the road was like for their boys, and relief that there are some things I will never have to reveal and explain.

Jim Fleming, whom we met in 1980, and who, after years of us dealing with well-meaning buffoons and inept and venal swine, taught us that you could make a decent living in the music business and still keep your moral compass. He is a true friend, and over the years has become like a brother to me, a term I don't use lightly. I must pay tribute here as well, to others at Fleming Artists, who over the years have helped me along my way. Karla Rice, Susie Giang, and Cynthia Dunitz have gone far beyond the limits of what might be expected from a booking agency, and have all become part of my much-loved extended family.

My good friend, John Templeton, who, aside from building and taking care of my amplifiers, and sharing my disturbed world view, has given me endless and patient help in untangling the mess that was the

14

manuscript. I began this project without the vaguest idea of what I was doing, and about a year ago, I presented John with a terrible scramble of mis-labelled files and random chapters, all written as they came to me, in no particular order, and stored on an elderly Lenovo laptop with a crumbling and cranky hard drive. John was able to sort the whole mess and save me from throwing myself in front of a bus in frustration when it all got too dire.

There are others... Archie Fisher, Scott and Sue Merritt, Scott Alarik, Bill Richardson, all of whom lent an ear and gave me advice and encouragement. Thanks as well, to some of the characters who were part of the story...David Woodhead, Jim Morison, Jimmy Ogilvie, and David Eadie, who I only recently tracked down and re-connected with after over 30 years of not knowing if he was even on the planet. We have compared notes on the stories in this book to some degree, and it's a little scary how poorly the details and memories line up. I can only attribute that to time, alcohol and the vastly different perspective that results from standing 10 feet away on the other side of the singer. I have taken care to not let his recollection of events alter my own.

Finally...

This is a really long book. I was horrified to see just how big it was the first time John printed it out, and I did my best to edit it down. I removed most of the "F" words. That lost 50 or so pages. I then took out all the sex scenes, which took care of a paragraph. (We were after all, a folk band.)
But the fact remains that this is a huge and unwieldy thing, and I am sorry if the endless detail gets to be too much after a while.
Eulogies are typically awkward and inadequate. How do you sum up a person's life, particularly when they were such a large part of your own? You can't do it. Not in the allotted 10 minutes at a church service, and certainly not here...even after 700 some pages. So while I could have tried to edit it down further, or given it to a stranger to streamline, I decided to just leave it all in, and you can decide what to read and what pages to flip past.
My best advice is to try reading this in short doses. It's a heavy bugger and you don't want to sprain something. You might find that a small room in your home best serves as a place to drop in on the story once or twice a day, depending on your dietary habits. And at some point you might be grateful for the all the extra paper.

CHAPTER 1

"There are no career moves in folk music." Utah Phillips.

Somewhere on the coast of Connecticut.

Pissing rain.

We had driven up from Baltimore through a young hurricane two days before, fleeing a truly horrible and pointless and even by our standards, humiliating gig.

We'd landed in this seedy flop house of a 20 dollar a night motel about 3 in the morning.

Three guys in one room with two single beds.

It was all we could afford. More than we could afford really, but we were shaky and depressed, and we needed to get our bearings.

We needed to mend our fences.

We needed to get our ducks in a row.

"I need a couple days of not listening to the two of you assholes belly-ache," said Stan.

Whatever.

We needed the room.

We'd made an extra bed by pulling the top mattress of one onto the floor, hauling it into a corner, and throwing a sleeping bag over it to hide the archipelago of stains left by previous occupants.

We had taken everything out of the van for fear it might be stolen, and had dragged it into the room with us. All the guitars and amps and our suitcases and other gear, and even the spare tire for some reason, had been piled in a corner next to the television.

We had attempted a hand laundry, and now ragged threadbare jockey shorts, faded souvenir festival T shirts, and mis-matched socks hung everywhere around the room, dripping water on the floor and fogging up the window glass.

There was a game show on the TV with the sound off.

A half loaf of white bread sat on a dresser with some cold cuts, along with the remnants of a pound of cheddar, a tub of margarine, and a jar of mustard.

16

"There are no career moves in folk music." Utah Phillips.

The room looked like two warring bands of hillbillies had met on this
spot, fought briefly, and then left.
The three of us, Stan, me and David Alan Eadie, who was then serving
out his sentence as our bass player, were all stretched out on top of
unmade beds, noses buried in our books.
Stan was balancing an ashtray on his belly, and alternately smoking a
cigarette and drinking a beer, and working his way through one of the
Horatio Hornblower novels.
David had been reading, but was now laying on his back, staring
bleakly at the ceiling and blowing smoke rings at the light fixture.
He had developed a party trick where he could blow one very large
smoke ring, and then send a dozen or so smaller Cheerio sized rings
through it.
I found it pretty impressive, but by now we had been on the road for
weeks and I was very nearly brain-dead. Anything would have amused
me.
I was on the floor, on the improvised bed, re-reading a Travis McGee
novel for the umpteenth time, and working on a glass of Teachers
scotch.
None of us had spoken for the better part of two days.
We were tired, and we were broke.
We were pissed off, and sick of each other's company, and the gig in
Baltimore had left us stretched to nearly breaking point.

Our so-called agent had booked us into a Baltimore folk club.
It was our usual deal, 50% of the gross, with a 3 dollar ticket, or as Eadie
put it, "Fuck all on toast. Bring your own bread."
We'd arrived in at the address given us.
It was in a filthy garbage strewn barrio of attached 7 floor walkup
apartments. Large groups of sinister and dangerous looking kids were
lurking around the doorways.
There were trash fires everywhere, and acrid smoke was drifting across
the street.
All of the apartments seemed to have at least a couple of broken
windows, and doors, when they were present at all, were hanging off
their hinges, or plywood had simply been nailed across the entrance.
Angry spray painted graffiti was everywhere.
It looked like a battle zone, and we were scared shitless.

"This can't be the place," I said.
Stan was looking at the contract and peering anxiously at the street
numbers.
"I think it might be. You guys stay with the truck. I'll go look."

"There are no career moves in folk music." Utah Phillips.

He opened the driver's door, slid out of his seat, stood up, and lit a cigarette. He looked around and then hitched up his pants and marched off, trailing smoke over his shoulder.
I locked the door behind him, and David and I huddled in the van and waited.
And waited.
We waited some more.
Neither of us said much.
David lit a Camel, and I took a careful swig of my dwindling supply of scotch.
God only knew when I'd have the funds to get more.
More time passed.
We could hear shouting down the street but couldn't locate the source; the buildings making any loud noise like a gun shot or a plea for mercy echo wildly.
        "Probably a just couple of kids fighting over a chicken." David said.
I began to seriously worry about Stan's safety.
He was a big guy, but he had been gone a while now, and maybe the shouting had been connected to him.
I imagined him in chains and manacles, being prodded through the filthy streets by feral urchins carrying torches and sharpened sticks to be displayed in an iron cage as a spoil of war.
Christ, what if he simply disappeared?
What would we do?
I looked at the ignition switch next to the steering wheel.
Jesus, he had taken the keys with him.
We had no way of escaping.
I looked in the passenger side rear view mirror.
Were there suddenly more kids around us than before?

Stan reappeared about half a block away.
He was marching quickly with a fresh cigarette in his mouth and a grim look on his face.
A small lumpen troll like figure in a shapeless dress trailed along behind at some distance.
I kept a careful eye on the gang behind the van, and when he got within a few feet of us I unlocked the door. Stan got into the driver's seat, slammed the door shut, hit the lock, blew out a lungful of smoke and then sat quietly for a minute or two, staring out the windshield and getting his breath.
We waited.
It didn't look as if good news was coming.
It wasn't.

"There are no career moves in folk music." Utah Phillips.

Stan said, "We're screwed. There is no gig. She told me that there was no point in renting a hall or doing publicity, because no one knows us anyway. No one's gonna come."

There was a silence while we digested all that.
Jesus.
We were truly screwed.
We were almost completely broke, and many miles from home, and what was to be our major "anchor gig" had turned to shit. The small troll like person was hovering outside the van, shifting her weight from one foot to the other, wringing her hands and waiting.
  "Who's your friend?" I asked.
  "That is our promoter." Stan said.
The poor creature.
She was clearly anxious about something, either her having screwed the pooch on this show, or perhaps the ever growing number of hoodlums milling about the street and edging closer to the van. There was probably a Black Market ring of kids in town who roamed the streets kid-napping stragglers and harvesting their organs, selling them to hospitals for transplant, or to Doberman trainers for dog treats.
Fuck it, I thought. She's on her own.

  "So, what do we do?
Stan ground out his smoke in the ashtray, and said, "She told me we can still do a show. She said she can call up all her friends, and we can play in her living room and they'll pass the hat. We'll at least make something."
David spoke up from the back of the van. "The last pass-the-hat gig I did was in Sharbot Lake. The hat got stolen."
  "So what do we do?"
Stan leaned back and closed his eyes for a moment.
  "Christ, I don't know."

What we did was hump all the gear, the five guitars, my guitar amp, David's bass, the suit bags, my violin and flute, nearly everything we owned and feared losing up six creaking flights of stairs into the lumpen troll like person's over-heated and cramped little apartment. We brought up David's bass amplifier, which was a sinister looking black thing with winking red lights. It weighed about a 100 pounds, and was the size of the monolith from Stanley Kubrick's "2001: A Space Odyssey."
Our host had whined and complained about it all the way up the stairs. She paused on a landing behind us.

19

"There are no career moves in folk music." Utah Phillips.

"I don't like electric guitars," she called up to us. "Folk music should be acoustic."

"Fine," said David, turning around. "I'll carry the goddamned thing myself."

The woman drifted off to make some phone calls while we set up for the show.

"There's lots of stuff to drink on the sideboard," she called from the kitchen.

"My friends left it. I don't drink so help yourself."

The sideboard was covered in dozens of oddly shaped bottles, mostly strange red and blue cordials and off brand spirits, what Archie Fisher had once termed, "Cooking Whisky."

There was a half-bottle of some strange viscous yellow goo from Holland, called "Advocaat."

"Snot liqueur," said David. "Stay the hell away from it. It goes down easy, but man, it hurts coming up."

What else?

Oh my God. She had a bottle of Lemon Gin.

No one drinks Lemon Gin. No one, unless you are a 16 year old girl who is planning on mixing it with Lime Rickey and then puking out your immortal soul for a couple of hours in the Girls' washroom at the high school dance, after which you are found in your parents' front yard, minus your best tube top, it having peeled off and floated away in the night air as you were hanging out the back window of your friend's car, painting the door on the way home.

You are found unconscious on the front lawn the next morning, as your neighbours drive by en route to church, your remaining clothes and hair so matted with dried vomit that Mum and Dad have to leave you under the sprinkler for a few hours to rinse off before allowing you by stages into the house through the garage.

At least that was the tradition in my neighbourhood.

There had to be something for a civilized person to drink here.

Wait. Look at this. A jug of Teacher's Scotch, seemingly untouched by human hands.

A whole blessed gallon.

It was even my brand.

Come to Papa.

I broke the seal and we had some drinks and waited.

We could hear her plaintive voice in the next room as she made her phone calls.

Apparently, we were going to have an audience after all.

"Alright boys, let's do this," said Stan, and we opened our suit bags

20

and changed into our habitual stage gear of pressed white shirts, jackets and ties.
I have no idea why.
Maybe we thought one of her friends would turn out to be a famous concert promoter who would be dazzled by our sartorial elegance and offer us riches beyond the dreams of avarice.
Maybe it was like putting on armour.
More likely, it was just pride.
She hadn't done her job, or held up her end, but dammit, we would.
I don't know.
We just did it.

The troll like person came back into the room and said she had called all her friends and soon we would have an audience to play to.
She launched once more into her defense of why we were in this fix.
     "Well, nobody knows you here, so there was no point in advertising, and I didn't see any point in renting the room and an expensive sound system..." and on and on.
So just why the hell had she booked us in the first place?
We all just looked at her and her voice finally trailed off.

We had a couple more drinks, and made some more awkward small talk.
We were starving too, and according to the contract, dinner was included in the deal, but we couldn't see ourselves eating anything that came out of that filthy kitchen, so we just drank and waited.
Stan kept a vigil by the window, looking down at the van. The chances were very good that it would be gone by the time we were finished the show.
Presently there was a knock on the door and all of her friends came in, and they were both drunk.
Legless.
Introductions were made. Nobody seemed to be able to make eye contact.
Neither of them looked like a world famous concert promoter. They both looked like they had been thrown out of the local Greyhound track for violating the dress code.
All of her friends sat down and immediately passed out on the couch, and turned into a pair of snoring farting beasts.
The woman looked pointedly at her watch.
Time to start.
This was just...grim.
It was not the first time we had outnumbered our audience, but that had been in the days when Stan and I had been in a 17 piece band, complete

with two drummers, two bass players, and a sitar player, not to mention the interpretive dancer in white face and a tight black leotard.

Now there was just three of us.

This was truly humiliating.

Unless you counted the cockroaches rattling the pots and pans as they raced around in the kitchen, we outnumbered the spectators by a factor of...oh shit. I decided, for the sake of my pride, to count the cockroaches as audience.

Our host got the full show too.

We stood, three abreast, in our usual order. Stan in the middle, David on his left, me on his right, and we went through the whole opening of our show, complete with in between song patter and clumsy dance moves as we sang "The Xerox Line."

We in turn seemed to be getting a bit of a show as well.

She was sitting cross-legged on the sofa, staring fixedly at all of us in turn and I became aware that her nether garments had come adrift.

It looked as if she was hiding a monkey or a small poodle under her smock. Or perhaps she was related to Ernest Borgnine. She was growing more flushed and intense by the minute as the skirt rode higher up her thighs.

Clearly, something else was going to be required of us.

We played for about an hour, and called it a day.

All of her friends woke up and drifted off into the night, scratching and yawning. One of them, the man, paused briefly and shook his right leg, perhaps to free a trapped testicle. He miscalculated and left us a gift that now hung in the room in a small poisonous cloud.

"Christ, everyone's a critic." said David, waving his hand back and forth.

Holding our breath and averting our faces, we hurriedly packed up our gear, and David and I began humping it down the six flights.

I prayed that the van would still be there, and not just a smoking empty hulk up on cinder blocks, as was more likely the case.

Stan opened delicate financial negotiations with our presenter.

Of course, there was no money.

Not now.

Not ever.

Not even the 50 per cent of the six dollars that had presumably walked in the door with the brace of wildebeests in piss stained sweat pants.

"They're my friends. I couldn't charge them admission."

She began to babble that food and lodging was part of the contract. We could stay with her. We had to stay with her. It was...she lowered her eyes shyly, required.

"There are no career moves in folk music." Utah Phillips.

Why she chose this moment to insist on obeying the letter, if not the spirit of the contract I don't know, but as we continued to drag our stuff down the stairs she began to get more strident and insistent.

"I've got a bed. At least one of you can stay here."

By "bed," I assumed she referred to the sweaty tangle of soiled rags and knotted tomb wrappings I had glimpsed through the half open bedroom door as we had arrived.

She was getting really distressed, standing by the door and once again twisting her hands.

"You can't leave me here like this."

I was the last to leave her overheated little love nest, and as I did, hooked my finger through the handle of the jug of Teacher's. She had worked her way down the stairs, was now standing on the landing outside the front door, yelling threats at Stan, who had fired up the van. I ran up behind and squeezed past her.

"Excuse me...sorry...coming through."

"You'll never work in this town again!"

I fled down the steps, taking them four at a time, squealing "RUN AWAY! " like the Knights of the Round Table in the Monty Python movie.

I vaulted the iron gate at the bottom of the steps with the whisky bottle in one hand, and leapt out on to the street.

The van was already moving with the side door slid open.

David was hanging out the front passenger window and yelling in a loud and theatrical voice.

"RUN! OH RUN LIKE THE WIND! AS YOU LOVE THIS LIFE, LET YOUR FEET HAVE WINGS!"

He fell back, laughing like an idiot.

It had clouded over while we were upstairs and the wind had come up. I was hit in the face with a gust of warm rain. The incoming storm had overturned the barrels of burning trash and the fires had now spread along the streets, and smoke and steam mingled in the air.

I heard a siren in the distance.

Christ. Had she called the cops?

I threw myself into the back of the van and Stan jammed it into a violent skidding stop to make the door slide forward and slam shut.

Luggage and clothing and books and a Slazenger tennis racket (where the Hell did that come from?) and sleeping bags, and anything else that hadn't been tied down showered over me.

Then Stan floored it again and we roared down the street past the clusters of hoodlums and the piles of burning filth and the stripped down abandoned cars.

"There are no career moves in folk music." Utah Phillips.

We careened down a series of side streets, mostly on two wheels, laughing maniacally.
We made the ramp on to the highway and blasted out of town, heading North.
The whole bizarre scene, and our narrow escape kept us laughing for a few miles up the coast, then reality reasserted itself, the rain picked up, and the storm swept over the van.
We made the trip up to Connecticut in grim silence.

So, two days later we were still in our fetid little hideout, reading, sleeping, and trying to recover.
The mess in the room was piling up to the point where we were becoming a biohazard, visible from space by satellite.
And still, no conversation between the three of us. Just an occasional grunt, a throat clearing, or some other staccato male noise.

David had finished his smoke and resumed reading his Flashman novel.
But after a few minutes he tossed it aside and sat up. He swung his legs over the side of the bed, and reached once again for his Zippo lighter and Camels.
He was wearing only a T-shirt, jockey shorts and white tube socks.
He shook out a cigarette and then sat for a while tapping it against the package, staring absently into space.
Finally, he put it in his mouth, lit it and inhaled deeply.
He sat there for a minute or so, smoking and still staring blankly.
Then he rose from his perfumed bower and began to thread his way through the piles of debris on the floor toward the window.
He parted the blinds with a finger and studied the world outside.
Outside the weather was still of Biblical proportions. Sheets of rain lashed the parking lot, and I could see the broken MOT L sign bravely blinking off and on in the storm.
He took another drag on his smoke and blew it out, and then, in his best Bogart accent said,
     "When do you think the heat'll be off us Mugsy?"

These days, in the age of the Internet and social networking, and the Folk Alliance, and a half dozen festivals every weekend, and iTunes and free downloads, and every kid in the world being able to write and record a CD on their laptop and get it out to the world with a glitzy bio and the assurance that they are going to be the NEXT, next, big thing, (and they sometimes are, for about two minutes,) it is hard to imagine just how foolhardy and misguided and naive we were back then, in the early to mid-70's, thinking we could go out and play original acoustic music for a living.

There was no living to be made.

We didn't really find that out or accept it for a long time.

There were no gigs.

Nothing for someone who wrote their own songs, cared about the writing, and wanted to put it over in a non-showbiz way, and in the face of complete indifference from the Industry.

If you were a cover band, or, as they called them in those days, a "show band," you could play lots of places, as long as you had a tuxedo with a ruffled shirt, and could sing "Feelings," during the bride and groom's big slow dance. It helped if you had a taste for bitter drunken bridesmaids in orange chiffon who felt they were getting even with someone by having a knee trembler with you in the cloakroom at the local Kinsman Hall.

There were dangerous gigs in rural villages and northern mining towns, in horrible pissy-smelling tap rooms with the "Ladies and Escorts" signs over the door, as long as you were a country act, had a pedal steel player, knew the words to the "Green, Green Grass of Home," and were able to diplomatically turn down the drunken girl who had stood in front of the bandstand and ripped open her pearl buttoned cowgirl shirt as a prelude to courtship, and do so without offending her large and surly boyfriend.

"You sayin' you don't think my girlfriend is purty enough for you?"

There was no good answer to that question.

If you said "Yes," you got savagely stomped into cat meat.

If you said "No," you got savagely stomped into cat meat.

There's no winning with shit kickers.

If you knew "The Wild Colonial Boy" and "the Wild Rover", and "Danny Boy," and were willing to wear matching plaid shirts and leather vests and Greek fisherman's caps, and could sing in a fake Irish accent, and were willing to embrace the idea of having a liver the size and weight of a truck battery, you could get a gig in a college pub, where they served yards of ale, and first year English majors and mechanical engineers mingled freely, and held after hours pole-vault vomiting contests in the parking lot behind the dumpster.

The poor professors would be there too, sodden drunk, passed out and hopeless in their food- stained knitted ties and corduroy jackets, pissing into their Hush Puppies.

Knowing all the words and most of the chords to "Fox on the Run,"

"There are no career moves in folk music." Utah Phillips.

got you a weekly gig at the Central Tavern in Lucan Ontario, as long as sweaty polyester didn't give you a rash, and you had no sensitivity to penicillin.

But back then, if you presented yourself as a "singer-songwriter," you needed to be able to sing "Fire and Rain" and "Bad, Bad Leroy Brown," and yes, "Feelings."
Everyone had to sing "Feelings."
If you tried to explain that you only played your own songs you were met with puzzled silence or anger and outright violence.

It wasn't like today, where there is some little room in nearly every town, even if it is just an open mic at the local coffee shop, where you can get out and be heard and work up a few moves, learn how to tune your guitar while on stage, and tell a few jokes, and develop your curve and your fast ball, and maybe gather a bit of a following.
Back then there was nothing.
Just rumours.

"There's a place in Boston, but they have no money."
"There's a great gig in Ann Arbor, but they have no money."
"A guy in Edmonton has a place, but how do we get there? There's nothing in between Edmonton and Toronto, and he has no money."
And so on.
There was the Mariposa Festival on the Island in Toronto, but it was geared more towards showcasing what might now be called "real" folk music, ie, the non-professionals who had learned songs and tunes as part of their lives and had no pretensions to being in show business.
It was there one could still see giants like Elizabeth Cotten, and Mississippi John Hurt and Bukka White, Jean Carrignan, and Ola Belle Reed. The festival was (bless them) vehemently against anything smacking of stardom, after a few nasty experiences with concert goers getting out of hand when someone famous turned up.

There were a handful of little clubs in Ontario. Grumbles in Toronto. L' Hibou in Ottawa. The Riverboat in Yorkville, but you had to be an established act with a record deal to get a night in most of those places. The initial folk revival was ten years in the dim past, and was the object of much humour and derision. People and tastes had moved on.
So what to do?
You watched and you waited, and played where you could, and you tried to make it count, and you hoped that somehow, somewhere, someone would notice, and things would improve.

CHAPTER 2

In the Beginning

I'm not sure just how useful a great load of early family history might be to the more immediate story, but some of this might provide a bit of context, so for what it is worth here goes...

If this becomes tedious, and it probably will, you can skip ahead a few pages to where the sex begins. That's the good news. The bad news is that livestock were involved, and I expect (and hope) that it will be disappointment to read.

Our mother's side of the family, the Harts, have lived in Canso, Nova Scotia for centuries. That at least is what we were told as kids, and I am sure it seems that way for their neighbours.

The old Hart house on Union Street, on the waterfront east of the harbour turned 200 officially in 2012.

My maternal Grandmother, who rejoiced in the name Letitia Narraway Hart, married a handsome and flashy Englishman named Sidney Bushell, who had come to Canso to work for the Commercial Cable Company.

Canso was the western terminus of the Transatlantic line that connected Europe and North America. There were a great many men who emigrated from Britain to work as telegraph operators in Canso. Our grandfather arrived from Kent, after first having some adventures in South America.

As my mother told the story, he had met and romanced a young woman there, and when it looked as if Nature had taken its inevitable course, he was called home to avoid any awkward entanglements and embarrassment to the family.

The young South American woman and her child presumably were left in the lurch. Strangely, my mother claimed she caught a brief glimpse of the man who would have been her half-brother at the Owen Sound folk festival many years later.

What are the odds?

There were two Trans-Atlantic cable companies in Canso, the

Commercial and the Western Union. The Western Union office was
located in Canso near the harbour, in what was called Irishtown. The
Commercial Cable office was in Hazel Hill, three miles west of Canso.
It was a beautifully designed brick building, at the left side of the
road leading into town. After the cable traffic ceased in the Fifties, the
building was closed and left to fall into disrepair.

For decades various schemes were put forth to give it a new use, but
nothing ever came of it, Canso traditionally being given the short end of
the stick when it came to government programmes. As I write this, the
building, now sadly fallen to a near ruin is slated for demolition.

My grandparents settled down to life among the other ex-pat Brits who
worked for the Cable company, and who largely kept to themselves as
a colony, the way Britons have done for centuries the world over. For
all the contact and traffic between the Cable families and the local fisher
families, it might as well have been India, or Hong Kong or Ireland.

When we were kids, Stan and I were told in no uncertain terms to keep
away from the locals as we were from a different world, and a different
kind of family, and well above the common herd, with better manners,
better breeding and an aspiration to higher things.

As my Dad once put it, "Only God and the Bushells see the little
sparrow fall."

Or, as the kids from the fisherman families expressed it in their taunts,
when our mother was a girl, "Ha Ha. Bushells say "penis" for cock."

Apparently lacking even the merest vestige of a scrap of a scintilla of
self-control, my grandfather set about turning my grandmother's uterus
into a human PEZ dispenser and sired 12 kids with her, and though
by the standards of the day he was reasonably well paid, with all those
mouths to feed the family was terrifyingly poor.

Housing was provided for the workers, in lovely big frame houses,
many of which still exist in Canso and in Hazel Hill, where our mother
was born. There is a side bar to the story of the houses. They were
designed and prefabricated in England, and then shipped across the
water and assembled in Canso and in the Azores, where the Cable
Company had another station outpost.

If one goes into the attics of the Canso houses one finds they are heavily
braced to withstand high winds and bad weather, but with almost no
insulation.

These are the houses that were to be sent to the Azores where
hurricanes and typhoons regularly roar through.

The workers in the Azores got the less sturdy, but better insulated
houses meant for Canso.

One could see the gentle guiding hand of a committee in the planning and execution.

Canso has been occupied by Europeans since the early 1500's.
"Canseau" as it was then spelled, referred to the small archipelago of
islands off the mainland.
It was a fishing center where ships from Spain and France and Britain
and Portugal would collect to process and salt down their catch before
taking it back to Europe.
Naturally it became a hotly contested area, and there still remains the
ruins of a small French fort which was built in the 1700s on Grassy
Island, at the mouth of the harbour.
That fort was a major player in the battle for Louisburg in Cape Breton.
The town struggled for life back then, and has pretty much struggled
for life ever since. It took several tries to get going, partly due to harsh
weather, and mismanagement, and also due to the displaced and
disgruntled First Nations sweeping in on occasion and taking a swift
hack at the settlers.
The Americans didn't help one damned bit either.
John Paul Jones, the privateer, and great hero of the War of
Independence, raided the place twice and burned it down both times.
Part of George Washington's regiment came north and torched the place
again just about the time it was being rebuilt.
The early history of the town reads like a bad folk song, a sad litany
of fires and ship wrecks and drownings and disease and famine, and
violent depredations before things finally sorted out and peace reigned
long enough for more permanent civilization to be established.
Around 1812, as another war was warming up, the Harts, a merchant
family with a small fleet of ships, were able to acquire the large house,
which now looks out over the harbour. My Grandmother was born in
that house, and she recalled looking out her bedroom window around
1900, and seeing schooners moored side by side in the harbour, so
closely that one could walk across the harbour merely by stepping from
ship to ship.
She said it was a forest of masts right to the horizon.
Years passed.
Wars came. Men went away.
My great uncle Lee Hart was killed at Vimy Ridge.
His sister, my great Aunt Elsie, kept his uniforms on dress dummies
in her bedroom upstairs at the Hart House. The dress dummies scared
five kinds of shit out of me, when as a boy I was sent up stairs to fetch
a spool of thread or a pack of smokes, and ran into the two headless
uniformed figures standing at attention in the dark room.
I still have a couple of his books, which were sent back with his

personal effects after he was killed. They are the poetry of Shelley and Byron, published in special Officers' Editions, suitable for trench warfare, when it was realized that killing one's fellow man was no longer the genteel pastime it had once been. Merely pulling the lace hankie from one's sleeve and wrapping it around the book to protect it from the dew was no longer enough. These are bound in a sturdy oilcloth wrapper, which buttons around the volume to keep out the mud and blood and mustard gas.

As our mother told the story, her parents had something of a difficult marriage.
Times were tough, and made tougher just by the sheer number of kids. Grandma's brother, Scott Hart, took it upon himself to have "a little chat" with my grandfather about perhaps dialing down his activities in the marital bed, or at least using protection, as my poor grandmother was getting worn down to a nub with endless pregnancies.
He offered to get in a supply of "French Letters", or as they no doubt called them in France, "English Letters."
Grandpa was outraged.
"Condoms? Condoms? That's no good. It ruins it for the man."
He had a rather enhanced sense of self to go with that air of entitlement.
One morning, again according to my Mum, Grandma came into the kitchen, furious that someone had not flushed the toilet after what was obviously a hugely cathartic event.
"Who in this family would leave such a disgusting mess behind?"
There was an embarrassed silence around the table, and then Grandpa cleared his throat, and said, "I guess that was me."
"You? You did that? Why on earth?" She was outraged.
He shrugged.
"It was such a nice one, I thought everyone might like to have a look at it."
Thank God there was no Facebook back then.
Grandpa wrote poetry, and had published in magazines before and during the Second World War.
Many of the poems are celebrations of the joys of home life.
Invariably inspiration arrived on the heels of some domestic disaster.
The porridge pot would explode, or a diaper would overflow, or there would be an outbreak of Dengue fever, or someone would have forgotten that the chimney sweeps were due that morning, and the house would have filled with clouds of airborne soot.
At that precise moment Grandpa would feel the need to put his thoughts down in verse and he would throw his scarf around his neck, grab his hat, and be out the door and on his bicycle.

"The Muse is on my shoulder," he would call out, pedaling furiously.

Some hours later he would return, much refreshed, after a walk by the sea, and perhaps a bit of light lunch at some fisherman's cottage, and waving a piece of paper, like Chamberlain with his "Peace in our Time" speech, ready to read his latest ode to the joys of domesticity.

Grandma would be standing, covered in soot and porridge and baby shit, listening as patiently as she could.

Being a man, particularly an English man of that period, he felt there was a strong line of demarcation between what was Men's work and what was Women's work. In short, neither he nor the half dozen or so of his strapping sons did a lick of work around the house. That was for the daughters, and Grandma. It was made worse when he and Grandma would be preparing for a rare evening away from the house and kids. Grandma would have had to cook and clean and iron for him, and the kids, and then set about to get dressed herself. Meanwhile Grandpa would be sitting downstairs, having thrown on a freshly washed and pressed shirt, which had magically appeared, and he would play what he called "hurry up" music on the piano in an effort to move her along. How she was able to keep from smothering him in his sleep is beyond me.

It may have been from his line that the music gene was passed to Stan and me. Grandpa was by all accounts an excellent singer and pianist. Mum recalled to me that Grandpa would stand in front of Stan's crib when he was still a toddler, and sing bits of scales and chords, and Stan would be able to complete them.

Grandpa was a huge influence on Stan and me particularly, in that we had before us a living breathing example of how one could document, romanticize, and glorify the beauty in one's life through music and poetry, and in the process avoid anything even remotely approaching real work.

Our mother, Valerie, was born in 1929, the third youngest of the twelve, and pretty far down the food chain. With so many mouths at the table, alternate sources of protein had to be found, and she recalled muskrat being a frequent staple in her diet.

She said that she never had a glass of milk that had not been made from powder, and diluted until you could see through it until she was living away from home. As is the case with most folks who grow up poor, she was never quite able to let go of the habit of thrift, and neither Stan nor I got to taste real milk until we began going to school. Ironically, lobster, which was in good supply, was considered to be poor people's food, and Mum recalled how the fishermen's kids would halt a few hundred feet from the school every morning and empty the lobster meat from their sandwiches, then put the slices of bread back together, and at lunchtime pretend to be eating baloney.

One morning, Mum came out of the house on the back road in Hazel Hill, and a large shadow was moving across the trees and lawns. She looked up and saw that it was the Hindenburg. It had arrived that morning and had been leisurely floating around the town, most likely taking surveillance photos of the harbour and the islands, which protected it. The war was only a few years off. I wonder now, if any of those photos made it back to Berlin, and perhaps having survived the war, are now in some dusty archive?

Canso later became a staging area for the great convoys, which kept Britain supplied during World War II. Mum once told me the story of how when the fleet was assembled and ready to set off under the cover of night, the whole town would turn out in the evening as the ships got up steam, and walk up the high hill where the Star of the Sea Church stands.

There they would watch as the camouflaged and blacked out fleet threaded its way past the islands towards the eastern horizon. There were local boys on those ships, and the people in the crowd would be standing anxiously, watching and praying as the convoy moved away. Just past the headland, the German U Boats were waiting, and the townsfolk would see the flashes of light as the first torpedoes struck the convoy. The dull boom of the explosions would roll over the water sometime later. The U Boats would circle and follow all the way across, and that fleet which had set out from Canso would be reduced to just a handful of battered stragglers by the time they made Britain.

With the outbreak of war the small town was now overwhelmed with thousands of sailors and soldiers and airmen who were waiting for the convoys to assemble.

Something had to be devised as entertainment for the highly trained and restless and above all, horny young men who were now at the peak of physical condition, and looking at an uncertain future.

It being Canada, it was decided to build a curling rink. Somehow, it wasn't enough.

Dances were organized, and Mum and her sisters were busy little social butterflies.

Mum's diary from that time reveals a very active and happy young woman.

Two years ago as I write this, I was told about an old wooden hut from the cable company which had been moved down to the waterside at the "Tickle" just west of Canso.

I was walking by it one afternoon and the gentleman who was converting the hut to a summer place kindly offered to take me in to show me around.

"There's something I want you to see." he said.

We stepped through the door and there were thousands, literally thousands of names and signatures and cartoons scrawled on the walls of that hut. They covered every inch of every surface, not just the walls, but the floor and the ceiling too. It was overwhelming.

Young men from all over the country had scratched perhaps the only evidence of their time on earth on these walls before going away, and never returning.

The Royal Hamilton Light Infantry. The "Rileys" who had suffered so badly at Dieppe.

The Cape Breton Highlanders, with whom my uncle served.

The Royal Winnipeg Rifles.

The Vandoos.

All the storied regiments. So many young men from so far away. They had all been in this room and had all sailed away from this town. What had become of them?

I was looking at all the names with a lump in my throat.

"Thank you for showing me this."

The gentleman said, "That's not what I wanted to show you." He pointed. "Look down there, just at the bottom of that board."

I bent down and peered closely, and there was my Mum's signature and the date.

"Valerie Whitman Bushell. August 21 1944."

Christ. She had written this on her birthday. She was just a young girl, with her whole life ahead of her. I could imagine her, in a washed out and faded hand-me-down dress, kneeling and scrawling her name in that familiar, nearly unreadable crabbed handwriting.

My parents had been failing over the last few years previous, and in the course of Gail and I taking care of them, we'd had the usual uncomfortable conversations about what they wanted done with their estate and their remains. I was reminded of the story about Bob Hope, who, as he neared his hundredth birthday was asked whether he wanted to be buried or cremated.

"We never discussed it, Dad," said his son.

"I don't know," said Hope. "Surprise me."

Mum and Dad both wanted cremation. Mum wanted to have her ashes scattered on a beach about a mile west of where I now was.

Dad, for reasons of his own, which were never revealed, wanted his ashes scattered about 30 miles away, on another part of the coast entirely.

Mum's choice had been her favourite place to go, both as a child and all through our growing up years, and well into her old age. She would hike down the shore with her sisters, cousins, and nieces and they would settle in at the little cove for an afternoon of building driftwood fires, making tea, and swimming and sunbathing in the nude. All of which was just fine, except they all took many inappropriate photos, and insisted on bringing them home and showing them to us.

"Look at this one. Isn't your Aunt's gall bladder scar healing nicely?"

"JESUS, MUM. STOP IT."

"And your little cousin so and so is really starting to blossom out."

"AAAAUUUGH!"

"Oh, it's just a picture. Grow up."

There are some things you can never un-see.

They would lay naked on the rocks, drinking tea laced with rum, and gossip amongst themselves until some poor fisherman in his open boat would come up the channel to check his lobster pots, at which point, Mum and her kin would all leap to their feet, and begin jumping up and down, waving brightly coloured beach towels, and yelling, "DON'T LOOK AT US! WE'RE NAKED OVER HERE! NO...OVER HERE! WE'RE STARK NAKED! DON'T LOOK!"

By now, the fisherman was on his back, clawing at his eyes, and his retriever would have leapt overboard and begun swimming frantically back to town.

It was that very part of the shore where I had scattered her ashes that afternoon, and I had been walking back when the gentleman stopped me to show me the wall with her signature.

The timing of the two incidents was extraordinary. I had no words to say, really, as I knelt and looked at the signature.

The man was standing behind me, jingling the change in his pocket. He cleared his throat and said, "Yup. There's your Mum." He paused.

"Under a couple hundred sailors."

Ah.

"You knew her then?"

Well done, Mum.

They also serve who stand and wait.

Our mother moved away to Amherst at a very young age to work at Moss's jewelry store there, where she at least had a chance to get regular meals that had come from a grocery store, rather than being pulled from a snare.

Her first glimpse of our Dad, Al Rogers, was when he marched by as part of the scout troop that paraded before the King and Queen in New Glasgow, during their 1939 tour.

Her second encounter was some years later, at the jewelry store, when he came in to buy an engagement ring for another girl. Guess it didn't work out.

Dad had served in the Air Force during the war, mostly being sent around the country to train in various western towns, like Calgary and Prince Albert. He never saw action overseas, thankfully.

He spent the last eighteen months of the war training as a gunner and radio operator when he wasn't trying to conduct amateur field research on women's anatomy.

He never saw much action there either.

At war's end he signed up for trade school in Port Hawkesbury, and got his ticket as a bricklayer.

The Rogers side of the family arrived in North America pretty early on, having been forced out of England for religious reasons.

John Rogers was burned at the stake in 1555 for refusing to embrace Catholicism.

He had a wife and 11 kids, who could have used having him around, but dammit, he also had his principles. As he was being tied to the stake, he was given a last chance to renounce his Protestant faith and embrace Catholicism. The story was that he held his hands out to the flames, and rubbed them as if enjoying the warmth, while his wife and soon to be orphaned and destitute kids looked on.

My wife Gail read this in the 1936 New England Journal of History years ago, and said, "Well, this explains a lot."

The Rogers moved to Connecticut and founded a cult of ultra-conservative Quakers called the Rogerenes. They settled in West Hartford, and near New London, and there is still a Rogerene cemetery in Mystic Seaport, Connecticut.

They were not popular, and were eventually hounded out of New England, (for pig stealing, as the New England Journal of History told it) and settled in Wolfville, Nova Scotia, where they began to multiply and spread out of the valley.

Dad's father, Stanley Rogers, met and courted Juanita Tupper, a niece of one time Prime Minister Sir Charles Tupper. Sir Charles held for many years the record for having served the shortest term as P.M., until Joe Clark and Kim Campbell came along and re-set the bar for unpopularity. According to our Dad, Sir Charles was known locally as "The Cumberland Ram," a reference to his uncontrollable horniness.

He was shipped off to England for a time, if only to give the local girls a breather, but soon was sent back, most likely in a cage, having gone through the flower of English womanhood like a priapic devouring flame.

Grandpa served in World War One, in the cavalry briefly, then in a variety of roles. As boys, Stan and I heard vague stories about Grandpa being attached to a unit called "The Mounted Machine Guns," which were motorcycles with side cars equipped with large caliber Brownings, whose job it was to roar out of side roads and annoy German motor convoys as they drove past.

I don't know if the stories were true, although being boys, we loved the idea.

Grandpa came home, married Juanita, and sired eight kids.

When the Second World War began, he lied about his age and headed back across the water.

I don't know if it was patriotism so much that made him go, but rather an innate restlessness and need for diversion. He was found, as my father told the story, in the highlands of Scotland, at work cutting timber with the Forestry Corps on some rich widow's estate. That by itself would have been fine, but he seemed to feel his duties extended to other services up at the big house. Grandma got wind of it, and had his wandering ass sent back.

Our father was born on Christmas Day, 1925, in Great Village.

He was delivered by Anne Murray's dad, Doctor Murray, of Springhill Nova Scotia. Soon after, the family moved to a tiny crossroads village called Millstream in the woods near Stellarton, where Grandpa set up a large saw mill.

Dad told about his boyhood and adolescence as a series of thrilling near-death experiences involving guns, runaway horses, motorcycles, and uncooperative farm girls with fortress-like undergarments. It sounded like a cross between the Adventures of Tom Sawyer, and a L'il Abner cartoon.

It wasn't all fun though. There was one bitterly cold winter day when Dad's left hand drifted too close to the giant circular saw he had been feeding logs into, and the air was suddenly full of severed fingers. He was looking in horror at his now fingerless hand, and one of the other workers quickly collected them, jammed them into a gunny sack filled with snow, packed more snow on top and said, "You gotta get into town as soon as you can."

They bound up his hand to take him to the doctor, but it was so cold none of the trucks would start, so Dad had to run the 14 miles into Stellarton with the sack over his shoulder and nearly fainting from the pain. They managed to successfully re-attach the fingers, and he never had any sort of impairment from the accident, just a faint white scar across the four fingers.

There was another guy who was less lucky. Once more, standing next the big saw and feeding it logs, he was telling Dad a story over the roar of the machinery and gestured a little too broadly and the saw took all the fingers off. And once more they collected them, and he went into town and had them re-attached. A couple months later he was back at work, his hand still bandaged. This time he was on the other side of the blade, and someone came over and asked how it had happened. And with the other hand he gestured and said, "I just went like this..." ZING... and the other hand was now just a stump.

Grandpa was a fair man, and had kept the guy on part pay during his convalescence, but this was too much.

"I'm sorry, but I have to fire you. You're too stupid to keep around."

Dad's older brothers all had motorcycles of some kind, and for a while after the war, he had the use of a four cylinder Indian. Wonderful machine.

He made the tactical error of attaching the sidecar one day. It was Sunday, and he was supposed to be at worship.

He cruised down the street and couldn't quite negotiate the turn at the corner where the church was. A sidecar has a different kind of physics, and he lost it and hurtled up the low steps leading into the church and crashed through the doors into the midst of the congregation, for whom his older sister was playing organ.

The bike had a faulty magneto, which made it unpleasant to ride in the rain, but the sidecar was handy during hunting season to bring the deer home.

He was still too young to legally drive when he sent away for his license. You could get it through the mail in those innocent and trusting days. He got a job driving the local family doctor, Old Doc Chisholm, as Dad always referred to him, in a huge 20's vintage McLaughlin Buick, with a straight 8 engine and giant wooden spoked wheels that came up to his chin.

Dad told me that his eldest brother Emerson managed to figure out the secret to wind generated electricity all on his own. He got some old car batteries, some pulleys, and other bits and pieces, hooked them up to rickety old windmill, and strung the lines, and they were the first family in the valley with electric light.

My grandparents spent their last years in Oxford NS.

They had a wonderful old frame house, with a secret bedroom at the top of the stairs, which was where Stan and I slept. It was accessible through a tiny door, held closed by a carved wooden turnbuckle, with an old thread spool for a doorknob. Once you had made yourself very small and stepped through that door and down onto the floor, you were standing in a full-sized room with an old iron framed double bed. It felt like magic, like a C. S. Lewis novel. There was a grate on the floor, through which warm air from the kitchen rose to keep things cozy. It was also useful for listening in on the adults, after you had been sent to bed.

The other feature of the room was about 40 years' worth of National

Geographic Magazines, with which we spent many a long and
instructive hour. There is probably a whole generation of men for whom
the sight of a pair of yams sets off an immediate physical response.

Mom and Dad married in Amherst in 1948, and soon moved to Ontario
to look for work.
The post war building boom was on, and yet they had a real struggle to
get by. They lived briefly in Hamilton, with Dad's older sister Audrey.
She and Mom did not see eye to eye on anything, pretty much, and
the folks soon relocated to a little house trailer on a pig farm outside of
Smithville, where Mum was happier.
Later on they moved to a trailer park at the corner of Lake Avenue and
Barton Street, in Stoney Creek.
Work was still largely seasonal, and they were barely making it. Stan
had arrived by this time, and things must have been dire.
Dad would have to walk or hitch hike into Hamilton once a week to
the unemployment office on King William Street, and get into line for
an hour or two, to pick up his cheque for 9 dollars. There was only one
person on duty at the window, and Dad mentioned one time that it
might speed things up a bit if they added more staff. The guy behind
the glass tossed the envelope at him and said, "Don't bite the hand that
feeds you, boy."
Dad would then walk or hitch the 15 miles back to the trailer, picking
up some bread and a jug of corn syrup on the way. Mum would be
huddled under the covers with Stan in the tiny frigid trailer, trying to
keep warm. She didn't want to waste precious fuel for the heater.
Things eventually did pick up. Dad got a steady job at the Steel
Company of Canada, as a full time shift worker, and they felt confident
enough to apply for a Veteran's Land Act mortgage.
They bought a little piece of land in Tapleytown, outside of Stoney
Creek, and began to build a house together after work. They worked
on it from pay cheque to pay cheque, using salvaged lumber mostly,
pulling huge hand forged spikes out of old hardwood boards. It
was horrible, brutally hard labour, and after pulling and carefully
straightening and saving the nails, they would stack the wood, hoping
it wouldn't get stolen before they used it.
After Dad finished his shift at Stelco they would hammer another
section onto the little house.
They bought a car.
It was a 1928 Model A Ford, with no roof, but a powerful heater which
blew hot air right off the manifold. They would put Stan in a sort of
papoose hung from the remains of the convertible roof and tool around
town. There were no safety regs in those days. Once, Dad had to make

an emergency stop, and Stan, hanging in the little papoose, swung around and around the supporting bar like a circus trapeze artist. He was wound up so tight that it took a half hour to cut him loose and free him. He never made a peep.

They were still living in the trailer on Lake Avenue when I came along. In stark contrast to Stan, who had been the most placid and happy child ever, and who had to be wakened for meals, I spent the first 10 months on this planet screaming like the dive siren on a wartime Stuka.

Just screaming.

Night and day.

Screaming.

Without so much as pausing for breath, by all accounts...just... screaming.

I can't remember what was bothering me.

We moved into the house in Tapleytown before it was finished. Probably the sleepless neighbours in the trailer park had appeared at their door with a petition.

There was no roof on the house as yet, except for the bedroom that Stan and I shared. The rest of the house was mostly open to the sky, with a big smelly canvas tarp over the kitchen. Mum told the story of me watching starlings flying about the kitchen while I was eating my porridge, and laughing myself sick.

There was no toilet in what was to become the bathroom, just a large "honey bucket" which had to be emptied into a hole dug in the back yard. A neighbour of ours, Mike Gushie, had the same arrangement in the house he was building, except he had five kids and the system was prone to overload. One freezing winter night he got up for a pee, and found the bucket perilously full. Cursing, he picked it up, and very carefully started edging his way to the door. Just as he stepped on to the large iron grate over the furnace, the handle let go and the contents exploded into steam all over the hot metal below, and the place was uninhabitable for weeks.

Stan was five and a half years older than me, and started school right around the time we settled in to the new house. It was a tough and polyglot little neighbourhood. Poles and Ukrainians, all sorts of new refugees were living around us, along with a smattering of German immigrants, who were not popular for obvious reasons. The Germans in our neighbourhood always contended that they had never been Nazis."Vee hated Hitler," they always said, and yet there was one guy who proudly displayed his Waffen SS uniform in a glass case in the hall. Their kids made playing soldiers difficult. They were always trying to re-write the script and change the ending.

We were all poor. Most of the families were barely scraping by.

Everyone had a big garden and everyone canned food for winter. We all wore hand me downs, and nothing ever got thrown away. We wore our rubber winter boots until we outgrew them, and all the kids learned how to use a rubber patch kit for bicycle tires to repair their boots, or failing that, insert a plastic bread bag into the boot.

Stan and I were allowed to mingle with the kids in the immediate area of the survey where the houses were being built, but beyond there we were not allowed to go. Our sphere of influence extended from an old and rickety building called the "Men's Club" on Mud Street, to the south of the village, which was where we all got mass vaccinated for chicken pox and polio, to as far north as a woodlot called Norton's Bush where we gathered hickory nuts to supplement the family's diet.

Stan and I never could figure out why we were forbidden to go further until one day we hiked the extra quarter mile to Green Mountain Road to visit the small farm there.

When we walked into the barn we found one of the older boys standing on a stool behind a heifer with his pants around his ankles and an earnest expression on his face.

I had no idea what was going on. Nor did Stan, I believe, but we knew instinctively we shouldn't be seeing this. Stan took my hand and said, "Let's go home, brother," and he frog marched me back down the road.

Having grown up poor in Nova Scotia, our mother was well versed in finding ways to save money. We ate nothing store-bought or prepared except for coffee, peanut butter and margarine. Margarine came in a large soft plastic bag.

It was white, with a big dot of yellow colouring which one had to mix by hand. I remember sitting with Stan on the back step, it being our job to labouriously squeeze the bag for what seemed like hours. It was nasty stuff.

Coffee came from the sweepings from the bottom of the grinder at the Dominion Store in Stoney Creek. They had a deal with the manager there, who kindly let them collect it once a week and take it home for free. We had homemade brown bread, and cookies and cakes, and we never went hungry, but we weren't living rich either.

Dad was always coming home with some new attempt at getting protein into our bodies. Baked beef heart stuffed with stale bread and onions was a pretty frequent meal.

Head cheese.

Horse meat too.

I hate to think of it.

Milk was always powdered skim and came from a 40 pound bag kept in the cupboard. We had real milk delivered by horse drawn wagons back then, but it was not for drinking. Cooking and coffee only.

Even the bright foil wrapper from the top of the milk bottle was saved and made into Christmas decorations.

Until we finally got the plumbing connected drinking water came from the 5 gallon galvanized jerry can which Dad filled every week from the hose at the Sunoco station at the corner of King Street and 20 Highway in Stoney Creek.

All of our clothes were homemade. Mum had a sewing machine and I don't think I ever had a pair of store bought pants until I was in my early teens.

CHAPTER 3

Bullying

One of my clearest and most disturbing memories of those days was how Stan would come home from school bleeding from his nose or mouth, nearly every day, or so it seemed to me. He had skipped a couple of grades, and was always the youngest and smartest and the largest kid in class.
He paid for it.
The other smaller and quicker and meaner kids would gang up on him and pummel the crap out of him. It didn't help that he was pudgy, either, at least by the standards of those days.
The bullying continued right into his teens, and he bore the scars of it, one way or the other all his life.
Photos of Stan smiling show him with a gold front tooth. That was a souvenir of having his face pushed into a drinking fountain in Grade 9, some hours after a confrontation in the parking lot which Stan thought had been settled. He also had a permanently enlarged pupil, from when a kid fired a dart gun point blank into his face. They thought for a time that he would lose the eye, but the doctors managed to save it, and he wore a Medic Alert bracelet in case he got brought into a hospital unconscious and someone noticed the enlargement and began drilling into his head looking for a blood clot.
He got his ass kicked pretty much daily, and the chief result of that was to give him a lifelong hatred of bullies of any sort. Any situation where he felt threatened or cornered would elicit a terrible and swift and violent reaction, and the rush of adrenalin would render him scarily and psychotically strong.
Dad, who had boxed some in the Air Force, came home one night with some boxing gear; two pairs of 16 ounce gloves, a speed bag, and a 200 pound heavy bag, the latter of which he hung up on a stout chain in the basement. And most nights after school both Stan and I would be taken downstairs and given some lessons. The speed bag teaches timing and reflexes, and... well... speed. The heavy bag gives you endurance and punching power. It's exhausting to hit someone for any length of

time, and you need to build up tone. Sometimes the difference between winning or losing a fight is just being able to remain standing a few seconds longer than the other guy.

The first time Stan and Dad faced off for a practice round, Stan managed to land a lucky and early left to Dad's jaw, and a second later Stan was unconscious on the floor, Dad having reacted instinctively and dotted him a good one on the chin with a right uppercut. At least that's what I think it was. The punch was too quick to see with the naked eye. Dad was embarrassed and contrite, Mum was furious, and Stan was determined to never let it happen again.

He worked out with the gear every night, and made progress, to the point where one evening, when something was bothering him he went down for a session with the heavy bag, and as I watched he hit it with a series of terrifying round house punches, and with a final right tore the thing off the rafters and sent it flying end over end into the furnace room.

Dad took care to not have any more practice bouts after that.

So we both picked up a few basic skills over the months, and learned that while slipping a punch was best, taking a punch was not the worst thing in the world, and you could push through the pain and carry on. Neither of us would ever, no matter how hard we worked, be able to go up against a real fighter, with a real fighter's reflexes, but just those few lessons put us ahead of the kids at school, and that was all that mattered. And as the years went by we also picked up some tricks that weren't in the Marquis of Queensbury rule book.

The two of us were hitch-hiking home from Hamilton one winter night. We had been stuck at the corner of Highway 20 and King Street in Stoney Creek for maybe an hour and were both chilled and shivering. We ducked into the P and G Chinese restaurant, known locally as "the Pig," for a coffee.

We were both huddled in the booth when a half dozen young guys came into the room.

They were some of Stan's old tormentors from public school, and seeing him there, they decided to push him around once more for old times' sake. They crowded around us and began taunting him, calling him "Pumpkin Head," which had been his nickname in public school, partly as a result of him having an oversize skull, and also because of an ill-considered choice Mum had made on his behalf for a Halloween costume one year.

He took the abuse and threats for a couple of minutes, just sitting and staring down at the table, but then pushed his coffee cup away and stood up.

And up.
And up.
My, how he had grown.
I could see the concerned faces of the guys as they began to reconsider
their situation.
He pointed to the exit.
   "Outside. All of you."
He herded the bunch of them out the door like a flock of nervous ducks.
I was briefly delayed as I had to search my pockets for enough change
to pay for the coffee, and by the time I got out the door, to either back
him up or pick up the pieces, Stan was standing by himself in the
middle of the lot, breathing heavily and looking at what he'd just done.
They were all down, bleeding, with broken teeth, broken noses, and
at least one broken arm, and Stan now began paying special attention
to the last one who was holding desperately onto the guy wire from a
hydro pole as Stan kicked him repeatedly in the ribs.
I can't describe the shock.
I had never seen this thing unleashed before. I managed to pull him
away, and we left them there and marched the mile and a half up the
hill to Green Mountain Road where we stuck out our thumbs again.
That fear and the reaction to being cornered never went away.
Years later we were walking back from a show at Smales Pace
Coffeehouse, one night in London. It was about 3 in the morning and
the headliner's performance had morphed into one of those wonderful
quiet sessions after the audience left, with a bunch of other musicians
sitting around with wine and coffee and other stimulants, passing the
guitar back and forth, and trying out their new songs.
It had been a lovely evening.
I was too young to drink, or use anything else. Stan kept a close watch
on me. But he had a nice buzz, and he was smiling gently as we walked
along. We were both quietly singing the chorus to David Bradstreet's
new song, "Beresford Street."
We drifted down towards Maitland Street, where Stan was living, and
we could see two drunks were coming towards us. They were leaning
into each other, nodding and laughing about something. As they passed
by, one of them said "Howdy Tex," an obvious reference to Stan's giant
black Hoss Cartwright hat.
It was innocent enough, just a dumb joke, but even the suggestion of
any kind of aggression was enough to set him off.
Stan dropped his guitar and whirled around and grabbed both of them
by the throat, and lifted them up, one in each hand, to pin them against
a tree, their feet about a foot off the ground.
He held them there while they began the process of choking to death,

and stared into their faces for a minute or so. The two of them were struggling helplessly, and kicking and turning red.

"Uh Stan..." I said.

Stan continued to hold them there.

Jesus.

This was getting desperate.

"Stan...maybe uh..."

He wasn't hearing me.

Presently he leaned in closer to them and in a terrible quiet voice said, "What did you say?"

He held them for another beat and then threw them both across the sidewalk, onto the street where he began kicking them along as they scrambled to get to their feet.

The two managed to stagger off, coughing and retching, and Stan reached out for the guitar case which I'd picked up. We continued home, this time at a pretty good clip.

Stan burst through the door, took the stairs two and three at a time, and went to the fridge, got a quart of home brew, popped the top and poured out two glasses.

Lit a smoke and sat at the kitchen table, breathing deeply for a few minutes, staring into space. After a while he crushed out the smoke, drained the glass, and came back from where ever he'd gone. "I hate that shit." he said quietly, and went in to the living room to make up my bed on the sofa.

It was that fear and hatred of bullying which was to lead to so many fights and altercations with our audiences years later when we began playing the shit hole bars that made the bulk of our gigs. In those situations we always made sure that we had the other's back, although as Stan was older and bigger it mostly fell upon him to be my protector a lot of the time.

He must have been kept busy, because I was an annoying and mouthy little shit right from the get go.

Even at a tender age I was given to making off kilter jokes which no one but me seemed to find funny.

There was a morning in Grade One when the teacher had left the room for something, and of course the class erupted into a seething mass of laughing shrieking hyper active demons, all running about the room and throwing black board erasers and balls of crumpled paper.

"She's coming back!" someone shouted, and we all scurried back to our seats and assumed wide eyed and innocent expressions as the teacher stormed back in.

She was furious.

"Who was making that noise?"

Silence.
She glared about the room, taking in the mess we had made.

"Who did this? Someone had better speak up and confess, or I will march the lot of you down to the principal's office and you will ALL get the strap."
Still no response.

"Right. I am going to count to ten, and the persons who did this had better confess or you will all be punished."
We sat, immobile.

"One... two... three..."
The tension was awful.

"Four... five... "
We were all looking out of the corners of our eyes, wondering who was going to crack and rat out the others.

"Six... seven... I'm waiting."
It was no use. I had to do something.

"Eight..."
I couldn't take it.

"Nine..."
I broke.
I stood up and came to attention.

"I AM SPARTACUS!"

CHAPTER 4

Nova Scotia

1957. Dad got a new car.

It was a white Ford Fairlane four door, with a pale blue interior. A beautiful machine. We had to celebrate, and our little family made the ritual trip down to the Stoney Creek Dairy for ice cream cones.

I remember sitting in the back seat with the window down, and my orange flavoured cone in my right fist.

It was a lovely sunny day and we were all happy. Dad was in a great mood. It was his first ever new car.

He decided to take a really good run at the little rise on the road home. You could get air-borne if you hit it at the right speed.

"Oh Al, be careful. "I heard my mother say. We were really moving. Dad had a little grin on his face, and we hit the hill and achieved lift-off. There were no seat belts in those days, and I became a weightless little space monkey, and as I somersaulted above the back seat I planted my orange cone right into the perfect and pristine cloth on the inside roof. We never got the stain out.

None of which is important, except that I spent a lot of time looking at that stain, laying in the back seat, as we began to make regular trips to Nova Scotia.

It seemed like any time Dad had a couple of extra days off or got a few dollars ahead, we would load up and make the long, frenzied non-stop drive through New York and Maine back East to visit the relatives.

Mum would make a bed for me and Stan on top of the suitcases on the back seat floor, pack some cheese sandwiches, and off we'd go.

We'd make a few quick stops in Oxford to say hi to members of Dad's family, and then press on to Canso to see Mom's folks.

Her Dad was in failing health, and was confined to a wheelchair. My grandparents lived in a large frame house on Water Street in Canso, with a view of the harbour and the big wharf where the boats still brought in their catch.

One of my earliest memories is from some years before, getting lost in the rhubarb patch in the front of that house. I might have been 18

47

months old, and I was frantically pushing past the thick green stalks, under the broad leaves, as if in some old Tarzan movie, yelling for help. I think it was my Aunt June who rescued me. Two large hands came down through the top of the rain forest, and lifted me up into the sunlight, and I can still remember seeing the wharf and the bright sunlight on the harbour beyond.

Our grandparents' house was a big dark and spooky place for a small child, with endless stairs and un-lit halls, and rooms full of old furniture, and shelves crammed with musty books with dry brittle pages. Stan and I would search the book cases for something to read, and then we would hunker down and try to make ourselves invisible, with the Uncles sitting around the living room, talking in that polite but disinterested way men do when they have nothing in common but a difficult and contentious set of in-laws.

Meanwhile, out in the kitchen Mum and her sisters and Grandma would spend hours boiling eggs, baking biscuits and bread and cookies, and cooking stew and baked beans to take on a picnic to Glasgow Head, at the far eastern tip of the peninsula.

After some hours of preparation, during which time heated arguments would erupt over the proper way to make a deviled egg, and the Uncles had all wandered off or fallen asleep, the picnic would be pronounced ready and the whole massive expedition would be launched.

My poor grandfather by now had Parkinson's disease, and it was a difficult job in those days to get his wheel chair loaded into the car. A fleet of cars would be loaded down with baskets of food and billy cans, and water jugs, and deck chairs, and sweaters and blankets, and what seemed like a hundred kids, and the convoy would trundle slowly and painfully down the road to the stony causeway that led to the beach. One of the overladen cars would inevitably strike a beach rock and begin to leave a trail of oily goo, like a wounded bug. We'd all pour out and search for driftwood as others would argue how best to build and light a fire. Someone would arrange the blankets, and erect the little camp tables, and set out the chairs and the food would be brought out. The kids would be called in from exploring the shore, and lunch would be served just as the fog began to roll in, and the landscape would disappear, and the whole world became dead and grey and damp. We'd pack all the food and baskets and blankets and chairs and camp tables back up, drown the fires, and heave the whole unwieldy load back into the cars and slowly and silently grind our way back into town. The kids and the Uncles would eat lunch around the dining room table, while the sisters continued their turf war in the kitchen, as they began the process of cooking dinner.

Stan and I would disappear with a P.G. Wodehouse novel, or something by Kipling, or maybe an ancient back issue of "Boy's Own" magazine, a vaguely homo-erotic illustrated publication in which pure and high minded lads with bee stung lips and muscular thighs seemed to spend an awful lot of time wrestling and sweating on the emerald green rugby fields of dear old England, while kindly old headmasters in caps and gowns smoked pipes, and cried, "Bravo," and "Oh jolly good," from the sidelines, while waiting to escort them to the showers.

Our uncles, Lee and Norman, or Bim, as he was called, had guitars which they had built themselves, real store-bought guitars being too expensive. It was Lee who built Stan's first instrument. It was a little birch plywood number with frets made of brass welding rods, which we passed to and fro in the back seat of the Ford, on the long drives to Canso.

Parties down East were pretty much do it yourself affairs. There was no record player, so if you wanted music you had to make it.

I have early memories of the big people in the kitchen sitting around singing and talking, while the uncles belted out Hank Snow and Hank Williams songs along with other tunes of the day, while quarts of beer got opened, and steamed clams and lobster and fish cakes and biscuits got loaded on to the table. The parties went on pretty much every night in the summer, or so it seemed to me.

The pace of the social whirl caught up to some after a while.

"I hope I pass out early tonight," Lee was overheard saying as things got underway. "I need the sleep."

My Aunt June's first husband, Sam Jarvis, was a short-ish quiet man, with thick dark hair, and when he was younger, astonishing matinee idol looks. He played guitar and sang too, but was often over shadowed by the larger and louder Bushell brothers. Sam had been in the navy during the war, on convoy escort duty, and had seen hard service.

He had been terribly wounded, both physically and emotionally. He spent the rest of his life trying to deal with the pain and the memories that would never leave, not to mention an indifferent government bureaucracy that never acknowledged his service, much less compensated him for his injuries.

Back in those days there was no talk of PTSD. If you were lucky enough to come back from the war at all, you were expected to simply get on with your life and shut up about it.

Often times at the parties, Sam would disappear from the room where everyone was laughing and singing and dancing, and I would find him, maybe in a spare bedroom or at the bottom of the stairs, sitting with his guitar, strumming quietly with his thumb pick, and singing Jim Reeves songs to himself.

It was lovely. So lovely that I would not interrupt him by attempting to join in. There was no sense of him trying to be a "performer." He was simply singing for the joy of it, and the magic of being able to step into the world of a song, and the sound of someone doing that is one of the most beautiful sounds in the world.

He was a kind man, and funny and sensitive. He and June were endlessly generous to me and Stan, and we were to spend a lot of time with them in later years, sitting around their kitchen, playing and singing. It was June who first suggested to Stan that he should write more about the Maritimes, which led to much of the music on the first album, and Stan and I both spent hours trying to assimilate Sam's guitar style. It was no use though. He had magic in his hands.

There were other contrasts in the music being played at the parties. Mum's oldest brother, Arnold, fancied himself an opera singer. He had inherited his father's sense of self-importance and entitlement, and being nearly 6 foot 10, had no trouble making his presence felt. He was listening impatiently one night as one of his brothers was yodeling a Hank Snow song. He interrupted and said, "You call yourself a singer. Pfft. None of you are REAL singers. Here, if you think you can sing, let me see you try this."

And he stood up, threw back his head, and let out a long and loud and quavering baritone bellow which lasted the better part of a minute. Everyone in the room was cowering and waiting for it to end. Two miles away in Chedabucto Bay, a pod of humpback whales was looking nervously around and saying, "What the HELL was that?"

He finished and sat down.

"There," he said. "Sing THAT note."

"Which one?" asked Bim.

Music for us wasn't just on the radio, it was what one did for fun. It seemed like everyone we knew wrote songs; parodies of hits, original songs, and chronicles of local events. The concept of making sense of one's life through music and verse was for us not a foreign one right from the start.

For Stan first, and me later, the hook was planted and set during those trips to Canso.

CHAPTER 5

Radio

We lived in the little house in Tapleytown until it was finished, whereupon it was sold, and we moved to a new house which we'd had built in Woodburn, a few miles away. It was slightly larger, and Stan and I both had our own rooms.

We were moving up in the world. We got a big floor model Stereophonic record player and radio for the living room, to replace the ancient RCA floor model radio we'd listened to for so long. My first memory of listening to music was from that old RCA radio, sitting head to head with Stan, on the floor, in the dark in our flannel jammies, long past our appointed bedtime, as we tuned into the big broadcasts from Wheeling, West Virginia.

The smell of the old dusty cabinet, and the hot tubes warming up the glue stays with me all these years later. I still use tube amplifiers in my shows now, and inevitably every night there will be a moment when I turn my head and the smell of the glue and the hot cathode tubes reaches me, and I am back in that room watching the yellow light from the radio dial shine on my brother's face as he is teaching me how to sing sotto voce harmony with the Everly Brothers.

The new stereo came with a box of free records, "cut-outs" mostly, unsold stock that got tossed in to sweeten the purchase. They were all over the place thematically, a bunch of old Carter Family collections, some records by Jimmy Rodgers, "The Singing Brakeman," Burl Ives, Handel's Messiah, all kinds of stuff. We loved almost all of it.

There were a lot of original cast Broadway recordings, like "Gigi." We didn't care, it was all music to us, and caught our attention the way the stuff on the radio couldn't at the time. The radio then was full of "Bobbies." Bobbie Vincent, Bobbie Rydell, and Bobby Curtola, and we hated all of them.

It was a bad time for popular music as far as we were concerned. Elvis had joined the army a few years previous, and had come out with his nuts cut off and a little bell on a ribbon around his neck.

The Beatles and Bob Dylan hadn't yet arrived and what was on the

radio just made us queasy. Syrupy strings, whiney quavery voices, and
gooey vapid lyrics. We detested it.
The other music, even the Broadway stuff, had more grit.
Through osmosis, listening to our original cast recording, Stan was
eventually to learn the whole of Gigi, and in later years, I was treated
to a performance of the entire show by him and our then bassist,
David Eadie. David must have had a similarly odd upbringing. Their
performance of "I Remember It Well," with Stan taking the part of
Maurice Chevalier, and David singing the Hermione Gingold part, but
in the character of a hissing Nazi Gauleiter nearly gave me a hernia.
Stan started it off.

"It was a Monday…"

"IT VASS A TUESDAY…" David corrected, holding his cigarette the
German way, and narrowing his eyes, trickling smoke from his nostrils.
We were driving from nowhere to somewhere else, in Ohio one night,
and boredom had set in, and they continued the duet as we drove south
on I-75.

"OH YES, I REMEMBER IT WELL…"
I was in the back seat of the van, helpless with laughter.
What really got our attention in those early days were those Jimmy
Rodgers records, and the Carter Family collections. Of all the music that
influenced Stan, at least in those very early years, you can trace back to
Jimmy Rodgers and Mother Maybelle that solid, rock steady rhythm
guitar style he developed.
Neither of us were ever able to precisely replicate Maybelle's driving
sound, the "Carter Scratch," using a thumb-pick and two finger picks,
no matter how many hours we spent listening and playing along, but
we gave it our best.
I remember the two of us, sitting next to the clothesline pole behind the
house in Woodburn, passing a borrowed Sears Silvertone archtop back
and forth, trying to get the riff to "Bear Creek Blues."
The guitar was a pig to play anyway. It had a neck the size of your leg
and towing cables for strings, but Maybelle's guitar part was just brutal.
"Ding ding dah dang dah dang guh duh dang. No. That's not it…try it
in D. Nope. That's not it either. Here, let me try." And so on.
We never got it right.
But I also remember standing next to him through all those years of
crappy or non-existent monitors, and sound systems that were never
meant for music, but were more suitable for addressing Ku Klux Klan
rallies, and Stan's timing never faltered.
He had a killer right arm, and the band became a relentless machine,
and you can thank Mother Maybelle for it.
There was a terrible urgency to the old songs as well. People bled and

died and were mourned in those songs. Storms rose and ships sank.
Lovers were parted forever by war or misunderstandings or death. It
affected us deeply. These weren't just made up Tin Pan Alley tunes,
churned out to make a buck. These were real chronicles of actual lives,
and their stories and voices spoke to us across the years.
Finding a decent guitar in those days was a real trial.
The little homemade birch number wasn't much more than a kid's
guitar, and the instruments we lusted for in the Sears catalogue, (once
we'd managed to get past the ads for the bullet bras and ladies' corsets,)
were out of our range.
I don't think Gibsons and Martins were even on our radar, back then.
We had the use of the old Sears arch top for one summer, but it would
have to be returned eventually, and anyway, the strings were an inch off
the fingerboard.
Stan got a job baling hay later that year. He spent weeks on the back of
a farm wagon, catching the bales in mid-air as they flew towards him,
and then piling them. Then he had to load the whole damned thing into
a hay loft in the stifling summer heat, and after that rattle out to the
field to do it all over again. It was hot and nasty and dirty work.
I've done it myself. It's no fun. By the end of the summer he had red
and swollen eyes, and a persistent cough from the dust, and his hands
were shaped like claws, calloused and crooked. Guitar playing was out
of the question.
Still, he hitch-hiked into the city one weekend, and spent the whole of
his saved wages, 80 dollars, on a big German-made Dreadnaught, made
by Hoyer.
It didn't sound great.
It had a laminated top and plywood back and sides, and had apparently
been finished not in lacquer, but by running it through one of those
machines they used to have in the bus terminal for "Plasticizing" your
ID cards.
As the saying went in our family, it was "Not much for looks but Hell
on strong." It was what we both learned on, and it was the guitar that
he played on his first gigs around Hamilton, at the church coffeehouses
and hoot nights.
Radio changed completely for us around 1963, or '64, and the years
following up to about 1970 were wonderful.
Suddenly the hated Bobbies were gone, and a whole other world was
opening up to us.
We weren't even remotely interested in what had been on the radio
before then. It was just vapid commercial pap, the sonic equivalent of
airline food. You were presented with it and told it was good. Everyone
around you was consuming it. It must be okay. But you instinctively

longed for something else, if only you could find it.

We still got the big country music signal from Wheeling West Virginia, at night, but Motown radio began beaming in from Detroit around this time, and the local Canadian stations were now pumping out great stuff, and there didn't seem to be any format or pattern to what was getting played. It all sounded wonderful and exciting.

On any given day, at any given hour, just by turning the dial, you could still hear the Isley Brothers, and then Otis Redding and Carla Thomas, singing "Knock on Wood," and Sam and Dave, singing "Hold on I'm Coming," and then with another turn of the dial have Ferlin Husky and Johnny Cash. And still further up the dial, Mozart, Beethoven and Stravinsky. Another twist, and then, holy shit...Wilson Pickett.

Stan learned and sang "The Midnight Hour." It was beautiful. His voice was perfect for it.

We heard the new single, "They'll Know Me by the Stones I Throw," from a local group, Levon and the Hawks. They later became The Band. We could hear The Yardbirds, and Aretha Franklin.

Aretha Franklin. Her voice could give you a heart attack and set your hair on fire.

Years later, Stan and David Eadie and I briefly toyed with putting her song "Respect," into our set list. Stan sang the pure living hell out of it, but David balked at having to sing "sock it to me sock it to me sock it to me," as they did on the record.

It was a shame. We sounded great.

Ian and Sylvia. Such a singular and iconic sound. Such great songs and harmonies.

Mitch Ryder and the Detroit Wheels. "Listen to that damned guitar," Stan said one afternoon. "That is a Telecaster if I ever heard one. I've got to get one of those someday."

He did a great job on covering the "Devil with a Blue Dress," medley when he played bass a few years later in the little high school rock band.

We heard Odetta. We couldn't believe a human being could have that voice. And we would have stared at you in disbelief if you'd suggested that she would one day become a dear friend.

B.B. King.

Handel's "Water Music," and "The Royal Fireworks Suite."

The Rolling Stones.

Johnny Rivers.

Louis Prima...a voice like a saxophone.

Judy Collins was on the radio, with that pure voice and extraordinary arrangements that went way outside the folk genre. There was one recording of hers particularly, an arrangement of four songs about

Marat Sade, that we couldn't get enough of.

Howlin' Wolf. His voice sounded like stones being ground together.

And Jim Reeves singing his hit, "He'll Have to Go." It had one of the all time great opening lines for a song. "Put your sweet lips a little closer to the phone. Let's pretend that we're together, all alone..."

Chuck Berry. You could still hear him on the radio, and he was still on fire. Still dangerous. Still crazy.

Jerry Lee Lewis was out there, and he was still crazy too. Hillbilly batshit crazy.

Little Richard. He was crazy in ways you couldn't even begin to imagine.

Gordon Lightfoot. There's a big one. He just popped out of nowhere, seemingly, fully formed with his high clear tenor voice, and that signature trio sound of Red Shea on guitar, and John Stockfish on bass. It left an indelible imprint on us.

Mozart's "Magic Flute." Haydn's string quartets.

Beethoven's "Kreutzer Sonata." The "Pathetique.'" All the symphonies.

Joan Baez. That voice. That perfect flawless voice. And one of the best guitar players we'd heard.

We had Woodie Guthrie records from the library and we listened to him singing "Roll on Columbia," and the other Dust Bowl Ballads, like "Pastures of Plenty," and "The Ballad of Tom Joad." Again, as with the music of the Carter Family, people were living and bleeding and dying in those songs. Money was changing hands in a back room somewhere, and hungry families were paying the price because their poor dad didn't know the secret handshake. Cops were being paid off by mill owners, and workers were being clubbed to death for trying to unionize, and kids younger than us were dying in terrifying arranged accidents. I remember the two of us bent over the turntable, listening to Woody's song about the Italian Hall in Calumet Michigan in 1913. Children dying by the dozens at a Christmas party just so the mine owners could save a few pennies per ton of copper ore. Stan's face looked drawn and haunted, and he sat back and said nothing for a long time. How could this happen? Neither of us had any answer.

Johnny Mathis.

Stan loved him. He picked me up one day, many years later, to go to a gig, and as we drove along he said, "I had a great time last night."

"What were you doing?"

"Oh, Joe Zizzo and I went down to the Collins Hotel for a few beers, and they had a trio in there doing a "stump the band" thing. You request a song and they have to play it for you while you sing. The prize is a 40 pounder of Canadian Club."

"Bleah."

"Never mind. You'd drink it if you had to. Anyway, I requested "Misty," and they played it, and when I was done the place went nuts, and I won the booze."

"Good for you. Did you think to bring it along for your thirsty brother?"

"Never mind. Anyway, the band leader came over during the break to give me the rye and sat down and said, "Okay. We know you're a ringer. Who are you anyway? So I had to tell them I did it for a living. They let me keep the booze, but I can't go back now."

He was pleased as hell with himself.

We listened to Paul Robeson. Again, how could a human have that voice? Where did it come from? And we'd heard about the blacklist and the price he was made to pay for his political beliefs. It didn't make sense.

Patsy Cline. She had been gone for years but the records were still magic. Such a lonesome and hypnotic late night sound.

The Supremes. The songs. The voices. The harmonies. That incredible band.

And Leadbelly. Kids today are made to listen to Children's Entertainers, playing carefully sanitized songs that have no doubt been run past a committee to ensure they're safe and full of whole wheat goodness. We were listening to a guy who'd done time for murder.

Chet Atkins.

Eric Burden and the Animals.

Cisco Houston.

Roger Miller. We loved him. Such great crazy lyrics, and he seemed to be having more fun than anyone had a right to. Stan and I spent a night once in the back of the family camper on the way to Nova Scotia, playing every Roger Miller song we knew. There were dozens.

The Righteous Brothers...such soulful singing, and those epic, massive sounding records.

Les Paul and Mary Ford.

Martha and the Vandellas. Just what the Hell was a Vandella?

Roy Orbison.

Serge Prokofiev.

Just a few twists of the FM dial during the day would give you all that. It was magic.

At night you could switch over to AM radio and hear far away broadcasts from the deep South as they came in on a wave skip. It might be the same music, but because of the distance and the interference from other close-by stations, you could also hear the faint ghosts of emergency weather reports warning of tornadoes outside of St. Louis, or Tulsa, and call in shows with angry veterans complaining about "all these hippies, and dammit, this isn't the country I fought for," and frantic fire and brimstone tent preachers outside of Chicago, with a wild, sweaty gospel band tearing it up in the back ground, while someone got out the box of rattlesnakes. It all sounded so far away, but urgent and exciting nonetheless.

All of it...all those strange and myriad voices got churned together and mixed up into a great musical Tower of Babel, as you lay in bed in the darkness with your ear pressed to the tiny transistor radio, trying to tune in the signal and maybe hear "She Loves You," just one more time that day before you tried to get to sleep.

Oh yeah. The Beatles.

Jesus.

The Beatles.

We were like most of the western world that February night, sitting in front of the TV, waiting for the Ed Sullivan Show.

I listen now to that moment, when Ed says, "Ladies and Gentlemen... The Beatles!" as the crowd screams, and just before you hear Paul count them in, and they begin to play "All My Loving," it is for me like the last few seconds before the first atom bomb test at Los Alamos. We had no idea just how big this was going to get, but everything before that moment was "Then."

Everything after it was "Now."

To this day, I can still remember exactly where I was, what I was doing and even the clothes I was wearing, whenever a new Beatles single came on the radio for the first time.

Every new song, every new album was a massive leap forward for us. I recall us standing next to the record player, watching the disc go around as we listened to "Tomorrow never knows," the last track of "Revolver." Stan and I spent ages trying to figure out how they were getting the sounds they were making. Good luck with that one.

Pete Seeger had a very low key and cheaply produced TV show on PBS back in the mid-sixties, when he was still suffering from the same black list that came close to breaking Paul Robeson. Thanks to Pete, a whole new universe opened up for us. He had as guests, The Greenbriar Boys, and the Beers Family, and the New Lost City Ramblers, and Mississippi John Hurt and Jean Redpath. This wasn't the cleaned up version of folk music we had heard from the Kingston Trio, or Peter Paul and Mary, or even Pete's old group, The Weavers, all of which had left us cold. Once again, these were songs from another time. The melodies and words were raw and primal, and they still had the power to grab us by the throat and speak to us.

Ronnie Hawkins did a show at Stan's high school. Ronnie had moved up to Canada from Arkansas and ran what amounted to a school for rock and roll guitarists in Ontario in those days. It was like a triple A ball team.

Once you had some seasoning in his band, you knew how to play all night, and drink and fight and screw strange women, and there was a chance to move up and see if your liver and immune system could survive in the bigger leagues.

A lot of guys passed through that band. Some of them even made it out alive. A couple of the guys were from our area. Robbie Robertson was from the "Rez," the Six Nations Reserve, near Brantford. Richard Manuel was from Stratford, so it wasn't out of the realm of possibility that they might play a dance at Saltfleet High school.

Stan told me how someone started giving Ronnie grief over his new radio jingle for Wildroot Formula Three hair oil.

"Why'd you do it Ronnie? Why'd ya sell out?"

Ronnie looked down from the stage, covered in rhinestones, with sweat and hair pomade running down his face.

He laughed.

"Hell, if they give me enough money, I'd sing about Kotex."

He was a hero to us. We'd heard stories about how he had walked into a Rolls Royce dealership in Toronto, and dropped a shopping bag full of cash onto the floor in front of the prissy salesman who had dismissed him out of hand a few hours before, when he had first come in to kick the tires and toot the horn of the Silver Wraith he fancied.

"There ya go, sonny. 40 Grand."

"But sir..."

"Oh, and by the way. What is your commission on this sale?"

The little twerp gave him a figure, and Ronnie bent down and counted out some bills, and stuffed them into his own pocket.

"Too bad for you. That's what you get for being rude, junior. Have it washed and ready for me in an hour."

We loved him.

The Motown revues started coming through town and Stan came home one night, looking like Moses after seeing the burning bush. He had just been to a small church hall, where he had seen live, and not 15 feet away, Martha and the Vandellas and Wilson Pickett, among others. Stuff like that changes you forever.

CHAPTER 6

Bob Dylan

Our cousin Iris owned the first two Bob Dylan albums.
She would arrive with a bottle of wine, and she and Mum would stay
up late, and drink, and listen and try to parse the lyrics. Stan came
down one morning, to find them both asleep on the rug next to the
stereo with the needle on the record still making a rhythmic scratching.
Not passed out, as he would later tell the story.
Just asleep.
We all as a family had a bad habit of deliberately substituting one word
for another in conversation, for the sake of being funny. This led to
misunderstandings.
Some years later, in an interview, Stan told the story about finding Mum
passed out on the floor, having listened all night to "The Free Wheelin'
Bob Dylan" on the turntable.
    "Yeah, my Mum used to lay prostitute on the floor, listening to Bob
Dylan."
He was of course, substituting the word "prostrate" for the sake of a
joke.
The reporter dutifully wrote down how "Stan Rogers' mother at one
time, prostituted herself for Bob Dylan." The editor missed it, and it got
printed.
Our more conservative neighbours weren't happy about it. Mum wasn't
real thrilled either.
Through Iris we got tickets to see Bob Dylan play at Massey Hall. Stan
and I were actually being allowed to go.
I had never seen live music before, outside of my Grandmother's
kitchen. I had never been to Toronto. I had never been in an apartment
building before, or an elevator, or ridden a subway, or done any of the
things we were now doing.
I was out of my tiny mind with excitement. I remember every detail of
that night. We got to the Hall, and took our seats, in the balcony, three
rows back, stage right.
We had of course been hearing the big controversy over Dylan going

electric, and the riots that were following him at every show. The format of the concert was that he would come out and do the first hour solo. There would be a break, and then there would be a set with the band, whereupon the audience would follow the script that the press had written for them, and dutifully go berserk.

Tonight was no different.

He came out and did an hour of songs like "Blowing in the Wind" and" Masters of War," and "Desolation Row." The "good stuff."

It was beyond quiet in the room. If you closed your eyes you would never guess there were a couple thousand other people huddled worshipfully in the dark, hardly daring to breathe. It was just you and that voice and that guitar, and those lyrics.

The only words he spoke that night were when he was wrestling with the tuning on his Nick Lucas Special.

"Durned guit-ar won't tune." It got a huge laugh.

After the break we all came back in to see the drum kit and the Fender amps on stage.

There was a lot of muttering. The band came out with Bob, wearing Ray Bans and slick looking suits.

As soon as they hit the first chord the place erupted.

Crumpled up programmes rained down on the stage, and people were on their feet yelling and booing. A guy behind us in a tweed jacket was screaming "FALSE PROPHET!" repeatedly, and flecking the back of my Dad's coat with spittle.

It was a riot, just as the papers said it would be, and it all must have been very satisfying for the pretentious nitwits who were later interviewed outside the hall in front of the cameras. But right now, Dad was grabbing my arm and saying, "Let's get the hell out of here."

The band was still playing this wild ecstatic noise. People were still screaming abuse at the stage.

I recall one guy in the front row furiously trying to pull the seat out of the floor, in order to throw it, I suppose. I'm not sure some of the less evolved among us weren't flinging feces.

Dad and I left Stan and Mum in the concert room, and made our way to the lobby.

People were weeping, and hitting each other, yelling and being carried out bleeding, on stretchers. Two guys with bad facial hair were standing nose to nose screaming into each other's face, right in front of us. One pushed the other and the second guy pushed back, and then they were on the floor, wrestling and beating each other bloody.

Police, some on horseback, others on foot with drawn truncheons, were everywhere, and I could hear sirens outside.

TV camera crews in the lobby were lighting the whole thing up beautifully.

Through the walls I could still hear the deep thump of the bass and drums, and the chanting of the mob. I was standing holding my Dad's hand, thinking to myself, "THIS... IS... GREAT."

I decided at that moment, and I'm not making this up, that I wanted to be a musician.

It wasn't a need to be the center of attention, or the desire to be the object of so much weird and obsessive scrutiny. It was the words, and the music and the heart-stopping sound of loud guitars thumping against my chest.

It was a life changing moment, and I have thought about it a lot over the years that have followed, trying to examine why it had meant so much to me. As I later came to understand it, it was the sound of an artist who simply didn't care what people expected him to do or be. He was going to do this regardless of whether anyone was listening or approved of it. It was the sound of that most precious thing in the world, someone telling the truth.

CHAPTER 7

The Predators

I'd guess it would have been around 1965 when I came home from school one day, and as I approached the front door I could hear a deep thumping subterranean pulse coming from the house. What the hell was this?

I opened the door and a loud and booming wave of sound was coming up from the basement and rattling the windows. The cat was racing around the house, looking like he had just come out of the spin dryer. Mum was walking around the kitchen with a set look on her face and wiping down anything within reach with a dish cloth.

"What's going on?" I shouted. She shook her head, and waved me away.

I ran downstairs to the basement, and there was Stan and three other guys. Two guitars, and a drummer. Stan was on bass.

This was new.

When did he start playing bass?

Up to now he had only ever played acoustic guitar and French horn in the high school band.

And now this. They were playing "Slow Down," by the Beatles. I still have no idea whether they were any good, but they were loud, and I'd never heard electric guitars that close before. I was transfixed. They worked their way through a few more numbers, and then Dad came home from work and it was time to enter into some negotiations.

Would Stan be allowed to play bass for the band and do regular gigs if he kept up with his homework, and his share of chores around the house?

He was going to start doing chores? And homework? Wow.

How he was going to manage that with a band to play in was beyond me, but Stan swore he would hold up his end of things.

After many more promises and a final audition of The Animal's version of "House of the Rising Sun", as the "folk part" of the band's repertoire, the deal was struck, and Stan was now the bass player in a rock band.

Stan had a cheap Japanese copy of a Fender bass to start. It didn't last long.

The cat leapt up and broke the head stock one day after practice. I don't know whether it was by accident or design, but it was after all a damned cat, and by definition a conniving and treacherous little shit. Stan borrowed a better one, a real Fender Precision bass, with the big Fender Bassman amp to go with it.

He fell in love with the sound. He liked to stand in front of the speaker cabinet and turn it up to the point where his pant legs were flapping, and everyone else in the house was seized with a sudden urge to run for the bathroom to evacuate their bowels.

The band needed a name. They were called "The Livingstones" before Stan joined, and they toyed briefly with "Stanley and the Livingstones," but cooler heads prevailed, and I think Mum eventually came up with "The Predators."

The band was doing all the current stuff on the radio. "For Your Love" by the Yardbirds, "Paperback Writer" by the Beatles, and "Devil with a Blue Dress," by Mitch Ryder. A guy named Jack Mathews was the pretty boy lead singer. He got the ballads.

Stan sang the screamers, from the Ray Charles and Wilson Pickett catalogue.

They began to play school dances and little church hall gigs within a 30 or so mile radius of Hamilton. On Friday afternoons after school the station wagon would pull into the driveway and Stan would load his bass and amp into the back, and they'd set off. He'd usually arrive home sometime after 2 or 3 in the morning and crash out and be up again, fresh and rested around noon the next day. They acquired a lead guitarist after a couple of months, a guy named Paul Solenkovich, if memory serves, and he was terrifyingly good, at least by any standards I had back then. He wore a pair of Ray Bans, owned a beat up old Telecaster, and had nailed the stinging ear piercing sound that the guy in Mitch Ryder's band had developed. Together they all sounded terrific.

I got to see the band play one Fall afternoon.

They had a gig at the Binbrook Fair and as it was only about 12 miles away, I decided to hitch hike over and catch the show. Normally it wasn't that hard to get a ride back then, as I was local, and everyone knew me and picked me up anyway. But time was wearing on, and after an hour I still hadn't got a ride and I was worried that I might miss the show, so I began trotting towards Binbrook, and then turning around and sticking my thumb out as I heard cars approaching. Still no luck.

Presently I heard the sound of a large diesel motor coming slowly along. I turned and saw that it was Keith Edwards, our neighbour from across the road.

Keith and his wife Marge were wonderful people; sweet and kind and generous, and deeply Christian in every good sense of the word. In spite of that I was welcome in their home and allowed to play with their kids, and their eldest son Jim was my best friend at the time.

I was glad to see Keith as I knew he would stop for me. He never missed a chance to do a favour. I was less happy to see he was driving his brother in law's tractor and hauling a large manure spreader full of about a thousand gallons of semi liquid pig shit.

He slowed and stopped very carefully, and the horrible mess behind him surged forward and came close to spilling out the front of the spreader. The smell was appalling, but I reasoned once we got moving we would be upwind and I wouldn't get my clothes impregnated with the stink.

He gave me a hand up and I had to stand next to his seat, holding on to the high fender, and we set off, again, very slowly and carefully. There was no point in trying to talk, the noise of the motor was too loud, so we just rolled along together, Keith every once in a while catching my eye and giving me his kindly smile.

Lovely man.

After a few minutes though, we both heard the prolonged blast from a car horn behind us. I looked back and it was a guy in a massive Cadillac convertible with Florida plates. He was the archetypal "Ugly American," heavy, red faced and sweating with a set of golf clubs beside him in the front seat, and he was stuck behind us as the road was too narrow to pass. He was beating his fist on the horn and yelling hysterical obscenities at us.

"GET OFF THE DAMNED ROAD YOU STUPID FARMER! C'MON, MOVE IT YOU ASSHOLE! SOME PEOPLE ARE IN A HURRY! WHAT THE HELL IS WRONG WITH YOU?"

There was nowhere for Keith to pull over. He pushed down on the gas a bit, but the tractor was not built for speed. He waved in an apologetic and friendly manner to the guy behind us, and kept going. I knew the swearing was getting to him, as I had never known Keith to ever use bad language, or speak unkindly to anyone.

Or as my own Dad put it, "Keith wouldn't say shit if he had a mouthful."

The guy kept on.

"GODDAMN IT YOU FUCKING HICK, PULL OVER AND LET ME PASS!"

More furious and prolonged honking on the horn.

The abuse continued, and Keith was beginning to look grim, but there was nowhere for him to go on this narrow hilly road.

"GET OUT OF THE FUCKING WAY YOU STUPID MORON!"
Keith flinched and shook his head. Perhaps he was worried about my
tender sensibilities.
It was at that moment the lever which controlled the roller on the
spreader gave a loud clank and it shifted forward, and the air behind
us was filled with a couple of hundred gallons of well matured liquid
pig shit being propelled backwards at a high rate of speed.
I heard a scream, suddenly choked off, and Keith very quickly grabbed
the lever and jammed it back into place.
I looked back at the Cadillac, and it was at the side of the road about a
hundred feet behind us, covered in a glistening black layer of pig crap,
and the driver was standing next to it waving his arms frantically and
looking like an overweight Al Jolson in a shit stained Hawaiian shirt.
Keith didn't look back. He kept on going, saying nothing. I continued
looking at him, as the screams from the driver faded in the distance.
   "Oops," he said quietly, after a while. That was all.
   "Oops." He repeated.
And as I kept looking at him out of the corner of my eye, about a mile
later, I could see the tiniest of smiles, barely visible, at the corner of his
mouth.
We arrived at the driveway of his brother in law's farm, and he stopped,
and I hopped down and thanked him for the ride. He smiled again, and
waved and turned down the long lane.
There was nothing I could say.
This man, whose kindness and generosity was a watchword in our
little village, whose true Christian values were an inspiration even to
hardened heathens like me, had just meted out one of the most perfectly
executed acts of justice I had ever seen in the form of a quarter ton of
well-matured high velocity shit mist. But the more I thought about it
the less likely it seemed. I hadn't actually seen him touch the lever, and
anyway this was Keith, one of the most patient and forgiving men I had
ever known.
Then it occurred to me.
Maybe what I had just seen was in fact the real live actual power of
prayer.
That was a hell of a thought.
I watched this beautiful kindly man trundle off with his load of hog
squeezings, and wondered if there might be something in this religion
stuff. Being able to call on God to smite someone like that held a real
attraction.
I turned and began walking quickly towards Binbrook. I still wanted to
catch the show, but I also had some thinking to do.
I got to the Fairgrounds and paid my way in, and found Stan and the

boys in a stiflingly hot tin hut on the infield in front of the grandstand. They were trying to get away from the noise and tune up. Stan was holding his bass up, with the horn against his ear, and the head stock pressed against a metal locker. It gave the instrument some added resonance, and in later years became our main way of tuning in noisy bars.

He turned to me.

"You made it."

"Yeah. Listen, Stan, you'll never believe what I just saw happen..."

"Later, okay? We got a show to do."

"Alright, but..."

"And where the Hell have you been? You smell like a pig farm."

"Well that's the thing, I ..."

He waved me away and followed the other guys.

"Do us a favour will you, and stay downwind."

And he and the boys went outside and climbed the stairs to the stage in front of the grandstand.

I stood in the shade nearby and watched. It looked like tough going. Nobody could hear a thing up there and I could see them every few minutes reaching back to crank their amps up a few more notches. It was no use.

They were working through their set, trying to be heard over the noise of the Midway and the screams from the Tilt a Whirl. There was also a large Ferris wheel across the park, the other side of the racetrack, and it was doing a brisk business.

Stan was deeply into his big soulful solo bit, a Ray Charles song, and at one point he sprayed a bit of saliva over the mike.

It connected the circuit between his gold front tooth and the whole 10,000 watt sound system. There was a huge flash and bang, as the electricity arced across to his open mouth and he gave an almighty scream, and danced away from the mike, tripped and fell into the drum riser, knocking the whole kit over and sending the drummer off the back of the stage.

The crowd thought it was part of the act, and went nuts.

It was just about then that someone at the top of the Ferris Wheel lost their battle to the nausea incurred by ingesting a days' worth of licorice Twizzlers and cotton candy and caramel coated popcorn, along with corn on the cob and jaw breakers, not to mention semi-raw boiled hot dogs with onions mustard and sauerkraut, all washed down with gallons of Grape Fanta. The air was now filled with a sour purple cloud, which floated downwind towards the stage and the bleachers, and I was treated to the sight of a thousand or so frantic shit kickers screaming and running, desperately trying to shed their skins. The show was over. Stan and the lads quickly unplugged and ran for the shelter of the tin hut.

I left before the contagion floated over my way, and got back out on the road to hitch hike home without saying goodbye. It had been a full day for me.

The band got more gigs, and the pace of the lifestyle started to tell on Stan. He was falling down on his share of the chores, and his marks were suffering. He had always been able to do his homework on the bus, but now he needed that precious 40 minute ride for sleep. The crunch came one morning, when Mum had to keep calling upstairs to hurry him along to get ready for school.

He wasn't responding.

The bus was due in about 15 minutes, and he was still in bed.

Mum wanted us out of the house so she could maybe slip back upstairs for a little nap. She was never a morning person.

She called up again. "Stan! Get up before I come up there with the yard stick!"

She had an inch square hard wood yard stick, with edges like a razor, which she kept in the broom closet in the kitchen, and which was the final arbiter in all disputes in those days.

"Alright! I'm up!"

There was a series of thumps.

He was up. I could hear him walking around in his room.

His door was partly open, and as I went by on my way to the bathroom I pushed it back to say good morning and ask him how the gig went last night. He was still laying in bed.

His eyes were closed, and desperate for a couple more minutes of sleep, he had hung his legs over the side, and was stomping his bare feet back and forth on the floor so it sounded like he was up and getting dressed.

I heard a throat clearing behind me.

I turned. Mum was standing at my shoulder watching, with Excalibur in her hand.

His days with the band were over.

CHAPTER 8

High School

Stan and I were different in many ways, our approaches to music being one of them.

For Stan, music was a means of attracting attention and getting approval from his peers, particularly in his last years of high school, where he looked and felt largely out of place. He began losing his hair early on, and his ego took a terrible beating. He was shy and awkward anyway, but being an oversized and chubby 17 year old with horn rimmed glasses and a comb-over must have been hellish.

If he was at a gathering and was having trouble fitting in, he could always find a quiet corner and pull out the guitar, and within a few minutes he would have a circle of listeners around him, and it became a performance. It was easier than having to come up with something interesting to say to a girl, one on one.

He began attracting a crowd of other would be singers and guitar players and a couple of times a week there would be jam sessions in our living room with as many as a dozen kids with guitars and mandolins, and Stan leading them through most of the songs.

He organized a folk club at school, and performed at most of the school assemblies. His repertoire was at odds with what his music teacher might have wanted. The music teacher was a bitter and angry old man who was himself follically challenged, and wore a rich and luxuriant chestnut brown toupee that crouched on his bare skull like a frightened woodland creature. He wasn't hiding anything from anyone, particularly when he got behind the wheel of his flashy little convertible. As he drove out of the school parking lot, the wind would catch it, and the whole mess he had epoxied to his skull that morning would lift away and hang down below his shoulder blades. If you squinted your eyes, it was like watching a re-enactment of the Zapruder film.

The kids called him Rughead.

He didn't care much for Stan, particularly after an ill-advised wager he had made with him one day in class. The teacher was talking about the various instruments used in the classical orchestra: The bassoon, the violin, the French horn, and so on, and Stan raised his hand and said, "And the guitar.

No, the teacher insisted, there was no guitar in classical music. They went back and forth a bit and then Rughead said that if Stan could prove the guitar was used in classical music and bring in a list of compositions, he would buy him the records.

So Stan wrote in to the local radio station and got back a long and helpful reply with the names of a couple of dozen composers and their works which featured the guitar. It amounted to a lot of LPs. Stan took it in to school, read it out in front of the class, and got 2 weeks of detentions for being insolent.

There was one school concert where Stan got on stage and sang a Leadbelly song.

The opening verse went,

"Black Girl black girl, don't you lie to me,
Tell me where did you sleep last night?
In the pines, in the pines,
where the sun never shines,
And I shivered the whole night through."

He followed that with "Just like Tom Thumb's Blues," by Bob Dylan, and when he got to the line, "They got some hungry women there, and they really make a mess outta you," Rughead darted out onto the stage, clamped his hand over the strings of Stan's guitar and said, "That will be enough Stanley." And gave him 2 weeks of detentions.

Some people shouldn't be allowed near kids.

My own approach to playing was a bit different.

I was awkward and useless in social situations as well, but I didn't feel any need to perform in public. I had enough unwanted attention from the older kids who had decided I was a 'faggot', simply because I played flute, wept when the English teacher read Shakespeare aloud, and wore a three piece denim suit which my mother had made for me, onto which I had sewn large red velvet stars, finished off with a kicky pair of Stan's old white band uniform shoes, now painted silver.

Rather, I kept to my room and simply put my head down and tried to learn what I felt I needed to know. I also had dreams of being a painter, and had an easel set up in my room, with a swivel chair.

When I came to a stopping point on a painting, (I was terrible, by the way,) I would turn the chair around and switch on the tape recorder and lay down the guitar and vocal track for a song, and then begin adding flute and violin overdubs. Music for me was an alternative to dating.

I never took my flute or the violin to school, and there was only one
other kid who shared any interest in playing an instrument.
His name was Ray, and he came from a bad home situation. Both his
parents worked, and both of them drank, and Ray mostly had to raise
his little brother by himself.
So there were many afternoons where Ray and I would sag off classes,
and go back to the loft over the garage where his family lived and baby
sit his kid brother. Ray would put on a Blue Cheer record, or MC5's
"Kick out the Jams," pour himself a shot of gin, and we would try to
play along on Ray's Dad's guitars.
Ray was a piece of work. He was stoned most of the time I knew him.
Pot in the mornings, before classes, and maybe a little mescaline or even
a tab of acid as the day wore on.
Evenings were enlivened by some PCP and then a nightcap of vodka
mixed with the free 2 ounce samples of Nyquil the drug store gave out.
I watched him one day during final exams when he slid out of his
seat and began creeping around the floor, and grabbing at something
I couldn't see, and then getting back into his seat for a while and then
repeating the procedure.
    "What the Hell were you doing in there?" I asked as we left for his
house.
    "Ah man, I dropped a tab of acid before the exam and the letters
were sliding off the page and I had to keep picking them up and putting
them back."
He passed the test too.
One afternoon we were hitch hiking from Saltfleet High School where
we went, to Orchard Park some miles down the road where all the drug
dealers were. Ray was hoping to score some pot.
It was a warm and cloudy day, with a gusty wind, and you knew it was
going to rain soon.
Ray had taken a couple of hits of acid before we set out, and as we stood
at the corner of Grey's Road and Highway 8 he began to describe what
he was seeing.
The cars were apparently all walking on their rear wheels, like in the
old cartoons we'd seen on TV.
Presently a very old and beat up station wagon pulled over to give us a
ride.
It was a wreck, with bald tires and a loud squealing sound coming
from under the hood, as the power assist belts slipped. The back of the
wagon was boarded up, covered in tattered pieces of stained cardboard
and packing tape.

The driver looked no better. He hadn't shaved or washed or changed his clothes in some years. Ordinarily Ray and I wouldn't have got in, as we'd had a few near adventures with similarly grizzled old guys who had a habit of diving off the highway onto a side road and whipping out their wrinkled old peckers as a way of saying hello. However, it had begun to rain pretty heavily, and we were willing to lower our standards, at least in the matter of transport.

My reflexes were better at the moment, and I dove into the front seat, and the derelict driver took Ray around and shoved him into the boarded up back of the car. He slammed the gate shut and got back in, put it in gear and we set off.

Getting soaked with rain had not improved his odour. He smelled like a wet donkey.

We had driven maybe a mile or so, and the rain was coming down pretty hard, when there was a loud yell from Ray in the back.

"OH GOD! PLEASE DON'T! "

There was a loud thump, and the car lurched to the right.

"PLEASE NO! OH GOD, DON'T!"

What the hell was going on?

Once again, Ray yelled.

"NO! LEAVE ME ALONE! AAAAHHHH HELP ME!"

The old guy behind the wheel seemingly hadn't noticed.

I was worried about Ray, but I felt awkward about saying something like, "You'll have to pardon my friend, but he has a head full of Purple Microdot acid."

There was more banging and more screaming. The car was getting more and more difficult to keep on the road, and after a few minutes of frantic yelling and thrashing in the back, I turned to the driver and said, "Uh, maybe you'd better let us out at the next intersection. I think my friend isn't feeling very well."

The guy shrugged, put on the turn signal and pulled over to the side of the highway, and stopped.

He said, "I guess he doesn't like the geese."

We got out and opened the back gate.

Ray came scrambling out, eyes wild, pouring sweat, covered in red welts, and his hair and clothes covered in shit and feathers, and with a half dozen large and angry geese hissing at him and trying to snake their heads out to bite him to death.

Ray and I ate our lunch every day under the bleachers next to the football field, with a handful of other losers. We were a sad and pitiful bunch. One guy secretly kept an iguana in his back pack, and had to have been the only 15 year old boy who ever failed sex education. The others were similarly lacking in any social skills, and we all crouched

under the seats like a group of frightened mice and mostly avoided eye
contact as we unpacked and ate our sandwiches.

Ray didn't have sandwiches. He had a a Dr Pepper with a shot of
vodka, and a couple of packages of Hostess Sno-Balls.

I wonder if they still make them now. Two pink coconut covered cakes
in the shape of a snow ball cut in half. They might have had a cream
filling. I never found out. My lunch was a virtuous bran muffin and a jar
of yogurt I had made myself, pretentious little twerp that I was.

"How can you eat that shit?" I asked Ray one afternoon.

"What shit?"

"That crap. The Sno-Balls."

"They taste great," he said, "and best of all, they feel like a tit."

"What?"

"A tit. They feel just like a girl's tit."

He held out the package and said, "Here, try it."

The other guys all stopped chewing, and looked over at us.

Ray said, "I'm not kidding. Just like a tit." He shook the package at me.
"C'mon."

I didn't touch it. It felt like I would have been crossing some sort of
boundary. It wouldn't have mattered if I had anyway. I had no frame of
reference, nor was I likely to.

But the rest of our little group, a few minutes later was lined up, waiting
their turn to fondle Ray's lunch with a faraway look in their eyes, after
which they returned thoughtfully to their seats. Ray popped his snack
into his mouth, now that it was thoroughly soiled and its reputation
forever ruined, and washed it down with the last of his luncheon
cocktail. He belched and the bell rang for the end of the period.

Next day, every one of those guys under the bleachers had a packet of
Sno-Balls.

I had to find another place to eat my yogurt. None of them had the best
table manners, and it was hard enough to watch some of these guys eat
their food, without there being a session of prolonged foreplay.

The last I heard of Ray was a few years after we all left school. He had
been involved in a police chase in a borrowed car, and he had driven
through a small frame house near our home at a speed estimated
somewhere north of 110 MPH and coming out the other side, continued
on through a field and hit an apple tree. The car was launched into the
air, cartwheeled a hundred yards of so, and after it came to a rest, Ray
got out, completely unscathed, and fell down laughing helplessly as the
cops put the cuffs on him.

CHAPTER 9

Port Dover

It was a beautiful summer night on the shore of Lake Erie.
Stan and a friend were living in a trailer near Port Dover, that year.
Port Dover is now mostly known for the big Friday the13th biker rally,
which happens every Friday the 13th.
No matter what kind of nut freezing, pecker-shriveling weather it
happens to be, the bikers turn up. Thousands of them.
Bikers are tougher.
Bikers are different.
Bikers don't care about the weather.
Bikers are not that smart, actually.
Port Dover was then a grubby little fishing town, still trying to cling to
life, catching ever smaller numbers of the feeble and sickened fish that
lived downstream from the industrial murk that poured into the water
from Ohio.
There was also a small carnival near the shore.
Some rusting rides and a circle of tiny, patient ponies waiting to carry
the next load of snottering midgets around for the parents' cameras.
There were hot dogs, fries, burgers, and the smell of smoke and grease
mingled with pony poop. Paradise
It was also the place where the migrant teen workers would collect
every night, to spend their pay after a long day in the tobacco fields.
Working in the tobacco fields was a rite of passage for a lot kids around
the country back then.
They lived in tents and in barns, and in the huge old mausoleum on
Highway 6 outside of town.
During the day they'd pick the tobacco, then clean up as best they
could, and head for the bright lights and the beach, which was where
we were at the moment.
There was Stan and his buddy Bill Jurgenson, and a couple of other
guitar players, all sitting around the fire.
There was no driftwood on the shore, so we had to burn some old
railroad ties.

There was a lot of bad tarry smoke and it was not so romantic, but hey, it was a fire, and we were okay.

I was better than okay actually.

Stan had carefully poured me a half glass of beer mixed with ginger ale, and said, "There, make that last. You are only getting the one."

I was all of 14 maybe.

But here I was sitting up with the older kids.

There was music. There was firelight.

And there were girls. Lots of girls, all too old for me, but I was sitting right next to one, at that very moment. And she was wearing a bathing suit.

And in that bathing suit were actual breasts. Real live breasts, and, if the legends were true, nipples.

I was one happy little kid.

The breeze was coming in from the south and I could hear the waves as they gently rolled the dead fish onto the shore.

One of the guys was singing an Eric Anderson song, "Thirsty Boots." The others around the fire were chiming in. Guitars, soft voices in harmony, the fire crackling and sputtering as the creosote flared up, it was a beautiful quiet moment.

Suddenly, the idyll was ruined by the sound of about fifty Harley Davidsons as they roared over the hill and spilled down towards us. Oh Jesus.

"Quick. They'll see the fire," someone hissed, and we made frantic efforts to douse the flames, but by now the railroad ties were fully ablaze, and we were clearly visible in the ugly smoky light.

Jesus, what were we going to do?

We had heard stories of what bikers did to young and innocent girls. We'd seen the movies.

More to the point, I had heard stories of what bikers did to young and innocent boys with cute Prince Valiant haircuts.

I had dreamed of someday having a serious romantic relationship, but not like this.

The bikes did a half-circle pincer movement to cut off our escape. Our only way out now was to run into the filthy stinking lake, and that wasn't going to happen, not even to avoid what was coming.

I wondered, what would my new biker boyfriend would call me? Would it be a cute name?

There was no escape. We were doomed.

Stan was carefully putting away his guitar, and even more carefully strapping his large chrome Hamilton guitar capo over his fist, like brass knuckles, preparing to sell our lives dearly.

The bikers were assembling in the darkness away from the fire light, milling ominously about and moving in for the kill.

They were just a darker shadow against the black night.

Stan reached out to make sure where his girlfriend was. "Stay near me. If it gets bad, run for town."

I could hear whimpering in the darkness, an annoying high pitched keening sound.

Stan said, "Garnet, shut the fuck up."

The bikers were coming closer.

I could hear the jingle of the chains, and the dull clonk of the souvenir human skulls they had around their waists.

Closer…closer.

They were still advancing.

Ah shit, we were all going to die.

They stopped for a moment, still just outside of the ring of fire light.

Then the leader stepped forward into the flickering glow.

He was terrifying, covered in matted hair and dark blue smeary prison tattoos, with chains and filthy stinking leather made from the skins of deadly feral hogs he had no doubt killed with his bare hands.

He looked at Stan, who was presumably our leader, as he was the biggest of us.

There was a long silence.

The fire was still hissing and giving off foul-smelling steam from where some of us had frantically pissed on it.

Then the leader of the bikers spoke.

He said, (and I swear, this is the truth,) "Can you play Michael Row the Boat Ashore?"

CHAPTER 10

Rubbers

It was later that summer, after the big kumbaya moment with the bikers that Stan came home one afternoon with a new girl, whom he'd met in Port Dover.

Damned if I can remember her name, but she was pretty-ish with short dark hair, and older than Stan by some years.

There was a mean spirited saying back in those days which ran, "If you can't get a girl, get a nurse," which I took to mean that nurses were "easy." I don't know that they were "easy" or whether they were so used to the obscene processes of the human body that nothing much could disgust or repel them. This new love was in fact a nurse, and Stan had been getting some advanced anatomy lessons. The steam was rising out of his pants.

Stan was obviously head over heels with her, and Mom's hackles and radar immediately went up.

The happy couple came in, lit up cigarettes, and Stan, with his new love perched on his lap said, "Can you guys stand to hear some good news?"

Mum visibly stiffened in her chair, and said cautiously, "Okay. Shoot."

"We're getting married."

I don't recall Dad making any immediate comment, but Mum's response was to pick up her tobacco and rolling papers, and very carefully and calmly set about to rolling a smoke.

She normally could turn one out in about 6 seconds, but this one seemed to be needing a lot more attention.

She finished it and picked off the ends, and lit it, took a deep drag, and blew the smoke up to the ceiling and then, carefully pinching a bit of tobacco off her lip, looked up said "Any particular reason?"

I bolted out the door and ran over to the neighbours' house.

This was too good not to share.

Stan's friend Pat was at the kitchen table when I burst in the door.

"Stan's getting MARRIED!"

She said nothing, but stood up and grabbed her cigarettes and lighter,

opened the fridge and snagged a bottle of beer, and ran out the door, across the lawn, and into our house.
I followed close behind.
Pat had already grabbed a chair, opened the beer and lit up by the time I arrived.

"What the fuck do you think you're doing?" She was coughing and laughing.
Pat was the only person who could get away with the "F" word in Mum's presence.

"We're in love." Stan said, a bit put out I think, by this lack of support from his old friend.

"Love! You're not in love." Pat turned to my mother, "He's just getting his ashes hauled!"
She looked back at Stan, "You didn't knock her up did you, you stupid bastard?" Thereby giving voice to Mum's worst fears.
No they weren't pregnant, just deeply in love.
The upshot of the whole drama was that yes, Stan was in fact of legal age to get married, and was free do so, but would be leaving the house not only without the parents blessing on the union, but without anything but the clothes on his back.

Dad said, "You can take that guitar when you've paid back the loan on it."

"What!"
Oh dear.
This put things in a different light.
The two young lovers left pretty soon after that.
Mum didn't invite the girl to stay for dinner, and I don't recall that we ever saw her again.

It was around this time that our cousin Steve began visiting regularly, and although he was only a year or two older than Stan, he was miles ahead in worldly experience, having joined the Navy at an early age. He had seen the world, or at least the soft white interesting bits that haunted our dreams, and our parents, realizing that Stan was now of an ardent and developing nature, decided to enlist Steve's aid in trying to manage the monster that had been let out of the cage.
No one wants to talk with their kids about sex.
Actually, Mum was more than willing to have a go at it, but that would have been too weird and uncomfortable. She had a tendency in all things, to get bogged down in needless detail, and both Stan and I would have wound up in a monastery for the rest of our lives if she had attempted to have "The Talk" with us.
And Dad was painfully shy about the whole subject.

The sum total of his Fatherly advice to me was over the phone once
from Sault Ste Marie, where he was working, where he counseled me
that in the unlikely event that I ever found myself in bed with a girl,
that it would be best if I "try to ejaculate over the side of the bed."
Grateful for that wisdom Dad. Without it I wouldn't be here myself.
At any rate, the folks held a committee meeting with Steve.

I don't know if Steve ever actually sat down with Stan and had a frank
talk about a gentleman's responsibilities regarding contraception. I do
know that one day after Steve left to get back to his ship, a large box of
Navy Issue "condoms, sailors, for the use of," had appeared on Stan's
dresser.

By large box, I mean a full gross. 144 rubbers, all rolled up and wrapped
in a little cardboard sleeve with a flap, looking like a small envelope,
hence the old name "French Letter," I guess.

A gross. Was this what they issued for weekend leave? No wonder
Steve was so thin.

My friends and I enthusiastically broke into the box, and began to
examine the rubbers.

They were not the sort of boutique condom one finds today, thin and
sleek, "ribbed for her pleasure", lubricated and sealed in bright festive
looking foil, like a party favour.

These were serious government-issue, and built to last under the
wear and tear of difficult and dangerous battlefield conditions. They
were ugly and evil smelling, and a pale translucent yellow, like an old
person's toenails.

No special lubricant, just a thick dusting of what might have been corn
starch or talcum powder, to keep them pliable, and which probably did
just that back when they were made in preparation for the Gallipoli
landings. But by now the talcum had over the years changed from a
powder to a nasty mixture of grit and small pebbles like drywall dust,
and the condom was not even remotely something one would want to
place on the part of the body where resided so many sensitive nerve
endings, not to mention the greater part of the adolescent male brain.
I was the first to put one to use.

I raced down the hall to the bathroom, and rolled one over the bath
spout, and turned on the water. In minutes, it changed from an
ugly wrinkled sausage casing to an enormous and frightening pale
ectoplasm that lay quivering and undulating in the tub.

By the time I got the water shut off, it was over the sides of the tub, and
looked like one of those poor creatures one sees now on reality shows
who have to have a wall knocked out of their single wide trailer, so the
fire crew can load them out to be taken to see Richard Simmons.

I poked cautiously at it with my finger. I was able to push in maybe a foot and there was no sign of it breaking. I made a fist and smacked it lightly in the mid-section. Nothing. I moved closer and did a quick left right left combination. Still nothing.

I tested it further, and poked it repeatedly with the sharp tail on the end of my pocket comb.

It was impervious.

Jesus.

My friend handed me my mother's sewing scissors and said, "Try it again," I jabbed the scissors into it and there was a sharp bang and the monster disappeared, and about 20 gallons of water spilled onto the floor, which we hurriedly cleaned up, while the rest went down the drain.

Whatever happened, no one was going to pregnant with these things. They had probably been used as life preservers during the Battle of the Atlantic.

The box disappeared into Stan's personal effects on his next visit home, but not before my friends and I had snagged a handful each, and, as was the custom, placed them ostentatiously in the change purses in our wallets, where they soon wore the much coveted tell-tale ring on the pockets of our jeans, which announced to the world that we were a dangerous and virile bunch of 13 year olds, and ready for action at a moment's notice.

A couple of years later, Stan and I were having a coffee together in the kitchen on Maitland Street, in London.

"Remember those rubbers that Stevie brought us a few years ago?"

"Yeah, what about them?

"Well, have you ever tried using one?

I had only conducted that one experiment regarding Fluid Dynamics versus Tensile Strength, but didn't want to show my inexperience.

"Yeah, I tried them out, have you?

"Yeah. Jesus. I brought a girl over from the York Hotel a couple of nights ago, and you know, one thing led to another, and she asked me if I had any protection. So I remembered those Navy rubbers, and got the box out of my closet, and tried to skin one on.

Ouch, I thought.

"And?

"Well, I'm not built like a bull or anything but they're really tight, and thick, and it took me ages. And once I got the damned thing on, it immediately started choking off the blood supply, and I've suddenly got this purple eggplant flopping around in front of me, and the girl is killing herself laughing, and I'm panicking, and the pain is like you can't imagine, and I'm running around the room looking for my buck knife."

"Aw Jesus. Not a knife."

"And the thing keeps on swelling and the pain is killing me, and now I'm terrified, thinking about gangrene. And I finally run naked down the hall to the bathroom and start rummaging frantically through the waste basket trying to find a used razor blade..."

"NO! NOT A FUCKING RAZOR BLADE!" I shouted.

"...and I start trying to hack at the ring at the base of the damned thing, but I can't see it now, my dick is so swollen around it. I'm yelling in pain, and the damned girl is still down the hall laughing her fool head off. And I'm standing there, stark naked in front of the sink, slashing and hacking, and I was finally able to pull the ring away and cut through it, and get the damned thing peeled off, and I look up, and Mike and Tim and their girlfriends were all standing in the doorway, watching."

"Jesus. What did they say?"

"Oh, you know Mike. He just said, "Why are you trying to cut your penis off Stanley? You might want to use it someday."

"Bastard."

CHAPTER 11

Bill Powell

Stan used to tell the story of his first paid solo gig.

"I was 15 years old and played all night for ten bucks and a bottle of wine."

The story grew a bit in the telling.

What actually happened was that Dad took Stan down to the Ebony Knight Coffee House, which was run by Bill Powell, and Stan did three songs.

Dad lurked in the back of the club to make sure Stan was able to leave without being importuned by a drug addict, or some horny sailor, or one of those Beatniks with their jazz cigarettes. After Stan's set they packed up, and Dad drove them home in the pick-up, and Stan went to bed. He had school in the morning.

There was no wine.

And there was definitely no ten bucks. Not in any club Bill ran.

I don't know how he met Bill Powell, but in those days, it was kind of inevitable.

If you were involved in the arts, and were working under the radar of anyone who cared, you were going to meet Bill. He was the son of a local politician, Bill Powell Senior, and was evidently intent on breaking his parents' hearts by being a Beatnik artist bum.

He's a big guy, about 6' 4", and solid with it.

He hasn't changed much over the years, thick reddish brown hair, a beard, and a cigarette permanently attached to his lower lip, and a shirt that he has never learned how to button.

He lived in the top floor of the Anne Foster Building, a 6 story condemned wreck, across from Gore Park in Hamilton, right downtown.

His studio was a huge open space, with big floor to ceiling windows facing North, and a collection of broken down furniture, and stacks of paintings, some finished, and others in progress.

There was a steady stream of musicians, sculptors, painters, actors, some barely getting by, and some not at all, and medical students and nurses, and drag queens, and university students who passed through the door.

You never knew what sort of scene you were going to walk into. This was what passed for the Twi-light demi-Monde in Hamilton.

A rabble of misfits and rebel-wannabes, and unemployed drifters, who were always on the scrounge, trying to get something happening using other people's money. And yet it never felt dangerous or unwholesome. Bill, of course, was the son of the future Mayor, and was smart enough, and kind and respectful enough, to not want to embarrass his Dad with any sort of scandal. So was all somehow largely innocent, at least what I was allowed to see of it.

Drugs were verboten, and I think there was a tight rein on any predatory behaviour.

This, although grizzled and world weary bohemian perverts mingled freely with dewy eyed and innocent flowers like myself who were looking for something beautiful and grand and mysterious and above all, artistic and meaningful within those walls. I never heard of anyone being molested, not unwillingly, anyway.

Throughout all of this, the daily and nightly parade of the lunatic fringe, Bill sat at his easel, toying with his brushes, moving colours around on the canvas, and watching, his head tilted, eyes half-closed against the cigarette smoke, while some gullible nurse would be stretched out shivering on the sagging day bed, having been tricked once again, dammit, into posing nude.

The pipes would be banging and the pigeons fluttering at the window, with snow drifting outside. You would hear the clank and whir of the elevator as it made its slow progress up to the sixth floor, and the door would open, and some new drama would burst into the room...

A couple of drag queens having a loud and very public fight.

A doctor between shifts at St. Joseph's Hospital talking about someone in Emergency with a new and even more unlikely explanation as to how some foreign object had ended up lodged in his rectum.

"A flashlight, for Chrissake. A fucking flashlight jammed up his ass, and he says he has no idea how it might have got up there. Jesus. I ask you. Last week it was a Barbie Doll. We managed to remove the doll okay, but it took ages to fish out all the damned accessories."

A failed part time actress having a swooning hissy-fit over the venality of the local little theatre director.

"I don't care. I am NOT going to play the part of the mother. I'm not that goddamned old. He can take his new little tramp girlfriend and go fuck himself."

Another guy coming in with valuable foreign crafts and trinkets he had purchased from non-English speaking sailors down at the dockyards, using worthless Canadian Tire money as currency.

Stan rushing in with an idea for a new song, and hurrying over to a corner to scribble it down. Someone else sauntering in with an overcoat filled with much needed shop-lifted groceries.

It was great. Dinner and a show.

Stan recalled how he and Bill one evening started picking up the now tame pigeons that lived on the window sill, and brushing glitter and powdered paint onto their wings. They ended up with a gaudy flock of feathered drag queens, which were then released to fly down to the street and importune passersby for bread crumbs.

"You could see the drunks walking along, suddenly being confronted by this little acid hallucination." he said. "They'd scream and run to the other side of the street.

It was Bill who gave Stan some basic skills to survive in the city with no money.

The court house was where you could get the best cigarettes. You would hang around the halls, waiting for a recess, and inevitably the jury would get called back in, just after they had lit their second smoke. The sand-filled ashtrays could then be harvested, and a day's worth of almost new cigarettes were yours for the taking.

There was also "ketchup soup." You would go to the downtown MacDonald's, and grab up all the little packets of ketchup. Boil some water, add some dry pasta, and then the contents of the packets, and voila, there was dinner.

Bill was and is, enormously kind, and was capable of extraordinary generosity, and yet had the predatory instincts of a Carney, and the sharp eye of the born con man. He could sell pretty much anything to anyone, and in time was to become one of the prime movers and shakers on the local Arts scene. And he was founder of the Festival of Friends, by means of his ability to impress local council with his vision, and his knack for getting governments and businesses to throw money at him.

He has many friends, and many on the other side too.

Very early on in my nascent career, I realized just what a polarizing guy he could be.

I joined the Musician's Union.

I was maybe 16 or so, and this was a proud moment for me. We came from a staunchly loyal union family.

I paid my entry fee, held up my hand and took the oath, and then the union secretary gave us our indoctrination speech.

He was a "Union" guy straight out of an Elia Kazan movie. He was heavy set, with greasy slicked back hair, and a single enormous eyebrow. He wore an ill-fitting and shiny suit speckled with dandruff, and had badly pock-marked skin. He looked more like a guy who would kneecap you for not paying a loan on time than a sensitive musician.

"Now, listen up. Listen to me. You guys are now officially all Union Musicians now. Dat means you gotta responsibility to NEVER, EVER, play for less than Union scale. I mean it. Not ever, not for whatever reason. Some guy comes up to you and tries to offer you less than Scale, or he tries to gyp you outta what's rightfully yours, you call me immediately. I'll take care of that guy PDQ. Y'unnerstan'? Never."
We understood. But...
I raised my hand, "Uh, excuse me, uh, yeah, but like, what if you have a friend who has a coffeehouse or something like that, and he wants to give you a gig, and he can't pay you, but it's good exposure, or maybe he wants you to do a benefit for the club, so it can keep on going and he'll be able to hire you in the future...and ...uh..."
I stopped.
The Union guy was starting to swell visibly, and his face was clouding over.
He wheeled around, and put his finger about an inch from my nose.

"Don't ever, EVER let me hear that you bin talkin' to Bill Powell, ever again. You hear me? I'm SERIOUS. You stay the hell away from him and all his Beatnik faggot buddies, or I'll kick your ass from here to breakfast. You hear me? Now get the hell outta here, all a ya."
I told Bill about it later that day, and he airily waved away my concerns.

"Don't worry about him. The Union knows I'm kind of a special case. "
And he was, and he is.

Inevitably, it was partly because of Bill that I did my first paid gig. I had played a show with Stan at the local Catholic High School that spring, but as Stan was flipping me a few dollars out of his own pocket, it didn't really count. Our act was one of a dozen or so that day, and at one point the Mother Superior came up to the stage, and asked if we knew how to play Tom Lehrer's "Vatican Rag."
Well of course we did.
There was another gig, which involved walking around downtown Hamilton, playing as we went along, "like Wandering Minstrels," as Bill put it. But there was no money. We were doing it to add colour to the cityscape, and for the exposure, of course.
That's right. The "exposure."
The highlight for me was the little boy who came up and asked if we could play the theme song to the TV show, "Batman."

Stan and I looked at each other. He shrugged. "What key?" he said.
Bill and his partner Lynne had set up a tent theatre at Confederation
Park, on the shore of Lake Ontario, east of Hamilton.
There was a cluster of camping trailers and pup tents surrounding the
Big Top, where the shows took place. It was a real live circus tent, with a
stage, a backstage crowded with props and smelly unwashed costumes
on hangers, boxes of ratty wigs, and out in the house about a hundred
threadbare seats. The director was a man we only knew as John Dee, a
hyperactive little guy with a goatee, a comb-over, and an ascot.
Stan had got hired on, likely through his connection with Bill, and they
put on the usual light theatre fare that goes on all over the country in
little community theatres everywhere.
They did "Charlie's Aunt," with Stan playing the part of an elderly
English Army Major. They did "Come Blow Your Horn." Stan played
the lead in that one, the same role that Frank Sinatra had in the movie.
There were all the usual clichéd characters roaming about the place.
There were fresh faced and under dressed ingénues, and older,
predatory heavy eyed ex- leading ladies, now reduced to "character
roles," and who tried to bolster their self-esteem by trolling the
younger male cast members and having the odd quick knee trembler in
the dressing rooms between acts. Nothing like a quick rattle to settle the
nerves before your big soliloquy.
There were nervous high strung young men who were trying to deal
with the realization that their lifestyle was never going to be acceptable
in the main stream. "Nature's Bachelors," as my grandmother called
them.
There were old heavy-set male actors with whiskey breath, and
smoker's cough; "Where's the stage, what's the play?" types, who were
on their last go round.
One of them actually did make the big exit, on stage one night.
He had a massive coronary and hit the deck, dead as a mackerel.
Someone actually had to make the announcement, "Is there a Doctor
in the house?" so they could convincingly swarm around his body and
pretend to work on him while they loaded him onto an ambulance, so
no one's night out at the show would be spoiled.
John Dee finished out the evening reading the actor's lines from the
script after the gurney had been wheeled off the stage.
One night during a thunderstorm, lightning hit the tent and a huge
flash exploded down the center pole of the tent, and set fire to the
stage. It was quickly extinguished, and they carried on as if nothing
happened.
The show had to go on.
There were any number of hangers-on, like myself, and I was there

nearly every night. I loved the whole thing, not enough that I ever wanted to try it myself, but it was strange and exciting, and the potential for real disaster and drama, both on and off stage was like heroin to me. I kept going back for more.

I was playing flute back in those days, and carried it with me everywhere.

It wasn't just that I needed the practice, but I had some vague idea that girls would be attracted to a musician, so I was always off under a tree, trying to work out something by Yusef Lateef, or Roland Kirk or Jethro Tull.

Turns out girls liked guys with guitars.

Flute was "kinda faggy" apparently.

Actually, girls didn't even care that much for guys with guitars, so far as I could tell.

Girls seemed to like guys with cars and jobs, and haircuts, and the ability to sustain a conversation past muttering "hello" into one's armpit.

I had none of those things.

And so, the summer wore on, and someone noticed Stan and me under a willow tree one day, playing "Locomotive Breath," by Jethro Tull.

John Dee thought it might be a nice touch to end the night with a short concert.

Stan would go up first, alone, and work through his best repertoire of originals, and then launch into his big performance piece, which was a showy and over the top version of St. James' Infirmary Blues.

Then he'd invite me up and we finish off with something lighter.

I was scared to death but I loved it.

One night, as things were being packed up for the evening, Mr. Dee stopped me in the passageway behind the stage.

Stan and I had just finished our little show at the end of the night. I had helped him wipe off his grease paint with a much used and filthy towel, and now I was hurrying out to where I could hear yelling and swearing. One of the many fleeting off-stage romances was coming to a noisy and messy end in the parking lot, and I wanted to see how it all concluded. Mr. Dee grabbed me as I hurried along, and said, "Here. You've been a big help around here lately," and gave me ten bucks.

In retrospect, it was probably more a gesture towards all the fetching and carrying I had been doing these past weeks, but I took it to mean that I was getting paid for playing.

I went outside and watched as one of the male actors stormed off to the parking lot and jumped into his car and left hot smoking divots of black rubber behind him as he peeled away.

The fight between him and his now ex-girlfriend had drawn a good

crowd, and there was a smattering of applause, and calls for an
encore as we listened to him wind it up through the gears out towards
Centennial Parkway.

Someone handed me a cold beer, and I took it. I was way too young to
drink legally. I had tasted beer before, sipping from my Dad's bottle as
a kid, but this was the first time I had ever had an actual drink, and as
that tiny amount of alcohol entered my system, I suddenly felt better
than I had ever felt in my life. Wow.

I walked over to a picnic table and lay down on top of it. The stars were
shining dimly through the industrial haze over the city. I finished the
last of the beer. This stuff was wonderful. No wonder it was so popular.

I was relaxed.

I was happy.

I had just played a gig, and I had actually been paid for it.

And I was drunk.

I was a Professional.

CHAPTER 12

Jackie Washington

It was also through Bill Powell that I met Jackie Washington.
Old Jackie is gone now. We lost him about two years ago, as I write this.
How to begin with him?
He was possibly the kindest and gentlest man I have ever met.
He didn't seem to be able to hate, even after all the terrible things that
happened to him as a black man growing up in Canada before the War.
He came from a large family in the North end of Hamilton. They were
all musical, and Jack was to see the last of the old vaudeville players, as
he and his brothers demonstrated yo-yos in between sets at the Capitol
Theatre.
He met everyone, and remembered everything.
He had a working repertoire of around 2000 songs, most of which
he kept in his head. Songs from the great American songbook...The
Gershwin's, Duke Ellington, and Hoagy Carmichael.
All the great black bandleaders and musicians came through Hamilton
in those days. They weren't allowed to stay in any hotels, so they would
be billeted with the local black families. Jackie met them all, and got to
play with them. He told me once of how Duke Ellington came to play
the Burlington Golf and Country Club, and of course no one in the
black community was allowed in to see them, as the club was restricted.
No blacks allowed.
But it was an open air gig, and the trees surrounding the golf club were
soon full of hundreds of black people, standing in the branches in the
darkness, listening quietly to their hero, as the whites-only audience
glided around the dance floor.
Jack worked at the race tracks at Woodbine and Fort Erie as a hot
walker, one of the lowest jobs at the track. He made extra cash
handicapping the races. He had a reputation for picking winners, and
would get swarmed by the rich punters on race day, looking for a hot
tip.
He worked as a porter on the CPR, and had a shoe shine stand.
All those years he played with his brothers and as a solo. And it was

only around the time of the first Folk boom that he started to make regular money as a musician, doing openers for people like Gordon Lightfoot at the Riverboat, and other clubs around the province. By then he was a middle aged man.

I started seeing him at Bill Powell's club "Knight II" on Augusta Street in Hamilton when I was about 14 or 15. Bill was managing Jack back then, and he played the club a lot. He wasn't like the other people I was seeing on stage then. He wasn't the sensitive moody introvert we all modeled ourselves on. He was sweet and funny and spent much of the time on stage joking with the audience and telling stories. It wasn't a performance so much as a celebration.

One of his quirks was that he only played the black keys on the piano. It made life difficult for a wannabe like myself, trying to play along with him, but he was endlessly patient, and when he saw me struggling he'd stop and launch into another story.

His left hand on the guitar was a miracle of nature. He could play a different inversion of a chord with every down stroke. I ran into Gamble Rogers, years later, at the Owen Sound festival. He was sitting on a bench, staring into space and looking transfixed, or as if someone had struck him on the head with a brick.

I went over and touched him on the shoulder.

"You okay?"

He shook his head, re-focused his eyes and came to the surface. "Oh I'm better than okay. I've just been to Church. I just got back from school."

"Huh?"

"I just spent an hour watching Jackie Washington's hands on the guitar. That man is a gift from God. I have never seen anything like it. I feel so grateful that I have been allowed to hear him. Just humbled and grateful."

He stood up, took hold of his guitar case, gestured with it, and said,

"I'm going to do some more work with this thing," and walked away.

Gamble was a pretty damned flashy guitar player himself, a fiery and terrifying finger picker, like Doc Watson on crystal meth. It felt great that a total stranger, and someone as good as Gamble recognized it too, that he could see just how wonderful Jack was.

Jackie was not just an extraordinary guitar player. When he sang, his vocal phrasing reminded me of Billie Holiday.

When he met you, he would ask when your birthday was, and then file it in the back of his brain.

The morning of your birthday, he would call and wish you the best, and just laugh it off when asked how he did it.

"I just remember, that's all."

Jackie Washington

We were up at the Northern Lights Festival in Sudbury. It was the year Stan wrote "Barrett's Privateers" at an after-hours session. There was a nice buffet laid on for the musicians backstage, with lots of salads and fresh fruit. We had waded in, and were making pigs of ourselves. Our diets were bad enough in those days that the danger of scurvy couldn't be ruled out.

So we were gobbling down as much as we could, and stuffing our pockets with bananas and nectarines. It occurred to me that this might set up unfortunate and unrealistic expectations among members of our audience, but screw it, I was hungry. Jackie was next to me, nibbling on some grapes and holding forth like the royalty he was.

He had the best stories, and we all tended to cluster around him whenever we had the chance.

I stood up to get some more watermelon, and Jackie caught my arm, and said in a low voice, "Garnet, could you get me a piece of that while you're there?"

"Sure Jack."

I brought back a plate of watermelon, and set it in front of him.

"There you go."

"Thanks. I love to eat it," and then he leaned forward and looked around to make sure no one was listening. "I just hate to be seen carrying it." And he fell over laughing.

He and I were sharing digs at the student detention centre on the campus where the festival took place.

I came in pretty late that night, and there was Jack, in Jockey shorts and a tee shirt, and white tube socks. There was a line of young women stretching out of the room into the hallway. They were all holding notebooks and pencils, and Jack was standing on his bed signing autographs.

I've no idea what he had been doing before I arrived, but it had been a big hit.

I found a really spectacular old Gibson guitar in a music store in the east end of Hamilton one day maybe 20 years ago. It was a massive electric arch top, a model ES-300, the Jayne Mansfield of the guitar world. I had no use for such an instrument. It is suitable mostly for jazz or maybe rockabilly music, but it called to me simply for the same reasons that Jayne Mansfield might call to a man of her generation. It was blonde and spectacular, with exaggerated curves, and merely being seen in its company gave one an enhanced status even if you couldn't live up to it. So I bought it and kept it, and felt vaguely guilty about having something so lovely when it wasn't getting the attention and respect it deserved.

Then one day I saw a Sing Out! Magazine article about Jackie, and in

90

it there was a picture of him from 1952 holding that very guitar. It is an extremely rare model, with only a handful made, particularly in the blonde finish, and the chances of there being two of them in the same town were very small.

I took it to a show that Jackie and I were sharing one night and pulled it from its case.

"Recognize this Jack?"

"My Gibson girl!"

I handed it to him and he strummed it briefly and then turned to Gail, and said, "I'm am so happy to have this back in my hands again, I am going to play a special private concert for you."

And for the next hour or so he looked right into her eyes while he played Gershwin songs and Cole Porter tunes for her.

Magic.

In the last years of his life, he was busier than ever. Mose Scarlett and Ken Whitely began recording and touring with Jack, and he was having a great time, traveling around the country in comfort, and playing to big audiences.

Other good things happened too.

He received an honourary doctorate from McMaster University.

He was in a wheelchair by this time but he insisted on standing up and walking ever so slowly across the stage in his cap and gown to receive it, his jaw set with pride.

The clueless stuffed shirt academic who got his award after Jack referred to him in his own acceptance speech as "Jackie Robinson."

Gail and I were in the audience, pissed off and embarrassed but when I looked over at Jack, he was once again leaning over, laughing and wiping his eyes.

He had always been too heavy, and diabetes was making things difficult. He lost a leg to it.

Gail and I went to visit him in hospital, the day after the surgery. He was sitting up in bed, and telling jokes. You could hear his laugh all the way down the hall.

"How are you doing Jack?"

"Oh I'm just swell. I'm getting fitted for a new leg at the end of the week."

He took my arm and pulled me in to whisper. "I'm getting a white leg. They offered me a black one, but I said no. I always wanted to have a white leg. There were a lot of places that I used to get thrown out of. At least now I can get a foot in the door."

Gamble had it right. He was a gift from God.

CHAPTER 13

Trent University

After his summer at the tent theatre it became evident that Stan's post-secondary education had come to naught. He'd taken a shot at the school of dentistry at McMaster, but his aim was off.

He'd spent most of that year in the student union building, playing euchre, and the rest of the time playing guitar, and helping with the folk club.

He did some articles for the student paper, including an exclusive interview done backstage with Gordon Lightfoot.

I'd love to have that one back.

It would have been something of a curiosity piece, but it got lost somewhere over the years.

He played a few gigs at the Ebony Knight, and did an opener for a strange double bill of Doug Henning and Murray McLaughlin at McMaster. I still have the ticket stub somewhere. It was 2 bucks to get in.

In the end he just had to bail on school, and Dad with characteristic brevity put an ad in the paper.

"For sale: Full set of 1st year dentistry textbooks. NEVER USED."

He spent some time treading water, and worked at odd jobs, here and there.

He worked at K Mart for a few weeks as a clerk, and also, as the announcer who called, "Attention, K Mart shoppers" over the intercom, and alerted people to the specials.

The manager didn't like it when he tried to improvise and tell jokes.

There was a brief time when he went door to door as a Filter Queen vacuum salesman.

That didn't work either. He sold exactly one machine,

It still works.

He was a Fuller Brush salesman for a couple of weeks.

There was one scheme, briefly, where he was going to be the Ringmaster

in a small circus, wearing an actual by God, cape and top hat.
It wasn't what he wanted, but he would get to sing a song or two with
the house band, mostly Frank Sinatra stuff and Johnny Mathis.
It was sort of show business, but nothing ever came of that.
He spent a few weeks with another theatre group in Montreal, but his
French was not up to being on stage. He mostly played some incidental
music and as he told us in a letter home, he was learning how to read
music for guitar. The job paid nothing though, and he had to bail.
He was running out of options.
Work was hard to find.
He was desperate.
Something had to be done.
He got another student loan, and he went back to school.

Trent University is in Peterborough Ontario
I think at the time it was a small liberal arts sort of place. Stan described
it as less of a school and more of a spa resort on the Ottonabee River.
He was taking Sociology, which was the fastest route there was to a
degree and a job back then, without having to actually do any work.
He settled into residence, piled his books in a corner, and started
seeking out the other guitar players.
It was at Trent that Stan met Nigel Russell.
Nigel was the best guitar player we had yet met.
He had assimilated a lot of the Doc Watson guitar style, and could sing
most of the songs from the first Tom Rush albums, "No Regrets" and
"Galveston Flood," and other stuff like that.
He had sort of an act, and the two of them threw in their lots to form a
duo.
Nigel had it in him to be charming enough, but he was a bit of a liability
as a sideman.
Soap and water to him were in his words, a "bourgeois affectation." He
must have bathed occasionally, or he would have begun to decompose.
But it was a rare event.
The house had to be fumigated and the sofa cushions and the bed
clothes all had to be washed or burned whenever he and Stan visited
home.
The first time he and Stan came to stay for a weekend, he drifted in
behind Stan, a curly haired guy with a raffish mustache and a cigarette,
looking suitably world weary, and sporting a sweatshirt that said "69...
Breakfast of Champions."
It fell to Stan to try to explain to our Mum what that meant.
They did click as an act though, and began to hitch hike around the
province and into Quebec playing the small clubs.

Stan was using his friend Bill Jurgenson's Gibson J-45 at the time,
having no professional grade guitar of his own.
It being Bill's precious instrument, and a "real" guitar, Stan was
naturally protective of it.
Stan told me of standing under an overpass on the 401 highway one
trip, trying to catch a ride to Montreal. He was covered in ice and sleet
and frozen muddy splatter from the trucks, shivering, teeth chattering,
with his winter coat tightly wrapped around the guitar case.

After a couple of months it finally became evident that the world of
academe was going to have to rub along without either Stan or Nigel.
They had yet to complete a course, or attend a class, or actually do
much of anything beyond smoke dope and drink beer, and try to figure
out how Mississippi John Hurt played that solo in "Candyman."
That, and bird dog the girls.
Nigel was working his charms on a succession of gullible English
majors who either had no sense of smell, or sufficiently low standards
that they were willing to give him a tumble before, and breakfast
afterwards. Stan had a serious girlfriend at the time, a quiet and sweet-
faced girl named Gillian, who lived with her folks back in Hamilton.
It was a big deal for him, and he wrote a lot of bad and turgid love
songs for her.
I am still in touch with her brother occasionally, and he recently told me
that in spite of Stan being a largely unemployed, wastrel fuck-up, their
family loved him for his kindness, and the sweet attention he paid to
their grandmother, even hitchhiking over to their house and visiting her
when Gillian wasn't around.
It was through Gillian that he began to get seriously involved with
the Anglican Church, the two of them having met, I think at Camp
Canterbury Hills, in Ancaster.
She was a camp counselor, and Stan spent a summer there as a cook.
He went so far as to get baptized and confirmed in the High Anglican
Church when he was about 20 or so. It was a serious and considered
move for him.
We'd had no religious upbringing of any kind, and while he didn't talk
about it much around me, Christianity was to remain a big part of his
life for a while anyway.

Stan and Gillian used to take me along on dates, for no reason that I
could discern, other than that they were both kind people, and I was a
confused and lonely misfit kid.
We three went to a dance at McMaster University one night.
A Caribbean steel drum band was playing, and I was thunderstruck at

what a good dancer Stan was.
Of course I had no real frame of reference beyond old Gene Kelly and
Fred Astaire movies.
But to my eyes Stan was light and graceful, and absolutely confident,
particularly for a guy who looked like a water buffalo in polyester
slacks and desert boots.
The band was playing "Spanish Eyes" as a samba, and he swung and
floated Gillian around the room like she was a thistledown, all the time
wearing a look of complete bliss.
I couldn't believe it.

CHAPTER 14

Stan and Nigel

His tenure at Trent was coming to an end.

He had washed out of most of his courses, and the residence really didn't fit his needs anymore.

He and Nigel needed a place to rehearse, and the guys who were actually trying to do some work resented the noise. And so they moved out, into a tiny ugly run down two bedroom shack covered in red insul-brick.

It was a couple of miles out of town, in Millbrook.

The car situation was dire.

They couldn't even walk to a store for groceries, or at least being pudgy out of shape guys they were unwilling. Once again, Dad opened his wallet, and they bought a clapped out grey VW Beetle which they christened "the Pearl." There was some sort of complex paper agreement whereby Dad retained ownership of the car until the loan was paid, but for Stan and particularly Nigel, that was just a formality. The loan was never re-paid, and later, when the duo split up, the Beetle somehow morphed into a Triumph motorcycle for Nigel.

Dad never saw a cent.

And so they worked on their act.

Stan naturally assumed the role of front man.

Nigel was the quiet sideman, mostly, although he was given to the occasional quiet cutting comment, when Stan's flights of rhetoric got to be too much on stage.

But it was getting to be a relatively polished act, and Stan's songs were starting to improve.

It was around this time that he wrote his first really good one, called "Turnaround," a wistful and perfect little gem about one half of a couple moving on while the other half is left behind.

For the rest of the songs he was still trying to find his style.

It was mostly a pastiche of all sorts of influences.

There was Lightfoot, of course. You couldn't have aspirations to be a musician in Canada and not be influenced by his writing and singing

96

and his sound. Nigel as a sideman was also heavily influenced by Red
Shea, the guitar player in Lightfoot's peerless trio.
There was a bit of early Bob Dylan in there for a while, but you had to
look really hard to find it.
Stan had bought and used a harmonica holder for about a week back in
1964, but that was that
It just wasn't him.
You could listen to the duo play and hear bits of Tom Rush, and Eric
Anderson, and Fred Neil and Jerry Jeff Walker.
We loved Fred Neil. Stan spent hours with his records, particularly "A
Little Bit of Rain," trying to train his voice into Neil's impossibly deep
range. He was a mysterious character for us. We couldn't find any
reliable information on him at all. He was rumoured to have been part
of the Greenwich Village scene back in the early days, and had been
courted by the major record labels after his song "Everybody's Talking"
had been covered by Harry Nilsson for the movie, "Midnight Cowboy."
The word was he had said no, and had moved out of their range to
Florida where he was spending his time with dolphins. We loved the
story and hoped it was true. As much as Stan wanted success and fame,
the idea of having the nerve to just say no, and pull the plug and do it
on your own terms had tremendous allure.
Jerry Jeff Walker was to remain one of our big heroes too.
We wanted to be like him, an easy going and amiable and pleasantly
stoned self -described fuck-up. "Just getting by and getting high's my
stock in trade," as the song went.
Jerry Jeff's music made up a large part of the duo's repertoire back then,
and our trio's repertoire a couple of years later.

There is an odd little side bar to the Jerry Jeff story.
One summer we were all staying in our Uncle Prescott's cottage at
Halfway Cove, Nova Scotia.
We kept seeing a guy on a motorcycle with a guitar case strapped to the
sissy bar on the back.
We could never catch him.
We would be just coming into Canso for an evening party/jam session,
or heading out to the shore, and there would be the biker, pulling
smartly away in the opposite direction.
This went on for a couple of weeks, and then we never saw him again.
It was frustrating.
Cut ahead a couple years to Trent University, and Stan and Nigel
had somehow managed to get Jerry Jeff Walker hired for the Student
coffeehouse. This was a huge coup, and they wanted everything to be
right. They scored some weed, got a bottle of off brand tequila, and

managed to draw Jerry Jeff into a post-show jam session.

It was a dream come true for them.

Some hours went by, and then Jerry Jeff started playing one of our Uncle Lee's songs.

Stan stopped him, and said "Wait a minute. Holy shit. Where did you learn that?"

Jerry Jeff said, "Aw...a couple years ago, I was in Nova Scotia and Cape Breton, just tooling around on the bike and I fell in with some guys on a road crew. We had some beers and one of the guys taught me that song."

"That was you!" Stan said. "Jesus. We kept seeing you everywhere. We never could catch up to you. Damn."

And of course there was Ian and Sylvia.

Stan and Nigel's big tour de force back then was their note for note take on Ian Tyson's "Four Rode By." I remember them spending any spare moment trying to get the fiendishly difficult guitar break right.

People say they hear a lot of Lightfoot in Stan's music, and of course it's in there, but I think there were a handful of songs by Ian Tyson that really pointed the way towards what would eventually become his style. "Four Rode By" had a sense of place and history to it, along with a driving rhythmic urgency.

"Four Strong Winds" has such pathos and an only hinted- at back story. I always felt Stan's song "Turnaround" was written as a companion piece to it.

And "Summer Wages" for me, is one of the best written Canadian songs ever.

It drops you right into the story with that first line.

"Never hit 17 when you're playing against the dealer, for you know the odds won't ride with you."

We loved the eye for detail in the lyrics.

"So I'll work the big boats in my slippery city shoes, which I swore I would never do again." There was so much defeat and shame in it. Such economy of writing.

I think in the midst of all the other extraordinary and wonderful music that was around in those days, that was the one, the ground zero, where so much of Stan's later writing emanated from.

You could steer a straight line through the perfect detail and heartbreak of "Summer Wages," and the heroic sweep of Lightfoot's "Great Canadian Railroad Trilogy" back to Tyson's to "Four Rode By," and end up at the well spring of what Stan was later to create.

But for the time being, really good songs like "Turnaround" were few and thin on the ground.

The duo's repertoire consisted of a lot of covers and a handful of Stan's bad first attempts.

He was searching for something that would distinguish them from the rest of the acts out there toiling in the clubs, and of course he would latch on to anything that was currently popular on the radio and try that style on like a shirt, to see if it fit.

It's what we all do.

He had a brief and disturbing period of sounding very much like Elton John, circa "Your Song."

It drove our Dad wild particularly, that Stan was no longer using his light baritone, as it was then, but Elton John's high nasal tone and inflection.

Stan got a ticket to see Cat Stevens at the old Hamilton Forum, and for a while all of his new songs had a full stop and start with big flourished chords like "Peace Train."

This of course was before Cat Stephens' conversion to Islam and his subsequent support of the Fatwah on Salman Rushdie.

"Peace Train," my arse.

He went through a brief James Taylor period. That didn't last.

Joni Mitchell's music took hold of him and in truth, never let go.

Her use of open tunings and free meters crept in whenever Stan had some bee in his bonnet, and he wrote a number of really bad songs using her style. Invariably, when he was trying to make a point about something he would drift into an open G tuning, but played in the Key of C, and the results were mostly tragic.

The only songs that survived from that period of influence were "So Blue," from the Turnaround album, and "Half of a Heart," from the ill-fated "From Fresh Water."

Years later, when we recorded "So Blue," we threw caution and taste overboard and deliberately tried to make it sound as much like "Court and Spark" era Joni Mitchell as possible.

We justified it in that she was actually mentioned in the song.

For myself I never really fell under the spell. I had problems with her vocal delivery.

Her vibrato in the early years sounded like a French ambulance.

However, her "Hissing of Summer Lawns" record got a lot of play years later, when Stan and I lived together in Brampton.

I think one can trace the form of "Northwest Passage" directly back to her song, "Shadows and Light." They are not terribly alike but they share DNA. More on that later.

Looking back at those times it occurs to me that somehow so much other popular music by-passed Stan, and he kept resolutely to his own path.

Consider that Cream, and Jimi Hendrix and the Who and the Rolling Stones were out there, as he was trying to find his way, and their music never touched Stan's in any fashion.

He was of that precise generation for whom the opening notes of "Sunshine of Your Love" would usually have another man reaching to crank the radio volume control, and miming Ginger Baker's drum entry, but it seemed to go right past him.

It only has occurred to me as I write this. Interesting.

To be sure he did listen to it, but it was never to influence his own music except second hand through me, years later, when I began sneaking power chords and distortion into the mix.

But I'm getting ahead of myself.

Stan and Nigel had heard about a folk club in London, Ontario called Smales Pace and had made the trip down to see if they could get a spot on the bill as the opening act, with an eye towards an actual paying gig in the future.

Smales Pace was run by a trio of brothers with a love for folk music, coupled with a fiduciary death wish.

It was located on Clarence Street in London Ontario, in what was once an old Bell Telephone building. It was a long L shaped room, seating maybe 80, with a low stage in one corner near the kitchen door.

It smelled wonderful. The air was filled with the scent of ginger bread and cinnamon, and hot apple cider and cloves, and the patchouli and strawberry oil that the waitresses wore.

Stan and Nigel had a good first gig there. They did their top drawer material, hoping to make enough of a splash to get a night of their own later.

They played "Four Rode By, "and "Turnaround," and a terrible, ostensibly funny ragtime song of Stan's called "The Fat Girl Rag."

Even by the non-politically correct standards of the time, it was offensive and mean spirited. But they snuck it by and it stayed in the repertoire, to the extent that when they finally did land a brief recording deal with RCA, it became their first single.

They did well enough though, that first night at Smale's Pace, and got invited back to play again, with the possibility that they might get a whole night of their own someday.

They were a hit.

Visually they were a little out of the norm too, which might have helped with their impact.

Nigel looked normal, beyond the appalling reek that fumed off him, but

Stan was still wearing his stage gear from his brief stint with Tranquility Base.
The folkies had never seen anything like it.

The Tranquility Base gig was a brief anomaly in the story.
Stan had come home one day, during his hiatus from school, and before he'd hooked up with Nigel with the news that he'd got a job with a "real band."
A real band, with actual money and solid bookings, and a manager and overhead, and everything.
We were all thrilled for him, until he named the act.
"Tranquility Base."
Ah Jesus, no. Not that.
I was appalled and shocked. Even my parents were taken aback.
Tranquility Base was a bad, light-weight pop show-band with pretensions to Art, who had played at my high school the year before.
The entire student body had sat in sour disgust, and butt-clenching embarrassment, as they went through their whole smarmy act, culminating in a long "Tribute to the Beach Boys" medley, while the lead singer wobbled his fat ass, and did the Twist.
It wasn't just the bad music, although that was a lot of it. It was watching the interplay on stage and seeing that they were laughing at the audience, thinking we couldn't see, and because they were somehow too good for this gig.
Fuck 'em, I thought, and walked out with the rest of the students.
What was Stan thinking?
He was probably thinking that it was a paying gig, doing music of a sort.
And in any case there had been a line-up change.
The annoying fat arsed singer was gone, and well, after all, it was a gig.
AND! It came with a whole new wardrobe.
Stan had to have a stage persona.
He had to have a look that defined him as a character on stage.
He didn't fit in with the rest of the band physically. He was six foot four, forty pounds overweight, and prematurely bald. So they kitted him out in a huge black cowboy hat, black slacks, tucked into knee high English riding boots, all topped off with a thigh length black felt cape.
Where they got all this stuff in his size is anybody's guess.
The hat alone took up an acre of real estate. Stan wore a size 8, for God's sake. They were having to divert air traffic.
But there he was, in the front door one night, having hitched up from the city one rainy night, wearing the whole ensemble. Who the hell would have had the nerve to pick him up, I wonder?

He swept in and made his grand entrance with a freshly lit cigarette in a long holder.

There was a new camera slung from his shoulder.

With the hat and the boots, he was over seven feet tall and looked like a cross between Hoss Cartwright and Quentin Crisp.

The gig with Tranquility Base didn't last long.

The wheels were coming off the band, and Stan, as much as he liked the regular money, was fed up with the bad pop music, and the weird band politics.

One of his last gigs with them was New Year's Eve in Sudbury Ontario, for the Miners Ball.

It was a formal affair.

As Stan described it, "It was like being trapped in a room with several thousand booze maddened penguins."

CHAPTER 15

Moving To London

Stan and Nigel's little ménage in Millbrook had broken up.
It had cost a fortune to heat the house, and Millbrook was in the precise
geological middle of nowhere as far as the music world was concerned.
Nigel found other digs and Stan was couch-surfing in an apartment on
Summerhill Ave in Toronto. Not being in close proximity to one another
made it harder to rehearse, and pretty soon the duo began to lose focus
and drift apart.
Stan came in from a solo gig one night and bumped into a hippie-
looking guy in the hallway.
"You a guitar player?" the guy asked.
"Yeah."
"Come on in." And he took Stan down the hall to another door.
It opened and three very tall scruffy guys were lounging around with
guitars, an autoharp, and a banjo. The air was thick with dope smoke.
The tall scruffy guys were the Good Brothers, and the guy in the hall
had been James, of "James and the Good Brothers" as they were known
back then.
"Care for a toke?"
"Uh...well yeah, sure."
One of the guys reached for a briefcase, took out a huge block of
hashish, carved off a chunk the size of an ice cube, and said, "This
should do us for the evening."
That was the last of Stan's memory of the event.
They became friends, and the Goods started playing regularly at Smales
Pace around the time that Stan moved to London.

He began bunking in with two brothers from the Annapolis Valley in
Nova Scotia, Mike and Tim Curry. Tim was going to Western, I believe,
and Mike was doing something with the world of Physics. I think Stan
might have told me years later that Mike was part of the team that
designed the guidance system for the Cruise Missile which was being
built in London at the General Dynamics plant.

They were both quiet and amiable and liked to play guitar and sing.
Mike had a more formal background in music. He had briefly been a
choir director, or had dated a choir, or something like that. They both
had pleasant tenor voices and they both liked the old Maritime ballads
and fishing songs.
It was from them that Stan learned "The Maid on the Shore," which we
recorded on the first album.
Mike was one of those fussy guys with a pipe. He had a collection
of expensive briars and leather pouches of whatever mixture he was
currently smoking, and a clanking collection of little tools to clean the
pipes. And during conversations he would pull out the pipe, and begin
to labouriously scrape and scratch and peer down the barrel, rapping it
against the table, blowing into it and making little quacking noises.
It was hypnotic, and presently all talk would cease, and everyone in
the room would be watching, and after a long while the pipe would
be deemed clean enough for use, and be carefully loaded up, and a
wooden match brought to the bowl, and he'd finally light the damned
thing.
And everyone in the room could finally relax and begin to talk again,
whereupon he would knock the dottle out of the bowl after a few
draws, and once more begin the whole cleaning process.
It drove us mad.

Tim and Mike and Stan decided they needed bigger digs, and moved
out of the high rise they were in to a two bedroom upstairs apartment in
the 500 block of Maitland Street.
The brothers shared one room mostly, while Stan had a room to
himself...mostly.
The sleeping arrangements were pretty flexible, depending on who was
entertaining a guest at the time.
Eventually there was a fourth member of the household.
Willie P. Bennett moved into the large hall closet at the top of the stairs.
He had been sleeping on the stage at Smales Pace before this, dossing
down after the staff had gone home and the doors were locked.

It was a typically ad hoc, BoHo lifestyle.
There were a lot of late nights. A lot of dope, a lot of people coming and
going, all night parties, girlfriends coming in and leaving in a huff. God
knows how the Curries managed to get any studying done.
The communal living arrangement made it so that Stan didn't need a lot
of cash to make the monthly nut. Once he'd made rent and his share of
groceries and beer-making supplies, he was free to read, listen to music,
write, drink beer, smoke pot...take a nap...wander around London...

smoke pot...hang out at the York Hotel...drink beer...smoke pot...take a nap...
It's a Man's life, I tell 'ee lad.
Stan made reference to this period of his life years later, in the song, "Working Joe."

What made the whole time in London so important to him was the crowd of other like-minded players who started to hit town.
Some of the musicians who came through had already gone national with their careers, guys like Bruce Cockburn, Murray McLaughlan, and Valdy.
Others were fated to remain forever local and obscure, but all of them were trying develop a career outside of the mainstream, to raise their game, and find a means of creating something good and lasting while largely being ignored by the music industry.
There were a lot of really creative people, and they all had an effect on us.

David Bradstreet was a handsome scoundrel with a really wonderful voice, powerful songs and a great polished stage act. There was talk that he was being "watched" by the major labels.
Doug McArthur had a bunch of tightly written songs, and a really funny in-between song patter that threatened to take over his whole act.
Willie Bennett was writing good stuff, and screwing up on a pretty much daily basis.
He was one of those sweet vulnerable people whom everyone longed to help, and who had a serious and pronounced self-destructive streak.
Typically, just around the time he'd got a song covered on David Wiffen's major label record, and was getting cover stories in magazines, and being seriously looked at by the suits, he disappeared into a lame local bluegrass band, and stayed there until the attention died down.

David Essig was up from the States with a degree in economics he had no use for, a big Gibson guitar, a lot of flashy instrumental prowess, and a bunch of dark and funny songs. Sort of Steven King meets the Stanley Brothers by way of Robert Johnson.
It was Dave who first got the idea and the wherewithal to start his own record label a few years later, called Woodshed Records, and he began releasing his own stuff and producing and recording people like Willie P.
There were others who drifted in and out of the scene.
There was a trio called Lazarus up from the States, Bill Hughes, Gary Dye, and Carl Kessee.
They had a debut album on Bearsville Records which had been

produced by Phil Ramone, whom they'd been introduced to by Peter Yarrow. It was a simply made and yet lush-sounding record, with just the three guys on guitar and bass and keyboards, and it was a textbook of vocal harmony, and a big influence on the sound Stan and I would later develop with the trio and unsuccessfully attempt to record.
Bill was the songwriter in the band, and had one of the most pure and strong and beautiful voices I'd ever heard. He was an ex-child prodigy violinist-turned guitar player from Texas.
He was deeply Christian, and the songs from their first album reflected that, but the beauty of the harmonies, and their extraordinary arrangements allowed even hardened heathens like myself to overlook it.
Bill's overt Christianity was contrasted by his wild and dissolute lifestyle.
It was Bill who made Columbian Marching powder fashionable in London, and gave Stan his first taste of it.
The trio sounded great, and they dressed great, and they were the closest thing we had to rock stars in those days.

Colleen Peterson and Mark Haines came in with a bunch of great songs and a funny act with a lot of flashy playing.
Biff Rose came up from the States.
Watching him was like being on the sidelines at an Italian car rally. You were going to see a lot of brilliant work, but secretly you were mostly there for the inevitable crash and explosion, and you were going to wish you had a camera. Wild and funny songs, blinding skill on the piano; he was just ...crazy.
I watched him one night at the club.
He apparently had been up for a couple of nights in a row studying the exports of Peru.
He came out of the kitchen, wandered up on stage with a massive tumbler of whisky, and proceeded to play and sing and talk in a bizarre stream-of-consciousness rant for about two and a half hours.
It was brilliant, but it was also starting to get a little scary.
He was playing a lot of songs from his new album called "Uncle Jesus and Auntie Christ," going into wild speeded-up Lord Buckley-inspired verbal riffs, interspersed with bits of Beethoven and Cecil Taylor style dissonant jazz. It was hard to follow.
Presently, he stopped and looked around for a bit, as if seeing the audience for the first time, and then carefully got down from his chair.
He crawled very slowly on all fours to the couple sitting at the side of the stage, and in a loud stage whisper said, "How long have I been up here?"

The guy looked at his watch and said "About two and a half hours."
"Jesus."
And he crawled back to the piano, and re-took his seat, and played for
another hour or so.
Stan was there every night when he wasn't working himself, taking it
all in, and I was coming in on the bus every weekend.
I loved the whole scene, although I was too young to really be part of it.
Stan was really generous to let his kid brother hang around so much,
and he looked out for me as well.
We were at a post-concert party with the Good Brothers once, and as
usual it was degenerating into an out-take from the movie "Caligula."
There was a big crowd...a lot of noise, a lot of drugs, and a lot of music.
I had just come back from a trip to the bathroom, having had to make
my way past a couple celebrating their new-found friendship on a
mattress on the floor.
The guy had his pants around his ankles, and they were racing for the
finish line, his ass going like a fiddler's elbow. The girl was wearing
only cowboy boots and had her feet in the air, whipping the guy with a
rolled up magazine and yelling "Ride! You son of a bitch! Ride!"
I had to choose my moment, judging the rhythm of the guy's ass, and
on the down stroke leaped over them and through the curtain.
I was just regaining my seat, when the door opened and a crowd of
really seriously tarted-up women came in.
They didn't look like the girls from the folk crowd.
No patched and embroidered jeans. No long printed hippy skirts, with
sandals.
And they were wearing bras. Serious push up bras, requiring a lot of
steel reinforcement and advanced engineering skill. They were dressed
in long satin gowns with high heels and piled up hair, and giving off
clouds of actual perfume as opposed to the Strawberry oil the women at
the club wore.
Where the hell had they come from?
I was trying not to stare.
Stan came over and sat down.
   "So...what do you think?...like what you see?"
I didn't know if he was trying to set me up on a date. I wasn't ready for
what looked like the Big Leagues.
   "Well, I uh...Jeez...I dunno. Yeah...I guess they're...I mean the one in
the red...she's kinda..."
   "A man...she's really a man, you poor sap."

It was around this time that Stan met Paul Mills, another local guitar
player.

Paul had been working at Proctor and Gamble, and his gift to the world from that period was the formulation of Rose Lotion Vel, or Lemon Pledge, or something.

He was a tall guy, with curly hair and glasses, and an actual Martin guitar, a rarity in those days, who'd spent much of his young life trying to assimilate the playing style of Doc Watson.

There was a whole legion of guys out there around that time, each with a guitar they carried everywhere they went, a well-worn set of National finger picks, and their own version of "Doc's Guitar" which they could pull out and play at a moment's notice, and pretty much kill any party. And for every generation there is a certain tune that you will hear being played at any hour of the day, in any music store you happen to walk into. It's always some poor pimply guy and he sits, head down, playing the same thing over and over, while looking around furtively to see if anyone is impressed.

It's like a bird call. A way of saying "Hello...Here I am. Is anyone listening out there?" And after a while, some other spotty herbert will wander over with his guitar and they will put their heads together and spend the rest of the day comparing versions of that tune, while their poor girlfriends sit on an amplifier wishing they were somewhere, anywhere else. Eventually the girls leave to find a bar where they can form a support group, drink Margaritas, and dream of meeting someone with a job and a few social skills.

Back in my day the tune was always Davey Graham's "Anji." I spent perhaps 10 years working on my own bad version.

Then it was "Doc's Guitar."

Later came the opening bars to "Stairway to Heaven" (there is actually a fine for playing that one in most stores.)

Nowadays I suppose it's Green Day's "Time of Your Life," or the opening bars to "Sweet Child O' Mine" by Guns and Roses, or something I wouldn't recognize now, being so far out of the loop.

But I digress.

So Paul had a collection of riffs and licks, and a reputation within a 10 block radius anyway, of being a flashy player. He and Stan became friends, and for local gigs Paul would sit in with Stan now that Nigel was no longer on the scene.

But Paul was leaving London soon.

He had a job waiting at the CBC, as a producer for an up-coming radio show called "Touch the Earth" with Sylvia Tyson hosting.

It is difficult to over emphasize just how important that show became. Not just the exposure it gave performers to a national radio audience, but as well for the financial and moral support it gave Stan and many others over the years.

It was exposure and money, and a feeling that you were legitimate, a professional.

Being on the show gave you an excuse to call the parents for a reason other than to borrow cash. They in turn could call their friends and family, and on the night of the broadcast they would be sitting around the radio, all over the country, and thinking perhaps you weren't quite the washout they had feared.

Of course you had phoned everyone you knew.

And hopefully they were all now listening to the recording Paul had produced of you, and then the interview with Sylvia, and you had somehow arrived.

You still weren't making any money beyond that pay cheque from the CBC, but no one had to know that.

Paul made sure everyone got on that show, and in those days, before independent record companies, the appearance on "Touch the Earth" was a calling card. It could translate into a gig at a club in another city and you could get a little further from home, and eventually develop a loyal following outside of that one narc who was always parked on the street outside your house.

Paul also produced a series of extended play recordings which got regular airplay nationally and which could be purchased from the CBC. This, long before anyone dreamed of having a recording deal of their own.

In later years, the CBC during Paul's tenure recorded live at all the major folk festivals in Canada. Peter Gzowski hosted those evening shows, and suddenly there was a folk music scene again in Canada.

In the interests of full disclosure, it must be said that Paul and I did not get along, pretty much right from the get go. He didn't like my playing, and I didn't like his. Nor did I like his production, for that matter, either at the CBC, or in later years with our recordings.

And we just didn't click on a personal level.

But I don't think Paul has ever had the proper credit for what he did for the acoustic singer-songwriter scene in Canada, and the way it grew while Touch the Earth was on the air.

There were other forces at work in the sudden emergence of a Canadian music scene; the new Canada Content rules for one, which dictated that stations play at least 30 per cent of home grown talent, which left record companies scrambling to find new artists. And so it might have happened had he not been there, but not in the same way, and certainly not as quickly. Most of us would have had to pack up and get real jobs had Paul not lent so much support as keeper of the public teat.

And while he has in the years since Stan's death dined out on his association with Stan, while at the same time negating my role in the music, he has to my knowledge never laid claim to being such a positive force elsewhere in the folk world, and I'm saying it here for the little it is worth.

CHAPTER 16

Cedar Lake

The scene around London continued to grow. The little club was
becoming a magnet for songwriters. Stan was there, drinking it all in,
and he was writing all the time.

He said there was a lot of pressure to come up with new stuff.
The shows at Smales Pace would often devolve into long after-hours
jam sessions and it was important to have something new to trot out.
The scene by itself was competitive, and Stan personally was more so.
He was still batting barely a hundred in those days. For every 10 songs
he wrote there would be 1 that might stay in the set list for more than a
few weeks. But that was fine, he was listening and learning, and trying
to figure out what made a song or an act work.

In the meantime the club was really busy and everybody was coming
through.
Valdy was getting to be a national name by then, and was really too big
for the room. He came in for a multiple night run, and as Stan told it, he
did a different show every night.
He never repeated a song. It was a hell of a feat, and it threw down the
gauntlet for the rest of them.

The club needed a new entrance, something to keep the cold air from
blasting into the room every time the door opened. They had no money
to pay a construction worker, so of course Stan generously volunteered
the services of our Dad for free.
Dad was typically good-natured about it, and Stan and I both had a
small hand in helping out.
We were sitting around the table after lunch break one day, and John
Smale began complaining how he had been maneuvered by some big
city agent into booking a guy from the States who had a major label
record coming out, and John had been pressured into guaranteeing
more than he could afford to lose if the show didn't sell well. And
tickets weren't moving. The guy was a complete newcomer.

111

Luckily, a few weeks later the big time agent called and canceled.
"Something has come up."
John was off the hook.
Next week "American Pie" hit the radio, and that guy from the States
had a number one song and people started calling for tickets to his now
canceled show.
Showbiz.

Someone came up with the idea of doing a big concert at Alumni Hall in
London to show case the artists who were playing Smales Pace.
There would be a lot of acts on the bill, a sort of indoor festival.
Everyone would get equal time and equal billing, and everyone would
be on stage together for the duration of the show, adding harmonies or
whatever else seemed to fit.
It was to be called Cedar Lake.
There was one initial concert that went off pretty well, and about a year
later another one was launched. The really big news was that it would
be recorded by the CBC for national broadcast on a show called "the
Entertainers," and Paul Mills would produce it.

My parents and I went down to London to see the show.
Dave Bradstreet, Doug McArthur, Willie P. Bennett, Steve Hayes,
Lazarus, Stan, Dave Essig, and the Whitely brothers from Toronto were
there, with Jim Ogilvie on bass and Ian Guenther on violin to sweeten
things up.
Guenther had been an original member of Lighthouse, but I knew him
more from his playing with Fraser and DeBolt and Bruce Cockburn,
and on this particular night, David Essig. He was to be a huge influence
on my own playing, in that he played behind singers with classical
technique and tone. There was nothing of the Irish or Cape Breton style
in his approach and I loved it. I was just beginning to learn the violin
and what he was doing opened a door for me. I have never in my life
been able to force myself to learn an actual fiddle tune, and to this day
never pick the instrument up unless there is a singer in the room. His
approach to playing became a template for my own.
The live show was wonderful, and the later radio show, heavily edited,
was good as well, with the exception of a pretentious and inexplicably
weird voice over written by Bill Howell.
Bill Howell was from Nova Scotia, and had published a book of
poetry called "The Red Fox," and was now doing odd bits of writing
and production for the CBC, both in Toronto and in Halifax. He was
hyperkinetic and loud and mostly drunk whenever I saw him, and
wore the regulation poet's uniform of brown corduroy jacket, and Hush

Puppies. Paul had likely brought him in on the project to add some needless context and pointless narration to the music, and to once more support a friend.

As the broadcast opened, the narrator intoned, "The house lights went down, like the ghost of a childhood, at eight o'clock."

What?

It continued through the rest of the show, and had no relation to the music being played.

I think Bill just wanted to insert himself and a bunch of pet lines into the show, but it was awful. At one point during the broadcast I was just winding up to throw a cushion at the radio, when my Dad grabbed it out of my hand and threw it himself.

None of which is important, except that Bill in later years took refuge full time from the real world as a writer at the CBC, and then later as head of Radio Drama, and he and Stan became friends and collaborators.

It was Bill who later kept hiring Stan and the band to write and perform songs and incidental music for projects he wrote and produced at CBC Halifax.

He helped keep us alive, and he flattered Stan by taking him seriously as a writer, not just a songwriter. He acted as a foil for Stan, and gave him a lot of encouragement to try different styles of writing.

Stan unveiled a new song that night, called "Pharisee."

It was sweet little tribute to the other guys, and how he felt about the whole scene in London.

The audience loved it, and to us listening at home, our applause-o-meter registered that it got the best reaction of the night. The others could disagree, but it didn't matter. What mattered was that Mum and Dad were proud of him. He was on the radio, and Mum had called everyone in her family to make sure they were listening.

A few months later, some bright spark decided that the Cedar Lake idea could be expanded. More concerts could be organized. It could be a gimmick, a new thing to sell to the little festival scene that was growing up in Ontario back then.

And over a period of months a loose aggregation of songwriters formed who called themselves Cedar Lake, and they started to get booked here and there. One of the gigs was a free event in Hamilton, in the summer of '73 I believe, which rejoiced in the name of "It's Your Bag Day."

The artistic director was Diane Patterson, a red haired thirty-ish working mother, whose second marriage, as I later learned from Stan, was wobbling badly, and looked to be heading for the ditch.

Stan introduced me to her one afternoon, as we rehearsed at Bill
Powell's club on Augusta Street in Hamilton. She clattered in carrying
a clipboard and an armload of papers, and came way too close into my
personal space. She looked me up and down, said "Hmmm...not bad,"
and then barked out a maniacal laugh.
It was a laugh, to quote P.G. Wodehouse, like a troop of cavalry going
over an iron bridge. She walked away still laughing, and disappeared
into the back office.
My tender teen aged sensibilities were hurt, delicate little flower that I
was.
  "Who the hell was that?"
Stan was still looking at the door she had gone through. I saw the
expression on his face, and thought, Whoops. What's this?
Long story short, after a protracted and loud, and on-and-off again
courtship, during which time Diane got divorced, followed by a
tumultuous period of living together, and then a nearly two year
break-up, and much shouting and broken crockery, Stan and Diane got
married.
But I'm getting way ahead of the story.

It was also around this time that Stan had attracted someone's attention
at Vanguard Records. Vanguard Records. We couldn't believe it. They
had actual folk singers on their roster. Legends. Great people, like Eric
Anderson, and Mississippi John Hurt. Joan Baez recorded for them.
This was amazing.
Stan and Paul went down to New York City, and met with various suits,
and did a demo of sorts, but they couldn't see eye to eye with the other
parties, and they came back empty, and the Vanguard deal died on its
ass.
Stan sent me a letter from New York while he was still hopeful.
It read in part, "Well kid, all the long years of sacrifice and heartbreak
are over. I've finally made it. The demo sessions are going great, and
we'll be recording in earnest in a few months."
The sheer naiveté of the letter was breath-taking even then. The only
real long years of sacrifice had been lived by our parents, and anyone
else whom Stan had put the bite on for a loan.
What the hell, he was so young.
The only enduring thing to come from the Vanguard experience was
that Stan's mistrust of big labels grew deeper, and the songs which he
foolishly signed over to them in a typically cynical big label publishing
deal got farmed out to some other artists.
The Country Gentlemen, a bluegrass band in the States recorded
"Guysborough Train."

Stan was thrilled, despite never seeing a cent in royalties.

As the months went by the Cedar Lake concept had now somehow become an actual band, and amazingly for me, I was to be part of it. I was still in my last year of high school.
Gord Lowe, who wasn't part of the original shows as far as I recall, seemed to be the prime mover behind this new enterprise. Gord had been around for a while.
He had a huge voice, somewhat reminiscent of Fred Neil, and had been around the Yorkville scene, and further afield, once getting a gig opening for the Doors at Boston Gardens, at least according to Gord.
He had also recorded as part of a duo with a young woman, whose name escapes me, but I did for a while have the record, and played it for my Mum. She liked Gord's voice well enough, but wasn't impressed with the other half.
Upon meeting Gord, Mum held the album up and said, "I hope the screwing you were getting was worth the screwing you got."
Neither of my parents had much in the way of a filter for their thought processes.

Cedar Lake was to have a Manager, and a secretary, and a road manager, and a booking agent, and a full time sound engineer. We were "going to do it right." We had watched other bands and had learned.
There was another local band at the time called The Perth County Conspiracy, a loose collection of free thinkers, musicians, part time herb farmers, poets, and free form dancing girls in tie dye based in Stratford Ontario.
They were getting well known around the province, and seemed to be having some success, but to our eyes they were a bit on the dis-organized side. The irony and arrogance of that assessment became clear to me much later.
We were going to be more professional. We would have staff.
How we were going to pay everyone did not seriously come up for discussion, but given that we had about a dozen regulars in the band, plus this unwieldy support crew, chances were that there were going to be too many pigs for the teats.

We played the inaugural Home County Folk Festival later that first summer, and my main recollection of the show was standing on stage and being handed a note which said that Richard Nixon was going to resign the next day. Apart from that gig I don't believe there was ever a show where we did not outnumber the audience. After our Sunday night concert, the director, Walter Grasser came back stage with a little bonus cheque for us, 200 dollars, over and above our negotiated fee. It was a sweet gesture, but I remember the band and the management having a long and bitter fight backstage as to who should get the money. Management thought it should go to outstanding bills. The musicians all thought it should be divided amongst ourselves. It meant an extra 10 or 15 dollars each. And besides, we were musicians. We'd got into this lark so we wouldn't have to worry about bills.

In retrospect, the band was one of those really goofy ideas you can have when you are young and naïve, and suddenly everyone is excited and on board, and the whole thing just starts rolling, and it looks somehow plausible.

For myself, I was out of my tiny mind with excitement that whole year leading up to me getting out of school and going out on the road. I still had a few more months of school to get through but I figured the work would magically take care of itself. I was in a real band, with all the guys I had been listening to for years.

I hadn't been able to shut up about it.

People took to avoiding me even more.

I was failing Math.

Who cared? I'd been failing Math my whole life. I was in a BAND.

The last day of school, I walked down to the shore of Lake Ontario with my two best friends, Doug and Robert, and we shared a bottle of bad Italian sparkling wine. We talked about our dreams, what our futures might bring, and wondered where we might all be in ten years.

Ten years later, Stan would be gone, and I would be in complete shock, and trying to pick up the broken shards of my life, but right now, it all looked very bright and shiny.

We finished the wine, hugged, and promised to keep in touch, and I hitch-hiked home.

I dumped my books in the hallway, and next morning got my flute and my fiddle and a shoulder bag with a week's worth of clothes, and hitch-hiked up to Burk's Falls, in Northern Ontario, to catch up to the band bus. I found it under some shade trees, by the river.

It was a beautiful sunny day.

Someone was playing guitar on a picnic table.

I could smell reefer smoke on the breeze.

On the beach near a small tree, a couple of women were sunbathing, topless.

Wow. Only 24 hours before I had been an ink-stained wretch of a school boy.

Now this was my job.

Life had suddenly expanded.

There had been a near tragedy that morning.
As Doug McArthur told the story, he and Stan decided to take a canoe
out on to the river.
They shared a reefer, got the canoe launched, and swung out into the
middle where the current was strongest and the paddling for two out of
shape hippies would be easier. The sun was out, life was good, and they
were now moving along at a pretty good clip. There was a breeze now,
keeping the black flies at bay. They shipped their paddles, and leaned
back to relax.
Maybe another little smoke would be good.
Presently Doug, noticing that they were now fairly rocketing along,
turned back to look at Stan who was sitting with his eyes closed, a
blissful expression on his face.
Doug said, "You know Stan, I wonder. Do you suppose it's called Burk's
Falls because..."
and they came hurtling around a bend in the river, where there was
a cloud of vapor and a loud thundering roar, "BECAUSE THERE'S A
FUCKING FALLS?"
And the two idiots had to paddle for their lives for about half an hour,
frantically backing water, and scrambling for the nearest bank.
They just made it before the current took them into the abyss, and were
now laying in the shade, sweating, exhausted and limp.
That night at the hall, we played for two teen-aged girls, and the janitor,
and his dog. As gigs went it was a nice dog.
We played a couple more places on that first trip. They were all tiny
towns, with no one living there who might have had even the slightest
interest in watching a stoned and drunken rabble of unrehearsed
hippies.
We had a discussion one afternoon, where Gord Lowe outlined our
game plan and mission statement, which was that we were going to
take the music of The People (I could tell by the way he said it "People"
was in capitals) out to The People, (whoever the Hell "The People"
might be,) and stay away from the cities.
In retrospect, we might have been better off playing shows in towns
where there were some people, (even if they weren't "The People,")
who might actually buy a ticket.
But for those first few shows that summer I was happy just to be there,
and to float along, while someone else took care of the details and did
all the work.
We had an old school bus which we had painted a calm and soothing
dark green one afternoon in my parents' driveway. Someone had ripped

out all the seats and replaced them with easy chairs and a day bed and a sofa. There was a brass bed in the back behind a beaded curtain, and a wood stove.

The wood stove was a great idea, on paper.

In practice, not so much.

Any wind blowing past the chimney of a wood stove adds to the draft, and increases the heat generating capacity. Try taking one out on the highway at 55 miles per hour.

It looked like a scene from 12 O' Clock High where Gregory Peck is trying to put out an engine fire by flying faster.

I remember laying on the floor of that bus one night that summer, after we'd finished yet another secret show where the people on stage outnumbered The People out front.

I was sprawled on top of some embroidered cushions, with a beer in one hand, and a reefer in the other. It was a sweet and mild summer night, and I could see the moon through the tree branches as they flashed by outside the window. There was a cool breeze blowing in, and the light from the kerosene lantern was making crazy shadows as it swung back and forth.

I thought, "I'm going to do this for the rest of my life."

Idiot.

We played in South River, near Huntsville Ontario.

The band bus was parked at an old lodge in the woods.

It was a massive and lovely run down resort hotel. There were huge fireplaces, suitable for roasting oxen, and gleaming wood floors, and an enormous kitchen. Inexplicably, we had the run of the place, and there were about twenty of us infesting the joint, with, as far as I could tell, no supervision.

There was Stan, me, Gord Lowe, Frank Wheeler, Doug McArthur, our resident idiot George Kinsman, Willie P. Bennett, and Jimmy Ogilvie on bass, and Ma Fletcher, our Sitar player.

Yes, we had a Sitar.

Of course we did.

We were joined for this run by Rick Taylor, his brother Lucky, and their own bass player, Mike Gardner.

Rick and his group were the anomaly in the mix.

In sharp contrast to the flaccid post-hippie music we were making, Rick and his guys were rehearsed and tight, and thoroughly dangerous on stage.

Rick had the only electric guitar in the band, a little Gibson Melody Maker, and his music was bluesy and dynamic, and they regularly

wiped the floor with the lot of us..
They even looked dangerous, dark and swarthy, with unruly hair
and Zapata mustaches. They all looked as if they should be wearing
bandoliers and laughing derisively at Yul Brynner in a dusty
windblown border town.
I don't think we had Peter Po that trip.
Peter (I never learned if Po was a real name) was what was called in
those days, "an interpretive dancer," and he was a regular feature at the
side of the stage when we did festivals. He was barefoot, wore a semi-
transparent black body stocking and danced free form, wearing white-
face make up. I find clown make-up creepy, so I tended to give him a
wide berth. But he was undoubtedly very fit, and the leotard was very
tight, and he did have his own fan club among the throngs of brightly
dressed female propeller dancers who collected at the side of the stage.

We had our "support crew," which mostly consisted of various
girlfriends who were funding much of this project out of their own
pockets, in return for which they got to...wait for it...SLEEP WITH
MUSICIANS! Hurray! Everybody wins!

We had Sandy MacDonald, our red haired lunatic of a Scottish sound
engineer, who comprised about a dozen people just by himself, if you
counted all the voices in his head, fighting to be heard. We also had
some ex-carneys, who, in a breath-taking bit of gamesmanship had been
persuaded by Gord Lowe to donate time and labour and free transport
to this low rent circus.
Our numbers were rounded out by a few of the inevitable drifters and
head cases who tend to collect around any poorly organized enterprise
such as ours, like white cells around a urinary tract infection.

We were supposed to be rehearsing, but it was a beautiful place, with
woods through which to wander, and a lake by which to dream, and
a pristine and unsullied stream for George Kinsman to piss in. I think
most of us went in with good intentions, but within minutes the concept
of rehearsal went out the window, and the whole thing degenerated
into a drunken bacchanal.
Later that first night, we were awakened by cries of "Fire!"
It was the bus.
We ran out to the yard where people were pulling smoldering bedding
out of the bus and beating out the embers on the gravel drive. Willie P.
and Rick Taylor had decided to sleep on the bus, and Willie had fallen
asleep with a lit joint in his hand.
Rick woke up.

The place was full of noxious smoke.

He crawled over to Willie.

"Willie ...wake up...We're on fire...Wake up ...Come on, let's go."

Willie P. shook him off, rolled over and muttered, "Fuck it man."

Rick dragged Willie out of the bus by his heels, and raised the alarm. The bus took no lasting harm, and after we had finished stamping out Willie we managed to get back to sleep.

The next day was much the same, except we did have the show to do. We played to the cleaning staff and a handful of stragglers, then went back to the lodge, and resumed the party. I packed it in sometime in the small hours, and went to sleep, only to be awakened by our manager having noisy and exuberant sex with his girlfriend across the room.

It was too much for my tender sensibilities, and I decided to camp out on the floor downstairs.

I went into the kitchen for a glass of water, where Willie P. and Rick were smoking a chunk of hashish. They were hungry too, and dipping crackers into the five gallon drum of health food peanut butter that we had brought as part of our provisions.

It had a two inch layer of yellow oil on top, and they had to plunge their hands through it to get to the peanut butter. They were covered in goo. It was dripping off their chins, running down their elbows and onto their pants.

Willie said something that made Rick choke with laughter, and Rick spat his mouthful of food out into his hand, and mashed it into Willie's hair.

Willie retaliated, and when I left, the two of them were facing each other across from the bucket, each digging up handfuls of peanut butter and plastering it over the other like spackle.

The sun was just coming up, and I took my sleeping bag out to the screened in porch and climbed into the hammock.

I had just got settled and was drifting back to sleep when the hammock broke away and I crashed to the floor.

Sometime later that afternoon, we assembled those who were able to stand, and loaded up into the little convoy of vehicles that would take us back south.

Lenny, our resident carney, had just installed a rebuilt engine in his panel van.

It was important to nurse it along and break it in gently for the first few hundred miles. Sandy was driving, and one of residents in his head, apparently the winner of the 1958 24 Hours of Le Mans, kept urging him to go ever faster.

"Sandy. Slow down. It's a new motor. You'll over stress it."

"Oh we're just fine. I always like to break them in this way."

"Sandy. Slow the fuck down. It has to be broken in gradually. Take it down to 55."

Sandy gunned the motor in response. "We're fine. I've been doing this for years. I used to..."

BAM!

And we coasted to a stop on the side of the highway, leaving pieces of hot twisted metal and a smoking oil slick in our wake. Stan had been sitting on the engine cowling, and the explosion lifted him a couple of feet in the air, and he did a somersault and landed on his ass on the floor.

The van was full of oily smoke, and we all hurriedly bailed out.

Stan unbuckled his pants and began frantically searching his groin for shrapnel wounds.

Lenny was staring sadly at the wreckage of his van, and Sandy was trying to open the hood to begin fixing whatever the problem might be.

"Leave it Sandy."

"No, it's okay. I'm sure it's just something minor. I'll have us up and running in no time." And he got the hood unlatched and threw it open, whereupon the fresh air ignited the hot oil on the manifold and the whole thing burst into flames.

"Just a minute, I've seen this before. I know what to do." He ran off into the darkness.

It was clear the van was going no further tonight. Calls were made, and eventually our manager and some other people came back up from Toronto to rescue us. We continued on for about half an hour or so, and then things went very wrong in front of us.

Cars were spinning out of control, and a pick-up truck with a camper was rolling over and over into the ditch. We piled out and ran to help. There was a Volkswagen with its roof and windshield caved in. The two women in the front were covered in jagged glass and blood. They were barely recognizable as people.

Stan ran up, looked inside, turned and ran three short steps, bent over from the waist and vomited. He wiped his mouth, and then turned back and grabbed the handle and tried to open the driver side door.

The handle came off in his hand.

The door was badly twisted, and jammed.

He threw the handle away.

He grabbed the door itself, and placed his foot against the frame, and heaved and ripped it off its hinges and threw it into the ditch. Other drivers were stopping too, and a woman stepped in front of Stan, pushed him aside, said, "I'm a nurse, let me in," and began attending to the bleeding driver.

Cedar Lake

We ran over to the truck camper.
It was upside down in the ditch, and a man and a woman were being attended to on the embankment. The hatch to the camper was flapping, and I could hear kids' voices.
We pulled the hatch the rest of the way off, looked inside, and there were three frightened but miraculously unhurt children in their night clothes, crying.
I shimmied into the camper, and began to hand the kids out through the opening to Stan.
There was a terrified dog too, also seemingly unhurt.
 I got him out as well.
There was a heavy smell of gas, and I looked up and saw fuel running down the walls of the camper, and I realized I was soaked with it.
Time to go.
Stan was leaning in with his hand out to pull me free, when I saw a guy bent down next to him with a lit emergency flare, peering in at me.
I pointed at him, and said, "Stan."
Stan turned and looked and with one hand grabbed the flare, and with the other decked the guy.
BAM.
Dropped him like a bullock.
Stan threw the flare well away and pulled me out of the camper, throwing me about ten feet away in the other direction from the gas soaked truck. He then helped the guy he had just clobbered to his feet.
    "Sorry about that," he said, brushing the dirt off him.

We finally made it to Toronto, and from there I hitch-hiked home to shower and change my clothes. I had some minor surgery on my foot scheduled for later that morning.
I entered the doctor's office, and got up on the table.
It had already been a full day.
    He said "So how was your weekend?" and I burst into tears.

We did a gig at the Stoney Creek campus of Mohawk College, the next week.
It was the student lounge, and it was full of kids, not one of whom gave a rat's ass about anything we were doing.
We were just an annoyance, a distraction from the real business at hand, which was getting blitzed. The management refused to turn the TV off above the stage, and at one point while Stan and I were playing, an empty beer bottle came whirling out of the darkness, and shattered against the wall, narrowly missing us.
The show was notable only for one thing.

Stan and I won the award for "Coolest Mom."
Mum and Dad came to the show, and sat gamely through it.
We were just embarrassed.
The kids were yelling filthy abuse at us when they noticed us at all.
I worried that Dad might take things into his own hands and smack one of the little bastards upside the head.
Mum noticed a kid sitting by himself at a table. He had a huge bag of dope spread out, and was vainly trying to roll a reefer. God knows why, he was already so stoned as to be helpless.
He was struggling with the papers and trying to glue a couple of them together, but it was useless. He had sticky scraps of paper stuck all over himself.
The more he struggled the worse it got. Mum went over and sat down next to him and pushed him aside. She had rolled her own cigarettes most of her life. It took her about ten minutes to roll an ounce or so of pot into dozens of perfect little joints. She finished, and then gathered them up, and dropped them into the plastic bag.
She said something like "There you go", and went back to sit with Dad.
The kid had no idea what had just happened.
The hand of a kindly and benevolent God had just intervened in the form of a little blonde haired lady, and he was now set for the weekend.

There was no money playing with the band.
None.
So I was working for my Dad a bit that summer, helping him on some of the little bricklaying jobs he had. He didn't really need a labourer, but it was a way to get me out of the house and in his words, "Blow the stink off." I was depressed and unhappy with the lack of success we'd had so far, and was perfectly capable of staying in bed till suppertime.
Dad and I were driving down to the job site one morning, and he asked me what I wanted to do with my life.
Oh Shit, I thought. Here it comes. This is it. This is "The Talk."
   "Your Mother and I have saved up enough for you to go to college, if that's what you want."
I thought about it for a bit.
I knew that they were dubious at best about the idea of yet another son falling into the abyss.
I should really think about doing something meaningful with my life.
I took a breath.
   "Thanks, but I'd really like to see how the band goes. Maybe give it another try, see if we can do something with it."
I imagine he was scared for me, having watched Stan floundering for the last couple of years. He was probably nervous about his bank

balance too.

Stan was constantly coming up short and hitting the folks up for loans which were never repaid.

He finally spoke.

"Well, your Mother and I talked it over, and we thought that might be what you want. So we thought that if you want to make a good try at this, a really good try, and not just screw around and waste your time, we would make that college fund available to you."

He continued, "If you need an instrument, or can't make the rent, or something else comes up, you can borrow from that money, as long as you put it back. Think of these next four years as your college education, and try to learn everything you can about the business."

I was dumbfounded. Thunderstruck. This was generosity on a level I'd never imagined.

"Jeez Dad, I don't know what to say."

My voice wasn't working too well.

"Whatever you do, don't take some shitty job that you hate, just to pick up a pay cheque."

He paused and then continued.

"Like I did."

What?

I turned to him.

"You mean you don't like your job?"

Dad snorted.

"No. What's there to like? Getting up at 5 in the morning, to stand in a trench with a foot of water in the bottom, and have some asshole foreman yell at you in Italian, and have to throw 10 inch blocks around all day in the pissing rain?"

Now I was ashamed. Unbelievably, it had never occurred to me or Stan, as I found out later, when I told him, that someone would make that kind of sacrifice, and never complain, just to raise a pair of ungrateful and lazy kids who were capable of eating twice their weight every day.

Stan was dumbfounded when I talked to him a couple days later.

He looked away from me for some minutes.

When he was able to speak his voice was thick and shaky.

"I can't believe that he would do that for us."

"I know. They should have drowned us at birth."

I had to do something after that.

I applied for a job as a labourer at the Steel Company.

The doctor listened to my chest, took my pulse, and then fondled my nuts for a bit.

It seemed to going on for a while.

"Um...Is this where I'm supposed to cough?"

"Excuse me?"

"Shouldn't I be turning my head and coughing?"

"Oh...right. Yes. Cough for me."

I coughed, after which he let go of my wedding tackle, and I pulled up my pants, while he made some notations on a form on his desk. I wondered if I'd come up to whatever personal standards he had.

He looked up at me. "This is a goddamned dead end job. What the Hell are you doing trying to get hired for this kind of crap?"

I mumbled something about wanting to make a lot of money and save up to buy a place in Nova Scotia someday.

"You'll die first. Guys come in here with the same stupid idea all the time and they never leave. They stay on, and every year they get more hopeless and broken down. Before they know it they're 50 years old and need help getting out of bed."

He said he was going to recommend that I not be hired, for my own sake.

"You can do better than this."

I pleaded with him, and he relented.

My first day at work consisted of crawling on my hands and knees, in the tunnels under the still burning furnaces, and drag out buckets of ashes in heat so intense that the sweat burned right off your skin. They found me, face down and unconscious in a foot of coal ash about an hour into the shift, and carried me hand over hand up a three storey ladder. When I came to and was able to speak, I pulled out my ID card and handed it to the foreman. I quit right there, and went for a shower, and called my Dad who came down in his pickup truck to take me home.

It was about 3 in the morning.

We were driving through the industrial wasteland of the north end of Hamilton.

The air was thick with Sulphur, and there were fires everywhere. It was like driving through Mordor.

"So you quit, huh?"

I was ashamed and depressed.

Why couldn't I do this for them?

"Yeah...I quit."

There was a silence, and then Dad uncharacteristically punched me playfully in the shoulder.

"Feels great, doesn't it?"

I took a job as a waiter at a wretched bar called the Carleton Tavern at the corner of Main and Wentworth Streets in Hamilton. It is just around the corner from Grant Avenue where Dan and Bob Lanois would later build their studio.

The bar was and still is a shit hole.

It was a hold-over from the old fashioned southern Ontario Taverns where drinking was not something you did for fun. It was man's work. It had a "Men Only" drinking room, with the "Ladies and Escorts" on the other side.

Concrete floor, cinder block walls, murky pebbled glass windows, and an overwhelming smell of cigarette smoke, stale beer and piss.

It wasn't an evening out, it was a sentence in the Gulag.

It had a limited menu. Pickled eggs and some sort of grey Polish sausage floating in a murky brine, looking like Lorreena Bobbitt's keepsake collection.

Sour smelling draft beer, a couple kinds of bottled beer for the effete snobs, and rye and rum.

Scotch was for sissies.

Mixed drinks more complex than rum and coke were "for faggots."

At 11 30 we would open the doors, and the regulars would all file in, looking shaky and pale.

They would sit and watch the Price is Right, along with the clock, and wait for noon, when we could legally serve the first beer of the day. At 11 55, Gord, the three hundred pound bartender who collected snuff porn, would start drawing draft beers and arranging them on the big aluminum trays, 33 to a tray.

All eyes were on me as the clock ticked down. At the stroke of noon I would grab a tray, and dash down the right side of the room, dealing out two at a time.

Run back for the second tray, and deal them out along the other wall. Run back again and get the third tray, and start collecting money, making change and handing out more beers.

When they had all got six beers in them the tension level of the room would go down, and they could all settle in to a quiet day of sipping and smoking, and coughing and farting, and falling asleep and puking down their shirt fronts while watching "As The World Turns."

Those mornings and afternoons were relatively pleasant.

We just had our little flock to tend to, and they were all too old and broke-dicked to be much trouble.

Evenings were another story.

The Red Devils and Satan's Choice were frequent customers, and a bunch of guys from the Rez, in Brantford did a lot of extra-legal business there as well. Pot, speed and motorcycle parts from Midnight Auto Supply were all available if you knew who to ask.

There were hookers there as well, who, if they weren't on the street turning tricks congregated in a shivering and anxious flock in the corner. There were some older whores there too. Probably none of them were much more than 40 or so, but the life they had been living had made them look like they'd been pulled from a crypt. There was a particularly loud and obnoxious one who liked to grab me by the pony tail and pull me in as I bent down to serve her drinks. I couldn't fight very well with a full tray in my left hand, and she would jam her filthy old tongue into my ear, swirl it around while I struggled helplessly, and then let me go and cackle along with the rest of the Ladies knitting circle. I should have known better than to get near her. When I first met her she'd introduced herself as being "semi-retired," but, and here she grabbed me by the essentials and squeezed hard while I made wounded puppy sounds..."I still like to keep my hand in the business."

Gord took me aside and showed me some ugly but useful tricks which he recommended in the event of a fight. Basic stuff, like how to safely execute a head butt.
It's tricky if you don't know how.
You apply your own forehead sharply to the other party's nose, and not the other way around. Breaking your own nose is considered bad form. Follow it with a swift knee to the groin, and you have the guy's attention.
    "The main thing to remember, if something starts up, is get to me and keep your back against mine. It's the only way we can take these guys on, just the two of us."
I was 18, and not even legal to drink, myself.
What was I doing here?
Around 7 PM the trade got a little heavier, and the room got louder, and the little kids would start wandering into the bar in their nightgowns, crying and wondering where Mommy and Daddy were.
Often as not, Mommy and Daddy were at that moment bent over the hood of a police car, being hand-cuffed, or in an ambulance in restraints. I was frightened all the time, and took it out on the guys I was having to manhandle out the door.
After six weeks or so, I was deliberately giving them more than they needed or deserved to get the message across. I took a guy out in the alley one night, and after I threw him into the wall, picked up a garbage can lid and began lecturing him that, "This...WHAM...sort of ...WHAM...bad WHAM...behaviour...WHAM...will not be...WHAM... tolerated...WHAM...any more...WHAM."
He managed to get loose and run out of the alley, and at that moment I thought, "I'm gonna get killed doing this."

Or I was going to kill someone else.

I tossed the lid aside, and went back into the bar to give my notice to Big Gord. He was talking to a guy who wanted to take some time off work, with pay, at the Steel Plant.

They'd worked it out that if the guy could somehow get into the plant with a broken leg, and fake it so it looked as if it occurred on the job, he would not only get a vacation, but Workman's Compensation would kick in too.

"I want 100 bucks." Gord said.

"Okay."

"And another 100 if your Workman's Comp comes through."

"Shit. Alright."

Gord dragged a chair over and grabbed the guy's leg.

"Just put that up there. I'll be right back."

He went behind the bar, and got the Louisville slugger that he kept to settle wagers and political disputes, and came back over. He looked at me.

"Hold his leg down."

"Uh Gord...I need to talk to you."

"Hold it down for Chrissake. I don't wanna fuck this up."

God forbid.

So I held the guys leg down, and Gord said "Ready?"

The guy nodded, and closed his eyes, and the bat came whistling in. There was a hideous crack and a scream, and the guy pitched over backwards.

"Someone call him a cab. He needs to get to work," said Gord, laughing.

We got the guy up onto his chair again, and he peeled off some bills, sweating and moaning, and handed them to Gord.

The cab arrived and I helped him into it, and went back in to give my notice.

Twelve hours later, I was on the highway outside of Halifax airport, with my guitar, and holding my thumb out, on my way to my Uncle Prescott's little house in Halfway Cove.

I stayed there by myself for nearly three months, doing little else but walk the shore, build driftwood fires, and play guitar by the wood stove.

Most days I could go down to the shore in the evening, and buy a nice pair of mackerel for a quarter, or if I was lucky, a haddock to bake in the oven.

I stayed until I couldn't stand my own company any more, and took the train back to Ontario.

Stan had written a letter inviting me to come live in the basement of the little condo where he had been living with Diane Patterson and her three young kids for some months. Her divorce was close to being finalized and the two of them were deeply in love. It made no sense for Stan to keep living in London. So I moved in and made a pallet on the floor next to the furnace. They wouldn't charge me rent or board. As Stan said, "It doesn't cost anything to throw another potato into the stew pot." Easy for him to say, as Diane was the only person bringing home a regular pay cheque.

A few weeks after I came back I made a little nostalgia trip to the Carleton Tavern, and there was now a row of large caliber bullet holes in the front of the stainless steel bar.

Gord said, "Some guy came in looking for you about a week after you quit, and emptied a .45 into the bar and left."

Timing is everything.

The band was still going, more or less.

There was still no focus to anything. It was difficult to motivate most of these guys, not that it was my job. It was just frustrating. Trying to sort them into any cohesive functioning unit was like trying to shovel fleas, or organize the NDP. We never rehearsed.

Luckily, most of them still had highly impressionable and gullible girlfriends, who held down jobs and took care of the bills.

There was no real need to work hard, but we did need a steady gig somewhere, if only to maintain the pretense that we were full time musicians.

I don't know who made the initial contact, but we ended up parking the bus at the Aberfoyle Flea Market, on Highway 6, south of Guelph. I say "We," but at that point I was only nominally part of the band.

The two brothers who ran the Flea Market, Howard and Peter, had somehow fallen under our spell, and had bought into the idea that what the place really needed to put it on its feet was a coffeehouse.

There was an old abandoned slaughter house on the property Concrete floors with channels for the blood to drain off and run away, and huge iron hooks hanging from the ceiling. There was still a giant iron cauldron for scalding the hair off pigs.

Very cozy.

We did some basic carpentry. Built a stage, and a sound booth and a small apartment for visiting musicians to doss down in.

Stan did most of the actual work.

He enjoyed building things, and unlike me, who'd had some actual experience as a construction labourer, he showed a real and unexpected talent for it.

I mostly stood around and handed him tools, and held the other end of the tape measure.

We left the traces of the building's former role as they were. It was too much work to eradicate them, so we decided that the iron hooks and blood channels were just part of the charm.

We called the club "The Slaughter House."

Perfect.

I could just imagine some guy in a smoking jacket putting down his Meerschaum pipe and tossing aside his New Yorker magazine, and saying, "It's poetry night at The Slaughterhouse. What say you, pet? Shall we go?"

There were other performers who came through the club, but it was miles from any potential audience, and most nights the club was host to some variation of the Cedar Lake rabble. You never really knew who was going to turn up for the gig.

The main value of the place for Stan and me was that Howard and Peter paid 2 bucks an hour for whatever construction work we did there.

It wasn't much, but it got us through that lean winter.

We felt like the club was something worth working on. It at least gave us some focus, but it was an odd place.

Howard and Peter were weird guys.

They had an inexhaustible supply of hash.

The story I heard was that their seriously Bohemian parents were touring North Africa, and mailing home Care packages of Blonde Lebanese, and other delicacies of the Mysterious East.

The brothers had a trick with a large homemade brass hookah, and an oxy-acetylene welding rig.

Place a chunk of hash on the bowl, suck on the oxygen tank for a bit, so you could hold your breath longer, and then light the hash. Play the oxygen on the burning chunk of hash, and then suck hard on the hookah. The dope would be vapourized and in your system for days. I never had the nerve.

My one experience with the shit they were inhaling did little but fry my brain to the point where it seemed like a good idea to put on the large Flea Market mascot outfit, the one with six arms, each with its own large white glove, and a top hat, to wander in traffic for some time up and down Highway 6, being blown around by the wind from the passing trucks.

We held a big Thanksgiving dinner that Fall at the club.

Someone got the idea to stuff the turkey with a marijuana dressing.

"It's an herb. It should work."

It was okay, just a little odd tasting.

It may be the only thing the band accomplished, inventing a
Thanksgiving dinner that gave you the munchies.
I slept that night in the giant cauldron.

The winter went by.
There just wasn't enough work to sustain all of us.
Go figure.
The sad part was that it took us so long to accept it, even when the math
was staring us in the face. Stan and I began rehearsing a bit with Jimmy
Ogilvie, the bass player.
Maybe a trio would be more manageable.
Cedar Lake was going nowhere, and the music was amateurish and
disorganized and an embarrassment. There was a surreal discussion one
night, where someone expressed the idea that just because they didn't
know a song shouldn't mean they not be allowed to join in.
    "But you don't know it."
    "Yeah, but that shouldn't mean that I'm not allowed to play."
    "But you haven't learned the song."
    "It's not fair, I want to play along."
    "But you won't rehearse."
    "It's not fair."
The final straw for me was one night when we set up to do a show, and
George Kinsman arrived with a pedal steel and amplifier.
    "I didn't know you played pedal steel, George."
    "I don't, but I'm gonna learn."
    "Right here?"
    "Yup."
    "Right now?"
    "Yup."
    "On stage?"
    "Yup."
    "At a gig?"
    "Yup."
And he made a complete disaster of it as one might expect. Horrible
tuneless caterwauling accompanied every song that first set. But it
was okay. Within the band rules one couldn't be excluded for being a
talentless nitwit. I was proof of that most nights, but now George was
setting the bar even lower.
I looked out at the little audience.
There might have been 12 people out there, sitting at their tables,
smiling gamely at the noise, and I just snapped.
I packed up my fiddle and flute, and left the stage, just as it was Stan's
turn to lead a song.

131

He was calling me as I walked out, but I said nothing. I just left.
Jimmy came into the bus where I was packing my gear a few minutes later.
I turned to him.

"What are you doing?"
He shrugged.

"I'm out of this too. It's just embarrassing."
His girlfriend, Gail, had just had their child, and he needed something else to do.
This was no life for an adult.

Stan hung on for one more gig.
He had more of an emotional investment in the band, they were his friends, after all.
But in the end he couldn't take it anymore either.

Stan had had another major life change, as well, after all these months in Aberfoyle.
His loud and stormy relationship with Diane had finally ended.
Living in their basement, I had been an uncomfortable and unwilling witness to the dissolution of the relationship.
I think from her side, she was growing rightfully disenchanted with the reality of living with a shiftless and lazy ass musician, no matter how much love there might be between them. She had three kids, and a brutally demanding job, and Stan was not holding up his end very well. She would come home from an exhausting and emotionally stressful day at the hospital, and find not only that no dinner was waiting for her or the kids, but the breakfast dishes were still rotting in the sink, and Stan had accomplished little but smoke pot, drink three quarts of home brew, and organize his schedule so as to watch 5 episodes of Sesame Street in a row. And it wasn't as if I was picking up the slack in terms of the house keeping.
Arguments would break out, resulting in Stan yelling, "That's it. I'm out of here!"
And he would frenziedly pack up his suit bag, grab his guitar, bash his way through the front door, and charge up the street, as the two of them exchanged insults between the front porch and the curb.
Diane would slam the door and go into the kitchen, muttering to herself, trying to get the kids' dinner ready and there would be a heavy knock at the door.
Stan would be on the step, still breathless and angry, but now embarrassed.

"I need bus fare."

This comedy was enacted on a pretty regular basis, with Stan never making it much past the end of the block. He would stand there, furiously puffing on a smoke, and considering his dwindling options. Finally he would walk back and begin negotiations to make his way back into the house.

In the end, I think it was Diane who for the sake of her kids, and her own sanity turfed his ass out the door for good.

As the old joke went, "What do you call a musician with no girl friend?" Homeless.

The three of us, Stan, me, and Jimmie Ogilvie decided to throw in our lots, and live together, and work on being a trio.

CHAPTER 17

Brampton

We rented a house in Brampton. I don't know why we chose Brampton, except that it was cheaper than Toronto, and still readily accessible by train. And Jimmy's brother in law lived there, and he had a job, and a credit card and a car which could be borrowed.

It was a large four square Craftsman style place, built most likely just after the First World War, with two storeys, a big front porch and a deeply shaded yard on Albert Street. The train tracks were about 75 feet away. Clattering decrepit freights and high speed commuter trains roared by every 10 or 15 minutes. We stopped hearing them after the first couple of hours.

We moved in and set up the house.

Jimmy and Gail contributed almost all the furniture, as Stan had left Diane with little more than his guitar and suit bag.

I had a table and a chair and a single bed which my cousin Juanita donated from the motel she ran with her husband Paul. It didn't bear close inspection, but it was free, and I was rather less fussy about things back then.

We were all pretty excited.

It was a lovely house, as I remember it, airy and spacious, with three big bedrooms, and a huge beautiful bathroom that had a claw foot tub I could lay full length in, and float. Stan took the large back bed room and paneled all four walls with bark which he'd peeled off a dead elm tree in the side yard. It was ugly, and damp and smelled bad.

"I love it. I think it's great. It's like living in a tree." he said.

Wonderful, except there were a million little bugs living in the bark and they all seemed to have an insatiable curiosity about the wider world, and an overwhelming urge to broaden their horizons. There was a tiny stampede down the hall all the time emanating from Stan's room, and I was kept busy shoveling them back in and closing the door.

Jimmy's partner Gail was concerned for her new baby's welfare,

"I've got a baby to feed here. I can't let her go hungry just because you assholes aren't making any money." This being said as she swung two large green plastic garbage bags of Perth County Home Grown from her shoulder on to the floor.

It was a lot of pot. Maybe three bushels before it was cleaned.

We had no moral qualms about selling pot.

Hard stuff, cocaine and smack was another matter, but pot was just pot. Hell, our parents kept a couple of plants growing in the back yard for the neighbourhood kids. So, the three of us spent the first night in our new house cleaning, weighing and bagging about 30 pounds of weed into small sellable portions, mostly dime bags. It was fun in a communal sort of way, picking out the seeds and stems, carefully weighing the baggies, and stacking them on the big dining room table. It made an impressive pile.

We opened a case of beer and worked well into the night, and went to bed at last, tired and pretty stoned ourselves, but with the knowledge of a good job well done. Next morning, about 8 A.M. I was going down stairs for a glass of water when there was a loud knock on the door.

I opened it, and there were two cops standing on the porch. The one on the right was holding out a search warrant for our address, dated for that day.

They were looking for the previous tenants who had ripped up the nice parquet floors, sold them, and done a midnight skip on the rent.

"Sorry, Officer, we just moved in last night. Those guys aren't here anymore. I guess they did some damage, and the landlord is looking for them. Would you like to come in and call him? You can use our phone."

They were looking over my shoulder, past me into the dining room.

The cop on the left said, "No, it's okay. If they aren't here, we'll try somewhere else.

He looked back at his partner and raised his eyebrows.

The other guy shrugged.

"Really, come in and use the phone. I have the landlord's number in the kitchen.

"No, we have his number. We'll come back another time."

"Are you sure?"

We had been raised to be respectful of cops, and I was trying to be a good boy.

"It's no trouble at all. I was just going to make some coffee. Why don't you come in?"

They kept looking at each other and then past my shoulder.

They seemed confused.

"No thanks sir, we're good. Have a nice day.

"Thanks, you too.

And the two nice policemen left.

I shut the door and turned away to continue my errand, and saw Stan,

sweating and gibbering   and flapping his hands at the top of the stairs.
  "What's wrong?"
  "WHAT WERE YOU THINKING!!!!"
  "What?"
  "THE POT!!!"
  "The pot?"
Oh.
Yeah.
The pot...
It was still piled on the table, a couple hundred small bags of it, and
clearly visible from the door, along with the scales we had used to
weigh it, unused baggies, and the other impedimenta of the drug
dealer's trade.
There was still a thick stinking cloud of smoke hanging below the
ceiling like a weather system.
Why the cops had not come in and arrested the whole lot of us and put
us away, and why Gail and Jimmy's daughter didn't grow up in the
care of Children's' Aid, while Mummy and Daddy rotted in a prison
cell, I don't know.
It occurs to me now that they might have been put off by my
appearance. Being confronted by a scarecrow in a tattered brown terry
cloth robe which looked as if it had been looted from a monk's tomb,
and whose hair was standing out as if having been electrocuted, with
some weapon no doubt concealed in the folds of his garment, and who
was now repeatedly inviting them in for coffee and maybe a nice chat,
seemingly unembarrassed by a fortune in illegal drugs on the table
behind him, they simply might have decided I was too much looney for
their pay grade.
In any case, we never saw them again.

Stan did some basic math and realized that with heat and hydro, and
four people and a new baby to feed, we needed about 1400 dollars a
month just to make our nut.
He was sitting at the big table in the dining room, with piles of paper
covered in scribbled figures. No matter how he added it up it was a lot
of money.
I was proud, we must be a successful band, if our bills were that high.
He began going into Toronto every couple of days, to lurk around the
halls of the old "Kremlin," the main CBC offices on Jarvis Street.
It was a wonderful old relic, that building.
Formerly a girl's private school, it now was a warren of narrow
hallways with uneven floors and dank, cramped offices, and small
studios where legends of Canadian Broadcasting still sat and read the

news of the day. There was little security back in those days and the place was overrun with hangers-on, under medicated mendicants and rightful claimants to various thrones.
As the great Max Ferguson once told us, there was a guy who was known to the staff as "the Moon Radiant" who wandered the halls dressed in a long white robe and a protective tin foil hat.
He would drop in regularly and tell anyone within earshot about his plans for interstellar flight. It was all possible if he could only get the proper funding, and did you by the way, have any spare change?
Occasionally one would be confronted with a man dressed in a heavy wool top coat, wearing gloves and a large fur Russian hat.
It might be 90 degrees outside, but the costume was the same.
He presented himself at the desk of a young producer one morning and the guy burst out laughing. The man in the top coat unwound the wool scarf from his face and was revealed to be Glenn Gould. He lived in deadly fear of catching a cold and dressed that way no matter what the season. Ironically, it was a cold or the flu which was to kill him years later.

Stan was just part of that throng of job seekers.
He would spend the early part of the day buttonholing people for a job writing, and then let Paul Mills take him across the street for a lavish tax-payer funded lunch and 3 or 4 double Manhattans.
He wrote a lot on the train in to town.
   "I noticed all the businessmen, getting into their seats, and opening their brief cases, and going to work. I figured what the hell, I can do that too. So I opened my brief case and wrote a song on the trip."
He would pick up a discarded newspaper on the train, and look through it for some story that might be worked into a song. Nothing he wrote on those trips into town withstood the test of time, but he was learning discipline, and we were amassing a larger catalogue of original tunes.
There were only a couple of listening clubs available to us in those days, Fiddlers Green, and Shier's, which Ken Whitely ran out in Scarborough.
We played Shier's one night, with Raffi as our opener. Raffi had not yet struck kid's music gold, at that point.
He was just another guy out on the circuit, with a shy and loopy patter in between songs, and a voice reminiscent of Kermit the Frog. Decent guy though, and he loved Stan's song, "45 Years," and I remember watching Stan writing out the lyrics for him, and running through the chords after the show.
Colin Linden turned up that night too.
He was about 14 at the time, a somewhat formal and anxious and

diffident kid, with scarily nice manners, who bowed, doffed his hat, and called me "Mr. Rogers," and told me he was planning on spending the winter "woodshedding" to get his blues chops up.

Strange obsessive young boy.

It was a year or two later that Raffi made his first kids record.

He recorded it in Dan Lanois' basement studio in Ancaster, with Ken Whitely producing.

I think their original choice for a fiddle player couldn't make it, so I got the call, and by the way, could I bring my flute along too? I went in and did a couple of tracks, for which I got paid the dazzling sum of 35 bucks. That was okay, I guessed, except that a few months later, Raffi called me and needed my help to fudge his expenses for tax purposes. Was it okay if he told them I was paid 175 dollars instead?

"Are you sending me more money?"

I was currently starving.

No, just cooking the books, apparently. Everyone did it I guess.

That first record really took off, somewhat to our surprise.

We couldn't figure out the concept of kid's music.

When we were kids, we listened to Leadbelly, and Jimmie Rodgers and Beethoven. Scary guys who would cut you if you looked at them wrong. This sounded like musical cream of wheat.

But what the hell, Raffi did well with it, and he did get around to recording "45 Years" sometime later, after the second kids' record had hit the million mark and he was now seriously pigeon-holed as a childrens entertainer. I think he wanted to remind people that he was still a "legitimate artist."

In one of the worst career miscalculations I have ever seen the album was called "Adult Entertainment," and the cover was a picture of Raffi, looking coyly at the camera, and holding a flower, on a background made up to look like the classic "Plain Brown Wrapper" from a porn shop.

It was more than a little creepy, and for a guy who was now known worldwide as the preeminent kids entertainer it was ill considered, and wildly inappropriate.

Apart from the shock value of the cover, the album got no attention, and it dropped out of sight pretty quickly. I still have a copy.

It is not for sale.

Fiddler's Green Folk Club was in a condemned and falling to bits two storey house in Toronto, and was run by a condemned and falling to bits group of ex-pat Scots and Englishmen, along with a lone Jew from Hamilton. The concert room was set up in what had been the living room.

There was a minimal sound system, some cushions on the floor, a handful of chairs, and a tiny stage, about four inches high.
The Friends of Fiddler's Green were (mostly) sober and hard working as they all had real jobs and families, but crazier than a bag of mice.
They performed traditional songs from the British Isles, solo acapella pieces, and great chorus songs and sea chanteys and instrumentals.
Grit Laskin was the odd man out, a Jewish kid from Hamilton. He was working as an apprentice luthier in Jean Larrivee's guitar shop. He played about a half dozen instruments.
Ian Robb was from England. He sang and played concertina, and wrote some excellent songs.
He ran an electron microscope at a hospital in Ottawa.
Jim Strickland was a Scot.
From what part of Scotland, I have no idea.
English did not appear to be his first language anyway, particularly when he was singing.
I am no doubt being typically unfair, given my own language skills were habitually impaired when I was in his company. He had a supply of the best single malt and was more than generous with it. I doubt that he could understand me either by the end of the night.
I think he worked at an investment office. God help Bay Street.
David Parry was from England. He was tall, red haired, handsome and vague, charming and funny and truly eccentric. He did extraordinary and beautiful recitations, and worked at the Museum of Man, I believe, in Ottawa. Most sadly, he died some years ago. It was a shock to all of us. His son now plays with Arcade Fire, and his daughter Evelyn is a successful poet and story teller herself.
Lawrence Stephenson was also from somewhere in Britain, again, I'm not sure where. With all the regional accents in the band, it felt a bit like the U.N., and I'm no Henry Higgins. He was also red haired and friendly, and wildly exuberant.
Lawrence played fiddle, and had a job spilling drinks onto expensive equipment at the CBC.
Alistair Brown was from England, and taught school in London Ontario, and sang and played concertina with the group.
Tam Kearney was from Glasgow, with all that that implies.
He was loud and fat, and wildly, obscenely funny. He had no sense of boundaries or good taste. He was a short rotund Billie Connolly in overalls, and he worked in the Toronto sewers
Go figure.
No joke was too tasteless, and nothing was sacred, or out of bounds.
We were having breakfast at his house one morning, having slept on his floor after a gig at the club. Tam's then wife, Margot was busy making

breakfast. Sausage, and eggs, and bacon, and ham, and beans, and fried potatoes, and black pudding, and toast and porridge, and tea, and scones and smoked kippers, and whatever else Tam might need to get through till lunch, and Stan made a vaguely flirtatious remark to her. She laughed coquettishly and slapped him on the shoulder, and Tam looked over the top of his newspaper, and said, "I wouldnae bother Stan, it's like throwing a sausage doon the Holland Tunnel."

I saw Tam one morning at a festival some years later.

He was walking from his motel room towards the restaurant, and saw a young woman standing in the door of her room brushing out her long hair.

"Good morning darling," he called out.

"Hello."

Tam altered his course to come closer.

"It's a lovely day."

"Yes, it is a lovely day."

He moved in still closer.

"How about a wee kiss?"

I think the woman was a bit taken aback with the over familiarity, and perhaps searching for a gentle way of turning this strange man down, said, "Oh no, I haven't brushed my teeth yet."

"Right then, how about a blow job?"

Tam and I watched as she stormed into the restaurant and demanded that this pervert be arrested and put away. She told the story to the room full of performers who knew him and they all burst out laughing. The Friends were all really funny guys, but they were serious about the music, and what they performed had a kind of urgent primal power. Old songs about death and starvation, and love and betrayal, and war and revenge, and incest and murder and other aspects of home life they had left behind and now missed, having left England's green and pleasant land.

They were all perfectly reasonable people... alone. They were friendly and generous and polite, one on one. Even Tam had a sweet and romantic and sensitive side, which he took great pains to hide. But together, they were loud and outrageous and unstoppable, and they appeared to have no sense of shame. I once watched them sing "Swing Low Sweet Chariot" at a festival in front of Odetta. That by itself was fine, except they sang it accompanied by disgusting and inappropriate hand gestures. Odetta was outraged and told them off in front of the audience for perverting a beautiful and precious song, and turning it into a cheap high school joke.

They took the scolding meekly enough, but when it was their turn to sing again, they launched into a song called, "I'm a Wanker."

"I've wanked over Paris.
I've wanked over Spain.
I've wanked in an omnibus.
I've even had a wank on a train."
Chorus:
"I'm a wanker, I'm a wanker.
And it does me good like it bloody well should.
I'm a wanker, I'm a wanker,
and I'm always pulling my pud."
You could always tell what stage they were playing on at festivals, by the herds of mothers frantically running away covering their kids' ears.

The club was run loosely on the British Isles model. Some floor singers would get up and do a spot, and then there would be a break, and the featured act would do a set. Tam was usually the MC, and this gave him full rein to stand at the back of the room and make jokes and direct cutting remarks to whoever was on stage. He was funny and relentless, and obscene, and you quickly learned to sink or swim.
The Friends were wonderful harmony singers. They had combined the chantey style of singing with the Appalachian shape note tradition. At festivals and parties we would find ourselves drawn to wherever they were, usually standing in a circle, leaning in slightly, and singing close and complex harmonies, long chords that changed and morphed and interwove constantly. It was beautiful and moving, like being inside a pipe organ.
The other side of them was just a kind of roaming anarchistic bedlam of elaborate practical jokes. No one was safe.
Grit had bought a Volvo.
It was his first decent car, and he was very proud of it.
    "It gets fantastic mileage." he said one night, showing it to us out in the parking lot.
    "I've been driving it for weeks now, to and from work, all over town, city driving, you know, stopping and going, and the gas gauge has barely moved. It's wonderful.
It went on for a month or so, Grit extolling the amazing mileage he was getting, to anyone who would listen.
    "How's your car Mister?" Little kids would call out to him, giggling, as he went into the club.
I don't know how it all fell out, but it was eventually revealed to him that Tam, for weeks, after a long day at work in the sewers, had been filling a jerry can of gas, and getting on a series of buses, and making the hour long trek over to Grit's house to sneak up and fill the tank.
I watched them one day, at the Home County Folk Festival, in London,

as they came running en masse through the crowd. The boys had been on their way to do a Mummers play performance, and it had come on to rain.

Ian was wearing a green dragon suit that covered him from head to toe. The rest were wearing odd costumes made of long strips of coloured paper.

They were frantic, running in terror, and laughing helplessly in the pissing downpour.

"What's up?" I said as they ran by.

"Pre-glued wall paper!" Jim Strickland shouted, gasping.

I think it was that weekend that they unveiled the parody of "Barrett's Privateers" that Ian wrote.

It was called "Garnet's Home Made Beer."

It was a tribute to a party gone terribly wrong in the Brampton house. We had decided to throw a celebration that winter, during the brief lull that fell between the obscene over indulgence of Christmas and the prolonged and brain paralyzing debauch of New Year's Eve. In advance of the party I brewed about 20 gallons of what I fondly imagined to be beer. Stan helped me bottle it, and we put it in the cool room off the back porch to mature.

We had been using the same yeast for years, and it had become pretty resistant to alcohol, so we knew the final result would be around 8 per cent by volume.

It was nearly lethal to anyone who thought they were just drinking beer.

The day of the party arrived.

We had invited maybe forty or so guests, expecting maybe twenty to show. Near as we could count about eighty people showed up. Things quickly got out of hand.

Our personal stock went up among our male friends when the 1974 Penthouse Pet of the Year arrived. She was married to a friend of Jimmy's, and apart from being physically spectacular in ways we'd only heard about in the myths and legends told in hushed voices around campfires, Avril London was a really smart and funny and down to earth person. Another sharp lesson in feminist theory for us. Apparently it was only men who were automatically rendered stupid by large breasts.

Ian Robb and his wife Val, who was then about eight months pregnant arrived, and I handed Ian a glass of my creation.

"Here, you're English, you guys like beer. Try this."

As he tells it, he took a sip and said, "I think your camel is pregnant," and handed the glass back to me, and withdrew the hem of his garment. I was a little hurt, but thought, fine, all the more for us then.

Sometime later, a harmless water pistol fight had inevitably escalated and I was rounding the corner at the bottom of the stairs with a bucket of ice water, chasing someone down.

Ian and Val were at the foot of the stairs just turning to wave goodbye. They just got in the way, your honour. That's all.

Val got the full force of the bucket right in the face and all down her front. Why she didn't go into labour right there is a mystery, but the outcome of that incident was that she only began speaking to me maybe a decade later. I don't think she has it in her to hold a grudge, she's far too kind. I think she just couldn't bring herself to trust me for a very long time. I still think she is carefully checking to make sure my hands are empty when I see her.

In any case, Ian got a lasting revenge, and that song is like the mark of Cain for me.

The wreckage from the party took ages to clean up. We were sitting around the evening of the next day, and could hear faint voices under our feet. I wondered if it wasn't some alcohol induced delusion. Was this the beginning of delirium tremens? The voices kept moving around, and we were trying to figure out what the hell was going on. Stan went out to the big pantry in the back of the house and lifted the trap door that was under the carpet. There were three grubby and soot stained faces peering up at us like rescued coal miners, or damned souls looking up from the Abyss.

These guests had found their way to the basement through the nearly inaccessible trap door, and had "fallen asleep." The basement had no light in it at all, and they woke in a kind of sensory deprivation tank. They'd had the good manners not to relieve themselves on the basement floor thankfully, and had managed to find the sump drain and use that.

We pulled them out, gave them some coffee, and sent them on their way.

None of us had the faintest idea who they were.

CHAPTER 18

Montreal

Mike Regenstrief had a club in Montreal, called The Golem.
It was in the Jewish Students' center at McGill, and he had booked us for a weekend.
Sort of a weekend, as there could be no performance on the Sabbath.
We were to play the Friday night, take the Saturday off, and then come back Sunday.
We still had no car in those days, so borrowing the use of Jimmy's sister in law's credit card, we got a clapped out American Motors Gremlin, an aptly named little piece of shit, from Rent a Wreck.
It was cramped and ugly, and when asked to go left or right, it had to give long and sober thought before responding, and even then it tended to waver and reconsider.
It had no heater.
That didn't really matter anyway, because the temperature went down to around -50 degrees the day we left. Minus 50 Fahrenheit, or Celsius or Kelvin, it made no difference at that point, the scales all merge. No heater could compete. It was like driving through an abyss on the far side of one of Jupiter's moons.
We arrived in Montreal and the streets were empty. No one was foolish enough to go out in this weather. You could die in moments. Dire wolves from the forest north of the city had probably invaded and were roaming the streets, looking for the sick and the lame and stealing their pants.
We got to the gig, set up, and waited.

Mike is a quiet friendly guy, and he was giving us a reasonable guarantee, unheard of in those days.
The Golem was in the Hillel House, the old Jewish Students' Center near McGill.
It was a large red brick building with a small common room where the concerts took place.
It was a nice club, verging on legendary, mostly because of Mike's

inspired and eclectic booking policy.

We'd heard one story about Frank Wakefield playing there.

Frank was a famous bluegrass mandolin player, enormously gifted, but bat shit crazy, who, according to the story, had had a massive nervous breakdown and was no longer able to play. After a year or so, he'd one day had some sort of divine revelation, took up his mandolin and composed a tune called, "Jesus Loves this Mandolin Picker: Number 1." As Frank told the story to Rolling Stone magazine, suddenly his abilities came back and he vowed from then on to name everything he wrote, "Jesus Loves This Mandolin Picker: Number 1 or 2, or 3, or whatever. So Frank arrived at the Golem, and began his show.

"This here's a little tune I wrote called "Jesus loves This Mandolin Picker: Number 17," and off he went.

"This next tune is called "Jesus Loves This Mandolin Picker: Number 45."

And so on.

He was looking out at his audience a bit uncertainly from time to time. They were mostly young Jewish men, with Yarmulkes and sidelocks, sitting attentively and applauding politely after each numbered opus of "Jesus Loves This Mandolin Picker."

Finally Frank paused, and shading his eyes against the stage lights said, "Y'all look like Jewboys. Are Y'all Jewboys?"

There was an awkward silence, and then one of the young men said, "Yes Mr. Wakefield. We are all Jewboys."

Right now things were not looking too good for us.

We all kept looking at the clock. It was nearly show time, and nobody had come through the door.

We sat in silence, listening to the radiators clank and groan and bang. At least it was warm, and our muscles were beginning to un-clench from the terrible drive.

About five minutes before show time, a couple, followed by one lone straggler pushed through the door, and began peeling off their winter gear.

It took some minutes for them to unwrap and unwind various mufflers and parkas and sweaters, stamping their feet, holding their frozen ears, and moaning softly.

So we had an audience. We did the show, packed up and left.

Jimmy had a couple of friends up in St Sauveur des Monts, north of the city, up in Kate and Anna McGarrigle country.

They ran a little vegetarian restaurant there, called "The Crossed Carrots," and we were staying with them for the weekend.

We headed north.

The cold was like nothing we had ever experienced. It took over your whole being, your every thought.

None of us had winter coats or hats.

In desperation we had unrolled our sleeping bags and we all trying to huddle as much as we could in the cramped space of the shit box Gremlin.

Our breath was frosting over the inside of the windshield, and so while Jimmy drove, Stan scraped a peep-hole in the glass with the borrowed credit card. It was like driving by periscope.

After about an hour or so we arrived, and Jim's friends, whose names, sadly, I have forgotten pulled us out of the cold into their kitchen.

They were lovely people, kind and welcoming, and they had a big pot of soup on the wood stove.

It smelled heavenly, and I could feel tears start in my eyes. We weren't going to die.

The room was warm and snug, and fresh bread was coming out of the oven.

We hurried back out to get the guitars out of the cold.

Stan came in with his suit bag and threw it onto a daybed, where it shattered into a hundred razor sharp pieces. The vinyl had frozen as if it had been dipped in liquid nitrogen.

Jim came in with the guitars, and Stan opened the case of his Guild to check on it.

Bad move.

There was a prolonged crackling sound, as the temperature differential hit the lacquer on the guitar, and it broke up and slid off like river ice in the spring.

There was no finish left on the guitar. It was all in the case, looking like stripper glitter.

We spent the next day sitting with Jim's friends, playing music with them, drinking their wine and eating everything in sight.

At one point I looked out the window to see a man pushing along on cross country skis.

"Jesus, that guy must be crazy. He's going to die out there."

Our host spoke up.

"No, that's Jacques Rabbit, our local hero."

Jacques was then nearly 80 years old and was credited for popularizing cross country skiing in Quebec and Canada..

He was to live to a ripe old age, going out every day...in the winter at least...and skiing until well into his nineties.

The second night of our run at the club was no better.

A few brave and frozen souls stumbled across the threshold.
The cold had gotten worse if anything, and most of them kept their coats and hats and mitts on.
When they applauded their hands only made a muffled sound so they stamped their feet as well.
We could only see their eyes.
We played to a total of 13 people over the 2 nights.
Mike gave us the full guarantee, although it probably meant he was going to live on Matzoh wafers for the rest of the month.

CHAPTER 19

Noel Harrison

It wasn't all terrible.

A few weeks later we got a call from CBC Halifax.

They wanted us to appear on the Noel Harrison's "Take Time" television show.

We were to be flown out for several days of rehearsal with the house band, with a final taping before a small studio audience.

The show was sweet and quiet and low key, very much like Noel himself.

He was the son of Rex Harrison, who was one of the last of the old Hollywood legends.

Noel had drifted around a bit in his life.

He had been the captain of the British Olympic downhill ski team for a while, and had done some theatre here and there, although being the son of a Hollywood star, it was difficult.

He'd had to turn down a lot of clumsy and insulting requests to reprise his Dad's role in small regional productions of My Fair Lady.

He recorded a couple of albums in the 60's, as did everyone seemingly, and he had a small hit with Leonard Cohen's "Suzanne," and a larger hit with "The Windmills of Your Mind," the theme to "The Thomas Crown Affair."

He had a couple of seasons as the male co-star on The Girl from Uncle, and after that landed a spot as a regular guest on Hollywood Squares. His career was foundering, and as he told me in later years, he was unhappy, and lacking a direction. He met a smart and beautiful young woman named Maggie, who was working on a sailboat as a deckhand. They fell in love and bought a Winnebago, and the two of them went out into the desert east of Los Angeles to take many drugs and live among the iguanas and scorpions for a year, and find themselves, you know, like everyone did in the 60's.

Their expedition took them to Nova Scotia where they fell in love with a farm in the Annapolis Valley. They moved there and began to have kids.

Noel was one of the most naturally charming and well-mannered people in the world, with a great gift for self-deprecating stories, and an innate kindness and decency.
He tended to downplay his abilities, and felt himself to be only modestly talented as a singer. Much like his father he'd mostly speak the lyrics of songs, rather than sing them, but he so obviously loved what he was doing it was a joy to watch and listen to him.

The real test of a person's kindness is how they treat others who are ostensibly "below" them; waiters, cab drivers, and chambermaids.
Noel was unfailingly polite to and keenly interested in everyone he met. We had the pleasure of sitting on a resort balcony with him one summer night as a very formal and white gloved waiter brought us many martinis, which of course Noel was buying.
It was an elegant and posh sort of place, and Stan and I had no business being there.
Nor did Noel if one judged by his appearance.
He was wearing ripped and faded jeans and canvas boat shoes, and an old sweatshirt with the sleeves hacked off.
The waiter was a one of those rigid Jeeves types, and was probably taken aback at having to serve a bunch of hairy raggamuffins, but by the end of the night Noel had drawn out from the man his name, the names of his wife and kids, and his whole life story, and when we got up to go back to our rooms he left the man a lavish tip, and they hugged like old friends.

That night he told us about an incident from his boyhood.
He was living in the south of England with his mother, during the height of the Battle of Britain.
One warm sunny afternoon he could hear the sound of over stressed aircraft engines and gun fire in the distance, but coming rapidly closer.
His Mum shouted to him to come inside, but Noel stayed out to see the show.
All at once a Messerschmitt 109 came roaring over the trees, followed closely by a Hurricane with its guns blazing.
Pieces of cowling were exploding off the front of the German plane.
It had one wheel down, and it was trailing smoke. They flashed over the house and disappeared past the trees on the other side of the yard. There followed a massive explosion, and a ball of orange flame blossomed up into the sky.
The Hurricane came back over the house, and executed a victory roll.
A moment later the pilot brought the fighter down low and flew slowly past Noel as he stood in the yard. He caught Noel's eye, and then

snapped a smart salute before opening the throttle and roaring off back to the battle.

Noel had his feet up on the railing and we could hear the raccoon family we had let into our rooms busily tearing into the pizza boxes, and then going into the bathroom to wash the leftover crusts in the toilet.

He was holding his martini glass by the stem and twirling it slowly. His eyes were far away and he had a sweet reminiscent smile.

"I think that was the best day of my life, you know...as a kid, anyway. The only way it could have been better was if the pilot had come down and handed me a puppy."

I think to a large degree he felt over-shadowed by Rex.

And who wouldn't?

I met Rex years later, while playing with Noel at Tommy Makem's Irish Pavilion in New York, and he was a terrifying and cranky old man, very much aware of his own legend and gravitas, and with the look of a debauched and dyspeptic old eagle.

I had Gail with me for the trip, and she and Noel and I spent Father's Day backstage with Rex in his dressing room on Broadway, where he was starring in a production of "Aren't We All?," with Lynn Redgrave and Jeremy Brett and Claudette Colbert.

We drank Dom Perignon and I told Rex lurid stories from Hamish Imlach's life, while Gail and Lynn Redgrave discussed the problems of persistent uterine infections in thoroughbred broodmares.

Rex was sitting back in his chair, dressed in a beautiful silk Hermes robe, and giving us expert advice about Champagne.

"Oh, this Dom Perignon you brought along is all very well and good, but rather overrated in my estimation. I much prefer the Tattinger '79 vintage. There is a store on West 64th called "Garnet's Liquors." He paused and looked at me. "Your name is Garnet too, you're not related? No? Too bad. Oh well. Never mind. Anyway, they will sell you case lots of the Tattinger for 12 dollars a bottle. Well worth the trip."

At one point the phone rang, and Rex's dresser answered it and then brought over the receiver.

It was Rex's wife, his seventh, I believe.

Rex took it, and there was a brief and tense conversation, and he ended it by slamming the phone down and saying, "Women! I hate them all. They remind me of my agent."

As we made our goodbyes, the evil old man took Gail's hand and leaned forward and ever so gracefully kissed it.

Anyone else these days who tries to kiss a hand looks like a complete

twat, but for Rex it was an effortless and practiced move, borne out of long years of breeding and privilege, and being... well...Rex.
He was all the while looking up at her with his hooded eyes as if to say, "I know it, my sweet, and you know it too. Not today perhaps, not tomorrow, but someday. Someday I will make you mine."
It was an astonishing performance.
We parted outside in the alley next to his limousine, in a throng of autograph seekers, and as the car glided away, Gail said, "Wow. I just got Rexed."

Noel was very respectful and subdued about his Dad.
He mostly seemed to be just happy to get along in his life, and be in love with his wife, and raise the kids.
He appeared to have no need for the limelight. Perhaps he was just resigned to forever being in that long shadow.
Children of famous folk have a hard job.
The parent's particular gift or talent is never completely passed on, and the opportunities are never the same, and if they are bent on trying to make it in the same discipline as their parent they will always suffer by comparison.
It can be very sad to watch.
In Noel's case he seemed to have come to terms with the whole thing, and he had learned the difference between humility and shame.
His television show was all about the song writing and the joy of connecting through music.

So we flew into Halifax, and arrived at the studio, excited as hell.
This was a big break for us.
National TV.
The green room next to the studio was Bedlam.
Everybody was staggering, rat legged drunk. They'd just found out that their option had not been picked up, and this was the final season.
Damn.
My first glimpse of Noel was as he came into the room, a reefer in one corner of his mouth and a bottle of cheap tequila in either hand, arms outstretched in apology.
But rehearsals went well.
Stan and Noel taped a good interview, a one on one about the writing process, and we were to do the taping of the show the next day. Next morning we ran through the tunes with the house band, and blocked out some camera shots.
Then we had to go into make -up.
This was new.

We were in the dressing room changing our clothes, and we were all standing pantless, Jimmy as usual was going commando.
The door opened, and the makeup artist swept in.
"Well hel-lo there." he said, admiring Jimmy's wedding tackle.
He put a hand on his hip and struck a pose.
"I'm here to make you all beautiful. Who wants to be first?"
We all frantically scrambled into our jeans, and lowered our voices an octave.
"I'll go first." said Stan bravely.
God, we were hicks. Still labouring under the stupid myth that a gay man will want to have sex with anyone, no matter how unattractive and stupid and beastly.

Stan got into the chair.
Jim and I sat down to wait and began pointedly flipping through Penthouse magazines and talking like John Wayne.
The make-up guy put a cloth around Stan's neck and took a step back, considering.
"Not a lot to work with here." he said.
I don't know if he meant Stan's hair, or just his appearance in general.
In any case, he began to layer on foundation and then some ghastly orange mixture, and then went to work on the bags under Stan's eyes.
He decided that Stan's almost none existent mustache needed some help, and with the aid of eye shadow, and some mascara, and possibly some Bondo, gave Stan a weird and ghostly Trompe L'Oeil creation in brown.
It was unsettling.
Jimmy took no time at all to make beautiful, but I was in the chair for the better part of an hour as the makeup guy troweled over the damage from the excesses of the night before.
First some foundation, and then rouge to give my cheeks some much needed colour.
He then pulled my long blonde hair back and braided it.
After that he went to work on my eyes with heavy mascara and eye liner.
He redrew my eyebrows, and I now looked permanently surprised.
When I got out of the chair I looked like Heidi might have appeared after spending a couple of seasons working the steam rooms and massage parlours on the back streets of Geneva.

The show went off without a hitch, no disasters, for once, and we celebrated later with the crew.
Next day, I caught the train back to Ontario, and Noel took Jim and Stan

to the airport.
He led them to a grassy hill away from the terminal, and popped open
a cold bottle of Champagne for their breakfast, lit up a cannon-cracker
sized spliff, and got them helplessly addled for the flight home. What a
lovely man.

Noel began touring in Ontario fairly regularly after that.
The TV show had helped with his profile, and he was picking up some
really nice gigs. Stan and I and David Woodhead, who had replaced
Jimmy Ogilvie by now, became Noel's semi-permanent backup band.
We played that resort in Huntsville where he had bonded with the
waiter, and the Astrolabe in Ottawa, and many other gigs we never
could have got ourselves.
We would open the show with our own set and then back up Noel.
His repertoire consisted of Jacques Brel songs, old World War One
music hall stuff, like "How're ya gonna keep 'em down on the Farm,
after they've seen Paree?" and George Formby tunes, along with John
Denver songs, and tunes by Willie Nelson and Jerry Jeff Walker, both of
whom he had spent some time with while living in Texas.
Except for the John Denver stuff, which we despised on principle, it was
all fun, and we loved him.

Noel passed just last year, as I write this, having split from Maggie some
time before.
We had kept occasional touch with him over the years.
He came to the O'Keefe Centre in Toronto, with a production of
"Sullivan and Gilbert," a comedy about the light opera composers.
It was wonderful to reconnect, and he was still the same sweet and kind
man I had known.
Gail and I met him for dinner after the show.
He was making a decent living in the theatre, with that sort of typical
light fare we had seen his Dad play in years before.
Lots of doors slamming, mistaken identities, with slim ingénues
running about the stage in their underwear, and bronzed young men in
striped jackets and boater hats, stepping onstage through French doors,
carrying a tennis racket, and crying, "What Ho!"
He was having a good time.
His next gig was going to be playing the director in "Noises Off."
        "Oh God...you'll be perfect for that."
        "Thanks, I'm even doing "My Fair Lady" now."
        "Really? Isn't that awkward for you?"
        "No, the old man is fine with it. He told me to have fun with it and
to take the money and run."

I said, "You know, Stan always used to say, "Take the money and get the fuck out of Dodge."
Noel laughed.
"Oh, I do like that."
He raised his glass and clinked it against ours.
"Here's to him, then. Take the money and get the fuck out of Dodge."

CHAPTER 20

The Stampeders

Incredible luck.

We had not one, but two gigs.

We had a weekend at Smales Pace, in London, and to sweeten the deal, somebody had set us up to do an opener for the Stampeders in the gym at Strathroy high school west of town. They were touring behind their big hit single "Sweet City Woman," and were taking a full rock and roll show out into the boonies, and it required a big crew, with semis and limos and all the other accoutrements of the rock and roll lifestyle to do it.

Stan and Jimmy and I arrived in a borrowed Mini.

Three tall guys and two guitars, and a bass amp, and fiddle and flute, and all our luggage, in a Morris Mini. We pulled up in the shadow of the semis in the parking lot, and got out.

It took a while and some extra hands to uncoil Jimmy from the back seat where he had been curled up like a moth larva.

We pulled him out and he spent a few minutes massaging his limbs, trying to get the blood flowing again.

The Stampeders road crew strolled over to say hi.

The roadies were all nice guys, which was good, as they were all huge and terrifying, with arms like tattooed Virginia hams, and earrings made from the teeth and finger bones of their vanquished foes.

They made Stan and I feel dainty.

"Where's your gear?" someone said.

"In the car."

"What car?"

Stan gestured with his hand.

"That car."

"That car?"

"Yup."

"You guys are on tour in that? It's not a car. It's a fuckin' roller

155

skate."

"It's just a weekend out," Stan said a little defensively.
The bunch of them doubled over laughing, and a large flat cart was
rolled over, and four of them each grabbed a corner of the Mini, lifted
it up and set it onto the cart. They pushed it through the double doors
into the hall and wheeled it in front of the stage.

"There ya go."

I never was much of a fan of the Stampeders music.
I only ever knew that one single, but it wasn't aimed at me so it didn't
matter that I didn't like it.
What did matter was they were all nice guys, particularly for emerging
rock stars, and they treated us well during the little time we spent with
them. They made sure we got a sound check first, which was un-heard
of courtesy for an opener, and then proceeded with their own.
There was a lot of fussing about the timing of the drum solo. Everyone
had a drum solo in those days. The Stampeders' drummer at some point
would switch to cloth mallets soaked in lighter fluid, and the lights
would go out, and well, it was all very impressive, I'm sure. A couple of
roadies had to be on hand with fire extinguishers in case the drummer
accidently self-immolated.

There were no seats in the gymnasium. It was a cross between a rock
concert and a high school dance.
The doors opened and the crème of Strathroy's youth culture poured in
and they were already gunned. All of them.
They came through the doors, staggering and lurching and reeling,
looking as if the Last Trumpet had just sounded, and the Dead were
now rising to meet and accept their Final Judgement.
High school hadn't changed much in one respect since I had left.
Gilbey's Lemon Gin mixed with Fresca still seemed to be a rite of
passage.
Before the show there had been scattered pairs of girls out in the
parking lot. One would hold back the others hair while she bent over
and blew lemon scented vomit out her nose and whimpered, "Never
again." Then they'd reverse position.
Farm boys were already having shoving contests that would inevitably
lead to them breaking their knuckles on each other's foreheads by the
end of the night. It was going to reduce their sex lives by about 50 per
cent.

"Just like the old days." Stan said, as he smoked a pre-show
cigarette and watched by the gymnasium door.

"Yup. The classics never die."

156

We went on and began to play.

We were just wrong for the crowd.

They hated us, and rained trash down on us for the duration of our set. At one point, Stan, in an effort to connect with the mob said, "So, what do you guys like to do for fun around here?"

A young girl in tight jeans staggered up to the stage. She had an unruly left breast which had just managed to free itself from her tube top. She thumped the stage with the flat of her hand to get Stan's attention, and yelled, "Take Acid!" and then her knees buckled, and she hit her chin on the lip of the stage, and fell down unconscious.

Well that's nice, dear.

Her friends grabbed her by the wrists and dragged her out into the hallway, her tube top finally being rolled down to her waist by the friction of the floor.

She's someone's sweet old Grannie by now, dandling the little ones on her knee, and reminiscing about the good old days.

We finished our set, and now had to carry our gear out through the gauntlet of the mob, and be pelted with more used Juicy Fruit gum, potato chip bags, empty beer and coke cans, and a couple of (thankfully) unused Kotex from the dispenser in the girls' washroom. That last one hurt.

Someone had decided it was worth investing10 cents to show us how much they hated us.

We loaded up. Stan went back in to collect our cheque. We'd made 100 bucks, and we peeled out of the parking lot and headed for London. There were tornado warnings on the radio for a hundred mile radius, and at one point we had to make a wide detour to avoid where we could see the telltale flash of power lines being ripped off poles out on the dark and ugly horizon. We didn't want to be crushed by falling cattle or a grain silo that had been launched out of a barn yard like an ICBM, and was now returning from orbit. It was a scary drive.

We made it to the club, and were greeted by the manager, Bonnie Boydell, who had a plate of sandwiches and a bottle of scotch waiting for us in the dressing room.

I'm pretty sure that gig at least went well, but typically I have no memory of it as a result. It seems easier to remember the disasters. I do recall just how happy and grateful we were to get out of the storm, to see an old friend, and the food and the scotch waiting for us, and to smell the scent of cinnamon and warm apple cider, and the patchouli and strawberry oil, and hear the murmur of the audience sitting out in the darkened concert room, waiting patiently for us to arrive. We were home.

CHAPTER 21

Secret Agent Man

I don't know where she came from, but somehow we had got ourselves an agent.

She was a thin blonde-ish chain-smoking creature from Toronto, and as she may still be with us, I will not reveal her name. I don't think there should be any statute of limitations on prosecuting war criminals and child molesters, but there's not much point in tormenting someone after all these years just because they were greedy, self-serving and incompetent.

I don't know why she got the job.

I would guess that at the time we were just so thrilled to have someone interested in what we were doing we didn't think to check if they were good or capable or honest, and she was none of the above.

We had an initial meeting with her, and she laid down some ground rules. "I get 20 percent of gross income, and all my expenses. Phone, hotels, and airfares."

Hotels? Airfares? Where the hell was she going?

"I'll need to be reimbursed immediately for any capital outlay. And I need to be able to make expenditures without consulting you."

What?

"I don't want to have to check with you on every little thing. It takes up valuable time."

How were we going to afford this?

Her last instruction to us came as she handed Stan her business card.

"This is my private phone number. DO NOT give it out to anyone."

"So how the Hell is she supposed to work for us, if no one is allowed to call her?"

Stan and I were walking through the ankle deep slush on Yonge Street down to the Elizabeth Street bus terminal, some 20 blocks away, to go home.

Stan shrugged and said, "I guess we make the first contact, and then we get her to phone the club and make the deal."

"But if we're still finding the gigs and making the contacts why are we paying her? We're doing all the work."

"I guess she can negotiate better fees."

"But we're paying her 20 percent of those fees and her travel, and who knows what else. What do we do if she decides she needs a car, or a nice little house in the suburbs?"

He didn't answer. We were both depressed and deflated, after our initial euphoria.

We got to the terminal and caught the bus back to Brampton.

She did get us a gig though.

Two weeks in a basement bar on Queen Street, a couple blocks east of Yonge.

The winter Olympics were on, and we were not allowed to turn off the row of TVs that hung over the stage.

We could turn the sound down however, which made for a few surreal moments, when the audience, apparently watching us intently, would burst into wild cheering in the middle of a song.

We would find out later that it was just in response to some Austrian downhill skier cartwheeling end over end down the course at 60 miles per hour, arms and legs in the shape of a swastika, to crash through a snow fence.

We hated missing that sort of thing, and arranged to have a smaller TV pointed back at us next to the monitors, so we at least would have some idea of what was going on.

There was a nicer, more upscale lounge above us.

A couple of burnt-out head cases were playing that room, and we had to share a dressing room with them. One of the head cases was a semi-famous guitarist who had played with pretty much everyone in the world, and was currently drinking himself to death with the royalties of his one big co-written radio hit.

The other was just a mess, a local guy who'd had a brief dalliance with a major label, and was cruising on what little name recognition he still had.

They were both staggering, rat legged drunk the whole time we were around them, and the semi-famous guitarist was at the point where he could no longer play his own guitar parts. They'd hired a young kid to take care of that.

One night, the semi-famous guitarist was missing in action.

It was about a minute to show time, and frantic phone calls were being made back to the house they shared. No one knew where he was.

The dressing room door opened, and he breezed in with his guitar and banjo cases.

"Where the Hell were you?"

He threw the cases up onto the counter and said, "What are you guys worrying about? Everything's under control."

He was obviously already blitzed, and trying his best to hide it.

"I've never missed a gig in my life."

He then opened the cases with a flourish, and we could see they were both empty. He shrieked, and then turned and ran out the door and up the stairs to flag a cab and go home to get the missing instruments.

An hour later, we were relaxing after our first set, and the guy crashed back into the room, wild eyed and sweating, grabbed the empty cases he had left behind and ran back out.

A couple of nights later, I went down to the dressing room to retrieve a capo for Stan, and found the two of them, their pants around their ankles, getting serviced by a couple of decrepit Queen Street scrubbers. I stopped, and began backing up and babbling apologies.

"That's okay Garnet. We're almost done here." the guitarist said.

He gave a little gasp. "Stick around. They'll do you too."

I left a Garnet-shaped hole in the door, like in a Bugs Bunny cartoon.

A few people started coming in to actually listen to the show.

One night we were sitting at a table visiting with a couple of friends, and a handsome and well-dressed older man came over to our table and introduced himself.

As soon as we heard his voice we knew who it was.

It was Max Ferguson.

Max Ferguson.

We couldn't believe it. He was a legend of Canadian Broadcasting, one of the last of the announcers who had once made the CBC such a respected institution all over the world.

He was wonderful. Kind, and funny, and still very much the revered grand old man of CBC radio.

It was exciting to sit and listen to that so familiar voice at such close range.

He was a great story teller.

He would light a smoke, pick up his drink, swirl the ice around a bit, hold it up to the light, and then take a sip. Then he'd throw one leg over the other and lean back and talk, always in that deep beautifully modulated voice.

Always perfectly dressed in a dark blue blazer with brass buttons, and grey slacks, and with an actual by God, silk ascot at his throat. He was one of our heroes, and we had listened to him all our lives.

He had started out in London Ontario, just after the War, working
for a commercial station, and then moved to CBC Halifax as a junior
announcer and spare wank for the jobs no one else wanted to do.
He had been assigned the hosting job for a morning country music
show being broadcast out of Halifax. As he told the story in his memoir,
he was furious, having a deep loathing for the sappy and sentimental
tripe that was country music in those days. The songs, as he said, all
had titles like, "I Tapped Upon the Hearse Window, Grannie, But You
Did Not Look Out."
Worried that someone he knew might recognize him, at the last
moment he disguised his voice as that of a crusty old cow poke named
"Rawhide," who spent his time making fun of the singers whose
records he was playing.
     "And that was Furlined Husky, folks. We all wish him the very
best as he moseys off down the canyon on his faithful horse, into the
glorious sunset, where he will no doubt be blinded by the light, and not
see the deadly 500 foot drop in front of him."
Max had been trying to get fired that first morning, but the switch board
lit up after the broadcast and the character and the show took off, and
he was stuck with it. In later years he broke away from the country
format and began playing music from his own eclectic library. He also
began writing and performing small topical comedy skits, staying in
character as "Rawhide," and using other characters he invented and
played himself.
In his memoir, Max described how one morning he performed an
elaborate scene where a character named "Grannie," a foul mouthed
and violent pensioner with criminal leanings attacked and grievously
injured a small pet spider owned by another character.
During the attack a pompous and egotistical CBC announcer character
named "Marvin Mellobell" tried to intervene, and at the same time
describe the fight to the radio audience. Max, still in character as
"Rawhide," wrung his hands and called for help. Max did his own
sound effects, and to give the illusion of the spider being beaten to a
pulp by Grannie's umbrella, he slowly crushed an empty strawberry
box in front of the microphone. It was a very busy few minutes for Max.
Next morning and for weeks following, the mail was full of sympathy
cards for the spider and loving gifts which listeners had sent in,
including boxes of live flies, in case he got tired of hospital food, and at
least one tiny knitted sweater with eight arms.
Because he was going out live and using as a script only a few scribbled
notes on the back of an Export "A" cigarette package, the censors
couldn't keep up with Max, and there were times when he would do
a skit on the morning show, and later that day be attacked on the floor

of the House of Commons by whatever worthless stuffed shirt he had
been lampooning. He became a national hero.
And now, here he was, and we were thrilled to think he liked what we
did.
He was there most nights.
A few years later, when our records started coming out he was a big
supporter.
He played us a lot on his national show. Just a sweet and charming and
gentle man.
He passed recently, as I write this, and I was appalled and ashamed
that his death rated barely a mention, well down the list on the evening
news, from the Corporation where he had done such beautiful and
ground breaking work.

The Queen Street gig wore on, and we began to notice that the bar was
running out of a lot of stuff, and not replacing it.
The sound guy slid over behind the table one night, as we were taking a
break.
He leaned in and said, "I think you guys better make sure you get paid
in cash tomorrow night. This place is closing for good, and the sheriff is
going to lock the doors."
So the next night while Jimmy and I helped the sound guy load his
equipment out in advance of the bailiff, Stan had a long and earnest
conversation with the manager, and we did in the end get the cash,
almost all of which was handed over to our Dad, to pay off a small
portion of our loan balance.
The rest went to the secret agent, so we were still broke.
Jimmy was coming down with a flu bug that night which would keep
him on his back for the next few weeks. He hitchhiked through the
snow back to the house with his bass and amp, and Stan and I ended
up at some expensive apartment with the secret agent, and two of her
depraved friends.
The friends were bleached blonde, and vulgar and skinny and loud,
and expensively dressed, with leather pants and wolf fur coats, and
diamond rings you could hold the Stanley Cup on.
They were both very tanned, and very drunk, and coked to the gills.
I couldn't figure out what they did for a living. That was revealed some
time later.
There was a long and surreal discussion about Stan's career that night,
wherein one of them seriously suggested that what Stan really needed
to improve his image and get ahead was a pair of two hundred dollar
designer jeans.
The taller one stood up and modeled for us. "See? Gucci."

She spun around a few times, threw out her arms, and then fell back
into the sofa, giggling inanely.

"See what they do for the figure?"

Two hundred dollar designer jeans.

What Stan really needed was two hundred dollars, and as for his figure,
for Christ's sake, he was tipping the scales at about 270 pounds just
about then.

The women were tiresome and loud, and I left to hitch hike back to
Brampton.

Stan stayed behind, and somewhat to my disgust, the taller of the two
career girls became a feature in his life for a couple of months.

She and the shorter one would turn up on our doorstep after a night
on the tiles and want to be served breakfast. They would have been
working a convention west of Toronto, and after a busy shift in the
world of mergers and acquisitions would be hopelessly addled on coke,
and in need of a place to freshen up and rinse their mouths.

The shorter of the two developed an interest in my fair white body, and
began phoning from time to time inviting me over to her lair. I never
had the nerve or the desire.

One afternoon Stan knocked on the door of the bathroom where I was
relaxing in the tub with a book, and handed me the phone.

"It's for you," he said with a nasty smile.

Oh Christ, it was her.

"I've got a jeroboam of champagne here, and I just filled the
bathtub with peach Jell-O. Why don't you come over?" She then made
a suggestion that would have made Caligula call for the police, and I
nearly dropped the phone into my bubble bath.

I came out a while later and handed the phone to Stan.

"Don't ever do that again."

"Not interested?"

"No. Not now. Not ever. If she calls again tell her I've moved to Fire
Island with a guy named Lance."

I got back to the house in Brampton that night after the Queen Street
gig, to find Jimmy sweating and shaking and puking out everything he
might have eaten in the last two years.

Multi-tasking.

There was no food in the house except for what was my staple in those
days, Red River cereal. About 89 cents for a box that would last about a
week.

It was dull stuff.

It had to be cooked for an hour or so, and it tasted much like the box

it came in, and even after an hour on the stove it was still like eating a
warm bowl of wet sand.

I made a pot of it, forced it down and went to bed.

We were given another booking.

It was a weekend in Quebec City, playing at a small college.

We spoke no French, the audience spoke no English, and the gig was
chiefly memorable for the drive home.

We were creeping along the westbound 401 just outside of Kingston, in
a rented Dodge Pacer which was the colour of a blow fly and about the
size and shape of an anal suppository.

Jimmy was driving, and the road was slick with freezing rain.

The cops and emergency crews were out in force.

There were wrecks everywhere.

Jimmy was hunched over the wheel, and we were debating whether to
pull in to a rest stop, to wait out the storm.

Stan said, "I heard the Good Brothers got caught in a snow storm
on the 401, and pulled into the rest stop and made a couple of hundred
bucks, just by opening up their cases and playing for the truckers."

"Doesn't sound like much fun to me."

"Yeah but we could use a little extra cash."

We could have used a lot of extra cash, but the idea was repellent to me.

"I'm not playing 'Fox on the Run'. Not for any money."

The road was a frictionless surface.

Jimmy was just trying to keep it between the ditches where the other
drivers seemed to have decided to park, apparently at random, and in a
great hurry.

I was squirming around in the back seat trying to find somewhere to
put my legs, when I noticed a large dump truck behind us.

We were doing about 40 miles per hour.

The dump truck was doing maybe 41 miles per hour, slowly gaining
on us, which would have been okay, except that he was out of control,
spinning slowly and elegantly in a stately 360 degree ballet.

He kept inching closer. Soon he was only a couple yards off our bumper,
rotating like a 30 ton curling stone.

"Uh, Jim."

"I see him." Jimmy was peering at the rear view mirror. "I see him. I
just can't do anything about him."

There was no safe way to move out of its path. If Jim turned the wheel
at all it had to be done slowly or we would go into a helpless spin
ourselves.

We continued along, watching the monster float ever closer, and then
there was a slight bend in the road to the left which we were able to

follow. The truck, in accordance with Newton's Second Law, kept straight, as the road curved out from under it, slid into the ditch, and disappeared down a gully. I could see the tops of trees whipping back and forth as he plowed through about a quarter mile of forest, and gradually came to a halt.

We made it back to Brampton in one shaky piece to find that the pipes in the house had frozen and burst while we were away. The place was full of steam and icicles, and Jimmy's partner Gail had taken the baby to away to the house of a friend to keep warm.

It was a tough winter.

The food situation was dire

Gail was breastfeeding her baby, Felice, which meant that she herself had to eat.

Her parents were up on the North shore of Lake Superior.

Her Dad, Mr. Nyman, was a commercial fisherman, and Gail and Jimmy · went up North for two weeks to show off the baby to the grandparents, and to ice fish.

They came back with a pick-up truck load of home-canned whitefish and trout, and smoked salmon.

That with the eggs and bread we got through the five finger discount at the Dominion store kept us alive until Spring.

The secret agent got us an audition for a club called Egerton's near Ryerson University.

A paid audition. 50 bucks, to play an hour long set.

Stan was either staying at Paul Mills' place or with the young CBC production assistant he was currently seeing, so Jim and I caught the bus into Toronto, and humped all our gear along Yonge Street from the Elizabeth Street terminal.

We had the bass, the bass amp, the speaker cabinet, and my flute and violin.

We had to walk some 25 blocks through a blizzard.

Neither of us had winter coats, or proper shoes, just sneakers. This wasn't the music business, it was a Dickens novel. We got to the club, brushed off the snow, hooked up with Stan, did the set, and he collected the money.

Our agent took the 50 bucks from Stan, and shoved it into her bra.

"I need new drapes."

We played a gig at a club called "The Bitter Grounds," on the Queens University campus.

It was notable only for two reasons, in that Shelagh Rogers, who would

later work for the CBC, was our sound person, and the club closed its
doors for good the night we played, due to declining revenues. It was
just one of an endless number of clubs to which we administered the
death blow in the coming years.

Apart for that show we had no work, and the rent was coming due, and
there was a phone bill on the hall table and nothing to pay it with.

Mum and Dad had made it clear that they weren't a bottomless well of
largesse.

I applied to a gas station one afternoon for a part time job, but was told
to get lost after it was revealed I had no idea how to operate a cash
register, a gas pump, or even an oily rag.

CHAPTER 22

Jimmy Leaves The Band

Rescue arrived in the form of a CBC recording gig, courtesy of Paul Mills.

In those days the Corp was doing in-house, extended play recordings, which would then be broadcast on the national and local services, and could be actually purchased by mail-order.

They gave much-needed exposure to a lot of artists back then, and the sessions paid money. Actual coin of the realm.

Stan had done a couple of them a few years previous as a solo, and it was now it was the trio's turn at the public tit.

The morning of the session our borrowed car broke down, and I don't recall how we got to Toronto, but we arrived at the studio late and scared, and anxious and embarrassed.

The room was full of seasoned studio veterans.

A guy named Jack Zaza was on accordion this morning, but he also played another dozen instruments.

John Capek was on piano.

There was a session drummer named Brian Leonard, I believe, and David Wilcox was on acoustic guitar.

There were also about 16 or so string players out on the floor, smoking, chatting idly, and reading the paper, and getting paid Union scale for it. The clock was ticking. Shit. This was awful.

Paul was livid, and tearing out his hair as we loaded our gear in.

We set up as quickly as we could, and got going.

I was not up to play yet, as I was ostensibly going to lay down my flute and violin parts later.

Stan and Jim were out there though, and it started going wrong immediately.

The arranger, Mylan Kymlicka, had taken it upon himself to change the keys of the songs, as well as the arrangements, and Jimmy, his nerves in rags from lack of studio experience, and the terrible start to the day was having trouble.

"45 Years" had gone from B flat to A, and Jim kept missing takes.
It shouldn't have been a big deal, but Jim had been thrown an
unexpected curve, and unlike the other players in the room he had no
idea how to read a chart. And all these pros were sitting there, watching
and waiting. They kept having to stop and retake, and the morning
wore on.

Stan was okay. He had only to sing. He wasn't even playing guitar
today.

Paul, as producer had determined that Stan's signature guitar part
which Jimmy was used to cueing off of would be replaced with a more
generic part played by David Wilcox.

It no longer sounded even remotely like the song we knew, and Jim was
sweating bullets.

Another fluffed take and Paul called a halt. Stan left the room to look for
the washroom.

I followed Paul out into the big room to take Jimmy a coffee and try to
buck up his spirits.

Paul went over to Jack Zaza, and in a low voice I heard him say, "Do
you have your bass with you?"

"Yeah. It's out in the car."

"Get it, would you?"

Paul and Jimmy had a short whispered conversation in the corner of the
control room. Jim's face fell, and he turned and left the room.

Stan came back, and Paul explained that we needed to get moving.
Jack would play bass on the song.

Stan shrugged and nodded. He knew we were under the gun.

I realized that my presence was surplus to requirements for the
moment, and wandered down the hall to see if I could find Jim.

There was no sign of him, and I gave up and sat in a lounge, watching
the live in-house feed from the studio where they were taping "Mr.
Dress-up."

That day, the story line was that Mr. Dress-up and the puppets, Casey
and Finnegan, were making soup. Mr. Dress-up was wearing a Chef's
outfit, complete with tall white hat. He was waving a spoon like a
baton, and leading the puppets in singing "the Soup Song." It was
going well, until Ernie, AKA, Mr. Dress-up flubbed a line, and they had
to stop and retake.

And he got to the same place and flubbed the line again.

And again, they had to re-set and start over, and he once more he blew
the line.

He whipped off his hat and threw it at the camera, and then grabbing
the two puppets with a pair of tongs, threw them into the stock pot, and

began to stir vigorously.

The two suddenly naked hands mimed shock and surprise, and ran off camera, and the whole crew broke up.

God help them if this somehow went out live, on the network. A lot of traumatized kids were going to need therapy.

I went back to the studio. They had just finished a successful take of "45 Years", complete with a rich syrupy layer of Mantovani-like strings. It was awful. This was everything I hated about commercial radio, not to mention Paul's approach to Stan's music. I had to leave.

I bumped into Jimmy on the stairs outside.

"Jesus, Jim, where did you go?"

He was wiping his eyes on his sleeve, and his voice shook.

"Tell Paul that Jack can do the whole session. I'm quitting the band."

"What? Jim you can't quit. It's just one song."

"It's not just one song. I've nearly starved to death and done every shitty gig that's been thrown at us for the last year, and now that something good comes along that I really want to do I get replaced. Fuck it. I've had enough."

And with that he went out the door and disappeared. He had left his bass and amp behind.

Shit.

I went back into the control room.

They were now running through "Make and Break Harbour."

Paul was sitting, listening intently, and smoking.

He looked up at me.

"Stan was looking for Jim."

"Jimmy's gone."

"Gone?"

"He quit the band. He was pissed off about being replaced."

"Jesus Christ. Do me a favour. Don't tell Stan until the session is over."

"Yeah. Right. Okay."

They got through "Make and Break Harbour".

There was some discussion about whether to have Jack do a really cheesy and ornate accordion track. Thankfully they didn't in the end.

I assumed that by now it might be time for me to go out and put down my own tracks. I was still reeling from Jim's news, and having very little experience in the studio was shaking pretty badly.

I was warming up a bit next to the piano, when Milan Kymlicka came over shuffling the orchestral scores.

He was a fat little guy with greasy pomaded hair and an even greasier smile. He paused as he went by and smirked at me.

"Not today," he said. "Some other time. Maybe."

Sneering little shit.

So I was out too.

I went back into the control room where Stan was having a tantrum about Jimmy having gone missing.

"How dare he just walk out in the middle of a fucking session? That's it. He's fired. The fucking nerve."

Paul was sitting and smoking and staring at the floor. It had been a tough day for everyone.

"Just wait until I see him. He'll..."

I spoke up.

"Jimmy quit."

"What?"

"He quit. He quit the band."

"He what?"

Stan wasn't comprehending what I was saying. I let him have both barrels.

"He quit because the fucking arrangement got changed, and he had no time to re-learn it, and Paul replaced him with Jack, and he felt humiliated, and you didn't stand up for him, and he's sick of the whole fucking thing. He's tired of starving, he's tired of the shitty gigs, and I don't know where he's gone. He even left his gear here."

I ran out of breath.

As I was ranting, I felt an overwhelming desire to quit too.

This was stupid. This was no way for an adult to live.

We were getting nowhere. Fuck it.

Stan's face reddened and crumpled, and he began to cry.

"He quit? We need him."

"What do you mean, need him? You just fired him a minute ago."

Stan was a mess. He prized loyalty above everything, and now he had been disloyal to Jim.

Paul took us to the Pilot Tavern in Yorkville, and fed us dinner and many many drinks.

Stan couldn't stop weeping.

At one point he literally had his head down on the table, sobbing.

I was fed up. The waiters were keeping a respectful distance and I was having trouble getting served.

I was pissed off at Paul, even though I understood his decision. He was under the gun.

He'd had to make the call, and given the situation it was the right call.

He was working with a massive budget and had to justify it probably on a daily basis to his bosses.

I disagreed then, as I do now, about his take on what the music should sound like.

He never had any interest in what the band was trying to do, and continued to make it clear over the years that he considered us to be amateurs.

In retrospect, I doubt that he ever had the intention of using me or Jim at the session. Certainly the parts that I had worked out for the songs wouldn't have fit in with the treacle that Kymlicka had poured over the final arrangement. Paul probably thought he was doing us a huge favour when he put us on the contract so we could get paid too, but we weren't needed or wanted, and in the end it was just humiliating.

As we helped Stan walk out to Paul's car I wanted more than anything to leave too. To get out of this horrible life we were living. To have a future, to stop sponging off my parents.

I wanted to know where my next meal was coming from, but watching Stan, this wasn't the time or place.

I resolved to give it another 6 months until he recovered from this hit, and then bail.

It was pretty quiet around the old homestead, the next few weeks.

Jimmy had the kindest and sunniest of personalities, but he was hurting, and feeling defeated and betrayed, and rightly so.

He had gone right out after quitting the session, and signed up for a trade school course in printing.

And no amount of begging or apologizing would make him come back.

He was out, and for a while we worried that we'd lost a friend.

CHAPTER 23

Feelings

A few weeks after Jimmy quit, Stan and I got a three night run in the
Student Union building at the University of Western Ontario.
It was a typical bar gig, in that we were having a miserable time,
getting paid almost nothing, and the audience, when they noticed us
at all, hated us. We were working our way through our set of originals,
interspersed with some other obscurities written by our friends,
steadfastly refusing to play anything that anyone might actually want
to hear.
There were lots of sensitive white male songwriters on the radio in
those days.
James Taylor, Jim Croce, Dan Fogelberg, John Denver. They were all
wildly popular, and we hated all of them on principle.
We refused to unbend and learn to play any songs which anyone might
actually recognize, and which might have made an audience warm to
us.
We had our pride, after all.

It was tough going.
The P.A. was terrible. It was a 50's vintage Bogen system, tube powered,
and between its natural tendency to go into overdrive, and the power of
Stan's voice, the speakers were coughing blood.
The kids were simply ignoring us and concentrating on getting plowed.
There was a pool table on one side of the room, and a shuffleboard
table on the other, where a bunch of drunks were having a noisy and
exuberant contest, which at times involved throwing the pucks at each
other's head.
There was a hockey game on the TV above the stage, which as always,
we were not allowed to turn off.
Stan and I were both broke, and couldn't afford the price of a beer
ourselves.
As I said, a typical bar gig.

Where were these little bastards getting their money?
It was barely 9 o'clock and they were all hammered.

It was halfway through the second set, and we were playing "Make and Break Harbour".
There was a large table full of kids to our left, maybe twenty feet away.
They had been getting steadily drunker and louder as the night wore on.
It was hard to compete, or to be heard over the shrieks and yells and the crash of glass.
We had just started the song, and I watched as one of the kids got up and left his friends, and wobbled over to the front of the stage, which was only about a foot high.
He stopped and stood in front of Stan, who was sitting down, singing with his eyes closed.
The kid was holding a slip of paper out, about a foot from Stan's face.
Stan still had his eyes closed, and didn't know he was there.
I didn't know what to do, so I just kept playing along.
The kid now shoved the paper into Stan's face and rattled it violently.
Stan opened his eyes and started back from the kids hand, but still kept playing his guitar, vamping on the D chord
The kid moved in closer, and shook the paper in Stan's face again. Being next to the microphone the noise filled the room, and probably sounded like the last thing Vic Morrow ever heard.
Nothing had yet been said, and they remained in that position for a few seconds, Stan strumming the D chord in 3/4 time, as the paper was once more shoved at him
The kid clearly had an agenda.

Stan finally gave up and stopped playing, and took the paper.
He read it, flinched, paused for a moment, and then said, "I'm sorry sir, we don't play "Feelings."
I loved the "sir." The kid looked all of 15.
  "What?"
  "We don't play Feelings."
  "You don't play Feelings?"
  "Well, no, but if..."
  "You call yourself a fuckin' musician and you don't play fuckin' Feelings? Jesus Christ."
He turned and addressed the room.
  "This fuckin' guy says he doesn't play Feelings for fuck's sake. What kinda fuckin' asshole calls himself a fuckin' musician and can't play fuckin' Feelings?"

The kid was radiating outrage, and clearly was just getting the
bit between his teeth for an extended philosophical discourse. He
continued.

"I wanted him to play Feelings for my girlfriend's fuckin' birthday,
and he won't fuckin' do it. It's only the most popular fuckin' song in the
whole fuckin' world, and this fuckin' asshole says he can't fuckin' play
it.....what kind a fuckin'..."

Stan cleared his throat and broke in, "Sir, if you would like me to
dedicate a song to your girlfriend, I'd be happy to play something just
for her."

The guy turned around, and said, "Fuck you, asshole. I want
Feelings,"
He kicked over a chair and walked back to his table.
He sat down, but he wouldn't let it drop, and continued his harangue.

"Fuckin' guy. Ask him to play a..." he turned and yelled over his
shoulder, "SIMPLE FUCKIN' REQUEST, AND HE JUST SHITS ALL
OVER ME."
Stan was sitting quietly, breathing deeply, and crumpling the paper in
his left fist.
He let it fall to the floor, and began playing again.

"Second verse." he said to me.

We soldiered on for another minute, but our art lover would not let the
matter drop. He was sitting with his back to us, and loudly addressing
the rest of the people at his table.

"Fuckin' guy calls himself a musician...It's my girlfriend's fuckin'
birthday."

Stan had a vein on the side of his forehead, which would grow and
swell in times of stress.
It was a good barometer of his mood.
If you were smart, you kept an eye on it, and at a certain point, learned
to shut the hell up, or get to a safe distance before something exploded.
Right now, his temple looked like a map of the Amazon River Basin as
seen from space, and his face was a deep red.
Oh Shit.

"Please shut up...please." I was praying.

The guy was not letting it go. "Probably couldn't play it anyway. It's
way better than that shit he's doing."
Stan stopped playing and put his guitar carefully down beside his chair.

"I'll be right back."

"Stan. Uh, maybe we should..."
He held up his hand to silence me.

174

He stood up, and slowly climbed down from the stage, and walked over to the table, where our hero was still expounding on his thesis. He hadn't noticed that the music had stopped. "Ask a guy a simple fuckin'..."

And then Stan had the kid by the scruff of the neck.

He pulled the kid's head back a couple of feet and then smashed his face down into the table.

WHAM!

There were screams, and bottles and glasses jumped and broke and scattered everywhere.

He pulled the kid's head up, looked him in the eye, possibly to make sure he had his attention, and then drove his head repeatedly, maybe five or six times into the table again.

WHAM! WHAM! WHAM! WHAM!

He then pulled him into a standing position, still holding him by the neck.

The kid's face was pouring blood.

Stan reached down with the other hand and grabbed a fistful of the guy's nuts, and hoisted him up, and carried him like a battering ram across the room.

The kid was barely conscious, and only feebly waving his arms.

Stan got to the emergency door and swung the body back and smashed the kid's face against the crash bar.

The door burst open and Stan brought the limp form back once more, and then with a heave consigned him into the outer darkness.

I could hear trash cans falling over, and the sound of breaking glass.

Stan pulled the door shut, wiped his hands on his pants, and walked back across the floor. He climbed back on the stage, sat down, picked up his guitar, and looked out at the shocked and silent room.

For all any of us knew we all might have just witnessed a murder.

The room was eerily quiet except for the sound of some girl weeping, and Howie Meeker raving about a dubious off side call on the TV.

Stan glared at the audience for a few moments, getting his breathing back to normal.

He leaned over and dug a flat pick out of his pocket, and snapped it a couple of times between his fingers.

Finally he spoke quietly into the microphone.

"Anybody else in here want..."

He leaned forward. "FEELINGS?"

Silence.

"No? Alright then."

He looked over at me..."Let's go back to the top...a one two three..."

175

Unaccountably, no police arrived.
The room emptied within the brief time it took for everyone to drain
their beers, and we spent the rest of the night playing to a collection of
beer stained tables and overturned chairs.

CHAPTER 24

David Woodhead Joins

My recollection is that we first met David Woodhead at the CBC, at the old Studio 4S.

He was doing a session with his band, the Perth County Conspiracy, a loose collection of artists, poets, actors and musicians who were based in Stratford Ontario. Skinny guy, medium height, with thick-lensed wire rimmed glasses, a mustache, and long brown hair in a loose pony tail down past his waist. He was making whale noises using the volume control on his bass as part of the sound track to a spoken word piece. Stan and I were behind the glass in the control room, and Paul Mills who was producing the session leaned over and said to Stan, "You should really think about grabbing this guy. He's good."

I was still smarting from the debacle over Jimmy's leaving, and was loathe to take any advice from the guy who I felt was partly responsible. Still, there was no doubt, the kid could play. I say "kid" because he looked about 12 at the time even though he is older than me by some years.

It was worth a shot, if he was available.

We had a meeting and David agreed to give us a try, although he wasn't interested in any sort of exclusive commitment to us as a full time member. He had a lot of musical interests, and while he liked what we were doing well enough, there was a lot of other music out there he wanted to be free to try.

We were okay with that. Chances were we couldn't support a third guy full time. We weren't able to support ourselves yet.

So we had a new bass player.

And we had an actual decent gig for a change, an appearance on the Bob Ruzicka show at CBC Edmonton.

We were to fly out and begin rehearsals that week, but first we felt we needed to bond with the new guy. The CBC had sent us fat per diem cheques which we cashed and began spending as soon as we got them. We took David out to Le Coq D'Or on Yonge Street, to see "Martin Mull

and his Living Room Furniture," as his act was then called.
The waitress came over to take our orders.
Stan and I ordered our usual, everything behind the bar with a beer on
the side, and David, when pressed, ordered Kahlua and milk.
    "I'm really not much of a drinker."
    "Jeez Stan," I leaned over and whispered, "I don't know if this guy
is gonna work out or not."
Stan bolted a double amber rum followed by a pint of draft beer, and
raised his hand for the waitress.
    "We'll whip him into shape. Don't worry."
What he really meant was we were going to break his spirit, ruin his
health, and turn him into a slobbering degenerate like us.

Martin Mull was terrific. Really funny, and a surprisingly good
guitarist.
He did a strange number called, "Talk Dirty to Me Baby," which
featured a slide solo played with a plastic baby bottle on a ukulele.
Stan and I got wrecked, David sipped his Bosco, and next morning we
flew to Edmonton.

The Bob Ruzicka show was a little odd.
As I understood the story at the time, and I may be getting it wrong, he
was a dentist in real life, who co-wrote some songs with Valdy and had
managed to have a couple of near hits. Because he hated touring he had
managed to wangle this little show about songwriters. He insisted that
there be nothing "show biz" about it. No theme music. No annoying
and rehearsed patter, no live audience, no glitz, no glamour. Nothing
resembling what passed for entertainment back then.
As I remember it took place in a stark space consisting of some white
boxes, and a bit of dramatic lighting. It looked like the set from a high
school production of "Waiting for Godot."
Bob himself was a quiet and decent and earnest guy, and he and Stan
got along fine, and the show was okay within those weird parameters,
but watching it on the tube some weeks later, it looked less like
entertainment, and more like an autopsy in search of a body.

We came back east.
The ménage in Brampton was falling apart.
With Jimmy having left the band, things were awkward, and he was at
school full time.
Gail, his partner, was still rightfully pissed off about how he had been
treated, and was largely silent with us. Stan was busy in Toronto,
pitching songs, and continuing his studies as a freelance gynecologist,

so I decided to move back to Hamilton to be closer to my parents' bank account.

We began serious rehearsals with Woodhead.
He proved to be not just a wildly inventive bass player, but was depressingly adept at playing anything with strings. He wasn't a particularly strong singer back then, and so our harmony vocals were a bit on the wobbly side, but he was and still is one of the most gifted and hardworking and beautiful players I have ever heard.
Sweet guy too. Endlessly curious about the world, and with a really quirky sense of humour, and an endearing air of innocence about him. We knew it couldn't last.

He was living in a houseful of other hippies in Cabbagetown, on Winchester St. a few blocks off Parliament.
Stan and I began to trek in a couple of times a week to work on repertoire.
We were on the streetcar one evening en route to rehearsal and as we rattled along the car began to fill with excited young boys all in strange costumes and wearing black and white face paint.
There seemed to be hundreds of them packed into the aisles and hanging from the rails.
    Stan said, "What's all this in aid of?"
It turned out they were all going to see some band called KISS at Maple Leaf Gardens.
We had never heard of them, but the young lads gave us a pretty good description of the act. Loud guitars, huge explosions, heavy Japanese Kubuki make up, platform shoes, and leather costumes. They had a fire breathing bass player with a foot long prehensile tongue who also puked out gallons of presumably fake blood. It was rock and roll played by cartoon super heroes.
Stan listened for a bit and then shook his head and began to lecture the mob of young guys about how badly they were being taken in by mere showbiz trickery.
    "All the explosions and fireballs are just to distract you from the emptiness of the music. You're being taken for a ride."
The kids were looking covertly at each other, embarrassed at the diatribe. Who the hell was this old guy? Why was he trying to spoil their evening out? And just what the Hell was this "folk music" crap he was banging on about?
    "Just remember, the louder the music, the less it has to say. Try to keep that in mind as you listen tonight."
Under any circumstances it was an annoying and pretentious lecture,

but coming from an apparently middle aged man dressed in patched
and faded jeans, a stained T shirt, and carrying a battered guitar case, it
was a wonder that the kids didn't kick him to death with their platform
shoes. The streetcar went completely silent as he droned on, and then
we stopped in front of the Gardens, and the doors opened and the kids
all piled out screaming and laughing as if they were escaping from
prison.

The doors slammed shut and now it was just us and an older guy in
construction clothes.

He was three seats ahead of us to our right, and in the silence that
followed the kids' exit he said over his shoulder, "I'm twice your age,
and I hate this modern rock and roll crap. And even I think you're fulla
shit." Stan was hard to stop once he'd got the bit between his teeth.

Somewhat ironically, Troy Greencorn, the man who would later found
the Stan Rogers Folk Festival in Canso, is himself a life member of the
KISS army, Stan's music being unknown to him before his wife Jennie
introduced him to it.

There exist pictures of Troy in full KISS drag, dressed as Gene Simmons.
I'm sure he would love to share them with the world.

Tell him I sent you.

We continued up Carlton Street in silence.

The streetcar stopped again, and a lone passenger got on, a slim young-
ish man with a shoulder bag full of pamphlets and a happy and eager
expression on his face.

He sat down in front of the construction worker for a minute or two,
and then turned to him and said, "What would you say if I were to tell
you that Jesus loves you very much, and is coming back some day very,
very soon?" He pulled out a tract with a large picture of Jesus ascending
into Heaven in a pink nightgown and offered it to the guy. The big
guy had had enough of zealots by this time apparently, and said, "I
wouldn't say nothin.' I'd just kick your fuckin' head in."

There was a short silence.

The young guy put the pamphlet back in his bag, and said, "Oh," and
turned around.

At the next stop he got off and a few blocks later it was our turn.

We got to David's house and set up for rehearsal. He was sharing
the house with a bunch of other musicians at the time, and the front
room was filled with guitars and keyboards and amplifiers and tape
machines, with mics and cables strung everywhere. Wonderful place.
David greeted us, got us each a coffee, and then said, "I have a couple of
records I want to play for you. You have to hear this," and put a record

on the turntable.

It was Jaco Pastorius' solo album.

Stan and I listened for a minute or two and then just stared at each other.

It in a lot of ways was like hearing Jimi Hendrix for the first time. It was a sound you had never heard before, but once you did, it sounded so right that you couldn't imagine it not existing. David was himself an extraordinary and dazzling bass player, who was already doing things we would have thought impossible on the instrument, but Pastorius was taking it to a whole new level, and I had the feeling at the time that a whole new world had opened up for David.

Certainly, his playing became even more fluid and he took to inserting odd pushes and accents and unexpected inversions into the chords of the song, along with clusters of harmonics. It was wonderful to see him take what Pastorius was doing and put his own stamp on it. He wasn't copying him, it was more that he'd been given permission to stretch out and find another sound of his own.

I don't know.

I'm sure David would have his own take on it if you asked him. All we knew was that we were working with someone whose capabilities were far beyond our own, and in his effort to properly serve the music Stan and I were playing, David was having to seriously dial it down in terms of his technical flights of fancy. It was like hitching Secretariat to a plow. I got to watch the nightly tug of war between him and Stan. We had arranged "45 Years" so that Stan played a little guitar figure for the opening, and on the second time through David was to come in with an answering figure on the bass. Stan wanted something a little more reserved than what David's restless nature desired. And so every night on stage Stan would lean over to him and tell him to just "play it straight," and every night David would come in with yet another brilliant but inappropriate flurry of notes that took his left hand the whole length of the fret board. He would then look over at me with a bright and mischievous smile, while Stan would sing the first verse from between clenched teeth and the vein in his temple would swell.

The other record David played for us that evening was by Paul Brady and Andy Irvine. They were members of the Irish group, "Planxty," and the record was another game changer for us, and a huge influence on Stan's writing, and the sound we would begin trying to build.

He was still mostly working on personal songs, or "navel gazers," as he called them.

The results were largely hit and miss, and he was still very much working his way through a bunch of influences, trying to find a

combination of sounds that he could bang together and make his own.
The songs on the Brady/Irvine album were a mixture of new and
traditional, and they blended seamlessly with each other.
The record opened with an astonishing arrangement of a tune called
"The Plains of Kildare," a variant on the old song, "Stewball." We'd
heard a dreary three quarter time version of the song from Peter Paul
and Mary years before, and it had left us cold, as all of their music did.
But the version that Brady and Irvine came up with left us breathless.
It changed time signatures a half dozen times over the course of 4
minutes, and had so many skipped beats and dropped bars as to be
impossible for us to follow. There was a heavy Balkan influence there, a
music which we had never heard before, and it was powerful and wild
and hypnotic.
Brady's version of "Arthur McBride and the Sergeant" in later years
became very much like Richard Thompson's "Vincent Black Lightning,"
a touchstone for a thousand players who all felt compelled to do their
own bad version of it.
Ours was just one of them, and we gave up trying to play it after a
while, except at parties. The guitar part is impossible for mere mortals.
The whole record is one of the few flawless recordings I have ever
heard. The songs, the arrangements, and the pacing were perfect. The
spirit of it, if not the actual sound became the template for the approach
we would later attempt as a trio, and dream of trying to record. The
closest we ever came to it was the "Between the Breaks" album, with a
small unit of musicians all bringing a variety of sounds and influences
to a set of very strong songs, without relying on faceless and sterile-
sounding outsiders and studio trickery. I ran into Andy Irvine a few
years ago and tried to tell him what a huge impact it had made on me
and Stan, and he just looked confused and abashed.
Archie Fisher was standing nearby at the time, and Andy looked over at
him, and said, "He's having a laugh, isn't he?"

Rehearsals with David continued and we took him out on some local
shows, and then, wonder of wonders, we had a couple of weeks of
actual paying gigs coming up on the East Coast.
Life was looking up.
Idiots. We should have known.

CHAPTER 25

Labrador City

It was a miracle. We had two gigs, nearly a month's work.
One gig was in Halifax, once again, working for the CBC.
Bill Howell over at the Ministry of Poetry had written a series of radio performance pieces... I don't know what else to call them...and had commissioned Stan to write some songs to accompany them.
It was an interesting idea, building a song cycle based on, but not actually quoting from an already existing series of poems.

Stan and Bill had done a number of projects using that idea, and the results could be hit and miss. There was what Bill called a Folk Opera, based on the '76 Olympics, called "So Hard to Be so Strong."
For that Stan wrote a song called "Front Runner," which made it onto the Turnaround album a few years later. Another song, and the best one, to my ears, to come out of that project was "Second Effort," a tightly written little piece on the heartbreak of going home and facing the folks, and oneself, having fallen short of all expectations. I played it last night, as I write this, in Roanoke Virginia, and it still twists something inside me. The line about the old man pouring a drink, and then asking what the tears are for, was all too close to the truth for Stan.

Another project gave us "Delivery Delayed," one of Stan's most beautiful and perfectly realized songs, which gets mostly lost or ignored by those who only seem to remember "Barrett's Privateers," or "Mary Ellen Carter."
There was another, less successful radio piece called "Orders for a New Day" about the changing role of the Canadian military, the only survivor of which was a mandolin/flute instrumental we improvised on the studio floor one morning, called "Plenty of Hornpipe." It found its way onto the Fogarty's Cove recording.
One of the really valuable aspects of these commissions, was that they forced Stan into overcoming his considerable natural inertia.

He had it in him to be a truly lazy bugger at times, and commissions like this would propel him off the couch, and kick him into a furious and sustained burst of creativity.

The down side for the band or anyone else working with him was that he typically left writing it all down all till the last minute. He would read, and research and assimilate information, stare out the window, let it all percolate, sometimes for months, until it was done, and then finally put it on paper, in some cases in the back of the taxi on the way to the studio.

"I know what I'm going to say, I just haven't written it down yet," he said to me one time, as the clock wound down to our studio deadline.

I was having a panic attack over the session.

"Do you think perhaps, you know, just maybe, you could give us a hint? Some sort of clue? I have to play this stuff later. It's hard to figure out my parts, when I haven't heard the damned song yet."

Stan waved his hand.

"Don't worry. I know what it is going to sound like, it's just all in my head. You'll do fine."

It drove us mad.

But now we were once again going to be up to our snouts in the public trough.

Lovely CBC money, and hotels, and per diem, and drunken producers with fat Government expense accounts, who would take you out for dinner and wine, and insist on picking up the cheque, as long as you were willing to listen to their sodden ramblings all night.

All we had to do was get through a two week club date.

Right.

The secret agent had found this one.

I have no idea how. Or where. Or why.

A couple of Czechoslovakian brothers had opened a disco in Labrador City, Newfoundland.

"A disco? A fucking Disco? What the hell are we going to do in a disco for Christ's sake?"

We were buying her lunch, as we found out later when the bill arrived, while she gave us the details of the gig.

"You'll do fine. The brothers are great guys, and they love folk music. You'll play three sets a night in between the recorded music. It's Newfoundland. Your kind of people. They'll love you."

Our kind of people.

Right.

A disco.

Stan and I were staring at our plates, hating the whole idea, but knowing we couldn't afford to refuse. We were broke.

She snapped at us.

"Listen, it's a great gig. 1500 bucks for the two weeks, and hotels, and airfare, and it gets you out to Halifax."

It didn't get us out to Halifax. It got us to Labrador City, a frozen and windblown collection of small frame houses and ugly crooked single wide trailers, perched on the edge of a vast abyss where once there had been a mountain.

Some US company had come up and blasted out about 200 square miles of the planet and turned it into raw ore, which was then shipped back across the border via a rail line which was no doubt built free of charge for the company by a grateful government who could then trumpet their job creation record, meanwhile, giving the company a free ride in terms of forgiven taxes and a complete pass on environmental regulations. The toxic tailings were left to run into the nearest river and kill anything within a hundred or so miles downstream. It's the Canadian way.

I was told years later that the director of the Canadian branch of the company was none other than that great patriot, Brian Mulroney.

I have no idea if that is true.

If I'm doing him a disservice by wrongly laying this particular bag of burning dog shit at his doorstep, too bad. It was only because he hadn't got the chance.

We took the gig.

There was an enormous sound system in the club, but it was for recorded music only.

We couldn't connect up to it. We had to rent our own PA.

After further negotiations we got a promise that we would be reimbursed for the rental, so we went to Len Kozak's, chose the cheapest and lightest one he had, and packed it up.

A small mixer, 2 cabinets, and 3 microphone stands with mics and cables. It pumped out a mighty 100 watts or so.

Our transportation didn't include airfare from Toronto, only from Montreal, so we had to figure out a cheap means of getting ourselves and all the gear to Dorval airport.

In those days one could get what was called a "drive-away."

If a vehicle had to be delivered to some part of the country, you'd have the use of it, so long as you got it there in a timely fashion, and in its original condition. It didn't always pan out that way.

There were occasional abuses.

I have dear friends, now living in Arlington Ma., who once upon a
time engaged to deliver a drive away Mercedes from Boston to San
Francisco, back in the early 70's. It must have seemed like a good plan
at the time, but that car saw a lot of America.
Minnesota, New York, New Hampshire, North Dakota, Georgia,
Colorado, Vermont, Louisiana, and in no particular order, before finally
coming to a burnt-out smoking rest in the Mojave Desert. They had
neglected to check the oil, and the motor had run dry and seized into a
solid block of precision built pig iron.
German engineering was no match for hippies with mushrooms.

We got a white Ford van, and loaded all the gear into it, and parked it in
front of Dave Woodhead's house, ready to leave in the morning.
Early the next day we threw our bags in and mounted up.
Stan turned the key.
Nothing.
The van was dead, and no amount of peering at the motor, and
checking the oil, verbal abuse, or kicking at the tires would revive it.
The drive-away company had nothing to replace it.
They weren't a rental place. You had to take whatever was there. We
were screwed.
The dead van was towed away.
Calls were made. Money was borrowed. And we got a taxi to Union
Station and humped all of the equipment, our guitars, David's
amplifier, and the whole goddamned sound system plus our pitiful
battered luggage onto the train for Montreal.
We were still okay for time.
Our flight wasn't until next morning.
We were going to make it.
We sat on the train trying to ignore the hateful looks of the people
whose path we were blocking with all our gear. We got to Dorval, and
labouriously unloaded everything, and got another cab to the airport.
We were nearly out of money.
We spent the night in the Airport, taking it in turns to sleep on the pile
of gear, so no one could steal it. The restaurant prices were ridiculous.
We couldn't afford to eat.
We were up early to check in.
   "You are seriously over the weight limit sir. We need an extra 200
dollars to put your equipment on board."
What?
I stood by our pile of dunnage and watched as Stan walked over to the
line of pay phones and commenced making calls.
After a couple of minutes he came back and we had to search through

our collective pockets to get enough change to continue calling.
He tried the club. No answer.
He called our secret agent. She seldom rose before noon, and mostly kept her phone turned off.
No answer there.
Time was passing.
Stan came back to the counter and wrote a cheque for the overweight charge, and our gear was allowed onto the plane.

"I hope no one gets in the way of that cheque when it ricochets off the ceiling," he said, as we walked away. "You could lose an eye."

Our flight was called, and we filed onto the plane and took our seats. The plane pulled away from the gate, and began to taxi toward the runway.
Stan looked around to see where David was, and David was not on the plane.

"Where's Woodhead?"

"I dunno. He was right behind me a minute ago."
Stan leapt to his feet.

"David?"
No answer.

"DAVID!"
Nothing.

"STOP THE PLANE! STOP THE PLANE!!!! MY BASS PLAYER ISN'T ON BOARD!!!"
The flight attendant hurried over.

"Sir, you must take your seat. We are about to take off."

"STOP! STOP THE GODDAMNED PLANE!!!!! "
Stan brushed past the flight attendant and began pounding on the cockpit door.

"I'VE LOST MY BASS PLAYER!!! STOP!! WE HAVE TO GO BACK!!"
The co-pilot came out, and he and the flight attendant tried to lead Stan back towards his seat.
Good luck with that, I thought.
We were no longer moving down the tarmac.

"Sir, you are in direct violation of Federal air safety regulations. We could have you arrested. You must sit down. Right now."

"MY BASS PLAYER ISN'T ON THE PLANE! WE HAVE TO GO BACK TO THE..." and he stopped, suddenly.
David was sitting at the back of the plane, watching the whole drama. He smiled and waved.

"I'm right here Stan." he called out.

He had been carefully stowing his amplifier head under the seat, and digging a model train magazine out from his pack when Stan had missed him.

Order was restored, and I could see the police cars turning back from their interception course outside my window. We took off and Stan went back and tore big strips off David for being invisible in the line of duty. He stormed back to his seat. A few minutes later he got up, went back to David's seat, apologized, and with his last 2 dollars had the flight attendant bring David a Kahlua and milk.

So David at least got breakfast.

We were on our way.

Downtown Labrador City was a collection of ugly concrete office blocks in the neo-Gulag style so popular in boom towns, surrounded by about 50 miles of badly broken roads.

Battered and blown out muscle cars, and huge mud covered four wheel drive trucks roared around the roads every night. It was like a cross between NASCAR and the Paris to Cairo Rally, through muskeg and scrub forest and moose pasture.

Teenagers, with little else to do would get shit-faced, and crowd 6 or 7 into the car, and race the entire circuit every night, yelling and whooping and puking out the windows, and the lights from the police cars ambulances and the tow trucks lit up the sky for hours after the bars closed.

We were taken to the club.

It was in the basement of an ugly two storey cinder block office building with a potholed gravel parking lot. Above the door was a sign saying "The Take 5 Club. Newfoundland's Finest Disco Bar." I may have been behind the curve in terms of Newfoundland's cultural evolution, but when I thought of Newfoundland, Discos didn't really spring to mind. I had a more traditional, perhaps clichéd idea, of little smoke filled clubs with floor singers, and accordions and fiddles, and tall glasses of ale. The whole John Travolta white polyester jump suit thing just seemed at odds with what I'd been led to believe.

We met the owners.

They were friendly enough, but as mystified as we were as to why we were there, and being paid fifteen hundred bucks to destroy the carefully cultivated mood being created by 10,000 watts of pre-recorded industrial strength dance music.

There was no hotel. It was a boom town and rooms were at a premium, a premium which the club owners weren't willing to pay for three guys

in ragged jeans and T shirts, and barely a winter coat between them.
We were to be billeted at a local boarding house. Not even a real
boarding house, just a nice middle aged couple with two bright and airy
spare rooms on the second floor.
We weren't allowed to stay in those rooms.
We were given a dank windowless cell between the furnace and the
laundry room, in the basement.
It was like a sensory deprivation tank.
We would go to sleep and lose all track of time, emerging some days,
around three or four in the afternoon, confused disoriented and
starving.
That first afternoon, after we had set up our pitifully inadequate gear at
the club, Dave and I went back to the black hole to catch a nap.
Stan had spent some time chatting up the two brothers back at the club,
and had managed to wangle 100 dollars as an advance so we could eat,
along with a bottle of bar scotch so we could drink.
Prices in the town were ludicrous.
A simple breakfast of bacon and eggs would run 12 dollars.
We invested in some bread and mustard and a loaf of Maple Leaf
baloney. Newfy steak.
Between the lightless airless room, and our diet, it's a miracle we
weren't found dead of asphyxiation.
After the first week, the lady of the house decided we were okay. We
seemed more or less harmless, and she relented, and we were moved up
stairs into the real bedrooms.
An exorcist and a crime scene remediation crew were called in to
freshen up the room we'd just vacated.

The gig itself was all that one might expect.
The doors would open, and a couple hundred young mine workers
would crowd in, already drunk, and the first record would hit the
turntable. The sound was deafening, and they would each hit the glass
dance floor and begin to convulse to the music as much as their ruined
cerebral cortex would allow. The lights under the floor pulsed, drunken
women screamed and shrieked, and fights erupted. Glasses shattered,
and the bouncers began their constant gliding through the crowd, like
mean ass burly sharks.
The mine had to offer huge sums of money to get people to come
up and work in such awful conditions, and live in such a frozen and
isolated shithole, and the kids were making the most of it.
They were all slobbering rat-legged drunk, right from the opening bell.
We realized that the glass dance floor had probably evolved not as an
artistic statement, but more likely to facilitate the cleaning up of the

blood and vomit and piss that was raining down onto it every night.
So the music would blast out for an hour or so. The crowd would
dance like broken spastic marionettes, and then it would all come to a
grinding halt.

Donna Summer would be cut off in mid orgasm, and in the ensuing
silence the three of us would drag out our crappy and useless sound
system, and set up the mikes, as the sullen and confused cultural elite of
Labrador City watched.

Stan would introduce us with some nervous and lame jokes, and we
would begin.

About 15 seconds into the first song the crowd had taken the measure of
us, and simply turned their backs and resumed drinking and screaming
and fighting and puking and pissing.

We finished the set. We pulled the gear back into a dark corner, and
scuttled off in shame.

And the real music started up again, and the dance floor once again was
full.

An hour later, the same stupid scene played out. The disco stopped to
cries and shouts of complaint, and we dragged our junk out onto the
glass floor. We played another hour long set, while the crowd got ever
drunker.

Once again, we would drag the gear back into the shadows, and sit on
the back steps outside, next to the kitchen dumpster.

There was no dressing room. If it was raining we would hang out on the
concrete staircase leading to the second floor.

We would wait for the final shift, which would be around 1 a.m., and
once again we would go through the whole process, dragging the
speakers out onto the now filthy and slippery dance floor, setting up the
mikes, as the now thoroughly pissed off crowd yelled abuse and insults,
and we'd run through the final set.

Tear down the gear, as the disco once more resumed, and walk in
silence the mile or so back to the boarding house. Stan would build a
couple of baloney sandwiches, using the washing machine outside our
cell as a table, and crack open a couple of beers.

We had discovered O'Keefe's Extra Old Stock.

It was a local beer, previously unknown to us.

It was about the same price as regular beer, but had a really high alcohol
content, which was what we needed.

It also gave you violent explosive diarrhea, and breath like a cannibal
bat, but life is a trade-off.

We were all tired and depressed, stuck in this horrible town, playing to

a roomful of degenerates, who were at best indifferent to our lame ass
act.
We heard that minutes after we left that first night, some guy had his
throat ripped open with a broken bottle. He and some other guy had
squared off on the dance floor, and in true movie hero fashion one of
them had slashed at the other holding a broken quart bottle by the neck.
Somewhat to his surprise no doubt, he'd connected perfectly, and his
opponent went down with a torn carotid artery, spraying blood in a
hissing arc over everyone's shoes.
It took him about a minute to bleed out and die.
The Czech brothers were upset by the incident.
　　"Son-a-beech. We run nice place. This give us bad name. We told DJ
to turn up and play louder, so no one notice. Son-a-beech."

We had two weeks of this to look forward to.
There was nothing to do during the day.
We slept a lot. There was no sense of time in our airless fetid dungeon.
David began making unauthorized field trips to the mine. He would
walk a couple of miles out to the pit, and sneak through the fence, and
collect rock samples and drag them back to the room, where he would
carefully sort and label and then store them in his leather Gladstone
bag.
What he was saving them for, we had no idea.
I think he just needed something to do, any kind of project, to keep his
mind off the nightly ordeal.
Maybe he saw a fight coming, and was stock-piling material for a
barricade.

Stan spent his days writing long epic letters to a woman from California
named Louise, who was currently a guest of the Canadian Government.
He had met her a couple of months before during a weekend in
Kingston, when we were asked to play an afternoon concert in the
Women's Pen, and they had made a deep and personal connection.
Every day he would bundle up about 20 pages of sexual frustration
and unrequited longing into an envelope, bash his erection into a
manageable size so he could trudge into town, and stuff the whole
unwieldy mess, minus the erection, presumably, into the mailbox.
I had the poor taste to point out to him a number of times that he could
be more gainfully employed writing the music we needed for the
upcoming CBC project, but he just shrugged it off.
He was lonely and miserable, and he needed this contact, however
fragile and tenuous.
He would come back from mailing the letter and sit down and begin

another. It was heartbreaking to watch.
And then every night we would walk the long mile back to the Take 5 to once again wow the kids.

I was sitting at the bar one night during our break, and a tiny blonde girl climbed up onto the stool next to me. She looked as though she should be modeling perky little sweaters in the Sears catalogue, or wearing pigtails and a pleated shirt in a badly lit adult movie about the adventures of a young girl and her favourite teacher.
She was a bulldozer operator, making about 20 dollars an hour, a fortune in those days.
She introduced herself, and said "You know, I've been watching you guys play all week. You're okay and all that, but you'd do a lot better if you played something we liked."
I had no answer for that. The logic was irrefutable.
"We don't know anything you'd like."
I excused myself, and went outside to sit by the dumpster.
Stan was already there, in the midst of yet another letter to Louise.
I sat next to him while he scribbled away, snuffling and wiping his eyes, and I watched a pair of beavers working on their dam in the little stream behind the club.
The sun was nearly down, and the light on the water looked like polished copper.
It was relatively quiet.
Only the huge throbbing grind of the bass from the disco could be felt through the wall. Neither of us said anything.
There was nothing to say.

We bought what was purported to be some pot from one of the wait staff.
It was pathetic stuff. It didn't look or smell like the nice green fragrant home grown we knew back in Ontario. It looked like some naturalist had collected an old bird's nest in a baggie.
It had little effect, mostly light headedness, and a vague nausea from the weed killer it had been soaked in.
I never did like dope very much. It mostly made me anxious and confused and stupid, and I was getting along just fine in that department, anyway.
Nonetheless, we smoked a lot of it.
We were depressed and feeling trapped.
We just wanted some sort of oblivion, and the drink prices here were beyond our reach.
Our depression grew to the point that one night Stan and I made a

detour as we walked home from the gig. The RCMP station was on a hill overlooking the town and the surrounding valley. From the front steps we could see the entire fifty mile course where the kids held their nightly races. We could hear faint sirens, and see maybe a dozen or so crash sites where the police cruisers were doing a brisk business.

Ambulances were racing back into town from all over the darkened night landscape.

We sat on the steps of the police station, and in a fit of stupid and self-destructive bravado, pulled out the bag of weed and rolled a couple of cannon cracker sized spliffs.

Blazed them up, and sat and watched the emergency crews race back and forth in the distance.

A cruiser pulled up at the bottom of the steps, and an officer got out, and very slowly and painfully started up towards us, hauling himself along the guard rail with one hand.

His head came up as he caught scent of the smoke billowing into the night air, but he continued right past us, without a pause.

He looked haunted and bone weary, and there was dried blood down his pant leg and all over his shoes.

He spoke as he went by.

"You two fellers better go home and get to your beds. We got bigger fish to fry than you tonight."

We literally couldn't get arrested in this town.

The next morning, we heard that a Korean show band called the Seoul Society had been among the casualties from the previous night.

Three members of the band were killed outright, and the rest were in hospital with a variety of serious injuries.

Stan was devastated.

"It could have just as easily been us."

He began doing nightly announcements from the stage at the opening of every set in an effort to raise money for the survivors, and he visited them every day in the hospital.

They were thousands of miles from home. Literally half a world away from their loved ones.

It haunted him, and he spent hours every day with them, reading to them and trying to help with getting word back to their families.

The second last night of the two week run, the wait staff took pity on us and invited us to an after show party.

It was the first human contact we'd had.

It was just an innocent gathering, and we were having an okay time,

happy in the knowledge that we had only one more night. Three more sets in this shithole, and then we could get paid and leave.
Forever.
Someone handed me a reefer and I took a hit.
It wasn't the local bunk weed that we were used to.
It was something else.
Something horrible and deadly and toxic, and within seconds I was helpless.
I carefully climbed off my chair, and got down on all fours.
I didn't know where I was.
I knew I was going to be violently ill, and the polite thing would be for me to find a bathroom. I dimly reasoned that if I followed the baseboard along the bottom of the wall, I would eventually come to a toilet, which is what I did.
 I crawled, following my nose, past people's feet, around potted plants, behind the sofa, past the cat box. I briefly considered using that, but I apparently still had some standards, and continued on, just following the wall.
Eventually I got to the bathroom, and spent the next few hours puking up my immortal soul.
Just before dawn we left the party, and Stan walked back to the boarding house with me, keeping well ahead in case anyone might see us and think we were together. We arrived and he went in to his room, and I sat on the back porch and watched the sun rise. The little dog who lived in the house came out after a while and kept me company as I sat and occasionally retched in a spasm of dry heaves.
I decided that maybe pot wasn't for me.

We finished the gig.
We had never once connected with any member of the so-called audience.
It had simply been a nightly endurance test.
We did the last miserable set, and for the last time piled our sound system into the corner where it would be picked up and shipped back to Toronto.
We found out later that Len Kozak had to spend a fortune to get his own sound system back.
It took weeks.
David and I sat at the bar, and waited as Stan went into the office to get paid.
The noise in the place was intolerable, with thumping bass, and screams, shouting, glass breaking, and chairs and tables being knocked over and broken.

K.C. and the Sunshine Band were singing "That's the way (uh huh uh huh) I like it."

We waited some more, and then Stan came out from the office.

He didn't look good, and we realized that some new humiliation was about to be enacted.

The long and the short of it was that the pay cheque had been sent, per the secret agent's instructions, to her.

Not us.

To her.

In Toronto.

We were a thousand miles from home, and completely broke, with no way of leaving.

Next morning, we got the husband at the boarding house to give us a ride out to the air strip.

We checked our baggage through, but there was hitch when I was told that I could not carry my violin case onto the plane.

It was suddenly, after all these years, too big to fit into the overhead.

There was a heated discussion at the counter, and we finally agreed that if I would leave it with the baggage handler, he would hand carry it onto the plane for me.

It made no sense, but I could live with it.

We hit another snag, when the handler at the counter tried to lift David's Gladstone bag full of ore samples.

"What the hell do you have in there, rocks?"

In any case we did manage to get on the plane, Stan this time keeping a careful eye on David's whereabouts.

We began to taxi down towards the runway, and I realized that my fiddle hadn't been brought in.

I leapt out of my seat.

"STOP THE PLANE!!!! STOP THE PLANE!!!   I DON'T HAVE MY FIDDLE!!"

"Sir, please sit down and we will..."

"STOP THE PLANE!"

I was up and pounding on the cockpit door.

It opened, and I could see the two tired and pissed off crew members glaring over their shoulders.

Not this shit again.

"Sir sit down, or you will be arrested."

"I DON'T GIVE A SHIT. THAT BASTARD BACK AT THE COUNTER SAID HE'D HAND CARRY MY FIDDLE ONTO THE PLANE!!"

195

There was a 10 minute delay, and I could hear while messages went back and forth between the tower and the cockpit.

"He says there is a fiddle behind the baggage counter. Yup. Yeah... okay."

The pilot turned around and said "If you will kindly wait in your seat sir, the handler will bring your instrument out."
And so we waited and watched, as the asshole baggage guy strolled out a quarter mile across the tarmac, smiling and idly spinning the case by its handle around his finger, and tossing it in the air and catching it.
The door was opened, and the ramp was partially lowered.
The flight attendant crawled out on her hands and knees, grabbed the case, crept back in, hit the retract switch, and slammed the door shut.
Locked it, and brought my fiddle to my seat.
She opened the overhead, placed it inside, slammed it shut, and we took off.
Amazingly, after my violent outburst, she apologized, and brought me a large complimentary drink for breakfast once we were in the air.

We flew back to Montreal, and caught another flight to Halifax, collected our per diem cheques, checked into the YMCA to save money, and had our first non-baloney meal in weeks.
We were to begin recording the next day.
The next week was a daily frenzy of trying to make sense of whatever Stan had written the night before, or that morning.
He would sometimes sing the bits and pieces to us in the back of the cab, on the way to the studio. David would be madly scribbling minute notes and making charts for himself.
Sometimes we didn't hear the songs until we got there.
And sometimes I would be sent out onto the studio floor to aimlessly noodle around on the flute, with a spooky tape delay to add atmosphere, buying precious time while Stan wrote in the corner.
One morning the cab arrived, and as we loaded in, the driver said,

"Which one of you is the fiddle player?"

"That would be me," I said.

"I used to work with a fiddle player, years ago."

"Yeah?"

We weren't that interested, but tried to be polite.

"I played piano."

"Uh huh, who with?"

"Don Messer."

Jesus. This was Waldo Munro, the guy who had pretty much defined a whole style of music back in the day, with perfect rhythm and great big moving bass chords, and a lightning right hand, and now he was

driving a trio of losers to the very studio where he had once worked for years.
Bloody Life.

The night the sessions ended, Stan had a massive and complete breakdown. We were visiting family, and after dinner he was having a much needed tub bath. While he was relaxing in the hot water he had drunk perhaps a pint or so of neat gin.
I was in the next room, and heard a sob, and then all the pain and frustration of the last few weeks, and his life in general came out and he was weeping like a child.
He was huge and pink and slippery, and I wished I'd had a gaff-hook, but I managed to get him out of the tub. I got him dried off, and he dropped onto the bed and slept into the next afternoon.

The one song that survived from those sessions was "Louise's song."
Stan played it on the studio floor one morning, reading the lines off the page as the engineer got the levels adjusted, and I sat behind the mixing desk, wiping away tears.
It was beautiful and sad, and full of longing, and with a lovely turn around between verses.
Poor bastard, I thought. What must he be going through?

CHAPTER 26

Recording Fogarty's Cove

A year or so previous we'd decided we needed a demo recording of
some sort to send out to presenters.

The only records we had as an example of Stan's writing were the
singles he had done with RCA a few years before, but they were pretty
awful, and anyway it was impossible to get copies from RCA.

There were the CBC Extended Play recordings Stan had done with Paul
Mills producing, and they had at least gotten Stan's name out a bit, but
with the ornate arrangements and lame orchestrations, they weren't
what we wanted to present to the world either. We needed something
that sounded like us.

Bob and Dan Lanois had built a small studio in their mom's basement
in Ancaster.

It was handy for us, as Stan was still living in Dundas with Diane at that
point.

The studio was small and cramped and not terribly well equipped
compared to other larger studios, but Bob and Dan both had a lot of
enthusiasm and dedication and they made it work.

There were egg cartons on the walls to deaden sound, and a small
apartment sized piano was in the corner. There was a collection of
pretty cheap microphones, but they were constantly trying to upgrade
and learn as they went along.

Great guys.

Weird guys, but great guys.

It wasn't until some years later when I read an interview with Dan that I
found out that he'd had kept his drug stash in the toilet tank.

I never thought of looking there.

I think we recorded 3 or 4 songs there, and the result was a tape
we could at least mail out to clubs along with a couple of positive
newspaper reviews, and hope they'd take the bait.

Some months later after we'd moved to Brampton, Paul Mills played the tape from that session along with some other things we had done at the CBC, for Mitch Podolak.

Mitch was a short, fat furry chain-smoking ex-political shit disturber; (an avowed Trotskyite, for God's sake,) originally from Toronto. He was currently trying to overthrow the government by getting it to finance a folk festival in Winnipeg. Presumably the worker's paradise would come later.

Picture a truculent hairy rhino with black rimmed glasses, and a deep sense of grievance, wearing the same black T shirt day in, day out, and ill-fitting jeans that never stayed up.

He favoured the sartorial double whammy of belt and suspenders, and yet his pants were still always sagging southwards, revealing an obscene plumber's cleavage.

Mitch was also a dyed in the wool folkie.

His heroes were Woody Guthrie, Pete Seeger, the Weavers, and Uncle Dave Macon.

He hated anything electric.

He claimed to hate singer songwriters as well, at least the sensitive and mopey navel gazing mob that currently infested the airwaves. He was vulgar and loud and with a deep seated paranoia about the government whose money he was using to further his causes.

He was obscenely funny, and fiercely loyal, and breathtakingly, embarrassingly and overwhelmingly generous, and he habitually carried the remnants of his lunch in his beard.

Sitting across from him in a restaurant was a trial.

He was perfectly capable of sending a steak back a half dozen times for being too well done.

He needed it barely warm from the cooler.

Actually, if he could have eaten some poor cowering beast right off the truck he would have.

That was bad enough, but his concern and high regard for the worker didn't extend to over stressed and under paid waiters, and he would get increasingly testy with the long suffering server who had the temerity to offer him a steak of insufficient rareness. It was embarrassing to watch.

I turned to him once during a late night nosh at Nate's in Ottawa, when he had sent the steak back a fourth time with an insulting and abusive message for the cook.

"Mitch, I know this because I have been a waiter. Do you have any idea what they are doing to your food right now? What sick perversions they are now performing on this thing you are going to put in your

mouth?"
He looked up from his plate of schmaltz herring.
"They wouldn't dare."
"Haven't you ever read Portnoy's Complaint? I guarantee you
Mitch, there is a guy back there right now who is getting even with you
by fucking your dinner."

He was to become one of Stan's best friends, as well as one of his most
loyal supporters.
He and his wife Ava opened their home in Winnipeg to us, and we came
and went at will over the years. He and Stan would sit up all night,
arguing and plotting and laughing as Stan nursed a glass of rum, and
Mitch would criticize him for it, all the while wreathed in pot smoke.

The phone rang one day in the house in Brampton, and it was Paul,
telling Stan to come into Toronto to meet Mitch at Paul's house.
That evening Mitch made Stan an offer.
If Stan could write more songs like "Make and Break Harbour," and
"Fogarty's Cove," and less of "that navel gazing shit," he would be
willing to put up the money for a record.
Paul would produce.
Wow. And holy shit besides.
We began to assemble a band for the recording.
David Woodhead would play bass.
He recommended Jerome Jarvis, an old friend from his Perth County
Conspiracy days, for drums and percussion. We knew Jerome from our
days playing with Noel Harrison. We liked his playing a lot.
Grit Laskin and Ken Whitely came in as the utility infielders, guys who
could get around on about a dozen instruments between them.
I was ostensibly in on fiddle and flute, and Paul would play guitar.
John Allan Cameron made a brief guest appearance on fiddle and 12
string.
If nothing else, we could stick his name on the back of the album cover
in big letters, as a "special guest," and maybe sell a couple more records
to the unsuspecting.

We found a comfortable studio outside of London, called Springfield
Sound.
It was a converted school house in Mennonite country, and it offered
a full service, with a kitchen, three squares a day, and showers and
sleeping quarters.

Stan got busy and wrote a few more Maritime sounding songs.

They weren't really what he was interested in writing at the time, but we wanted the record deal.

My belief is that had Mitch or anyone else come to Stan with money and a promise to front a recording, provided he write a bunch of Be-bop jazz tunes, or an orchestral piece in the style of Arnold Schoenberg, he would have got busy and done it. And the history of Canadian music might have looked a lot different. We really wanted that record deal.

In any case, he came up with what I perceived as filler, "Watching the Apples Grow," and "The Wreck of The Athens Queen."

They both sounded much the same. They were ersatz rollicking clones of "Fogarty's Cove," and we never liked them enough to play live.

There was also "Acadian Saturday Night," which Stan had written after seeing Doug Kershaw on the television.

It never felt right either.

More filler.

We wasted the better part of a morning in the studio trying to get a take of the song, but in the end had to abandon it. It just wasn't us.

We resurrected "Plenty of Hornpipe," a little instrumental, which as Grit pointed out, was not a hornpipe at all, and which had been written for one of Bill Howell's projects at CBC Halifax.

"The Maid on the Shore" had been learned from the Curry brothers in London.

We got a pretty good arrangement of that. Music for me is about tension and release, and I loved that the song went along for a couple of minutes, building the story before the whole band jumped in.

We hid a little joke in the song's instrumental section by playing a few bars of "the Cutty Wren," which we had learned from an Ian and Sylvia record.

"Giant" was written, according to Stan, because Paul had said we needed something "weird" for the record. I believe it was the first time that he had tried writing something using the DADGAD tuning.

The really odd and special one for me, and the sleeper of the bunch, was "The Rawdon Hills."

I think people forget that song in the midst of the other more obvious pieces on the record.

It's a strange song, inspired as Stan said, by a dryly written government document on the short lived gold rush in Nova Scotia during the last century.

God only knows where he got that sort of reading material. Bill Howell, most likely.

But it has beautiful and poetic lyrics, and a slow dreamy melody which was enhanced by the extraordinary guitar solo that David Woodhead played.

David had a sweet little Regal guitar made sometime back in the 20's or so, which he had acquired at a yard sale.
It had a small sound, but like everything else in David's hands it was wonderful.
I managed to wreck the first take on David's solo.
I was sitting near him on the floor of the recording room and he asked if I would take a picture of him while he played, using his camera.
In the control room the click of the shutter sounded like a snare drum.
We had to roll the tape back and try again.
The song became one of my few favourite moments on the record.
"Finch's Complaint" had started out life as a song, but the tune didn't gel for any of us.
I think it might have been Paul who suggested that Stan do it as a recitation.

And of course there was "Barrett's Privateers," which was already taking on a life of its own, despite having been written as a joke, a one off, at a party in Sudbury.
That story has been told before, but I will run through it again for the sake of being complete, and because I was actually there to see it happen.
We were up in Sudbury, at the Festival Borealis.
We had taken the train up for the gig, being still without a reliable vehicle.
The show went okay, and things degenerated into the usual sing around with the Friends of Fiddler's Green in a large meeting room at the Student Detention Center where we were being housed.
As Stan told the story, he wanted to have a song of his own to lead. He disappeared for what seemed like a half hour at the most, and then returned with a sheaf of papers in his hand.
    "I have a new song."
    Tam Kearney said, "Ah fuck, no, Rogers is gonna make us all cry again."
    "No, no, it's not like that this time."
He stood in the middle of the room and started the song, and the rest of the guys all clustered around him.
Kearney was standing on a chair, reading the lyrics over Stan's shoulder, and they of course got it immediately.
And the damned song caught on in a way none of us ever expected.
I have been told stories of people hearing that song in bars all over the world.
Saigon, Berlin, Barcelona. It just kept turning up.
One fellow told me how he had heard the song in Australia, in a bar in

Alice Springs.
He came back to Canada, and decided to look for the record as soon as
he got off the plane in Toronto.
He ran into an old school chum at Sam the Record Man's on Yonge
Street, and he was looking for the same song, having heard it in a bar in
Lisbon earlier that week.

And then there was "45 Years."
It along with Barrett's, was the most popular song in the repertoire back
then, and there was no way we weren't going to include it, in spite of
it not sounding traditional, and the fact that Stan and Diane were no
longer together. I had also been present at that song's birth a couple of
years before in Nova Scotia.

Dad's younger brother Prescott had bought a small house on some land
overlooking Chedabucto Bay in Halfway Cove, Nova Scotia.
The story went that it had been built sometime back in the 1830's of
wood salvaged from a ship wreck.
I don't know about that, but certainly by the time Prescott found it, it
was very old and run down and creaky.
It had a rough pine floor and an old green enameled wood stove, and
no plumbing.
There were two small bedrooms, a front parlor which served as a spare
bedroom, a main sitting room, and a summer kitchen.
There were iron beds with rough, smelly lumber camp blankets.
The ceilings were very low by modern standards, and the taller among
us had to walk at a crouch, as if auditioning for the part of Quasimodo.
Up the hill was a good spring with clean cold water that made
wonderful home brew.
Dad and Prescott were thrilled with it.
Mum and Prescott's wife Mabel were less so.
To them it represented not a holiday so much as a more primitive and
difficult place to do housework.
Oddly, from our point of view anyway, they felt compelled to rigidly
adhere to the same strict schedule of daily and weekly tasks they had at
home even though they were ostensibly on holiday.
"The Boys," ie; Dad and Prescott, would grab a coffee and a muffin, and
a chunk of cheese in the morning and bolt out the door to drive down
the shore to look for other places to dream of buying, leaving "The
Girls" to cook and sweep and clean, and to laboriously haul and heat
water for laundry, because it was Monday, and Monday was laundry
day, come what may.
The lack of a bathroom was an issue as well.

The outhouse was cold, and damp and drafty, and located on the other side of a tangled and wet and over grown orchard.

It made their lives miserable.

For the "Boys," they were content as men generally are, with nipping around the corner for a quick pee.

Other more arduous functions were simply to be borne manfully, and for "The Boys," who had grown up little better than savages in the wilds of Pictou County, a smelly and rickety outhouse was a step up in the world.

This was living.

Finally Dad and Prescott relented and set about to build a large and spacious two holer about twenty paces from the house.

It was an ambitious project.

It featured a magazine rack, and a large picture window through which to enjoy the view of the Bay.

An extension cord was brought in from the house for a reading light and a space heater.

Like all jobs undertaken by Dad and his brother, the actual work was secondary.

More important was the art of standing around, talking idly and scratching, taking surreptitious pulls at a rum bottle, munching on apples, and balancing carefully on one leg to facilitate easing out long and elaborate farts.

Mum and Mabel stayed well away and mostly muttered between themselves.

After a couple of days of intense work it was finished.

The girls were called out to inspect it.

The boys of course, had to pose with it for pictures.

Mum and Mabel were watching from a few feet away, as the boys reveled in a job well done.

"Well, what do you think of it?" said Prescott.

There was a pause, and then Mabel turned to Mum. Mabel was dressed as always, immaculately, with hair and nails and make-up perfect, and in this situation completely at odds with her surroundings. In all the years I had known her, I had never found her to be the least bit rude or vulgar, just a sweet and quiet and kind person, whose manners would have done credit to Royalty.

She leaned in close to Mum and said, "Let's live in that and shit in the house."

So, in this kind of tense domestic situation it wasn't the best time for Stan to descend unexpectedly into our midst with a new girlfriend. She was introduced to us as Diane Patterson, a soon to be divorced mother of three from Dundas.

Mum was nonplussed.

Aside from the fact that beds were...ahem...limited (and just where were two unmarried people going to sleep?) there was the added work of looking after a strange guest in a difficult and contentious atmosphere.

There was also simply the fact that Mum and Diane didn't get off to a terribly good start.

She was boisterous and somewhat "forward" as my grandmother might say, and with a sharp barking laugh.

She had as well a somewhat richer command of the vernacular than Mum might have wished.

In short, she swore like a longshoreman's parrot.

Mum on the other hand, had that keen sense of propriety and correct behaviour which comes from being raised in abject poverty, in a family which considered itself well above the common herd, if not actually of Royal blood.

She was my Mum, and I loved her, but she had it in her to be a crashing snob.

The relationship was probably doomed from the get go.

Who was this strange and loud person?

And where had Stan found her?

And what were her plans for him?

And did she really have three kids and a couple of ex-husbands for God's sake?

There was also a serious age difference.

Stan proudly bragged to Dad that he was dating an "older woman" some nine years senior to his twenty three.

She was as close in age to Mum as she was to Stan.

Stan was just a kid, and an immature and shiftless one at that.

But he was obviously smitten, and was walking about with a fatuous smile and visible waves of heat rising from his groin.

There were furtive whispered discussions between Mum and Mabel in the orchard, out past the new outhouse.

Just what was he seeing in her?

Part of that became clear the next day as we were sitting out on the hill drinking tea, and watching the bright sunlight shift and change on the face of the water below.

It was a perfect day, warm and cloudless.

Stan and Diane had grabbed a quick bite of breakfast and had disappeared after what must have been a long and agonizing night of behaving themselves in the spare room.

The other inhabitants had no doubt been listening tensely for the first

dreaded sound of a creaking bed spring or a stifled gasp of pleasure.
The couple had managed to maintain a chaste silence though, and the
folks were now relaxing in the sun.

All was well for a time, until from the woods on the hill above us
came a series of ungodly piercing screams and obscene imprecations
mixed with urgent and hoarse baritone bellowing and a lot of rhythmic
crashing.

Oh Dear.

This was awkward.

Mum and Mabel sat upright and rigid with set expressions, as the
shouts and cries of encouragement came echoing down the hill.

Mum was embarrassed and outraged.

She didn't allow the "F" word to be used under her roof.

And while this was technically more of an al fresco event and not under
her roof, that word was now being conjugated in a number of new and
creative ways, and Mum was not one bit happy.

I don't know how long it continued.

I saw Prescott surreptitiously glance at his watch, he being naturally
competitive, but I never thought to ask him later.

It sounded as if events were racing to their frantic and inevitable
conclusion when there was a huge roar of outraged pain from Stan, a
pause, and then shrieks of laughter from Diane.

What the hell was this?

Had he sprained something?

Had she cut off a souvenir?

We heard more yelling and swearing from Stan and more laughter
from Diane, and then she appeared from out of the trees, flushed and
staggering, while trying to rearrange her clothing.

She was helpless with laughter.

"WE WERE UP ON THE HILL SCREWING," she yelled rather
unnecessarily.

She continued, "AND A BIG RED ANT BIT STAN RIGHT ON THE
BALLS."

Poor Stan was up on the hill, out of sight but still audible, and we could
see the tops of the trees shaking as he thrashed about in the brush like a
stricken beast.

Dad and Prescott flushed and stared out at the bay, trying to keep from
laughing.

It was touch and go.

The slightest show of amusement or sympathy would have meant
instant death from the wives.

Mum and Mabel silently got up and walked into the house to slam doors and violently bang saucepans around for a while.

It was a bad start to the relationship between Mum and Diane, and as much as they tried over the years to mend things and make nice it never went well.
It was hard to watch.
There were many things that she and Diane had in common.
Intelligence, a strong work ethic, and a deep love for their children.
They also both loved Stan, and that brought them into conflict and competition.

Later that same day the two young lovers decided to drive down the shore to sight see.
Stan came to Dad to borrow the truck.
Under normal circumstances this might have been refused as Stan was then a novice driver, and at the best of times prone to distraction.
However the little cabin seemed rather more crowded than usual today, and so Dad gave him the keys, and they hurried off.
They had unfinished business.
As Stan told me later, they ended up at a small beach in Cole Harbour, past Whitehead.
Events unfolded, and they found themselves in the back of the camper vigorously testing the trucks suspension.
Stan claimed he fell completely in love with her when, during a pause in the festivities, Diane leapt out of the stiflingly hot camper and ran, sweating and stark naked into the water in full view of the startled drivers going by on the road.
It certainly spoke of a certain joie de vivre, and feeling the need to enter into the spirit of things, he ran naked as well, into the water after her.

She left to go back to Ontario a couple days later.
Mum and Mabel were relieved.
Stan was heartbroken and distraught.
He took long walks down to the shore at Halfway Cove to smoke and stare at the sky and to dip his parts into the water to extinguish the flames.
He was in a bad way.
I found him one afternoon at the table in the little house playing guitar and scribbling in a writing tablet.
I don't recall precisely, but it probably didn't take him much more than an hour to complete "Forty-five Years."
The whole story (minus the red ant attack,) is there for the listening.

I had also been present at the birth of "Make and Break Harbour."
The three of us, Stan, Jim Ogilvie and I had been in Halifax a few years
before, working for the CBC.

Bill Howell had put together a series of poems and spoken word pieces
about the inshore fishery, and wanted Stan to contribute some new
songs.

Whatever I might have felt his faults were at the time, and I had
dismissed him earlier as just another drunken loudmouth poet, I don't
think it is possible to overestimate Bill's role in kicking Stan into action,
and getting him to write in new and different ways back in the early
days.

Bill was extremely supportive and generous, and Stan was flattered by
Bill's attention and high regard. Bill was after all a published poet, and
an important one, if Bill's opinion counted for anything.

Before we were due in Halifax we had a couple of nights playing at
the Scarecrow in Kingston. It was one of our favourite places, and we
were beginning to build a bit of a following. We had to catch a train to
Halifax after the gig, and rather than wait at the station with our gear,
we dragged everything over to the Plaza Hotel around the corner. We
piled our stuff under the shuffleboard table and sat down and ordered
a pitcher of beer. We were in pretty good spirits. We'd had a couple of
decent nights, made some money, and had an overnight train ride and
another gig, and CBC money to look forward to. The beer came. We
clinked glasses, and drank. There was an old fellow across the room. He
had watched us come in with our instruments, and after we got settled
into our second drinks he came over and said hello.

He looked about a hundred years old and was dressed in very worn but
clean and carefully mended clothes. I wondered if he was going to hit
us up for a free beer.

"You boys musicians?"

"Yeah."

"I used to play for a living too."

"Really? That's great."

"Yeah, I played for a few years with the Benny Goodman
Orchestra."

Huh?

"Benny Goodman? You?"

"Yup. Tenor sax."

Wow. I wondered what had happened. Maybe he was bullshitting
us. He looked like he was currently living in a cardboard box under
a bridge. It was then he opened his wallet and showed us a couple of
cracked black and white pictures.

"That's me." he said, pointing to a slim and handsome dark haired guy in a white jacket just behind Goodman on the bandstand. He then shrugged and said, "Well, it was me."

Stan said, "Would you like a beer?"

"No, thanks. I'm good. Just wanted to say hello and wish you boys luck. You think you're on top of the world right now. Just keep in mind it doesn't always last."

He turned and walked away.

I looked around the room. The Plaza was a grim and dirty all nude strip bar, where the tired and bedraggled dancers were mostly there to help supplement their biker boyfriends' incomes. Hardly the top of the world. All the same it was a scary warning. We ordered another pitcher and a couple of shots apiece to go with it.

We caught the train a couple of hours later, and arrived in Halifax the next evening, not more than a few hours behind the published schedule.

So we had a couple of weeks' worth of work from Bill, and he very generously allowed us to stay at his house, around the corner from the Lord Nelson Hotel.

Stan decided he was going to make dinner for us all one night.

He had a specialty, something he called "Canterbury Beef."

It was nothing more than a large overcooked roast, with garlic slivers stuffed into it, and about four bottles of red wine carefully poured over it during the course of the day.

Just before being served, the wine sauce would be thickened to the consistency of pudding, a Cabernet flavoured Jello. We all left him alone for the day while he wrestled with his masterpiece, and came back later as he was putting the finishing touches on the dish.

He tasted it.

"Needs more wine, I think," he said, and he poured in another half quart, then tilted the bottle up and sank the rest of it himself.

"Never cook with a wine that you wouldn't drink," he said, wiping his mouth on his sleeve, and belching. This of course, meant nothing to me.

I had never met a wine I wouldn't drink, and I was damned if I was going to waste it by pouring it over food.

Dinner was served.

There was a period of silence as we filled our plates and glasses.

I took a bite of the beef.

"Well?"

Stan was looking anxiously around the table for our reactions.

"Did I do good?"

I was no gourmet but to me it tasted like he'd stolen a saddle from the
Bengal Lancers down the street and had boiled it in Absorbine. But we
all were careful to make the appropriate noises of approval. The dishes
were cleared away, and Stan said to Bill, "I got some work done today,
when I wasn't busy in the kitchen."
He pulled out the Guild, and spread some pages out on the table.
He tuned up briefly, and then sang "Make and Break Harbour."
Holy shit.
I was thunderstruck.
Even Bill was quiet for a few moments.
It was and is still, an extraordinary piece, one of those rare songs that is
capable of freezing time.

So beautiful and simple and powerful were the words, that it wasn't
until years later that I realized, and only after it was pointed out to me,
that the song mostly doesn't rhyme, and only the chorus follows any of
the rules of rhyme and meter that Stan ordinarily adhered to so strictly.
Someone said "Let's hear that again."
Stan knew as we all did that he'd got hold of a good one.
Jimmy and I got out our instruments.
We couldn't wait to learn it, and play it, to step into that little world.
This was a song with the ring of truth.
We had seen firsthand the effects of our governments' stupid and short
sighted policies surrounding the inshore fishery. We had only to look
out the window at Halfway Cove to see whole fleets of Russian and
Portuguese trawlers combing Chedabucto Bay clean of anything that
moved, with no protection for the people who lived there and whose
livelihood was being destroyed.
It would have been a surprise had he not written about it. All the same,
when it did come along it was an extraordinary moment.

I still play the song from time to time, and I never do without
envisioning the calm bright evening waters being parted by the bow of
the little boat, as it threads its way through the rocky islands that shelter
Canso Harbour.
And I still see those little boats, and the islands, and the extraordinary
light beyond them, from the kitchen window of the small house that
Gail and I bought there a couple of years ago. Only moments ago, as
I write this, I took a break and watched Mike and Juanita Dort, our
neighbours from across the street, bring their Cape Islander in, and in
one perfect and graceful motion swing it around the jetty and bring it
alongside to touch the dock as gently as the goodnight kiss of a sleepy
child. The show-offy bastards.

Odd thing, to live inside a song.

I don't remember where the CBC studios were where we recorded those projects. I know we did some sessions in the old main building at the corner of South Park and Sackville across from the Public Gardens. It was where Max Ferguson had got his start just after the war, and having listened to him for years and then making friends with him, and having read his memoir it was wonderful to walk through the halls and look out the windows up at the Citadel and feel his presence.
There were other secondary studios closer to the harbour, in a run-down warren of office buildings and warehouses, and I think that was where we did most of the work.
The one we used most was three narrow flights of stairs above the street, and it was small and cramped and filthy, with dust and used coffee cups everywhere. The recording console was an old green enameled vacuum tube powered relic from before the war with huge Bakelite knobs and VU meters that glowed yellow in the dark. The studio had no air conditioning, and it would overheat and the circuit breakers down the hall would give a loud bang and the lights would go out. We'd have to shut down and let it cool. There were a couple of channels which would only work if you wedged wooden matchsticks into the control slider. It was a mess. It reeked of history and bad wiring, and I wish I had it now.
Our engineer was a smallish dark haired guy, with a massive upper body development, the kind you only get from weight lifting or using crutches for many years. One of the rare times he got out from under the console I noticed he had a large black leather shoe on his right foot. It was built up maybe 3 or 4 inches to compensate for his withered foot.
We were on our way to the studio one morning, and it was raining a hard relentless downpour, that hurt if it hit bare skin. Stan and Jimmy and I were in a cab. Me and Jim in the back, Stan up front with the driver.
We turned the corner onto Sackville and we could see our engineer, whose name I have forgotten. He was stumping along in the downpour with his head down and his shoulder raised against the wind.
God, it was a miserable day. The poor bastard. Stan rolled down his window and a blast of rain blew into the cab. He leaned out and yelled, "Hey there."
The guy stopped, and I could see that perhaps he thought we were offering him a lift.
But Stan banged the flat of his hand on the door and yelled, "We got a busy day ahead. Get moving. Come on. Shake a leg."
He rolled the window back up and we carried on.

Jim and I looked at each other.

"Uh... Stan?"

"Yeah?"

"That guy. He has a club foot."

"Huh?"

"He's crippled. He has a club foot. And he's in the pouring rain. And we just drove by him and YOU JUST TOLD HIM TO SHAKE A LEG."

"OH JESUS CHRIST." Stan yelled at the driver to turn around, but we were on a one way street, and by the time we had circled the block back to the Public Gardens and then turned right the engineer had disappeared.

Stan spent the rest of the drive to the studio holding his head and moaning and rocking back and forth.

"Oh God. I never noticed. I swear I never noticed."

Poor bastard. It was the kind of faux pas that could follow you around for the rest of your life. In Stan's case it often did, and he developed an unfortunate reputation for being coarse and insensitive, and uncaring, and he was none of those things. Well, coarse maybe. And maybe a tad insensitive at times...But he had the kindest of hearts and was appalled at what he'd done.

I spent a lot of time back in those days going around behind him, and telling people, "He's not really like that. He's a really good guy."

I expect he might have been doing the very same for me.

I hope so.

I needed it.

The engineer was pretty good about it when he had hauled himself up the stairs, and shook the water out of his rain coat. He waved away Stan's abject apologies.

"Its okay. Don't worry about it."

But Stan spent the rest of the sessions fetching the guy coffee and tending to his every imagined need.

Bloody Hell...where was I?

Oh yes...the album.

We rehearsed around Toronto for some weeks, in advance of going into the studio, and the record was starting to take shape.

It was a shape we weren't always happy with, but Stan was adamant that Paul was the Producer, and once we went into the studio he was boss. I didn't argue...much...but at the time I felt, as I feel all these years later, that the producer is not the boss, but rather the hired help.

And I personally was off to a rocky start as Paul wanted me off the

212

project, right from the get-go.
He had hired another fiddler, Bernie Jaffee, to come in and play the
songs without, I believe, consulting Stan, and certainly not me.
I didn't know that he'd been rung in until he turned up at the studio the
first morning.
Bernie was at least twice the fiddler that I will ever be, in that he came
from a traditional music background, but he wasn't an accompanist,
and he didn't get what the songs needed.
The poor guy had to come in at the last minute and try to put his parts
together and he was having trouble. It was embarrassing for both of us,
particularly when Paul sent the two of us downstairs so I could teach
him to play the parts I had worked out for the songs.
Once more, I was ready to quit.
I kept remembering the debacle with Jimmy Ogilvie the year before.
To try to be fair to Paul, he was trying to get the damned job done, and
within the tiny budget he was allowed, but this was just stupid, not to
mention insulting.

That first morning in the studio started out in an interesting way.
Stan was sitting in the main room in front of a microphone, checking
levels, when a telegram arrived for him.
    "Who's that from?" I asked.
Stan said nothing, just turned away to read it.
He then smiled and folded it into his shirt pocket.
I never pursued the matter, but I think it was most likely from Diane,
who might have got word that Stan was now getting off his lazy ass and
actually learning how to work, and wanted to wish him luck.

We were behind schedule almost immediately.
Stan's old Guild guitar was barely okay for live stuff, but once we got it
into the studio, under intense scrutiny, it fell way short.
It kept going out of tune, and nothing would make it stay.
We lost the better part of the morning until Gord Lowe drifted in and
offered his Epiphone Texan for the job.
It sounded great, and why not? It was the same model guitar that the
Beatles used; the one you hear in the opening bars of "Yesterday."
Stan balked.
He wanted to play his own damned guitar.
In the end, he did use the Guild for a couple of songs, most notably
"Make and Break Harbour," but for the rest the Texan was used and it
saved the session.
What also saved us was how well the rest of the guys played.
David Woodhead was wonderful and inventive as always, and Jerome

was coming up with great little percussion ideas, like step dancing on a
piece of plywood during "Maid on the Shore," and a tiny triangle part
in "45 Years."
And Stan was a one take wonder.
His vocals were pretty much flawless, and all done live, on the fly.
We decided to have him do all the harmonies in the interest of saving
time, as none of us were either really up to the job, or confident enough
to go out and do them, given the time constraints.
The only song we all sang was "Barrett's Privateers," and we never got
the parts or the mix right.
David was not a particularly strong singer back then, and his rather
high and wobbly voice was up too far.
   "Why is the cabin boy so loud?" he complained when he heard it.
But Stan was remarkable.
Given how green he still was, relatively speaking, and the pressure
he was under with his first record, he had enormous confidence and
enthusiasm, and pulled off all his vocals seemingly with no effort.

We still were lacking most of the fiddle parts and Bernie had gone
home.
While I was happy for Stan, for myself I was fed up.
We had all been recording or hanging around in the studio waiting to
record for the better part of 72 hours.
I was sleep deprived, and jittery with too much coffee.
I left the studio for some air.
A while later Stan came out as I was sitting sulking out on the front
steps.
It was about 5 in the morning, and I was watching a Mennonite drive
by, his black buggy being pulled by a sweating and typically starved
horse.
I was stranded.
I couldn't leave.
Stan sat down next to me.
   "You're up."
   "Huh?"
   "We need you in there."
   "For what?"
   "Overdubs, come on, we're running out of time."
Shit.
   "Paul doesn't want me in there."
   "Well, he wants you in there now."
Fuck him, I thought.
   "Come on, please. We need to finish so we can start mixing."

214

I went in, and got set up.
Paul's voice came over the talk back.
    "We need to start mixing in an hour."
Great.
I was nervous anyway, and now the pressure was really on.
I managed to stagger through the parts, but I felt then, as I do now, that
I sounded nervous and unsure. Even though I knew the parts inside
out, it was tough to play when I also knew that the guy behind the
glass, the so-called "boss," didn't want me on the project.
I thought, well that's that, I'm done with this.
Playing live was one thing, but this was too humiliating.
I finished my overdubs and went downstairs, and sat with Mike Curry,
who was around for moral support for Stan.
He had a bottle of Remy Martin, and he very kindly poured a large
measure for me.
I sat and drank and moped while Mike fussed with his pipe.
Neither of us said much.
The mix got done by nightfall I think, and Stan had given birth to the
first record.

Sometime later, I'm not sure how long, we took the final mix to play for
our parents.
It was like bringing home a report card. We were anxious that the folks
be proud of it, or at least pretend to be.
Mitch was there, as was Paul, and we sat through that first full listening
in their living room.
It sounded okay, for the most part, and Mum and Dad made polite
noises.
What I mostly remember was the shock, when Paul turned to Mitch and
said, "The next record, I'm gonna get that guitar out of his hands." By
which I took him to mean that Stan's playing also wasn't up to Paul's
standards. That was just absurd and beyond insulting.
I was furious, and my already dodgy relationship with Paul never
recovered.

I still don't know, even after all this time, what he thought Stan's music
should sound like.
Certainly not like Stan and I had envisioned it if you judged by the
arrangements we developed together in the band.
And over the years whenever Paul had got a free hand and a
larger budget, he seemed bent on eradicating any trace of the band
and the sound we spent so much time developing by hiring slick
session musicians, and loading the songs down with cluttered up

arrangements, and syrupy strings. Witness the confused and treacly mess that is "From Fresh Water."
It wasn't folk music as we saw it, and it certainly wasn't Stan.
Moreover, it wasn't the trio that went out on the road and helped sell that music every night.
There was a massive disconnect between what we presented live and what Paul seemed to think the music should be, and over the years that followed it drove a wedge between Stan and me and whoever else was in the band at the time.
But Stan was nothing if not fiercely loyal, and he largely went along with Paul's ideas, even though we both had real reservations, not to mention fights and firings and resignations throughout all the subsequent recordings.
Paul likely saw me as an impediment to the process, incompetent and too green to be in the studio with what he considered to be real musicians.
I'm sure he was right.
Certainly as a novice in the studio I would have welcomed more support, as opposed to the dismissive attitude I had to deal with, not just for that first record, but for all the ones that followed.

Stan and I shared more than just DNA. We had the deep musical bond that only siblings can have, and I spent every night on stage trying to find the heart and the center of those songs, and the communication between us was almost telepathic. None of that counted when we got into the studio, where Paul called the shots.
My only explanation was that by this time he had spent years in the studio at the CBC, in an assembly line atmosphere, and there were only so many hours allotted for the job, and the most efficient way to do it was to bring in the team of guys he knew could depend on. Fair enough.
The result to me sounded slick, highly proficient, and utterly devoid of life.

This will all sound petty and confusing for someone who is simply a fan of those wonderful songs, and is grateful for the records, and I know Paul would have a different view of his role in things.
But it was to be a continuing crisis for me and Stan for every album we made, and it came to a head during the final days of recording "From Fresh Water."
Stan had to try over the years to negotiate a difficult path between the two of us, and he never succeeded, and the music and the records and our relationships suffered for it.

But for now we did have a first recording.

The cover as Stan envisioned it was to be a warm sienna brown.
I think we felt it would look friendly and somehow "more folky," like
whole wheat bread.
Then we came up against the realities of the manufacturing process.
Back in those days, with what was called "the four colour process," the
machines would have had to be completely rinsed out every time we
made a pressing.
Brown was going to cost an extra couple of cents per copy, and it simply
wasn't in the budget.
We weren't aware of this until we frantically opened the first box to
view the album for the first time.
Wow.
What the hell had happened?
It was and it remains an ugly and lurid almost hunter orange.

CHAPTER 27

The Trapper's Festival

We got booked into the Trapper's Festival in The Pas, Manitoba.

It was the first gig we'd had in the months following what amounted to a break down for Stan.

He'd left the big house Brampton and had moved back in with Diane in Dundas after we'd recorded Fogarty's Cove, and it looked to her as if he might be finally learning to pull his weight financially.

But the economy was in tatters that year, with unemployment hovering around the 10 per cent mark. Gigs were even harder to find, and in desperation he had gone up to North Bay with a friend to install drywall during the day, and play in a bar during the night.

I didn't come along. The budget wouldn't support it. Actually, I don't think there was a budget.

They were mostly playing for drinks and tips.

Stan discovered Bacardi's 151 Proof Rum there, and he'd made the mistake of thinking he could drink it straight, as he did with ordinary rum, and managed to scald and destroy the tissues of his esophagus and stomach.

He came back 30 or 40 pounds thinner and was unable to keep down or digest food.

He had been concerned enough that he had checked in for a colonoscopy. As he told the story, he'd been inflated to the point that when they removed the probe he flew around the examining room like a party balloon.

He was going to need some time off.

I was getting odd jobs that winter through a friend named Morrie Gold, who owned a deli in Hamilton.

It's worth a minute to talk about Morrie.

Morrie had spent WWII on the run from the Gestapo, with a price on his head. He was captured at one point, and as they were marching him to the car partisans threw a grenade. It was better to take the chance that Morrie might die rather than have him give away any secrets during interrogation. The Germans were killed and Morrie was able to slip away and escape by jumping into the river.

He lost his family in the Holocaust, and after the war taught hand to hand combat in what was to become the Israeli army. After that he went to Argentina and worked as a gaucho, or so he claimed. He was pretty evasive about his time there however, and I always wondered if he wasn't chasing escaped Nazis.

He could ride though, and for a little round shouldered man with a pot belly he was terrifyingly tough. He settled down in Hamilton after meeting and marrying a former Chicago chorus girl named Jean. She was loud and blonde and lovely, and the very soul of kindness.

I was sitting at a table one day, eating the bowl of chili Morrie had given me in return for loading bags of horse feed into his truck, and two young kids with Mohawks and leather jackets with chains hanging from them came into the deli.

They both had Swastikas painted on their jackets. The whole place went silent. I could see elderly men and women all around the room who were having bad flashbacks. I was just getting up from my seat to throw the kids out when Morrie came out from behind the counter with a meat cleaver.

In seconds, before I could get there to assist, he had thrown the two of them out onto the side walk and had cut the Swastikas out of the jackets. He stood over them with the cleaver as they cowered on their backs and begged for mercy. He shook the patches in their faces.

"Come back and talk to me when you find out what these mean." The cops arrived but did nothing when the two little shits demanded charges be laid.

You don't mess with the guy who makes the best free pastrami sandwich within walking distance of the station.

Morrie got me another short lived job with a friend of his who hired me to load bananas in warehouse.

It wasn't that hard a job, in that the bunches of bananas were only about 40 pounds a piece, but they did have spiders. Black spiders about the size of a child's hand, who luckily were dopey from the cold and the bug spray. They would drop down on your neck, and struggle sleepily inside your shirt, growing more active as they warmed up, but they never bit, and their legs were soft, and covered with thick fur like a bunny.

I picked up a few dollars here and there shoveling snow after blizzards. I would walk a couple of miles to the North end of town and with a few dozen or so other desperate souls would be issued a shovel and spend the day clearing sidewalks for a couple bucks an hour.

Tough winter.

So I was glad when word came that Mitch Podolak had got us booked
into the festival and I could call myself a full time musician again.
In the penurious state we were in following the long lay-off, we had to
once again borrow train fare from our parents. The festival was paying
well though, and we knew at least this time we would be able to re-pay
the debt and still have some left over.
So we rattled our way out to Winnipeg, to stay at Mitch's house until
we could catch the charter flight up to The Pas. The flight was on an
old and noisy twin prop commuter bus with wings, and the seats were
little more than benches. Heat in the cabin was almost non-existent and
we couldn't see out the windows. They were completely frosted over.
We huddled in our seats and wished we'd had better winter coats the
whole trip.
The festival took place in the dead of winter.
It was a way to stave off boredom during the long nights, and
make suicide a somewhat less attractive option to living in The Pas.
Winnipeg is hellish enough in the winter. But hundreds of miles north
of Winnipeg and in almost permanent darkness, it is only a matter of
time before you wake up one January morning and begin to mentally
calculate just how many neck ties you own, and whether there are
enough to string together and throw over the rafter in the basement that
keeps calling to you.
We put down in The Pas, and it was around minus 20 Fahrenheit in the
bright sunshine.
"It's a dry cold," someone said, "You won't feel it after a while."
True enough, after a couple of days we were walking about town with
our coats unbuttoned just like the locals.

The town was jumping.
There were dozens of concerts.
Whole plane loads of musicians descended on the place.
There was a PBS film crew up from the Twin Cities doing a
documentary.
The on camera "Talent" was a racy-looking young woman, who,
although not dressed terribly provocatively, exuded some sort of high
power pheromone which had most of the horny rabble of musicians
drooling into their beards and acting like idiots, trying to attract her
attention.
She appeared to be used to it though, and was able to ignore them, even
when a guy named Dave threw himself on the floor in front of her at
the airport, and grabbing her leg, shouted that he was feeling faint and
could she provide mouth to mouth resuscitation?
She carefully stepped on his hand and walked away.

We had dinner and stayed the first night with a lovely couple, whose name I've forgotten, sadly, but they were extraordinarily kind and generous to us, and the man was an inventor, who'd designed and built an acoustic pedal steel guitar out of old bicycle parts with a top made from an old piano sound board.

It was a strange little contraption, particularly for a man who didn't play, but it sounded wonderful, and I wish I had it now.

Next day, we got installed in our hotel rooms, and the deliveries of free alcohol started.

The festival was sponsored by both a brewery and a distillery, and they were doing their best to get the word out.

I was lying in bed, reading a brochure on the town, when the door opened, and some men walked in with cases of beer.

"There, that should do you for today."

I sat up, "Huh?"

But they were already gone.

I went back to the brochure, and a moment later two guys walked in with bottles of rye and rum and scotch.

"There you go," and off they went.

Wow. Breakfast in bed.

And so it continued, for the whole week we were there.

It would have been rude not to at least make the effort to drink it, but Jesus, it was hard work.

Apart from the daily delivery, there was also a free 24 hour supply in the hospitality room just below us.

How did these people cope?

Stan and I were rusty from not playing for a while, so we had to do some rehearsal together.

We found out that we were also expected to find other folks to play with, and form little temporary ad hoc bands.

We hooked up with an old school harmonica player.

He wasn't one of those annoying guys you run into with a leather belt full of harps, a crumpled fedora, and a need to mindlessly noodle around everything anyone happened to play whether it was appropriate or not. This guy was a classical player, like Larry Adler or Max Geldray.

He was wonderful, and we did at least one show with him.

We also hooked up with a truly odd bass player.

He had a musical comedy act, in which he played solo bass, sang, and played trumpet, all at the same time. He was a really eccentric guy, even by our generous standards. And he was not only getting through his daily ration of booze from the sponsors, he was haunting the hospitality

221

suite, and the bars and scrounging from the rest of us.
He never seemed to sleep.
I wonder what museum his liver is in.

By the third morning, Stan and I were nursing Olympian hangovers
We stumbled out into the bright winter sunlight.
We were both in that precarious state of alcohol poisoning where some
kind of food, say a soft boiled egg, and buttered toast sounded good for
a few moments, and then waves of nausea would strike, and the world
would tip sideways and spin away.
It was touch and go.
We were walking down the street, going from car to car for support,
looking for a nice safe diner.
We made it to a corner, and saw a crowd of First Nations women
gathering around a large dark shiny pile of something we couldn't
identify. It was about eight feet high.
The women all had long bright knives, and when a whistle was
blown they all leapt forward and the air turned into a red mist. We
had wandered into the middle of the muskrat skinning contest, and
the shiny pile was maybe a thousand or so dead rats. Guts and other
viscera were being thrown all over the parking lot.
A minute or two later, Stan and I found ourselves leaning heavily on
a lamp post, and each other, and as he straightened up and wiped his
mouth, he turned away and said, "Maybe a little nap first."
We kicked some snow over our indiscretions, and wobbled back to the
hotel.

Later that same day we tried again, and were heading towards the
downtown area, where we saw another crowd gathered. This time we
knew enough to approach a little more slowly.
It was the flour packing contest.
There was a pickup truck filled with 50 pound sacks of flour, and
women were backing up to it to be loaded up, using a leather and
wooden frame strapped to their bodies. From there they would slowly
and painfully stagger across the parking lot to the finish line. It was an
astonishing feat of strength and will.
We were both big guys, but we could never come close to lifting the
flour, let alone carry it over the course.
And what did these women win?
Not a giant cash prize.
Not an all-expenses paid vacation in Florida.
They won...the flour.
They got to take the flour home with them, and be able to make enough

bannock to perhaps survive until spring.
The winner carried just under 700 pounds of flour on her back for a
distance of 100 feet.
It was heroic. It was epic.
It was roughly equivalent, in those days, to carrying a Canadian folk
festival director away from a dim sum brunch.

There was a party in one of the bars that night.
Various pick up bands were there, working through their repertoire,
and the Lady from PBS was shaking it on the dance floor. She was still
like a drug on the brains and libidos of the numbskull musicians.
There was a crowd of them trying to join her on the dance floor to
slow dance and propose marriage, or failing that, lure her into a corner
for a quick knee trembler. I was sitting by myself, nursing a beer, and
thinking about going back to my room to sleep when she was across the
table from me. She leaned in.
"So what does a girl have to do to get your attention, anyway?"
Huh?
"You playing hard to get?"
"Uh, I was just having a couple of beers, and thinking about calling
it a night."
"How about calling it a night with me?"
"Huh?"
"Let's get away from all this, shall we?"
Wow, apparently I too had some overpowering charm which worked
even from a distance.
I must be careful, and not misuse this power.
I was going back to my room anyway, and I could give her the bad
news where it was quieter, away from this din.
We walked out of the bar and across the street to the hotel, and she
outlined her plans for the rest of the evening in graphic and explicit
detail.
It all sounded pretty stimulating, not to mention good for the
cardiovascular system and the endocrine glands, but I was never one
for intimacies with strangers. I wasn't even comfortable being naked by
myself. She was annoyed and embarrassed, having made the pitch and
then being turned down, and she flounced out of the Lobby using bad
words.
I took my noble self to bed.

I was awakened about 9 the next morning by thunderous pounding
at the door. I staggered over and opened it, and looked out past the
security chain. It was Dave, the guy who had been most intent on

winning her favour.

"OKAY YOU BASTARD…I WANT ALL THE FILTHY GORY DETAILS, YOU SON OF A BITCH. IF I CAN'T HAVE HER I WANT TO KNOW JUST EXACTLY WHAT SHE WAS LIKE. DID SHE SCREAM AND CALL FOR DADDY? DID SHE CLAW YOUR BACK AND YELL OOOOH FUCK ME HARD BIG BOY? COME ON YOU BASTARD, I WANT IT ALL."

I opened the door and saw he was with the delegation of idiots from the night before.

They all pushed past me into the room.

One of them got down on his hands and knees and looked under the bed.

"Where is she?"

Dave said, "Come on. I want every filthy detail. Complete play by play."

"What are you talking about?"

"The chick from Minneapolis. The TV broad. Where is she? What did you end up doing to her? What was she like?"

I was briefly tempted to tell them she'd had an extra breast, webbed feet, and a small vestigial tail, but it might have inflamed them even more.

"Nothing happened."

"What?"

"Sorry guys. I told her no."

There was a silence.

Then, "You told her …NO?"

"Are you fucking kidding me?"

"Are you some kind of FAG?"

"Guys, I just didn't feel right about it. I think she'd had too much to drink. She probably would have regretted it in the morning."

There was a longer silence, and the lads filed out muttering.

I had failed them.

Dave was crushed. He spent the rest of the week at the festival getting steadily drunker, and making ever clumsier come-ons to any woman who was literally within shouting distance.

The main object of his desire, the TV producer, was still on the scene. I caught the odd glimpse of her doing stand ups on the sidewalk in front of the hotel, but I didn't see her in the company of any other guy. Poor thing. I had probably spoiled her for other men.

Dave kept trying and he kept striking out. He was a mess.

"Poor bastard," said Stan, watching him. "He's gonna die of terminal hard-on."

The last evening we were in town, we went to an after concert party at the home of the nice couple who had put us up that first night. In contrast to the noisy and raucous circus we'd been in all week, it was a sweet and quiet gathering in the basement of their home. Just a few guitars and some harmony singing.

Dave arrived late and it looked like he had finally found love.

While everyone else who lived locally was dressed in parkas and wool sweaters and mukluks, Dave's new friend was wearing stiletto heeled shoes, with a red satin dress. She was a tribute to centuries of selective breeding, and the miracle of stretch fabric. The hem of the dress was slit up to here, and the neck line was plunging down to there. And that was pretty much it. She had no under garments. You couldn't look directly at her.

I didn't know if she was a professional or just a gifted amateur, but you could drop this woman into any village, on any continent on the planet, and no matter what the culture, she would raise the hackles on every woman in the room. She would have been exactly what Doctor Strangelove had been envisioning in the last moments of the movie, when he was talking about repopulating the world.

She had long dark hair, huge dark eyes, and lips like a catcher's mitt. And her name was, I swear to God, Ruby.

Dave was in a frenzy of lust, and looked as if he might try to close escrow right on the spot, but Ruby evidently needed some courting too. So I was wrong. This was not just a simple business transaction.

Dave got ever drunker and finally passed out under a pool table around 4 A.M.

Ruby waited around for a while, hoping he would wake up, but after a couple of hours she'd had enough.

She left.

We were all just cruel enough to wait for Dave to wake. And as the sun was coming up he groaned and stirred, and rolled painfully over onto his side. He raised himself up, hit his head on the underside of the table, yelped in pain, and fell down onto his back.

He made another try and managed to roll out from under the table.

He sat up, holding his head and looking around.

"Where's Ruby?"

Stan was waiting with his guitar. He hit a chord, and quoting from "Ruby," the old Kenny Rogers song, everybody in the room sang as one,"She took her love to Town."

The festival reached its inevitable and depraved climax on the plane trip home.

All of the musicians were in an advanced state of alcohol induced psychosis, and the cranky old twin prop cattle car we were on looked

like it had been flying upside down by the time we reached Winnipeg.
Trash and empty bottles, and abandoned clothing were everywhere.
One of the fiddlers, not me, was wearing panty hose tied around his
head and playing gypsy music.

The poor flight attendant had given up and left the drinks cart out in
the aisle to be pillaged, and had locked herself in the forward toilet.
Our last sight of the lot of them was as we left to catch a connecting
flight to Toronto.

They lay in a pile on the slowly revolving luggage carousel.

There were suitcases broken open and spilling out filthy laundry
and ashtrays and hotel towels and bedding. Guitar cases and other
wreckage were piled around them. They had somehow managed to
bring what was left of the drinks cart, and it was upside down, wheels
spinning slowly.

They were still playing, still trying to sing, struggling helplessly against
the mild centrifugal effect of the carousel, and from a distance it looked
like a large and ugly and badly broken music box.

We went home.

The album was due out in a week or two.

CHAPTER 28

Fogarty's Cove Music

We had a little run of Eastern Ontario after the Trappers Festival. There was a bar in Ottawa, and then we had a weekend in Kingston at the Scarecrow. We were talking up the album, and people were wondering how they were going to get a copy. It's not like we had any chance of getting the album into the stores. There was no system of distribution for small fry like us, and it was too much trouble for stores to keep track of what little they might sell of an independent artist if we tried to deal with them directly.

What to do?

I don't know how we hit upon the idea, but Stan began announcing from the stage that if folks wanted a copy of the record they could give us their name and address and we would get our Mum to send it along with an invoice, or failing that, they could write to her directly, or call her at home. And here was her info...etc.

Jesus.

What were we thinking?

Without any prior consultation with her, we had committed Mum to working out our distribution problem. A few weeks later we presented her with a bale of napkins and paper placemats and cigarette packages with peoples' names and addresses scribbled on them, and left her to sort the whole mess.

A truck brought a pallet load of albums to our parents' door, and Dad loaded them into the basement.

And then Mum began the process of learning, and in many ways, inventing the art of independent music distribution. She had no template. She was making it up as she went along.

She had to source out mailers, and get in a Post Office scale, learn how to fill out Customs forms, and work out currency exchange and a myriad of other things. Eventually the business was to take over what had already been a pretty full and busy life.

And as the business grew, the local Post Office was obliged to hire on

3 more workers just to keep up with the flow. She began to accumulate a network of distributors, as chains like Sam the Record Man and A&A Records began to sit up and take notice of the growth of the independent music scene in Canada. More important to her was the vast network of private customers who began to send orders in the mail.

With every personal mail order she would include a little hand written note, and there began an enormous correspondence between her and what became the tens of thousands of customers who thought of her as a friend and pen pal. Pictures began to arrive of births, and christenings and weddings, as folks kept her in the loop about what was happening in their own lives.

Stan and I began to get people coming up to us at shows with messages from Mum, telling us to make sure to eat well and not drink too much. In the midst of everything else she had devised a way to nag us from a distance.

She learned something called "double entry book keeping" and along with making sure all appropriate taxes were filed and paid, she kept a tight grip on the money that was coming in, which more than once saved our asses when we would be in some far off town and the van needed an engine transplant or some other life-saving surgery.

Typically, when she began to get requests from radio stations for play copies, she was able to get the stations to pay for them. Any other company would have seen free copies as the cost of doing business, but Mum saw no reason that they shouldn't pay at least the cost of the postage, if not full retail on the album.

In short, she loved it, and she loved the world into which she now had an entree.

Stan made sure she and Dad always had full back stage access at festivals so they could hang out with people they only knew through their music, and they made lifetime friends with many people they'd only previously known from the radio.

Family run businesses can often run into trouble as egos and agendas get in the way, but in all the years that Mum took care of Fogarty's Cove Music, I don't recall any serious disagreements between Stan and Mum about anything. From where I was it seemed to run smoothly and without a hitch.

Stan and I would come off the road and he would proudly dump the wad of cash and cheques onto the dining room table, and they would count it together, and then Mum would open the books and show us where we currently were, and how much had come in that week from mail orders and the small stores she loved to service. They were proud of each other, and what we were accomplishing, and they were thrilled with the whole process.

I have read in recent years interviews with the person who ended up with Fogarty's Cove Music after Stan died, and comments about how the company under Mum's control never would have made it as the Canadian record industry grew; that certainly we would have sold out and signed with a major label, as we were nothing more than a "Kitchen Operation."

I can say for certain, based on conversations Stan and I had just weeks before his death that it never would have happened. We loved working as a family.

And as for it being a "Kitchen Operation," it's easy to stand and sneer from the sidelines, but I never saw anyone else in that kitchen helping. Mum and Dad did it all.

CHAPTER 29

First US Tour

I think it might have been the spring of 1976.
We had a short tour of the US eastern seaboard.
Not a big one, just a handful of dates scattered over a couple of
weekends and about 2000 miles of driving. It had been set up by a
woman who would later become our regular agent for stateside gigs.
She was well meaning, and sincere, and more importantly honest, but
the gigs we were doing were without exception a mess. The routing was
terrible and there was never any money. On the other hand she wasn't
making anything from us either.

We had wanted to take Dave Woodhead, but the money just wasn't
there, and besides, we were going to be travelling in Diane's brown
Honda Civic, and the two of us were enough of a load.
We packed the car, and Stan threw in a thermos of rum laced coffee and
we left after midnight.
Stan did all the driving as I had yet to get my beginner's permit.
The first show was in Hartford Connecticut at the Sounding Board
Coffeehouse.
We arrived about 8 in the morning at the home of the Domlers, the
couple who ran the club.
Stan in particular needed a nap, and we were shown to the guest room
which had only one double bed. Stan, his need being greater, took that
and crashed out. I spread my sleeping bag out on the braided rug and
curled up like a pet dog.

The show went fine.
We had a good turnout, far better than we had expected.
There was a lovely moment, when we played "The Band Played
Waltzing Matilda."
Eric Bogle's great song had just arrived in North America the year
before, via Archie Fisher, and it still packed a tremendous punch.

It had not yet been forever devalued by having thousands of whiskey
sotted Irish bar bands belt it out to rooms full of glass-waving drunks,
as their "big moment" in the set.
It is still a great song, but like Michael Smith's "The Dutchman" it
has lost its shine, after having been fondled and frotted and soiled as
it passed through the grubby mitts of every handless Liam Clancy
wannabe on the planet.
We got through the first verse and went into the chorus, at which point
every voice in the room lifted up in harmony.
There were several lovely soprano voices in the back, and it was sweet
and utterly moving, and all at once Stan and I both had something
wrong with our voices.
We came to a full stop.
    "Give us a minute," Stan said, "That caught us by surprise."
We sat for a moment, and got our composure back.
Stan began singing the second verse, but his voice was less sure than it
had been before, and we both had to make use of our shirt sleeves when
we finished.
At the end of the show, the audience stood and sang "Will Ye No' Come
Back Again?" to get us back for the encore.
Sweet people.
There was an awkward moment, though, after the show, when Bill
Domler came over to pay us.
    "I deducted a third of your fee because you didn't bring the bass
player."
What?
    "There is only the two of you, so that's what I'll pay for."
We were strangers here, and didn't know how to handle this.
We'd drawn a good crowd, and thought we'd done a good show.
This felt wrong.
We looked at each other and then Stan took the envelope with the 120
dollars in it.
We thanked him as politely as we could, not wanting to burn any
bridges, but it was a jarring end to the evening.
Stan came up to me a few minutes later, as I was packing up, and said,
"I don't know if this going to be weird or not, but there is a couple over
there, and they have a little motel out on the coast and they've invited
us to stay over. It's a free room and they'll feed us in the morning. The
alternative is to sleep on the floor at Bill's house."

Fine. It sounded okay.
Stan took me over to meet the couple.
They were Gene and Barbara Bellows, and they were to become good

and supportive friends.
Gene was from Newfoundland, a restless self-made man who had got
an education at the University of Toronto simply by walking into classes
and taking notes for four years.
He didn't see being unable to afford school as an impediment to
learning what he needed to know.
His wife Barbara came from an old and respected New England family,
(they owned the lake where "On Golden Pond" was filmed,) and Gene,
being the soldier of fortune that he was might not have been the partner
they had envisioned for her.
It was a true love match though, and they were smart and kind, and
extraordinarily generous to us in the years to come.
The "motel" was actually a beautiful guest house called The Bee and
Thistle Inn in Old Lyme.
It was full of antique furniture and four poster beds, and smelled of
beeswax, wine sauce and old New England money.
It was the sort of place we never could have afforded.
It was in the sort of neighbourhood we should have been chased out of
by a police escort.
They made us welcome that night, and in later years, opened the place
to us as a base of operations whenever we toured down there.

In the morning, Gene cooked us sour crème and artichoke heart
omelets, and then took out his Rand McNally Atlas and mapped out the
best route for us to get down to Norfolk Va. where we were playing in a
couple of days.
"Stay off I-95. Take 84 past Danbury to 684, go south, and then turn
west to the Tappanzee Bridge. Then south on the Garden State Parkway
and pick up I-95 again south of Philly. Take the 895 ring road at
Baltimore and when you get to Route 50 outside of DC cut East through
Annapolis, and you can catch the road to the Bay Bridge Tunnel to
Norfolk."
He handed us the Atlas with the route marked out.
Hugs and handshakes in the parking lot, and then we were off.

Somewhere around Philadelphia the weather started closing in.
Big fat flakes of wet snow started to fly up against the windscreen, and
soon we were in a blizzard.
We kept going.
Stan was hunched over the wheel, peering through the storm. It was as
if someone was standing on the roof of the car shaking a burst feather
pillow over us, and the windshield wipers weren't up to the job.
We passed into Delaware.

There was no snow removal equipment, apparently. It was just piling up, and the little car was not liking it.

Stan was fighting with the steering, and muttering to himself.

"I've used rubbers with more tread on them than these tires have."

A moment later the car went into a spin, slipped off the road, and we were plunging down a long embankment.

Stan was doing some very fancy heel and toe work with the pedals, and fighting the wheel to keep us from flipping as we careered down the long snow- covered hill towards a small brook.

We came to a stop just a few feet away from it and a few moments later we got out, sweating, pale and shaking.

We looked up at the highway we had just left, and realized we were screwed.

We were maybe 40 or 50 feet below the road now.

We would never get back up there without help, and we had no money to spare for a tow truck, even if such a thing could be found.

We were doomed.

The snow was getting deeper.

Maybe someone would find us in the spring, after the wolves were done with us.

We just stood there, stunned at the enormity of the disaster, and then a voice was calling down to us.

"You boys need a tow?"

We looked up and there was a trucker who had seen us leave the road.

He was uncoiling a long cable, and he threw it down the hill.

Stan crawled under the car and hooked it on, the trucker turned on the winch and we were back on the road in a few minutes.

It was a miracle.

The trucker waved off our fervent thanks and drove off.

God bless that guy, wherever he is.

We pressed on into Maryland, and finally we knew we couldn't go any further.

The snow was up to the bottoms of the doors.

There were no plows at all, and it was getting dark.

The road had disappeared and Stan was simply steering between the telephone poles and light standards on each side of the road. Our world had dwindled down to a tunnel of white, seen through the ever diminishing clear space in the wind screen.

When we were younger, Stan and I had both read a book by a Danish explorer named Peter Freuchen, who had traveled and lived among the Inuit of Greenland in the early part of the 20th Century.

There was one story where Freuchen had been buried in an avalanche,

and was sure his time had come. He had no way of digging himself
out. As he lay in the frozen dark, under tonnes of snow, he remembered
kicking aside a frozen Husky turd a few days before, and had noted at
the time how hard it had become in the 40 below temperatures.
Being an inventive sort, and not having much else to do to pass the
time, he removed his pants and had a crap. He then carefully fashioned
a crude digging tool, and then waited for it to freeze hard enough to
chip his way to freedom.
The story must have been on both our minds, because when I said,
   "Much more of this and we're going to need a shit chisel," Stan
merely nodded.

We came into Elkton Maryland, and by now we'd had enough.
There was a motel on the left.
Stan steered us slowly and carefully into where we thought the parking
lot might be, and we went in to the office.
In the few seconds it took for us to get from the car to office we were
covered in snow, and the pair of us looked like a couple of Yeti.
An enormously fat man in a stained sweatshirt was sitting behind a
filthy desk, with a shotgun under his right hand.
As we came in the door his right hand moved carefully to the trigger
guard, and he said, "What kin I do for you fellas?"
We got a room.
12 bucks for a double.
We loaded our gear out of the car.
The room was everything a 12 dollar a night motel room in Elkton,
Maryland could be.
But it had heat, and two beds, and we unrolled our sleeping bags on top
of them.
Nothing was going to induce us to sleep between those sheets.
The bathroom worked though, and in the midst of all the filth and
squalor it had a brand new Sony Trinitron television bolted to the wall.
Stan turned it on to get a weather report, but there was only one station
and it showed nothing but re-runs of Batman.
But we were okay. We were out of danger, we were dry and warm, and
we would try again tomorrow.

We needed supplies, and the two of us struggled out across the parking
lot, and looked carefully both ways, for all the good that did. It was a
white out. We took a deep breath, hooked our arms together and ran
across the road to a shopping plaza.
There was a liquor store there, and we went in and realized that things
here were different from home.

Here, in one store, you could conceivably buy a small caliber handgun, a box of shells, and a six pack of Pabst Blue Ribbon and still get change from a twenty.

Stan moved in close to me and said very quietly, "Jesus, I can just see some guy finding his wife with his best friend, and dragging them in here and throwing a twenty on the counter and getting the guy behind the counter to set him up."God damn it Linda Sue, and you, you sonavabitch Dean, I trusted you. BAM BAM BAM, and then walking out with his beer. What kind of place is this?"

We got some beer, some bread and cold cuts, and a bottle of cheap scotch, and got back to the room, and settled in for a night of Batman. At one point during the evening, I went in to the office to make a collect call to our parents, who might have been watching the storm on the tube, to reassure them we were out of danger.

The big guy behind the desk kept the shotgun pointed at me the whole time.

Next morning, Stan brought me a shovel from the office.

"Do me a favour and dig the car out will you? My back is giving me grief."

Ordinarily I might not have believed him but the beds we had slept in were in keeping with the rest of the ambience of the room.

They didn't just sag like hammocks. They were more like something one would hang in a tree in the woods to keep your supplies from marauding bears.

Stan and I had actually had to link arms together to climb out that morning.

I went out to the first snow covered hillock I found and commenced digging.

After maybe 10 minutes of shoveling I uncovered a fender.

It was dark blue.

Damn. Wrong car.

I tried the next one.

Wrong again.

Shit.

Got it right the third time, and we loaded up and got under way.

The snow had stopped, and the sun was out and as we headed down the peninsula to the Chesapeake Bay Bridge Tunnel, the air turned milder.

We were playing a little place called "Ramblin' Conrad's," in Norfolk. It was run by Bob Zentz. He was a nice guy, and a pretty good songwriter.

The deal for the gig was 50% of the gate, no guarantee.
It was a three dollar ticket, and maybe 6 or 8 people showed up. Even with my poor math skills, I knew this wasn't good. We went back to Bob's house after the show, and stayed up most of the night while he played us records, showed us some new songs he'd written, and nearly finished our scotch.
We crept out of the house about 5 in the morning, loaded up and went back North across the Bay Bridge Tunnel.
We had a long drive ahead of us.
The next show was that night in New Hope Pennsylvania.
It looked like about a 7 hour run in favourable conditions.

We were hungry.
Really hungry.
Ravenous.
    "I could chew the ass off a dead skunk," was how Stan put it.
Funds were low, and we kept on going, sustaining ourselves with the anticipation of the wonderful breakfast that was waiting for us up ahead at a restaurant called "Stuckey's," on the Maryland side of the Bay/Bridge Tunnel.
There were billboards everywhere, advertising the great 99 cent eggs and bacon and toast and home fries breakfast special.
It looked wonderful on the sign, and we kept going.
There was another billboard.
God, it looked good. Bacon and coffee, hot and strong and black, and eggs, bright yellow and sunny side up. Crunchy toast with the butter running. Crisp home fries. God, and only 99 cents. We could afford to order a couple each.
We could imagine the place. A quaint little diner converted from an old Airstream trailer, full of interesting locals and a pert waitress in a starched cap and a spotless uniform with her name, "Dottie," stitched on the breast pocket.
She'd call us "Hon," and "Doll," and bring us endless re-fills of coffee, and maybe a free piece of warm apple pie with a chunk of cheddar cheese on the top just because we were nice boys and far from home.
We both felt faint.
    "Can you wait 'til we get to this place? It's still an hour away."
    "Yeah. It's a great deal. I can hang on until we get there. I'm starving though."
    "Yeah, me too."
Well of course, anyone who has been to the South, knows what we were presented with when we finally got to Stuckey's.
It turned out to be a gas station with a tacky gift shop, and a grubby

fly blown lunch counter where truckers huddled over plastic plates of
something we couldn't identify as actual food.
We didn't care at this point.
We were hungry. Whatever standards we might have once had were
gone.
Stan put a forkful into his mouth.
His face went blank and he grabbed a handful of paper napkins and
spat into it.
      "Jesus. What IS this?"
The eggs were like the results of an alien autopsy. The bacon had
evidently not come from a pig, but some other species of animal, likely
a mutant creature that was being bred in the backwoods by a family of
hillbilly moonshiners who probably regarded it as not-too-distant kin.
The home fries looked like they were second hand.
The toast was cold and limp, and after carefully sniffing a slice, I
decided I'd rather eat a used field dressing.
We got up and walked out.
We were crushed, and faint with hunger, not to mention furious, being 2
dollars out of pocket.
The Honda was now blocked in by a dump truck.
We had to go back in and ask around the groups of truckers who were
wolfing down their 99 cent breakfast specials if they could let us out.
One of them came out and pulled his rig a few feet forward.
He hopped down from the cab and said, "What's the matter boy? Thet
little tater bug of yours too much for ya? Haw haw haw."
He hitched up his pants and went back in to finish his feast.
We got back on the road.
I went back past the restaurant last year.
The place is still there, still open.
Unaccountably, no one has torched it.
And it is still offering the same breakfast special, literally.
I think it is still the same two plastic plates of greasy poisonous swill we
left uneaten on the counter all those years ago.
      "Someday, Goober, someone's gonna eat this shit. We'll just keep
putting it out until they do."

We were playing a joint called "John and Peter's Place."
It was just up the river a few miles from where Washington crossed the
Delaware.
We had a long way to go, and our stomachs were still empty.
Snow had re-appeared, and the road was getting bad again.
Jesus, where were the plows?
This was stupid.

How can they live this way?

Do they just wait for it to thaw?

And... HOLY SHIT! We were off the road again, spinning end for end down a long embankment towards a large metal culvert.

We hit something under the snow, and came to an abrupt stop.

I smacked my head against the windshield.

We sat in shocked silence for a few seconds and then Stan said, "Are you okay?"

"Yeah." I felt my forehead. "Got a bit of a bump, but yeah."

Reaction and adrenalin set in and we both began to shake.

We got out to look at the damage, and almost at that same moment, a voice once again called down from above us.

It was another kind trucker.

He was laughing at us.

"That looked real exciting. You boys okay?"

He too had a cable and a winch, and he too waved off our thanks as he drove away after carefully and expertly pulling the Honda out from its grave.

Back on the road, we crept along carefully for the next few hours, scared that if we ran off the road again we might be stuck forever.

We had to run out of Good Samaritan truckers some time.

I looked at my watch and then looked at Gene's atlas and made some rough calculations.

We were just going to make the gig if nothing else horrible happened.

The snow kept falling.

We got to New Hope and found the address.

We pulled into the parking lot behind the place and went inside. It was a low ceilinged bar, circa 1750's, full of people drinking and laughing and keeping warm from out of the storm.

Loud music was playing.

Actually, as I looked closer, it was full of men. Just men. Good looking guys for the most part, all carefully groomed and well dressed.

Many of them were dancing.

Dancing?

"Uh...Stan."

"Yeah?"

"Um...This looks like it might be a..."

"Yeah, I know."

We both needed a pee.

We went into the washroom and stood at the urinals, the usual male ritual, eyes front, just taking care of business.

The graffiti on the walls were all variations on a theme.

"Jason sucks dick."
"For a good blow job call Bobbi."
"Adrian is a cock sucking whore."
And so on.
We stood, silently reading.
We finished up and went over to the sink to wash our hands.
"Looks like a friendly enough place anyway." said Stan.

We came out of the washroom and the manager came up and
introduced himself.
"I've been calling your agent all day, trying to cancel because of the
weather. We can't do a show. It's a snow emergency."
"But we just drove up from Norfolk. We had an accident. We..."
Stan ran out of words. He waved his hands helplessly.
We didn't know what to do. The guy looked at us, and realized I think,
that we both were at a low ebb.
"Tell you what. You can still play. I can't do the original contract, but
we'll pass the hat. You'll do fine. Folks here are really generous."
We had gathered as much from the washroom wall.
"Okay."
We had no other options.
"What hotel are you in?"
Hotel? We couldn't afford the YMCA.
We could barely afford to sleep in the car.
"We don't have a hotel."
"Okay, look. It's a little untidy, but you can sleep in the office
upstairs. It's just that I'll have to lock you in for the night after the
show."
Fine.
We lugged our gear upstairs, and the office was a disaster.
It was beyond filthy.
"This is a little untidy?"
Stan and I were looking in vain to find a clean place to set our bags
down.
There were piles of paper everywhere, broken furniture, wads of some
kind of thick matted animal hair, little hillocks of dirt, like sweepings
from a barn, and just years of accumulated crud piled up past the
window sills.
"There should be a sign, saying, "George Washington shit here.""
And there were piles of cocaine.
Everywhere.
Mounds of it, on the desk, and on magazines. Untidy lines of it,
chopped and scattered over large pieces of broken mirrors.

There were dozens of bricks of it wrapped tightly in plastic, stacked in the corner behind the desk.
Somebody was either supplementing their income or was having trouble with their energy levels.

"I wonder if Hunter Thompson is the co-owner?"
We were too tired and depressed to be shocked much at this point.
I started piling broken chairs and other junk out of the way, and Stan worked with a broom for a while, and we managed to clear a place to sleep.
There was a sagging and filthy daybed, and he lay down on it and put his forearm over his eyes.
I sat down in a captain's chair and waited for the room to stop spinning.
Neither of us had eaten since the night before, and I felt whoozy.
After a while, I realized Stan was crying.
The stress of the last 72 hours was getting to us both.
The storms, the near death experiences, the bad food. Hell, NO food, and now the disappointment that we'd just been handed had overwhelmed him and he was sobbing quietly.
It was hard to listen to him.

"Uh...Stan...?"

"Stan?"
He cleared his throat.

"Yeah."

"I just want to thank you for all this."

"What?"

"All this. The tour. These gigs."

"What the hell are you talking about?"

"It's just that when you and the other older guys are all sitting around, telling war stories about how hard it is on the road, I've always felt bad, because I didn't have anything to add. I didn't have any stories of disasters, and I felt kinda left out, and I just want to say thanks. Now I've got some stuff to complain about. You've given me so much. It means a lot to me. Really."
I looked over and he was giggling and crying at the same time with his arm still over his eyes.

"Glad I could help," and we both burst out laughing.

"Why don't you try to get a nap for half an hour. I'll wake you up."
I unwrapped his sleeping bag and threw it over him.
I actually tucked the poor bastard in.
He'd had a hard day.
He fell asleep almost instantly, and I went downstairs.

Outside, the snow had stopped, and the air was quiet and clean, and the streets were hushed.

I went up the street, found a narrow iron bridge, and made my own personal crossing of the Delaware into New Jersey, found a liquor store and spent 12 bucks on a bottle of Glenmorangie.

It was more than I could afford, but we both needed cheering up, and besides, 12 dollars for a bottle of 12 year old whisky was a bargain.

It meant the Scots were only charging a dollar a year for storage.

I took it back to the club, went upstairs, woke Stan up, and we had a quiet drink and then went down to play.

The gig was okay.

The patrons were kind, and fairly generous, and we had a good meal after the show.

We were feeling a bit better, but still had the shit-hole upstairs to look forward to.

There was a very thin and twitchy blonde woman behind the bar, who had been bringing us drinks on the house, in between trips upstairs to the office.

She came over as I was finishing my burger, wiping her hands on a towel.

She put her elbows on the bar and leaned in.

"Need a place to stay tonight?"

I wasn't sure of her intentions.

"Like, um...sleep on your couch?"

"No."

She moved in closer and grabbed my collar.

"I was thinking of kidnapping you and dragging you back to my place, and we could have some fun after I tore your clothes off."

Oh.

"Uh...well that sounds really nice, but I'm here with my brother."

She let go of me and pulled away.

"I'm not into that shit. Just you and me. I might let him watch, but he can't join in, and he'd have to sleep on the couch."

Oh my God.

"I didn't mean, like, uh... jeez...I'm really sorry. But I'm... uh... We're staying upstairs tonight."

"The office? That place is a dump. Come back to my place. You can sleep on the couch if you want. It's okay. I won't attack you."

"Thanks anyway. I'd better stay here with my brother."

"Okay, if you change your mind, I'll be here for a while."

"Thanks."

A few minutes later, I felt a hand on my left shoulder.

It was one of the guys from the audience.

He was a big strapping fellow, sporting a carefully trimmed mustache, a

Jane Fonda hairdo, and a cloud of industrial strength cologne.

"Need a place to stay tonight?"

God, I had never been so popular.

"Thanks."

I cleared my throat and lowered my voice about an octave.

"Thanks. But I'm going home with her."

He looked over at the bartender and sniffed.

"Oh...Her. Okay, suit yourself, but if you change your mind, I'll be here for a while."

The bartender had overheard the exchange and looked over at me with a raised eyebrow.

I said, "Sorry, I..."

She nodded and waved me away.

"It's alright."

Stan was sitting a few stools away from me, working on his third or fourth beer, and his second cheeseburger.

He raised his glass to me.

"I think you're gonna like it here. You're a woman of mystery."

"Thanks a lot. And fuck off."

I went upstairs and hid until the place was locked for the night.

After everyone had gone home Stan and I went back down to the bar.

The owner, who really was a decent guy, albeit with an apparent chronic sinus problem, told us to make free with the bar.

"Help yourselves. It's on the house."

We had read a passage in David Niven's autobiography, how he and Errol Flynn had gone on a bender, drinking according to the flags of the nations, using various coloured liqueurs to achieve the proper effect.

"What's Albania?"

"No idea."

"Argentina?"

"Let me think."

We had resolved to up the degree of difficulty by proceeding alphabetically as well.

"Bolivia?"

We thought we remembered that one.

"It's got green on the flag."

Stan fetched the bottle of Crème de Menthe and a tall glass.

"Fine, what else?"

"Canada?"

"Got it. White rum and raspberry cordial."

"Whoa."

"Denmark?"

"I dunno."

"Damn. I wish we had an atlas."

We looked at each other.

"Gene's Rand McNally. It's still in the car."

It was a worthy project, but we were tired after the hideous day, and finally gave up around Venezuela.

In any case we didn't know what the flag of Zimbabwe looked like.

Next morning, I felt like a dead cat had been nailed to my face.

We slowly and tediously assembled what was left of ourselves, the day manager came in, and we were released into the morning light, to once more dig out the car and begin the drive to Godfrey Daniels' in Bethlehem.

Godfrey Daniels' is still going after all these years.

Back then it was run by Dave Fry, and Cindy Dinsmore, and it immediately felt like home.

Walk in the door and there was the smell of cinnamon, and nutmeg and hot cider, and weapons grade coffee.

There was a counter to your right as you came in off the street, where they served coffee and soups and home baked bread, and the kind of pies normally seen only in Norman Rockwell paintings.

The concert room was in the back. It seated about 80.

Upstairs was the apartment that Dave and Cindy shared with a couple of cats, and in the front room there were some bunk beds for the performers.

We had drawn a modest but friendly audience, and it was a nice end to a bumpy couple of days.

We were not familiar with the liquor laws in Pennsylvania, which allowed folks to bring their own beer and wine, so long as they didn't get shit-faced and unruly.

It made for a relaxed and convivial atmosphere while playing, where a kindly member of the crowd might crack a beer and hand it up to the stage during the show if he thought you looked dehydrated.

We loved it.

We loved the room, and the volunteers who ran it, and the neighbourhood was great too.

The club is on 4th Street on the south side of Bethlehem, and back then it was decidedly down market, mostly students, Italian working class families, and a growing influx of Latino immigrants.

It was a neighbourhood where folks sat out on their front steps on warm summer nights and called greetings across the street, and kids could play in safety.

There was a little tavern right next door to Godfrey's.
It was another one of those perfect American joints which we grew to
love.
It was long and narrow and dark, with a bar on the right, a pool table in
the front, and a pretty good juke box.
The juke box didn't get a lot of use mostly because there was a truly
eccentric bartender there who kept her own Seabreeze record player
behind the bar, out of reach from the public.
She was about 6'3" and skinny, with a massive dark Afro style hair-do,
and crazy eyes.
Occasionally she would simply unplug the juke box in mid-song, and
then, over the howls of protest tell everyone in the room to shut up as
she needed to listen to something.
Invariably it was "Astral Weeks" by Van Morrison, and smart drinkers
learned to get their orders in early, as all service stopped while it
played.
At least all sane service.
As the record played she would commence a bizarre free form dance
which had nothing to do with the actual music, but rather something
else only she could hear.
She would sing along with the record using a Rolling Rock bottle as a
pretend microphone.
When she did get around to actually serving you, the price could range
from 50 cents for a double shot of Jack and a beer chaser, to 7 bucks for a
mere 8 ounce draft.
It was all arbitrary and made no sense, but we loved the show.

There was a great little chrome diner down the street which stayed open
late, where you could find some ballast for your belly after a night of
thin American beer.
I walked into the little place one night and had my first hot Italian
meatball sandwich.
This was not on the menu anywhere in Canada.
Spicy meatballs, caramelized onions, roasted red peppers, thick
marinara sauce and melted cheese, all wrapped in a crusty roll.
It had all the food groups.
I bit into it and I broke into a sweat.
It was life changing.
I wolfed it down, paid the bill, and ran as fast as I could back to the club
to get Stan.
He was by himself at the counter in the club, drinking a beer, and
writing post cards.
  "Come with me."

"What?"

"Come with me, right now."

"I'm having a beer."

"So drink it and come with me. I promise you, you'll thank me later."

I frog marched him down 4th Street and ordered two more sandwiches. He took up the first one, carefully peeled back the wax paper it was wrapped in, took a huge bite, chewed briefly, and then stopped, and I swear his eyes teared up.

"Well. What do you think?"

"Mumph."

"What?"

He shook his head. "Mumph... Mumph."

He banged his fist on the counter, and shook his head again, chewing and crying.

"Mumph."

"Yeah...I know." I patted him on the arm.

"Second one is yours too."

I left him there.

It was a great crowd that hung around there in those days.

In the years to follow, we spent a lot of nights sitting up after the show, jamming with the locals, and telling jokes and drinking Rolling Rock until sun up.

John Gorka was one of the volunteers back then.

He did sound for us a few times.

We didn't know he sang and played guitar, and had dreams of being a songwriter.

Back then he was just the quiet and sweet and bunny-like guy with soulful eyes and dark curls, who stammered and stared at his shoes while he talked to you, and who made our guitars squeal with feedback.

Stan and I went back there a year or so later with David Eadie and the sound check was a disaster.

John was busy in the sound booth to the right of the stage, turning knobs this way and that, and sincerely trying to help, but we were tired and grumpy, and the band had probably just had a crisis on the drive in.

I think the band broke up at least three times in the parking lot down the street from Godfrey's over the years. It had nothing to do with the club. We loved the joint. It's just that we all quit or got fired about once a week.

There was another wail of feedback as we tried to get Stan's guitar in the monitor.

Stan put down his guitar and stomped into the sound booth and

pushed John aside.
  "Out of the way, Frodo. I'll do this."
I watched as John trotted out the door.

Stan never did figure out how to get to the club the same way, all those years.
We would always approach it from a different direction, and somehow the club kept migrating back and forth across 4th street.
It drove us mad.
John, with his perfect eye for detail, wrote our little problem into the chorus of his song for Stan, years later.
The song is called "How Legends are Made," and John was the only guy to get the story right, out of the hundreds of sincere but painfully bad tribute songs that were written after Stan died.

  "So long.
It was nice meeting you.
But how do you get back to Route 22 from here?"

Good song.
Great guy.
I still love playing that club.
I still love those people.

CHAPTER 30

Mariposa 1977

There is a picture, somewhere in the family collection of my Mum, with Utah Phillips.

I haven't seen it for years, but in my memory, Utah is sitting on a picnic table, wearing the floppy leather hat he favoured in those days.

He isn't wearing a shirt, and his Korean War tattoos are still dark blue, and well defined.

He is restringing his big blonde Guild guitar that has the silver dollar glued to the head stock.

He doesn't have the full beard of later years, but rather an impressive set of mutton chops, and he's looking a little uncomfortable as Mum has just been sitting on his lap, wearing her pink stretch terry cloth jumpsuit.

Dad is not in the shot.

Presumably he was holding the camera, or out of the frame, waiting for his turn to sit on Utah's lap.

No reason to mention all that really, except that Mariposa 1977 was the festival where I met Utah, and a handful of other singers and performers who were to change Stan's life and mine in so many ways over the next few years.

Utah had come back from Korea, as a young man, traumatized by what he'd seen and done there, and determined in his own words, "To never again relinquish the right to decide for myself who the real enemy is." He drank too much in the years following, and mostly drifted around the Pacific Northwest, riding the rails, and collecting stories from the old generation of hobos, itinerant workers and other lost souls and refugees who lived in the twilight of postwar America.

A Christian Anarchist/Pacifist named Ammon Hennacy, who ran the Joe Hill House in Salt Lake City rescued him from the streets, and helped him sober up, and stop brawling.

"You have to stop drinking and become a Pacifist," Hennacy said to him.

"Why?"

"Because you're a lousy fighter. If you were winning it wouldn't matter. But I'm tired of having to patch you up every night."

Utah became a pacifist, and like Hennacy, joined the Wobblies, the Industrial Workers of the World, and spent much of the rest of his life on picket lines, singing, protesting, and raising money for various causes and the community around him.

His pacifism extended beyond simply avoiding bar fights.

He declared that as a white man, he had arbitrarily been given the weapons of power and privilege which were never available to women, and people of colour and other disadvantaged groups.

He refused to take any advantage of being what he had no control over from then on, and worked for justice and equality for everyone for the rest of his life.

Like Hennacy, he refused to pay taxes which might be used to support the war machinery, and he never registered any of his songs, as he said they weren't written by him, but had arrived through him.

He was a wonderful songwriter, but had only decided to become a traveling singer and performer at the urging of Rosalie Sorrels, after he had run for office in the state of Utah under the banner of the Peace and Freedom Party.

He lost, and was subsequently black listed from working in that state.

He went to Saratoga Springs New York, to hang around Café Lena, and write and work on his stage moves.

He was one of the crankiest, and funniest and most generous people I have ever met, with an unwavering moral compass, and a highly developed sense of outrage, and an innate gift for verbal irony and cutting invective.

He also had a lot of slick guitar moves, and an extraordinary stage patter that was equal parts

Circus barker, political rabble rouser, with some W.C. Fields and Foghorn Leghorn thrown in for good measure.

I often imagined him as one of the characters in the old Pogo comic strip, whose personality was revealed not by just his speech, but by how it was lettered in the drawing.

We had never seen anyone capable of doing a full set of comedy, and stories and poetry.

The songs were in effect, bookends to the rants and jokes and tall tales.

He was enormously well read, and endlessly curious about the world and the people around him.

Getting to whatever town he was playing, he would hit the library and

the museums and the coffee shops and try to get a handle on what was
going on locally.
What politician was doing some good, (a rarity,) who was a thief, who
was in trouble, who was in who's pocket, and what cherished landmark
was being torn down to make way for some rich greed head's pet
project.
The local news would be woven into the stage show, and he kept careful
records of what he said and played in every town, so as not to repeat, or
get stale when he came through again.
We had never seen someone work so hard to make it look so easy.

Stan and I were taking the small ferry over to Toronto Island one
morning that weekend, and we were sitting with Utah as he threw
small bits of bread to the ducks which had learned to follow the water
taxis.
We were impressed, partly by his kindness to animals, and also by
the fact that he had food to spare. We were still competing with the
squirrels in Queen's Park.
Utah was idly ripping up the bread, tossing it to the little flotilla of
birds, and occasionally dropping little pearls of wisdom.
    "My Grandmother always used to say, if at first you don't succeed,
to hell with it. She also told me that poverty is its own reward."
He was chewing on what I thought at first was a thin brown cheroot,
but it turned out to be licorice root.
    "It's sovereign stuff for cleaning the teeth, freshening the breath,
and improving the digestion."
    "It's good for making tiny logs for model railroads too." Dave
Woodhead said from his seat.
David is an ardent model railroader, and Utah turned to stare at him,
for once, speechless.

A group of elegantly dressed African women were seated around us.
They were wearing long colourful robes, and exotic head dresses and
wild tribal jewelry made of silver and coral and other bright stones.
I assumed they were singers from some village in the Congo, or Mali,
and had been brought over at great expense to play the festival.
Sure enough, they spontaneously broke into a song, but it was an old
African-American spiritual.
It was beautiful, and incredibly moving to hear those voices so close
and all around us.
It was like being inside some wonderful instrument, like a pipe organ.
Stan and I both were moved to tears, and bowed our heads, and simply
listened.

The song finished, and I wiped my eyes and turned to the woman closest to me and said very slowly and loudly, "Thank you. That... was... wonderful."

"You're very welcome. I'm happy you liked it."
She had no trace of an accent.

"Oh. You speak English very well. Where did you learn?"

"From my Mother and Father."

"And... where... do... they... live?"
I was still speaking loudly and slowly, so as to be understood, as if I was talking to an ex- governor of Alaska.

"New York City."
Stan leaned in close and said, "Smooth move, Bwana."
I had never heard of Sweet Honey in the Rock.
Still, even by my normal standards, I was being unusually stupid.

We had heard some bits and pieces of live recordings of Archie Fisher before this weekend, but had never met him.
There is a picture of him from that time, on the cover of his Man with a Rhyme album; handsome, tanned and windswept, cigarette in the corner of his mouth, looking rakish, and planning mayhem.
We met backstage in the performer's area, sat down across from each other, and he and I immediately traded guitars, he checking out my Larrivee, and me looking at his Fylde. I realised that his guitar wasn't tuned the normal way, and it was there that Archie showed us around the DADGAD tuning that was partly responsible for his songs being so mysterious and alluring. Stan had used it once before on the first album, but after seeing Archie up close it was to become a big part of our sound. And Archie's singing and writing were to leave indelible marks on Stan's own singing and his approach to writing songs, not to mention my own, in later years.
There was no chance we would ever be able to emulate his life style. His back story was epic... the stuff of legend.
He'd been born in Glasgow at the start of WWII, and ran away to sea and was ship wrecked off the coast of South America when he was just a teenager. He was briefly engaged to the heiress to the Guinness fortune, and spent time in India photographing tigers, and fooling about with a sitar. He once told me, "You've never really done it until you've done it in a Howdah on the back of an elephant."
I have ridden more conventionally on the back of an elephant, and been nearly thrown off by the animal's 10 foot stride, but have never had the opportunity for any other activity. Scotsmen are made of sterner stuff.
Archie and his sisters, Ray and Cilla, became major movers in the Scottish folk revival, and Archie was responsible for developing a

whole new approach to guitar playing and song writing, using alternate tunings and traditional songs and poetry as a starting point. The young Bert Jansch followed him to gigs, soaking up whatever he could. Archie has never had any gift for self-promotion, and as a result has never received the credit he is due for his talent and influence on generations of singers and guitarists. He has become one of my very dearest and most cherished friends, and I simply cannot imagine my life without his music and presence.

Heady stuff for a man who, as his friend Hamish Imlach put it, "Had his first job working as a turkey wanker on a poultry farm."

We took to him immediately, and spent most of that weekend in each other's company.

We were sitting on a workshop stage at one point, and noticed that a great many of the women in the crowd who were sitting with their arms around their knees were not wearing underwear beneath their long hippie skirts. It was quite a show.

Stan was sitting on my right, his face impassive, checking out the view from behind his sunglasses. He leaned over and said, "I keep thinking of pictures of Savannah, Georgia".

"Huh?"

"Spanish moss."

Archie, on the other side of me leaned over and said "I'm counting 12 right now. How many do you see?"

"Um...8. Can you point the others out?"

"I could if I stood up."

Later that weekend I saw a quite beautiful young mother.

She was tall and striking with long red hair past her waist, and vivid blue eyes.

She was playing with her little blonde daughter in the dappled shade beneath the trees. They made a lovely picture.

Here was a chance to wind up Archie.

I found him stretched out beneath a willow, smoking and watching the soft sunlight filter down through the branches.

He said, "So, been walking about checking out the talent?"

I said, "Oh yeah. There was a real stunner out by the swing set. Long red hair, blue eyes."

Archie sat up and looked suddenly alert, and said, "Yes? Red hair and?"

"And she was beautiful. Really built too. Hair past her waist. Legs up to there. Amazing body."

"Really?"

He was coming to point like a setter.

"Oh yeah. Fantastic. You should see her."

"Well. Right then. Where do I find her?"

't, smoothed back his hair, and re-buttoned his shirt.
_..u over by the swings."
"Right then. I'm away, see ya."
"Yeah, with her two year old daughter."
He stopped.
"A daughter?"
"Yeah."
He sat back down, pulled out his cigarettes and lighter, and lit up.
He lay back and blew smoke into the air.
"I've already met her then."

It was at Mariposa that we met the Red Clay Ramblers.
They were five guys from the Carolinas, all extraordinary players with
seemingly odd musical backgrounds.
They were all multi-instrumentalists, and could change on the fly, in
mid song, going from guitar to fiddle to trumpet to bass and back.
Great songs and quirky arrangements.
They would be in the midst of a long set of fiddle tunes, and suddenly
switch gears into a ragtime song, then come to a full stop, play a few
dozen bars of Mozart, and back to the fiddle tunes. Then a bit of doo-
wop, then a Carter Family song, all within a span of 5 or 6 minutes.
They killed us.
They had a couple of wonderful albums, "Hard Times", and "Merchants
Lunch", and we listened to them endlessly.
Funny guys too.
Stan and I walked in on them years later, in Calgary, as they were
working on a synchronized swimming routine in the hotel pool.
They were actually sort of good at it.
Hairy, but good.
It was kind of disturbing, and we left pretty quickly.

Giants walked the earth in those days at Mariposa.
Rufus Guinchard was up from Newfoundland.
The Balfa Brothers from Louisiana.
Joseph Spence.
Taj Mahal.
Blind John Davis.
Ola Belle Reed.
Jean Carrignon, the great Quebecois fiddler who had played with
Yehudi Menuhin, but still had to work for a living as a cab driver in
Montreal.
Johnny Shines, who had played and traveled with Robert Johnson was

there. Seeing him was seeing a figure from the Bible. Suddenly Noah was sitting in front of you, talking about what it was like back in the old days before the rain started.

We met John Allan Cameron that weekend. He was standing at the end of a dock, next to David Bromberg, wearing a pale blue T shirt that read "You're only as good as your last gig."

John Allan became one of Stan's dearest friends and biggest supporters. It was the weekend Stan met Tom Paxton, and they too became friends. It was the weekend I met Eugene O'Donnell, my favourite fiddler of all time.

He was a tiny man with thick white hair, like a kewpie doll, who had won the all-Ireland step dancing championship so many times as a young man, they finally asked him to stay home and give someone else a turn.

He specialized in the sweet and slow Irish airs, played with wonderful classical technique, and a rich warm tone.

He was my hero of violin, and I knew all his recordings by heart, and he was patient enough to let me play along, one afternoon as he practiced under the trees.

Lovely man.

It was the year that Pierre Bensusan unleashed his dazzling guitar technique, and his bee stung lips, and brown doe eyes onto an unsuspecting world.

He was a breath-takingly good player, and raised the bar for all would be finger pickers in North America.

He had a weird effect on women.

They would see him, and something would happen to their inner ears, and they had to, simply just had to lay down and loosen their clothing.

He boasted to me that he had slept with over 80 women so far on his tour.

He'd only been over for a couple of weeks. He was raising the bar for everyone.

I heard a story about him some time later, how he had done a concert in the Midwest, and afterwards all the hot players had raced over to where he was being billeted, to set up and lay in wait for him.

As the story was told to me, all the players opened their guitar cases, put on their finger picks, tuned up, and watched the door.

This was their big chance to go up against the new gunslinger.

And so they waited.

They waited some more.

After a couple of hours the beer ran out, the pizza was gone, and people started to drift out into the night and go home.

Finally, just as the host was wondering whether to call the police, and report a missing French Algerian guitar god, the door blew open, and there he was.

He had a bottle of brandy in one hand, and a handful of Brandi in the other.

He'd found some floozy in a satin dress somewhere, certainly not at the folk concert, not wearing those shoes, and was now eager to celebrate his new found friendship.

He waved the bottle vaguely in the direction of his room, and said, "I go to bed now."

He then lurched across the floor, kicked the door open and flung his new love inside.

Kicked the door shut, and for the next couple of hours it sounded like someone beating a carpet with a baby pig.

It was at Mariposa in 1974, I think, that I first ran into Ramblin' Jack Elliot. I was standing next to a side stage, watching Stan play his concert, and waiting to join him for the last few tunes. He was singing Tom Rush's version of "Galveston Flood" with his guitar on his lap and using a kitchen knife as a slide, when Jack walked up to me, shook my hand and introduced himself, and as he did with everyone, begin a stream of consciousness monologue, seemingly without taking a breath. "Well, uh, hey now, how yuh doin'? I been up for the better part of a week now with no sleep, and damned if I can figure out where the Hell I am supposed to be right now. I was doing a show in Hong Kong, and I remember a plane and then some palm trees...I thought it was Singapore, but I guess maybe that was Hawaii...seemed like it anyway, those girls were all wearing coconuts, and now I'm supposed to be in Toronto, but where the Hell is it? It's a city isn't it? I saw the airport. Oh wait...there it is over there. Huh. Look at that. I never knew it was out on an island like that. Say what? You mean we're on the island and the city is on the shore?...Well now, that makes more sense. I like what that fella is doing, playing the guitar with the kitchen knife like that. Sounds real good. I saw Brownie McGee do that a few times. We played a show together in Glasgow back in...oh...Hell, maybe '68 or so...people love their Indian food over there...That's your brother huh? And you play the fiddle? Woody played the fiddle a bit too, not a lot of people know that, but he did. Anyway, nice meeting yuh. I gotta go and find my guitar. It's gotta be around here somewhere..."

And off he went.

The next time I ran into him was in 1989, backstage at the Winnipeg Folk Festival. I was waiting in line for lunch and heard that familiar high pitched voice. I turned around and there he was, wearing that big dove grey cowboy hat and the neckerchief, and talking as always, 18 to the dozen to some startled random stranger.

He might have sensed he was being watched, as he turned and looked at me. He gave a start and yelled, "Garnet! Garnet Rogers! My God, where the Hell did you come from?"

He ran over and tried to lift me off the ground in an crushing bear hug.

"It's so good to see you man. How the Hell have you been?"

"Jack, it's great to see you too. I just can't believe you'd remember me. We met for maybe 5 minutes back in the early 70's."

"Hell yes, Toronto wasn't it? And that big fella with the kitchen knife and the guitar. Well you know me and my brain. But yes, I remember you good. How you been?"

So it was old home week, and I was pretty chuffed to be greeted so warmly and in public by a legend. A crazy legend, but a legend nonetheless.

"Listen Jack, I'm so happy to run into you. I'm just going to get some lunch and then you and I are doing a workshop in a couple of hours. I'll see you then okay?"

"That's great buddy." He slapped me on the shoulder. "See you then."

We shook hands and off he went.

Maybe 40 minutes later I was in the performers' parking lot, getting a guitar out of the Volvo, and I noticed Jack pulling a guitar case out of the back of his truck camper, 3 cars over.

He also took out a large and highly illegal .50 calibre Sharps buffalo gun, which he had picked up in a flea market somewhere, and had felt no pressing need to declare to Canada Customs when he crossed the border.

As well, a young couple, a man and a woman emerged, looking sweaty and disheveled and confused. He had evidently picked them up hitch-hiking a few days previous, somewhere in North Dakota or Montana, and after stowing them in the back of the truck had forgotten about them, and had brought them across the border without any sort of paper work or ID. They had no idea where they now were, or how to get back home, and the young woman was pretty upset with her boyfriend in general, and Jack in particular.

It was at that moment that Jack looked over at me and once again, gave a start.

"Garnet! Garnet Rogers! Where the Hell did you spring from?"

And he once again ran over and tried to crush me to his bosom.

"My God, it's so good to see you again after all this time. How the Hell are you?"

255

I said," Uh, yeah Jack, it's wonderful to see you too, but I was just
talking to you, maybe half an hour ago in the performers' area."
He let go of me and looked a bit embarrassed, but recovered nicely.
    "Yeah, that's right. So..."
He cleared his throat.
    "How you been since then?"

It was wonderful to watch the old blues players.
Not just their playing, but how they conducted themselves in the world.
They all had immense presence, and dignity, and mostly kept to
themselves between workshops, sitting in the deep shade beneath
the willow trees, like a pride of lions with their black suits, and stiffly
pressed white shirts, skinny black neck ties, and carefully brushed
fedoras.
They all wore wildly coloured argyle socks, and beautifully polished
shoes.
In short they all looked like a million bucks, whereas we looked like
about 37 cents in loose change and pocket lint.

They would sit in a group, sipping from time to time from pocket flasks,
watching the young women go by.
One would lean over to another and say something, and they would
collapse, coughing with laughter, and wiping their eyes.
Once in a while one of the pretty hospitality volunteers would go
over to the little group with her clipboard, and announce that the next
workshop was in 15 minutes, and would they like a ride over?
    "I need money before I play."
    "Oh, everyone gets paid on Sunday after the last performance."
    "I'm not playing until I see the colour of your money."
One of the other gentlemen leaned over, whispered something, and they
both broke up laughing.
    "But sir, the payroll trailer doesn't open until Sunday. You'll get
paid then."

Stan and I drifted over the better to watch and eavesdrop.
This was what they call "A Teaching Moment."
    "No pay, no play."
    "But sir, the performers all get paid after the show."
    "Nope. I do not play unless I have the CASH, Missie, in my pocket."

These were guys who had seen a lot more grief and nasty venal shit
than we (with luck) ever would. Years of traveling as unwelcome
intruders in their own country, and not being able to sleep in decent

hotels, or any hotels period. Not being served in restaurants, living on baloney sandwiches in the backs of cars.

Knowing they had no recourse, if anything, a dishonest club owner, an overzealous cop, or just some good patriotic Southern Christian in a white robe happened to take a dislike to them.

They had learned their lessons, and it didn't matter how much peace and love and patchouli oil was floating around. They had been burned too many times.

The volunteer would keep trying to move them, and meeting a blank wall of resistance, would eventually give up, and run to find the Festival director.

Negotiations would begin again.

Finally, the director would bow to the inevitable, pull out a roll of bills, and begin to calculate. "Five workshops, and an hour long concert divided into your fee equals..."

And the portion of money owed for that next workshop would be counted out into the gentleman's hand where it would be carefully recounted, folded into a diamond studded money clip, and safely tucked into a pants pocket.

He would then pick up his guitar case, and say, "All right Missie, let's go do it." He would readjust his hat, climb into a waiting golf cart, flash a triumphant gold toothed smile at his buddies, and be taken away to scare the pure living shit out of the white kids.

Stan turned to me and said, "It's as good as a play."

CHAPTER 31

Owen Sound

In the mid 70's, for a while, at least, it seemed as if all one needed to start a folk festival was a guy with an ever so canny sense of how to pry public money out of the hands of the government, and who had a collection of stained and faded oversized T shirts, rampant facial hair, and a weakness for all you can eat dim sum buffets. That, and a collection of eager and greedy friends who were all standing around waiting for their turn at the Public Teat.

It helped if you could find a site which was beautiful but difficult to get to, subject to flooding, and directly in the path of of whatever hellish weather system a vengeful and capricious God might send along.

In other words, Tim Harrison was starting a folk festival in Owen Sound.

I don't recall what year it started, but we were there at the beginning. It was a pretty ad-hoc affair. I think a couple of the stages at least were farm wagons, and the main stage was a Main Stage in name only.

It rained. Of course it rained. It was the tail end of summer, and it was a folk festival. There was a story making the rounds that after a few successive years of week-long monsoon-like downpours surrounding the Winnipeg Folk Festival, the Manitoba Farmers' Association sent the festival a letter of appreciation for breaking the drought and saving the wheat crop.

What I remember most from that first weekend was the giant vat of chili cooking over an open fire in the performers' area behind the Main Stage. It was a huge iron cauldron, lent out no doubt, by a local farmer, as he wasn't currently using it to scald pig carcasses.

A volunteer was using a canoe paddle to stir it, but the pot was so deep that much of the solid matter went straight to the bottom and burned. The top mostly consisted of cold rainwater. Not even hippies would eat it.

Still, the festival managed to struggle through that first year, and came back next year a bit bigger and better organized.

We were no longer being billeted with volunteers, but were put up in a huge resort cabin complex outside of town on Highway 6. It was somewhat down at heel, but back in the day it had had been built on a grand scale, with a main office, a restaurant, a work out room which we affected not to notice, and an indoor Olympic sized swimming pool, along with the biggest fireplace that I had ever seen next to it. You could roast a steer in it, and still have room for Joan of Arc.

It was the perfect place for after concert debauchery.

The only person to make proper use of the pool was Michael Lewis, a singer/piano player who had moved up from the States to Ontario. He was completely blind, but astonishing in his ability to get around on his own and tour for a living. He came into the pool room and carefully worked out the dimensions of the pool, and then, laying aside his white cane, dove in and swam the length of the pool completely under water, without coming up for breath. He spent the next hour or so doing lengths, like a hairy porpoise, while the rest of us merely paddled about.

Chopper McKinnon was on his back, with a massive cannon cracker spliff in his mouth, and a tall can of Harp Lager balanced carefully on his rather large belly. He was moving his hands just enough to keep under way, and there was a large plume of smoke coming off him.

Stan looked at him and said, "He looks like one of those little Channel steamers from the Second World War."

He was right. I could easily imagine a flight of tiny Stukas swarming in and dropping bombs on him.

There was a ballroom off the side of the pool where we set up for late night sessions.

There was a low stage, and someone had brought in part of a sound system from the festival.

There was a drum kit, and various performers got up to try their luck at it, the way one might try the mechanical bull in a roadhouse. As it turned out none of us were drummers, and we proved it that night. To quote Stephen Fry, we had "all the hand/eye coordination of Lord Nelson."

Stan borrowed my Telecaster and amp and began trying to play "The Midnight Hour," but he'd taken a little too much beer on board, and got hopelessly lost in the middle section where the horns are supposed to come in.

Michael Smith, who wrote "The Dutchman," that sweetest and gentlest of songs, turned out to be a rock and roll monster. He knew all those old songs. He took the Tele out of Stan's hands after a while, and tried to show him how it went, but at this stage in the proceedings, he wasn't able to play them either. Nor could anyone else. There was a complimentary bar just off the room and it was doing big business. It was taking a toll on everyone's motor skills, and the jam session became a loud and ugly trainwreck. The next morning Dave Essig walked by me, and in passing said, "We must do whatever we can for the sake of the planet and our children, and our children's children, to ensure that never again will folk singers have access to dangerous electric guitars."

It was that year that they managed to get Bruce Cockburn for the festival.
He was still affordable as he had not yet hit pop radio success, and was still playing only solo acoustic guitar.
As always, Stan and I and the others had furtively looked over the evening concert schedule to see where we were in the bill, and consequently where we were in the pecking order. You wanted to be on after sundown, and get the benefit of the stage lights. The later you were on, presumably, the bigger a deal you were.
Cockburn was nowhere to be seen on the evening concert lineup.
"What's going on?"
Stan was searching the list as well.
   "I don't know. He's here in his camper. He didn't cancel."
Huh.
We looked over the festival schedule and discovered that Cockburn had opted out of doing a show at night on the big stage. He was playing an hour long concert on a workshop stage at 1PM on Saturday.
The more we thought about it, the smarter it looked. Evening concerts on the main stage were all well and good, but on a late summer night, with the cold damp air coming off the lake behind you and freezing your ass off, and the stage lights in the front and overhead cooking the other side, tuning was a nightmare. And you only had 30 minutes to get across the dozen or so songs you had planned.
Bruce was going to have a whole blessed hour in the warmth to play a relaxed and intimate set.
That afternoon the other stages closed, and Cockburn set up and played in the bright sun with a light breeze coming off the lake.
I don't recall what songs he was featuring back then, but the concert made a huge impression on me in another way, and I came away from it moved to the point of tears.
There was something else at work here, besides the deeply spiritual songs and the terrifying guitar prowess.
It was the sense of humility and the act of turning away from the glamour (whatever glamour there might be at a folk festival,) and simply serving the music and the audience. He was presenting the

songs with no fuss, and no fanfare, while the rest of us were all clamouring for attention. It was beautiful and humbling, and a huge life lesson, and the memory of that feeling has stayed with me ever since.

I had the temerity to approach him later that night, after Stan and I had finished our frozen and out of tune set.

He was walking slowly up the low hill to where his truck camper was parked away from the cabins. He was at the festival with his then wife, Kitty, and their lovely young daughter.

He stopped outside the camper to finish his beer, and I walked up.

"Excuse me, Mr. Cockburn."

He turned around.

"Bruce."

"Excuse me?"

"Bruce is fine."

Wow. Bruce. We're on a first name basis here.

"Uh, thanks. I just wanted to say, I saw your concert today and it was great, and I'm a big fan of yours, but I felt like today there was something else going on, and it changed the whole way I think about music, and performing, and the reasons for performing. You were just up there playing the songs. No glitz, no show biz. No flash."

He smiled and said, "I thought I was being pretty flashy."

"Sorry."

Jesus, I was making a hash of this.

"It's okay. I know what you mean."

"Anyway, I want to do this too." I waved my hand vaguely at the scene below us. "To play...To tour and play music for the rest of my life, and what you did today answered a lot of questions I've had for a long time, about the real reasons for doing it, and about, well, you know, humility, and how empty show business is, and other stuff, and I just wanted to say thank you."

I was getting a lump in my throat. This was a big deal for me, and I was trying without any success to articulate something I had not yet sorted in my own mind.

He was absolutely still, and watching me very carefully. He was probably rethinking his decision to park where people could find him, and wondering if I was going to sever a body part and offer it to him as a token of my love.

A woman's voice came out from the camper.

"Bruce? Is that you? It's getting late."

"Just a minute."

He held his beer up to the light to see if there was any left, and then tilted his head back and drained the last few drops. He lowered the

bottle, looked at me again said, "Thank you. That means a lot."
Stuck his hand out, and we shook, and then he turned and climbed the
few steps to the camper and got in. He stuck his head out the door and
said, "Thanks again. Goodnight."
He probably spent the next half hour piling his camp stove and other
assorted gear against the door while I walked back to the party room.
Didn't matter. I had got the chance to thank him, however inarticulately,
and I took it.
The next night, I was sitting on the sofa by myself in front of the giant
fireplace, quietly playing guitar, and out of the corner of my eye I
sensed someone sit down next to me and begin playing along. I looked
over and it was Bruce. It was a lovely and kind thing for him to do, to
acknowledge a young kid that way, by treating me as a peer.
I haven't always liked his music in the years since, and I was one time
responsible for having Utah Phillips nearly sabboutage Bruce's tour bus
by jamming potatoes up its tailpipes, as the stinking noisy thing idled
back stage at the Kate Wolf Festival, but that concert and that moment
afterwards have stayed with me some 40 years later.

There was another night there, years later where we watched Odetta do
her main stage concert after the traditional Saturday night tornado.
Owen Sound is right on the edge of the path where storms come up
from the Midwestern States. They cross the border just north of Windsor
and continue along, bringing hail and wind and lightning and dropping
Chevy trucks, grain silos and dead cattle out of the sky as they go.
Communities from Grand Bend to Barrie are in a constant state of
being rebuilt. From early July to the beginning of September, insurance
adjustors in the area watch the sky and listen to the weather reports,
and mentally calculate whether the starting cord on the lawnmower
will be long enough, if they pull it out of the engine, to wind around
their own necks and tie to the water pipes in the basement ceiling,
before they kick out the chair.
Odetta came out with her sparkling sequined robes and the beaded
head dress, and her old Epiphone Texan, with the stick of incense
threaded through the strings on the headstock, and began to sing. The
night had gone calm and peaceful in the wake of the storm, and the
stars were out. The moon was rising full behind us, and she took a
breath and began to sing of all things, "Kumbaya."
I was standing hugging Gail under my right arm, with Stan on my left,
and I heard Stan's sudden intake of breath.
    "I don't believe it."
I couldn't either. The song was a cliché. A joke. What could she be
thinking?

But that voice. My God, that voice.
    "Someone's singing Lord."
To the audience, "Sing it with me."
    "Kumbaya."
    "Someone's singing Lord."
And out of the darkness a couple of thousand voices floated up.
    "Kumbaya."
    "Someone's singing Lord."
A wave broke softly on the beach behind the stage in perfect rhythm.
    "Kumbaya."
Another wave broke with a faint whisper.
    "Oh Lord, Kumbaya."
And so it continued. A line sung, the sound of a wave breaking, the voices of the unseen crowd chiming in. And then another line, and another, until she finished and we simply stood there. Unable to move. Unable to speak.

CHAPTER 32

Ye Old Chestnut Inn

It was Dennis Ryan who got us what became our regular bread and
butter gig in those days.
Ye Olde Chestnut Inn in Fredericton NB.
Fredericton was a pleasant little town, deeply shaded by tall elms,
beside a broad river.
There was a small college there.
It was a quiet and genteel place.
The kind of town where one might like to put down roots, get a job, and
raise some kids, live out your life among kind and decent neighbours
and age gracefully into an honoured retirement.
That was the town.
The gig was a shit hole.
More precisely, it was one of those rowdy Olde Oirish Pubs that were
beginning to raise their ugly heads everywhere back then.
They were all built along the same general plan; some architect's idea
of what a "Local" looked like back in the Old Sod. Dimly lit, with fake
wood paneling and flocked wall paper and the cluster of pewter mugs
hanging over the bar, and dart boards on either side of the stage. Dart
boards. Yeah. That's a great idea. Get a bunch of students pissed to
the tits, so they can barely find their own mouths to pour the beer in,
and then hand them sharp objects to throw at the targets next to the
musicians.

The tables all had a pattern of deep semi-circular dents on the tops
from the beer mugs smashing into them during the inevitable nightly
rendition of "The Wild Rover."
"And it's no nay never, BANG BANG BANG BANG! No nay never no
more..."
The place smelled of stale beer and piss with a faint overlay of vomit,
and menthol scented urinal cakes, and was completely and utterly
devoted to pulling every last dollar out of the students' pockets, and

converting it into necrotic brain tissue.

If you were well known, and had the right repertoire you could do the gig and survive, and it paid what was good money back in those days. 750 bucks for a week and free beer.

And there was a reasonably clean band house to stay in.

Ryan's Fancy could do it in their sleep. They were seasoned, and tough and really good and they played what the people wanted to hear.

We did not.

Denis very kindly put in a good word for us, and we got the gig solely on that recommendation.

We didn't belong there.

We didn't play any of the standard repertoire.

We insisted on playing all our own stuff, and the audience either loathed us or just ignored us completely and devoted themselves to the nightly task of getting crushed.

We decided we needed to be louder.

Stan and I each rented 50 watt Yamaha amps, and stuck little nasty-sounding Barcus Berry pick-ups onto our instruments.

That, along with a couple of MXR Phase shifter pedals would be enough to get their attention, we thought. We were wrong.

We were at best a vague irritant, a barely heard obbligato to the sounds of screaming and yelling and vomiting and the breaking of furniture.

Three hour long sets a night, and the only interaction between us and the audience was when some English major would stand up on a chair and scream, "PLAY THE WILD ROVER YOU FUCKING LOSERS!!! and then fall backwards into the crowd.

Ironically, it is the same sort of enthusiast who now will scream, "SING BARRETT'S PRIVATEERS, YOU FUCKING LOSERS!! in other Olde Irish pubs all over the country now.

I wonder what Stan would have thought of that.

We were there with Dave Woodhead, and he wasn't having any fun either.

He not only had to contend with the violent drunken rabble he was playing for, he had to contend with the violent drunken rabble he was playing with.

Stan and I were not handling this very well.

The smartest thing for a young band to do when they arrive at one of those hellhole gigs is to make friends with the bouncers. Buy them drinks, or drugs or call girls, or whatever they need, because at some point something is going to go very wrong, and you are going to want these guys at your back.

We had a couple of bouncers at the Chestnut. One, a black guy, who called himself Pepper, and a white guy from Newfoundland, named Salt.

"Salt and Pepper. Get it?" Yeah yeah. We got it.

They were decent guys though, serious weight-lifters, and above all, merciless and tough after a decade or so slapping the shit out of Poetry majors from 8 till closing.

We were doing three sets a night, six nights a week, and there was never a moment when we felt like we were reaching anyone in the audience. They hated us, or at best were completely indifferent.

Every once in a while one of the drunks would rise up from the mob and start in on us, yelling abuse and being egged on by his buddies. We tried various tactics.

"Hey there, would you like us to dedicate a song to your girlfriend?"

"I don't have a girlfriend."

"Your boyfriend?"

"Fuck you asshole."

"Your favourite hand?"

If you played it right, the guy would get obnoxious enough to attract the attention of Salt or Pepper, who would swiftly move in. The young idiot's face would turn white, and he would become very attentive and eager to please as the lads stood him up and escorted him from the room using some variation of the Newfoundland Death Grip.

There was one night when Stan bought a guy a yard of ale if he would promise to be quiet.

That only led to everyone acting like assholes so they could get a yard of ale too.

Eventually, it got simpler just take them outside for a bit and reason with them away from the light behind the club, and then walk them back in, sit them down and get a bar towel filled with ice.

"Here, hold that against your nose. That'll stop the bleeding, and it won't swell as much. Okay? Now we have to go up and play again. Would you like us to dedicate a song...?"

It got tiresome, and we quickly grew to hate everything about the place.

We began departing from the usual set list and throwing in a few songs here and there which we had never actually rehearsed, just for fun and diversion. I think in football it is known as "Calling an audible," changing the play on the fly. One night, Stan turned to us and called out

"High Ground in E Minor."
Woodhead and I both knew the song in theory, and we did a quick run through of the chords behind Stan's back while he did the intro.

"This is a song written by our good friend David Essig, and is based on a book called "Various Persons named Kevin O'Brien," by a guy named Alden Nowlan."
There was a yelp from the right hand corner of the room, but I figured it was just the usual bar noise from some guy waking up from a nice restful nap to find his neighbour had just pissed down his back as a joke.
Stan counted us in and we played the song. It was a bit of a train wreck, but no one noticed, and it went well enough that I knew it was going to be in the repertoire for a while. While we were playing a smallish man began struggling towards the stage, frantically pushing aside chairs and stepping on peoples' feet. He had a beard and wore a corduroy jacket with leather patches on the elbows and a checked shirt with a knitted tie. I decided he wasn't likely to be violent. Dressed as he was, he was most likely the local NDP member. He stood in front of us and seemed oddly excited.
We finished the song. No one had noticed or reacted except for the bearded man.
"That's ME! THAT'S MY STORY!" he said.
It was Alden Nowlan.
We'd had no idea he was within a hundred miles of the place. It was just happy coincidence.
We finished the set early, and Stan and Alden went back to the table to drink a few beers and talk.
He'd had no idea that there was a song floating around out there based on his novel. He was thrilled. He started coming in regularly. We played the song every night for him, and he and Stan had a lot of long talks in the corner during the breaks.
We knew his writing, and it was good to meet an author whose work you admired and have him turn out to be a pleasant, if somewhat depressed character.
He had grown up in New Brunswick, and had had a terrible hardscrabble upbringing.
He'd quit school after grade 4, to go to work and help support the family, and was largely self-educated.
He was currently a professor of English at the University of New Brunswick, and would come in most nights after a hard day of trying to teach the rest of our audience to read without moving their lips.
He'd put back a dozen or so beers and listen for a while, and then leave before the last set, looking tired, sad and defeated.

It had to be tough work.

The low point of the gig came the last night of the two week run.
We were working our way through the second set, and during "Make
and Break Harbour" eight people at the large table at stage right started
slowly and loudly gang-clapping out of time.
I could see Stan's face getting redder.
Dave was keeping his head down and simply doing his job.
I looked at the table of idiots. They were all staring at us, smiling, and
clapping, trying to drown us out, or throw us off.
Bastards.
I took it for as long as I could, but then something snapped. It had been
a long two weeks and we'd put up with a lot of needless abuse.
I put my electric fiddle down against the amp, where it began howling
with feedback, and
I ran across the stage and dove full length onto the table.
I slid the whole way down, scattering the glasses, and got my hands
around the leader's neck and began choking him to death. He fell over
backwards, and I followed, landing on top of him and pinning him to
the floor.
I could feel hands grabbing at me from behind, but I shook them off and
began beating his face bloody.
Suddenly I was picked up and lifted into the air.
Pepper had picked me in a snatch and jerk move, and was now carrying
me over his head across the floor.
He dropped me on the other side of the bar, leaned over and said, "You
stay right here. I've got a job to do. I don't want to see you move."
I stayed put and watched the two pros clear the room.
It all got sorted out after a while.
It turned out they weren't trying annoy us.
They were trying to ...wait for it....CLAP ALONG WITH US. Jesus. I
couldn't believe it.
    "WHAT?" YOU WERE DOING WHAT?"
    "We liked you guys." said one of the women, sobbing. "We were
just clapping along with the music."
    "No, you weren't. You were out of time. You were clapping in 4/4
time. The song is in 3/4 time. It had nothing to do with the rhythm of
the song."
    "We didn't know, we're not musicians."
Oh man. This was awful.
I had just tried to murder someone for being rhythmically challenged.
I spent the rest of the night apologizing to everyone in the room.

The real disaster happened the next morning, when I walked into the kitchen of the band house looking for coffee. David was furiously packing his gear and muttering to himself.

"In all my life, I have never seen anything so unprofessional. So stupid. So dangerous...so..."

"What are you doing?"

"I'm going back to Toronto. I'm catching a train in about an hour. I refuse to put up with that kind of behaviour. I'm quitting."

He was stuffing jockey shorts into the amplifier head.

I sat down.

There was nothing I could say.

Even sorry was just useless.

"Sorry."

"Sorry? SORRY?" He slammed his suitcase shut, whirled around and glared at me.

His face worked for a few moments, and he made as if to say something, and then simply turned and went out the front door, furiously waving off my offer to help.

Right on cue, a cab pulled up, and he threw everything into it and drove off without so much as a backward glance.

I went upstairs and woke Stan with the bad news.

He wasn't the least bit surprised.

We knew we wouldn't be able to hang on to David right from the start. He was talented, and gentle and sweet, and we were loud and drunk and angry and in a continual state of fear about when the next disaster was going to happen.

We knew it was driving him crazy.

It was driving us crazy.

Even on our best days it wasn't a good fit for us or him.

Still, it hurt to lose him this way and to have lost what little respect he might have had for us, or at least for me.

We managed to patch things up a bit some time later.

He is a professional sideman after all, and we did offer work, but he would not tour with us again and neither of us could blame him.

He had been in on some of the worst gigs Stan and I ever did, at least to that point.

It was no life.

In later years he and I sorted things out, and he has remained a treasured friend, and one of the best musicians I have ever been in the same room with.

CHAPTER 33

Turnaround

Fogarty's Cove had been out for about a year maybe, and was getting uniformly good reviews both sides of the border.
It was selling well too, particularly for a first effort on an independent label with zero budget for advertising.
The CBC had picked it and was playing it nationally in Canada, and there was some airplay in the States as well.
We were touring farther afield, and Stan was even getting some TV work.
John Allan Cameron, God bless him and rest him, was a huge supporter and did a lot to get the word around. He shared a manager with Anne Murray, a guy named Leonard Rambeau, and took Stan into the office one day to pitch Stan as a song writer for Anne's next record.
As Stan described the meeting to me, he stood in front of Rambeau's desk and sang a handful of songs while a bored Rambeau flipped through his Rolodex and took phone calls.
After 3 or 4 tunes he waved his hand and said, "That's enough. There's nothing we can use here." And Stan was dismissed.
He was crushed, having gone in with visions of royalty cheques dancing in his head.
It had been completely typical of John Allan to have gone out of his way to support a friend and try to advance his career with no thought of anything beyond doing a good turn.
He was a lovely sweet guy, who worked harder than anyone we knew.
He was the first the only person we had met with an actual rehearsal room.
It was in the basement of his home in Markham outside of Toronto.
The room had one wall covered by a huge mirror, in front of which John Allan played and worked on his step dancing moves.
He actually practiced facial expressions and playing to the video camera he'd had installed.
He had a nationally televised variety show on CTV, and probably

against the wishes of his production team, brought Stan in to play.
The show was a typical network variety show, all very upbeat and fast
paced to the point of being frantic, and carefully scripted by writers
who had apparently had never heard actual human beings speak. Stan
looked really awkward in a hideous pinkish beige polyester suit he
had bought at George Richards Big and Tall Shop that morning. George
Richards would have been the only place where a guy of his size and
height could have found a suit several sizes too large. It was bunched
up under his guitar strap, and it looked as if he was moonlighting from
his regular gig as a bell ringer.
The poor guy came out, nervous as hell, but game to make a go of
it, with sweat running down his face and leaving ruts in the heavy
pancake makeup they had plastered on him.
He shared some awkward and inanely scripted dialogue with John
Allan, and then launched into a tune.
I was not part of the show. I watched from home.
There had apparently not been enough in the budget to have me along.
Paul Mills was there though, inevitably, and a fiddler from the house
band, The Cape Breton Symphony, stood in for me. It was probably just
as well. The tunes they wanted Stan to play for the show were the hyper
fast, "Raise your glasses mateys," genre that I loathed listening to, hated
playing, and which I spent a lot of time trying to steer Stan away from
writing.
Stan gave it his best, but I don't recall it doing us any real good.
Still, it was something on the resume.

We wanted to do another record.
Stan had a backlog of older songs which had not made it on to the first
record as they didn't fit the Maritime theme.
Stan talked with Mitch, who once again agreed to foot the bills, and we
began to assemble the players.
Paul Mills would once again produce.
We still had David Woodhead to play bass, although by this time he had
left the band as a regular member.
At David's urging we hired his old high school friend Bob Cohen for
electric guitar.
Ken Whitely came in again, on piano and Hammond organ.
Gordon Lightfoot's drummer, Barry Keane was rung in. We were
chuffed about that. Having a member of Lightfoot's band was like
getting the seal of approval.
Ken Bloom was hired on to do everything.
We had met Ken Bloom at the Winnipeg Folk Festival the year before.
He was an ex studio hot shot from Los Angeles, as the story had it,

who'd had enough of the scene there and was now getting back to his
roots in the folk world.

He was a serious over achiever. He not only played a dozen or so
instruments, but he had made many of them himself. He had a set of
Northumbrian small pipes which are by themselves difficult enough
to play, but he had actually made them himself, turning the damned
things out on a lathe.

He hunted with a black powder rifle which he had also made on a lathe.
He traveled with his own espresso machine which he (of course) had
made...wait for it...on a lathe.

I don't know if I ever saw him drink alcohol.

Presumably he had yet to master the art of growing his own barley and
building a still.

He was a gannet too.

He could eat more at one sitting than any three people.

Odd guy.

He was so proficient on so many instruments that one had to keep an
eye on him, as he could take over a project out of sheer enthusiasm and
force of will, and just because it was there.

The album went off the rails pretty quickly.

Stan had wanted to call it "Big Blue Lake," after a song he had written
as a lament and rebuke for the demise of Cedar Lake.

As was often the case when Stan had an important idea he wanted to
convey, he had gone deep into Joni Mitchell mode.

The song was a disaster, with pretentious and confused lyrics, and
pseudo jazzy chords so derivative of the Mitchell style that for once
Paul and I were in complete agreement.

I hated it, and had refused to play it on stage, and Paul, bless him,
didn't want to proceed with recording it.

Stan was sitting out in the recording room with his guitar.

Once more he'd had to stop a take as the guitar had gone out of tune,
and the band was swimming around helplessly trying to find the center
of the song.

Paul pressed the talk back button.

"Uh, Stan?"

"Yeah. What's the problem?"

"Have you really thought whether this song is going to fit on the
record?"

"What do you mean?"

"You know, stylistically."

"I want to try a lot of different things this time out."

"Yeah, but this one is kinda..." Paul paused.

Fuck diplomacy. I leaned over and spoke into the talk back.

"It's a bad song."

"What do you mean, it's a bad song?"

Paul and I went out into the recording room.

"What is it supposed to mean anyway?

"It's about Cedar Lake. You know that. You were there."

"Yeah, I was. But this doesn't sound like you."

Paul said, "It sounds like bad Joni Mitchell."

"Well, yeah. There are elements of her style, but..."

"And what the hell does the chorus mean?"

I recited the lyrics.

"It was dream when it was started.

Now it's become a way of life

They we be open hearted,

Maintain an open mind

And live on trade with neighbours

And be a simple kind of gypsy farmer."

"Yeah? So?"

"Just what the Hell is a Gypsy Farmer? It makes no sense. Are they supposed to be planting crops and moving on?"

He sat there, pissed off and embarrassed.

He lit a smoke, sucked in a lungful, blew it out and looked at me. "You got something better?"

"You know I don't. But you do."

"Like what?"

Paul spoke. "I don't know, but you can do better than that."

So the song was out.

Stan was angry, and we now were embarked on making a record with no title song.

Moreover, we had wasted the better part of a day running it down before we killed the damned thing.

We had worked up an arrangement of Archie Fisher's song, "Dear Dark Eyes," only Stan kept referring to it as "Dark Eyed Molly," and so it appeared on the cover.

Ken Bloom, having no Irish harp to play, and being without the means to build one on the spot played a Ukrainian instrument called a bandura on the track.

The song was to be the opening cut at Mum's behest, her theory being that the rest of the album was so potentially jarring to listeners familiar with the first record that at least this would draw them in.

We had picked up a traditional song from Newfoundland called "Oh No Not I," via Ian Robb.

We were playing a lot with different styles, and this song was a nod to
Steeleye Span, to whom Stan had taken to listening.
Ian was less than impressed with our arrangement.
We came off the stage one night at a festival having just performed it,
Stan and I both plugged in, and playing through hideous sounding
phase-shifters, and he pulled back from us, making a cross with his
fingers, and said, "Oh No…Not you."

Stylistically we were all over the map.
"Front Runner," a survivor from the old CBC folk opera about the
Olympics was included.
It wound up with a weird country arrangement, featuring Ken on a
German guitar zither for God's sake. A guitar zither. Why not?
He had one.
He could play it, so of course it had to go on the track.

We disappeared completely down the rabbit hole with "So Blue,"
another song unabashedly stolen from the Joni Mitchell style book.
It had been written on the CN train, The Ocean Limited, as Stan was
coming back from Halifax a couple of years before, when he and Jimmy
Ogilvie and I were in Halifax working on one of Bill Howell's projects.
It made reference to his then impending break up with Diane, and the
woman in London who was waiting in the wings for him.
The recording of that song got completely out of control.
Ken Bloom and I ended up building a woodwind section with
overdubbed soprano Saxes and flutes. Bob Cohen was copying Larry
Carlton's volume swell guitar, and during the hugely complicated mix
down we all ended up with fingers on various sliders on the mixing
console.
As the song ran along it looked like a race for the finish line.
Fingers kept creeping forward, and eventually Stan's voice was
drowned out almost completely.
The finished recording made it sound as if he was singing on a traffic
island at rush hour.

"Second Effort," another holdover from the Olympic folk opera came
out relatively unscathed.

"Try Like the Devil" was from our days in Brampton, and the terrible
two week gig in the basement club on Queen Street which the secret
agent had found.
It was recorded live off the floor, with Stan out there with the full band.
The first take came to pieces when he over extended himself, blew out

his vocal cords and spent the next 10 minutes bent over coughing.
He had a smoke and a glass of rum, and nailed it on the second take,
meanwhile cracking us up by doing an impression of Joe Cocker's
spastic stage moves as he sang.
He and I went in, just the two of us, about a week later to add some
background vocals to the song. During the drive I sang to him my idea
for the vocals on the chorus, and we did it together.
Stan's voice is the impossibly high one you hear on the record. I turned
to him after the take and said, "How the Hell did you do that?"
He merely shrugged. He'd just hit a note that only dogs could hear. "I
dunno. I just did it."
I also got to snarl my way through the harmony at the end of "Oh No
Not I."
One of the better moments on what was generally acknowledged to be a
pretty uneven record was "Song of the Candle."
Stan had written it back during his days with the Curry brothers in
London.
It was definitely a period piece, but it still holds up.
He told me that the line about the "waitresses in passing," was a
reference to Laura (then known as Susie) Smith, who had worked as
a waitress at Smales Pace back in the day, and who was the object of
considerable interest and speculation among the horny layabouts and
wastrels that infested the place, Stan included.
Laura herself covered the song years later, not knowing then that she
was part of the story.
I asked Ken Whitely to play the quiet church organ bit during our
recording and he did a great job.

There is a lovely moment on the record, as Side Two opens, where you
hear Stan take a breath and then the song begins. The song is "The
Jeannie C," and it appeared one day after a weekend gig near home.
We were playing a sweet little club near Jarvis Street in Toronto, called
the Nervous Breakdown, just the two of us.
I had been listening pretty obsessively to John Martyn for a couple of
years now, and had brought a tape of Sunday's Child into the van to
listen to on the drive into Toronto.
One track particularly, "Spencer the Rover", had taken over my brain.
It was a haunting and beautiful piece about madness and redemption. It
was a traditional tune, mostly sung as a dreary dirge by drunken Morris
dancers after a long day of demonstrating the famous English sense of
rhythm.
I had heard it before and it had never made any kind of impression on
me.

John Martyn had taken the song and made it magic.
The combination of his voice and his mysterious open tuned guitar,
and Danny Thompson's extraordinary bowed bass turned the song into
one of those pieces that stopped time. You wanted to sit and hold your
breath while it played out so as not to break the spell.
Stan didn't seem that impressed by the tune or the whole record.
Martyn's at times heavily distorted guitar, and slurred, almost
unintelligible vocals were at odds with Stan's taste.
He listened and merely said, "Hmmph," when it was over.
Still, a couple of days later Stan brought "the Jeannie C." into rehearsal,
and I found the songs to be strikingly similar. The time signature,
the tempo, and the guitar turnaround between verses, all sounded
somewhat the same.
Way different songs though. Stan was no plagiarist.

There were a couple of extra verses to "the Jeannie C." initially, and
while Stan did sing them live at first, we cut them out in the interest of
fitting the song onto side one of the album when we came to record it
And that version of the song is what we performed from then on.

Stan was confronted about a year after we recorded it, at the Folk
Legacy Festival in Connecticut.
A woman came up to him and took issue with the fact that he had not
performed the song the way Gordon Bok did.
    "So what? It's my song. My way is the right version."
    "Yes, but Gordon Bok performs it correctly with all the verses."
    "But I wrote it, I can do whatever I want with it."
    "But that's not the way Gordon does it."
Jesus. Folkies.
He just managed to restrain himself, and walk away.

We ran into a bit of difficulty later, during our show, when Stan
introduced our version as "The Official version, no matter what Gordon
Bok or his evil minions might say."
    "So," he said, laughing, "suck this back Bok."
There was a gasp, a sudden intake of breath, in the audience.
A number of people accosted me afterwards, outraged. One of them
said, "I can't believe your brother said that."
    "Said what?"
    "That thing he said."
    "What did he say?"
    "That thing."
    "What the hell are you talking about?"

276

There was a furtive glance over the shoulder.

"Your brother said, Suck my cock, Bok."

"No he didn't."

"Yes he did. I heard him."

"No he didn't. I was standing right next to him."

"No, that's what he said."

"You're out of your mind. I was right there. It didn't happen."

"No, I heard him."

There is no reasoning with people.

Some dumb ass mis-hears something, repeats it, the story gets distorted further with repeated telling, and before you know it, you've started a religion, and century's later people are being killed in service of the one true God.

I don't think we ever successfully squelched that story, and the rumour persisted for some time that Stan and Gordon Bok were at daggers drawn.

When Stan and Gordon finally met a couple years later, they arranged a small tableau for the benefit of the people who wouldn't let go of the story.

It was backstage at the Owen Sound Festival, and Stan affected to see Gordon for the first time.

"BOK!"

Gordon turned around.

Stan yelled, "It's time Bok. I'm coming for you. It's time for you to pay."

Gordon wheeled around like a gun fighter, and the two slowly advanced toward each other, waving their arms, shaking their fists, and yelling threats and curses at each other.

Someone yelled, "Call security."

They got to within a few feet of each other, and just as the big guys in the black shirts arrived, Stan and Gordon reached out and embraced, and then began to waltz across the sand.

I doubt that it helped.

There is probably a small cult of idiots out there who now believe Stan never died, but had a sex change, and is now living in Gordon's boat house in Camden Maine.

When we did record the song, I was determined to have a fretless bass on the track.

Dave Woodhead, who played bass on the rest of the album, didn't play fretless at that point, or wasn't available.

Bob Leth, the engineer, knew a guy and made a call.

Dave McManus came in, listened to the track twice, and nailed it on the

second run through, using a battle scarred old Fender Jazz bass.
He did a beautiful job.
Lovely, and thanks very much, and we'll see you next time.

"Good player." Stan said. "It really makes the track."

Bob said, "Yeah, he doesn't play much bass these days, he mostly
plays piano. He's really into Chopin. Did you notice the scars?"

"Yeah, a little bit."

Dave had some shiny scarring around his eyes, back then, nothing
major, but it was there if you looked, and his eyebrows were very faint.
Bob continued, "He was playing in a power trio a few years ago, and
taught himself how to do a fire breathing act. He would hold a shot
glass of lighter fluid in his mouth while he did his bass solo, and
then light it and blow it out in a ten foot long flame. The kids loved
it. Anyway, they were getting better and better, and the shows were
getting bigger, and the fire breathing thing got more elaborate. He got
to the point where he was sucking back an eight ounce glass of lighter
fluid and holding it in his throat while he did the solo, and then he
would flick the lighter and blast off a huge sheet of flame. It was really
impressive."

Stan said, "I'll bet."

"Yeah, finally, they got a spot at Maple Leaf Gardens, opening for the
Who or Zeppelin, or someone, and Dave decided to sacrifice his bass on
stage. He was gonna burn the whole thing.
He got a couple of extra strength Kotex, and soaked them in Varsol,
and taped them to the back of his guitar. Then he tossed back the
lighter fluid and did the bass solo. Took out his lighter. Flicked it, and
WHOOSH! he just exploded into a fireball. The Varsol had soaked
down to his knees, and up into his shirt, and he was now lurching
across the stage completely ablaze.
Everything was on fire. He said all he could think about was that he
had a mouthful of lighter fluid, and he didn't want to swallow it. He
panicked, and blew it out his nose, and through the flames he could see
17,000 kids on their feet going YYYYEEEEAAAHHH!, and pumping
their fists.
The roadies eventually stamped him out, and hosed him down, and got
him to the hospital.
He was standing there in the emergency room, with little wisps of
smoke still coming off him, shivering uncontrollably.
He was only wearing his scorched underpants, and a borrowed trench
coat.
He was going into shock, and he was telling the emergency
room admitting nurse the whole story, in a long sort of stream of
consciousness sentence."

"Well, I play in a band… and I do a thing with spitting out lighter fluid after my solo, and I decided to burn my bass, and I got this Kotex…and I…" and so on.
He went through the whole story, as she typed it out, and when he finally stopped, she slammed the carriage of the typewriter back and looked at him, and said, "You Asshole." He quit the band after that, but he kept the bass, and just pulled all the frets out of it. That's what he used today."

I have no way of knowing if the story is true, but it's what we were told, and it's what I intend to believe.

We were nearly done, and still had no title, or title song.
Mike Curry was fooling around with my guitar one night after dinner and sang "Turnaround" in his light and pleasant tenor.
As Stan told the story, he didn't recognize the song until Mike told Stan that Stan had in fact written it.

"That's your song you idiot," was how it was supposed to have gone.
Not true.
Stan never forgot anything like that, and besides, he and I had taught the song to a friend in Ottawa the month previous.
Good story though.
At any rate, Mike did a lovely job on it, and Stan went upstairs after dinner and laid it down.
That was the record.

It was around this time that Stan and Diane decided to marry.
There wasn't a lot of money to lash out for a big wedding so they held the ceremony at the house of Stan's friend Joe Zizzo in Smithville, Ontario.
It was a small gathering, and the ceremony included Diane's three children from her second marriage.
Very movingly, they pledged to accept Stan as their Dad, and in fact took his last name.
The minister was a wee handful.
Diane, having been through the turnstile a couple of times before had had trouble finding a minister willing to perform the ceremony. The guy they came up with was a white haired Unitarian minister about the size of a jockey.
As best man it fell to me to pay him for his services.
I handed him the envelope, and asked him if there was anything else I could bring.

"Yes, Whiskey, a double. And keep 'em coming."
He kept me busy.
It was lucky he was so small. It would have been hard to carry a normal sized man to his car, get him strapped in, and help him turn on the ignition so he could drive home.

The wedding day was significant for other reasons.
Mitch had just told us that week that with the pressures of starting a new folk festival in Vancouver, he would no longer be able to act as our executive producer.
He was closing down the record company.
We now had an unfinished and unpaid for record, and no idea of where to go.
We were broke.
I was living once more on my old stand-by of Red River cereal and little else.
The other musicians were calling wanting to know when they were going to be paid, and Stan was trying to start a new life with new responsibilities, three of them to be exact.
The day of the wedding he and I were at Mum and Dad's house, and we had a talk.
Mum agreed to shell out for the new record, paying all the costs so far, session fees and Paul's Producer fee, and she as well promised to pay for the mixing and manufacturing.
She and Stan had been in discussion with Mitch, and he agreed to sell to her and Stan the rights to the album "Fogarty's Cove."
So we had a new executive producer, and a new record company.
We were saved.

There was another touching moment an hour or so later, when Dad took Stan aside and handed him a new school kid's slate.
    "What's this?" said Stan.
    "It's a clean slate." said Dad.
    "I know but what is it?"
    "It's a clean slate. I am wiping out your accumulated debt. You're starting a family and you'll need to think about them."
This was big news.
Stan had been putting the bite on the folks for years now, and had never even come close to paying a tithe of it back.
It had to be a serious sum of money.
Stan held the slate in his hands and began to snuffle and wipe his eyes.

In another family this might have been the signal to hug and say "I love

you." But we didn't do that sort of thing in our family.
We used a complex and confusing code to say it, and you had to watch carefully for the signs or you'd miss it.

CHAPTER 34

Kingston: David Alan Eadie Joins The Band

Stan and I were doing a long weekend at the Scarecrow, in Kingston, Ontario.

It was a vegetarian restaurant/coffeehouse, on Princess Street, downtown.

You would come up a long flight of stairs, turn left at the top and enter a large sweet smelling sun-drenched room.

There were wooden chairs and tables with checkered table cloths, and raffia-covered wine bottles with candles, and little vases filled with flowers.

There was a small stage in the corner by the windows, overlooking the street.

It was run by a quiet and funny hippie fur ball named Bram Fisher. He was a great guy, hardworking and smart, and he always got the crowd out for us.

It was those weekends at the Scarecrow that made you feel that this wasn't such a bad way to pretend to make a living.

You'd turn up around 6 PM and have a quick drink around the corner at "the Plazoo," as it was known locally.

Go back and play to a full house, and then have a few beers after.

Wake up next day, wander down town to the club and get breakfast.

The room was wonderful in the mornings, full of light and the smell of baked goods and coffee, with an overlay of fresh coriander and cumin.

John Martyn or Van Morrison would be on the sound system, and there was always someone to talk to.

Thomas Handy might be in the corner, cigarette in one hand, and maybe his twentieth black coffee of the day in the other. He was conducting ground breaking research on the long term effects of nicotine and sleep deprivation on the human brain.

David Eadie would come in.

He was in the 5th year, maybe, of a four year philosophy course. Or it might have been English Lit. It could have been Etruscan Pottery for all I know. He was having a pretty good time with the student Boho lifestyle, drinking coffee and playing guitar and casting an appraising eye over the young and insouciant first year English Majors who collected in flocks on the street corners downtown in their Birkenstocks, T shirts and painter pants. He had the use of a Sunfish sailboat on the weekends and didn't seem to be in any hurry to leave.
He said he was biding his time until a position opened up in the Philosophy Department at General Motors.
Both Thomas and David were really good guitarists.
Thomas was something of a local hero, having once been in a band called "the Kurds of Whey." And David carried in his wallet a review of one of his own gigs at the college coffeehouse, where the reporter at the Whig Standard had referred to him as "one of Queens University's better blues men."

"Look at this." He held it out to me, giggling.

"It sounds like the halls are full of guys with berets and sunglasses, standing around waiting for the next box car leaving town."

So, coffee in the morning, then out for a stroll around the town.
Check out the book stores for a while.
Drift down by the lake and watch the sailboats.
Then up to the bar in the Holiday Inn for the mid-day Martini special, and more staring out at the water.
Then back to the club for more coffee, and a chat with the boys.
Dinner, then play to a full house again.
After that, more beers at the Plaza.
Then off to bed and get up and do it all over again.

One afternoon Bram came to our table where Stan and I were visiting with David and Thomas, drinking coffee and listening to Astral Weeks on the house system.
He sat down.

"Would you guys be interested in playing a set at the Women's Prison? There's no money in it, but it's part of a programme we're trying to run to help the inmates, a kind of community outreach thing." Well sure. It sounded a little weird, and potentially scary, but we didn't have anything else planned that day, aside from Stan giving me my daily drunk driving lesson over on Wolfe Island. We had been given of late to taking a bottle of cheap sherry over to the island on afternoons, so I could get some much needed time behind the wheel, and learn the nuances of the high speed four wheel drift and the bootlegger's turn well away from any traffic and potential spoil sport cops. I could afford to miss a day in aid of a good cause.

I had visions of a cold grey stone building, damp and dark, with beaten down inmates and a lot of hard-faced wardresses standing guard, and that is more or less what we got.

We got checked in, and were given a thorough search, after which we re-adjusted our clothing and went through the big door.

The cliché of hearing that big door closing, and being terrified it will never open again is true.

C.S. Lewis, in his book "The Screwtape Letters," once had a demon refer to Hell as "The Kingdom of Noise."

That is prison. Just a long drawn out echoing cacophony of pain.

It is all hard surfaces. There is nothing to muffle the sound.

A set of keys dropped on the concrete will clatter and echo for days.

A cry or a sob or a shout will go on forever.

We were both shit-scared.

We were following the guard up the stairs, and we could hear the far off sounds of doors slamming, people yelling, and our own echoing footsteps as we lugged our gear to the concert room.

I was trembling and my guts were turning over.

I had been trying to match Thomas Handy cup for cup, drinking black coffee all day at the club and I was wired and queasy.

We stopped at the top of the stairs, and the guard opened the door, and we looked in.

It looked like the scene in Castle Anthrax, in "Monty Python and the Holy Grail."

The room was glowing with warm candlelight, and there was the scent of perfume.

We could hear soft music, and about 40 beautiful ex-drug mules in long gowns were now standing and looking intently at us.

This was unexpected.

We went in, got introduced and sat down.

Stan made the obligatory joke about a "captive audience" and we started to play.

It was all going fairly smoothly, albeit a bit awkward, perhaps. I'd never realized how much of our repertoire back then leaned on the themes of freedom and wanderlust and the joys of home.

And of course, the subtext to all of this was that whatever we were playing we were able to walk out of this room when this was over.

None of the women could say the same, not until they had done their minimum seven years.

Still, we plowed on, and our audience was being politely receptive.

Presently, I became aware of a serious problem in my lower GI tract.
Perhaps it was the two or three gallons of strong black coffee I'd had
before coming here.

Maybe it was an advanced case of nerves.

Or it could have been the excesses of the last few nights of post-show
debauchery, and the nasty green beer they served at the Plazoo, but I
was suddenly seized with terrible Apocalyptic cramps.

I began to pour sweat, and my heart was racing.

Something dreadful was taking place down below. Fire in the engine
room. Oh God, this was bad.

I had to find a bathroom, and soon.

I leaned over carefully, trying not to disturb whatever was trying to
claw its way out of me and touched Stan on the knee.

He was in the middle of an intro.

"Stan. I gotta take a break. I'm not feeling so hot."

He looked over at me where sweat was dripping in rivulets off my
nose and chin, and said, "Jesus...you okay?"

"No. I'm not okay. I need a break. Right now."

So Stan turned back to the audience and said, "We have one more
for you," ONE MORE? ARE YOU CRAZY? "...and then we're gonna
take a short break."

One more. Jesus.

I was dying.

So we did the last song, and I leapt up and ran over to one of the male
guards.

"Quick. I need a bathroom. Right now."

He took me down a long corridor through several doors, all of which
had to be carefully unlocked and then re-locked after he had searched
labouriously for the right key on the chain.

I was walking stiff legged, like a speeded up robot, sweat cascading
down my body and urging him, sotto voce, "Come on. For God's sake,
COME ON."

We came to another locked door, and he once again began sorting
through the key chain, taking one out, looking at it carefully and trying
it and then muttering, "No, that's not the one. Huh...Darn it. Maybe this
one."

"Have you ever thought of maybe colour coding them?" I asked
between gritted teeth.

"No, that would take too long."

We finally got to the washroom, and it was a big room with a toilet in
the middle of the floor, plainly visible from the corridor through a large
window under a bright fluorescent light.

"This is it? Don't you have something private?"

285

He turned and looked at me. "Private? This is a prison. There is no privacy in prison."

Jesus.

This was awful. But something terrible and life-changing was about to erupt in about 10 seconds, whether I wanted it to or not, and I wanted to have my pants down when it happened.

So I put away my girlish modesty, and went in, unbuckled and sat down...

When I was about 8 years old, a large truck carrying a bunch of plate glass windows and several long aluminum ladders spun out of control and overturned on the road in front of our driveway.

It had been going along at a pretty good clip, being chased at the time by a police car with its siren on, and slid for maybe a hundred yards or so, scattering its load over the road and the field next to our house and then cartwheeling several times into the neighbors' yard.

The violence and the volume and the duration of the whole incident was very much like what I was now achieving.

After some minutes I looked up from my labours, and saw a crowd of pale and frightened faces at the window. Guards and several inmates. I waved them away feebly, and wished that there was at least a light switch in the room.

Sometime later I got back to the concert room in a much reduced condition, and found Stan talking to a tall beautiful woman with long dark, almost black hair in a thick braid that reached literally to the floor. This was during the period we were still living in Brampton and Stan was currently single.

The woman's name was Louise, and they were to become an item, a long distance item, but a serious item, almost immediately.

"Feeling better?" he said.

"Yeah. Just great."

I was exhausted.

We went back to our places and resumed playing, but the audience was somewhat smaller now. A few of the members had witnessed my solo turn down the hall, and some of the magic inevitably, had gone from the situation.

It was at the Scarecrow that the genesis of the stage show took place. To this point I had not been doing much other than playing violin and flute, and waiting more or less patiently while Stan went into long-winded flights of rhetoric while introducing the songs.

The intros began to take on a certain familiarity after a while, and it was at the Scarecrow that I first began to open my big mouth, if only out of

ill-concealed boredom rather than any idea of adding to the show.
Stan would be in the middle of some long story, and I'd make a snotty
comment.
It would get a big laugh, and Stan would be brought up short, and give
me a withering glance and then carry on.
Again I'd make some little jab at him, and it would get a laugh and I
could see Stan was starting to get pissed off.
The vein in the side of his forehead was beginning to grow and turn
red. Always a bad sign.
But I was getting big laughs, and I was enjoying showing off, and it was
hard to stop.
We broke after the first set and Stan frog-marched me out onto the
balcony and backed me up against the rail so I was hanging over it two
storeys above the dumpster in the alley.
"Look asshole. What the hell do you think you're doing up there?
You're undermining me and I don't need it. Just keep your goddamned
mouth shut."
I didn't know what to say.
It's difficult to tell someone that they are boring you and everyone
around them rigid, particularly when they are holding you over a ton of
wet kitchen garbage and threatening to break your jaw.
"I was just trying to help, you know, make a few jokes."
"Well you're not helping. You're putting me off my stride up there.
You're making me look bad."
The fire door banged into us and Bram Fisher came out with a big smile.
Stan hurriedly put down his fist.
Bram said, "What a great set, guys. The humour stuff is fantastic. Really
good. You're really doing great tonight." He patted Stan on the shoulder
and went back inside.
Stan let go of my collar, and took a breath. He looked around and
waved his hands.
There was a silence, and then he said, "Okay. Jokes are fine. Just quit
making fun of me."
Fine.
So we went back in, and did the last set.
Stan's case for me shutting up was not helped the next day when Bram
came into our room waving a newspaper review of the show which
raved about the jokes and between song patter, as well as Stan's songs.
And that became the pattern of the shows from then on.
Stan would play straight man to my character as a cynical and
somewhat brain damaged asshole.
I did learn to dial it down though, and not make fun of Stan so much.
David Eadie was a fan of the band, and he and I had become good

friends over the last few years or so.

Thin guy, medium height, and good looking, with dark hair and pale eyes.

He looked a bit like a cross between a young Mick Jagger and that old picture of Charlie Patton, the blues singer.

He'd been wearing a three piece tweed suit with the pants tucked into Wellies when I first met him in Hamilton a few years previously. He'd started out eccentric, and over the years had embraced his inner nuttiness.

In the first year I knew him in Kingston he moved about 14 times.

At one point he was kipping out in the upstairs hallway of an old house in the student quarter a few blocks from downtown. He had a narrow army cot full of used plates and other crockery under the blankets on either side of where he slept. He would take a sandwich to bed, and eat it while reading, and then tuck the used plate away under the sheets for later.

He was finally ending his studies at Queens and looking towards the future after school.

"Are you guys still looking for a bass player?"

We were walking down Princess Street on our way to have high tea at Chez Piggy.

Chez Piggy was the little cafe that Zal Yanovsky of the Loving Spoonful had opened after he fled to Canada after turning States' evidence in the wake of a serious drug bust.

They did it up right. Warm scones with clotted cream and Earl Grey tea in large Minton china pots.

Somewhere, other guys were playing football, or working on cars or oiling their guns.

David and I were having high tea.

"A bass player? Yeah, sort of. Why?"

"I'd like to try out."

"Really?"

"Yeah."

"Okay. Do you have a bass?"

"No, but I can borrow one, and learn."

"But you don't play bass right now?"

"No."

"Okay, let's talk to Stan when we get back to the club."

We sat for the better part of an hour and drank tea, and watched as Zal Yanovsky dealt in his own way with various delivery men and suppliers.

At one point we heard prolonged yelling, a crash, and then saw the poor delivery guy being chased out of the kitchen by Yanovsky who was wearing a Savoy Hotel chef's hat and apron and brandishing a real live meat cleaver.

The delivery guy bolted out the door into the alley and Zal came back in, perfectly composed, still holding the cleaver, and walked over to our table and asked us if we needed more hot water.

We found Stan a few hours later.

He was at the club, exhausted and red eyed.

He had smoked a joint that morning and then laughed himself sick for a couple of hours at a Cheech and Chong double bill matinee at the movie house.

We talked over the notion of David joining the band, and Stan was up for it.

The fact that David had neither a bass nor currently played one, did not seem to be an impediment.

We both liked him.

"We'll keep the position open for you, until you're ready."

Great.

We now had a bass player, at least in theory, and David had done the impossible by completing a University Arts degree and having a job waiting for him when he got out.

We gave him a couple of records to rehearse to and left town.

A few months later we were back, and we set up in David's living room for his actual audition.

He had a cheap Japanese copy of a Hofner Beatle bass with a string missing, which he plugged it into his stereo.

He was a really good guitarist.

Bass is a whole other thing.

He was nervous anyway, but his playing was way too busy, and we had to coach him to play more simply.

Stan had had some experience in the high school rock band, and gave him some pointers.

I for some reason, had learned how to play a close copy of Dave Woodhead's nearly impossible bass part from "Fogarty's Cove."

I'm not a bass player. It was more of an idiot savant circus trick, but I was able to show David the tricky dropped bar in the chorus.

It wasn't a great audition, but he showed us that he could also really sing.

And he had a similar musical background. He liked a lot of the same stuff we did, and he knew the repertoire, having been to so many of the

shows. And above all, we were friends, and that counts for a lot in a band.
So he was in.

Rehearsal with David began in earnest as soon as he was out of school. First, he needed a decent instrument, and we went to Len Kozak's music store in Toronto.

There were lots of instruments to choose from. Fenders, new and old, all light and relatively easy to play. There was a nice Hofner Beatle bass on the wall, but it had too "thumpy" a sound, and besides, being associated with Paul McCartney, it had too high a price tag.

There was also an old Dan Armstrong bass, with a body made of clear Plexiglas. It had the added advantage of slightly magnifying anything viewed through it, and David, after seeing what it did for his groin once he had properly adjusted the strap, was all for it. But once again, it was too pricey and anyway the damned thing would not stay in tune.

So, out of all the basses he could have chosen, he somehow ended up with the biggest and heaviest and scariest one ever made.

It was a huge instrument, completely black, and apparently machined out of weapons grade plutonium in the waning days of the old Gibson factory in Kalamazoo.

It was called an "RD Artist", with active electronics designed by the Moog Corporation.

It was about 7 feet long and weighed in at about 40 pounds.

It was an evil and sinister-looking thing, and we christened it the BatmoBass.

It had a series of switches which, when hit in the right order, would activate some infernal device called a "compressor/expander," and the sudden added volume and mid-range would blow the clothes off the people in the first three rows, set fire to the carpet and leave shadows from the radiation on the back wall of the venue.

He played it through a large 100 watt Yamaha amp, also jet black, and that rig became an integral part of our sound.

During the last verse and instrumental part of "Witch of the Westmereland," David would hit the Warp Drive, and it sounded like a Steinway being abused by a large and angry Russian on stage left.

"Too Loud!!!" people would yell, covering their ears.

"We don't care!!!" we shouted back.

"Fuck folk music." Stan said under his breath, one night as we left the stage.
We loved it.

David was great for harmonies, too.

He had a real gift for finding the lower harmony against the tenor part I sang.

And as I tended to work out my harmony in advance, I could stake a claim to the easier part while David had to steer a difficult and sinuous path through the song, and we made his life miserable by making him sing odd intervals, and strange wandering lines, that made no sense by themselves, but which filled the chord perfectly.

It worked, and we rehearsed endlessly, looking carefully at dynamics and nuance and the juxtaposition of quiet passages and VERY LOUD ones that made the music so arresting.

It was around this time too, that we developed a repertoire of shanties and acapella songs.

Again, David knew the whole genre, and we took to singing and rehearsing those pieces in the van as we drove around.

We worked out sea chanteys and sacred harp hymns, and vile army and air force drinking songs.

David had a couple of Sam Cooke songs he liked to sing.

It became a big part of the show.

We had a lot of gigs back in those days in noisy campus bars, where the whole second set was acapella, and it made a nice break for us.

We could just stand there and sing and not have to worry about keeping the guitars in tune.

The other advantage was that it left us free to drink beer with one hand, and slap the shit out of hecklers with the other.

David's first gig with us was the Old Town School of Folk Music, in Chicago.

We had no vehicle at this point.

The Datsun wagon we had been touring in was in need of major surgery. It had been pretty much clapped out when Stan had bought it second or third or fourth hand from Gord Lowe, and the rings were gone, so we borrowed our Mum's pick-up truck.

It was a hot day. Really hot. Mid-west hot. And we had no air conditioning, so it was a windy and steamy drive along I-94.

We had taken a case of cold beer on board, to stave off dehydration and scurvy.

We got past Ann Arbor Michigan, and into farm country and we felt safe enough to crack open a few beers.

A young blonde woman came up beside us in a red Mustang convertible.

David looked over at her, raised his beer in salute, and took a drink.

She smiled, and he yelled, "Want one?"

She maneuvered the Mustang carefully over to within a couple of feet of the truck.

David popped open a beer and climbed part way out the window.

She took it, and blasted off over the horizon.

She came back about an hour later, for a refill.

Again, David leaned out the window while I held onto his belt, she grabbed it, waved thanks, and roared off again.

We drove along for a while afterwards in silence.

Then David sighed and spoke.

"She's got the lips that every folk singer dreams of."

"What's that?"

"One on the top, and one on the bottom."

It was in Chicago that we began to realize the music was getting out there and being heard in places where we had never played.

Mum had been busily sending out records to the few stations which played folk music, but we never thought about what effect it might have.

There was Bob Blackman in Lansing Michigan, who was a huge supporter.

Rich Warren at WFMT in Chicago had just begun to assist with a show called "the Midnight Special."

He played us a lot, particularly in advance of this gig.

We navigated our way into the Old Town part of Chicago, found the street where the venue was, and parked on the street about 3 blocks up from the School.

We carefully locked and then checked and re-locked the flimsy plywood cap on the back of the truck which held the instruments, and headed towards the address.

We were walking toward the venue, the three of us keeping close together.

This was the big city. We were hicks, and we were nervous.

We noticed a small gang about a block away as we walked towards the Old Town School.

They had zeroed in on us the way lions on the African Veldt will zero in on a group of weakened gazelles.

We could see them as we got closer. They were looking at us intently and saying nothing.

Stan said, "Boys, this doesn't look right."

The gang got closer and they began to spread out across the sidewalk, presumably to flank us and cut off retreat.

I could see Stan out of the corner of my eye, unbuttoning the sheath on the buck knife he always wore on his belt.

"Watch your back boys. If they surround us remember to stand back to back in a circle."

And then they were right in front of us, blocking our paths.

We stopped.

I was getting my feet planted and trying to loosen my shoulders when they all opened their jackets, and flashed us.

We leapt back.

They were wearing T shirts that said, "Save American Shipping. Stop Barrett's Privateers."

They all burst out laughing and morphed back from being the deadly street gang that had us nearly soiling ourselves, into the small and pudgy folk fans they actually were.

The show went well.

It was sold out.

We played okay, particularly given that it was our debut as a band, and David was lumbered with yet another nightmarish song to play.

Stan had just written the fiendishly difficult "Flowers of Bermuda."

 It was a wonderful song, but with all the dropped bars and accented beats, Stan had left himself nowhere to take a breath.

And the weird time signature made the whole thing a train wreck waiting to happen.

But we got through the show, and did pretty well if audience reaction was anything to go by.

Stan was just setting up for the final encore when a string popped on his guitar.

"Get me another G string."

"What, from your case?"

"No, I'm out. Try the store."

There was a small music store in the School, but when I ran off stage and down the hall the store window was dark.

Shit.

I went back.

"Sorry. The store is closed."

"Someone must have a string in this place. Find me a string."

Off I went.

There was a group of people next to the door to the concert room.

"Anyone here got a G string?"

"No. Sorry."

Damn.

"He can use Bill's guitar." someone said.

"Would Bill mind?"

People were grinning at me.

"No, Bill won't mind."

There were a lot of arch looks being exchanged.

There was a joke here that I wasn't getting.

"Who is Bill?"

"Big Bill Broonzy."

Bill Broonzy had left his Martin to the school in his will.

Big Bill Broonzy was one of our heroes.

If you handed Stan an electric guitar, he inevitably would play Big Bill's song, "Key to the Highway." His music was part of our DNA.

Someone came up with the guitar and I took it.

It was a Martin 000-28, from the 30's, I believe.

The strings were dead and rusty, and about an inch off the fingerboard, but this was Bill Broonzy's guitar. I had seen it countless times in pictures. It was a rare and valuable thing even without the provenance, and I took it up to the stage where Stan was waiting impatiently.

"Where's the string?"

"There is no string. The store is closed. You can use this."

"No. I hate Martins."

"You'll like this one. Here. Take it."

He shook his head. "No. Just get me a new string. I won't play that."

Keep in mind that this whole whispered conversation was happening in front of a capacity crowd who were waiting in the jungle heat of the un air-conditioned room.

I leaned in very close to him, and through my teeth I said, "Stop being an asshole. There is NO STRING. And I know you hate Martins, but this particular Martin belonged to BIG. BILL. FUCKING. BROONZY. Take the damned thing, and let's play the song."

In later years I got to tell Willie P. Bennett that his song, "Music in your Eyes," was once played on Big Bill's guitar.

I have no memory of the rest of the night...where we slept, or what else we did, or who we might have talked to.

That was the night we discovered the wonder of the all-night Chicago bar and Guinness on tap.

I suspect that we were taken to "Somebody Else's Troubles," or "The Earl Of Old Town," those two bars being the place where innocent out-of-towners were taken as a rite of passage, in much the same way as one would be "blooded" with the end of the dead fox's tail after the first hunt, or being ritually sodomized by the ship's crew when crossing the Equator for the first time.

It was a cruel and humiliating practice, but at the same time there was a danger that one might grow to enjoy it.

CHAPTER 35

The Dixie Flyers

Stan and David and I spent every spare minute rehearsing the summer that David joined the band.

We worked endlessly on the instrumental nuances and dynamics of the songs, going from very quiet to overpoweringly loud, literally in a beat. The songs were morphing and changing, and we were getting very tight and developing a sound that no one else out on the circuit had.

We got to unveil it one hot humid weekend in July. We were playing the Home County Festival in London during the weekend and we were also playing three sets a night all that week in Toronto, at the Groaning Board.

The Groaning Board gig was doing well, and there were line-ups down the block all night as people waited to get in and catch a set.

We had decided we were going to push the envelope a bit.

Rather than nurse our energy along to cope with the stress of the constant playing and the commuting between home and London, and then Toronto, and then back home every day, we were determined to just let it all out every time we played just to see how far we could take it before we collapsed.

We would finish a set trembling and exhausted and sweat soaked, take enough time to pour down a couple of beers, and then get up to do it all over again until well after midnight.

We'd pack up, and head home and crash for a few hours then reconvene to drive to London to start playing workshops at 11 a.m.

By 5 we would have to be done in order to blast down the 401 to Toronto and set up again for the evening shows.

I think it was Saturday afternoon.

It was typical Southern Ontario festival weather, hot, sunny and steamy with the threat of a thunderstorms and tornadoes, with occasional showers of farm machinery.

The pace of things was getting to us, and at one point Stan and I retired to the cool dim interior of a nearby bar to restore the tissues.

We had just re-ordered after the initial taste, and were starting to look around and take in our surroundings, when the door opened and the Dixie Flyers clattered in.

Stan groaned softly.

"Ah shit, there goes our peace and quiet."

The Dixie Flyers were one of what seemed like a hundred or so of the bluegrass bands that had sprung up like mushrooms in the wake of the success of the Good Brothers.

Their leader was a guy named Bert Baumbach, based on his ability to speak in what he fondly imagined was a Kentucky accent, and his being able to successfully hit the G chord in the Lester Flatt guitar lick 5 or 6 times out of 10.

They had an act of sorts, and a loyal and ardent following in the rural bars in Southwestern Ontario. They had matching suits and spoke fluent shit-kicker.

Bert caught sight of Stan, and whooped, "Hey there Stan-ley! How y'all dewin'?"

Stan hated being called Stanley, and Bert knew it.

"My name is Stan, Bert. Stanley is my grandfather's name."

The bunch of them came over and jostled around us at the bar.

It was like being accosted by a clot of sweaty orcs in sour smelling powder blue polyester, and sweat stained cowboy hats.

"My Gawd, Stanley," Bertie-Bob reached out and stroked the top of Stan's head. "Thet bald haid of yours feels just like my wife's ass."

The other geniuses all dutifully hyucked along with the joke.

Oh shit, I thought, here we go.

Bert's gonna die.

It's past time.

He's been asking for it.

Stan didn't give a shit about the bald joke.

It was just that Bert was being an asshole. He had made it his mission to annoy Stan for lo, these many years, and we were both feeling tired, and a little on edge, and this was as good a time as any.

I knew from experience how Stan reacted to bullying. Sudden savage and terrifying violence.

This was only mildly annoying, but the intent was the same as far as Stan was concerned.

This was the damned school yard, all over again.

I could see the telltale vein starting to grow and throb on Stan's temple, and resigned myself to the approaching explosion.

Let's just kill the son of a bitch, and we won't have to worry about him anymore.
I was checking out the positions of the other clowns, in case things went bad. I put down my glass and slowly slid off the stool, and got my feet planted on the floor.

Stan's right hand flashed out, and grabbed Bert's wrist and pulled it away from his head.
I could see Bert try to resist, but Stan was hideously, psychotically strong.
Bert was trapped.
Here it comes, I thought. Say goodbye to your arm Bert.
As Bert was struggling to get his wrist free, Stan leisurely reached up with his left hand, and felt the top of his head.
"My God, Bert, you're right. It does feel JUST like your wife's ass."
Bert's face turned red, and he made as if to say something, at which point, some dim, up till now un-used part of his brain kicked into life, and he thought the better of it.
Stan released Bert's hand, and Bert fell backwards into his buddies.
He readjusted his cowboy hat, and brushed himself off, and then turned, and he and the rest of London's cultural elite walked over to the other side of the room and sat down to sulk.

Stan was now looking down at his glass and trying to keep from laughing.
His shoulders were shaking.
"Good line." I said.
"Yeah. It's not mine, but I've been waiting to use it for years. Come on. We better drink up, we got a workshop in half an hour."
And we put back the last of our beers, and pushed away from the bar, and went back out into the sunlight.

CHAPTER 36

Chicago

After that first show at the Old Town School of Folk Music, Chicago
became a a really good market for us.
Ray Nordstrand and Rich Warren at WFMT were hugely supportive,
giving us regular play on the Midnight Special radio show. And word
of mouth was helping bring people in.

Fred Holstein and his brothers Ed and Allan opened a club on North
Lincoln Ave.
It was called "Holstein's." Go figure.
It was a different concept at the time. It wasn't a coffeehouse. It was a
listening room that served booze. In other parts of the country the idea
was anathema. Booze and music didn't mix. But this was Chicago.
People in Chicago liked to listen to music, and they liked to drink.
People in Chicago needed to drink.
Winter in Chicago is terrifying. It is cold enough to kill you in the time it
takes to walk between your car and your front door. Packs of ravening
wolves run through the streets of Chicago in the cold months. If you
slow down or show the least sign of weakness they will cut you fom
the herd and drag you down an alley, overturning the garbage bins and
then tear you apart behind a shed before you know what's hit you. The
last evidence of your existence on this earth will be as a frozen wolf
turd used as a puck by feral urchins in a pick-up game of street hockey.
So you need to drink and keep the blood warm and your limbs moving.
And of course in the spring there is the 2 month long celebration of St
Patrick, when all the amateur drinkers come out, and the river turns
bright green from the vomit being flushed into it.
Chicago in the summer is hotter than a lime kiln, and a frosty beer
might just be the one thing that keeps you from hauling out the semi-
automatic and hosing down the neighbourhood because it's 3 AM, and
the next door neighbour's dog just won't shut up.
And in the Fall, you're going to need something to numb the pain and
the Existential ennui as you watch the Cubs' inevitable slide into the

Abyss. The slide that in the Spring you told yourself wouldn't happen
this year. They had made a couple of good trades in the off season, and
the bull pen was stronger with that new Puerto Rican kid, and you had
a decent closer for a change, whose fast ball didn't take most of the day
to reach the plate. And the management was no longer pinning their
whole strategy on the long ball.
This year it would be different.
This year they had a shot at the Pennant.
This year, given some luck, they could go all the way to the Series.
It could happen.
Right.
Sure.
Choking sons of bitches.
Set 'em up, bartender.
So a folk club with a liquor license was just the thing.
Provided they didn't make the mistake of letting folk singers run up
tabs, they had an outside chance at staying solvent.
The bar and the concert room were both great.
The bar was everything a bar should be. Cool and dark, with lots of
brass and mahogany, and windows which were carefully shuttered
from an outside world that was too fast, too loud and had too much
sunlight. Generous drinks, and a friendly bartender, and one of the best
jukeboxes we ever found. You could plug in 5 bucks and get an hour of
Benny Goodman, and Van Morrison, and Lena Horne, and the Rolling
Stones and the Chieftains, along with bizarre oddities like Bob Gibson's
old 45 of "Marching to Pretoria." Stuff you usually didn't find on the
average box.
The concert room was long and narrow, with not the best sight lines
in the back, but it had a terrific sound system. And the stage was wide
enough for singers with sidemen like myself, who liked to roam about
and occasionally climb the walls and hang from the curtains.
It became a regular gig for us.
We were doing enough business to warrant 2 shows a night for a
weekend run. It was tiring, particularly as we tended to stay late and
socialize with other musicians who dropped by. Stan and Fred Holstein
spent a lot of nights trading songs particularly, and I remember Mary
McCaslin and Jim Ringer being there a lot as well. Jim was a really great
songwriter, a big guy with a gentle voice and a kind but rough and
battered face. He played a 10 minute long ballad called "California Joe"
for us one night. It just floored us. It sounded a hundred years old, or
as if it had been lifted from a Zane Grey novel.
   "You wrote that?" Stan asked.
Jim just shrugged and nodded.

"Holy shit."
Mary was a good writer as well, and might be the only person to ever
record the Who's 'Pinball Wizard' on frailed banjo. Stan used to sing her
song, "Going down the Road" occasionally as an encore. I think there
might be a recording of him singing it floating around on the web.

I was sitting at the bar one night after the show, having just ordered a
drink from Alan Holstein. It was supposed to have been just a double,
but it being Alan behind the bar, what I received was the equivalent of
taking my poor struggling brain and shoving it into a drawstring bag
and tossing it off a bridge with a brick attached, to drown in the river.
Next to me, a tiny woman was scaling the bar stool. It was a bit of a
struggle. She might have been 5 feet with her hands in the air, and the
stool was very tall. But she made the ascent without resorting to ropes
or pitons or a spotter, and got herself settled in. She took a breath and
pulled her cigarettes out of her purse and put them on the counter. She
called Alan over.
"The usual, Alan, thank you."
She then turned to me and held out her hand. "Hello, I'm Ethel Polk."
She had a hell of a voice. A wonderful whisky baritone, and, as I found
later as we talked into the night, a great and deep out of control laugh.
She was smart and funny as hell, and seemingly immune to fatigue. She
was extraordinary. She had worked for the Roosevelt administration
during the war, drumming up support for the UAW, and travelling all
over the country. In the course of her work and her life it seemed she
had met nearly everyone, and she was fascinating to listen to. After
a few hours of her pretty much matching me drink for drink, I had
to give it up and walk back to my hotel while I still could stand. She
said goodnight, and slid off the stool to find someone else with more
stamina to hang with. She was a mere slip of a girl back then, maybe
60 -ish. She is 98 as of this writing, still lovely and funny and interested
in everything. And aside from giving up smoking, she has not slowed
down or mended her evil ways in all the years I have known her.

Long nights and perhaps more fun than was strictly necessary.
You'd finally pack it in around 3 or 4 in the morning, and head back to
your digs.
I had taken to staying at the Comfort Inn on Diversey when I was in
town. I liked the place a lot. Like myself, it was a sagging wreck which
had seen better days. However, unlike myself it had been rehabilitated
by a couple of guys with an eye toward attracting the gay tourist
market. It was a lovely and welcoming little hotel, with an all-night

piano bar just off the lobby, where a chain-smoking human skeleton in a shiny dandruff-strewn tuxedo took requests from the die- hard barflies. And it had beautiful little rooms with high ceilings and double hung windows that actually opened. The owners had kept all the old paneling and fixtures, particularly the claw foot bathtubs, and the black and white subway tiles in the bathrooms.

Stan and I had walked over from the club after we'd had enough for the night.

"This place okay for you?"

He wasn't staying here. He was staying a few blocks away at a friend's apartment.

"Yeah, I like it fine. It's quiet, and it has a kind of a nice intimate European feel to it."

Stan looked over at the bar across the street, a place called "Chaps." There were a lot of well-groomed young men in front of it, with tight jeans and carefully tended moustaches, and Jane Fonda hairdos.

"Probably get a nice intimate European feel over there if you want."

"Thanks, I'll keep it in mind."

Stan and I would have drifted through the pre-dawn summer light towards our beds, past the warren of blues clubs that lined the street. Even at that hour they would still be open and jumping. A couple thousand people would be out, milling around with beers in their hands, and from one joint you could hear Etta James' voice blasting out the door, and then see Buddy Guy a couple of blocks away, standing on the roof of a car playing his Stratocaster, with a hundred foot cord trailing back into the club to his amplifier.

There'd be clouds of pot smoke in the air, and a couple of guys in white chef's hats and stained aprons would be grilling brats and knockwursts and serving them up on soft rolls outside the bars. They smelled heavenly after a night on the town, but I never had the nerve.

Stan had no fear of street meat though, and he would buy one and grab a handful of paper napkins. Onions, sauerkraut, and a big squirt of mustard. And he'd eat it as we walked along, leaning over as he walked, so as to keep his shirt clean. We'd reach the end of the block and he'd get another from a different vendor. Christ, and then another. I was grateful we weren't sharing a room. He was probably going to set fire to the sheets.

Couples were slow dancing in the street, hanging onto each other and laughing and smooching and talking quietly. Buskers were banging on crummy guitars for change, and skinny young guys were doing that trick with the cups and the little ball on a card table, hustling for a buck, and keeping an eye out for the police.

It was just a great long party, for blocks, with lights and colours, and half-dressed people of every race and background laughing and dancing and sweating, with every kind of music thumping out of a dozen different clubs.

People who lived here got to do this every night. What a place.

"I could move here, but I'd never get any sleep."

Stan was standing in front of a store, looking at his reflection, trying to wipe the mustard stain out of his beard.

"I know. I'm having about all the fun I can handle. It's kicking my ass."

I would come down to the lobby in the evenings, to wait for my cab, and see a bunch of handsome and elegantly dressed young men lounging around, reading the paper and talking quietly. They all had beautiful pastel coloured silk suits, and shoes that likely cost a year's wages for someone like me, and socks, socks for heaven's sake that actually matched.

God, to be so rich.

One of them noticed my violin case, and said, "Who do you play with man?"

It was unlikely they would have heard of us, so I said something like,

"Oh I just work with a folksinger. Are you guys musicians too?"

And with the sort of pride another man might reserve for saying, "I am a US Marine," he said, "We are the Tower of Power Horns."

I was sitting with royalty.

A couple years later there was a gig at the Fermilab Cyclotron on the west side of Chicago. We got booked in one summer as part of a double bill with the Red Clay Ramblers.

"We're playing inside a Particle Accelerator, boys." Stan said. "Our nuts are gonna glow in the dark after this."

We left late for the show, and as we drove out through the city to the suburbs, a massive downpour started. Streets quickly became flooded and we kept having to back up, grid over a few blocks and try another route.

Shit.

Now we were really late, and this was not the sort of gig you took lightly. Not that we ever took any gig lightly, but we had wanted to make a good impression here. Our new agent, Jim Fleming was with us that night, leading the way in his rented Buick. At one point Jim was racing along a street towards an underpass and evidently realised there was about 5 feet of water in front of him. A sane person might have pulled over and reconsidered.

Even Stan stopped the van when he saw it.

Jim was made of different stuff though. We watched as he hit the gas, and there was an almighty splash and a tidal wave, and then the whole car disappeared. The water closed over the roof, and the car vanished under the flood of paper cups and empty bottles and used condoms and other floating trash that was being carried along by the rain.

"Jesus Christ."

Jim could be under there drowning. He might be frantically beating his fists against the windows in the dark, trying to get out. The filthy water might be rising past his shoulders to the roof, and he was now struggling to keep his head up to catch his last despairing breath. He might need help, but I don't swim, and in any case I wasn't going to venture into that stinking soup for anyone.

"Fuck him, he's on his own."

Stan looked over at me. "What?"

"Nothing. Never mind."

Hell, I'd said that out loud.

A moment later the car resurfaced and Jim, feeling the wheels touch land again, floored it and carried on up the other side of the underpass. Miraculously, the Buick was still running.

Stan put the van in reverse, turned around in his seat, and began backing up, his tongue sticking out of the corner of his mouth.

Oh no.

"Stan, don't do it. We can cut over a couple of streets and catch up to him."

Stan stopped and put it into Drive.

"Stan."

"Hang on."

Ah shit, he was going for it.

He put the windshield wipers on HIGH and jammed his foot down on the gas. The van hunkered down, and then lurched forward, the rear wheels squealing, and the back end slewing around to the right and then to the left. He fought the steering wheel and straightened it out and we hit warp speed, and then the water was rushing up to us. There was a massive crash and an explosion of filthy diluted sewage burst over the windshield when we hit, and everything that wasn't tied down in the van catapulted forward and came down on top of me in the back seat. There were a few seconds where we plained along the surface of the water, but we were losing momentum and starting to sink. Water was coming up from the bottom of the sliding door.

We had just enough speed to get to the other side and have the rear wheels take hold before the engine was swamped. We pulled up next to Jim, trailing toilet paper from the backed up sewers. He simply waved and we took off again.

We found the Fermilab, and frantically loaded in through the rain. We had been booked to go on first, but being late, the Red Clays had filled in for us.

They finished, and we apologized profusely to them for being assholes, and then we ran out with our gear and did a quick sound check and changed our clothes during the intermission.

We got through the show okay, but it was a bit of an anticlimax after the drive.

It had been a long afternoon, and I wanted to get back to the hotel, but when I found Stan he was deep in conversation with a couple at the front of the stage. They were both dressed in pastel colours, like they had escaped from the Lawrence Welk show. It turned out they were a couple of Born Again numbskulls who had bought tickets and come to the show specifically to talk to him about what they felt was a problem with the lyrics to "Barrett's Privateers."

"We think it is wrong for you to blaspheme on stage. Instead of singing "God Damn them all," why can't you change it to "God Bless them all?"

You gotta be joking, I thought.

Surprisingly, Stan was listening to them politely.

He didn't take any criticism or suggestions about his lyrics from anyone, and yet here he was listening to these two idiots. I lost it and stepped in between him and them.

"What is wrong with you people? You don't like swearing? How's this? Go to Hell. Bugger off."

I clapped my hands. "Go on. Shoo. Get the Hell out of here."

They turned and ran out the door, and I grabbed Stan and said, "Come on. It's stopped raining. The van's loaded, and I'm not. I need a drink. I need several drinks, and something to eat. And then some more drinks after that. Let's get out of here. "

"Okay."

"And don't ever let me catch you talking to Christians again."

CHAPTER 37

The Burro

We were traveling around in an old Datsun 210 wagon in the early days
of our touring.
Stan had bought it from Gord Lowe who assured him that although
it was several years past its best before date, and somewhat rusty and
prone to sagging in the middle if you were foolish enough to open all
the doors at once, it was a reasonably cheap and sturdy little thing, and
Stan would be able to do most of the repairs himself.
Stan christened it "The Burro."
It was slow and cramped and grey, and given to stalling in cold
weather, until we were told about the little switch on the manifold
labeled "W" for winter.
You moved that switch to the side and it would direct warm air to the
carburetor, and save it from icing up.
We were at the side of the highway, outside of Halifax, in a sleet storm.
The Burro had been trying to climb an icy hill near the Bedford exit,
when it began to cough and lurch and then finally stalled and died.
Stan and I walked a mile or so through the sleet back to the exit, found
a pay phone, and made a frantic phone call to our uncle Prescott, who
had a car dealership in the Annapolis Valley.
It was beyond comforting to hear his calm and soothing voice.
He told us where the switch was, and we were able to move again.
Magic.
Eventually, the wretched thing needed a ring job or some other major
surgery, and Stan decided to re-build the engine himself, from the
ground up, with no real prior experience or training in mechanics.
We took it up to Gord Lowe's little place near Millgrove, outside of
Hamilton.
If we got into serious trouble, Gord might be able to get us out.
I say "we," but in the end it was Stan who did all the work.
He spread a blanket and started to tear down the engine, lining up all
the bits and pieces in neat rows on the ground.

My role was mostly to hover anxiously, and bring him the wrong tools, fetch coffee, and wring my hands. That was until David Eadie arrived, also ostensibly to help, but he and I just stood around making smart ass comments, and interrupting Stan with our plans to make an enormous pair of Batmobile style fins out of chicken wire and Bondo, and graft then onto the back end.

"It'll help keep the rear end stable at speeds over Mach 1."

"Do me a favour, you two idiots, and just keep out of the way."

Stan fashioned a winch out of some cedar poles and a block and tackle. The motor was pulled out, and was then completely stripped and reduced to its component parts. The worn-out whatever it was replaced and Stan started the long and careful job of reassembling the whole thing.

"The real trick," he said, "is to get it back together with no parts left over."

There were thousands of little sharp and fiddly bits and he seemed to know exactly where they all went, without as I recall, having to refer to any manual.

As far as I could tell, he seemed to be just inventing the internal combustion engine.

After a couple of days, we winched the motor back in, and he crawled under to tighten up various bolt thingy's, and dumped in some oil, and connected the gas line, and got in and inserted the key.

He looked at me.

"Here goes nothing." And turned the key.

And it started on the first turn, and caught, and sat there, quietly idling. Unbelievable.

He got out and went around to the front and bent over to listen to the motor.

He was desperately trying not to smile, as if having the car start on the first turn of the key was what he had expected to happen all along.

He picked up a rag and ran it along the fender as if to remove some imaginary blemish.

I was standing there with my mouth working, trying to speak.

David leaned over and said, "There will be no living with him after this."

Gord came out of the house with a bottle of Jose Cuervo tequila.

He said, "This calls for a celebration," and we all had a drink.

We had a few drinks.

And then a few more.

Typically I had not eaten in some days and the effect of the booze on an

empty stomach was predictable.
There was still a certain amount of standing around and admiring the
car to do.
Stan was permitting himself to smile now, and was accepting our
congratulations.
He got in and gunned the motor a few times, but it was running
beautifully, and needed nothing so far. The gauges all looked good. The
motor sounded like a sewing machine.
He let it down off the blocks, and busied himself with spraying WD 40
on all the hinges and belts, and then slammed the hood down.
I was in awe, for a while at least, but then the tequila began whispering
bad things to me.
Bad, bad things.
I noticed there was a motorcycle in the side yard.
It was a smallish Honda, or Yamaha.
Maybe 175 cc's. I walked over and sat on it.
  "I always wanted to ride a bike. Does this work?"
Gord came over.
  "Yeah, it's fine. You've never been on one?"
  "No. How does it work?"
So there was a bit of instruction, and I managed to kick start it.
Gord said, "Take it up to the end of the lane, and turn around, and bring
it back."
  "What if I don't get it turned around? What if I take it out on the
road? Are there any cops out here?"
  "Not really. About once a week the OPP come by."
Fine.
I was ready, and off I went, moving carefully through the gears, and
was quickly at the top of the lane.
I looked left and right, no cops.
I turned right out of the drive.
This is great, I thought to myself.
What a wonderful day.
The car sounds perfect.
Stan did an amazing job. Who knew he could fix cars?
I love this bike...I think I might have to get ...OH SHIT THERE'S THE
COPS!

The OPP had come over the hill, and seeing a lone nitwit on a bike with
no helmet, gave chase.
He had his circus lights on, and as I banged a U turn he hit the siren. I
was low over the handle bars, shifting frantically, and giving it the gas.
The common wisdom back in those days was that they couldn't arrest

you for a traffic violation on private property, so I was trying to get back
to Gord's front yard.

Just as I leaned into the left turn, skidding wildly towards the driveway,
the cruiser came up on my left, and I hit the right front fender, and the
bike and I flipped over the hood, and we cart wheeled across the road
and into the ditch, landing with a huge splash in about a foot of bad-
smelling water.

The cop came running over, hand on his holster, and stopped and
looked at me as I lay there with the bike pressing down on my chest.

"Are you okay?"

"Uh, yeah, I think so." I wiggled my toes.

Nothing felt broken. Just wet.

"I'll need to see your license."

Oh boy. This was going to be awkward.

"Don't have one."

"At all? Not even a car license?"

"No."

"There are no plates on that bike you know."

"Really?"

It hadn't occurred to me to look.

"So, no license. No plates. No insurance either, I guess."

"No. Nothing."

"Do you have any ID at all?"

I had a library card in my back pocket.

That was it.

I writhed around under the bike as best I could, and dug a hand into
my right back pocket and then handed him the dripping muddy card.
He shook the water off and looked at it and said, "This will take a while
I guess. Stay where you are."

Which I did, it never occurring to me to pull myself out from under the
bike and crawl to dry land.

I lay there, relaxing in the slime and duck weed, watching the bright
sky and clouds through the spokes of the front wheel as it spun lazily
around.

The large green frogs who had all leapt into the water upon my arrival,
were now cautiously poking their heads out, and carefully climbing
back onto the banks of the ditch.

What was I going to do?

Mum and Dad had often said that if we got into trouble with the cops
that we should never bother using up our one phone call on them.

"If you're looking for sympathy you'll find it in the dictionary,
between Shit and Syphilis," was how Dad put it.

Who was I going to call? No one from Gord's front yard was coming over to help me.

My brother and my friends seemed to be maintaining a strict policy of non-intervention.

I guessed I was alone here. I had never been the praying type. I had never yet felt the urge or the need.

But this might be a good time to open up delicate negotiations with the Almighty.

"OH GOD PLEASE PLEASE PLEASE GET ME OUT OF THIS I'LL NEVER DRINK TEQUILA AGAIN. PLEASE GOD DON'T LET MUM AND DAD FIND OUT I'LL NEVER RIDE A MOTORCYCLE AGAIN JUST THIS ONCE GOD OH PLEASE JUST GET ME OFF THE HOOK."

The cop came back after a while.

He was an older grey haired guy, and he was bemusedly leafing through a sheaf of papers.

The frogs all took fright again, and dove gracefully back into the water, as if doing an old Esther Williams/ Busby Berkley movie routine.

He looked at the first page.

"Well, there's a lot of good stuff here."

"Failing to stop for a police officer. That's a big one.

Resisting arrest. We don't like that.

Reckless endangerment. That's just another name for stupidity.

Assault on a police officer." He looked down at me. "That's the charge when you hit a police cruiser. It's a felony, by the way. That is jail time.

Um, let me see. There's more. No license. No plates. No insurance. No helmet. Some other stuff.

Oh, and you have two books overdue at the library."

He was flipping over the pages.

He looked at me again.

"How do you feel?"

"How do I feel?" My voice was starting to shake.

"How do I FEEL?"

My life was over. I was beyond screwed.

I was going to spend the rest of my days in a prison, being made to wear tube tops and satin hot pants, and getting passed around like a pack of cigarettes by huge ugly tattooed men with names like "Snake," and "Big Daddy," and "Fred the Impaler." I was going to have a really embarrassing nick name.

How did I feel? Jesus.

"I feel like an asshole."

The cop smiled.

"What is it you kids say these days? Go with the feeling?"

Great. I was dealing with a comedian. The bastard was enjoying this. The cop was now slapping the wad of tickets against his leg, considering me, as I lay there covered in green slime and farm yard run-off and tears.

"I did some checking up. There's nothing else out on you. You're not wanted for anything I know of."

"That's true, Officer, I've never done anything this stupid before."

"Well, I doubt that. But I think you might have learned your lesson. I'm going to let you off."

And he took the phone book sized stack of tickets, and vainly began trying to rip them in half.

Huh?

"OH THANKYOUTHANKYOUTHANKYOU..."

He raised a hand and cut me off.

"But listen to me. Walk the bike home."

And I did walk the bike back to where Stan and Gord and David were still standing, doing their best to look innocent of whatever sins they may have committed.

I found out later that Gord didn't actually "own" the bike.

He was "just holding on to it for a friend," and the serial numbers had somehow been worn away from the frame and the engine block.

CHAPTER 38

Photo Sessions

I have looked around various places, family archives and the Web, and it came as a bit of a shock to realise that there are only a handful of photos of the band in any incarnation, on stage or otherwise.

Similarly, there might be at most a total of half an hour of actual footage of us playing, or in some cases, lip synching.

It's sad. Now there are millions of photos and thousands of hours of live footage floating around on YouTube of anyone with a guitar and a need for attention. And as a performer one has to get used to the constellations of tiny red lights out there in the audience as people endeavour to record the moment rather than remember it.

But back in the 70's the best available technology was a Kodak 135 or a Polaroid Land Camera, the latter of which was mostly used to take ghastly bedroom souvenirs.

Stan and David Woodhead and I had had as our official promo shot a quick black and white snap taken as we leaned against the rickety garage behind Woodhead's house on Winchester St. It was the middle of the day, and we were all squinting and smiling against the bright sunlight, while dutifully holding our instruments up, so that people in the future would know we were musicians and not actually on our way to the Texas Book Depository.

The idea of a dramatically lit and artfully staged "8 by 10" photo taken by a professional in a studio was out of the question. That cost money. There are to my knowledge, no photos of the band when Jimmy Ogilvie was with us.

A shame too. He was a handsome devil.

It wasn't until David Alan Eadie arrived that we began to think about a "Professional" band photo. We met a guy in a loft on Queen Street in Toronto one day. He had all the proper equipment. Light meters and strobes and a Hasselblad on a tri-pod, but the shoot was a disaster. He had hired a young woman to spruce us up a bit. She brought along a case full of make-up and by the time she was finished it was lucky we had all brought gender appropriate clothing. We were all covered in rouge and powder and mascara and foundation. David and I both had what looked like Kohl eyeliner, and Stan's ghost of a moustache had been enhanced with eyebrow pencil to the point where he looked like a Pantomime pirate.

Our cause was not helped one bit by the fact that David and I had each bought new trousers for the shoot, and they were tight. Very tight. Painfully tight.

Stan took a look at us and said, "It looks like you're trying to smuggle Carmen Miranda through Customs." The pants, combined with the makeup sent out a very strange and disturbing message, and in the end we scrapped the whole session.

Our next attempt went a little better. Our friend Dave Essig had a good camera and a fine eye as well. He offered to do some shots for 50 bucks and expenses. We wanted to do something less formal this time with more of a Maritime theme, and ended up on the shore of Lake Ontario near Stoney Creek. There had been a massive die-off of smelt, and the beach was knee deep in rotting fish, and the air was poisonous and full of bloated flies. Other than the fact that we had to burn our clothes later, the shoot went okay. Stan had been working out religiously for a couple of months and had lost enough weight that he could actually suck his gut back into his pants. He looked pretty good, if a bit stern from holding his breath. David is on Stan's right, looking defensive and somewhat bee stung, and I was down slope from the two of them, looking typically addled, and in a world of my own, probably trying to remember who the other two guys were. Still, it worked okay as a promo shot, and was much better than the subsequent shots we tried in the apartment where I lived later that day. Those were all very serious and suitably moody and poetic. There was a series of pictures showing us drinking sherry (really) and pretending to read a newspaper article together. I have no idea why we thought that was a good idea. To prove we could read I suppose. Who knows what was going on on our heads? We hated the process.

Stan soon gained back the weight he had shed, and one night as we were setting up for our first gig in Ottawa in a bar owned by a pair of Lebanese coke dealers, one of them came up with the poster and looking pointedly at Stan's belly said, "Are we going to have to pay extra? There's a lot more of you than in this picture."

CHAPTER 39

Ryan's Fancy

We met Ryan's Fancy in Ottawa, back in the days when Dave
Woodhead was playing with us.

We'd been booked into a two night run with them, at an open air gig
called Camp Fortune, outside of town in the Gatineau Hills.

The shows were to be filmed for later broadcast.

They were good guys, friendly and funny and endlessly kind.

They were working on a variation of the Clancy Brothers play book.

Rebel songs, sea chanteys, and traditional Newfoundland ballads, with
some instrumentals thrown in.

They all wore matching outfits on stage. Jeans and Tattersall shirts, and
leather vests.

Denis Ryan was the leader.

He sang tenor and played penny whistle.

Fergus O'Byrne played guitar and banjo, and sang, and Dermot O'Reilly
played guitar and mandolin and harmonica and sang, and provided a
lot of the in between song patter.

Dermot liked his dram perhaps a little overmuch, and this is coming
from me.

He was one of those brilliant and wild and relentless guys who, no
matter how much drink he had on board never got sloppy or abusive, at
least not that I ever saw.

He would keep a steady patter of jokes, and songs and epic poetry, and
recitations going until long after lesser mortals had given up and gone
to bed, or passed out, or had driven someone else's' car home wearing
the wrong clothes.

They took us under their collective wings and put us into rooms and got
us life-saving paid gigs we never could have got on our own.

The first night's show was canceled because of rain, so we and the crew
all set up backstage and had a party.

Some of it might have been filmed.

God only knows what happened to the footage. Most likely it was

313

burned.

Next night we actually got to do the show.

Just before show time Stan was having fits, because Dave Woodhead had decided to go into Ottawa to have new pick-ups installed in his bass.

He was nowhere to be found until a half hour before show time, when he leapt out of a cab and raced to the back stage area.

Stan was furious, and was about to tear into him, but Dave was deliriously happy and excited about his modifications.

"Look," he said, holding the bass up, "EMGs. They're noiseless."

Stan took a breath, and said nothing.

It was impossible to be mad at a guy with the enthusiasm of an eight year old kid, and who played like an angel.

We went on and played and did okay, and then settled back to watch the boys.

We were tired by that time of the host of Irish Pub bands that had sprung up in the wake of the Clancy Brothers.

They all played the same repertoire, and they were mostly mediocre players.

It was largely for them a way to get paid to drink and travel and boink drunk girls, and that in itself was a fine old tradition. Many bands formed and got their start based on the very same impulse.

But for the most part, the music became a sad joke.

Ryan's Fancy were different.

They were pros on every level.

They were tight and polished and all of them could really play.

They were all walking textbooks of traditional Irish and Newfoundland music and they played a lot of new stuff from rising songwriters like Alistair McGillvray.

And they were rehearsed to the point that they could suddenly break away from the set list and go into a kind of freewheeling comedy act, take it as far as was safe, then a little bit more, and then reel it back in and return to the rehearsed part of the show.

They were brilliant.

That night, in the middle of their set, Dermot launched into a 20 minute riff on the herds of groundhogs lining the highway into town.

It was beyond funny, a surreal stream of consciousness rant, like an Irish Lord Buckley on speed.

It stopped the show.

Denis and Fergus wisely just stood back and let him run with the ball.

We were all awestruck.

It was one of the weirdest and funniest things I'd heard.

I congratulated him on the performance the next day, and he just stared at me.
"What?"
He had no recollection of the show.
It was just the booze, and his brain being on fire.

It was Ryan's Fancy who first took us into the Rebecca Cohn
Auditorium in Halifax to do an opener for them.
They had sold the place out, and didn't need us for support. They just
wanted to give us a shot at a real audience.
Our set was okay.
Just okay.
We were nervous, and having spent too much time in the bars we had
no idea how to tone it down and behave in front of normal people.
We were still trying to use the 50 watt amps and phase-shifters from the
bar act, and we overpowered the room's sound system.

The boys took us out on the road for a string of gigs.
We played the Y'Arc in Yarmouth, and some shows in Newfoundland
where Ryan's Fancy were worshiped as gods.
The whole time we were barely getting by. We were mostly an
interruption as far as the audience was concerned, but the boys were
wonderful and supportive, and they gave us a generous time slot on
stage, and a lot of good advice about playing the Maritimes.

Denis said one time, "Never ever announce your last song, boys, you'll
be playing to an empty room by the time you're done."
"What? Really? No."
"I'm telling you. Just do the show and then get the hell off stage.
They may want an encore, but if you announce the last song they'll be
out of there like you'd shouted "Fire.""
We didn't believe them until we were playing a small show in the
Church Hall in Little Dover, outside of Canso.
It was a year or so later. David Alan Eadie had now joined the band and
we were doing our own little tour.
Fergus was with us too, to run the sound system that Ryan's Fancy had
lent us, and to open for us, and to sing back up. His name was on the
poster as well, and he no doubt sold a lot more tickets for us than we
would have without him.
Did I mention that they were generous?

It was a strange room to play.
The Mums were all up front, with their knitting, minding the kids, who

were sprawled out on the floor with their toy trucks and dolls.
The men were all lined up along the back wall with their caps pulled
down over their faces, and their arms crossed.
Our show was going okay, except we weren't playing anything the
audience wanted to hear.
Stan was resolved to sing all the Maritime based songs, particularly
stuff like "Make and Break Harbour."
That was all fine except the guys along the back wall were looking at
their watches, and wondering how many hours of sleep they could
get before they had to get up and go out on the freezing water, and
actually live through the bone-numbing misery that Stan wrote about so
eloquently
It felt a little presumptuous, like preaching to the choir.
Presently, one of the fellows in the back spoke up, "Can't you play
something we all know? Like Hank Williams? Or John Denver?"
That last one hurt.
So we decided to call it a night.
Stan said, "Well, we have one more song for you here..."
And it was immediately bedlam.
The Mums in the front all started gathering up the kids' coats, and
saying, "Johnny come get into your snow suit. Leave your truck there,
and get dressed. Stop hitting your sister. Stand still till I zip you up. Pick
up your hat. Where's your mitts? Come on. Where did you leave your
other boot for God's sake?"
Chairs were being dragged across the floor, and knocked over, kids
were crying, and meanwhile, the men had all stampeded out of the
room and had fired up their cars in the parking lot.
By the time we finished the song, we were literally playing for Fergus
and the janitor, who was waiting to sweep up.
We were dumbfounded.
   "What the hell was that?" Stan said.
   "Bingo," said the janitor.
   "Told you." said Fergie.

The boys had a network TV show and they invited us to be on it.
Stan and David Eadie and I did a two week run at Ye Olde Chestnut
Inn again, and this time we managed to get through the gig without me
trying to strangle anyone in the audience.
Still, it was never fun for us, and we were glad to take the cash and
get on the road after the last show. We drove all night to Guysborough
County, and set up in our Uncle Prescott's little house in Halfway Cove.

We had a day or two to relax before Ryan's Fancy and the film crew got

there.
The day we arrived at the little house, we drove into Canso to say hi
to our Aunt June and Uncle Sam. June lent us their big cooking pot for
picnics on the beach, and gave us a loaf of her home made white bread,
still warm from the oven.
We bought a pound of butter, and then went down to the wharf to get
some lobsters.
We picked out three, about four pounds apiece, and went back to
Halfway Cove.
We built a driftwood fire, cooked the lobsters in sea water, buttered the
bread, and opened some quarts of Ten Penny ale.
It was a lovely evening.
The bay was calm, and the three of us sat and worked our way through
the feast.
We had only beach stones to crack the shells, and sharpened driftwood
sticks to pry out the meat.
After a half hour or so Eadie broke the silence. He sat back, belched,
wiped his mouth, looked over at Stan and said, "How yours, Og?"
After we finished the lobsters we boiled up the billy can, and settled
back with molasses cookies and driftwood smoke flavoured tea with
canned milk.
Stan and David sat back, lit cigarettes, and we watched the evening
light soften the hills across the bay with warm gold.
There are some meals that no restaurant can equal, and days that no
passage of time can dim.

A couple days later the lads arrived with their film crew, and the
director, Jack Kellum.
He drove around with us for a couple of days to scope out some sites
for filming, and discuss how the project would go.
We had gone into Springfield sound for a day a few months before to
re-record some tunes from the first and second albums using just the
trio so it would look more believable when we lip-synched the tunes for
the camera.
David Woodhead had done the bass parts as Eadie was not yet part
of the band, and now he was faced with trying to pretend to play
the typically difficult parts Woodhead had done previously. He was
nervous about looking foolish.
I was less concerned with him looking foolish, and more concerned
with the band's "artistic integrity."

    "Why the hell can't we just play live?" I asked Stan. "It's what we
do best, and the lip synching looks phoney."

317

"Yeah, I know, but it's what the other guys do, and it's what the director wants, it's what we're getting paid a shit load of money to do." He paused.

"And it'd be nice for a change, if we just DID WHAT WE WERE TOLD. ALRIGHT? "
Well yeah. Sure. Jeez. Okay.

So we spent the rest of the week standing on the sea shore, or on top of hauled up boats, or on the edges of cliffs, or up trees, pretending to play, as the crappy metal Tannoy speaker brayed out our pre-recorded tracks.
It just felt weird, and we suspected it looked weird too.
None of us were happy or comfortable with the process.
The shoots got progressively more surreal.
At one point during the shooting of "The Jeannie C," Stan was made to walk through wreaths of fog, waist deep in rain- soaked brambles, with raspberry canes shredding his jeans, playing guitar and lip synching, while the track was broadcast to him over the walkie-talkie stuffed into his pants pocket.
He was far above the town, in the bracken next to the Catholic graveyard next to the Star of The Sea Church in Canso. The camera was set up a quarter mile away, on the hill that now overlooks the main stage on the site of the Stan Rogers festival.

We did another location shoot in the boat shop in Little Dover.
It's mentioned in the song, and it made some sort of sense to have Stan mime that line in that very place.
A year or so before, Stan had been given a perfectly obscene hand tooled guitar strap by a friend.
It was disgusting and ugly and it depicted about a dozen couples doing whatever it is possible for a mixed and inventive crowd to do with various orifices and oversized swollen bits.
We had more or less gotten used to it, and tended to forget it was there. This made for some awkward moments when we did shows at schools, or when Stan sat down to play for kids in the children's' area at folk festivals.
At the boat shop that day, Stan was waiting for the shot to be set up, and the men would sidle up casually, and get a furtive look at the strap, and then return to work, grinning and shaking their heads. We were grateful for the use of the shop, and had brought a bottle of dark rum with us to ingratiate ourselves to the workers. In retrospect, it wasn't perhaps the smartest thing to do, to give booze to guys working with high speed saws, but no fingers were lost, and we finished the shoot and moved on.

318

We had another couple of days' shooting when I went to Jack Kellum, and finally tried to voice my artistic qualms about the lip synching.

"I need to talk to you about this miming that we're having to do."

"Yes, Garnet, what about it?"

"It looks really bad. Everyone knows it's fake. Why can't you just film us playing live? It'd be a lot better."

He was remarkably polite, given I had just impugned his artistic sensibilities, and shit all over his method of working.

"Well, you see Garnet, we have a very sophisticated audience, and they expect to see more than just a bunch of fellows sitting around playing."

"But it looks fake. It IS fake."

"Well that's what they're used to seeing, and that's what we give them. It makes for better TV."

"But..."

"Trust me on this. And anyway, you'll get to sing live in a couple of days, when we do Barrett's Privateers."

I left him there, and Stan who had just seen me talking earnestly to Jack, came over and grabbed my arm, and dragged me out of earshot.

"What did I fucking tell you?"

"I just..."

"Do you want to get us fired for Christ's sake?"

"It just looks stupid. It's embarrassing."

"Well, you're going to look stupid hitch hiking home, if you don't keep your trap shut."

I can take a hint as well as the next guy, so I let it go.

Next day, we got up early, and went down to the shore at Phillips Harbour just west of Fox Island Main. We were doing some shooting for "Fogarty's Cove."

Some bright spark had the idea that we three were to be rowed out to a small rock about a hundred yards off shore, and pretend to play there.

I said, "You gotta be kidding me. We're gonna stand on a fucking rock and..."

Stan glared at me, shook his head, and drew his finger across his throat.

David held up his bass and said, "This is an electric guitar for Chrissake. What am I supposed to be plugged into? A lobster?"

Stan turned on both of us. "For the last time, both of you. Just shut up."

So we got ready.

We loaded up and a small boat took us out into the cove, where we three shakily and carefully clambered out onto the little rock, and arranged ourselves in a row.

It was a very small rock, and the tide was coming in.

We were being crowded onto an ever shrinking piece of real estate, and there was a real chance that one of us would be elbowed into deep cold water.

"Let's just try to get this over and done with, please?" said Stan in an undertone.

The camera was ready, and the music started up, and we merrily pretended to play along like marionettes.

"Cut! That's great boys. Just give us a minute while we reset for the next shot."

We stood awkwardly out on our little island home, while they re-positioned the one camera.

I looked over at David.

"How you doing over there, Gilligan?"

David grunted and lit a Camel.

I sensed movement on the shore to our left, and saw that it was a local who had been attracted by the sound of the music.

He had a quart of Ten Penny Ale in one hand, and a cigarette in the other.

Apparently, breakfast had just been served.

"Holy shit! It's Stan Rogers! Hey Stan!"

The guy on the shore waved the bottle at us.

"Love your stuff! Give'r shit boys!"

He sat down under a tree and crossed his legs, and took a swig and a puff.

He gestured with his cigarette. "This is great."

Wow, a fan.

"Quiet on the set."

The crew was ready to go again.

David snapped away his cigarette butt and shifted his heavy bass.

"Okay. Here we go. And ...rolling."

And again the music blared out, and again, we jigged along, smiling like fools.

"Cut! That's good boys. Just making another change. Be with you in a minute."

The guy on the shore to our left was watching, concern and confusion on his face giving way to anger and outrage, as he looked back and forth between us and the Tannoy.

He stood up.

"Jesus Christ. That's not live. That ain't real. I thought you was actually playing out there, but you fellas are just fakin' it. Awww Jesus. That's terrible. That's just bad boys. Stan, I thought you were better than that. That's phony. That's just..." He paused, searching for le mot juste.

"That's just shit."

Jack was glaring daggers at me from the shore.

I'm sure he thought that this wasn't just some self-appointed arbiter of public taste, but a ringer whom I had bribed to make my point.

Stan was looking at me too.

"I swear. I didn't say a thing. I don't know this guy."

The guy on the shore wasn't letting it go either.

"Aww Jesus. People hate that kind of crap. You can always tell. That's just phony."

He turned to the crew in outrage, and waved in our direction. "That's just SHIT!!"

Two of the crew by this time, had crept up behind our critic, and seized his arms, and frog- marched him off into the woods.

We could hear him still yelling over his shoulder. "THAT'S JUST SHIT!"

I don't know what the guys on the crew did, but his critique was abruptly cut off. They came back wiping their hands, and we were soon able to resume.

We had to get this done.

Our rock was getting ever smaller.

"Okay...let's do this. Ready...set...rolling...GO!"

"THAT'S JUST SHIT!"

"Cut!"

The guy was back, perched up on a high jumble of rocks, silhouetted against the sun, declaiming into the cool morning air, and the two crew members ran off to deal with our critic once again.

By the time they got back, we three were huddled like frightened mice on a tiny bar of soap out in the cove, and we now had only a few minutes to get the shot done, and be rescued, and get the hell out of there.

"Ready! Let's..."

"That's ....just .....Shit!!!!!!"

We turned to look, and the guy was about a quarter mile away on a rocky outcropping, at the head of the entrance to the cove, his voice now just a faint wind-blown rebuke. "Thaaaaat's ......juuuuuuust ..... SHIIIIIIT!"

We gave up, and the lifeboat was launched, and we were brought in to shore.

The crew was standing in a half circle, looking at me.

"I swear. I never ever would put someone up to that. I was with you guys all day yesterday."

Jack reached into his pocket, and pulled out a roll of bills, and began peeling them off. Jesus, I thought, he's firing me. I'm being let go.

"Jack, I swear to you. Really. I have no idea who that guy was..."
He turned to Fergus and said, "I think we're about done for the day.
Why don't you and Garnet go get about 80 pounds of lobster. We'll do
some more scenery shots on the way back. I want to get a shot of the
Queensport Light. We'll wrap up and meet you back at the house."

What a great guy.
Anyone else would have clubbed me with a shovel and jammed me into
a lonely shallow grave back in the woods.
Instead he dropped a hundred bucks on a feast for us.
We broke for the day, and cooked up the lobsters, and by my count, Stan
ate seven.
The next day we shot some more footage for "Fogarty's Cove" at the
actual cove itself, just west of Fox Island Main. It went pretty smoothly
this time, as we were safely perched on some high rocks on the shore,
well away from the incoming tide and locals with deeply held artistic
sensibilities.
Later, we drove to Tickle, just west of the town of Canso, where Denis
lip synched "Fiddler's Green," as the fishing boats glided back and
forth in the channel. It looked lovely.
Stan decided that having a few seagulls in the background might be a
nice touch, and quickly rigged up a fishing line. Within a few minutes
he had jigged a half dozen Pollock or Mackerel and he began to throw
them in the air behind Denis to attract the birds. Within seconds we
were all running for our lives as flocks of the nasty creatures came
whirling out of the sky and turned our shoot into an out take from a
Hitchcock film.

The next day Stan did an interview with Denis on the hill above the
house, with Chedabucto Bay glittering blue in the background, and
then we set up for the live version of "Barrett's Privateers."
We grouped about the little kitchen table and actually had some fun,
jamming a bit with the boys while the crew rolled tape, and measured
sound levels.
We played a few Buddy Holly tunes (Dermot was a big fan) and then
we did an impromptu version of the "Mingulay Boat Song", or, as the
boys called it, "The 'Bongalay Meat Song."

Bottles were opened, and we started to film.
Again, the fact that we only had one camera necessitated numerous
stops and starts.
Stan would get a verse or two into the song, and then we'd have to
reset.

In the meantime, we'd all have a little drink, and of course then the continuity would be ruined.

Someone watching at home might notice that the levels of the bottles were different.

That would never do.

So they would be topped up and we'd start again. And once again we'd have to stop, and reset.

More drinks, more problems with continuity. More booze added, and so on.

The evening wore on.

I think it took nearly 3 hours to shoot that 4 minutes of film.

In the edited version, it becomes like time lapse photography of decaying flesh.

We change, in the space of mere minutes, from young men with brains, and functioning livers, and potentially bright futures, into slobbering red faced degenerates.

The moment the director yelled "Cut! That's a wrap," we all pitched forward, and crawled to our beds.

CHAPTER 40

The Winnipeg Folk Festival

I think it was around 1975 when word went out around Toronto and area that Mitch Podolak, the director of the Winnipeg Folk festival was arriving and would be holding auditions.
The festival had started the year before under modest circumstances but now was getting financial help from the Arts Council. Mitch was now able to look a bit farther afield for talent.

The auditions were held in a large cavern of a room down by the water front in Toronto, in what was to become the Harbourfront complex.
Stan told us we were likely shoo-ins to be hired. Mitch and Paul Mills had become co- conspirators in getting the CBC to throw some money at the festival. Paul put in a good word on Stan's behalf. The good word and Mitch's budget didn't extend to the trio however, so Stan did his first appearance at the festival as a solo, with Paul backing him up. Call it a win/win for Paul.
It seemed like every scruffy singer song writer with stars in their eyes had turned up at the audition. They each got to play a couple of songs, but I don't recall anyone from the event getting hired by Mitch with the possible exception of Willie P. Bennett.
Mostly what I remember from that night was Willie P. and Rick Taylor needing a quiet place to release their beer, and finding a massive white painted metal structure laying on its side in the parking lot. Evidently vandals had been at work. It was covered in coloured graffiti, thousands of bright scribbles. They climbed up on top and had their whizz, and that would have been that, except that the metal structure, as we found out later, was the final piece of the radio antenna for the CN Tower which was to be raised and affixed to the top the next day. From all over Toronto school kids had come down and signed their names to it. The day after the auditions, just before it was lifted up and installed, a coat of clear polyurethane varnish was sprayed over it to seal and protect the kiddies' signatures. It sealed and protected the signatures, and it sealed and protected the urine as well. So in effect what was for years

the world's tallest free standing structure, and the thing which still dominates the skyline of Toronto has had a faint pee stain at the top.

The festival took off in a big way. The CBC began doing regular live broadcasts from the site, with the evening Main stage concerts being hosted by Peter Gzowski, who was at the time the CBC's biggest radio star, if that isn't a contradiction in terms.

Peter did a great job. He was calm and prepared and pretty much unflappable on stage.

The only time I ever saw him lose it on the job was during his ill-advised foray into late night TV.

Peter didn't belong on TV. He was a radio guy and an excellent one. A legend. But he wasn't particularly handsome or charismatic. He was slow moving, with a bottle nose, horn rimmed spectacles, and a ragged moustache. He dressed badly and couldn't live more than a minute without a cigarette. He looked less like a TV star and more like your bachelor uncle who couldn't be left alone in the house in case he fell asleep with the Racing Form on his face and set fire to the couch.

Still, they gave it a shot for a season or two.

The show was called "90 Minutes Live," and being actually live there was all kinds of room for things to go very, very wrong.

I was watching one night when he had as his guests the comedian David Steinberg, and noted author Pierre Berton. Steinberg was on just because he was a smartass, funny and quick. Berton was there ostensibly to pitch his latest book.

They never got around to the book though. For some reason Berton had decided to bring along the newest invention for the busy and creative cook, the Cuisinart.

He set it up on a table and pulled out a bag full of vegetables, and began showing all the attachments, and jamming carrots and celery into the thing, turning them into a thick slurry. I don't believe he had any fiduciary interest in the success of the thing. I expect he just wanted to be a good guest and do something other than flog his latest history book.

Peter kept trying to lead Pierre back to the book, but Berton was relentless.

Steinberg was to one side, with his hands in his pockets, bemusedly watching the performance, and asked, "So, you like to cook?"

Pierre said, "Yes, I love to cook. It's my hobby."

Steinberg said, "Do you like to cook P- O -R- K?"

"Pork? Yes, we love pork."

Steinberg leaned in and said, "Did you know that P- O- R- K makes you S -T -U- P- I- D?"

Gzowski flinched and Berton did a double take. He was distracted for a moment, and made the mistake of removing the lid of the machine before it was stopped. He dug his hand in to bring out the shredded veggies.

There was a loud "CLANG" and Berton pulled out his hand. It was a mangled mess, and blood was shooting in an arc across the desk. Gzowski put his hand over his mouth and staggered off camera. Steinberg fell over laughing, and poor Pierre was bravely trying to carry on as if nothing was wrong. Blood was everywhere. I wonder now if the incident wasn't the inspiration for the Saturday Night Live skit about Julia Child.

Gzowski was still lurching around trying to act like a TV host, but it was no use. A stage hand offered a box of Kleenex to Berton. Gzowski grabbed it, pulled out a wad of tissues, covered his mouth and once again made a run for it to barf off camera.

They cut to a commercial and a second later David Eadie called me from Kingston.

"Are you watching "90 Minutes Live," right now?"

At the festival though, Peter was excellent. He made sure he was prepared. He wore a rumpled ash covered cardigan to ward off the night chill. He carried a clip board full of detailed notes so as not to forget names and other info, and had lots of little anecdotes to fill up any pauses stemming from technical troubles.

Interviewing you on the radio, he tended to be somewhat distant, but that was likely due to having a producer feeding him questions and information through his ear piece.

At the festival, though, he was relaxed and friendly, onstage and off, and the audience loved him.

The festival site itself was massive. Just getting from one workshop stage to another was an ordeal. To cut down on sound bleed from one stage to another, Mitch had placed them as much as half a mile apart. It was a great idea, but it was hard on the flabby and out of shape musicians who had to lug their guitars back and forth, hampered as well, by a chronic lack of a sense of direction. You would see small groups of them, out in a field, each holding a site map up and turning it this way and that, as if on an orienteering course. Fights broke out, people stormed off in different directions, and workshops would just be ending when some exhausted and bedraggled piper or fiddle player would stagger in, looking like a ghost from the Shackelton expedition, having staggered and fallen and crawled through every stinking swamp and duck weed covered slough within a 10 mile radius.

Mitch solved the problem by renting golf carts and organizing a cadre of volunteers called "Schleppers," who now could rocket wildly across the tundra from stage to stage, with poor hungover and enfeebled performers holding onto their sun hats and watching their precious and irreplaceable guitar go cartwheeling out of the back.

The weather never helped. It was either so hot that people were dropping from sunstroke, or so cold and rainy that often times performers were playing to an audience completely hidden under multi coloured tarps. Days would go by and hardly a soul would be seen. It was just a vast underground city of muddy refugees in rain soaked hippie sweaters. The whole place smelled of wet wool. And no matter what the weather, the Manitoba mosquitoes would descend in clouds. They are awful nasty things, about the the size of a starling, who would sweep in and rip out a chunk of your flesh and fly back to the trees and eat it like an apple, leaving you bleeding and anemic, and calling weakly for a medic in the mud below.

Stan claimed he had seen them fly in formation, like Stukas.

Bug spray was useless. All it did was add flavouring and strip the finish off any priceless vintage guitar it touched.

I remember standing on the Main stage one night, and I had a half dozen of the evil bastards on my left hand alone. We were in the middle of a song, and not wanting to spoil the show by waving my bow or flapping my arms, I simply stepped back from the mic and played what was for me, a wild and dazzling flurry of notes that were in no way suited to the song. Stan heard me, and shot me a dirty look.

We were on just before sunset. It had been raining non-stop since the Wednesday before the start of the festival; a cold, hard and relentless downpour. The area in front of the stage looked like a reenactment of the Battle of the Somme. Some helpful soul had spread bales of straw to soak up the water, but nothing helped, and now it just stank like a feedlot. The audience was nowhere to be seen, having taken refuge from the rain and the bugs under acres of tarps. Just as we were about to start the final song, there was a break in the cloud cover, out on the far Western horizon, as a cold front came in to scrub the sky clean. It looked as if a blanket was being rolled up, and the sun, now only a few degrees from setting was peeking through. The effect was extraordinary. We were suddenly warm, and everything was bathed in a delicious red glow. We were going to live.

All at once, the sea of tarps erupted into a mob of joyful and crazed hippies who were throwing aside their shelters, and standing up to greet the light. In a moment the air was filled with thousands of rain jackets, bright plastic ponchos, and Sou'westers.

Stan stopped playing, and we stood and watched. The world looked as if it were on fire, and the rain drops falling off the stage canopy were glinting like bright sparks.

The riot continued. The rain gear had come off and now the wet sweaters were being peeled off and tossed aside. Then the shirts. Hundreds of naked and hairy bodies were now dancing about in the warmth.

The three of us, Stan and David and I sat down on a riser and waited it out. David lit a smoke and handed the lighter to Stan. Stan lit up, and we sat and watched some more.

People were now singing and chanting.

I leaned in to Stan and said, "We must be careful, and use this power only for good."

That year, our Mum had decided she wanted to see the festival, and in her role as President and Executive Producer of Fogarty's Cove Music we felt we might be able to wangle the cost of a spare air ticket out of Mitch. Wanting to save money, and being of an evil and conniving nature, Mitch suggested to Mum that she might have more fun if she caught a ride with some other musicians who were driving out fom the east coast of the US. She liked the idea.

Stan caught wind of it however, and insisted that Mitch stump up for an air ticket. No mother of his was going to embark on a cross country odyssey with a pair of degenerates like Dave Van Ronk and Paul Geremia.

Shame. She liked folk singers, and she had a taste for cigars and whisky. It would have been an outing.

This was also the festival I believe, which took place in the middle of a beer store strike.

Mitch personally didn't approve of drinking, and forbade the use of any alcohol on site, other than what he would dole out backstage from a locked and heavily guarded road case, but he was a good and generous host, and people were going to need to unwind back at the hotel.

There were huge parties back at the hotel every night where performers and volunteers could mingle and socialize. It was a chance for folks to unwind, let go of the inhibitions, and maybe meet someone new. Perhaps drag them back to the hotel room and give that rain soaked clothing a chance to air out and dry. Beer was going to be needed.

As I heard the story, Mitch hired a large and mud covered farm truck, had it loaded with straw bales, and sent it south to North Dakota in the care of a couple of guys who had shaved off their moustaches, leaving only their beards. They wore wide brimmed straw hats and suspenders. No border guard was going to mess with a Mennonite.

They bought many cases of beer and then reloaded the truck outside of Grand Forks, with the beer on the inside and the straw carefully piled to hide it. A couple of runs like that and they were set. I didn't know if the story was true. I decided I wanted to believe it anyway.

I don't know if young performers now carouse and party the way we all seemed to back in the day. Maybe it is because I no longer drink and don't go to parties at festivals and simply don't see it. I don't go to that many festivals anymore period, so it is hard to tell. Mostly now, the only time I am in contact with large groups of young players is at some conference like the Folk Alliance, and I am unlucky enough to get jammed into an elevator with a dozen or so desperately eager young kids with pierced tongues, tattoos and dread locks, not to mention advanced business degrees, who push their promotional bumf in my face and tell me how they have achieved an exciting new synthesis of old time Appalachian banjo, Hip Hop and Tibetan throat singing, and they are doing a special 2 a.m. guerilla showcase in the stairwell which I'd be a fool to miss, and no, they've never heard of the Red Clay Ramblers, and I am barely able to keep from punching them in the throat.
Back in my day, it was easier to be an annoying little twerp simply by drinking too much.

The Winnipeg festival was unique back in the day in that they catered to every need and whim a performer might have.
I once boarded the chartered flight to the festival with no money at all on my person, thinking that when we got there Stan would pay me back the 8 dollars he'd owed me for some weeks now, and I'd be okay for funds. Of course he was too broke to pay the debt, and I was furious, but in the end I lacked for nothing.
We all had breakfast lunch and dinner provided on site, and on a scale we had never seen before. There was an enormous field kitchen back in the performers' area which served up scrambled eggs, and ham and bacon and French toast, and later roast turkeys, and baked lasagna and salads and hot fresh bread, and roast beef and salmon, steak and kidney pies and other things we'd only read about in books. It was enough food to feed us for a year, if we could just figure out some way of getting it home.

Mitch was smart in many ways, but one of his cannier moves was to throw massive after concert parties back at the hotel, for the volunteers. Bands which were actually playing at the festival would be hired to perform at the after-hours parties so the volunteers could hear the music they otherwise would have missed during the day. It was a smart way to get folks to volunteer, and it was a nice way to say thanks. If you were a star struck volunteer it was your reward at the end of a long day of fetching and carrying and putting up with needy folk singers in the heat and dust. You might get to meet someone whom you knew only from their recordings, and strike up an acquaintance, and maybe take it to the next level, and with an open bar you were able to drink enough to lower your standards.

For someone like myself, it was a chance to get ever so cunningly and quietly shit faced and wander about the hotel and check out the music that was happening in some of the quieter corners.

I once walked into Stan's room about 1 a.m. and he was hosting a session with Colleen Peterson and Steve Goodman. I felt no urge to go next door and get my fiddle. A fiddle was too loud, and it was more than enough just to listen. They had found that their voices all blended perfectly and they all knew a lot of the same songs. And if they didn't know the song they were able to pick it up quickly or were content just to sit and listen. Stan had something of a reputation as being loud and over bearing and competitive. And he could be. But in situations like this he was ever quiet and generous and supportive. There were other people in the room listening; Chopper MacKinnon, who helped Colleen on the road, and Stevie's manager as well. Bottles were passed to and fro, a joint or two got handed around, and the sound of the music ebbed and flowed, and when it was over, Steve's manager picked him up in a fireman's lift, Steve having pitched over and fallen asleep, and he carried him out the door to put him to bed. It had been a lovely night. All of the people in that room are gone now. It's a hard thought.

I was standing in the big party room the next night, drinking a beer, and watching a pick up band of fiddlers and banjo players bashing out an endless set of reels that all sounded identical to me, when an attractive young woman walked up. Her eyes were wet, and she looked upset. I had seen her around the festival site wearing a volunteer T shirt but didn't know her name. She had made a bee line for me, and was now standing in front of me wringing her hands and sniffling.

"Are you all right?"

"No, I'm not alright."

Ah shit. Now I was going to have to ask her. It was only polite.

"Is there something I can help you with?"

The tears were starting in earnest now. She shrugged and spread her hands.

"I love him, and he said he loved me, and now that we spent the night together, he won't even look at me and I don't know what to do."

"Um, who are we talking about?"

She stammered something I couldn't catch, and with that she broke down utterly, and launched herself forward and buried her face into my shirt. Not wanting to spill my beer, I drank it down, and then awkwardly put my arms around her.

She was sobbing so hard that her knees buckled and I had to hold her up.

Well this was embarrassing. People were walking by, catching sight of our little tableau, and then looking quickly away.

"Ah Jeez," I said, trying to be sympathetic, "That's awful. "

"Can you talk to him? He'll listen to you. Tell him I don't care about his wife. We can work this out. I love him and I just want us to be together."

"I uh..."

"Please, just tell him."

Tell who for Chrissakes?

And then it hit me.

Stan.

That worthless no good philandering bastard. Why else would she be confiding in me?

I had to get her out of sight. I pushed her away from myself. There was a small sticky suspension bridge of saliva and snot between us, and the wet makeup and mascara on her face had left an imprint on my shirt like the Veil of Saint Veronica.

I turned her around and marched her out the door and down the hall to the elevators.

The doors opened and I stepped in amongst the other riders with this sobbing human wreck. It was an awkward and silent trip up to my floor.

I got her into the room I was sharing with David Eadie, and she collapsed on the couch where she gave in completely to her grief and the full knowledge of her betrayal.

I didn't know what to do. I sat on the edge of the couch and tried to come up with some comforting words, but all I could think of was how I was going to kill Stan. He was bigger and stronger than me. It was going to take some finesse. No, wait a minute. Mum was at the festival that weekend. Maybe I'd just tell her and step out of the way.

It was at this moment David opened the door to our room. He took a look in and then stopped.

"What have we here?"

"Shut up. It's not what you think."

I could hear other people out in the hall behind him. He raised his voice unnecessarily.

"You could avoid all this disappointment if you simply read the manual we gave you. The female body is clearly marked on page 12. Stan and I circled it all the important bits in red ink."

"Fuck off."

He backed out and closed the door.

What to do?

The girl's sobs were subsiding and after a few minutes she fell asleep. I threw a blanket over her, and went off to look for Stan.

He was in the party room, drinking a beer and listening to the band playing apparently the same reel I had been hearing an hour or so ago. He turned to me and said, "Hi...how's it going?"

I grabbed him by the shirt and hissed, "You bastard. You worthless lying sack of shit." And then I pushed him out the door into the hallway and up against the wall.

"WHAT?"

"You know what I'm talking about. You son of a bitch. Well, let me tell you right now, if you want to be a sleaze bag on the road, that's your business. But I am not going to cover for you. This is your fucking problem."

He grabbed my wrists and pulled my hands off. Why he didn't belt me I'll never know. He didn't react well to threats.

"Just calm the fuck down and tell me what the hell is going on."

So I told him the story.

"And she's back in my room right now, passed out on the couch, and expecting me to help her, and just look at my goddamned shirt."

Stan raised his hands. "Look, I swear to you. Whatever happened, it wasn't me. I don't know what is going on either."

"Bullshit. Then why did she come to me? I'm your brother. She says she loves you. She expects me to help."

"I don't have the faintest idea. But I promise you, it wasn't me."

Yeah. Right.

I went back to the room but she was gone, and I didn't see her again for the rest of the weekend. Relations between me and Stan were strained for a while. I didn't know what to believe, and I was pretty sniffy with him.

A couple of months later we were back in Winnipeg, and a guy, one of the senior organizers at the festival, sidled up to me at a post-show party and said, "Hey Garnet, I just want to thank you for helping me out at the festival this summer."

"What are you talking about?"

"That night at the festival, with (he said her name), you know. She was pretty angry with me. And you kept her busy and talked her down and I was able to get away." He winked at me. "Thanks, man. I owe you one."

Huh?

Oh shit. It had been him. Of course. He was a well-known hound.

"Yeah, well, you know. Listen. I gotta go. I got something I need to say to Stan."

Being set loose in a strange city with unlimited food and booze was hard enough for some of us to handle, but for those who got into cocaine, it was a disaster.

Wille P. Bennett had gotten his nose into the stuff pretty deeply.

I don't know how he was able to afford it, as cheap crack had not yet come on the market. Coke was still a status symbol, a sign that you had were so successful that you didn't care that it made you more of an asshole than you already were.

I expect he had friends who supplied him.

There were a lot of suck-fish and hangers-on who collected around Willie over the years, who got some kind of sick thrill and imagined status by turning up with booze or coke or whatever, and getting him wasted, even when they knew he might be trying to keep away from it. He would have long periods of sobriety where he was the sweet and funny guy we loved. But it never lasted long enough.

Booze turned him into a loose cannon, and a loud and random mess, but at least he would eventually pass out and you could begin cleaning up the broken furniture and hosing down the floors. Booze, combined with cocaine turned him into the Thing That Wouldn't Sleep.

We were flying back from Winnipeg one Monday, following the festival, and I was seated next to him. I was a bit worse for wear myself, having had too little sleep and way too much to drink, and I was ready for my nap. Willie's brain was still on fire. He was slobbering drunk and yet unnaturally alert, with his eyes spinning in opposite directions. He sat down and then turned to me and grabbed me by the collar and said, "I haven't slept for 7 days. 7 fucking days."

"Well, we're all tired man, maybe put your head back, P., and close your eyes. Think nice thoughts."

Then I pushed him violently away. "Now leave me the Hell alone or I'll kill you."

I fell asleep immediately, and missed the breakfast service. The next thing I knew was we were beginning our descent into Toronto, and Willie was climbing onto my lap, choking me, and yelling, "YOU'RE A STAR! YOU'RE A BIG FUCKING ROCK STAR! LET ME BLOW YOU. PLEASE, I'M BEGGING YOU! LET ME BLOW YOU!"

I smacked him back and forth across the eyes, and managed to get my

hand under his jaw. I pushed him back into his seat. I had a fist raised.
"LEAVE ME THE FUCK ALONE. I'M WARNING YOU!"
He was still struggling, and thankfully a couple of flight attendants, one
male, the other female, were able to grab him and drag him down the
aisle to another seat where they buckled him in and cinched the belt
tight. I turned my head, and the seats around me for about 4 rows were
all empty. The passengers were huddled in the aisle at the back of the
plane, looking shocked and waiting for the drama to be over.
I shrugged.
"I don't even know that guy."

We landed, and Stan and David and I began walking towards the
baggage area. We were all whipped, and just wanted to collect our gear
and get the van out of hock in the long term parking lot.
"Where's Dave?"
Stan had stopped and was looking around.
"I dunno. He was right here a moment ago."
Jesus. What now? We began walking back and passed Willie P. in the
company of a couple of burly uniformed men. He was calmer now,
walking with his head down, scratching his head and yawning.
"Maybe they used the dart gun." Stan said.
"Yeah. That was a fun way to wake up in front of 30 or 40 people."
We found David.
He was standing at a small bar at the side of the hallway, talking
earnestly to an older man with a moustache, who was smiling politely
and nodding, and looking furtively around to see just where the Hell
was Security.
It was Eddie Shack, a former hockey player, and more importantly
a former Toronto Maple Leaf, and David was giving him an exact
blow by blow description of a brutal and expert body check that he
had seen Shack lay on someone behind the net in a game some 5 or
6 seasons ago. The swift surgical precision of it, and the depth of the
sheer mindless depravity had spoken to something in David's soul, and
it had apparently changed him forever, and he wanted to express his
gratitude.
"Dave, c'mon. We gotta go."
"Guys, this is Eddie Shack. Eddie Goddamned Shack. "
Eddie smiled and raised his glass.
He had nice eyes, for a killer.
"Hi there."
"Yeah, nice to meet you Mr. Shack. Come on Dave, we gotta move."
We grabbed him by the arms and dragged him away, and I imagine
Eddie reached into his pocket and clicked the safety catch back on.

CHAPTER 41

Between The Breaks Live

With David Alan Eadie in the band, we now had the template for our sound, our act.

We had great songs. We had a killer lead singer, who had one of the all-time God-given voices, and who was also a great guitarist with a unshakable sense of rhythm.

David was becoming a solid and inventive bass player, with a really evil and off-kilter sense of humour. I was on stage right with the fiddle or flute or electric guitar, spending most of my time in mid-air doing a disjointed post-hippie interpretive dance.

David and I could pretty much screw around with arrangements to our hearts' content.

Stan was remarkably generous about giving us free rein with the songs he brought into rehearsal.

The songs would often morph into something very different from Stan's original intention, and he was okay with that. Not just okay, but he actively encouraged it.

We had great harmony vocals, and we were funny as an act, and above all, we had developed as a band a really snotty attitude.

We knew we were good, and sometimes confidence will turn the corner when you're trying to win over an unfriendly or disinterested crowd.

With all due respect to the other wonderful musicians who laboured in the trenches with us over the years, the two and a half years with David Eadie were the most exciting and fertile period for the band. It was chemistry. We just clicked.

And while we were in all modesty, capable of brilliant stuff, we were also really volatile, and the wheels could come off on any given night, both musically and personally.

Stan and David particularly tended to strike sparks off one another.

It made for some great shows and some lousy ones. I wondered if sometimes people just came to see if we were going to make it through without coming to blows.

Speaking of Stan's generosity, I wonder if any other band leader out there ever paid himself the exact same money as the other people in the band, the way Stan did.

Whatever money came into the kitty was split three ways after expenses. That was the rule.

And the only time we deviated from it was the occasional really juicy gig where there was a little extra to go around, and he would shamefacedly ask if he could "skim just a little off the top."

We never objected.

Later there was some cash coming in from stage sales of the records, and he was able to skim a bit of that too, to give us Christmas bonuses. We had some discussions about him being too fair to us. After all, he had kids to think about. But he insisted that the band was what sold the act, and the songs and the records, and he couldn't have got anywhere without us.

Most people who came to Stan's music after he passed don't remember or even know that there was a band, or that it was essential to the whole creation of that sound, but Stan did, and he treated us accordingly.

We began talking about the possibility of doing a live album. It represented a whole other set of problems as opposed to working in the studio, but once the idea was on the table, I wouldn't let go of it.

My experiences in the studio with Paul as producer had left me with a real distaste for the whole recording process. I thought that with a live record at least, the core sound of the band could be preserved, with the addition of only a couple of outside players who understood what we were trying to do. This was the chance to have a try at replicating the spirit of that Brady and Irvine record we so loved.

We hooked up with Grit Laskin, who in addition to having built Stan's guitars was a good multi- instrumentalist. He played concertina, long neck mandolin, and Northumbrian small pipes.

Paul wanted to play guitar. David and I both objected on the grounds that Paul was a very busy player, who seemed bent on inserting every lick he knew into every song, whether it fit our arrangement or not.

He also had a very demanding full time job, and either couldn't rehearse or simply wouldn't.   But in the end he was Stan's friend, and Stan couldn't say no, no matter how intrusive David and I felt him to be. We managed to get a promise from Stan that Paul would faithfully turn up for rehearsals and learn the arrangements, and for the most part he did.

And so we were a 5 piece for the recording.

Bill Garrett would serve as production assistant, and on site recording supervisor.

We hired a mobile recording unit called 'Master's Workshop,' from a TV evangelist.

We had a week of shows coming up at the Groaning Board, and we started rehearsals at Grit's shop on Dupont Street.

Rehearsals went well, and I remember being struck by just what a powerful and beautiful collection of material we had to work with.

The core group of songs that we wanted to capture were by far the best Stan had written, and there were a couple of great covers.

Archie Fisher's "Witch of the Westmereland" had morphed from a quiet ballad into a wild and relentless juggernaut over the months that the trio had been playing it.

It had started life with us in the Key of D, as it was written, and I believe there exists in the WFMT archives of Rich Warren's Midnight Special show a recording of us playing it with all the verses in the slower tempo and lower key. But one weekend, at the Buffalo Folk Festival, I suggested we kick it up into the key of G, for my own selfish reasons, of course. It allowed me to use a bigger range on the fiddle, and it also drove Stan's voice into the very top of its range, and gave the song a greater urgency.

As we worked on it over the course of nearly a year, it had sped up, lost a couple of verses, grown tail-fins, added running lights, a four barrel carburetor, and had turned into a monster.

And every night, by the end of the song, when David kicked in the warp drive on the Batmobass, it was no longer folk music, but something else entirely, sort of acoustic heavy metal, and people were pinned into the backs of their chairs.

And that was just the first song, our way of saying, "Hello."

We had also worked up a do-wop version of Nigel Russel's song, "The White Collar Holler," complete with awkward white boy Motown dance moves.

We were including "Rolling down to Old Maui" from the acapella set we were currently doing.

We had learned it from the singing of the great Lou Killen, and Stan got a bit too close to Lou's accent and phrasing for comfort. No matter. We all work other people's turf from time to time. David had shown again his real gift for harmony, and his part in the song really kicked it up a couple of notches.

"Oooh...we sound ever so manly," he said, in a fey voice one day at rehearsal

Stan was writing at a level we'd never seen before.

One day he brought a new tune into the shop.

"What key are the small pipes in?" he asked Grit.

"F. Sorry about that."

"No, that's okay. That was what I thought." And Stan tuned into DADGAD, capoed up to the 3rd fret, and began playing "Harris and the Mare," a quiet and disturbing piece about violence, and the nature of right and wrong, and the evil choices that are forced upon otherwise decent people.

Stan's guitar arrangement was breath-taking, particularly for a guy who tended to dismiss his own skills. By the end of that first reading of the song, Grit had figured out his part, and the drones lent even more tension to an already scary story. Jesus, they were evil sounding little bastards, those pipes. David and I added penny whistle and flute, and we had an arrangement.

Stan had written some music for a CBC radio drama / documentary a few years back, and one of the songs, "Delivery Delayed," had always stuck with me. It was a beautifully written and moving piece, which had got lost in the shuffle, and never made it into the stage show, partly because it just wouldn't survive in the bear pits we were playing.

I brought it up one day in the van on the way to rehearsal, and just to please me, I think, Stan agreed to give it a shot for the live recording.

It still stays with me, after all these years, as one of the supreme achievements of his writing career, both musically and lyrically.

We also worked endlessly on "The Flowers of Bermuda," and finally had to accept that it would either come all right on the night, or the whole thing would be a loud and nasty train wreck. It was a bear to play. Stan had typically written in so many dropped bars and lost beats, and the band in turn had added such weird pushes and accents that in the end the song was beyond our abilities to perform, and Stan's abilities to sing.

There was no place for him to take a breath.

Maybe we could have an oxygen tank on stand-by.

We would either get it or not.

Then there was "First Christmas," a gut wrenching tear jerker, or a maudlin bit of over emotional drivel, depending on one's taste.

I have heard both opinions.

I have held both opinions.

It had come about when we were hired to do a CBC radio Christmas show a year or so before.

It was the "Touch The Earth" annual holiday special, and Stan wanted to do something a bit different from the ordinary cheerful Yuletide fare. It was going to be taped in Sylvia Tyson's Rosedale home, later that week.

David and I turned up at rehearsal a few days before the taping, and Stan played us the song.

He had been working all night, and was just scribbling out the words to the last verse when we came in the door. He barely said hello, and we each got a coffee and waited as Stan made some last minute changes to the lyrics. Then he picked up his guitar and began sorting out the chords. He fumbled about a bit, stopped, and then tuned his bass E string down to make a dropped D tuning. He lit a smoke, took a couple of puffs, and then put the cigarette in the ashtray. He blew the smoke up to the ceiling and cleared his throat.

"Okay. Here goes."

The first verse put a lump in my throat immediately, taking me back to those lean years when Stan would have hitch-hiked back home with an empty wallet the day before Christmas Eve.

He had always made it back, however broke, and our little family would be together for a few days, but you knew there would be a time in the future, for whatever reason, when there would be a face or two missing on the day.

As he continued singing, I thought back to my childhood and the Christmases we had celebrated as a small family.

We grew up knowing we were poor.

We aspired to be working class, given the fragile nature of Dad's job market.

Every year was the struggle to get enough work to qualify for "Pogey," unemployment insurance, over the winter months. And even when he had steady work we still lived poor.

Strange off cuts of meat, like kidneys, liver and heart. We never had real milk to drink, only powdered skim milk. We wore homemade clothes and carefully preserved and repaired hand me downs.

Nothing was ever wasted or thrown out. We made over and made do. I don't think either Stan or I had new store bought pants or shirts until we were well into our teens.

This was okay mostly, as Mum was an expert seamstress. She made the suit Stan would one day be married in. But there were some awkward moments, especially for any kid who just wanted to blend in and look like everyone else at school. It took me many years to recover from the terrible Jodhpur Incident of my Grade 6 year.

There was never money for extras.

Christmas was particularly hard for Mum and Dad as they wanted desperately to make it special, but Mum's need to save against the future made it difficult for Dad to make the grand gesture that he so longed for.

When we were very young, gifts were largely hand made, and as Stan and I grew older what we found in our stockings and under the tree were mostly the things we needed to get through daily life.

Toothpaste, deodorant, a set of new guitar strings, (Black Diamond, or Mapes brand, in the white box with the extra unwound strings,) pens and pencils, new school note books, new socks, and underwear.

The budget being what it was, the whole ceremony surrounding Christmas became the gift. The house would carefully vacuumed and scrubbed and polished during the weeks leading up to Christmas until every surface shone, and on Christmas Eve the decorations which had been carefully packed away and saved the year before would be brought out and placed around the room. But all of that would happen only after Stan and I had been sent to bed.

When Stan was 2 years old and just becoming aware of Christmas being an event he had decided that the tree was one of his gifts, and he was heartbroken when it had to be taken down and removed from the little trailer where they were living. So the next Christmas, Mum and Dad made a little ceremony out of decorating the tree in secret and unveiling it to Stan on Christmas morning as being one of his presents.

And that tradition continued for both of us all the years we were at home.

We would be sent to bed early Christmas Eve, even well into our teens, and listen as our folks stealthily carried packages past our rooms and downstairs to begin the process of wrapping them.

A copy of "Highlights from the Messiah" would be put on the stereo turntable, and it was at that moment for me that Christmas began, as we listened to the overture, and the sound of Dad cursing as he struggled to drag the tree in from the garage.

This would be the tree which he had assembled earlier that day, using spare branches and an electric drill, with a holiday bottle of Myer's Planters' Punch to fortify him and steady his hand. Stan and I would have been lurking on the other side of the garage door, listening in and enlarging our vocabulary.

Christmas morning we would wake well before sunrise, but would have to wait until we were called, making our beds in the meantime, and washing and dressing.

No mad pell-mell dash down the stairs for us, but a careful and sedate side by side procession, holding hands so that neither saw the tree before the other.

And then tea was carefully served from the pot that was used only on this one day, while we sat and remarked on the lights on the tree, and the candles burning around the room, and the fire on the hearth.

340

We carefully avoided looking at what was under the tree, having been warned repeatedly as always, that it was going to be a "thin year" this time, and not to expect too much.

I don't recall the phrase, "I love you," ever being used in our family as we grew up.
But we never felt unloved.
There was just that elaborate code that you had to learn to know what was being said. The carefully embroidered handmade shirts, the home made toy Esso gas station I was given one year when I was maybe four, the hand-knitted socks, the smoker's toothpaste Stan began receiving when he was 16, and that strange year when Dad and Stan and I all had decided privately that what the other guy needed most in this world was a new wood router. This in spite of the fact that none of us had even the vaguest idea as to how to use one.
Stan was habitually broke too.
After he left home for the first time, ostensibly to go to school, money was a persistent problem and he would arrive home penniless, and have a furtive and awkward meeting with Dad in the basement, in order that he might bring something to the holiday.
Oddly, from my perspective anyway, he was perhaps the most creative and careful gift wrapper I have ever seen. His packages were extraordinary, the patterns on the paper always lining up perfectly, and the ribbons and bows arranged just so.
I remember coming down the stairs with him one morning. He was carrying what was to be his gift to me, a beautifully wrapped LP, festooned with bows and curled ribbons. He shrugged embarrassedly and said, "These camel hair coats are hard to disguise."
It turned out to be a great gift, a Mississippi John Hurt record, and a set of National finger picks.
   "Listen to this," he said, "and you'll know everything you need to play guitar."
My gifts on the other hand, looked like they had been frantically taped together while acting out the storm scene from King Lear.

The tree always had the same decorations from that first tree they put up in the trailer on Lake Avenue the year Stan was born.
The same battered lights, the same tiny mercury glass bells and balls, the same tinsel which had been carefully removed from the tree every year and saved, and that same old silver star made of tin foil that Stan was now singing about, at the top of the tree.
Jesus.
And now here it was in a song.

I was a wreck.

I looked across the room at David, and he was a mess too.

He was trying to busy himself with lighting a cigarette, but I don't think he could see very well. He kept dropping his Zippo and when he finally got it going the cork tip was ablaze and making a bad smell.

The song finished, and Stan looked up from the page.

"What do you think?"

He caught sight of the two of us leaking tears, and wiping our noses on our sleeves, and said, "Oh. Okay."

He took a hit off his smoke and drank a slug of cold coffee as we struggled to regain control, and said, "That's the first time I have played it all the way through. I've just been working on the order of the verses and figuring out what was going to be the tune."

He paused.

"So, it's alright?"

No, you son of a bitch, it was ripping us apart, but we had to learn the damned thing, didn't we? Not only learn it, but learn how to get through it without turning into jelly.

Oddly, when we started running the song down to get an arrangement, it was Stan who then started crying, and we all came to a full stop.

The cumulative effect of the whole thing got to him. He had been so busy with the creative process, initially, that he wasn't really listening. In the end it took us the better part of the morning to get to the point where we could all play the song without it looking like we were in some New Age sensitivity training seminar.

We still had to studiously avoid any eye contact, even after a couple of days, and after the recording at Sylvia's house David and I rebelled and point blank refused to allow the song into the band's regular repertoire. But it was coming back for this recording.

We worked out an improved version of "Barrett's Privateers," with a little more bottom to the vocals than the original.

Grit found a part to sing pretty readily.

Paul Mills, whatever strengths he may or may not have had as a musician, was simply unable to sing on pitch. He mostly doubled Stan's part, and was warned to stay well off mic and not sing too loud.

We had a new show stopper with "The Mary Ellen Carter."

Stan had written it over a weekend when we were playing at James Gordon's Carden Street Café, in Guelph. Nice little place, and we had agreed to donate a night or two to help the club.

All clubs have to struggle, but the Café was very small, and further hampered by staffing problems.

At the time we were there, Jane Siberry was the waitress, and ordering
a simple cup of coffee might take an hour, as she was perfectly capable
of listening to your order, nodding as if she understood, and then
wandering back to the kitchen, returning a few minutes later with a
notepad, saying, "What was it you wanted again?" and then, realizing
she had forgot her pencil, going back to the kitchen. She would come
back some time later, and write down your order on her arm with a ball
point pen, having lost both her pencil and pad somewhere along the
line, and then drift back to the kitchen once more. She would eventually
emerge with the coffee, and on the way over to the table be distracted
by the piano on the stage, and taking your drink with her she would sit
down and begin to work on a song.
One would sit there listening to big random augmented Joni Mitchell-
esque chords as the coffee congealed and grew cold beside her. Finally,
you'd give up and go back into the kitchen and pour the coffee yourself,
and upon returning to the room find that Jane had now wandered out
the front door into traffic to stare at the sun for the rest of the day.
Ironically, she wrote a song, which I believe had as the title, "If I wasn't
such a good waitress, I'd be famous by now."

It was just Stan and me this night.
David Eadie was ill, and it didn't make sense for him to leave his sick
bed for a benefit.
I was upstairs, warming up the fiddle.
Stan brought the bones of the song into the dressing room, and sat
down with a pencil, and pad of paper.
"I've got a really good one going here," he said, scribbling madly, using
the back of his 12 string as a table.
He had made no mention of it on the drive up to the club. We had
motored along, much the same as we always did. He was just a bit
quieter than usual, that was all.
There has been a lot of nonsense written over the years, by various
people claiming to be in the know, about how Stan could write these
breath-taking songs in one long sustained crack of creative lightning.
It's true, they did look as if they were arriving full-fledged, but he had
generally been mulling them over in his head for some time before
that, trying out and discarding lines, sorting out the arc of the story,
and then, once he found the key to enter the story, he would put pen to
paper.
He didn't keep a notebook, like most writers.
I have more than 40 of them, large spiral school notebooks, full of bad
scribble, and stained with coffee and blood and tears of shame.
And to be sure, every writer lives for those gift songs, the ones which

do arrive like a sort of divine dictation. But to suggest, as some people
have done, that he wrote so many of those extraordinary songs in one
stroke of God given inspiration is just stupid. He simply kept them in
his head.
None of which is meant to take away from the beauty, and the power,
and the poetry of what he accomplished. We just never got to see
the process, that's all, except in small glimpses, and only if you were
watching carefully.
My final proof for his method of writing is that he rarely had to learn a
new song off the page when he brought it in to rehearsal.
He already knew it, as he'd been carrying it around for so long.
Writing it down was mostly a formality.
But I digress.

He sat with the guitar, alternately writing, and trying out chord shapes,
and finally had the song put together. This was around the time he
had acquired his 12 string, and he wanted to find a new voice for the
instrument, some way to make it his own.
He'd told me that Gordon Lightfoot had developed such a definitive
sound with his 12 string that one risked suffering by comparison every
time one picked it up.
He solved this by almost never taking it out of DADGAD tuning, and
keeping the capo on the fifth fret. It gave the guitar an enhanced high
ringing modal sound. It was distinctive, and it was powerful and it was
his.
Put a 12 string guitar into that tuning and key, and then just try not to
sound like him.
Hard work, isn't it?

We ran through it a couple of times, him on 12 string, and me on my
6 string, to sort out the beginnings of an arrangement, and then went
down to do the show. The song went over gangbusters, right from the
start, with Stan for this first time partly reading the lyrics off the page.
We finished the first set with it, and we went out for a couple of beers
down the street at the "Chooch," the strip bar across from the train
station.
It was a bleak and nasty place.
The women all worked naked. Not "nude," a word which implies
some sort of artistic element to the acts they were performing on stage.
The bar had no more art to it than a meat locker or an autopsy room.
We kept well away from the stage, as the dancers had a bad habit of
coming down onto the floor and interacting with the clientele. Some
poor virginal first year veterinary student fresh from Morden Manitoba

would be nervously sipping his first beer, with his back shyly turned to the stage, and a dancer would quietly approach from behind, and suddenly swing a leg over the kid's shoulder and straddle his face, while his friends all fell about laughing.
We wanted none of that.
We were just thirsty, and knew enough by now to keep well out of range of the woman whose act consisted of shooting ping pong balls across the room. She was incredibly accurate and we were tired of having to keep our hands covering the tops of our glasses.
We drank up and went out the door.

We went back, and finished the show.
We were all standing around afterwards, chatting, the two of us basking in the glow of having done a good deed.
Someone noticed a kid across the street, climbing on top of our van.
"Is that your van being broken into?"
We immediately dropped our drinks, and crashed through the door, yelling "Call the Police!"
Dammit, our van. The little bastard. He saw us and jumped down and took off down towards the underpass.
I caught up to him and tripped him up, and he pitched forward, went down and skidded to a stop on his face. We grabbed his feet, and dragged him back up the hill to the scene of the crime, and commenced pummeling him into a jelly.
The poor stupid kid was just drunk and stoned, and had decided to smash the driver's side window, and take our CB radio. I should have been grateful, I hated the damned thing.
There was no need for us to kill him, which is what we could have done had we not been lucky.
As it was, we kicked nine kinds of shit out of the poor little wretch, only letting up when the police arrived.
"He was, uh, resisting us, officer."
The one cop wasn't worried particularly. He prodded the kid briefly with his foot, and rolled him over. "He's okay."
They took down the details of the incident for the insurance report, and hauled the kid off.
We went back to the club to continue the party, but the nice warm hippie glow had faded from the evening. People wouldn't meet our eyes, and the room was soon empty.

Back to the recording.
Rehearsals continued well, and the day of the show a large truck full of gear rolled up in the alley behind the Groaning Board.

Cables got snaked in, mics set up, and we did a long and stressful sound check.

It was the days before even the most rudimentary acoustic guitar pick-ups, and monitoring was difficult. Feedback was a problem, and we all just had to listen very carefully, and trust that the other guys would hit their mark.

Everyone wanted to be next to Stan so as to hear him better, and it fell out that David and I had to shift over so the two less experienced guys could get in close.

I was able to manage as I had learned to watch Stan's right hand, and read his lips over the years.

He tended out of necessity to sing very close to the beat, and there was very little use of legato phrasing when we played live.

Back in those days of analog recording, a reel of two inch tape didn't last very long, maybe fourteen minutes, and we had to devise a talk back system so we could be warned about how much time we had left.

We couldn't afford to lose a take because a reel of tape ran out.

We only had 4 or 5 nights to get it right, as I recall.

Anything could go wrong, and we were nervous and keyed up.

We had a good turnout for the shows.

We always did well there anyway, but with a live recording the place was mobbed. There were lines down the block.

The Groaning Board was owned and operated by a guy named Harry Stinson.

He looked like Gollum in a three piece polyester suit.

Tall and skinny with sunken eyes, a sallow complexion, and an Adam's apple the size of my fist.

He is now a sort of Donald Trump wannabe real estate mogul in the Toronto / Hamilton area.

Back then, he was just a wormy looking guy with a room to play, and a fly-blown kitchen that not even we would eat out of, even though it was free.

I was told some years later by the woman who worked the door that she was under standing orders to skim two bucks off of every ticket sold to our shows.

I have no real way of knowing if this was true, but as our pay consisted solely of the door receipts, it was unconscionable, if it was.

His explanation, according to her, was that the room was so crowded, we would never miss it.

And we never did.

At least we never knew about it, which to him, I suppose was the same thing.

Traffic and security in the club was becoming a problem.
Stan asked his old friend Joe Zizzo, to run interference for us.
Joe was a firefighter, and could be relied upon to keep drunks and
hangers-on at bay when we needed our privacy to regroup and re-tune.
He was a really good guy.
He refused to be paid for his help. "Just take care of my beer tab." he
said.
Joe came to us one night during the recording with a story from his
work that day.
Some poor sap had fallen 17 floors to his death while at a wild party in
a high rise apartment in Burlington. A passing tenant noticed the body
flattened out in the parking lot, and had called the cops. They couldn't
determine the time of death as no one at the party really remembered
seeing him there, let alone when he went over the rail.
The cop in charge ordered that his wrist watch be examined.
Surely that would determine the time of death. There was a huge crowd
of shocked and curious on-lookers standing by as a young cop went
over to the tarp and lifted the guy's wrist up and looked at it, and then
dropped it.
He fell over laughing.
   "Sarge!!" he shouted. "It's a fucking Timex! It's still running!"
This was at the time when Timex had a big ad campaign about the
abuse their watches could take.
   "Takes a licking and keeps on ticking," as the slogan went.

The dressing room of the club was in the basement of the restaurant.
You had to go down a long sweaty concrete corridor with rat traps and
Warfarin everywhere, and piles of roach powder along the walls. Pull
the door open, and there was a low dimly lit room with mirrored walls
and ceiling, and a large red velvet covered water bed.
   "What the Hell is this?"
David poked at it cautiously with his foot.
It wobbled and undulated in a malevolent and sinister way.
Stan said, "Leave it alone. You might wake it up and make it mad."
We were all reflected a thousand times in the mirrored tiles that covered
the walls and ceiling.
What went on here?
It looked like the waiting room in an alien sperm bank.
God only knows what disgusting purpose Harry was putting the bed
to, but much like Harry himself it was a cold and ugly and repellent
presence in the room, and we wouldn't go near it.

This room was where we retreated between sets to discuss how things had just gone, and to allow Paul to change his guitar strings. He had some weird body chemistry that killed strings in about 2 minutes and rendered them dead and lifeless. He was under strict orders to never touch either Stan's or my guitars.

The first night was washout, much as we expected, partly from our own jitters, and also because of the table full of wives and erstwhile girl friends who insisted on sitting up front, and who NEVER SHUT THE HELL UP.

The person I was with at the time, who considered herself a songwriter, was particularly obnoxious, and as an aspiring singer herself should have known better.

"Tell her that she's not to come back after tonight." Stan said, after the disaster. "She can stay the fuck home. I don't ever want her in the room again."

"I already have. I'm sorry."

I was feeling sick, partly out of embarrassment, and partly from the migraine that was like a hatchet in my skull. I couldn't see out of my right eye.

We were under tremendous pressure.

The next day Stan and I were sitting at a table with a local journalist, having a beer, and waiting for some technical glitch to be sorted.

The reporter looked at his notebook and then at Stan.

"The first record was a Maritime themed project, and the second was kind of cleaning up your back catalogue. Is there any theme or direction with this one?"

Stan cleared his throat.

I piped up. "Heroes. This record is about heroes."

Stan looked over at me, surprised, I thought, that I had the temerity to jump in and speak at an interview.

He said, "Yeah, pretty much. All the songs are about heroes, or people forced to act or perform beyond what they thought they were capable of. Anyone has the capacity to be heroic given the right situation. It just takes the right set of circumstances."

The guy with the notebook took all of it down, and thanked us and left. We were called up to continue with the sound check, and Stan turned and said, "Did I talk to you about that?

"No, Sorry I jumped in."

"No, not that. Did I tell you about the heroes thing?"

"No. It just occurred to me as we were sitting there."

"Huh. I didn't think anyone had noticed."

348

That night was a little better.

There were a couple of good takes, and the crowd had really gotten behind us.

The place was jammed. It was difficult to get to and from the stage, and the crush of drunks and hangers-on downstairs was getting unwieldy. Everyone wanted to see the water bed after we had mentioned it on stage.

Stan's friend and CBC benefactor, Bill Howell was particularly a problem. He was there every night to be supportive, but he was also staggering drunk, and loud. He could not be silenced, and his apparent need to whoop like a coke addled cowboy in the middle of songs was costing us takes.

It is him doing the prolonged and annoying "Yee-Haws" at the end of one of the songs on the final recording.

Stan said, "I'll have a word with him."

But Bill didn't have it in him to shut up, and he was constantly elbowing his way into the dressing room to offer advice and encouragement during our much-needed quiet time.

It was a ticklish situation. Bill had shoveled large sums of tax-payer dollars our way over the years, and we didn't want to hurt his feelings. Stan took Joe Zizzo aside, and gave him strict instructions that no one could come into the dressing room while we were there. Not wives, not friends, no one.

"See to it Joe."

Joe nodded. "I'll take care of it."

"No one gets down here."

Joe clapped Stan on the shoulder. "Right. Got it. No one's gonna bother you."

I think it was the break between the second and third sets, and we were down in our stinking lair, conferring, safe in the knowledge that Joe was on the other side of the door keeping the mob away. Paul was snipping off the ends of his new strings.

"Okay, are we all set? We okay? Ready to go?" Stan was rallying the troops. "Let's go up and hit it."

And he tried the door.

It opened out into the hallway about an inch, and then was slammed shut.

What?

He tried again, and again the door was violently pushed back in his face.

What the hell was this?

He tried again, and once more the door was slammed shut.

"Try an opening spell, Gandalf." David said, giggling.

Once more, and this time Stan really put his shoulder into it. The door opened maybe 6 inches and then was pushed inexorably closed.
We heard a voice from outside.
"No one gets in to see the band. Stan's orders."
It was Joe.
"Joe. It's us. Let us out."
"Stan says no one gets in. You can't bother the band."
"JOE. Listen to me. This is Stan. Open the door. We have to go to work."
"I don't care who you are, Stan says..."
Jesus. We were trapped in this evil smelling dungeon with Harry Stinson's DNA, and possibly one of his recently discarded exoskeletons. What were we going to do?

"JOE! IT'S STAN! WE CAN'T GET OUT! YOU'RE BLOCKING THE DOOR!"
"My job is to see to it that no one gets in..."
"JOE!!! LET US THE HELL OUT OF HERE!"
We were all yelling and pushing and battering on the door with our tiny fists.
It was no use.
"JOE! LET US OUT OF HERE. FOR CHRISSAKE!!"
"Stan says..."
There was a pause.
"Stan? Is that you? Where are you?"

Joe had been suffering from dehydration, poor lad, and had perhaps been over medicated for the condition. He'd been resting comfortably in the corridor, his back against the door, feet braced against the opposite wall, steadfast and true.
He had no doubt been merely resting his eyes, when he felt the door move.
He had braced his sturdy firefighter's legs against the pressure, and nothing was going to move him. Certainly not a bunch of flabby folk musicians.
It took a while to get it sorted.
We managed to get upstairs with Joe trailing along behind us, weeping and apologizing.
"It's okay Joe. We're fine now."
"I'm just so sorry. I fucked up."
Stan put his hand on his friends shoulder, and said, "It's really okay, Joe. You were doing a great job." Stan giggled. "It was just in the wrong direction."

350

We threaded our way up to the stage to do the last set.

Stan had another friend who wanted to do the cover photo, one of those fussy self-important hobbyist guys with 10,000 dollars' worth of equipment, and not the least idea of how to use it. He spent the week thrashing around the room with lenses and meters and bags of extra film hanging over his enormous gut, knocking over tables and drinks with his tripod, ruining takes, and generally being a pain in the nuts. After running through a couple dozen rolls of film he still didn't have a usable shot. We were "difficult to shoot," he complained.
We were ugly, granted, but none of us were being difficult.
We finally had to pose for the shot, while the audience waited and watched. And that is what you see on the cover, a blurry and out of focus photo that looks like it was taken through a window that had been wiped with a used diaper.
Stan's unyielding loyalty to his friends was a liability sometimes.

The second last night, we felt like we had a decent recording. It wasn't brilliant, but we'd safely got through all the songs we wanted to have on the album.
The pressure was starting to lift, and Stan said, "Okay boys, we have it in the can. Tomorrow night is just for fun. Just for us."
I think most of the album was from that final night. We all played great, freely, and with a sense of abandon, safe in the knowledge, real or imagined, that we had already nailed it.
I have a distinct memory of playing the last few high notes on "Delivery Delayed," at the end of the night, and feeling the migraine suddenly leaving my body.
I could see again out of my right eye.
For me it is still the best record we ever did.

CHAPTER 42

March Break

We had a gig at a small liberal arts college in upstate New York.
It was one of the last of the legendary college folk clubs that had made
up the circuit back in the day.
The club was run by a scarily quiet young woman with long dark hair
in a braid down to her waist, who lived in a huge Victorian frame house
off campus.
She wore horn rimmed glasses, and a severe and very plain hippie
dress.
Her clothes said Grant Woods' "American Gothic."
Her finishing school accent said Miss Jane Hathaway from the Beverly
Hillbillies.
Her general demeanor screamed Edward Gorey.
I think the house might have been one of the perks for her running the
place.
It was nothing a student could afford. It was a vast and spooky old
mansion, with heavy ancient furniture, and high, ornately decorated
ceilings, with a long corridor upstairs that led past a number of
bedrooms to our quarters.
We arrived at the house and introduced ourselves, and she very quickly
retreated upstairs after showing us the kitchen and the large iron skillet
full of oily semi-charred eggplant on the stove.
   "Dinner is included in your contract."
There was a silence. "This is dinner?" Stan said.
He was looking around the kitchen.
I think he was searching for the rest of the menu. A lasagna perhaps,
a pot of beef stew, or maybe a large ox turning on a spit. He loathed
eggplant, not just as a food but on a deep philosophical level.
   "I'm a vegetarian." she said.
   "Yeah, but we're not. What are we going to eat?"
She gestured to the pan of blackened goo.
   "This is dinner. I can cook some rice if you'd like, but I don't allow
meat in the house."

She looked pointedly at the pack of Rothmans in Stan's breast pocket.

"Or smoking either." And with that she turned and left the room.

We couldn't face the eggplant.

I turned the burner off under the pan, and we went upstairs.

Stan was muttering loudly about "Fucking hippies and their goddamned NUTS AND BERRIES." His voice rose unnecessarily as we stomped past her room.

We stowed our gear in the big bedroom down the hall, got showered and dressed for the show.

We were hungry and pissed off, and things were not made better by her revelation at the college a few hours later that today was the first day of Spring Break.

"It's going to be a thin crowd, mostly just whoever didn't go home or fly down to Fort Lauderdale."

"What about the public?"

"We don't advertise off campus. It's just for the students."

Spring Break. Jesus. This was great planning.

Our agent had struck again.

The three of us were standing by the van behind a large grey building done in the Frank Lloyd Wright meets Albert Speer style so popular on US campuses.

"Perfect," I said, "We're playing to the handful of losers who can't even get invited back home for the holidays."

David said, "Mom, Dad, I'm coming home for the Break. Sorry dear, we rented out your room. You'll just have to stay there."

Stan had his hands in his pockets, and a lit cigarette held between his lips.

He was staring into space and absently rolling the butt around in his mouth.

I was worried that he was going to commit mayhem. We'd had a string of bad shows and something was bound to snap.

This was probably no one's fault. At least no one he could immediately lay his hands on and strangle.

The poor spooky girl running the coffeehouse for the college couldn't be blamed.

She was probably grateful to have the hole in the schedule filled when our agent called.

And our agent was doing the very best she could.

It just wasn't a very good "best."

Stan leaned forward and spat out the cigarette, and ground the butt out with his foot.

He breathed out a lungful of smoke.

"C'mon. At least we're working on a flat guarantee. This is one fuck

353

up we'll actually get paid for."

Well there was that.

The gig was in a large common room near the cafeteria.

There was no stage, no sound system, just a large empty space at the far end by the windows.

Three young girls were sitting together, quietly reading.

There was no one else.

The dark haired woman turned to Stan.

"The sound system and the portable stage are in a closet down the hall."

Fine.

We humped the gear down from the store room, built the stage, put up the sound system and did a sound check, all the time being covertly watched by the three young women at the other side of the lounge.

At 5 minutes to show time we realized that this was it. These three young girls were our audience, at least until they went back to their dorm.

Stan went over to them and cleared his throat.

He had a funny smile, and his eyes were bright and amused.

"Hi, I'm Stan. I'll be your folk singer for the evening."

Eadie and I both walked over and stuck out our hands, and introduced ourselves as well.

It was a little awkward, and the girls were a bit nonplussed at the weirdness of the situation, but we were too depressed to care. We were at least amused at the idea of introducing ourselves to the three girls, like waiters at the Ground Round.

We got up on stage and Stan took a deep breath, raised his eyebrows and said, "Okay boys, show time."

And we launched into our set.

We'd had worse gigs. At least the chances were that we weren't going to have to dodge beer bottles or beat the crap out of anyone tonight. The three young girls weren't that big. I figured if things got rough we could probably take them.

Our host sat to the side of the room.

She became our entire audience about a half hour into the show, when the three girls packed up their books and papers, got self-consciously to their feet, and skulked out of the room, holding their books over their chests, heads down and shoulders hunched.

One of them turned at the last moment, and waved and called out.

"Thank you, it was very nice," and fairly ran out the door. We gave up at that point and came down off the stage.

Our host came over.

"You're supposed to do two sets, aren't you?"
We all just turned and looked at her, and she retreated and went out of the room.
Stan looked over at the "No Smoking" sign and hesitated for maybe a second, and then lit up.
I was packing up my fiddle.
"Nice of that one girl to say Thanks like that."
David said, "Must have been a Junior Leaguer. They never forget their manners."
Stan was sitting on the side of the low stage looking at his cigarette, and massaging the back of his neck. He said, "You know why Junior Leaguers hate group sex, don't you?"
"No."
"It's writing all those little thank you notes afterward."
We packed up our gear, and took apart the stage and the sound system, and stowed it all carefully back in the closet down the hall.
We were ravenous, and very, very, thirsty.
The dark haired girl came back.
Stan said, "Where can we get a bunch of giant greasy cheese burgers and some"...he corrected in mid-sentence, "LOTS of beer?"
"I wouldn't know. There are many bars downtown. But I don't drink, so I never go there."
Stan stood up, and in a W.C. Fields voice said, "You don't smoke, and you don't drink. Do you eat hay?"
"No."
He flourished his cigarette like a cigar.
"Not fit company for Man nor Beast then."
There was an awkward silence, and then the young woman said, "I hate Robert Heinlein. He's a crappy writer and a sexist jerk."
Wow. She recognized the quote. Good for her. I hated him too.
I said, "Well, we're going out for food and booze. Do you want a ride home, or do you want to come with us?"
To our astonishment, she did want to come to the bar with us.
We found a nice warm place on a side street down from the main drag. Whatever faults America may or may not have, it has some wonderful bars, and this was one of them.
That great first Faces album was blasting on the sound system, and there were a couple of pool tables. And in the back there was a well-stocked bar with an open grill where a cook was alternately assembling giant burgers, shaking wire baskets of thickly cut French fries, and putting out small explosions and grease fires with a hand held extinguisher.
Heaven.

We found a table and sat down.

A waitress went by with a huge cheeseburger on a tray, about a pound of fatty meat, on a big crusty homemade bun, with all the trimmings. Stan stopped her.

"Three of those please, with the works."

"Gotcha. Three cheese burgers for this table. Any drinks?"

"No." He held up his hand. "Listen carefully. I want three of those cheeseburgers. For me. I don't know what these other guys want."

Oh.

She looked at David.

"Can I take your order sir?"

David pulled his bangs down across his forehead, whipped out his black pocket comb, and placing it under his nose, raised his hand in the Nazi salute, and yelled "YES!...CRUSH POLAND!"

She gave no reaction.

She just stood there waiting, no doubt planning how much phlegm she was going to put in our food.

David replaced his comb, and he and I gave her our somewhat more modest orders. "Cheeseburger and a side of fries. Vodka and tonic." David said.

I ordered a burger as well, and some fries, and onion rings, and..."Um... Let me see, better make that two burgers."

Our host was sitting apart from us just down the bar.

The gig had gone badly, but it was over now and it wasn't our fault. We were prepared to forgive the dark haired woman.

We were even prepared to forgive the eggplant and be friendly, now that the humiliation of the evening was over and the prospect of food and booze was before us.

We asked her to join us at our table.

"Ever had Wild Turkey? Jack Daniels? What are you drinking?" I asked her.

I had once seen a picture of Keith Richards holding a bottle of Rebel Yell bourbon, and when I realized the bar carried it, had made the tactical error of ordering a large.

America has a different concept of what "large" means, and as a result I now had a tumbler of brown poison the size of a waste basket in front of me, and it tasted like something you'd use to de-grease engine parts or to get rid of internal parasites.

Never mind. It was going to do the job, and a few beers would wash away the taste.

The young woman didn't want anything beyond a modest glass of white wine, and not very much of that.

She sipped it quietly while averting her gaze as our food came, and we began ripping into it like a pod of great white sharks.

There were a lot of grunts, and slobbering noises and low moans for a while as we tucked in.

Stan was having some sort of ecstatic meat-induced religious experience, and there was a fine spray coming off his side of the table.

"Keep your hands and feet away from his mouth and you'll be fine," I said to the girl.

I was feeling light-headed, partly from relief, and partly from about a quart of raw whiskey on an empty stomach.

David, having quelled the initial pangs of hunger, was looking through the local newspaper, in search of the hockey scores.

It was Spring, after all, and it looked as if the Leafs might once again get within dreaming distance of the play-offs, before they inevitably foundered and broke his heart once again.

He found the hockey results, muttered to himself, and then savagely balled the paper up and threw it into a corner.

Stan, having reached the end of his second burger, had slowed down a bit with his food, but was still occasionally pounding the table and raising his eyes to Heaven as he worked on the third.

They were great burgers.

David picked up another section of the paper.

He was looking at the club listings now.

"Guys...that band from England is playing in town tonight. I wonder if it›s a late show. Maybe we could catch them this time."

For the past few weeks we had been reading the papers and following the progress of a trio from Britain, who were on a guerrilla tour of small clubs in the North East that year.

We had come close to seeing them a couple of times, being on something of a parallel course, and the word was they were good.

We felt a kinship with them, as they were a trio, even farther from home than we were, and were also playing a string of nasty shit-hole venues while traveling in a van.

David turned to the dark haired woman and asked if she knew where the club was.

She did, sort of, and tried to write out directions for us but it was no good.

There is often a disconnect between Men and Women when it comes to giving directions.

Hers involved a lot of unnecessary information, involving the colour of houses, where cars were parked, and where people we didn't know used to live, and why their relationships hadn›t worked out.

We gave up, and said it was okay, we could probably find it on our own.

She got up and left, after quietly placing an envelope with our pay

cheque by Stan's plate. Strange and intense girl, but what the hell, she had in fact paid us.
That was something that didn't happen every day. At least not for us.

Stan threw aside the napkin with the scribbled directions, and we gave up once again on the idea of trying to see The Police, and ordered more booze and discussed ordering maybe one more burger each.
The poor girl was starting to haunt me.
She was less like a concert promoter, and more like a religious novice, or a spiritual penitent of some kind. She was spooky and weird, but probably a good kid at heart. I wasn't feeling anything approaching attraction for her. It would have been like dating the ghost of Emily Dickinson. Still, I felt bad for her when I considered how lonely a life she must be living as the manager of a folk club on this campus.
Nonetheless, being an asshole, I began to construct an elaborate and mean- spirited fantasy scenario for the other guys, as we sat sipping our drinks, belching contentedly, and dabbing with our fingers at the crumbs left over from our meals.
I leaned in.
"So here's the deal. If we get back to the house and she has a candle burning by the door, it's a signal. It means she wants one of us to go to her room. If it's two candles, and she has incense burning, then she wants two of us to..."
I launched into a vulgar and unnecessarily detailed description of what her personal needs might be.
Stan put down his beer, looked at me, and said, "Jesus. That's sick. Where do you learn that kind of shit?"
Eadie looked at Stan.
"Two of us huh? I guess you're sleeping alone."
"Fuck off."
I continued.
"And if she has a bunch of candles, and she's burning incense, and she's playing a Doors record, then all three of us are gonna have to, you know, gild our loins, and do whatever needs to be done."
David said, "You mean gird our loins."
"No, I think she's an Arts Major. She's gonna want it to look, you know...nice."
"Pervert."
I waved him away.
"Hey, I'm not saying I like it, it just is what it is. She's a young woman. She reads poetry. She has needs."
We drove back to the house, and parked. It was dark and quiet out in the yard, under the bare trees. We walked up the steps and I opened the

door. There were a dozen or so large white candles, big ones, burning brightly on the tables and the stairs leading up to the second floor. The air was thick with Jasmine incense, and there was vaguely oriental-sounding organ music coming from somewhere. A hypnotic and sinuous and sinister melody.

I looked back at Stan and David.

"Told ya."

At that moment a voice boomed out.

"THIS THE END..."

Jesus.

My knees sagged.

The Doors.

How had I called it so precisely?

I had just been riffing back at the bar.

I never imagined that some sick scenario like this could actually ensue.

We crouched, wide eyed, like frightened rabbits for a few minutes, while the music wound along, waiting for the nerve to sidle past her lair.

We crept silently up the stairs, and the music and the clouds of incense and the heat from the candles got ever more intense.

We got to the top, and could see that her door was open, and flickering light was spilling across the hall rug.

I got on my hands and knees, inched forward, and poked my head around the door jamb.

David and Stan poked their heads around at the same time. We looked like the Three Stooges.

It appeared there were a hundred or so candles burning around the bed-chamber, reflecting in the glass of the tall dark windows.

The air was shimmering with the intense heat.

She was lying motionless on her bed, long hair loose and carefully combed out past her waist, wearing a long white cotton night gown, and staring at the ceiling, her hands clenched in fists at her side.

We all simultaneously drew breath and screamed like castrati, and then leaped up and clattered away like stampeding deer down the long hallway to our room, and slammed the door shut. We frantically piled guitars and suitcases and most of the furniture against the door, still screaming and crying for help.

David threw open the window and stuck his head out and began to yell.

"Help! We're all going to be murdered in our beds!"

We were falling about, laughing like idiots and piling more junk against the door.

The next morning there was no sign of her.

The house was empty, and the front door was wide open. The candles
had all burned down and guttered in the night.
Why the house didn't burn down too, I have no idea.
No note.
No eggplant.
Nothing.
We loaded the van and drove to Boston where we had a couple of
nights at Passim in Harvard Square.

I think it was David who found the Passim gig.
    "It's run by a crusty old New Englander, a guy named Bob Donlin.
He has no money, but he'll let us have a weekend."
In those days, Passim was a card and gift shop on Palmer Street in
Harvard Square.
You would walk past the iron railing down some narrow stairs and
through the door.
The cash register was to the right, and to the left there was a hot and
crowded kitchen.
Bob was a stern looking older guy. Heavy rimmed glasses, and thick
greying hair, with suspenders and a belt over a large and incongruous
pot belly.
His wife Rae Anne was a tall, thin sweet-faced woman with curly
brown hair, and wide glasses.
She was one of the truly kind people in the world, as was Bob. He just
spent more time trying to hide it. Over the years I grew to love them
both.

The club was a mess. The toilets were rank, and the dressing room
existed in name only.
It was a cramped and overheated hole behind the kitchen. The kitchen
fan vented hot greasy air into it, and it was accessible by a narrow
corridor filled to the ceiling with empty boxes, kitchen supplies and
bales of unopened mail. You had to turn sideways and suck in your
gut to get to the room. The slightest touch would bring the whole
mess crashing down on top of you in a cardboard avalanche, and you
wouldn't be found until tax time, which for Bob, was apparently never.
He was eccentric.
I didn't find out how eccentric till years later, when I discovered an old
picture of him, slim and shirtless and handsome, standing with Jack
Kerouac and a young Allen Ginsburg.
    "Is this you Bob?"
    "Yeah, that was me, back when I was young and in demand."
    "Holy shit. You knew Kerouac."

"Knew him, hell, I grew up with him in Lowell. I traveled with him. I'm one of the characters in "On The Road."
Damn.

Bob was generous and fair and quirky, and really, really stubborn.
There was a story of him booking a very young Bruce Springsteen into the club, thinking he was getting a solo acoustic act. Bob watched as Bruce and a bunch of other guys began loading drums and electric guitars and amps into the patio below the street, preparatory to bringing them through the French doors and onto the stage.
Bob hustled over.
   "We have a strict acoustic policy here. No electric guitars. No amps. No drums."
Bruce insisted that he was not going to do the show without the band.
Bob said no. He'd thought he was hiring a solo songwriter.
There was a line of people stretching down Palmer Street watching the confrontation and waiting to get in.
Didn't matter.
Bruce insisted he was not going to play without the band
Bob still said no.
Bruce said yes, and Bruce was the Boss.
But Bruce was not Bob. And in the end Bruce and the band went home, and about 1300 pissed off Springsteen fans wandered off into the night.

The stage was and still is nothing more than a wide-ish window sill, just below street level.
There are some windows, stage left, looking out at ankle level on Palmer Street.
Looking into the club from the street, it has always seemed to me to resemble a museum diorama of the "Urban Folk Singer at His Daily Task."
At the end of the regular working day Bob and Rae Anne would tidy up the kitchen, pull the card displays into a corner, and then drag stacks of chairs out of a cupboard and set up for the coffeehouse.
Bob would work the door and man the barely adequate sound system.
It was a Shure Vocal Master. Tube driven, with six channels. State of the art maybe 10 years before the club opened. There must be some old timers who remember that staple of the coffeehouse scene. The mixing board had an "anti-feedback switch," which if activated took out all the high end frequencies and made your voice sound like an Irish Setter singing through a rolled up sock.
Rae Anne along with a harassed young waitress would get the coffee and food going, and the audience would be let in.

The opener would go on and do a strictly regulated 25 minute set. God help you if you went over your allotted time. At about the time when Bob felt you had two more songs to do, he would leave his place by the cash register and sit across from Rae Anne, hands on his knees, staring straight ahead. As you finished your second last song, he would leap up and scuttle down between the tables, catch your eye, and show you a finger. One more.

If you were foolish enough to go over that time, you were hard pressed to get back into the room.

Obey the rules and he loved you.

Go over your limit, and you were consigned to the outer darkness.

I once watched Scott Alarik do an extraordinary twenty five minute set. He got up on stage, said hello, and began playing some random chords. He hit the crowd with a joke, and got a huge laugh, and then he threw out another, and another, and within minutes he had them on the ropes. After 20 minutes he had yet to do a song. He was just up there riffing, and the crowd was helpless, and Bob was going nuts. He couldn't give him the "one more" signal when he had yet to do a song.

Scott finally did sing one tune, and got off stage at exactly the 25 minute mark.

Bob was seething. "Scott. You know I like you, but tomorrow night if you go..."

Scott raised his hand, and said, "Bob, the one thing I know is that if you get an audience laughing like that, you'd be foolish to stop."

Bob stopped, took a breath, looked at him, and said, "Yeah, okay... you're right," and punched Scott on the shoulder and walked away.

Stan and David and I began to pack the place nightly, and Bob would change the house between shows.

The heat and the humidity were incredible. We didn't like the air conditioner because it blew an Arctic cold front across the stage and put everything out of tune. So we all just sweated.

Us and the audience.

It was wonderful to finish that first show, and climb out of the club as the steam boiled out of the door and up the stairs and into the street in clouds.

You would walk past the crowd who were lined up waiting for the second show.

You would be soaked in sweat, and the night breeze would be cool, and it would lift your clammy shirt away from your over-heated body. And as you walked down to the bar in the square, to replace the precious bodily fluids you›d lost, you could look forward to doing it all over again in an hour or so, and you felt like a prince of the city.

We were getting good. Not to mention cocky. I remember standing on that stage, night after night, soaked to the knees, waiting as Stan tuned up for the last couple of songs, knowing that after an hour and a half of hitting the audience with everything we had, we were going to unleash the final punch.
We would be exhausted ourselves, playing way past our reserves of energy, but we were going to pull out the stops one last time.
There's no feeling like it.

Bob and Rae Anne had been tending the flame for folk music in the Boston area during the lean years, after the Club 47 scene of the early 60's had faded and gone away.
Every morning they would arrive at the club, which they had restored to being a card and gift shop after the show the night before, and set up for the lunch traffic.
Do lunch, clean up, and continue with the gift shop until late afternoon. They would break for their own dinner, and then stow all the displays and ephemera away, set up the concert room, and let in the first house. Do that first show. Run the bills through the cash register, and the dishes through the washer, sweep up, and then let in the second show. And afterwards, clean the whole place for the next day.
Most nights they didn't get out before 1 or 2 in the morning.
The pace must have been terrifying. They weren't young people.
They were a sweet and funny and gentle couple. I often would watch them from the stage, sitting together, across from the kitchen alcove. Rae Anne would be dozing with her head on Bob›s shoulder and he would be sitting ram rod straight, with his arm around her, gently stroking her cheek, when he thought no one could see.
They were kind and extraordinarily generous to me after Stan died.
Bob was one of the New England club owners who hired me having never heard me play solo, at Widdie Hall›s behest.
Even in those later years, he ran a very tight ship.
I would get booked for a weekend which meant 2 shows a night, plus a Sunday afternoon matinee which would be broadcast live on the radio.
The Sunday shows were more relaxed, and well attended, and Bob became concerned with the noise being generated by the kids who were being allowed by their parents to wander the room during the concert.
We were just coming up to show time one afternoon, and Bob got up to introduce me, both to the people in the room, and the audience at home, listening on the radio.
　　"I just wanna say that we appreciate people coming out on a Sunday, and we welcome the kids as long as they behave and keep quiet, and don't interrupt the performance. But if you have a child here

with you, please keep it under control for the sake of the performer and the rest of the audience."

He paused and took a deep breath. His eyes were blazing. "I'm not running A GODDAMNED BABY SITTING SERVICE HERE."

And then he held out his arm and said, "Please welcome Garnet Rogers."

He once sat me down for an hour after one of my early solo shows, and honestly and carefully critiqued my act as it was then.

"Garnet, you're doing good songs. They're not your own, and you gotta fix that, but you're smart enough to pick good ones. And they're mostly serious. That's good too. People like serious. And you're funny. People like to laugh. But if you're making fun of someone make sure it's you."

He had seen pretty much everyone come through over the years, and he was worth listening to.

The Passim shows were made more exhausting by the fact that we invariably stayed with Rick and Lorraine Lee who were married then, out in South Natick.

They had a wonderful old rambling frame house on a large lot near a conservation area, and it was to be a second home for us in the years we played the Boston area.

Rick, now sadly passed, played banjo and piano, and Lorraine, now married to Bennett Hammond, plays dulcimer, and more lately harp. The Lees had a huge repertoire of original and traditional songs and they were both tireless and relentless after-hours jammers. So we would finish our two shows at Passim, pack up and drive back to Natick, where they would be waiting with more refreshments and a small sound system and a tape recorder, and occasionally other local musicians, like Bob Franke. We'd play and arrange and record songs until the wee small hours.

They were wonderful and generous hosts, and they were a big influence on us musically, as well as for the extra stamina we developed playing for eight to ten hours a day, and mostly on a liquid diet.

We now had a couple of days off before a three night run at another Upstate New York college. We were at loose ends and wanted to find somewhere cheap to hole up.

We wound our way across country in the mild spring air to Lake Placid, New York.

"Placid. Rhymes with flaccid," Stan said.

David spoke up from the back seat. He had a bad habit of correcting our grammar and syntax. "Actually, flaccid is pronounced with the first C hard, like a K. As in flak-cid."

Stan said, "Well, I wouldn't know. I've never had occasion to use the word."

It was a big ski town, and reason dictated that there would be cheap off season hotels there, now that ski season was over.

We pulled into a decent place, snagged a room, and went out for a rare night on the town.

We found a big après-ski place full of rich young kids, all tanned and fit, and drinking their faces off.

We did not belong here.

These people were all young and privileged and good looking.

We were only relatively young.

Stan and David sat down and I went to get us some drinks.

David wanted a gin and tonic.

Stan wanted a double scotch and so did I.

The bartender made the G and T first, and then grabbed a tall glass about the size of an ice bucket, tossed in some ice, and then began filling it with booze. He had poured in nearly half a bottle before looking at me and raising an eyebrow.

"Jesus. That's enough. Thank you."

He said, "You wanted two of those?"

I looked at the drink.

"Uh, maybe just a couple of straws."

I took the drinks back to our table and gave David his gin and tonic, while Stan and I shared the scotch like a couple of kids with an old fashioned milk shake.

"Just don't blow bubbles in it, okay?" he said.

We had been there maybe a half hour or so, and were just beginning to unwind, when David grabbed Stan's arm and said, "Listen."

"What?"

"There's that song I was telling you about."

Over the noise of the crowd we could hear a very tight and spare sounding band playing an urgent and loping song in a minor key.

Who was this?

He pulled us over to the juke box to see what was playing, and it was the "Sultans of Swing," by Dire Straits.

We were all immediately hooked.

It didn't sound like anything else we had been hearing lately, and as the song faded with that final astonishing guitar solo, Stan put a five dollar bill in the machine and punched in the code for it to replay.

In those days, 5 bucks bought you a whole night's worth of music.

There were some complaints after a while, as the song went into its tenth replay, and we had to beat a retreat. We were no match for wiry downhill ski bums. We made a note to look for the record the next day, went back to our room, and racked up for the night.

Next morning we drove over to the hill where the Olympic ski jumping had taken place.
I don't like extreme heights, and I was not one bit comfortable up here.
Still, we were standing at the top of the jump, mostly enjoying the view and the warm sun, when I noticed out of the corner of my eye that Stan was ever so slowly starting to glide forward, so slowly that you had to really look to see it. He was moving down the gentle slope that would soon become the precipitous drop that would then become the ramp that would propel him like a rocket into the spring air to land somewhere over the Vermont border.
He didn't seem to be noticing.
He was enjoying his smoke, and squinting into the bright morning light.
    "Beautiful day."
    "Uh Stan."
    "That was fun last night."
    "Stan."
    "We have to find a tape of that song."
    "Stan."
He was moving just a bit faster now.
    "Dave, you said they're an English band?"
Now he was picking up speed.
    "Stan, look at your feet."
    "Not just a great guitar player, great drummer too. I loved what he was doing on the high hat."
    "STAN!"
He looked around and then down as he started to slide alarmingly fast down the jump, fighting for balance and wind milling his arms frantically.
The soles of his thin leather boots were like a frictionless surface in the crusty spring snow. He might as well have been wearing Teflon.
David was laughing, and yelling, "Head down! Put your head down and keep your knees together! Tuck in!"
Stan was sliding down past me now, really picking up speed, and I reached out with my left hand while holding onto the rail with my right.
    "Grab on!"
He managed to just catch my hand, and pulled me violently sideways. I lost my grip on the rail, and the two of us went down and spun crazily in circles as we flew down the ramp towards the end of the jump.

We might have been going 40 miles per hour, and picking up speed.
We scrabbled and dug in frantically, and were just able to grab on before
the end of the ramp as we slid closer to the rail on the right, and were
finally able to stop ourselves from hurtling into space.
It took us maybe half an hour to climb, sweating and shaking, up to the
top of the ramp where David was leaning wiping his eyes, and barely
able to stand.
It was a long and silent ride over to Potsdam New York where we had a
three night run in the student coffeehouse.

The student coffeehouse at SUNY Potsdam was a small and smoke-
filled grey concrete room, which held about 50 or 60 people.
As usual, the show wasn't advertised to the general public, not that that
would have helped us in those days.
We were just playing to a noisy crowd of indifferent students, who
smoked and drank and yelled and puked pretty much non-stop the
whole night.
The TV with the hockey game was on stage over our heads, as always,
and as always we weren't allowed to shut it off, or turn it down, or as
David wanted, to turn it around so he could watch.
Three hour long sets a night, with a 15 minute break in between.
At the end of the night, we drove over to the motel room we›d had to
threaten the student organizer over.
She›d claimed there was no provision for rooms in the agreement, and
we insisted there was, although we couldn't prove it as our agent had
once again neglected to send us a copy of the contract.
In the end, as a compromise, we got the use of a grotty flea bag of a
room, with two beds, a sofa and a stiff green tangled DNA museum of a
shag rug.
It was a mess, even by our standards, and I elected to sleep in the van in
the parking lot.

The rest of the gig is memorable to me only for the fact that Stan
and David and I had one of those sudden vicious band fights that
erupt every so often, borne out of nothing more than frustration and
depression, and road founder.
We were sitting in a diner, having breakfast the next day, listening to
"Far Away Eyes" by the Rolling Stones on the juke box, and I decided
that David was eating his eggs in such a way as to deliberately annoy
me.
   "Stop that."
   "Stop what?"
   "Eating like that."

He opened his mouth and rolled a huge wad of eggs and ketchup and
fried potatoes slowly from one side to the other.
Then he swallowed and smiled.
  "Like what?"
  "You asshole. Stan make him stop."
And so on.
Words were said, and food was thrown, and Stan had to intervene, and
I think I was sent to another table to finish my meal.

I was sitting in the van with my guitar later that day, listening to "Le
Roi Renaud" from Pierre Bensusan's "Pres de Paris" album on the tape
deck, trying to figure out what key he was in, and David came out of
the flea pit room to resume our philosophical discussion.
I was fed up and simply slammed the sliding door closed and locked it
from the inside, hoping he'd get the message and leave. He went back
to the room and got his own van key, and re-opened the door and the
debate. Once more I slammed it shut and once again, he opened it. This
was stupid. It went on for a couple of minutes, slamming and opening,
until Stan, wakened by the continual rumbling and crashing of the door
came out and enacted closure on the debate.
We went back to the club and did the gig.
That night was no better than the night before, and we got into the van
afterwards and drove back to the filthy room.
During the drive something again was said, and then something
else, and one thing again led to another, and once again Stan had to
intervene, and presently we all three found ourselves in the parking lot
waving Buck knives at each other, and yelling about table manners, and
why it is important to not chew with one's mouth open, and the napkin
was there for a reason, God dammit.
It took a while to sort it out, and after we'd made up, we finished
the day by having a knife throwing contest in the motel room, with a
large target drawn on the stained paneling over the beds, using a half
finished lipstick we'd discovered behind the TV.
The couple in the next room who had been endeavouring to set a new
land speed record for noisy sex complained to the manager, and we
finally gave up and went to sleep.

Many years later I was playing an outdoor festival in Potsdam, and a
fellow came up to me and said "I was a student at the college years ago,
when you and your brother played there."
I looked at him.
Really?
He seemed so old.

How could he have been a student back then?

"What I really remember is that you guys never once let up. I was the only person listening out of all those noisy assholes, and you guys never once dogged it. You gave it your best every set, every single night."

Wow.

Well, thanks for noticing.

You never know.

CHAPTER 43

The Atlantic Folk Festival

Stan hit it perfectly, paraphrasing Hunter S. Thompson.
"This is what all folk festivals would have been like if the Nazis had won the war."
We had driven over night from Fredericton, to play at the Atlantic Folk Festival outside of Halifax.
We had stopped off the night before to see one of our favourite bands, Barde, play a show at Ye Olde Chestnut Inne.
We had met Barde a couple of years before at the Owen Sound Folk Festival.
We had never heard of them, and being the competitive dicks that we were, were somewhat miffed to see them on the bill as the Saturday night headliners.
This was the plum spot, and Stan and I lurked around the side of the stage to see just who these interlopers might be.
They were visually arresting anyway.
They looked as if they had just escaped from some institution and had dressed for the gig by running through back yards and pilfering laundry from clotheslines as they went.
The accordion player in particular looked like an unmade bed with a mass of dark curly hair spilling out of the bolster.
They started the first tune of their set slow, with a solo fiddle, and mandolin entering a few bars later.
Then the accordion, then a tin whistle, and then all hell broke loose and the place exploded in a mass of sound.
It was wonderful. The whirlwind lasted for maybe a half hour, and when it was over Stan had smoked maybe 20 cigarettes, judging by the butts surrounding us.
I was soaked in sweat, and my left calf had a cramp.
I had been dancing wildly in place. Well, perhaps "dancing" might be too generous a word. I looked as if I was being repeatedly tasered by an unseen being.
The audience was in shock.
We decided to forgive them for being so damned good, and they became friends, and we stole from them shamelessly.

Their show was so dynamic, so exciting and so over the top, and we did our best from then on to try to replicate the drama, if not the wall of sound they created.
They were comrades on the same insane road we had chosen, and we made every effort to see them whenever we could.

We hung out with the boys for a while, after their Fredericton gig, and then we filled the thermos with coffee and whiskey, and continued on to the Festival.
We arrived around 8 in the morning, and the sun was well up.
Someone should have been stirring.
It had rained overnight, and the grounds had been churned into thick stinking viscous goo.
We were creeping along slowly in the van, looking at the passed out revelers from the night before, as they littered the ground in one of the camping areas.
It looked like an accident at a nerve gas factory, or a tableau of Gettysburg.
There were bodies everywhere, lying face down in the mud, and no one was responding to us as we drove.
Stan was at the wheel, and David and I had opened the side door, and in slow rhythm were beating a saucepan and our coffee pot with spoons, and yelling,
    "Bring out your dead!" BANG!"
    "Bring out your dead!" BANG!"
a la Monty Python.
Everything was covered in mud, and everything stank of piss and shit and vomit.
There was no response to our yells.
We couldn't see a single living soul.
    "I don't like the look of this," said Stan, and wheeled the van out to the exit road.

We drove to the hotel near the airport to check in, shower and maybe catch a nap.
We made inquiries, and found out that an old friend of ours was already in the hotel, having checked in the night before.
We decided to look him up.
We were just what anyone would love to see at that hour. We were all wearing mirror shades and leather jackets, and none of us had bathed or shaved or slept for a couple of days.
We got to his room, and started pounding on the door, and yelling.
    "I KNOW YOU'RE IN THERE, YOU FILTHY PERVERT! COME OUT OF THERE AND I'LL FUCKING KILL YOU, YOU EVIL SON OF A BITCH!!!"
The noise was horrendous.

All along the hallway, doors were being opened. Someone would peer out and then the door would be hastily shut and locked.

We continued for some time, yelling and hammering and kicking the door.

The door opened a crack, and our old buddy looked out past the security chain.

He was a mess, sweating and disheveled.

"Oh Jesus boys...It's you. Uh, shit. Ah, listen, I'm kinda," He looked around over his shoulder. "Ah, Jesus. I'm kinda busy right now. Good to see you though. Let's uh...you know, maybe coffee later."

"Sure. Just wanted to say hi. Glad you're here."

"Yeah, yeah. You too."

And he closed the door, and we heard the dead bolt snap shut.

"Must have caught him on the can." Stan said.

We went off to our rooms for a shower and a quick nap, and I ran into our old friend a few hours later in the lobby.

He came up to me, grabbed me by the shirt and pushed me back into a wall.

"You evil bastards. I thought I was going to have a fucking heart attack this morning."

"Yeah. Sorry about that. It was stupid. But we've been up all night. We're not tracking so great."

"You rotten pricks. I ran into a flight attendant in the bar last night. She's getting married to a pilot today, and she wanted a last fling before the wedding. When you bastards started hammering on the door we thought you were her husband and his buddies, coming to kill me."

"Oh Jesus, no."

"Shut up." He continued. "And I was getting the blow job of a lifetime when you knocked. She nearly bit my cock off."

"Oh man. I'm really sorry. Ah Jeez. That's awf.."

He shook me violently.

"Shut the fuck up. That's not the worst of it. When I finally got rid of you bastards, I turned around and she was gone. She'd grabbed her clothes and jumped out the fucking window. Stark bloody naked, and left me hanging."

"Oh man. I'm really sorry. I guess we owe you one."

He pushed me away and let go of my lapels.

"Well I bloody well don't want it from you."

We decided to go back to the festival early that afternoon to see how things were shaping up, and get checked in with the organizers.

There were fleets of ambulances entering and leaving the grounds, their lights flashing, as we drove up.

We were waiting for a cop to wave us into the entrance.

I opened a beer and handed it to Stan.

"Ambulances, in large numbers. You know that's almost always a

bad sign."
Stan nodded and turned the CB on to the emergency channel to see if he
could get some news.
A knife fight.
Three wounded, one seriously.
Great.
We continued, and parked near the main stage.
As I got out of the side door of the van there was a guy standing next to
a tan Dodge Dart, and pissing through the open driver's window.
He was giggling inanely, and when he finished he zipped up, took a few
steps forward and then pitched onto his face and passed out where he
lay.
Stan and I decided to look for the performer's check in, and we left
David to guard the van.
We got directions, and followed down a long path through the woods,
where a guy was walking a pair of enormous Great Danes.
The dogs were crouching and shitting about six feet off the path, while
the guy stood upwind and looked innocently at the tree tops.
We found the performer's area, and got our badges and other bumf,
drank some coffee, chatted with a couple of the staff for a few minutes,
and went back to find the van.
On the way back we saw a couple, stark naked, just off the path, and
they were ardently celebrating their friendship, and thrashing around in
the undergrowth.
In their passion, they had rolled right onto the giant piles of Great Dane
shit, and were now both covered in a brown Harlequin pattern.
Stan and I moved well away from the path to give them a wide berth.
We were both a little shaken.
At this point in our lives we were used to seeing drunkenness, and
public nudity, and even occasional al fresco boinking at festivals, but
there was something perverted and out of control about this whole
scene.
There was an underlying feeling of sickness here.
Stan said, "Make damned sure you don't drink anything here that a
stranger hands you. This is just wrong."
    "No kidding."

We got back to the van, and let ourselves in.
It was stifling.
David was sitting hunched over in the back seat, pouring sweat,
and rolling a smoke from his package of Drum tobacco, and looking
anxiously out the window.
    "You okay?"
    "No, I'm not okay. Have you been seeing what is going on here?"
    "It's an oven in here. Why don't you open a window?"
He finished rolling the cigarette, pinched the ends off, and put it in his

mouth. "I'm not opening a window." He picked up his lighter and fired it up. "Not here. Not in this place. Not for any money."
He had a point. We weren't arguing.

We were huddled, smoking and sweating and drinking piss warm beer in the locked van when Brookes Diamond, the artistic director, came up and banged on the windshield with the flat of his palm.
We all jumped in alarm, and then got out of the van, toweling the sweat off our faces.
"Hey boys, welcome to the Atlantic Folk Festival. Looks like we're going to have a good one."
A good one.
Jesus.
He left us and we got back into the van.
The afternoon wore on, the sun came out, and some friends and family started showing up, and we ventured out of the van, and cooled off.
We were looking at the main stage.
It was enormous, built on a scale none of us had ever seen.
"Who the fuck designed that? Albert Speer?"
"Jesus it's high. What's that, about 40 feet?" Stan said.
"Dunno. Why would they build it so high? What's the point?"

It was late afternoon, and steam was coming off the rain-soaked ground
We were due to go on, and as we went up the stairs we could get a better view of the area in front of the stage.
It was filled with thousands of mud -encrusted bodies. Some just lying motionless in the sun, others milling about, staggering like they'd been shot, or auditioning as extras for a Zombie movie.
A few were engaged in a shoving match at one side of the crowd.
On the other side, an actual fight had broken out, and a couple of beefy security guys with bright orange vests were wading in, swinging sticks as the crowd looked on and applauded.
Everyone was swilling back the beer as fast as they could, and struggling and floundering through the thick stinking mire.
The grounds were covered with thousands of empty booze bottles.
Trash was piled everywhere, along with discarded clothing, lost shoes and used diapers.
This wasn't a folk festival, it was a staging of "The Garden of Earthly Delights" by Hieronymus Bosch.
We saw a large yellow Hertz rental truck at the back of the field, behind the audience with a banner that read, "Albert County Liquor Pigs."
"Maybe it's a book club." said Stan.
We tuned up and started our set, and made no headway at all.
With this crowd we had decided that subtlety was not going to work, so we mostly just ran through our loudest and most drunk-friendly bar set.
We started with a couple of chanteys and then went into "Fogarty's

Cove."

No one paid the slightest attention.

By this time in a show, even the rowdiest bar crowd would at least be turning towards us wondering what all the noise was about, and yelling at us to shut up, but this bunch seemed to lack even the slightest curiosity about what we were doing.

The audience was just drinking and pushing and falling and puking and yelling and cursing in front of the stage, those who weren't already face down in a coma.

We weren't even there.

News helicopters were circling over the crowd.

The air was throbbing with the beating of the rotors.

It was a perfect counterpoint to the scene below us, but it was making it impossible to hear on stage.

I looked over at Stan and David.

"You guys know how to play Ride of the Valkyries?"

Stan was trying to tune his 12 string, but the heat and humidity was making it fold up like rubber.

There was a prolonged pause as he turned away from the audience and held the guitar to the side of his head, trying to hear. I don't know why he was bothering. For all anyone could hear we might as well have been miming.

Something, desperation maybe, made David step up to his mike and say, "We'd like to dedicate this next song to the Albert County Liquor Pigs."

With that the whole place exploded into a riot.

The herd of art lovers in front of us started screaming and howling and jostling and trying to climb onto the stage.

Now we knew why the stage had been built so high. Safety.

It was Bedlam.

David and I backed away from the front of the stage, in horror and disgust and fear.

They were screaming incoherently like animals, piling up on top of each other like army ants, trying to swarm over us.

I was yelling frantically for security. There was none.

They were busy beating six kinds of snot out of some hillbilly at the side of the crowd.

"Why the fuck did you say that?" I yelled over to David.

"I was just trying to connect."

"Well don't ever do that again."

These animals were going to rip us to pieces and sodomize the remains.

Stan was...I have no other word for it... magnificent.

He put down his guitar and stalked over to the front of the stage where the herd was scrambling frantically to embrace us to their collective bosom.

He stood over them and looked down, with his hands on his hips.

He waited a beat and the crowd paused in their mad scramble to the stage.

He then spoke quietly into the mike.

"Are you the Albert County Liquor Pigs?"

"YYYYEEEEEAAAAAHHHHH!"

Stan moved a bit closer, leaned forward, and again, in a very quiet voice, said,

"Do you want to become the Albert County Liquor...PORK?"

They all stopped.

Silence.

I could see some of the revelers looking uncertainly back and forth at each other.

"Well? DO YOU?"

A small voice came out of the now frightened and cowering rabble.

"No."

And then still in this terrible deadly quiet voice, he said,

"Then stay the Hell off my stage."

I don't know how he did it.

There must have been something in his eyes that they recognized, and were very afraid of.

I had never seen it myself, and didn't want to see it. Not ever.

They all started meekly climbing back to earth and resuming their places in the primordial ooze.

We finished the set, left to a smattering of applause, and went back to the van.

Unlike most festivals of the time, there were no workshops here.

It was just a series of half hour to 40 minute concerts on the main stage. With no workshops to keep us busy, there was nothing to do but stand around and drink beer and try to keep well away from the drunken mob.

There was little or no shade to relax in on the site and only a few food concessions selling deep fried lard and grilled road kill on a stick.

And instead of a craft section on site, selling tie dye and trinkets and T shirts, there were only a couple of vans with spray painted murals on the sides, depicting large breasted warrior women waving large swords and having orgasms on Harleys.

All they were selling was bad smelling black biker leather, martial arts gear, and stainless steel and leather cock rings, in sizes ranging from Peter Pan to Godzilla.

Buffy Sainte Marie was due to go on in the evening.

She had been in and out of trouble with various governments for years due to her opposition to the Viet Nam war, support of First Nations' rights, and other causes.

We were under strict orders that there be no one in the performers' area when she arrived.

It wasn't ego.

She was simply afraid of getting killed.

We vacated the premises, and watched from a distance as a couple of white stretch limos came into the backstage area, and laagered in a circle.

Two huge black men in dark suits got out, one with an automatic pistol, and the other with what might have been an Uzi, and they quickly swept the place of stragglers.

They went back and got Buffy out of the second car, and she was hustled into the trailer that served as a dressing room.

She came out an hour or so later and took the stage with a large band. She was wearing her hair very long and loose, and she was dressed in white buckskin hot pants, and a white buckskin vest with long fringes. No shirt, and her white doeskin boots came up to her thighs.

She looked less like a political activist, and more like a pole dancer in Miss Kitty's saloon.

The band kicked into a funk influenced instrumental vamp, and Buffy began to stalk the stage in her six inch heels and announced that we were all present at the birth of a new art form. Something never seen or heard before.

"Welcome," she said, "to Pow Wow Disco."

The band stopped, and then the drummer and the bass player began laying down a massive slamming groove together, and then the horns and guitar kicked in, (they were a killer band,) and then Buffy began to sing in her native tongue.

We were having a beer with some of the members of the Albert County Liquor Pigs, and we all agreed pretty much that it sounded a lot like Parliament Funkadelic with Yoko Ono on vocals.

That weekend I was being made to bunk in with a junior member of an Irish band. A band whose name I've since lost.

"O' Tempora O'Mores," or something. "Sodom and Begorrah." I don't recall.

It happened that way, sometimes, and you just had to put up with a stranger's disgusting habits for the duration of the festival, as opposed to the disgusting habits of the guy you knew.

Whereas Eadie and I mostly spent our off hours on the road flossing our teeth, and watching bad movies on TV, this guy had an unnaturally gregarious streak.

He was dragging a different girl back to our digs every few hours.

I found it awkward.

There must be some sort of rules of etiquette for being in the same room as a couple having sex, but I have never been able to find any sort of literature on the subject.

Is it okay to read?

Watch TV?
If I order a pizza, am I obligated to get enough for everyone?
Was I supposed to stand by with towels and hot compresses in case
someone got a cramp?
As a consequence I was spending even more time than usual at the bar,
if only to get drunk enough to pass out convincingly.
This guy was an animal, an extremely horny and undiscerning animal,
and my liver and I were beginning to tire of the pace.

"How do you keep them all straight? Don't you forget their names
the next day?"
"Ah no. You see, I have a system. I write their name on a slip of
paper, and put it in my shaving kit. Next morning I get up for a slash,
and there it is, and I can go back out and say, "Morning Veronica, or
Molly, or whatever. Makes me look good."
"They like it when you remember their name."
"Oh yes, the ladies love a gentleman."
The weak link in the system was that he never seemed to clean out his
shaving kit.
I crept past his bed one morning and went into the bathroom to look for
a couple dozen aspirin.
He'd had a particularly noisy and vigorous encounter the night
previous, and his new friend was evidently still buried somewhere in
the sweaty and DNA soaked tangle of sheets, unless, of course, he had
learned to snore and fart in harmony with himself.
There was no aspirin to be found, but there were dozens of little slips of
paper with scribbled names in his shaving kit.
I don't normally like to disturb another person's stuff, but this guy was
getting on my nerves, and when I was done it looked like someone had
held a ticker tape parade.
It made for an awkward morning.
The third night, I came in and he was just starting negotiations at the
foot of the bed with yet another girl.
What the hell was he doing? Holding tryouts for a softball team?
So, down to the bar, which was not really what I wanted as for once I'd
had enough to drink.
I had a couple of beers and then the bar closed.
I still didn't want to go back to the room, so I went down to the now
deserted hotel pool and fooled around in there for a while, but I
don't swim, and as drunk as I was I knew that I was flirting with an
embarrassing death. I had no wish to be found floating face down the
next morning, looking like Ophelia in threadbare jockey shorts.
I decided maybe a sauna would be good.
I was ingesting a lot of poison, and sweating some of it out might make
me feel better, or at least make room for more.
I stripped off and wrapped a pool towel around myself.

I had been sitting there for some time when the door opened and Buffy's two bodyguards came in.

They were both in the 300 pound range, and maybe 6 and a half feet tall. They were both naked except for the shoulder rigs and guns they were still wearing, and suddenly the room seemed very small.

Offhand, I can't think of a more enclosed and claustrophobic place than a sauna, with two enormous naked gym rats with automatic pistols and other intimidating weaponry.

They were friendly enough, though, and the meeting went as well as could be expected, given the kind of equipment they were packing.

I finally gave up, and went back to the room where our hero was still busy with the hurly burly of the chaise lounge.

"Don't mind me," I said, brightly, and quickly brushed my teeth and fell into bed. I turned out the light, and pulled the pillow over my head.

They continued their explorations, and presently I realized that in my haste to get to bed and pass out I had neglected to pee.

Oh Dear.

This was awkward. The lovers across from me didn't sound as if they were anything like nearing the finish line yet. This could be a while.

I lay there and desperately tried to think of anything other than my distended bladder.

This was terrible.

I had an idea.

I took a look from under the covers.

Damn.

The waste basket was out of reach.

I could neither reach it to grab with my toes, nor was I confident of the accuracy of my aim if I tried to hit it from a reclining position on the bed. I knew I could eventually get there, but I would need a few seconds to range in on the target, and that wasn't fair to the cleaning staff.

Don't think of water. Think of a desert, the sand, the dunes, the Nile River. Oh shit.

This was getting dire.

Get it over with, you priapic little bastard. Who the hell cares about her needs?

There was a pause in the action on the other bed. All was suddenly very quiet.

Were they done? There hadn't been the usual muffled screaming.

What was going on?

I heard the girl's voice. "Did I do something wrong? Did I hurt you?"

"No...I'm fine. It's just ...ah..."

"Then what is the matter?"

"Nothing. Nothing's wrong."

"Let me help."

"No, it's...uh."

"What are you trying to say?"

"This has...uh...this has never...uh, never happened to me before."

The lying hound.

I sat up and swung my legs over the bed to stand up and walk to the bog.

"He's lying to you miss. He said the same thing last night."

I went into the bathroom and slammed the door.

Outside I could hear the girl shrieking with laughter.

I came out much relieved, some minutes later, and she was gone, and the young guy was sitting on the side of his bed glaring daggers at me.

We were leaving the grounds the final day, and noticed a group of outlaw bikers were holding up the line into the festival.

This didn't look like security, it looked more like a shakedown. Just hassling the citizens.

Stan got on to channel 9 on the CB, and radioed in to the office.

"Are you guys using bikers for security out here at the gate?"

"No. They aren't part of the festival. We'll be right out."

Stan said, "Never mind. It's okay, we got it." He hung up the mike.

The smart thing to do would have been to let the security guards or the cops deal with it, but we were tired and hungover and in a seriously bad mood from this hellish weekend.

And we weren't smart.

One of the bikers had his head inside the front window of a car and was sticking his hand down the driver's blouse, fondling her breasts.

There was nothing she could do except sit there, crying in fear and embarrassment.

On the other side of the car, another tough guy was holding a purse upside down and shaking the contents out onto the ground.

Stan reached under his seat and pulled out a tire iron.

I reached under my seat and pulled out a tire iron.

David reached under the Cadillac seat and pulled out yes, a tire iron.

We each of us kept a tire iron under our seats in case of...um...a tire emergency.

Stan also had a "tire bat," an 18 inch long piece of hickory which had been turned on a lathe with an iron sleeve bolted to it. He had picked up at a truck stop in Gary Indiana. God only knows what its real purpose was, but Stan kept it under his seat for times like this.

You never knew.

"Let's go boys." Stan said, and snapped his cigarette butt out the window.

First things first. Bikers hate having people mess with their bikes.

You don't touch a bike without permission.

I think the first they knew of us was when Stan smashed the gas cap

and all the lights and pretty bits of trim off the one bike, and then kicked it over onto the side of the road where it began to leak gas.
The bikers turned around and Stan held up his lighter.
The bikers left the car and started towards us.
Stan clicked the lighter and looked meaningfully at the bike.
The bikers stopped.
It was then that a couple of RCMP cruisers came in with their lights flashing and skidded to a stop.
The cops leaped out and ran the bikers to ground, and had them cuffed in a matter of seconds.

We sidled back to the van with the tire irons behind our backs.
We got in and stowed them under the seats, and drove sedately past the cruisers and off the site.
We were about twenty minutes down the road and still feeling pretty shaky and sick from the unused adrenalin and the threat of violence, when Stan lit a smoke and cracked open the no- draft window.
He sucked in the smoke and then exhaled.
   "Nice to watch professionals at work. I kind of wish the cops had come a little later though. I was looking forward to seeing just how tough bikers are."
Jesus.
I was relieved the cops had come.
Stan had had his typical berserk reaction to bullies, and David and I as much as we hated fighting, had simply been following the rules of the road.
You always have the other guy's back.
But messing with bikers was a bad way to die.
Stan said, "Dave, do me a favour and get the percolator out and build me a coffee, will ya?"
David was smoking a cigarette in the back seat and looking out the window.
He looked sweaty and shaky and miserable too.
He leaned forward, opened the cupboard and pulled out the coffee pot, filled it from a jug of water, and plugged it into the lighter socket.
Stan said, "And maybe throw a big slug of Bailey's into it too."
Stan was in a great mood.
   "Yeah...I really would have liked to gone a few rounds with those apes."
David was spooning Nescafe into the little aluminum basket.
He had the cigarette between his teeth and was squinting and turning his face away from the rising smoke.
   He said, "It's okay boys. It's a long road. We'll have lots more chances to be stupid."

CHAPTER 44

The Kindness Of Strangers

It was January, and we were on a side street two blocks west of Lark Street, in Albany New York. We had been parked in front of the church which housed the Eighth Step Coffeehouse for about 4 hours. We were huddled in our sleeping bags, saying nothing to each other, just reading and smoking cigarettes and waiting. Outside, the plows had piled the snow nearly to the tops of the parking meters, and the temperature was around 10 below Fahrenheit. We had no money, no food, and about a half a tank of gas. We were freezing, and yet didn't dare turn on the motor to run the heater, in case we didn't make enough at the gig that night to fill up and get out of town to the next show. There were any number of warm and inviting restaurants to sit in along Lark Street, but we barely had the price of a cup of coffee between the three of us.
We could only sit and wait. We'd had a string of really bad gigs, and weather cancellations, and were now at the end of our resources, our funds and our tethers. And this show didn't look like improving things. Every hour or so Stan would wrestle his way out of his sleeping bag, get dressed in his parka, and climb out of the van to walk around the block to a deli to call the presenter on the pay phone. He would get the answering machine, lose his dime and come back to the van. We had soon run out of dimes.
We just had to wait.

Stan started the van up to clear the wind shield and warm us up a bit, carefully watching the gas gauge. The sun was going down behind the apartment buildings across the park to our west.
I looked at the door to the church. Still no sign of a volunteer or a janitor, or anyone.
It was now fully dark, the wind had picked up, and the thermometer was falling fast outside and inside despite the heater. Nobody spoke. Stan turned the motor off, and we sat in the dark not even able to read now, and waited.
Another hour went by.

We were beyond making a joke of this. We were in real danger here.
We had nowhere to go, and a person could die in this weather.
I looked out my window at the side mirror and saw now that a couple
of people were crouched in the stairwell outside the door of the club,
trying to keep out of the wind. Was this the beginnings of an audience?
I got out and walked over to where they were all standing, shivering
and gasping and stamping their feet.

"Are you guys waiting to get into the club?" There was a chorus of
muffled voices answering yes. This was good. The gig actually existed. I
went back to the van to report and to wait some more.
More people arrived. We now had about a dozen huddling in the cold,
but it was a quarter to 8 and there was still no sign of the presenter.
Presently a woman came trotting along the street and elbowed past the
small line of people and opened the door, and everyone pushed in. We
got out of the van and went down the stairs and ducked inside.

There was a cold and grim and dirty basement room with a scattering of
metal chairs and stained plywood tables. A low stage maybe four inches
high was pushed up along one stone wall. Ancient white paint was
blistering from the damp and falling off the walls onto the floor in piles
like eczema flakes.
Bare bulbs were hanging from the ceiling for ambience.
It looked less like a folk club and more like the sort of place where a
group of men might gather to empty their pistols into some poor wretch
tied to a chair while yelling, "Long Live Mother Russia."
The organizer was running frantically around the room turning on the
furnace and filling the coffee urn with water. She came over to me.

"I'm sorry. I'm so sorry. I forgot there was a club tonight."
"You forgot?"
We were nearly frozen.
I couldn't feel my feet, or anything for that matter.
My testicles had given up the ghost and I had no realistic expectation of
ever seeing them again.
"You FORGOT?"
"I said I was sorry."
Oh well then, that makes everything better.
"It's almost..." she looked at her watch..."Actually, it is officially
Showtime, could you guys just set up and play as soon as possible?"
Stan bristled.

"It's not our fault you're late. We'd like to warm up and at least get
a coffee."
"I know, I just need to get things started here. We can't run past
1030." So we brought our gear in through the snow, and hauled it down

the stairs, and set it up, and did a quick line check as the audience... all 12 of them, sat bundled in their coats and scarves and waited for the coffee to be ready. We went into the furnace room to change clothes.
It was very quiet.
I could hear the strange lowing sound that those large coffee urns make as they heat up, and some prolonged coughing from one of the audience members.
The furnace which had briefly been on, was now silent save for the ticking and clanking of cooling pipes.
I remember standing next to the furnace, ankle deep in ashes, and shivering as I tried to tie a knot in my neck tie with dead fingers. We couldn't look at each other.
We weren't going to make enough to get out of town. What the hell were we going to do? The organizer stuck her head in the door of our dressing room.
    "Ready to go?"
It was Showtime. We went out and did our two sets in front of what looked like the lost members of the Franklin Expedition. No one, including the volunteers, had taken off their outer clothing.
We then packed up, got changed out of our stage clothes into our cold weather gear and re-loaded the van. The audience had disappeared into the night. They all had seemed vaguely embarrassed by the scene.
Try as we might they couldn't be coaxed into any sort of enthusiastic response, although in all fairness, it is hard to clap with mitts on. The organizer handed Stan an envelope and then hurried off into the night, leaving a lone volunteer to lock up. We'd made about 40 bucks. Not enough to fix our current situation or make a run for home, but enough to allow us to sit in the all night restaurant on the Thruway and drink coffee and not be thrown out for loitering, and maybe, if we were careful, to make it to the next gig, if we didn't die of exposure in the interim.
We were coming out of the basement, having made a last sweep of the room to make sure nothing was being left behind when a man on the sidewalk approached Stan with an envelope in his gloved hand.
What was this, a summons?
    "I'm here as a representative of the audience," he said, rather formally.
    "Huh?"
    "We all held a meeting and decided you guys were too good for this room tonight."
    "Huh?"
    "You guys gave us a great show tonight, under terrible conditions. We decided you deserve better treatment than this, so we held a

collection, and this is for you." He held the envelope out to Stan.
Stan looked at it.

"What?"

The man continued.

"And there are three rooms waiting for you at the Tom Sawyer
Motel, and they're courtesy of the audience too. We all hope you can
put this behind you and come back some day."

We were dumbfounded. We had never heard of anyone doing such a
thing.
We all stood there on the sidewalk, our breath turning to clouds and
being whipped away by the wind. We were already starting to shiver
uncontrollably. The guy offered the envelope again, and Stan reached
out and took it, out of reflex more than anything. Given a chance to
think he might have tried to turn it down out of pride. For myself, I had
no pride left.
Stan stammered his thanks, and David and I joined in, and we watched
as the guy who had just helped save our lives turned and walked to the
corner, where he gave us a wave and disappeared. We got into the van,
and Stan tore open the envelope and counted the money.
120 bucks.
Jesus.
We were going to live.
We were going to eat. Stan started the motor, gunned the engine and
turned the heater to MAX, put it into gear, and pulled out onto the
street.

I could see the tears on his face as he made the turn past the park. I was
snuffling too. I looked back at David.
He was looking out the window and wiping his cheeks.
Christ, we were all a mess.
None of us could speak. We drove to the Tom Sawyer Motel, and there
were three clean and warm pre-paid rooms waiting for us.
Hot showers. Clean sheets.
There was even a bar, and we decided that we could afford a modest
celebration along with our first meal of the day.
We ordered food.
Drinks arrived.
Stan held up his Old Bushmills.
We all carefully clinked glasses. We didn't want to spill any.

"The kindness of Strangers," he said, and we tossed it back and
ordered another round.

I can't imagine that those wonderful sweet people knew just what they did for us that night. What that gesture represented to us beyond the considerable chunk of cash.
It went far beyond just saving us from a night shivering in a rest stop on the dark and windy I-90 highway.
We all got up the next day feeling like our luck had changed, that we had turned a corner.
Things were going to be okay.

As it turned out, the next night we played Phil Ciganer's little club, "The Towne Crier," a few hours down state, to maybe 8 people, and nearly froze to death getting there, in spite of Stan having wired a large piece of cardboard to the front grill of the van to help the radiator generate more warmth to the heater.
Phil is a lovely guy. Sweet, generous and quietly funny, albeit with a perpetual look of impending doom on his face as his beautiful little club always seemed to be on the point of folding up. It was located deep in the woods about an hour north of New York City and was nearly impossible to locate, either by performers or the audience. Phil once told me a a story about Pierre Bensusan taking a cab from LaGuardia airport to where he thought the club might be, and he and the cabbie spent nearly 4 hours on an fruitless quest driving through miles of narrow forest lined roads before he finally ended up at Phil's house, while the audience waited at the club some miles away.
Our gig was notable mostly for the fact that Claudia Schmidt had decided to hang around after her show the night before and do an opener for us, and then later join us during our own show to sing harmony.
Once again, the audience huddled in their seats, wrapped in their coats and scarves and mitts, while packs of ravenous wolves prowled and snuffled at the door outside the club.

CHAPTER 45

Road Food

Johnny Cash once wrote that people asked him "what was the difference between touring back in the 50s and touring now"? He said,
"Back in the 50s you couldn't get "Extra Crispy.""
I wouldn't know.
We never ate at KFC, except once.
Even as poor and broke and desperate and hungry as we habitually were back then, we avoided the obnoxious fast food chains that greeted us on the Golden Mile that was the arse end of every little town we drove into.
We once got dragged against our wills into a McDonalds in Edmundston New Brunswick, by our then bass player, the notorious "Klag." He was addicted to this stuff, and enthusiastically guided us through the menu choices. In the end I ordered a Big Mac. I took a brief sniff, and then I chucked it out the window of the van into the parking lot. A seagull swooped down on it, got a better look at what it was, and then checked in midair and flew away.
Someone told me once that Colonel Sanders used to drive around North America and check out his little franchises to make sure they were upholding his quality standards.
He would totter in with his polished black cane, and wearing the trademark white suit and the string tie, and introduce himself and then order a meal.
Then the kindly old twinkly eyed gentleman would sit down and wait for the manager to bring his tray over. As the story went, one time in the franchise near Hamilton, he picked up a drumstick, looked at it, sniffed at it, took a cautious bite, then put it back down and delicately wiped his mouth with a paper napkin.
The manager was waiting nervously behind the counter as the Colonel got to his feet and picked up the tray and carried it back.
"How was everything sir?"
The Colonel was quiet for a bit, chewing and swallowing the last of his chicken, and then he picked up his cane and began furiously lashing

the tray, the counter, and the cash register into pieces, finally breaking the cane into shards and throwing it across the counter where it hit the menu board and stuck quivering like a javelin.

"IT'S JUST FUCKING CHICKEN FOR FUCKSAKE. HOW COULD YOU FUCK IT UP?"

Our experience with Colonel Sanders was limited to the time we were turned back at the US Border in Detroit, in spite of having current visas and all the correct paperwork.

We had been on our way to a sold out show at the Old Town School in Chicago.

"Why are we being refused admission?" Stan asked.

The border guard looked at us from behind his mirrored aviator shades and said, "We don't have to tell you. Now get out."

We tucked our tails between our legs, and drove back across the Ambassador Bridge and went through Canada Customs, who had some searching questions as to why we had only been out the country for half an hour. We then got onto the 401 back towards home. On the way out of Windsor, Stan pulled over and got a Family Sized bucket of chicken.

When Stan was stressed he ate.

He got back into the van and put the bucket between his thighs and began wolfing down deep fried breaded chicken viscera and tossing the bones out the window.

"Want some?"

Ordinarily I wouldn't but breakfast was now long in the past. Yesterday morning, actually.

It smelled okay.

"Sure."

About 40 minutes later the two of us were pole vault vomiting at the side of the highway. It was windy out there in the flat fields near the Chatham exit, and we had to take care to stand well away from each other and not to hurl into the wind.

That was it for us and "Bucket in the Sky."

Finding a decent meal on the road with a reduced or almost non-existent budget meant long hours of slowly driving around some small town, and carefully sussing out the little grease pits and ramshackle cafes that lined the road.

Was the parking lot full? That might be a good sign, although on closer inspection it might just be abandoned cars or rubber neckers at a crime scene. And we found the myth about the best food being where the truckers ate was a lie. Truckers as a rule were in the last stages of toxic bloat, their faces mottled and ruined after years of bolting down cheeseburgers with a side of fries, bad coffee and a handful of white crosses for dessert.

Sometimes you just have to trust to luck and walk in.

We went into a place on the Indiana/Illinois border once, just north of Valparaiso, and sat down at the counter. We were in a hurry, so all three of us ignored the menu and just ordered coffee and cheeseburgers. The cook went over to the large black griddle and spat on it to see if it was hot enough. We were out the door in seconds.

"Cancel the hot dog." David said, quoting the old joke.

It was sometimes a good sign if there were a couple of police cruisers or ambulances parked outside. It suggested that the the owners had at least a passing acquaintance with the Board of Health rules. And with the cops there the van would be safe while you ate. Or it could mean something else. I once walked into a well-advertised "Family" restaurant in Osseo Wisconsin, to find the EMS crew working on a massive fat guy who'd had a coronary while eating his Sunday eggs and bacon and sausage and pancakes and homefries and ham special. The crew had torn his shirt open to the waist and were applying the paddles, and yelling "CLEAR!" and there would be a loud BAM, just like on TV.

The cops were standing there with notepads, taking statements from the other people at his table, while the waitresses ran about the room with trays piled high with eggs and a dozen kinds of fried meat, and the other diners held up their cups and called for coffee and more gravy. I was going to walk out, but I had actually stood in line to get in and now had an investment in time, and the next place might be just as crowded. I got a seat at the counter. I could at least turn my back as they carried the body out on a gurney, and the light was better to read the paper.

When my own "Heart Healthy" breakfast special arrived it was on a platter the size of a trash can lid, and the only thing that differentiated from the rest of the menu, and which made it "Heart Healthy" was apparently the slice of tomato, and the sprig of parsley on the side.

The best thing out there in the early days with Stan was the chrome diner.

There are still lots of them in places like New Jersey, but in other parts of the country you have to really look for them now. They are often ornate Emerald City looking places now, usually in the center of the town, and almost always run by a Greek couple and and a dozen or so of their dark haired kids. The menus are the size of the Sunday New York Times and are covered in plastic.

But back in the day, you could pull off say, the Taconic Parkway in New

York State, and in almost any town there would be a tiny aluminum clad diner with a counter and maybe ten or twelve narrow varnished wooden booths. The menu was printed on mimeograph paper, or posted above the counter. They were almost always clean and safe, and when you ordered a turkey club sandwich, the odds were that you wouldn't be facing turkey loaf, that slurry made from factory floor meat scraps, which was then baked and pressed into loaves. There was in fact, an actual roast turkey sitting on the table in the kitchen. There might even be dressing on the side if you ordered the hot turkey sandwich.

The menu changed a bit as you headed South.

Once we got into Pennsylvania, we were of course confronted with "Scrapple."

We'd heard of it. Stan and I had both read a biography of W C Fields, and apparently he'd had cases of it sent to him in Hollywood. It was all he ate. We decided it must be a delicacy.

We were in a diner on Market Street in Philly, and Stan ordered eggs, sunny side up and a side of Scrapple, with home fries and toast.

I didn't have the nerve. The name alone put me off. It sounded like the term for an obscure form of wrestling, as practiced in small isolated villages in Cumbria, and which involved a lot of grabbing of sweaty testicles.

It arrived and he took a tentative bite, and quickly put his fork down and reached for a paper napkin. He spat into it, carefully wiped down his tongue, and took a long drink of water.

"That good, huh?"

He shook his head and shuddered. "Never again." And this from a guy who a few hours later happily bought and ate a Polish sausage on a bun from a street vendor near the Liberty Bell. The sausage was swollen and grey, and looked like the aftermath of an assembly line accident.

It had been floating in murky oil slick- covered water that likely hadn't been changed since the Nixon Administration. Stan loved it, and would have ordered another, but wanted to save some room for a couple of giant mustard -covered street pretzels, and the inevitable cheese steaks at Jim's on South Street later.

The South had nothing to do with the Mason -Dixon line. You were in the South the first time the waitress called you "Hon," and grits arrived on your plate whether you wanted them or not. And you never did. I personally gave up eating paste in Grade 3. Or 4.

Travelling as a trio, it always seemed to work out that one of us would order something seemingly innocuous from the menu, and while the other two were served perfectly acceptable meals, the third would be confronted with some small disaster. Even if it was just draining the last of your coffee and finding that the dishwasher had missed the large wad of chewing gum from the previous user, or discovering the Band-Aid in your BLT.

We pulled into a joint off the New York Thruway once in Batavia and ordered, and when the meals came David's "Chicken and Biscuits" bore no resemblance to anything one might call food.

We were all omnivores, and not picky. David in particular was famished, having not eaten in an hour or so. Even so, he couldn't face it. Stan and I were hoeing into our dinners. David was just sitting there, lost in the utter despair that comes with realizing your one big meal of the day, which you had been so looking forward to, and needed so badly was something you wouldn't throw over a fence into a pig sty.

He looked for the waitress, but she was busy.

He picked up his fork and poked at the edge of whatever it was.

Maybe it tasted better than it looked. What the hell, give it a chance.

Stan paused in the middle of wolfing down his turkey club, looked over for the first time at what was on David's plate, and said, "Jesus. Looks like someone drained an abscess."

We met David outside a few minutes later where he was standing, smoking furiously and kicking stones across the parking lot.

Sometimes you lucked out.

We were somewhere in Vermont or New Hampshire one afternoon and we spotted a diner at the side of the road on the left. It was just your average little rural diner, except this one had an extension built on the side made to look like a small nuclear cooling tower. Someone around here had an odd sense of humour. We liked it already.

We had to stop. Stan hit the brakes and made a wide drifting turn into the gravel parking lot. He stopped, turned the motor off and we all got out and went inside.

There was a skinny middle aged guy behind the counter, wearing a baseball cap and a clean white apron.

"Help you boys?"

Three turkey club sandwiches, with fries on the side and coffee.

The guy got busy. It was midafternoon, and we were the only customers. We sat at the table and sorted through the pile of newspapers that had been left on the counter. David checked   to see how far the Leafs had dropped down in the standings today.

The sandwiches arrived and we realized this guy was an artist. It wasn't that they looked particularly different from your average run of the mill sandwich. Not at first glance. But this guy had found exactly the correct ratio of perfectly toasted bread to dark turkey meat, bacon and tomato and lettuce filling. Not to mention mayonnaise. It is a delicate balance, and can take years of discipline and careful and dedicated study to perfect. This guy had evidently spent his early years under the strict guidance of a master somewhere in Tibet, and now started his day with several hours of meditation and prayer and vigorous calisthenics before firing up the griddle. We ate every scrap within a couple of minutes, and then sat back as the guy came over and refilled our coffees.

"Anything else?"

"No, thanks. That was wonderful."

He gathered up the plates and took them away.

"Good. Glad you liked it."

David was looking at the big menu board over the counter.

The guy had gone back behind the counter and was polishing the green enamel on the Hamilton Beach milkshake mixer.

"Excuse me."

"Yeah?"

David said, "You look like the kind of a guy who'd make a pretty good meatball sub."

The guy paused with the rag, and looked very intently at David.

"I make the best meatball sub."

This sounded like a challenge. In my head I was hearing the theme from "A Fist Full of Dollars."

David said, "Well I guess we'll just have to see then, won't we?"

Christ. We'd just gorged ourselves. We had a gig to get to. C'mon Dave. Time's wasting.

Stan was busy picking his teeth with one of the little cellophane tipped toothpicks from his club sandwich. He looked at his watch. "Make that two."

What? Jesus.

Okay then.

"Make it three."

CHAPTER 46

10 Pound Fiddle

Stan and David and I had a gig at the 10 Pound Fiddle Coffeehouse in East Lansing Michigan.
Nice place, run by good and kind and dedicated people.
Consequently, I have no idea how or why we got hired there.
Stan and I had played there maybe a year before as a duo. It was during that weekend that I bought my first electric guitar. We were in Elderly Instruments and I had decided I needed an electric.
I had two choices near my price range.
One was a cheap Japanese copy of a Fender Telecaster for 150 dollars.
The other was an actual Fender Telecaster from 1954, for 400 bucks.
    "Jesus. They want 400 dollars for a used guitar? This other one looks brand new and it's way cheaper."
God, I was a rube.
If I had bought the original one it would now be worth in the neighbourhood of 15 to 20 thousand, whereas the cheap copy I went with is still worth maybe 150 bucks.
Live and learn.
In any case, I could barely afford the cheaper guitar. I had to give the store 50 dollars up front and they very kindly took a couple of postdated cheques for the balance.

Anyway, we were back at the club with the trio.
Arrangements had been made to house us all at a commune where a couple of the volunteers from the club lived.
Our hackles went up a bit upon hearing that. We'd had enough of dirty and incompetent Hippie Shit by this time
    "A commune? We're staying at a commune?"
The name of the place wasn't inspiring either.
    "Yes, it's a nice place. It's called Rivendell."
    "Rivendell? We're staying at a goddamned commune called Rivendell?"
The three of us were standing in the parking lot of Elderly Instruments,

393

where our volunteer sponsor, Carrie Potter was to meet us.
Stan was incensed.

"Great. Granola and nuts and berries for breakfast. And yogurt.
Yogurt, for Chrissake. It's spoiled milk with a fancy name. And there'll
be dogs too. Mutts wearing red kerchiefs around their necks, and
there'll be nowhere to smoke. They're probably all vegetarians too. Even
the damned dogs."
David wasn't happy either.

"They'll have a snotty little brat named Moonbeam or Travelling
Apple running around the place, and the cat box won't have been
changed since forever."
Stan was standing with a cigarette in his mouth, head down, hands in
his pockets, and kicking a rusted half inch bolt around the parking lot.
I wondered where it had come from.

"Is that off the van?"
Stan looked up.

"Eh?"

"Is that bolt from the van?"
He bent down, picked it up and looked closely at it.

"No." And he wound up and drilled it over the bushes next to the
parking lot. There followed a distant metallic clang and a shout. Oops.
It was a measure of just how pissed off he was that the sight of a loose
metal fitting near the van had not sent him crawling immediately
underneath to see if it was something precious and irreplaceable.
Stan was probably trying to figure out the logistics of getting us all into
a cheap motel, but the budget just didn't allow for luxuries like Motel 6.
It was 20 bucks we just didn't have.
We were stuck.
Carrie arrived, and seemed like a friendly and pleasant person, which
only made us more suspicious.
She hopped into the van, and we started to drive to our digs.

There were in fact, she told us, some ground rules we had to obey at the
Rivendell Commune.
There was no smoking. A relief for me, frankly. David was taking full
advantage of the availability of cheap unfiltered Camels at the moment.
They smelled kind of nice in the open air, but in the confines of the van,
and at the rate of maybe 5 an hour my clothes were beginning to smell
like they'd been dug out of a Turkish dung heap.
I could use the break.
It was, as well, a vegetarian household, but in our honour they had
unbent and made a special second lasagna with meat for dinner.
Okay, that was nice.

Above all, it was a seriously no nonsense Feminist house. Most of the residents were women.

There were a couple of men living there, but they were more highly evolved than usual, and one of them later took us aside and made it clear that we were to be very careful about saying anything that might be considered offensive.

We should have been okay with this.

We weren't completely stupid. Feminism was a common sense Human Rights issue.

We supported it in theory. Mum would have kicked our asses had we not.

We all just had a problem with taking instruction, and being told to rein in our offensive and testosterone driven humour didn't sit well.

Given any situation where the smart thing to do was to simply shut the hell up, we were all seized by a Tourette's like tendency to make the most inappropriate jokes, just to push people's buttons, and assert our independence.

In short, we were idiots, and doing the "smart thing" wasn't in our repertoire, so this could be a little tricky.

We arrived at the commune, a large airy late Victorian frame house shaded by tall maples.

It seemed clean and well organized, with a complete absence of the usual overflowing cat box smell.

Carrie got us settled into our rooms.

"The bathroom is down the hall."

"Do we have to sit down to pee?"

Great start, Stan.

She affected not to hear, and left us to unpack.

"Supper will be ready in an hour or so." she said over her shoulder.

We went downstairs, and David found the TV in the living room. There was a college football game on, and he settled in to yell obscenities at Michigan State, and hurl couch cushions and carved African fertility dolls at the screen.

Stan and I went out on to the porch so he could have a smoke, and I cracked open a couple of cold beers, and handed him one.

One of the male residents came out, introduced himself as Charlie, and sat down on the railing next to us.

"So...you okay living in a house like this? All women?" Stan said.

Charlie shrugged. "Yeah, its fine. We all get along, everybody pitches in and does their share. And it's a cheap way to live."

"Does the Women's Lib thing get on your nerves?"

"No. Actually I consider myself a Feminist, I couldn't live here otherwise. It's a pretty politically correct house."

"Do they make you sit down to pee?"

Jeez Stan, leave it alone.

"No, but I do insert a tampon into myself once a month, in solidarity with the women, just to understand what they go through." Stan coughed out a lungful of smoke, and bent over from the waist, and started choking.

Charlie got up and drifted back into the house, while Stan braced one hand against the railing, and with the other took off his glasses and wiped his eyes.

"I've never heard anything like that. Jesus Christ"

"Me neither. Holy shit."

Dinner was served.

There was a large salad, and vegetarian lasagna, as well as the promised meat lasagna for the carnivores. Lots of good food, warm garlic bread, big jugs of red Gallo wine. It was all delicious, and the folks around the table were friendly and interesting.

"We had a home birth here recently," someone said.

"Really? Did you all watch?"

"Not all of us. But it was wonderful. It's great to have a baby in the house."

Someone else spoke up, "We're going to have the Placenta Party next week. Too bad you're going to miss it."

"Placenta Party?" What's that?

"We kept the placenta, it's in the freezer, and next week we're going to thaw it out and we're going to make it into a dish, and cook it and eat it. It's a ritual in a lot of cultures, a way of connecting to the Life Force." I could tell by the reverent way it was said that "Life Force" was in capitals.

"You ...eat ...the ...placenta?"

The other male resident of the house spoke up.

"The placenta is the only animal protein that doesn't die in fear and pain."

"Yeah, but, you know, the placenta."

I couldn't get my mouth to work. "You eat... the ..."

Jesus.

I looked over at Stan, and he was having trouble keeping it together. He was dying to say something and was obviously wrestling with the better angels of his nature.

The conversation lagged a bit after that, and we mostly kept our heads down, and tried not to think about what we'd just heard.

Presently, Charlie spoke quietly to his neighbour.

"Speaking of the placenta, when I went down to the freezer to get the ground beef for dinner, I couldn't find it. A lot of the labels on the packages have fallen off. Everything is mixed up and mis- labeled. It's all just brown paper packages now. It's a mess."

He leaned in and lowered his voice further. "God only knows what these guys are eating."

There were three distinct clanks as our forks hit the plates.

I turned to Charlie.

"You don't know what kind of meat we're eating?"

"Not really, but I'm sure it's all perfectly good. It's all meat. Organic too."

Stan got up very quickly, nearly overturning his chair, and grabbed his cigarettes and lighter, and went out to the porch. David and I sat there, looking at our dinners, and saying nothing. The lasagna on our plates looked very red suddenly.

The residents of the house continued eating, and passing bread and pouring wine, and chatting quietly.

Stan came in a few minutes later, and sat back down.

He poured out a large tumbler of wine, and drank most of it down.

He looked at his plate, and then with the air of Sydney Carton stepping bravely onto the tumbrel, took a deep breath and picked up his fork.

He was hungry, and we had been raised to never waste food.

The gig went fine.

It was in a small wood paneled meeting room at the University.

There was a usable sound system and we only had a bit of flak from the sound bloke over David's bass amp.

We had a good turnout, and the audience liked to sing along.

We had been getting some regular airplay on local college radio by then, courtesy of Bob Blackman who worked at Elderly Instruments.

He had become a great supporter of us and had struck up a regular correspondence with our Mum in the course of her handling the mail order sales.

It was a great feeling to launch into the chorus of a song and have the audience already know the words. By the end of the show we were all feeling pretty chuffed and we still had a post-show party to look forward to.

Lansing had a huge population of folk musicians; fiddlers, and banjo players and guitarists, and most of them seemed to have come back to the house to drink beer and play and dance.

I was once more out on the porch, trying without success to get out of earshot of the army of banjos and bodhran players and clog dancers.

I was perched on the rail, drinking a local brand of beer called "Widemouth," in the warm darkness when Charlie once again appeared at my side.

He offered me a large kitchen glass filled with a pale straw coloured liquid.

"Try this. I make it myself."

I was disinclined to trust anyone in this house at this point.

"Yeah I make that stuff too. But then I flush afterwards."

"No it's okay. It's Moonshine. I have a still in my room, and it's perfectly pure."

He took a sip to show me it was safe.

Well. Okay then.

I took the glass.

"Thanks."

I held it up to the moon to take a closer look.

It was absolutely clear, and when I took a sniff it had a slightly sweet fragrance, like fresh cut hay.

This was the real thing. Wars had been fought for this. Men had died for this. Whole continents had been conquered because of this. Scotland hadn't fielded a decent football team since the 60's because of this.

I was in for a rare treat.

I looked at him.

"This place is kinda...you know... different."

"Not really. It's just you guys will apparently believe anything anyone tells you."

He was standing looking up at the night sky, with a bland smile.

"Huh?"

"That was just plain run of the mill lasagna you had for dinner tonight."

"Oh, you bastard. You mean...?"

His smile broadened.

"And the tampon?" You don't...?"

"You guys are so gullible. Don't tell your brother."

Wow. Game, set and match for the hippies.

We clinked glasses and I tossed back the drink, and my head exploded.

My dear departed friend Hamish Imlach once said, "I think I'm allergic to leather. Every time I fall asleep with my shoes on I wake up with a headache."

Next morning was tough.

I woke in something of a panic, not knowing how I had got where I was, and unable to feel or move my legs. It was a relief to discover that I had simply gotten them so badly tangled in the sleeping bag that it had cut off the circulation.

I was laying on my back, gingerly feeling my skull, trying to locate the marlin spike which some helpful soul had apparently used to nail my head to the floor so I wouldn't fall off the planet during the night.

The door opened, and Stan stumbled into the room.

He kicked my feet and then sat down heavily, and said, "C'mon. We gotta get out of here. It's nearly noon and we have miles to make."

Noon? Jesus. Where had I been?

He put a coffee next to my pillow.

"Ah God. Thanks."

"How do you feel?"

I lay with my eyes closed for a moment, hands still gently fingering my head, assessing the damage.

"I think there was definitely a second gunman on the Grassy Knoll."

"Well, get that coffee inside you and get moving. We're running late."

"Are those clog dancers still here?"

"What clog dancers?"

"Never mind."

He got up and tottered out the door like an old and broken man.

I managed to drink the coffee by carefully turning my head and pouring it into the corner of my mouth.

Jesus.

Whole parts of my brain were missing back to grade 3.

Charlie, the evil bugger, was making weaponized bathtub gin under the roof of this innocent looking hobbit house.

We managed to drag our sorry asses up and out of the house.

We said our goodbyes to the nice people, and got into the van and very carefully and quietly closed the doors and started it up.

None of us were ready for breakfast yet, so we worked our way out to Highway 69 in silence.

We were all feeling pretty seedy, and more than usually ashamed.

Hippies. We had been thoroughly gamed by Hippies.

People who lived in a house called Rivendell, for Christ's sake, had kicked our asses.

We were somewhere near Battle Creek when we stopped at a donut shop for take-out coffee, and we all began to feel slightly more human.

There is always that thin line with the kind of apocalyptic hangover we were all suffering.

The blood stream wants nourishment, but the stomach is having mostly second thoughts, not just about food, but maybe about leaving the current host entirely and finding a kinder, less abusive partner.

I felt like I might at least be able to eat and later barf up a poached egg if things continued to improve.

David spoke up from the back seat.

"Not a bad gig last night."

"Uh huh."

"Nice people."

"Yeah. Pretty good folks."

"We should maybe send the folks at Rivendell a little thank you gift for putting up with us."

"Yeah. We could do that."

"How about if we stop at a grocery store later, and pick up a case of Placenta Helper?"

By the time we reached the stink of Gary Indiana, we had managed to successfully eat and hold down some eggs and toast, and were all feeling a bit more lively.

I remembered the cassette tape Bob Blackman had slipped into my hand the previous night.

"I want you to hear this," he'd said. "I played this on my show last week and have been getting a lot of hate mail from listeners. There is a lot of outrage."

He didn't get any chance to explain further, as we had the gig to do.

I took the tape out of my shirt pocket and slipped it into the cassette deck.

"What's this?" said Stan.

"Dunno. Bob gave it to me last night and said we should give it a listen."

"Okay."

I turned up the volume.

There was a meandering instrumental intro and then some earnest and pretentious male voice intoning over it.

Stan said, "What the hell is this? The Moody Blues?"

And then a high and wobbly female voice started up.

It was the exact tune and some of the lyrics from Stan's "Northwest Passage," which we had released that year.

Stan looked surprised and then increasingly angry as it played.

"What the fuck is this?"

I looked at the paper that the cassette had been wrapped in.

"Some guy named Ashley Hutchings, and the Albion County Band."

We'd heard of Ashley Hutchings.

He was a member of one the various English bands who were constantly trying to inject what they fondly imagined to be rock and roll into endless dreary English folk dirges, as if playing all 400 verses of Tam Lin on out of tune electric guitars was just what the world had been waiting for.

"I'll fucking kill him. I'll drive his worthless little ass into the ground like a fence pole."

Stan was seething by the time we got to Chicago.

The song, apparently called "Wolfe" was now about the Battle of the Plains of Abraham, and not only used the exact tune of "Northwest Passage," but whole clumps of the lyrics reworked into the narrative.

This was not a folk process reworking of a song, such as happened with "Barrett's Privateers" within a year or two of its birth.

From Stan's point of view, and mine, this was a wholesale theft.

We got home a few days later, and through Bob Blackman got an address for Hutchings.

Stan wrote a pretty strongly worded letter expressing his displeasure about the lift, and some months later, got in return a pissy and tersely worded reply saying that Hutchings had never heard of this song Stan was claiming authorship of, nor had he heard of Stan Rogers, and please desist in contacting him.

A couple of years later Stan was over in England on a joint CBC/BBC project with the McGarrigle sisters, which was never released, and he went with the vague idea of searching out Hutchings and calling him out on it. I don't know if he had a clear plan. Perhaps a dawn duel across the Channel on the sands at Calais, with a brace of flintlock pistols. Or maybe a Mexican knife fight where the two competitors have their wrists tied together with a knotted kerchief.

Or more likely a just a quick smack to the back of the head with a garden shovel, and a hasty burial behind a potting shed.

Time didn't allow though, and perhaps Stan realized that it might be tough to leave the country with a murder charge following him.

The insult stayed with him though, and he never forgave Hutchings. Nor have I, when you get right down to it.

CHAPTER 47

New Jersey

We had a run of gigs on the East Coast of the States, set up by a woman friend of Stan's who had been doing our US bookings for a couple of years. She has passed now, and so I won't reveal her name or identify her in any way.

She was a decent enough sort, and she loved Stan, but she was terrible as an agent. She was good-hearted, well meaning, and hardworking, but the gigs she got us over the couple of years we worked with her were almost without exception disastrous, and it was wearing us down. She had set up that near-fatal first run for Stan and me a few years before, and later the dreadful Baltimore incident in the apartment with the troll like creature. And that pretty much set the pattern in terms of bad routing, terrible money, and sheer breath-taking incompetence. We were having a miserable time with her, and to make it worse she was the best we could find.

Stan had an interview at a folk friendly radio station in Teaneck New Jersey one morning.

David and I were surplus to needs. The studio was small and cramped, and anyway, we both had an ugly tendency to indulge in sarcasm when Stan had a chance to wax fulsome on the air.

He didn't want to take any chances with us in the studio.

"You guys can listen out here. We'll be going out live."

Great.

So Stan did the interview solo, and Eadie and I sat in the van, in the parking lot behind the building. We fiddled with the radio controls until we heard the theme music. (Why is it always a damned banjo?)

David lit a smoke, and I poured out a mid-morning dram to go with my coffee.

Stan came on after a while, and was being typically upbeat and enthusiastic about the tour, and the great reception we were getting everywhere. This didn't sound like our tour.

Who the Hell was he talking about?

We could hear him going into full Barry White mode, getting in close to the mic to emphasize the bass in his voice.

"Yeah, the whole tour has been sold out, and we've been getting standing ovations every night. It's been fantastic."
Who the hell was this?
Was he seeing another band on the side?

David flicked his smoke out the window into the bushes where it would probably start a deadly brush fire when we left.

"What a complete crock of shit."
I said "Jesus, yeah. Turn it off. It's embarrassing."
Before David could reach the radio, we heard Stan say, "You know, playing music is like sex, really, every night. It really is. That kind of intensity on stage. It's like you're making love to the entire audience. It's better than sex actually."
Jesus.
We looked at each other in horror.

"Turn it off. Oh man, before I barf."
David hit the switch, and we sat for a couple of minutes, mulling over what we had just heard.
He lit another smoke and did a French inhale, letting the smoke trickle up from his mouth to his nostrils, and blew it out.
He turned back to look at me.

He said, "Your brother?"
"Yeah?"
"He uh…he's had …um…he's actually had sex? Has he?"
I shook my head. "Doesn't sound like it to me."
Time passed.
We were getting bored.
I sipped my coffee and Wild Turkey, and opened a magazine which I had only read a dozen times.
David stared glumly out the window.
More time passed.
I looked at my watch. Christ, had it stopped?

Presently David turned around in the front passenger seat.
He said, "Okay, It's time to play Guess What Hit You."

"Ah shit, no. I hate that game."

"Come on." He pulled a quarter out of his pocket. "I'll toss you for first turn."

"God dammit."

"Come on. Do it."

"Guess What Hit You" was a pretty simple game, and our final

fallback position in times of extreme boredom.
One person would place a stolen Motel 6 pillow case over his head, and
wait.
The other would wallop the subject over the head with something, and
the victim would have to... guess... what... hit... him.
If you guessed correctly, it became your turn to be the hitter.
It wasn't a very good game, and there was an unfortunate tendency
for the violence of the game to escalate. We'd had to conduct serious
negotiations so as to enact an arms limitation treaty.
You could no longer use for example, a live animal.
And nothing dangerous, or wet.

I lost the coin toss.
I was first.
I put the pillow case over my head and waited.
WHAM!
   "OOWWWW! OH SHIT. That was your fist."
   "Nope. Guess again."
I waited.
WHAM!
   "AH JESUS! God damn it. That was a book."
   "Nope. Guess again."
My ears were ringing.
I was waiting for the next blow, when I heard the driver's door open,
and Stan said, "What the hell is this?"
I took off my hood, and saw David as he was straightening up from
hiding the tire jack handle under the seat.
   "Nothing. We had to turn the radio off to save the battery, and we
got bored."
   "So you didn't hear it?"
   "No, not really."
   "Shit. I thought it went pretty well, it was a good interview."

We still had a gig to do that afternoon. A matinee. We drove to the
address on the contract.
It wasn't a venue, as such. There was no club. Just a nice house on a
quiet residential street.
We pulled up and got out and walked around to the back yard patio,
where we could hear voices. We could smell barbecue smoke. Hell, this
could be okay.
Well, the long and the short of it was the promoter had either forgotten
about us, or had never known about us in the first place. There was no
gig, and he was expecting guests for a nice Sunday of watching football

404

on the tube.
Fucking agent.

I don't recall what sort of weird negotiations took place over the next
half hour or so.
I had gone back to the van, to sulk and plot a murder, but it fell out that
we actually set up our gear, and played a short set in the rec room, in
front of the TV, for a couple of bored and pissed off teenagers, and a
handful of mystified guests who were also not happy about missing the
big game
We packed up.
Stan collected some sort of fee, a pittance, really, and we left with our
tails between our legs.
There was an uncomfortable and depressed silence as Stan threaded
the van through the narrow streets out towards the Jersey Turnpike.
We weren't to know it at the time of course, but Bruce Springsteen was
at that moment probably only just miles away, getting ready to play
in front of a couple of thousand rabid fans and have just what Stan
had been talking about on the radio, three hours of tantric sex with a
sweating and ecstatic mob.
Maybe, in retrospect, that was why we were having such a miserable
time back then, Bruce was using up the entire world supply of fun.
There was none left for losers like us.
Stan guided the van into the toll booth and then out onto the Pike,
heading North.
I poured another shot of Wild Turkey and handed it over to Stan. He
nodded thanks, took a sip, grimaced and shook his head.
We were quiet for a while.
Then I said, "Well you know, this could be the next big thing. We could
just turn up at random, at people's homes, and play until they pay us to
leave."
Stan didn't say anything. He lit a smoke and hunched his shoulders and
stared fixedly ahead over the steering wheel. I think like David and I he
was fantasizing about killing our agent, and throwing her body into a
chalk pit.
There was another long silence.

I cleared my throat, and took a deep breath. "So... Like sex, huh?"
Out of the corner of my eye I could see Stan's face flush.
David spoke up from the back seat, where he was sprawled, staring
moodily at the ceiling.
    "If playing music is like sex, that gig was like a hand-job from a
drunken drag queen."

Stan looked back at him in the rear view mirror.
  "Well Dave, if you say so."

We drove to Connecticut.

CHAPTER 48

New London

A couple of days after the New Jersey disaster, we were staying with
Gene and Barbara Bellows at the Bee and Thistle Inn, in Old Lyme
Connecticut.
They put us up, and put up with us, in return for which we would play
an occasional concert for their guests.
It was a little odd, and it was awkward I think, for everyone in the
room. And I suspect Gene and Barbara only made the arrangement in
order that we wouldn't feel as if we were taking constant charity.
In any case, their very wealthy and no doubt mostly Republican blue-
blooded clientele, dressed in jackets and ascots, and pearls and twin-
sets had to endure from time to time a trio of loud and ragged scruffs,
singing in the corner of the dining room, or in some cases standing next
to their table.
A perfect accompaniment to the beouf en croute, and the vintage
Montrachet.

It was a very toney neighbourhood. Old New England money.
We were warned that if we were ever to run into a tall thin woman in a
red plaid hunting jacket and kerchief, walking at speed along the break
water, we were under no circumstances allowed to speak to her, or
otherwise annoy her.
Miss Hepburn liked her privacy.

We had a show in New London, not so far from the Inn.
Gene decided to tag along.
We got to the venue.
It was on a corner, downtown, surrounded by pawn shops and tattoo
parlors.
It was tiny saloon, with real sawdust on the floor. I had never actually
seen that before in all my years of close contact with saloons and their
floors. There was a low stage in one corner.
The so-called decor had a vaguely nautical theme, ropes coiled and

hung on the walls, and blown-glass fish net floats, and a couple of lobster pots nailed up on the ceiling. And it was a mess. Most of the chairs and tables were broken and over turned, as if Popeye and Bluto only moments before had taken their fight outside.
There was no sound system.
"I was told by your agent that you brought your own gear."
The woman manager was barely interested in us. She was leaning against the bar, smoking a cigarette and leafing through a newspaper.
Our agent had said that?
"We were told you'd have a full system." Stan said.
She shrugged without looking up from the baseball scores. "Maybe some of the other bars down the street will let you borrow some stuff."
She turned the page and we went outside.

"I've fucking had it. What the hell is she doing?"
We were on the street, and I was yelling at Stan, like it was his fault and not our agent's.
"She's a fucking disaster. We can't keep doing this shit. She's worse than useless."
I was fed up.
"Come on. She's not that bad." said David.
"What?" We looked at him in disbelief. He hated her the most.
"She's generous."
"Yeah, right."
"Yeah, she'd give you the scales off her back."
"Very funny."
We stood for a few minutes, watching middle aged and older men moving down the street.
They would hurry along, heads bent, and shoulders hunched over and then suddenly and furtively dive into the doorway of the porn theatre.
How had our agent found this place?
Stan said, "Let's play the damned gig, and then we'll figure out what we're going to do."

We split up and went to some of the other bars, and scrounged enough bits and pieces of gear to cobble together a sort of sound system.
None of the other bar owners seemed worried or surprised that their property was disappearing out the door.
Maybe our agent was booking acts through here regularly.

We set up and did a sound check.
The street outside was getting crowded and busy.
We were in the part of town where the sailors came to relax. This was

one stop shopping. Here, in this one block area they could get drunk, watch a dirty movie, get a tattoo, pick up a hooker and catch some dreadful disease, and be back on board in front of the Medical Officer for a penicillin shot before curfew.

It was getting toward show time, and we were having pints of Harp at the bar and waiting for the audience to arrive.

The only person to come through the door was Lui Collins.

We had met her some days before at another gig, and we'd all liked her. Tiny. No bigger than a fish dinner, with a bunch of good songs, and a real facility for open tunings. She was friendly and eccentric, but not disturbingly so.

We had offered her an opening spot at this gig, never knowing what a train wreck it was going to be.

This was embarrassing, but she took it all in stride.

Looking back, and remembering just how scared we all were in those days, traveling around a strange country, even as a trio, it was extraordinary that she had the nerve to do it by herself, a young woman on her own.

She pulled her guitar out of the case and did a quick sound check, simply by tapping the two mics and nodding, and then sat with us as we waited for someone to buy a ticket.

No one did.

What the hell. Gene was there. We'd play for him.

We opened the door onto the street to try to attract somebody, anybody, into the room, and Lui went on.

Some people drifted in. Not folk fans, just passersby, curious to see where the music was coming from.

Lui finished her set, and we went on, and a few more people came in. No one paid of course, and they weren't listening, but we could now pretend we had an audience.

It was mostly a bunch of drunks taking a break from the bedlam out on the street.

We could see groups of sailors, already staggering drunk, lurching past the window, being assisted by young women in miniskirts and very high heels, carrying the traditional suit case-sized purses of the hooker.

We were a little haven of calm away from the yells and car horns and fistfights.

We were finishing our first set when eight young men came into the room.

They were all very fit looking and tan, and dressed in perfect dazzling navy whites.

They walked in and started juggling. Just juggling, standing in a circle, using small red rubber balls.

"Who are you guys? The United States Navy Official Juggling Team?" asked Stan from the stage.

"Yup." said one of them over his shoulder.

Okay. They were harmless but a little distracting.

They began picking things up from all over the room. Anything small enough to lift and toss. And soon ashtrays, and empty glasses and Lui were flying back and forth past the ceiling lights.

We finished the gig, or whatever you wanted to call this horrible experience, and the manager presented us with our bar tab. 36 bucks. We'd made precisely nothing, even after Gene picked up the bill for our drinks.

We went outside.

Stan and I were sitting on a railing, watching the drunks and whores reeling past us.

It looked like a bomb had just gone off.

People were staggering and falling, and trying to get back up, bleeding and puking, and yelling random curses and threats. The flashing red and blue lights from the police cruisers were making it all look rather festive.

Down the street was a neon sign that read "Hygienic Restaurant." Stan gestured towards it with his cigarette.

"I wonder how bad the culinary standards have to be in a town when a restaurant's main attraction is that its Hygienic."

I shrugged. "I still don't know if I'd take their word on it." I'd decided that I'd be more concerned about the tattoo parlour with the mis-spelled sign. The consequences would seem to be more long term.

I was tired and nowhere near drunk as I needed to be for this sort of shit.

I turned to Stan. "You gonna make the call?"

Stan threw his cigarette butt into the piss-filled gutter and slid off the railing. "Yeah, let's do it."

We looked for David.

He was in the bar with his guitar playing a Fred Neil song for Lui and Gene, the juggling team, and the two young whores who were busy picking the pockets of the passed out sailors.

We grabbed him up to witness the call. Poor guy. He had loathed our agent. What little self-respect he and Stan and I had started out with was being eroded. He deserved to witness her firing, and get at least something out of this disaster.

The three of us went down the street to find a phone booth.

It was too small for all three of us to fit into, but Stan kept the door open

so we could hear him wake her up and say those words we'd so longed
to hear. "You're fired."
And the sailors, and the poor over-worked cops, and even more over-
worked whores were treated to the sight of David and me dancing in
a two man conga line outside the booth and singing, "Ding Dong, the
Witch is Dead" in falsetto harmony.

CHAPTER 49

The Folkway

Things picked up later that week.
We had a couple of nights at the Folkway in Peterborough, NH.
We had found it less than a year before, and it quickly became our home club.
It changed everything for us, how we felt about ourselves, what we were doing, and particularly, how we felt about New England.

We had nearly given up on the East a year or so earlier, after a terrible weekend in Brattleboro Vt.
We'd had a three night run at a folk club in an old converted barn on the outskirts of town. It was a decent enough place, a good room with a nice stage, and comfortable digs upstairs.
The owner hated us on sight.
We'd arrived flushed and excited, having discovered New Hampshire's tax free booze stores on the way to the club.
We unloaded the gear, and got settled in to the rooms upstairs.
She watched as we carried in a couple of gallons of scotch and vodka, and went back to her own house, probably to phone our agent to try to cancel the show, or the ATF to blow the whistle on us for illegal transport of massive quantities of booze over state lines.
We were sharing the bill with a tall handsome guy named Dick Pinney.
He was a good guitar player and singer and had a bunch of great songs.
He was pretty evasive about their origins.
  "Wow, who wrote that? Is that one of yours?"
He would change the subject, and we didn't find out until some years later that much of his repertoire was written by Greg Brown, with whom he had travelled a bit. He did have a funny story about doing a disastrous opening set a year before. His big show-stopper was "Coal Tattoo," a Billy Ed Wheeler song. He did it with a lot of flash and energy, and finished off his set with it, to a storm of applause.
He was walking towards the side of the stage, feeling pretty pleased with himself, and Billy Ed Wheeler, the main act, was there, glaring at

him.

"What the hell do you think you're doing boy?"

Turned out Dick didn't know that it was Wheeler's song.

The weekend was tough, not by our usual standards, in that we didn't have to beat the shit out of anyone, but we played mostly to the owner and the silent young girl who was at her side, and whom we'd been warned to stay the hell away from.

Nobody came, except for the Saturday, when we had 11 people all sitting at the same table.

"So...what's with you guys? Are you all out on a date together?" I'd had enough cheap scotch to loosen my tongue.

"Sort of."

Turned out they were (they claimed) all married to each other, and living in a commune outside of town.

I have no idea whether it was true, or if they were just yanking my chain, but they all held on to the same story. Why they were an odd number remained a mystery. Perhaps one was a spare, in case someone pulled a groin muscle or something.

The gig wore on and the owner continued to hate us.

We came off the stage one night, and she took me aside and pushed me into a corner. She was seething.

"I'm sick to death of all your goddamned macho posturing up there. I won't have it."

Macho posturing? Jesus. I was wearing a silk shirt, draw string linen pants, and ballet slippers, for God's sake. I looked like Oscar Wilde's sister.

Maybe it was the time spent playing the bear pits that we were used to in other parts of the country. When we got to a real club, we were just too loud, too aggressive, too stupid, and worst of all, too dumb to know it.

So we finished with that gig and vowed never to return.

Then we got booked into the Folkway, in Peterborough New Hampshire.

We were still pissed off and dubious about the whole concept of playing in New England.

Some goddamned hippie shit-hole, no doubt, out in the frigging woods. More fried eggplant, and more granola.

Stan was driving.

I was sitting in the front seat glaring out the window. He and I had had a fight about something, and we were currently not speaking forever.

David was in the back of the van doing the death scene from Camille.

413

He had the metabolism of a hummingbird, and needed food every hour or so.

Stan was in no mood to stop for anything, much less food, so David was having a hypoglycemic attack, and eating handfuls of sugar from the cabinet where we kept the coffee.

We coasted down the long hill on route 101 to the stop light, made the left turn onto Grove Street, and drove to the address.

There were a couple of large frame houses, with a converted barn, which served as the concert room. We parked behind the buildings in the lot up the hill, and got out.

Might as well see what kind of nightmare this is going to be.

Huh. It looked okay, actually. Nicely kept. There was a big stone wall surrounding a pleasant garden.

We walked down the hill and went through the gate.

There were fragrant herbs growing along the wall, and the big mulberry tree was in flower. Bees and bright butterflies were busy among the flowers nodding by the windows. We stepped through the French doors.

Inside was a lovely sweet-smelling and airy room. There were tables made from old hydro spools. A wood stove was at the right side of the room. Facing us was a low stage with a black board behind, showing the day's specials, written out in beautiful calligraphy.

Everyone was busy, and friendly and nicely dressed and competent. Everything in the room with the exception of ourselves, was bright and clean, and properly cared for. We could smell bread baking, and something being cooked in wine and garlic and butter.

There were flowers on the tables, and graceful waitresses in long skirts were moving around the room dealing with the last of the lunch crowd.

What the hell was this?

It must be some kind of trick.

A slender dark haired woman came into the room. "I'm Widdie Hall," she said, and shook hands with all of us. She had a strong dry grip, and a wonderful wide and luminous smile. "Welcome to the Folkway. We're so happy to have you here. You're sold out for both nights."

What?

It is easier, somehow to write about all the disastrous and crappy gigs we had over the years, and make them real.

It is nearly impossible to try to convey just how wonderful and perfect and unique the Folkway was for us, and for everyone who passed through its doors.

Widdie and Jonathan Hall had started it up a couple of years previous
to our getting there.
The club survived the break-up of their marriage, and Widdie carried on.

It is not just the passage of time, and the tendency to burnish the
memory of something that one loves that makes me feel such reverence
and longing for that place.
We knew it was perfect at the time.
We knew exactly how lucky we were to be able to play there, and to
have Widdie in our lives.
She was quiet and funny, with a great laugh, her voice roughened by
the Camels she smoked.
She was kind and thoughtful, and generous beyond any words I have to
describe. And the club reflected everything she was.
We never to my memory, had a bad night there.
The shows always sold out well in advance, and our days were spent
sleeping in, and then wandering down to a late breakfast, and then
maybe a pleasant stroll around the town.
The town itself was small and charming, with lots of good stonework
everywhere, and a river rushing past the old mill downtown.
Peterborough was the setting and inspiration for Thornton Wilder's
play "Our Town."

The place was full of eccentrics.
Every morning, I would be sitting in the garden, drinking coffee,
reading the paper and noodling around on my guitar, and hear the clop
of hooves and the silvery tinkle of a small bell behind me.
It was the guy who came in for his morning paper and groceries every
day, riding a tall dark bay horse, followed by his pet goat.

So it was a working holiday at the Folkway.
It required no real effort. We just had to hang around and wait for show
time.
We did good shows there too. The audiences were wonderful, and
actually listened attentively, and we learned how to dial it down a bit,
and play with a tad more subtlety.
Afterwards, repair to the bar, and carouse into the night, with only a
staircase between you and bed.
The Folkway was such a relief and balm to us. It made it possible to for
us to now face the terrible places we were still playing most of the time.
I remember leaving the club one morning, the three of us hung over
and cranky, with a wicker basket that Widdie had made up for us full of
wonderful roast beef sandwiches on homemade bread, and a thermos

flask of spicy and life restoring bloody Marys. She had even packed in a small vase with a rose.

We were going away to play another round of depressing shit holes, but we were okay. We were coming back to the Folkway in a week.

So we were back now, and Lui Collins was still with us. She had come along to do an opening set. Being a New Englander, the Folkway was her home club as well. I think everyone who ever played there thought of it as their own personal home club. We were no different, and once again, we had a full house and a great night. I woke the next morning to hear music being played across the alley from Widdie's house where I was staying. I hauled myself out of bed, dressed and went across the lane. It was Stan and Eadie and Lui, and they were wrapping up an all-night session, singing Greg Brown's "Rooty toot, toot, for the Moon." The words sound prosaic enough, but there was morning sunlight shining on the floor and the tables, and there was the smell of something delicious cooking, and a fresh cool breeze blowing the curtains in. And it was the first time I'd ever heard that song, and the three of them sounded so damned good you wanted to cry.

We played there a lot in the weeks leading up to Christmas every year, and I still have really strong associations with the holidays and the Folkway.

Widdie had a friend named Pat, who helped out around the gift shop, and decorated the club for the season. She did origami as a hobby. She made some paper stars for my first Christmas tree with Gail, and this morning, as I write this, thirty odd years later, we once again hung them on our tree, battered and as bent as they are.

It was at the Folkway where I proposed (in furtive whispers over the gift store phone,) to Gail.

It was at the Folkway where we heard the news of John Lennon's murder. I remember walking around the town the next day. People were in little groups everywhere, talking in hushed voices, unable to take in the terrible news.

And it was at the Folkway where I played my first ever solo show, a few weeks after Stan died.

Widdie probably sensed that I needed something to do to keep my wheels moving, and called our agent, Jim Fleming, and offered me the weekend that had been held for the trio.

Jim called and ran the idea past me, and Widdie hounded a bunch of other New England club owners into hiring me, none of them having ever heard me play solo.

And then she went to bat for me with Immigration, to get me a work visa for the tour, enlisting the aid of Odetta, who wrote a threatening letter to her Government. Good luck arguing with Odetta, boys. You're just the Federal government. She's Odetta.

And so I went down, ostensibly to say goodbye to folks, and thank them for their support over the years. In the course of the little tour, I realized that I did not want to leave the life.

After all the years of struggle, to have to say goodbye permanently to all of it, was too hard.

And so I kept on, and I might never have done but for Widdie's encouragement, and support.

The club remained a haven to me, as I started over.

I was again back to playing a lot of very hard and frustrating shows in places where I had to fight people's preconceptions at the very least, and outright hostility in many cases.

In the midst of all that I could still come back to the Folkway, and Widdie would be there with her welcome, and against all expectations, another sold out house.

I wondered sometimes, if she hadn't papered the town with free tickets.

I do know that she had a knack for always losing our bar tabs. "I can't find it," she would say as she sorted through stacks of paper. "You must have already paid, and you just were too drunk to remember."

Right.

She was absent minded in other ways.

I drove into town once, and stopped at the little grocery store downtown.

There were posters up everywhere for Claudia Schmidt, who was then living on Beaver Island in Michigan.

I tore one of the posters off the wall. It was obviously Widdie's work. She wrote in a beautiful stylized script. I threw it in the car and drove over to the club..

I got out of the car, and went into her house. She was at the sewing table, and when I walked in she got up and gave me a crushing hug. She always smelled of cinnamon. I held the poster out to her.

"Did the phone ring or something while you were doing this?"

"I don't know. I...oh shit!"

She tore it out of my hands, and smacked herself in the side of the head, and started laughing. She doubled over. "Shit. These are everywhere. Keene, Brattleboro. All over the place. Oh God."

The poster read, "Coming to the Folkway. Claudia Schmidt. The Queen of Beaver."

Widdie called some months later.

She had breast cancer.

She had a good doctor, and was outwardly confident that she was going to beat it.

But in the end, after a couple of years struggling with it, she knew she was losing the fight, and started making preparations to try to sell the club.

Gene Bellows came in to look the place over and make suggestions as to how to make the place more efficient and saleable.

"You could put in a time clock, make people punch in and out. You're losing a lot of money just by letting people wander in when it suits them."

"I couldn't do that. People would think I didn't trust them."

The next to last time I saw her was when Archie Fisher and I were playing there the summer of 1988. We were having a parting glass in the bar the following morning, and Widdie came in.

"I'm closing this place down in a few weeks."

I couldn't meet her eyes.

"Well, we've had thirteen wonderful years. It's time you shut down and started taking care of yourself, and fight this thing properly." I just couldn't face what was coming.

More to the point, I was unable to help her face what was coming.

I should have been a better friend.

A few weeks later I began thinking of Stan's funeral, and the hundreds of his friends who came from all over the continent, and who were in the same room for the first time. Wonderful and extraordinary people, who had been in our lives for so many years, in different parts of the world, and were just now meeting, and too late for Stan to have the pleasure of seeing them together.

I had looked around at the time and thought, "We should have done this while he was still here."

I called Jordi Herold at the Iron Horse in Northampton, and laid out the plan to him and his then partner, Carole Green.

I wanted to throw a party. A big concert with anyone who had ever played the Folkway, and have Widdie in the room so she could see at least some of the people who loved her, and whose lives she had changed.

It was my initial idea, but it was Jordi and Carole chiefly, who put the whole thing together with the help of Tom and Kathi Murri and Georgette de Friesse, and the concert took place at the Colonial Theatre in Keene.

Everything was donated, the hall, the sound, and dozens of musicians
showed up from all over the country, some from as far as California,
paying their own expenses. Flights, car rentals, hotels, everything. A
buffet was laid on, and a steel drum band played in the lobby.
Widdie herself wrote the programme notes, and they were
extraordinary. Typically funny and heart-breaking.
She referred to her up-coming career as a grass farmer.
We had no stage crew. There was no stage manager.
Performers simply milled about backstage, keeping an eye on the
posted running order, and when it was their turn to play, they would go
out and be assisted in setting up by the previous act.
The show ran something like three and a half hours. Everyone got two
songs.
There was talk that Widdie was too weak to come to the show, but in
the end she rallied, and turned up.
She joined us all on stage at the end, and stood for I don't know how
long, as the crowd gave her a tearful and prolonged ovation.
She had that same dear, deeply creased lambent smile that we all knew
and loved so well.
Later, she visited with the performers backstage, and sipped some
champagne, and then it was time to leave.
My last sight of her was as she was being carefully and tenderly
escorted down the alley behind the theatre, under an umbrella, to be
helped into the waiting warmed-up car to go home.

The club struggled on without her for a few more years, being run
by Widdie's mom and a dedicated group of volunteers, but with
Widdie's passing the heart had gone out of the place, and the lights had
permanently dimmed in our lives, and none of us were never the same,
and it finally closed.

CHAPTER 50

Ottawa

It's gone now, mercifully. Razed and bulldozed and scrubbed from the face of the earth that once groaned under its weight, but once upon a time there was a broken down hotel on Bank Street in Ottawa.

It was a remnant from the days of Ontario's antediluvian liquor laws when drinking holes had two entrances, and two carefully separated rooms.

There was one for "Men," and another for "Ladies and Escorts".

Presumably women were not able to handle strong waters without a chaperone.

God knows what they might do under the influence if left to their own devices.

They might want to vote or something.

Bars in Canada were cold grey cinder block rooms with no source of natural light except for some semi opaque industrial windows high up on the wall.

Drinking was men's work and done mostly in silence, as if they were doing penance, or under punishment in some grim Gulag.

The only sign that there was an outside world was the television bolted to the wall over the bar, invariably tuned to "The Price is Right."

The idea of bright airy patios, and cafes where groups of people might drink in the open and talk and laugh was anathema. It was something the French would do.

I don't remember the name of the actual hotel, but the club we were booked into was called "Shannon's Place."

I have been told since that it was owned at the time by Shannon Tweed, ex-Playboy bunny, and now pneumatic life partner to Gene Simmons, bass player for KISS, and who now serves mostly as a life support system for a scarily prehensile tongue on some Reality TV show.

Kind of creepy to have any connection, however tenuous, to that guy, but there you are.

The club was a cramped narrow room with a low stage at one end, and smeared dusty windows facing onto the street at the other.

There were small cigarette-scarred tables, and captain's chairs for the punters, and a bar along the wall to stage left.

It smelled like most of those old style taprooms did in those days, a mixture of stale beer, despair, cigarette smoke, and vomit and piss, topped with a faint soupcon of menthol- flavoured urinal cakes.

Looking at that last sentence, perhaps "flavoured" is not precisely the word I should use.

Stan was not well.

He had either picked up a flu bug, or was in the grip of food poisoning brought on by his habit of wolfing down whatever was presented to him in whatever crummy restaurant we could afford back then, and damn the torpedoes.

I tended to suffer fewer bouts of intestinal trouble, as I had a morbid fear of being heavy like Stan. As a consequence I approached my food rather more suspiciously, circling it warily, and poking at it repeatedly to see if it was safe before nibbling at it.

And in any case, I was mostly on a liquid diet in those days, and it was all safely distilled and purified before it touched my lips.

Stan had no such hesitations, and would order something off the menu which, at first blush might look perfectly safe, but would later turn out not to be dinner, but the Paris to Marseilles Bullet train.

He and everyone around him would pay a heavy price.

We loaded in, just the two of us, and the trouble hit just as we finished sound check.

He turned grey and sweaty, and bent over from the waist, and grabbed a table to support himself.

Even as young as he was, I thought uh oh, heart attack.

He was a good forty pounds too heavy, and smoked a pack and a half of Rothmans a day.

"You okay?'

"No. I need to get to a bathroom. Right now."

I ran for the manager of the club, and was given the keys to our room upstairs.

I grabbed Stan by the arm and led him up to the third floor.

He was in bad shape. He was hauling himself up the stairs by the railing, and puffing heavily.

Perhaps stopping at that parking lot hot dog stand in Smith's Falls and wolfing down three elderly grey-ish water logged tube steaks with mustard, relish and raw onions on our way up had not been the best idea.

Sweat was pouring off him in sheets, and he was in severe pain.

We got to the third floor and turned right at the top of the stairs.

We hustled down a long dark overheated hallway.
Radiators hissed and spat at us as we went by.
The walls were painted in some nasty green enamel which had no
doubt been left over from a job lot after an insane asylum had been re-
decorated.
The carpets had started out yellow, but were now stained and worn
and smelled of twenty years of stale piss, industrial cleaner and roach
powder.
I found the room we'd been assigned, and we had to step over the
unconscious form of some rummy who was sleeping it off on our
doorstep.
Stan staggered in, unbuckling his pants as he ran, and made it to the
bathroom and slammed the door behind him.
From the sounds of things he was staging a re-enactment of the Battle
of Trafalgar. I decided this was something I couldn't help him with and
went out of the room.

The passed out drunk hadn't moved, and I could see others sleeping as
well, scattered along the corridor in the dark.
It was creepy. It looked like a Holiday Inn as drawn by Gustav Dore.
I went back to the club downstairs, and waited.
It was near to show time, and Stan hadn't come back yet.
There were a few people sitting at the tables drinking quarts of Molson
Export, and smoking and chatting.
They weren't there to see us. It wasn't that kind of room.
We were to be background noise, or rather would be if the lead singer/
guitar player would only show up.

I went back upstairs. The bodies hadn't moved, and I again stepped
over the guy who was face down at our door, and went in to find Stan.
He was also passed out, exhausted from his labours.
    "Stan. Wake up. It's show time."
He stirred, and groaned and rolled over.
His eyes snapped open and he jack-knifed off the narrow bed and
hurled himself into the bathroom again.
This wasn't good.
I don't think it ever occurred to me, stupid as I was, to call a doctor or to
look for help. I don't think it occurred to Stan either.
He came out of the bathroom sometime later, still pale and shaky, and
we once again stepped over our human doorstop and went downstairs
to do the first set.

I have a good friend who claims to remember those shows we did that week, and he maintains they were great.

What I remember is getting most of the way through the first set, and Stan fleeing the room to again commune with nature.

"There's gonna be a short break folks. Talk amongst yourselves." Nobody looked up or responded.

I waited for a few minutes and then went up to check on him, and he was laying on his bed, knees drawn up under his chin, sweating and shivering.

"C'mon Stan, gotta go. It's time for the second set."

Again, he came downstairs, and we ran through the tunes.

I was having issues with our arrangement of Hank William's "Lovesick Blues."

Stan was usually pretty good about keeping songs in keys which were comfortable for a bad fiddle player.

He kindly stayed with keys like G, or D or A.

Once in a while he would slip into something like B flat, as in "45 Years", or "Second Effort," as it really suited his voice, but I managed to scrape by.

If he really wanted to play something in a terrible key like F sharp I could always pick up the flute or my guitar.

Our version of "Lovesick Blues" was in E major. Not a great key for the fiddle anyway, but he also insisted on modulating into F, at which point I gave up and simply sang a close harmony which resulted in the two of us doing a weird double yodel.

That double yodel at the end was too much for Stan's overstressed system, and he again left the stage abruptly and fled to our room.

He was a wonderful self-taught singer and always worked from the diaphragm, but in this case that had just been tempting fate.

I found him once again, sometime later, curled up on his bed and unconscious. I had to shake him awake again him for the final set.

It was not fun. People were getting drunker and noisier as the evening wore on, and the women sitting at the table directly in front of us were particularly a problem.

They, of course, had to shout to be heard over us and none of them had anything interesting to say. We both wanted to just get through this horrible night and be done with it.

And given Stan's delicate condition we really didn't want to attract further attention to ourselves.

He wasn't up to watching my back if things got ugly.

I should have left it alone, but it had been a hard night, and I'd had enough of the loud and inane chatter in front of us.

I took my mike stand, and carefully and slowly extended it until it was

right over the yapping and shrieking women.
Now everything they were saying was being amplified to the rest of the room, and it wasn't pretty.
One of them was in the middle of a long dissertation on her boyfriend's sexual shortcomings, and when she realized that her indiscretions were being broadcast to the room at large, she leapt up and overturned her chair.
"YOU SON OF A BITCH! WHAT THE HELL DO YOU THINK YOU'RE DOING?"
She was advancing toward me with murder in her heart and an ashtray in her hand.
This was difficult.
I couldn't hit her.
I put the microphone stand down and pulled the cable out of my electric guitar, and held it out to show her.
There was a loud buzzing sound from my amp, and I said "Get back. This thing carries a couple thousand volts. It's lethal."
She kept coming.
"I'm warning you. I don't want to hurt you."
She put her foot on the stage, I darted forward and touched the tip of the guitar cord to her forehead. There was a loud and reverberant BAM! from my amp and I shouted "YOU'RE DEAD!"
It was of course, harmless, just a loud noise from the amp, but it had the desired effect.
She shrieked and fell back onto the table, which overturned and spilled her onto the floor.
She thrashed around among the chairs, clutching her heart, and scattering glasses and broken bottles.
"I'M DEAD! I'M DEAD!"
Her friends clustered around her and helped her leave.
She was still weeping and yelling threats. Stan had taken his guitar off, and carried it out of the room through the door that led upstairs. He had some more business to attend to.
I shouted "That's it folks. Thanks for coming! We're here all week."
I packed up my gear and carried it upstairs.

I stepped over our mascot once more. It finally occurred to me to make sure he was breathing. He was, and I called it a day.
Next morning, Stan was not much improved.
He still couldn't keep anything down except for water, and then only a bit at a time.
He mostly stayed in bed except for sudden dashes to the bog.
Our hotel room was vile.

I doubted that it had been cleaned in my lifetime.

I was particularly wary of the bathroom, not just because Stan was making heavy use of it, but because I had heard stories about this sort of place.

One could easily catch the dreaded crabs simply by standing within three feet of the toilet.

There were family legends.

Our Dad had been visiting Mum during their courting days in Amherst, Nova Scotia, and while staying at the CPR hotel there had come away with a small personal menagerie.

He took his troubles to his older brother Doug, who had been overseas in the Armed Services during the Italian campaign.

"I was visiting Valerie on the weekend and I caught crabs," was how he phrased it, unfortunately.

It didn't raise Mum's stock one bit with her future brother in law, or Grandma Rogers, when the news got relayed to her.

Dougie told Dad to have a very hot bath, and then to shave the affected area thoroughly, and afterwards apply Varsol to his wedding tackle.

Yes, Varsol.

The result of course, was to raise such blisters and lesions that it was miracle that Stan and I were ever conceived.

Dad said it took weeks for the after effects to subside, during which time he was forced to walk like Tom Mix.

In any event, I was terrified of coming out of this adventure with a case of galloping dandruff.

Stan was rather monopolizing the bathroom anyway, but there were certain needs of mine which were not being met, and I was becoming increasingly uncomfortable. I'd had to let out my belt a couple of notches.

The gig itself just was something to be endured. We were making no headway with the audience. We were just trying to get through a whole show without Stan disgracing himself.

After three or four days though, he was starting to improve, and could keep tea and toast down, and he even started to look around and notice just how terrible our surroundings were.

The drunks in the hallway continued to pile up outside our door.

It looked like a giant cat was leaving them as gifts, like field mice.

They weren't guests, just down and out street people who had found shelter in the mostly unused corridors of the hotel, where at least it was warm.

Stan was sitting up in bed one afternoon, drinking tea, and nibbling around the edges of the toasted Western sandwich I'd brought him for breakfast.

I myself was under a lot of pressure now, having yet to dare the
bathroom after all this time.
"How are you feeling today?"
Stan swallowed and said, "Not so bad now."
He gestured with the sandwich. "This tastes pretty good. Thanks."
"That's great. Uh, any other, um, symptoms?"
"Like what?"
"You know like, uh...side effects?"
"What are you talking about?"
"From the toilet seat, you know."
"Are you talking about the Clap? Garnet, you can't catch the Clap
from a toilet seat."
He put down the sandwich, and despite his weakened state he
immediately went into Big Brother mode.
"We need to get you to a doctor right away."
"No, Dammit. I don't have the Clap or the Syph, or anything else.
How the hell could I catch that?"
"Well you can't catch it from a toilet seat anyway."
"I know. I know. Jesus."
Stan picked up his sandwich again and looked at it.
"I mean the other thing."
He put the sandwich back down.
"What other thing?"
"Well, uh, crotch crickets, tiny livestock, the big C."
"Crabs? Jesus. No. I'm fine."
Still he couldn't help switching on the bedside light, taking off the
shade and lifting the bedclothes and taking a thorough look.
He put the lamp back down and replaced the shade, and then he picked
up his sandwich again.
"I'm fine."
"Okay, good."
I stood up and headed for the bathroom door.
"You might want to take that sandwich into the hallway."

We played a lot of odd places in Ottawa over the years.
"L'Hibou" the legendary folk club, was pretty much gone by the time
I started playing with Stan, although I did get to play one set with him
there as part of a larger bill, early on.
For the most part we were playing bars.
Some of them were attempting to be listening rooms, and not quite the
shit holes we had spent so much time in elsewhere in the country.
There was a strange basement place, again on Bank Street, which was

run by two Lebanese brothers.

It had started life as a Disco, furnished in Early Travolta.

There were a lot of mirrors on the walls and low white leather couches in front of the stage.

I didn't take to the brothers very well, which was sad as they were very friendly to us.

We were getting good crowds in for them, and I think that endeared us to them somewhat, but they definitely had an underworld feel to them, and I found it unsettling.

They always had massive amounts of pot for one thing, all neatly packaged up in the office, and they were both deeply into cocaine as well, both on a personal level, and as an adjunct to their income.

Stan had a bit of a nose for the Marching Powder, and occasionally would take them up on their offer to get tightened up after a show.

But his budget barely extended to beer, and a coke habit was one of the last things he needed.

I never tried it. It scared the Hell out of me.

The two brothers had us over for dinner a few times during the years we played their club.

It was a vulgar and gaudy mansion, but the food was typically wonderful as Middle Eastern food is, and they took their duties as hosts very seriously and couldn't have been more generous.

But they were hard men, and there was an underlying sense of potential violence to them, enough that we never felt it safe to refuse their offer of hospitality.

They were also rude and dismissive of their wives, and they were thoroughly nasty to their servants.

I didn't like them at all.

However, the only untoward thing to happen to us during our tenure at their club was that a woman had her water break and went into labour on the white leather sofa in front of the stage one night, just as we started the first set.

"Shouldn't we call an ambulance?" Stan said from the stage.

No, she had been waiting too long to see this show. So she and her husband settled in and did their Lamaze exercises, as we worked through the set list.

It was a bit distracting having to sing over someone while she was yelling and groaning as her husband coached her along and said things like, "You're doing great, Honey," and "Breathe for me now," but we did the gig, and she hung on till the last song, after which she was loaded into a waiting ambulance, and we and the audience waved her off into the night.

I wonder where that kid is today.

It was at the Student Pub at Carleton where we met the guy who was
later to become our manager. He is still on the fringes of the folk scene
and I no longer have any particular wish to hurt or embarrass him,
so we'll call him...oh...Ronald. He was a short guy, about our age,
somewhat soft and pudgy, with dark curly hair and glasses. Picture
Frodo as a Rabbinical student.
He was the manager of the student pub, and he just loved us.
Stan and David Eadie and I had just finished our first set of a three night
run and he came up to the three of us, breathless and sweating.
"Do you guys have any idea just how good you really are?'
This was never a bad thing to hear from the guy who has hired you.
We were in our "dressing room," a narrow hallway where they kept the
empty beer kegs.
There were no chairs, just the barrels, a damp heap of dirty bar towels
and some piles of rat bait.
I was playing a song called "Howard Green" written by our friend Vin
Garbutt. I was hoping Stan might take to it and we could add it to the
repertoire.
Ronald burst in and began his pitch.
    "Have you guys ever thought about getting a manager and taking
this to another level?"
    David said, "There's another level?"
He was shocked that we had no management and no long term plan,
and we found ourselves talking to him over the course of the next
couple of days about the possibility of having him work for us.
It was good timing for all of us.
We needed a manager / agent and Ronald's position with the University
was coming to an end.

We should have twigged that something was wrong, when he told us
how he had acquired his vintage Martin D-18 of which he was so proud.
Evidently he had been following behind the touring van of a reasonably
well known Canadian Country star outside of Thunder Bay when a
guitar case fell off the top of the van and landed on the road in front of
him and cartwheeled into the ditch.
Another person might have picked it up and raced after the van to flag
it down. Not our Ronald.
He stopped, opened the case and realizing it was a really nice old
Martin put it in the car and kept on.
    "You didn't try to catch up to him or track him down?"
    "I've always wanted a Martin. Jeez. This was my chance."

This didn't bode well.

Nonetheless we had a lunch meeting with him on the Sunday following our gig, and Stan very sternly laid out some ground rules for our professional association.

We'd been screwed before.

Not this time pal. Things were gonna be different.

Stan opened negotiations.

"Okay. Here's the deal. You get 25 percent of the gross plus expenses."

David and I looked at each other in horror.

"WHAT?"

"The hell with him. Let me be the manager if that's what it pays."

Stan waved us away.

"He's an equal member of the band. I want him to feel like he's got a stake in this."

This was awful. We were making next to nothing anyway. How could we divide it further?

Ronald probably couldn't believe his luck.

We shook hands on the deal.

He had a terrible handshake.

It was like taking hold of a dead tulip. David and I both recoiled and wiped our hands on our pant legs, as did Stan.

There was some further discussion about what our respective duties were going to be, and how much money Ronald was going to be allowed to unilaterally spend on our behalf.

We picked up the tab for his breakfast and concluded the meeting.

Stan said, "Oh, and one more thing. You have to learn how to shake hands properly. Your grip is too soft. Make sure you work on that."

"Huh?"

"People judge you by your handshake. You gotta work on yours."

"Oh. Okay."

We left him in the parking lot of the restaurant and drove away.

I was depressed.

This was the guy who was going to represent us to the wider world.

Someone who would in effect steal a guitar from a professional musician, and shook hands like he was picking up cat shit with a Kleenex.

Stan and I drove back to Hamilton, dropping David off in Toronto en route.

The first invoice from Ronald came in a few weeks later.

It was a massive phone bill, along with some other charges for things like business cards and office supplies.

The first complaint about Ronald came soon after from Eric Perth, who managed the Rebecca Cohn Auditorium in Halifax. We had developed a good gig at the Cohn over the last couple of years, having first gone in as openers for Ryan's Fancy and John Allan Cameron.
Eric was a good man. A tough man, but fair and enormously kind.
He was about 5' 10", with a bullet head and a mustache and a bit of a belly, but it was what they call "hard fat," and he was still immensely fit, having been at one time heavy weight boxing champion of the Danish Navy. His clenched fists looked like they were made of beach rocks.
He was a sweet guy, and he and Stan became friends immediately. They both were loud boisterous guys who liked filthy jokes and whisky, and who used their vulgarity and loudness to cover up a softer and gentler side.
The Cohn had become a yearly event for us, our one good gig, and Stan would invariably spend hours after the show in Eric's office drinking single malt with him, smoking and discussing the world.
Years later, Eric was devastated at Stan's death and had a large portrait of him installed in the entrance to the concert hall.
He was a lovely man, gone now himself, and very much missed.

Eric called Stan one afternoon, and we learned that much of Ronald's enormous phone bill was from his almost daily calls to Eric, ostensibly to discuss the upcoming show which was already nearly sold out.
They weren't as Eric told us, to do with business, or about the show, but more along the lines of an annoying clinging girlfriend who needed reassurance and wanted to gossip.
Eric told Stan that if Ronald didn't stop calling and wasting his time he was canceling the gig.
Stan called Ronald and laid down some more ground rules.

There were more difficult times ahead for us with Ronald.
We had a series of shows booked in the States, and he neglected to get the paper work filled out and filed, even though he had a family connection at the Canadian Embassy, and it should have been a dawdle.
We were kept waiting on tender hooks, while a friend in Philadelphia made a bunch of emergency calls and got it sorted.
During the time he was in our lives, there was no gig he booked for us which we couldn't have got ourselves, and as in the case with the Cohn, a few he came close to losing for us just by being a pain in the ass. He was a drag on our meagre resources, and an annoyance besides, but it was either work with him or go back to doing the booking ourselves,

430

and we hated it.
We three had tried it for a while, and it was time consuming and
humiliating.
Just having someone to do it for us was a huge luxury.
We kept Ronald.

CHAPTER 51

Jasper

We had a week long run at the Astoria Hotel in Jasper, Alberta.
We had been on the road for the better part of a month, dragging our
asses through a tedious series of ill-conceived and poorly paid shows
around the west.
I don't recall the exact date, but one could look it up, as it was the year
the Montreal Expos came within shouting distance of making it to the
Eastern play-offs.
Or if you wanted to pinpoint it more precisely I am sure the RCMP
would still have Stan's arrest record in their files somewhere.

We were tired and dispirited, and nearly broke.
The gigs were going badly, there were huge expensive gaps in our
schedule, and the bills from Ronald kept coming in.
Between his enormous phone bills and office invoices he was proving
to be an expensive little bauble, and there had been several heated
discussions in the van about what to do about him.
One school of thought favoured keeping him on and holding a tighter
rein on his expenditures.
Another more popular idea involved burying him at a lonely crossroads
by the light of a full moon, alive or dead, we hadn't decided.
He had left a note attached to the contract for this show.
It read simply, "Relax".
At first blush the gig looked reasonable.
The lounge was dark, and lit with some neon beer signs, and it had the
usual assortment of faux colonial tables and captain's chairs arranged in
groups of four.
Beyond the intense stink of years of cigarette smoke it didn't even smell
too bad, just the usual industrial strength disinfectant, and a whiff of
mothballs from the urinals.
There was a low stage, and a fairly up to date sound system, and three
decent hotel rooms (by our standards anyway,) upstairs.
We were actually getting paid a fair wage for this as well, about 750 for

432

the week, and the young manager was friendly.

This might be okay, or, as Stan said under his breath as we climbed the stairs to our rooms, "Looks like the little twerp got it right for a change."

We were to do three hour long sets a night, which was about par for a pub gig back then.

We sound checked and then went back upstairs to watch the ball game and wait for show time.

When we came back down around 8 P.M. the bar was only about half full.

This was nothing new to us, particularly on a week night, but we noticed something about the patrons.

There were no women.

Not one.

It was all men.

Big ugly burly hairy men.

It looked like we had walked into a Bluto look-alike contest, and they were divided into two distinct and separate halves on either side of the room.

On our left side were workers from the CPR who were silently and morosely drinking beer and shots of whiskey while staring down the group on the other side of the room.

On the right were the oil field workers, "rig pigs" who were likewise drinking and glaring daggers at the railroad guys.

We found out from the manager that there was some deep and lingering enmity between the two groups, and the result was that after a long day of toil it was their custom to gather at the Astoria and drink and glare and make threatening gestures at each other from across the room.

I'm sure Diane Fosse could have made some sense of it, but we were mystified, and worse, in the middle of the line of fire.

It made doing the show harder too, because to try to curry favour with one half of the room risked alienating the other half.

It became clear that that didn't matter anyway, because as soon as Stan stepped up to the mike to introduce us the two formerly Balkanized groups became united in their dislike for the band, and putting aside their blood feud, started yelling abuse at us.

"Hey there, folks, we're the Stan..."

"FAGGOTS"

"Rogers band and..."

"FAIRIES."

"And we'll going to play a few..."

"ASSHOLES."

"Tunes..."

And much worse.

I could see Stan flinch and his face flush at the first volley, but we plowed on.

We had run into hostile and rowdy audiences before, but this was the first time we had run into a group that was in or above our weight class. Our usual tactic for subduing hecklers was not going to work here. In fact, not only were these guys as big as Stan, but they were vastly more fit, and any one of them looked like they could snap our necks. It made for a long first set.

We took a break, and went upstairs.

"What the fuck was that?"

We were all feeling shell shocked.

Stan was sitting on the side of his bed.

He lit a cigarette, and blew smoke towards the ceiling.

"I have no idea."

David was looking pale and angry.

He lit a Camel and turned the TV on.

The Expos were still hanging on in the late innings.

David slouched into his chair with his feet up and his arms folded, and stared at the screen, blowing dozens of tiny smoke rings across the room.

He said to Stan, "What was it you were saying about the little twerp getting it right for a change?"

Stan shook himself and stubbed out his smoke.

"I dunno. We're just going to have to muddle through. It's gonna be a long tough week though, boys."

He reached out for his bottle of Appleton's rum, and poured out a short drink, and took a sip.

"That big ugly guy stage left reminds me of the old Black Bart joke."

"Which joke is that?"

Stan lit another Rothmans, blew smoke up towards the ceiling and leaned back.

"There's this saloon in a little western frontier town. Guys playing poker, and the piano player is in the corner, playing "Camptown Races." Couple of whores sitting at the bar, the usual thing. The bartender in the saloon is polishing glasses and everything is quiet. Suddenly a guy runs in and yells, "Everybody run for your lives! Black Bart is coming to town!' And in an instant, the room is empty. Everybody in the place just runs like hell out the door yelling "Run for your lives, Black Bart is coming to town!" The bartender figures he can't leave the place unattended, he'll get looted, so he stays behind and keeps polishing glasses, and looking nervously out the window.

Outside, the whole town is stampeding in terror, and every few minutes someone pokes his head in the door and yells "Run for your life! It's Black Bart and he's coming to town!"

Finally the town is completely deserted, just armadillos and tumble weeds going by, and after about an hour, in the distance, he can see a huge figure approaching. As it gets closer, it turns out to be this giant ugly guy, about 6 and a half feet tall, covered in black curly hair and tattoos. He's riding a grizzly bear. He pulls up in front of the bar, ties the bear to the hitching pole, steps up onto the boardwalk, rips the doors of the saloon off their hinges and throws them away. Pulls out a couple of guns and shoots the shit out of the place. The place is full of smoke and broken glass. Then he sits down and yells, "Gimme a drink of whisky!"

The bartender pours out a shot and offers it to him. The guy knocks it out of his hand and yells, "No goddamn it. I want a REAL drink of whisky!"

The bartender pours out a tumbler full of booze, and brings it over. The big guy slaps it away, and yells "NO! You little pipsqueak. Bring me a real drink of whisky!"

The terrified bartender picks up the bottle and brings it over. The guy grabs the bottle and throws it against the wall.

"No goddammit. For the last time, I want a REAL goddamned drink of whisky and if you don't bring it, I'm a gonna tear off your arms!"

So the bartender goes behind the counter and rolls out a whole 20 gallon keg of hootch, and wheels it over. The big guy picks it up in both hands and bites the end off it, spits it out, and then drinks down the whole barrel. Gives out a huge belch and wipes his mouth.

The bartender is standing there shaking like a leaf, and says, "Is there anything else I can get for you sir? A bite of lunch perhaps?"

The big guy stands up, puts on his hat and says, "Naw, I gotta get the hell outta here. Black Bart's coming to town."

"Nice."

He smiled, picked up his glass, finished his drink, and then took up his 12 string and started tuning it.

He said to me, "Give me a G, would you?"

I blew a brief note on my flute and then put it back down.

He looked at his watch and squinted and said, "Ten minutes, and then we're back on."

Right.

I went downstairs in search of a beer, and ran into a couple of young guys in the lobby.

They had guitar cases, and when they saw me they headed me off from the bar and introduced themselves.

435

I have no memory of who they were, but the long and the short of it was that they had come to town hoping to get a gig opening for us for the week.

It was on the tip of my tongue to say, "Are you crazy?" but I could hear chairs being knocked over in the lounge, and someone shouting, "What the fuck are you looking at you son of a bitch?" and the sound of glass breaking.

"Let me check with Stan and the manager. I might be able to get you on for the next set."

"Really? Wow, Thanks."

I ran up the stairs and found Stan looking out the window at the mountains silhouetted against the evening sky, and softly singing Willie P. Bennett's "Country Squall" to himself.

He had his back to me, and I waited at the threshold of the room to hear him finish.

He sounded weary and lonesome, and the song was perfect, a brief respite from the world, a balm for the soul.

It ended, and he turned to pick up his 12 string and saw me.

"What's up?"

"You're not gonna believe this."

We went downstairs, and the two young guys were waiting with their guitars strapped on.

"You know we can't pay you," Stan said.

"That's no problem, it's an honour just to open for you Mr. Rogers." The poor misguided fools.

So, they went on and did a half hour in the bear pit, while we went back upstairs and watched the last inning of the game. The Expos were still in the running.

None of the three of us were baseball fans particularly, but we were so tired and so pissed off and bored that we were dogging it, not giving the gig our full attention.

We realised from the start that there was no way we were going to make any headway with this audience. It was just an endurance contest, with the promise of a modest pay cheque at the end.

We went downstairs and the two young guys were just finishing up. They sounded okay, and amazingly they were still full of enthusiasm when they came off stage.

"Really? We can open for you all week? Cool."

"Yeah," Stan said, "You can do 45 minutes tomorrow."

"Wow. Thanks."

We went into the lounge and got on stage.

I leaned in towards Stan and said, "Jesus, we are a couple of evil bastards, letting those poor kids do that."

Stan shrugged and smiled.

"It'll toughen them up. They'll thank us for it in later life, besides, I want to see how the Series goes."

The two young guys stuck around for our second set, and David and I hung out with them a bit afterwards.

We found them in the lobby, talking to a couple of blonde home wreckers who had probably been the hottest things going in Cochrane or Lloydminister before they had hit the road in an early Thelma and Louise act. They looked like 4-H queens gone rogue, in skin tight jeans and leather jackets, stiletto heels, and a lot of messy wind-blown hair. Both were chewing Juicy Fruit gum, and looking distractedly around the lobby, as the young fellows made their pitch.

"Yeah, yeah, we're opening all week for the great Stan Rogers band. You should stick around, there's gonna be a lot of good music. Maybe we could get some beer later and party."

These were the kind of girls who would have no interest in folk music ever, and anyway, there was something else going on here.

They were both edgy, and kept watching the doors.

"So you guys just breezing through town on the way to the coast?" I asked.

The taller one to my left snapped her gum, and said, "Yeah, uh huh. We were going to drive to Vancouver tonight, but the cops pulled us over for speeding."

"That's a drag. What did they get you for?"

"A hundred and forty miles per hour."

"Holy shit. What are you driving?"

"A Shelby Cobra."

"Wow. A real one? Not a replica?"

The Shelby Cobra was a rare and expensive custom built car back then, and the very thing if you needed to get from Edmonton to Vancouver in under say, 4 hours by road.

"Yeah."

"Wow. So what are you doing now?"

"We're just trying to decide. The cops seized the car 'cause we were going so fast, and we're kinda nervous 'cause it's stolen. We're gonna be in trouble when they run the VIN number."

She paused and cracked her gum, and finally looked directly at me.

"Do any of you guys have any money?"

She paused, reached up and ever so slowly ran a thumb along the upper edge of her tube top.

"At all?"

The two young guys were standing there looking awestruck, and I said,

"Excuse me, I have a show to do."

The wretched gig continued.

The next night was no better.

The two young fellows got to play for a whole hour while we sat in Stan's room and watched the game.

We eventually went down to do our three sets, and the tension between us and the drunks got worse.

Stan stepped up to the mike and said, "Well, we're back again folks..."

"FUCK OFF FAGGOT."

"Here at the beautiful..."

"HOMO."

"Astoria Hotel..."

"GET OFF THE STAGE YOU FUCKING QUEERS."

We'd spent enough time in the trenches to have a good stock of zingers, retorts, and one liners to let us deal with the occasional restless crowd, but we didn't dare use them here.

One wrong word was sure to set the whole room off.

So saying something like, "Save your breath asshole, you're gonna need it for your inflatable date after the show," was definitely not on the menu.

We just had to stand there and smile and grit our teeth and let them yell abuse at us.

"Four days to payday boys," Stan said over his shoulder as we dragged ourselves upstairs after the show.

He started singing the chorus to the old Mississippi John Hurt song,"Payday, payday..." and closed his door.

The days were little better.

We hated the town.

It wasn't the cute tourist trap it is these days.

Jasper was then (or at least as I remember it) a cold, snowy and windy outpost surrounded by bleak mountains which only gave me claustrophobia.

The mornings were punctuated by the sound of box cars being shunted back and forth in the switching yard.

It sounded like artillery rocketing through the mountains. It was a bad way to wake up.

I discovered that the hotel television only carried one channel, which for some reason showed nothing but re-runs of the Mary Tyler Moore show.

I mostly spent my days in bed alternately napping and reading, with the curtains drawn against the view.

I could hear strange voices in Stan's room next door one afternoon, so I put on my old brown terry cloth house coat and went over to see who it might be.

It was there that I first met Bill Bourne and Jim Morison, who were in those days traveling together as a duo called "Sweetgrass."
They had played this gig and were stopping by to say hi, offer support, and maybe play a few tunes after the gig.
Jim was to play bass for us some years later.
He remembers me coming into the room looking like Marley's ghost in a Phyllis Diller fright wig.

It was Friday night, second last night of the run.
Our young friends had finished their set, and were now sitting next to the stage.
We had taken to checking off the sets like markers on the wall of a prison cell, on the big dusty black slate next to the darts board.
  "Six more to go."
Stan adjusted his mike, and cleared his throat and said, "Hi there thrill seekers,"
  "GO FUCK YOURSELF."
  "We're the Stan Rogers band, and..."
  "FAGGOT COCKSUCKER."
  "We'd like to start out..."
  "EAT SHIT AND DIE, MOTHERFUCKER."
Right.
And a one and a two...
It was payday for the workers, and they were really pouring it back.
The guy we now thought of as Black Bart was sitting just to the left of the stage.
He had been there every night, and never once let up on us.
He was massive, and unlike his co-workers never bothered to clean up after a day spent pounding steel stakes into the ground with his fists, biting trees in half, and killing bears with his bare hands.
He just sat there in his filthy work clothes and steel toe boots, and drank and shouted insults at us.
It might have been getting on his nerves that we were not responding as we were expected to. Or maybe he had taken on more booze than normal, but he was getting more insistent and personal in his comments.
He was sitting in front of stage left, David's side, and he had his boots up on the edge of the stage.
This was clearly some kind of territorial challenge, even ignoring the fact that he was staring at Stan with a tight mean smile and giving him the finger.
It was near the end of the second set that I could see Stan starting to lose it.

439

Not being able to respond in kind was beginning to tell on him.
The vein on the side of his temple was up and throbbing, and he was missing chord changes and lyrics.
I went to the right side of the stage, and spoke to the two young guys.
    "If something happens, please grab Stan's guitars and take them upstairs.
They nodded, wide eyed, and I tossed them my room key.
I turned back to my mike just as the guy out front made a spectacularly rude and intimate comment about Stan's wife.
Oh shit, I thought, as I watched Stan stop playing and take off his guitar.
He put it down against the back wall, and I grabbed it and the 12 string and gave them to the young guys.
    "GO. NOW."
I hastily put my fiddle in the case, snapped the locks, and set it on top of the piano.
I turned back, and Stan had by now collapsed the mike stand so it was 3 feet of chrome steel with a 10 pound weight at one end.
He stepped off the stage, pulled it back over his shoulder, and set up like a baseball player.
The lout in the chair was looking away from us, and laughing with his buddies.
    I yelled, "STAN!" and he swung.
The mike stand came whistling down just as the guy turned back to face us, and he jerked his head away and the weapon missed him by a hair.
The force of the swing took Stan right around, and the base continued through the 10 inch thick concrete wall and exploded into the office, where it startled the hell out of the manager who was at his desk counting receipts.

The room got real busy after that, and I lost sight of Stan.
I did catch a glimpse of David.
He was occupied much the same as me, riding around the room on some guy's shoulders, like a jockey on a maddened Cape buffalo, as the fight that everyone had been longing for got into full swing.
I don't recall how long it lasted but my next sight of Stan was at the police station, some hours later.
He had been wrestled to the floor, hand-cuffed, loaded into a wagon, and taken away.
I had stayed behind as the wreckage was cleared away and the damage was assessed.
The hole in the wall was about a foot wide with cracks radiating out.
I could see a spray of rubble across the floor of the office. It looked

like a howitzer shell had blown through. There was broken furniture everywhere in the lounge, and the floor was ankle deep in glass and blood and spilled beer.

The manager was surprisingly cool about it.

Apparently it wasn't his first rodeo.

The police were less calm.

I had walked the mile or so to the west side of town where the RCMP station was and went in and introduced myself.

Stan was in a holding cell, pending charges.

I sat on a bench in the outer office, wondering just what we were going to do.

I knew from the warning Mum and Dad had given us years before that there was no point in calling home and looking for bail money.

Back by the cells I could hear more prolonged shouting and scuffling, a loud clang, and then silence. Apparently one or two of the revellers were still keeping the party alive back there.

The cop at the desk in front of me was sullen and brusque.

No doubt it had been a long night.

"What's going to happen with my brother? Is he okay?"

The cop shrugged and didn't look up from the forms.

"He's fine. But as soon as we get the other guy in here to sign the paper work he'll be charged with aggravated assault and attempted murder."

Jesus.

He flipped over a page.

"And vandalism."

Vandalism? That was just unfair.

The furniture wasn't broken deliberately.

And then I remembered the hole in the wall.

I heard someone call out, "We got him," and I turned as the big guy from the front row was led in. He was looking wet and bedraggled, but there was little other sign that he had been in a dust up.

I wondered how beat up Stan was.

The cop at the desk said, "Just sign this complaint and we'll start processing the guy who attacked you, and you can go home."

The guy in the plaid shirt was standing with his hands in his pockets. He looked down at the floor and shook his head.

"Nope."

The cop said, "Excuse me?"

"I'm not signing."

"What?"

"I'm not signing the complaint. It was my fault."

The cop came around the desk with the clip board and a pen.

"We need you to sign this so we can charge this guy."

"Not gonna."

The cops were standing looking at the guy in exasperation, and then the door to my right opened, and two more cops came out with Stan hand-cuffed between them.

He looked tired, and his clothes were filthy and he had been crying, but barring a scrape on his cheek, and a swollen lower lip, I could see no damage from the fight.

Maybe in the midst of the melee, he and his opponent hadn't actually landed many punches. While the rest of the room was going mad, they had presumably been merely beating their chests, roaring, and pulling down handfuls of twigs from the trees.

"Is this the guy who assaulted you?" said one of the cops.

"I refuse to press charges."

Stan's head came up and he looked at the guy.

What was this?

"I won't sign the complaint. It was my fault. I...I said a bad thing about his wife."

Stan said "No. It was my fault. I lost my temper and I could have killed you if you hadn't been so quick."

Our guy's face clouded over and his voice thickened.

He stepped a couple of paces forward.

"No. It was all my fault. I was ragging on you guys all week, and I had it coming."

Stan said, "No, man, it was all me. I should have handled it better."

Jesus, Stan, I thought, shut up.

He continued. "I just lost it, I've been on the road for weeks, I'm tired and I'm broke. I miss home...I haven't seen my kids..."

Here he broke down and started crying.

He hung his head down.

"I'm so sorry."

The other guy by now was weeping too, and the cops looked at each other, then at Stan's new buddy, and the cop with the clip board said,

"So you won't sign the complaint? We can still press charges on our own."

"I won't testify."

The cop tossed the clip board onto the counter where it slid and hit the wall with a loud smack, and said, "Fuck it. Cut 'em both loose."

Somebody freed Stan's wrists, and he and the other guy collapsed weeping into each other's arms.

One of the cops said, "Ah, Jesus Christ. Go on, get the hell out of here," and gave them both a push towards the door. "Fuck off. The both of you."

442

The two of them turned and went outside, still blubbering and
promising eternal friendship.
I was still on the bench.
One of the cops turned to me. "You need something?"
 "No, I uh..."
 "Fine. You can fuck off too."
I left the building and walked back to the hotel in the pre-dawn light,
and found our faithful openers still sitting in my room guarding the
guitars.
 "Thanks guys. I really appreciate it."
 "No problem. We're, uh, thinking that we might head out, maybe
find another place to... uh... you know... play."
I could hardly blame them.
I crashed out and woke mid-morning to pack and prepare to move on.
I hoped that our fee would at least partially cover the damage we had
done.
I went downstairs and found a very subdued and penitent Stan talking
to the manager in the lobby.
I went over and said, "I'm really sorry about all this."
I gestured to the room where the staff were sorting through the mess,
trying with little success to find chairs that were still in one piece.
Someone was dragging a bag of broken glass out the door.
There was a large pool of beer on the floor, and the place stank.
The manager waved off my apology.
 "Hey, don't worry about it. Shit happens you know? It's what
insurance is for."
Stan turned to me.
 "He wants us to stay on and finish the gig."
 "He what?"
 "Yeah, I like you guys, and besides that, this place will be jammed
tonight when word gets around."
Holy shit.
This was good news.
Sort of.
We weren't being fired
The bad news was that we still had one more show to do.
I needn't have worried.
By 8 o'clock the room was full, and all the guys who had been
hassling us all week were our best friends, now that some sort of ritual
bloodletting had been enacted. Black Bart, who had been on Stan's case
all week, and whom Stan had very nearly killed was there, buying Stan
drinks and proudly introducing him to all his friends as the "crazy
motherfucker who almost killed me."

The following morning we were to head south to Lake Louise to look up a friend before continuing on to Winnipeg.

The manager, who had to be one of the most easy going and forgiving people in the world, offered to drive David down and meet us there.

"It's a lovely day for a drive and I promised Dave a ride in the Lamborghini."

A what?

Jesus.

This guy could afford to be relaxed.

He and David disappeared in a roar of high octane supercharged exhaust, and Stan and I followed rather more sedately, but not before Stan's new blood brother came by to wish us well.

They gave each other a last hug.

"I love you man."

"I love you man."

Oh Jesus, more tears.

They wiped their faces, and Stan blew his nose, and gave the guy's shoulder a final manly squeeze, and then turned to me, cleared his throat and said, "Okay, time to saddle up."

Saddle up?

What, we're in a John Wayne movie now?

God, I pity women.

CHAPTER 52

Firing Ronald

We couldn't find our friend in Lake Louise.
It was full of tanned and buff ski bums and fuzzy blonde ski bunnies,
and we were decidedly out of our element. We did find a place to eat, a
big barn of a cafeteria that featured a hot beef sandwich for a dollar fifty.
"Sounds good," said Stan, "I could do with a decent meal after this
week."
We lined up, and got our plates and shuffled along the counter to where
a skinny kid in a T shirt and a purple Mohawk haircut was alternately
hacking at a giant rump of beef and blaspheming in a Cockney voice.
"Fucking job. Give me this piece of shit knife...won't cut worth a
fuck...sod this for a game of soldiers."
He looked up and glared at Stan, and gestured with the knife.
"And what can I do for you lot?"
"I'll have the hot roast beef sandwich...uh...please."
"Right."
He took the knife and savagely began to haggle off a slab of beef about
the size and thickness of a manhole cover.
He tossed a slice of bread onto Stan's plate and then loaded the beef
onto it.
Stan had to shift his weight in order to support it.
"Thanks."
"Potatoes?"
"Sure."
BAM.
"Gravy?"
"Absolutely."
SPLAT.
"Wow. Thanks."
"Sod it. NEXT."
Stan lurched off with enough food to keep Belgium for a week.
And now it was my turn. And then David's.
We ate it all, amazingly, and it was wonderful.

We were all feeling better.

The horrendous gig was over, and we'd got paid. Stan had miraculously avoided a stay in the slammer, and I had been spared some awkward questions from the parents, not to mention Stan's wife. Our bellies were full for a change, and we had a clear day for the drive. I got up to get a round of coffees, and Stan and David leaned back and lit up.

Life was good.

We briefly considered going back for an order to go, but we could now see the kid having a heated discussion with the manager, which finished with the kid repeatedly jamming the knife up to the hilt in the roast, while looking into the manager's eyes and shouting, "I QUIT, YOU FUCKING TWAT."

He undid his apron, balled it up, and threw it in the manager's face and then stormed out, and as he kicked the door open he yelled over his shoulder, "FUCKING TOSSER."

We decided it wasn't worth the bother.

We loaded up and turned the van to the East.

We had two more shows to do and then head for Ontario.

We had a couple of days in hand to make it to Winnipeg in a leisurely fashion, but that would mean a night in a hotel, and added expense.

So we poured on the coals, and held the van steady at 70 miles per hour, and made it to Mitch Podolak's house around three in the morning and crashed.

The morning ritual at Mitch and Ava's house started with a period of prolonged coughing as Mitch fired up the first smoke of the day, a hacking phlegm-laden obbligato to accompany the sounds of farting and laughing and showering, toilets flushing, and the two of them yelling at each other from various parts of the house.

It was chaos.

The smell of frying bacon would drift up the stairs, and then the front door would slam a couple of times, and then a couple more times, as various forgotten items were remembered and retrieved.

Outside there was more shouting, and then the cars would start up, and they would drive off to work in a squeal of noisy fan belts and tires spinning on wet leaves.

We would just be falling back into blessed sleep when the front door would again crash open, and Mitch would come back up the stairs coughing and hacking and wheezing and cursing and farting and muttering to himself as he looked for one more forgotten thing.

Then back down the stairs, and the door would slam again, and once more the car would squeal and grind its way down the street.

They were, and are, enormously kind and generous and wildly eccentric people.

Nothing was ever done quietly or in half measures.

They opened their house to us for all the years we traveled through the West, and Mitch, aside from having funded our first record, was a huge source of encouragement and criticism for Stan, and a fiercely loyal friend.

The two of them spent hours arguing and laughing and yelling good naturedly at each other.

Mitch called Stan "Baldy", and Mitch was "Fatty"; not wildly original, but on the mark.

They decided to have a contest one morning at breakfast.

Stan was carrying about 60 extra pounds at that time, and they determined to stage a race to lose the most weight.

There was a weigh–in, and the deal was struck, and the stakes were named, whereupon Mitch went into the bathroom for a couple of minutes.

We heard a flush, and then another, and then another, and then he emerged laughing, saying "Ha ha asshole, I just lost ten pounds right there."

He stepped back on the scales, and to my horror, he had.

I felt faint.

Stan and I decided to look for a cowboy hat for our Dad.

Mitch told us where the best store was, a couple of blocks from the corner of Portage and Main.

As we went through the intersection, the van began to gyrate and wobble wildly back and forth from side to side.

Stan looked concerned.

I said, "What the hell is that?"

"I don't know, but it can't be good."

I knew nothing about cars, but this sounded expensive.

My fallback position when the van made suspicious noises was to turn up the radio. I was just reaching for the volume control when Stan pulled over to the curb.

He got down and crawled under the van and came back up a minute later.

He dusted his hands, and lit a smoke and leaned against the left front fender, and said, "We're screwed. It's the drive shaft. The U joint is gone."

Jesus.

Stan called a tow truck and we waited at the corner of Portage and Main for about an hour.

It is a famously cold and windy corner, and it was living up to its
reputation. Garbage cans were rolling and tumbling down the street,
banging into cars which were unable to swerve out of the way. We
could see drunks and rummies being pushed along the side walk as if
by some giant unseen bouncer. Everything was covered in a fine layer
of dirt and pulverized pigeon shit, and the temperature was dropping.
We were frozen and numb and Stan had run out of cigarettes by the
time the tow arrived. It took us to the local Chev dealer, and then we
caught a cab back to Mitch and Ava's.
Replacing a U joint wasn't a complex job, but it would be two days
before we could get it back, and then we had to leave for Thunder Bay.
The earliest it would be ready was 1 PM the day of the show, and
getting to the gig would be a close run thing.
Meanwhile, we had a show to do in Winnipeg.
Mitch had put us into the Museum Theatre, across from the Hudson's
Bay Store downtown.
It was a nice place, and for a change tickets were selling well.
Except for the repair bill looming on the horizon, things were looking
up.
Then, the night of the show, as we were finishing the sound check,
Ronald himself appeared out of the wings.
He was wearing a new beige velour suit, which was a couple of sizes
too large, and made him look even more like a ventriloquist's dummy
than usual.
    "I thought I'd fly out and see the last couple of shows." he said.
He shook Stan's hand and said "See? I've been practicing my
handshake. Good grip huh?"
Stan instinctively wiped his hand on his jeans, and David and I left the
stage without bothering to try out the new sensation.
We went outside so he could have a smoke.
We were standing on the fire escape, shivering in the chilly wind and
David said, "So who the Hell is paying the freight on that little shit?"
"I don't know. I didn't invite him."
We confronted Stan a few minutes later, and he confirmed that yes, we
were paying for Ronald's last minute decision to fly out and see us play.
Stan had the bill for the suit as well.
I looked at it.
It was a lot of money for something Mortimer Snerd wouldn't be caught
dead in a ditch wearing.
This was not playing well and we were all pretty much fed up.
The gig went well though, and we had for the first time in Winnipeg a
sellout.
The extra money we made on the back end of the contract all went to

cover Ronald's air ticket and new wardrobe. So we were once again pretty much broke. The van was going to be ready tomorrow, and we weren't sure how we were going to pay for it.

I'm not sure what happened to sort it out.

I think that our Mum most likely wired the money to us out of record company funds.

In any event, Stan was able to get the van out of hock the next afternoon, and he arrived about 1:15 to load up and get us to Thunder Bay.

We had all the gear and suitcases piled in Mitch and Ava's front yard, and when Stan stopped we threw everything into the back.

A quick series of hugs all around to Mitch and Ava, and we were off.

Stan insisted on doing the whole drive himself, as he felt quite rightly, that he was the safest guy behind the wheel.

I don't think he dropped it below 80 the whole way, and the rest of us were kept busy watching out the front and back for the cops. I have little memory of that Thunder Bay show save for the sweeping power turn Stan made in the gravel parking lot up to the loading door. Some volunteers were having a smoke on the steps and as we came hurtling in, they scattered in every direction. Stan had timed the drift perfectly, and as the van rocked to a stop we were a mere three feet from the door. The van doors burst open, and we hit the ground running with guitars and amps and other bits of gear. It looked like a SWAT raid.

We were playing in an old community hall, and my only other memory of that show was sharing a sink in the kitchen with the lady who was trying to make coffee. I was having a shave, and it was close quarters as she filled the big urn.

"Try not to get your filthy and unwanted body hair in the coffee." she said primly.

Beyond that, nothing.

We played the show, got paid presumably, and loaded the van again to start for home.

It had already been a long day, and the drive across the top of the lake was still ahead of us.

It meant a night of trying to keep awake and watch for the deer and moose and other dare devil wild life that inhabited the woods, and who felt compelled to dart out in front of the van at the last moment.

There were also the truckers, who late at night tended to use the whole road, and coming around a corner you would have on one side a hundred foot drop into an icy black lake, and on the other side a wild eyed cowboy strung out on coffee and white crosses, driving a truck with the trailer behind him giving off flames and black smoke from the

449

seized brake caliper the driver had either not noticed or was too wired
up to care about.

It was tough on the nerves.

We made it as far as Marathon, and we were low on gas. As we studied
the map under the dome light, it became evident that there were no
towns within striking distance that might have a 24 hour station.

We didn't want to get stranded at the side of the road to have some
18 wheeler plow into us, or worse, have a tribe of overall-wearing
gummers come creeping out of the woods, and drag us back to their lair
to initiate us into the mysteries of hillbilly love.

We held a committee meeting in the van and it was decided we would
spend the night in the parking lot of the now closed gas station.

Sleeping arrangements were sorted out, and it fell to me to sleep on the
floor behind the front seats. David got the Caddy seat. Stan and Ronald
clambered up to the sleeping shelf at the back, and made a nest out of
the damp and moldering sleeping bags.

Ronald had a couple of reefers, and he and Stan got a buzz on while I
worked away on a bottle of nasty over proof Scotch that I had made the
mistake of buying.

We all dropped off after a bit, and when I awoke it was coming up on 6
AM.

The lights were on in the gas station, and the pumps were running.

Very quietly I crawled up to the front seat and started the van. I drove to
the pumps, filled the tank, paid the bill, pocketed the receipt, and pulled
out on the highway.

The others were still asleep, and technically I shouldn't have been
driving without a companion as I was still on a beginner's license. I felt
confident enough though, until about an hour or so later when I saw an
OPP cruiser following close behind.

I checked my speed. That was fine, but I could see him talking on the
radio.

We were being checked out.

Ronald was now awake, and crawled over David to join me up front.
That was better.

Now I was legal.

We kept on for a while until we neared Wawa.

Another police cruiser met us coming the other way and banged a swift
U turn and caught up to us.

What was this?

We were gliding down a long incline and I saw the sign for a Husky
station ahead. I needed a whiz and a coffee.

   "Anyone need coffee or a pee?"

There were groans from the back, and I hit the right turn signal and coasted into the lot of the restaurant.

The cruisers followed, and put their circus lights on.

A third cruiser came rocketing into the lot from the other direction and skidded to a stop in front of us, spraying gravel against the front of the restaurant.

He had his lights on too.

What the hell was going on?

I turned off the motor and opened the driver's door, and made to step down.

Someone shouted, "Keep your hands where I can see them."

I raised my hands, and very slowly put one foot on the ground.

There were three pump action shot guns with mouths like the Holland Tunnel pointed at me.

Now I really needed to pee.

"What's going on, Officer?"

"Who is in the van with you?"

"Uh, just me, my brother, our bass player, and our manager."

"That's four? There are four of you?"

"Uh, yeah. What is all this?"

"This morning a girl was kidnapped and raped at gun point by four men in a dark blue van like yours."

"Ah Jesus, no, when?"

"About 8 o'clock."

"Well we're a band, and we were in Thunder Bay last night and we gassed up in Marathon about 6 or so. I've got the receipt."

One of the cops moved a little forward along the left front fender of the cruiser, and kept the gun on me.

We had to be able to solve this.

We were innocent, and besides, I really, really, needed to pee.

I said, "What did these guys look like?"

We were a pretty disparate and motley crew, after all.

No way was there another bunch that looked like us.

I could hear groans and feel the van sway as there was thrashing behind me in the back of the van.

Stan was awake.

The cop said, "One of them is about 6 feet tall with long blond hair, and two others are short and dark, and the other is a big bald guy who looks about 40 years old."

Jesus. What were the odds? That pretty much described us.

It was at this point that the van door slid open and a very cranky and disheveled Stan came storming around the back corner of the van with Ronald in tow.

"WHAT THE HELL IS GOING ON HERE?"

451

The shotguns were all simultaneously shucked, and swung towards Stan, and he skidded to a halt and very slowly and carefully bent down and got on his knees with his hands in the air.

Good boy. Smart lad.

It all took about a half hour to sort out.

We showed the cops the contract and the poster from our show the night before, and I produced the gas receipt, and eventually we were accepted as being decent citizens, but not before an OPP helicopter swept in and scattered a couple of metric tonnes of dust and bird shit as it circled the area.

Somebody had neglected to call off the air strike.

Finally we were released, and I was able to get to the bathroom, and when I came out the other guys were sitting in a booth looking at menus, while the other patrons who had seen the whole thing play out watched us in complete and utter silence.

"Wow. Life on the road, huh?"

Ronald was enjoying the morning now that the crisis was over.

None of us said anything.

The experience with the shotguns had left us shaky and depressed.

This was the perfect ending to the whole rotten tour, a last kick in the nuts by Fate, and we were all feeling wrung out. What else was going to happen?

We got back into the van, and before Stan could start up, Ronald cleared his throat and said, "I hate to bring this up now, but do you think we could settle our bill?"

We all turned and looked at him.

What?

"I have to pay some bills at home and I was thinking of having you drop me off at the airport when we get to Sudbury. I'll need some cash for the air ticket."

There was a long and ugly silence, and Stan turned around to face front again, sighed, and in a low voice said, "Okay, what are the numbers?"

The long and the short of it was that by the time we settled Ronald's outstanding invoices for money we had never wanted him to spend in the first place, plus an air ticket to Winnipeg, booked at last minute, full rate, and a suit that a performing chimp might wear if he ran an escort service, plus his full price air ticket back to Ottawa, we each had about 140 dollars left in our pockets after a month on the road.

Technically, I was still in positive territory, as I had left home with about 80 bucks, but this wasn't really enough.

"Hardly worth the bother is it?" I said, dropping the cash into his lap.

"What?"

"A month on the road."

David counted out his share of the nut, and grabbed Ronald's shirt, pulled him sharply forward, and stuffed the roll of bills violently into the breast pocket. He then slammed him back into the seat, turned away and lit a cigarette.

Ronald said "Hey, come on, I work hard for you guys. This is no picnic for me either."

Stan put the van in gear and gunned it out onto the highway.

Nothing more was said until Ronald leapt out of the van during a rest stop, and ran across the road to buy us a bottle of scotch.

"Look at this," David said, as our manager dodged traffic in front of the LCBO.

"He's buying us a special treat."

Stan was rubbing his eyes, and flicking ashes from his cigarette out the no-draft window.

He looked over across the road.

"Yeah, that'll make up for everything."

I figured he'd invoice us for it later anyway.

We didn't fire him then, amazingly.

We kept him on for a couple more months over the winter, and finally broke the news to him over breakfast in a diner in Ottawa.

No one got hurt, but it wasn't pretty, and I heard years later that a mutual friend ran into him about an hour later and asked how the meeting went.

"Well, they didn't kill me." he said.

True enough. It was a test of our collective wills, and we should have been proud of the restraint we showed. But what it really meant was we were once again without someone to do the booking.

CHAPTER 53

The Philly Folk Festival

We got invited to play the Philadelphia Folk Festival.
That was the good news.
The bad news was they apparently had no money to pay, and for once,
David and I urged Stan to go down and do the gig alone.

"It'll be good exposure. There might be a lot of club owners at the
festival. They'll see you and hire you and we can come down another
time."
Stan was adamant. "I'm not going there without you guys. It's the band
or nothing. I'm going to tell them no."

We were on our way at that moment to play at Penn's Landing for
a week, on board the Gazella Primera, a 100 year old Portuguese 3-
masted barquentine which was moored semi-permanently at the bottom
of Market Street in Philly.
It had become a regular gig for us.
We played two shows a day, one in the afternoon, and one at dusk.
It was a little weird, as the tide went in and out. Sometimes we would
be looking up at the audience. Later in the day we would be far above
them.
The one constant was the summer heat in Philadelphia. There was no
shade on board, and the sun reflecting off the deck of the ship as we
played was near lethal.

The guys who worked the ship were all immensely fit young rich kids.
They were handsome, and tanned and smart, but we got along with
them pretty well anyway.
They liked the act, and we spent a lot of pleasant afternoons with them,
between shows, wandering the streets around Society Hill, drifting into
the little bars in search of the perfect juke box.
We liked the Khyber Pass on 3rd Street a lot. It had a huge selection
of foreign beers, and lots of polished wood and brass. The juke box
had Duke Ellington, and Benny Goodman, and Dave Brubeck, and the

Chieftains, and Van Morrison, and every Beatles and Rolling Stones single ever released.

Nice place.

We'd kick back by the dusty window facing the street, and order a couple of bottles of Old Peculiar, or a Whitbread's Pale Ale, plug a couple of bucks into the machine, and read the paper, and watch the shadows of people going by on the street outside.

I had once read a book in which a character said he "wouldn't mind if the whole world was indoors and semi-dark."

The Khyber Pass felt just about perfect that way.

The first night we ever spent on board the ship, things got a little out of hand.

Stan had got into some sort of beer and testosterone- fueled competition with one of the crew, and it led to a wrestling match between the two of them on the deck. Stan was a big guy, 6'4" and heavy, and he was a fairly experienced brawler.

His opponent was much smaller, but after years at sea, hauling on ropes and running the rigging in every kind of weather, he was much more fit than Stan could ever expect to be.

At the end of maybe 5 minutes, Stan was flat on his back, pouring sweat and blowing like a whale.

The guy from the crew was leaning casually on the rail, sipping a beer and accepting the plaudits of his mates, not a hair out of place.

Stan was game though, and wanted another go after a while. But I was concerned for his heart. He hadn't a chance against this guy.

I proposed leaving the ship and going on a pub crawl.

The details are a bit murky, but I do remember waking the next morning, feeling cramped and sore, and sick.

I rolled over to ease my back, and opened my eyes. Something was wrong. I wasn't in my berth on board the ship. I was out doors. I sat up and looked around and nearly fainted. I was eighty some feet above the deck, having decided the night before, apparently, to sleep in the crow's nest.

This was very bad. How the Hell did I get there? I hate heights.

I couldn't stay there, at least not for long. The beer I had consumed during our revels was urgently needing to be set free, and the mechanics of accomplishing that from this height were beyond me. Besides that, there were people scattered below me, sleeping on the deck. It wouldn't be polite.

I took a closer look at the people below. I hoped they were sleeping. There was a scary randomness to the way the bodies were positioned.

I looked over to where the US Coast Guard ship, The Eagle was moored.

Maybe a sniper had ranged in on us during the night.

Stan and Fred Oster, the owner of Vintage Instruments, and a now very conservative looking and respectable presence on PBS' Antiques Road Show, were both sleeping on their backs, head to head, on the broad wooden rail that surrounded the deck.
What had possessed them to pass out there?
One wrong move would give them a very nasty awakening, either hitting the deck or falling 15 feet into whatever it was we were floating on. It wasn't water, not by any standard we might use.
A dip in that harbour would likely result in an outbreak of boils, or chemical burns, or the clap.
I climbed very carefully and shakily down from my perch, and even more carefully woke the two sleepers by grabbing them and pulling them simultaneously onto the deck, and then raced to the head and raised the level of the harbour by a foot.

We were taking a break after the first show one afternoon, and Theresa Pyott, the Artistic Director of the Philly Festival came over and sat down beside me.
She was a pretty blonde woman, friendly and pleasant and funny. We all liked her a lot.
She took my hand and said, "We're all really excited to have you guys at the festival this year."
So I was going to be the one to deliver the bad news.
Damn it. I didn't want to hurt her feelings. She had only ever been nice to us, and here I was going to drop the big one on her.
    "Yeah, thanks, but we're not coming,"
    "Excuse me?"
    "We can't afford to come down on what you guys are offering, and Stan won't do it solo. We told him he should, but he won't come down without the band."
She looked confused.
    "What? You're turning down the Philadelphia Folk Festival?"
    "Yeah, I guess we are. I'm sorry."
    "Nobody turns down the Philadelphia Folk Festival. Nobody has ever turned us down. It's..."She paused, at a loss for words.
    "I'm sorry but we simply can't afford to come all that way to play for what amounts to nothing."
Theresa had now gone from confused to appalled.
    "You're not trying to tell me that you expect to make Money... from Folk Music?"
I lost my temper a little bit.

"Folk Music is not a goddamned religion. We didn't take a vow of poverty when we went into this. It just looks that way."
I was building into a rant.

"We're not lawyers or doctors, just fooling around with this shit in our spare time, on weekends like everyone else around here. This is what we do for a living, such as it is. We're serious about it, and we can't afford to play on what you guys are willing to pay us. I'm sorry, but we're going to have to give it a miss. Thanks anyway."
She was gob-smacked, and I was embarrassed and ashamed. She was a friend of the band, and only had good intentions, and I had let loose on her to the point of being rude.
She went off to talk to Stan, and I could see from a distance that she was getting much the same answer, couched a little less diplomatically, by the look of it.
She left pretty hurriedly.
In any event, they came back with a better offer, bless them, and we could now afford to come down and play.

So we drove south, later that summer, through a heavy rain that was sweeping through the dark hills of Pennsylvania.
It was the Thursday before the festival.
On the way we saw a car stranded at the side of the highway near Scranton.
It was night, and the car was in a bad place. It could cause an accident.
Stan slowly and carefully applied the brakes, and after much swerving and slipping on the wet pavement finally managed to come to a halt maybe half a mile down the long hill.
He put the blinkers on, put it in reverse, and backed up towards the car.
There was a lone woman standing forlornly by the dead vehicle, in the down pour.
Stan parked, and got out. He was immediately soaked in wind driven rain.

"Wait here."
"No, it's okay. We can help."
"You guys stay in the van. I don't want her to see the two of you and be scared."
What?
We were scarier than the six foot four bearded behemoth that was now marching toward her through the downpour and the lightning? All he needed to complete the picture was a couple of bolts in his neck.
We watched, as she dove back into her car upon seeing Stan, and locked her doors.
There were some negotiations through the window, and it developed

that we were going to tow this poor creature through the rain, another hundred miles or so to Bryn Mawr where she lived.

We had a 50 foot electrical extension cord, and it was wrapped around the front bumper of her car, and then attached to the back bumper of our van, and we set off.
It was a stupid and dangerous thing to do, and so typical of Stan.
Whatever happened, he was not going to leave some person stranded alone on a rain swept road in the dark.
We got up to speed, and she was having a lot of trouble with the steering, as there was now no power assist, or windshield wipers, and she tended to wander back and forth and creep up beside us as we coasted down the hills. The rain was torrential. It was like driving under the English Channel. Maybe three hours later we managed to get her to her own driveway.
We pushed her car up to the garage, and Stan stowed the now ruined electrical cord in the van, waved off her thanks, and we climbed back in.

We checked into the festival hotel late that night
We had nice rooms for a change.
It was a suite, overlooking the pool in the courtyard, with two bedrooms, a sitting room, and, OH MY GOD... A MINI BAR!
What a fantastic country. Hotel rooms that came with free booze.
This was the life. This was more like it. We emptied the thing within minutes. Two cases of beer, two bottles of white wine, a couple bottles of red, and a couple dozen of those little child-sized servings of rye and scotch.
Wow. What a great place.
It felt like Christmas morning.
Of course, like the rubes we were, we didn't realize that all of this stuff was automatically going on our bill, and in fact the mini bars would all be electronically closed as soon as the rest of the wastrels and ne'er do wells arrived sometime tomorrow. I guess the hotel had been burned before.
So we got blitzed and went to bed.
It had been a full day, and we were tired.

Next morning, the phone rang in the sitting room.
I just happened to be on my way back from the bathroom.
I staggered over and picked it up.
    "Hello?"
    "This is the festival hospitality room. You have a bill you need to pay."

"Excuse me?"

"You checked in late last night, and we are not paying for that room. We are only picking up the tab for the days you are playing at the festival."

"That's okay, we didn't expect..."

"And you also have a sizable bar bill that you need to pay immediately. The Philadelphia Folk Festival does not pick up any extra room charges."

"Uh, Okay. I can come down and give you cash or American Express Travelers' cheques. Whatever you need."

"We don't have any intention of paying for your alcohol."

"That's fine. We never expected that. I'll be right down. What room are you in?"

"We need payment immediately."

"Yeah, look, I understand. Just tell me where I need to go to give you the cash."

"We don't pay for bar tabs."

"Uh yeah. Look...uh... Jesus."

This was going nowhere. I could probably ask directions to the Hospitality Suite at the front desk. "I'll be right down. Okay?"

"You can't expect the Philadelphia Folk Festival to subsidize your life style."

Bloody Hell. Apparently my old Sunday School teacher was now a volunteer at a major folk festival.

I hung up and looked around.

Our lifestyle did leave something to be desired, judging by the state of the room.

The floor was littered with dozens of tiny empty booze bottles. It looked like the Keebler elves had staged an orgy.

The phone rang again.

"Hello?"

"This is the Folk Festival hospitality room. We need you to pay your room charges."

This was a different person now.

"Yeah, I know. I was just talking to someone else down there, and I'll be right down with the cash if one of you will just tell me where I need to be."

"We don't pay for alcohol, or any other incidentals."

Goddamn.

I hung up again.

This was stupid.

I sat down and held my head in my hands.

It was hard to think.

My brain was throwing itself against the inside of my skull.

Where were my pants?

Presumably I'd had pants when we checked in the night before.

I was going to need them if I was going to go downstairs and pay this bill.

I went into my room and found them, pulled them right side out and struggled into them. I buckled my belt.

There. Progress.

I wondered where my socks might be.

The phone began ringing once more.

Oh Christ. Here we go again. There was an unopened beer on the table.

I went over and picked it up. It was warm, but I popped it open and shot-gunned the whole thing anyway.

Ah. That was better.

I picked up the phone and spoke.

"Hello. Franz Kafka speaking."

"This is the festival hospitality staff. Is Mr. Rogers there? You have a room charge, and an outstanding bar tab."

I looked over at the desk by the window. Christ, we'd drunk all the wine too.

"Yeah, if you only knew. Look, if you just tell me where you are, I'll come down and..."

The door to Stan's room was wrenched open.

He looked out at me, squinting against the light.

"Who the Hell keeps calling at this fucking hour?"

"It's the festival. They want us to pay the room bill and the bar tab, but they won't tell me where to go."

"Hold on."

He disappeared back into his room, and came out a moment later, wearing a Tee shirt, and savagely pummeling his morning hard-on down into his jeans.

He zipped up, wincing, and grabbed the phone from me and said, "This is Stan Rogers. Who the Hell is this? Uh huh...uh huh...yeah. Room what? You wait right there. I'll be down in a minute."

He went back into his room for his cigarettes and lighter.

We went down the hall, and got into the elevator.

He was standing with his head lowered between his shoulders, breathing heavily, staring straight ahead with an unlit cigarette in his mouth.

He was barefoot, and mortally hung over.

I'd snagged a couple more warm Rolling Rocks before we left the room, and I offered him one.

"Thanks." He popped it open and drained it in one long gulp, sucking on the aluminum can so hard that it collapsed in on itself. The elevator stopped and the doors opened. Stan let out an enormous belch that echoed and reverberated down the corridor like the roar of the Balrog in The Lord of the Rings. He crushed the can in his fist and dropped it into the sand ash tray next to the door.

We got out of the elevator, turned left, and went down another hallway, into a room marked "Festival Hospitality."

"There's an ironic statement if I ever saw one."

Inside the Hospitality Suite, people were running back and forth, shuffling papers, stuffing envelopes and yelling into phones.

It takes a lot of coordination to manage a major festival.

Stan took the cigarette out of his mouth, planted his feet, and in a loud and terrible voice said,

"WHO THE HELL IS IN CHARGE HERE?"

There was a sudden and complete silence, and the lights flickered briefly.

Everyone was looking at the two of us.

"Can we help you?"

"Who the hell has been calling my room about a bar tab?"

A harassed- looking woman behind a table raised her hand.

Jesus. That was brave. I wouldn't have.

Stan looked truly awful.

His little remaining hair was sticking out from the sides of his head. His eyes were swollen and blood shot, and he had a large red pillow crease running diagonally down his face like a poorly healed machete scar. He had neglected to fasten his belt, and in his haste to dress, he had managed to put his shirt on both inside out and backwards.

He came slowly forward, and stood at the table, swaying slightly.

"How much is the room bill?"

His voice sounded like granite slabs being ground together.

"Excuse me?"

He cleared his throat.

"What is the sum total of my indebtedness to this organization?"

"One hundred and forty dollars, and eighty three cents...uh, sir."

"Fine. I will require a receipt."

He was being ominously formal.

This wasn't good.

The room was still and absolutely quiet, save for a ringing phone going unanswered.

He rolled the unlit Rothman's to the side of his mouth with his tongue,

as the poor volunteer looked frantically for a receipt book.
He cleared his throat and looked at the other woman behind the desk
who was helping with the search.

"We are the Stan Rogers Band, and we always pay our own way."
I looked over at him, startled. This was going to be good news for Mum
and Dad.
He reached into his pocket, and pulled out his lighter and lit the
cigarette.
Someone spoke up, "This is a non-smoking..."
Stan slowly swiveled his head around and looked at her through the
cloud of smoke.
Her voice trailed off, as Stan with his other hand reached into his pocket
and pulled out a roll of bills, and began to count twenties out onto the
table.
He leaned in toward the timorous lady behind the table as he did, and
spoke quietly and slowly, timing the cadence of his words with the snap
of the bills.

"Don't....you ....EVER.....fuck.....with ....my ....band ....again.....Now
would you please give me my change, and likewise my receipt, and
kindly leave me THE FUCK ALONE for the rest of the day."
The terrified woman flinched at each word, partly because of the force
and the threat in his demeanor, and likely also because of the fact that
he had yet to brush his teeth, and having just wakened after a night of
bingeing, had breath like the sweaty end of a leper's crutch.
She handed him the change, scribbled out a receipt, and Stan turned
and stumped slowly and heavily out of the room.
I followed as far as the door, and then, feeling that I could perhaps
leaven the situation somewhat, turned and said to the room at large in a
high squeaky Mickey Mouse voice,

"Yeah ...What he said."
I turned and raced down the hall to catch him at the elevator.
He was silent as we went back up. Just leaning with his eyes closed, his
face pressed against the cool metal of the elevator wall and sucking in
the life giving smoke.
We got back to the room, and he went directly into the bathroom and
had by my watch, a seven and a half minute pee.
He stumbled back to his bed, collapsed into it like a felled Redwood
and slept until noon.

We were a little miffed by what we felt was our poor placing on the bill.
We had been stuck in somewhere near the beginning of the show, early
Friday afternoon, when we wouldn't get the benefit of the Jumbo-tron
screen and the dramatic lighting.

We loaded up the van, and drove to the site.

There was a performers' shuttle, but we were feeling pissed off and anxious, and not a little snotty and aggressive, and being in the van together was a way of preserving our cohesion as a band, not to mention our thoroughly nasty mood.

We drove onto the site and were confronted by a volunteer in an orange vest, who said, "No private vehicles are allowed on site. You can't come in."

Oh boy. Here we go.

"We are performers."

"You don't have a parking pass."

"We weren't given one."

"You should have asked for one."

"Well, no one told us that did they?"

"You'll have to park over in the public lot."

Stan leaned out the window.

"I am getting sick and tired of dealing with you people. We are not going to carry four guitars, a fiddle, and a goddamned bass amp all the way from the parking lot, through a filthy swamp, and up that hill in this kind of stinking heat. If you think..."

He was interrupted by a volunteer supervisor, who had run up and pulled the parking lot person aside.

"It's okay. It's okay. He can come in. We'll fix him up with a pass. It's our mistake...sorry....sorry...sorry." She waved us along, and walked beside the van, past more security, shooing people from our path, and then very kindly got us set up in the backstage area.

There were more apologies.

The word had obviously gone out that a trio of psychos with a deep sense of grievance had descended upon them, and had to be placated at all costs.

This was good.

We opened our cases and tuned up, and then got back into the van, and sat waiting for it to be time to go on.

Stan and David lit up smokes, and we passed a bottle of Teacher's back and forth.

The inside of the van was sweltering.

We could have opened a window, but that might have invited some friendly soul to come along and try to engage with us. We didn't want that.

It was a little like waiting to "go over the top." We were nervous, but also itching to go out there and hammer on the crowd.

We got the call to go on, and we slid the door open and climbed out.

Stan turned around and looked at us

"We all okay?"

"Yeah. We're good."

He threw his cigarette into the grass, ground it out with his foot, hitched up his pants, and said, "Okay. Let's do it."

I started to giggle, and said, "Fix bayonets, men," in a deep voice, and we walked in single file to the stage, heads down, not looking to either side.

I suppose it would have been Gene Shay who introduced us. We didn't hear any of that.

My only memory of the set is that it was loud and frenzied, and we all spent most of that next half hour in the air, and as we finished the last chord, David and I spontaneously kicked the mike stands off the front of the stage and stalked off.

We walked back to the van, once again in single file, ignoring the other performers who were standing there applauding, and shaking off as well the stage hand who was grabbing at us and saying, "They want you back."

We packed up and got in the van.

Stan started it up and floored it, and burned a huge semi-circle in the grass and bucketed out of the back stage area out to the road, and from there to the hotel.

Some hours later, we were bulleting cans of beer from our balcony into the pool for the benefit of the swimmers, and the phone rang.

Eadie got it, and then handed the phone to Stan.

"It's for you," and went back to target practice.

Stan came back a minute or so later, smiling.

"What was that all about?"

He bent down, and picked up a full can of Rolling Rock, tossed it into the air and spun it end for end. He caught it, took careful aim, and then drilled it into the pool next to where Margaret Christl was floating at rest.

It missed her by inches, as he probably intended, and she yelped and disappeared under the surface.

He turned to us and said, "I guess we did okay tonight. They offered us another spot tomorrow."

I don't remember doing the second show.

I do remember watching Steve Goodman do his set.

There was a kind of modified traffic light on the main stage at Philly. Green meant go, Yellow meant you had 5 more minutes, and red meant get the Hell off, right now, no matter what you were doing.

People were pretty good about adhering to it. It wasn't fair to the other performers to do otherwise.

But Goodman was something else entirely, and he had little use for the rules.

And why not?

He knew he was under a death sentence, being in remission from leukemia. No matter how good he was feeling, he knew it was going to come back and he was determined to enjoy whatever time was left. He never whined, or used it to get sympathy.

He never mentioned his illness all the time we spent with him, but he was burning the candle at both ends, and using a blowtorch in the middle.

He got on stage that night, did a few songs, and the yellow light must have gone on, because he took his jacket off, and said, "Jeez...it's awful hot up here," and threw it over the light.

He began inviting guests up to play with him and soon the whole stage was filled with guitars and mandolins and banjos and trombones.

On the Jumbo Tron screens you could see his face in close-up. He was laughing, his eyes wild and bright as the chaos on stage grew.

It went on into the night, while the organizers tore out their hair and tried to figure out how to pull the plug.

Monday morning after the festival we were dragging our gear through the lobby of the hotel, and we ran into Scott Alarik. We'd met him during the course of the weekend, and recognized a kindred spirit. He had come up to us with a stack of business cards. He handed one to Stan, and Stan looked at it. It read "FFA."

"What's this?"

Scott said, "It's your membership card to the Fat Folksingers of America. That's the good news." He handed Stan another card. "The bad news is you have to tell Odetta she's also a member."

The guy had been on fire all weekend, and this morning it appeared as if he hadn't yet slept or slowed down. He was holding a huge glass goblet about the size of a fish bowl, filled with gin and tonic by the smell of it.

"You worried about Malaria?"

Scott gestured with the glass. "Can't be too careful."

He was going to catch a ride into Philadelphia with us, where we were to meet some mysterious guy who had a line on all the good gigs in the Northeast. Stan didn't have a name for him yet, but a woman named Wendy Grossman had promised to meet us there and make the introduction. This was the guy who could potentially change our fortunes in this part of the world and make the whole trip more valuable to us career wise.

Scott piled into the van with his bag and guitar case, and settled into the back seat with his fish bowl of gin.

On the drive into Philly he kept up a string of jokes, all wildly funny, and nearly all at Stan's expense. I could see Stan was getting pissed off, and I wanted to warn Scott to maybe dial it down, but Stan was a big guy. He could take care of himself.

We got to the restaurant where the meeting was to take place, and Stan got out and slammed the driver's door, and stomped off to find Wendy. I left David and Scott and hurried off after him. I found him at a table looking seriously annoyed, and watching as a waitress poured him a coffee.

"You okay?"

"Yeah. I guess. I know Scott's a good guy and all that, but I've just about had enough of him this morning. Which one of you invited him along?"

"Actually, I think it was you."

"Oh. Great."

"I don't think he'll be with us long. He said he had a meeting to go to this morning as well."

"He's not going to be around much longer if he doesn't shut his pie hole."

David and Scott walked in and sat down. Stan was only just keeping his temper. I could see he was going to say or do something, and I hoped nothing got broken.

It was then that Wendy came into the restaurant, looked at the four of us, and said, "Oh, aren't you clever Stan. You found Scott yourself. You didn't need my help."

That evening we hooked up with Steve Goodman and took him to Jim's Cheese Steaks, on the corner of South and 4th, in Philly.

It had been a couple of days since we'd had proper food.

The Philly Festival was notorious for its Saturday night performers' buffet.

It consisted of pork and beans and cut up wieners, and slices of fly-blown white bread with margarine.

Just that. Nothing more.

A concession had been made for the vegetarian crowd, in that there was another vat of just pork and beans, without the wieners.

We were none of us terribly fussy about food back then, but the Festival buffet left a lot to be desired, and we were all able to resist the lure of cold baked beans garnished with un-cooked chunks of industrial meat slurry.

Something else was required.

So we met up with Steve, and headed for South Street.

It was a wonderful neighbourhood. Tattoo parlours, and book shops and bars, cluttered head shops selling bongs and incense and rolling papers, and pawn shops with windows full of dusty junk, and crowds of people just milling around, and enjoying the scene on a warm and sultry summer night.

The air was full of incense and pot smoke and patchouli.

There were buskers and fire breathers, and guys doing card tricks on little tables, and drunks, and wild looking women wearing bikinis gliding by on roller skates, and cops on horseback, and a long line of limos, idling along the curb.

The uniformed drivers would be lined up out on the sidewalk, waiting to get into Jim's to order for their clients.

A lot of places claim to have invented the Cheese Steak, but we didn't care about the history.

We just liked Jim's.

It was and still is a narrow fronted building at the corner of South St. and 4th, with a great white and black and chrome facade. Sort of a Buck Rogers design of someone's vision of the future, circa 1930.

You would join the line, and wait.

There is a strict ordering policy.

Step up to the spot, and don't hem or haw or hesitate, or discuss your order with your friends, or ask, "What's good?" or the giant ex-linebacker with the 38 inch biceps will bark at you, and smack his spatula against the sign with the ordering instructions on the wall behind him.

"Read the damn sign, and get with the programme. There's hungry people behind you."

Right.

Two cheese whiz steaks "with extra whiz", and fried onions and fried sweet peppers.

You might as well order two.

The first one is going to go down in about 4 seconds.

And you know you're going to want a second in a while, and that line isn't gonna get any shorter.

Get two.

Slide over two paces to the right, and get your beer from the nice lady.

Slide over again, and pay for it all.

Grab a bale of paper napkins because the damned thing, no matter how careful you are, is going to leak juice all over you, and the feral cats on South Street will follow you home and tear you apart in an alley off Delancey.

Take your tray upstairs and snag a window seat so you can watch the zoo outside.

Stan and David and Steve and I got a window seat and dove in.
Nothing much was said for a while.
Stan finished both of his and was leaning on the window sill, watching
the street below and sipping his second Rolling Rock.
David and I briefly considered staging a cheese steak eating contest, but
I declined.
He was very thin, but was born with the ability of a circus Gannet to
pound down food.
I didn't have a chance. Hell, not even Stan could keep up with him. In
any case the world record at the time was 11. 11 damned cheese steaks,
eaten in one sitting by a local woman whose name is somehow not a
household word or taught to children in history class.
We ate our meal, drank our beers, and watched the passing parade.
It was wonderful and ever-changing.
There was a fire-breather doing a show on the side walk below, and a
juggler was at work half a block down. Two skinny women in cut-off
shorts and halter tops were flirting with the mounted policeman, (or in
this part of town, more likely his horse,) below our window.
Across the street another cop was checking the ID of a kid who had
been doing that trick with the cups and the tiny red ball, relieving
people of their money.
  "Sleight of hand, slight of mind," said David.

The conversation turned to bad drivers' license pictures.
Steve pulled out his wallet and said, "So I had to go down to the bureau
to renew my license one day and have my picture re-done. I'd been on
a bit of a bender with Holstein and some of the other guys in town, and
hadn't slept or washed or shaved for about 4 days. I was really hung
over and smelled like I was dead, covered in stubble, wearing a wool
hat and mirror shades. I stood up in front of the camera and I guess I
was waiting for the guy to tell me to take off the glasses and hat. He
didn't, and the flash went off and that was that. Couple weeks later I get
THIS." He opened his wallet and showed us the black and white photo
of what appeared to be a Mexican bandito in the last stages of tertiary
syphilis. "This is what I have to show the cops when they pull me over
for speeding now."

Nothing weird or outrageous happened that night with Steve.
Nothing went wrong or exploded, or otherwise self-destructed.
There was no yelling or swearing. No threats were made.
It was just a quiet evening, spent sipping beer, wolfing down some
grease, chatting, and watching the passing parade, in the company of a
really lovely and funny guy on a soft warm summer night, long ago.

CHAPTER 54

Return to John and Peter's Place

We had a weekend in Pennsylvania a month or so after the Philly festival, to capitalize on our appearance there.

The Cherry Tree in Philly, Godfrey Daniels' in Bethlehem, and a return to John and Peter's   Place in New Hope.

The Cherry Tree was a great club in a shaky old church hall on the west side of town near the University. It seated about a hundred or so on folding wooden chairs, with a decent sized stage and a pretty good sound system operated by a quiet and obsessive guy with glasses and an impressive mobile recording unit. I think he recorded all the shows that he worked on. I'd love to know where those tapes are.

You walked through the big church kitchen, which also served meals to the needy during the day, back to the big comfortable dressing room. Lots of room for friends to drop in and hang out.

We'd been getting steadily bigger crowds in recent months around the Philly area, partly due to our frequent shows at the Gazella Primera, but the set at the Philly festival seemed to have turned a corner for us. Suddenly we were doing two shows a night with a change of house. We felt like we were on a roll.

Next night we played Godfrey's in Bethlehem. Again a sellout, and we spent much of the night after the show drinking Rolling Rock, and playing tunes and telling jokes in the front room with the locals.

It was still the same warm and welcoming room it had always been, with the same sweet and lovely people. We were happy to be back.

The last night was our return to John and Peter's Place, where Stan and I had had such a miserable time on our first US run. We didn't want to go back, but it was a decent offer, and word was that it had improved. Sure enough, the piles of cocaine upstairs were gone, and the joint had been cleaned up a bit. It was still attracting a largely gay clientele, but with all the different musical acts coming through the audience was changing, and as far as we could tell everyone got along just fine. It was still cramped and dark, and the ceiling on stage was too low for me to play violin in any position but a crouch, but we did okay.

During a break we were reading the list of up-coming acts for the month.

David held the poster out to me.

"Look at this,"

Odetta, wow. This place was okay for lowlifes like us, but what the hell was she doing here?

Stan took a brief glance at the poster. "I guess she's trying to make a living," he said, and got up and left to get a beer.

It was a scary thought. She was a legend, and playing what was still essentially a road house, a dump. Could you ever make it out of having to scramble for a living? Apparently not.

It was depressing.

George Thoroughgood and the Delaware Destroyers were in for a weekend. That made some sense. The place would be jumping, and we kinda wished we could be there for that.

"Look at this," said David, holding up the poster. "Iron Goddamned Butterfly. How the...? "He waved his hands. "What the...?" Words failed him.

"They're here for 2 nights this week. Jesus."

Wow.

I went out to the front of the club to find Stan and show him.

He was drinking a beer, and talking to a guy who looked like he had just been tossed off the back of a Mississippi riverboat for card sharping. He was wearing a three piece white linen tropical suit, alligator shoes, dark glasses, and a Panama hat. He had a silver trimmed Malacca cane across his knees and a diamond pinky ring.

Holy Shit. It was Leon Redbone.

I shook hands with him, and said, "What the hell are you doing here?"

"I live here."

"In this town? But it's so cute."

"I'm a cute guy."

"Well I can see that."

I held the poster out. "Stan, look at this."

"Iron Butterfly. Holy shit."

We hung out with Leon a while longer, and then it was time to play a set.

We shook hands with him again, and went back on stage.

It wasn't planned, but we had to do it.

At the end of that next set, Stan began reading the list of upcoming acts to the audience. He did that a lot when playing a club, as a courtesy to the owners, and to maybe give a plug to whatever friend of ours might

be coming through. He got to Iron Butterfly and David began playing the bass riff. I joined in on the Telecaster with the distortion on my amp turned up to full, and Stan began singing "Inna Gadda Da Vida."
His voice was perfect for it.
We gave the audience the drum solo, and for maybe 5 minutes they bashed away on the table tops with their hands and beer mugs and assorted cutlery.
We took a break after that, and as we were getting a beer a tiny man with long curly dark hair and wearing a full set of black leathers pushed himself away from the bar where he was standing and came up and shook hands with all of us.

"Thanks for the plug, man."

"Excuse me?"

"The plug. You played our song. Thanks."

"And you are?"

"I'm Doug Ingle. I'm with Iron Butterfly. I just came in to see what the room looked like, and whether we can get the Hammond organ and the whole drum kit on the stage. It's gonna be tight. I don't know how we're gonna get the Marshalls in here."

"You're with Iron Butterfly, and you're playing this little place? How the hell did that happen?"

"Bad manager, and an asshole agent. This is the last string of gigs he booked for us before we fired him."
Well, we knew all about that sort of thing.

"Do you still do Inna Gadda Da Vida?"

"Oh yeah. We have to. We haven't changed our show since '67."
Wow.

"Anyway, thanks for the plug." He shook hands with Stan again. "Great job singing, dude."

CHAPTER 55

The Calgary Folk Club

I don't know how we found them.

It had to have been Stan who made the initial connection, perhaps through another club owner or promoter.

We were at the end of yet another hectic and depressing and unprofitable run through Alberta when Stan told us we were having dinner that night with a couple who ran a folk club in Calgary. They might want to book us in for a gig, and there was rumour that they could change our fortunes somewhat if we only had it in us to trust them.

Good luck with that.

We had just come out of the debacle with Ronald, and were in fact still paying for his sins on this tour. We were disinclined to trust anyone at this point. However, now that we three were doing the booking ourselves and having a wretched and humiliating time of it, we decided to give these folks at least a careful look.

Back then, email hadn't been invented, and most people didn't even have a working answering machine, and so booking oneself was difficult and confusing at best. You'd pace the room, and look at your watch, calculate the difference in time zones, and wonder if this might be the right moment to call. Most folk club presenters had day jobs, and you might call a dozen times with no luck before the phone was finally answered, and then it was usually a toddler who picked up.

"Hello? Is your Mummy there?"

There was only adenoidal breathing at the other end of the line.

"Hello? Can I speak to your Mum?"

Silence.

"Hello? I was hoping to talk to your Mummy. Is she around?"

"Mummy having a POOP."

"Oh, uh, could you let her know that I called and have her call ba..."

"Mummy poop... Poop Poop Poop."

And the phone would be dropped and the little monster could be heard running around in the background yelling, "poop poop poop...Mummy

poop."
There would follow the sound of a toilet flushing, and a distant voice
yelling, "Can't I have just one damned minute to myself around here?"
and then a smack, followed by distressed wailing from the child, and
after burning up precious and expensive minutes of long distance time
listening to the frantic mother trying to soothe and placate the kid,
you'd hang up and move on to the next target.
We needed help.
We met in a large dark Chinese restaurant. They introduced
themselves as Anne and Mansel Davies. They were a couple of ex-pat
Brits who were now teaching school and running the Calgary Folk
Club. Mansel was also a really good guitarist and he and his band,
"The Wild Colonial Boys," served as the warm up act at the club. They
were booking some nationally known acts into their room, and we felt
that if nothing else, we might at least get a gig out of this.
Beyond that, David and I were still deeply suspicious of anyone's
motives within the folk world. Stan had his doubts as well, but he
was tired and stressed, and sick of how haphazard the tour routing
now was. It was not unknown for us to be loading out after a show,
at say, Passim in Cambridge, with the idea that we were homeward
bound the next day, and one of us would let slip that he had booked a
couple of shows for us a thousand or so miles away. There would be
a mad scramble to check out of the hotel, and a frenzied all night drive,
arriving tired and breathless and with shattered nerves for yet another
badly planned and poorly organized gig. All of which we could have
avoided if we had someone helping with the booking, or had the three
of us at least been on speaking terms in the van.
The meeting took place between Stan and the couple at corner table.
David and I pointedly sat well apart from them at a separate table,
churlishly refusing to eat with them even though we were both
famished and broke, (and they were buying for Chrissake.) I was
determined not to be beholden to anyone. At this point in our lives,
having a potential agent buy us dinner was like being a low level
hooker on the street and having a sinister black limo with smoked glass
pull up to the curb and seeing a handful of large denomination bills
come out the window. You just knew that something disgusting and
repellant and painful might be required of you later on. Farm animals
might be involved. And pictures would surface. Ugly, awkward badly-
lit pictures.
I ordered a string of martinis with extra olives for ballast and roughage,
and to dampen the hunger pangs in my belly, and watched and waited
as they made the pitch.
First of all they wanted to book us into the Calgary Folk Club, at an

unheard- of fee, which was good news, but Annie also wanted to help put us into other venues farther afield in Alberta. She had a lot of great contacts and told us she could fill some of the deadly money-sucking holes in our schedule, those middle of the week nights when the three of us, broke and desperate, would crowd into a room for two and pull the top mattress off one bed to make three. The view from the pallet on the floor would be appalling as one could see all the terrifying crap that was left behind under the beds by previous guests, and subsequently overlooked or ignored by the over taxed cleaning staff or the forensic pathologists who had done a second rate job on the crime scene. Soiled underpants, stiff from dried bodily fluids, over-turned ash trays, used condoms, whiskey bottles filled with urine, (just how lazy and hung over must one be to make piddling over the side of the bed into a bottle a reasonable alternative to getting up and going to the toilet?) and in one case, about a hundred rounds of unspent ammunition. None of this of course held a candle to the worst room I ever stayed in, some years later, (in Camden, New Jersey, of course,) where I slept in a room covered in bloody hand prints and finger print powder, and where a chalk outline of the previous tenant had been drawn on the shag carpet where there was a deep pool of clotted blood between the bed and the bathroom wall.

But that's another story...

So what Annie was proposing sounded fine, but what was all this work going to cost us? Annie said she simply wanted her expenses covered, and that was it.

This didn't sound right at all.

"I don't like it. Not one damned bit. What's in it for them?" I said, as we drove back to the hotel we were staying in. The place is long gone now, but at the time there was a grotty strip bar at the corner of 16 AVE NW and Center Street in Calgary. It had become our base of operations while in town. It was full of rummies and drug dealers and down on their luck, disease riddled scrubbers, but we didn't know any better. Had we driven maybe 2 miles further west we would have found the "Motel Village," and had our choice of clean and decent rooms. Of course we couldn't afford clean and decent rooms, so call it a draw.

"They have to be working some angle. I don't know if we should trust them."

These people seemed decent and honest and smart and kind, and it worried the hell out of me.

"Something's wrong. I say give it a pass."

That night Stan and David and I sat in our flea bag room while the bass from the strippers' music thumped below us and talked over the proposal, with the result that we decided to give them a shot. We at

least would get a gig at the Calgary Folk Club. They could book us
a tour, but we needed to keep it all on the up and up. They had to
take a commission, and as well, they also had to keep careful track of
whatever expenses they incurred. None of us wanted to be once more
on the hook for ugly suits and last minute plane tickets. Nor did we
want to finish a trip owing a fortune in cash, or, in lieu of cash, some
awkward and humiliating favour, like having to play Paul Stookey's
"Wedding Song," at the ceremony for someone's daughter.

Long story short, it was Anne and Mansel Davies who were largely
responsible for the huge surge in our careers in the west. Our first tour
with them was successful beyond our wildest expectations, and from
there it went places we never could have imagined. Even better, they
became dear and treasured friends, and they opened their home in
Bragg Creek to us as a base of operations, and as a haven away from
the weirdness of the road. They both worked as teachers all day, and
Stan I got into the habit of making dinner for them and their sweet girls,
Shivaun and Erin, and as they walked in after a day's work we would
try to have something good in the oven, and a glass of wine waiting at
the door.

Stan came up with a typically over the top recipe for baked stuffed pork
tenderloin which became a favourite.

Take a couple of pork tenderloins, maybe one for each person. Make a
mixture of fresh pork sausage and onions and garlic and bread crumbs,
and form it into grenade sized balls. Wrap the tenderloin around the
mixture, and then wrap bacon around the tenderloin and pin it with
toothpicks. Bake in a 350 oven until brown, and then call an ambulance.
There was a variation of that theme which I would cook.

Take a couple of beef flank steaks, carefully butterfly them, and then
pound them flat with a mallet. Take a handful of bread and egg and
onion dressing and place on the edge of the steak. Carefully roll the
whole thing up, and once again wrap it in bacon and pin it with
toothpicks. Spread some tomato paste on top, a few sprigs of rosemary,
and bake until done. Serve with rice, and a salad made of plum
tomatoes and torn fresh basil leaves with Bocconcini cheese drizzled
with balsamic vinegar and olive oil.

We tried to help out a bit with the house work too, but there was one
awkward moment when the front door opened, and Anne and Mansel
and their daughters were confronted with the sight of Stan in his jockey
shorts and open terry cloth house coat, vacuuming the floor, and me
similarly dressed, only with a large bath towel wrapped around my
head, having just come out of the shower, and ironing the bands' shirts
while watching a quiz show on TV.

It made for an odd tableau, and I wondered if the kids would eventually had to go into therapy.

There were many nights were we might sit and talk around the table for hours after the dishes were cleared away, and work our way through 3 or 4 more bottles of red wine, and then brandy, and then coffee, and later a nightcap, while Mansel played us something on the newest addition to his guitar collection.

Wonderful, lovely and generous people.

The first tour that Annie booked for us, we drove out nonstop through the States after playing a show in Minneapolis at the Coffeehouse Extempore. We left directly after the show and drove overnight through the hills north of Minot, North Dakota, into southern Saskatchewan. There was a large open pit coal mine there. The devastation was beyond belief. The three of us sat in silent horror as the sun came up behind us and illuminated the piles of blackened filth. Stan shook his head and said, "Christ, the place looks like it's auditioning for the role of Mordor."

We got to Calgary in the afternoon of the next day, and landed on the door step of Tim and Patty Rogers, who were no relation to us. Tim helped run the Rocky Mountain Folk Club, if I recall correctly. Both Tim and Patty were quiet and funny people with a couple of charming and quirky kids, a son named Ben, and a daughter named Lisa. Tim told me in later years that no one could understand a damned thing any of the three of us said, having developed our own private language from listening to old BBC Goon shows all the way out. It was made worse by the fact that Stan and I had acquired a taste for some horrible caffeinated candy that was sold in truck stops. I forget the name, but they each contained the equivalent of two cups of coffee. We munched them like popcorn, and dropped them into the horrid ersatz swill that masqueraded as coffee in Husky restaurants. After a dozen or so your heart was racing like a demented squirrel in a cage, and your tongue looked and felt like a discarded bath house loofah, or a brisket gone way past its best before date. Speech was difficult, and they gave you breath like a cannibal bat. People learned to give us a wide berth.

That first gig Annie booked us into was a free noon time concert in the Devonian Gardens at the top floor of the TD building downtown. It was a large greenhouse holding a jungle of massive pre-historic looking plants. One kept expecting a Triceratops or John Diefenbaker to come trotting out from the bushes. As gigs went it wasn't terribly exciting, playing for a crowd of bored secretarial staff who were reading the paper and eating their brown bag lunches, but it paid us a whopping 500 dollars, and that alone had covered our expenses in getting out west, and then some. 500 bloody dollars. We were thrilled. Cautiously thrilled.

It got better.

We played to a sold out crowd at the Calgary Folk Club. (Very kindly, no one told us that all the Club's shows sold out well in advance.) From there we played The Rocky Mountain Folk Club, also sold out, and after that it began to blur. We had shows all over the province and they all went well. A week or two into the tour, we got a call from the Davies saying that they had taken a flyer on booking us at the last minute into the small auditorium at the college, and it looked like selling out, and was that okay?

What was going on here?

When all was said and done we felt like we had finally broken through as an act. We were getting a lot of radio play with local CBC, where Mansel had an "in." People knew the songs, and sang along. They laughed at the band humour, and for the first time in our careers, we had made a profit from a tour. We were actually going home with money.

We had a meeting with Annie to settle accounts and bring everything up to date. We also hoped to plant the seeds for another run as soon as we could manage it. We offered her a commission on the tour but she refused, and said merely that she could use some help with the phone bills. As for the rest of it, Annie said, "I was only doing my job." Their part in the story of our career has been forgotten and lost, if in fact anyone outside of our small circle was ever aware of it. They have never tried in any way to claim a special relationship with Stan in the years since his death, or, like so many others, try to cash in from their friendship. The fact is that they and Tim and Patty Rogers, along with Susan Casey and many others were good and generous and steadfast friends to us over the years. They played a huge part in our success, and we were sustained far beyond the borders of Alberta by their kindness.

CHAPTER 56

Canada Day on Parliament Hill

The CBC was doing a live coast to coast broadcast from Parliament Hill one July 1st.

I don't remember who else might have been on the bill, but it was a big show, with national exposure and a lovely government pay cheque.

The stage was set up near the Chateau Laurier, on the North side of the hotel.

It was handy as the CBC had its offices and studios in the Chateau which must have cost the taxpayers a fortune, but it was worth every penny as as far as we were concerned, as the Chateau had a couple of good restaurants and a really superior bar just off the lobby.

It was around this time that Margaret, the wife of our then Prime Minister, Pierre Trudeau, was making an unwelcome and unseemly splash in the domestic and international press.

There had been some speculation as to just why a man who was generally considered an intellectual would have paired up with a self-styled "flower child," nearly half his age, but the two of them did spawn a a number of kids, one of whom, at this writing, is the handsome and charismatic (albeit untested) leader of the Liberal Party who is poised to replace our current Prime Minister, Stephen Harper, who has all the appeal of an inflamed rectal polyp, and the personal charm of John Wayne Gacy.

In any case, while Pierre had been busy with affairs of state, Margaret had been seen cavorting in places like Club 54 in New York, and hanging about in Toronto with the Rolling Stones, and no harm in that, but there began to appear a lot of tabloid photos of her looking disheveled and even blanker than usual. There was talk of cocaine use and pot smoking. And finally there was a front page shot of her sitting with Ron Wood at some gathering, and in her haste to re-join the party from wherever she'd been, she had apparently forgotten her knickers.

Letters to the editor were written, and call in shows had a field day.

In the House of Commons, Ministers harrumphed, and desks were thumped, and after a few weeks Pierre called his errant bride home.

It was also around this time that Maureen McTeer had published a memoir, which among other things was written partly to counter the public perception that her husband Joe Clark, our former PM, was less like a confused and sleepy turtle, and was a much more vibrant and exciting person than he was perceived as being.

She even alluded to the fact that he was actually some sort of dynamo in the sack, and their activities in the marital bed went well beyond what one might expect from the leader of the Conservative party.

It didn't bear thinking about.

The point of all this is that a joke began circulating which went: "What do Margaret Trudeau and Maureen McTeer have in common? Answer: Every once in a while they both blow a little dope."

Not much of a joke, admittedly.

Still, a few hours later, as Stan and David and I were standing on stage waiting to commence our show, there was some sort of glitch and the satellite connection went down. The audience out front could hear us of course, but on the radio there was only silence, and the engineers scrambled madly to fix the problem. Back in Toronto, at the main studios, a deep voiced and authoritative announcer was no doubt saying, "One moment please," every few seconds over a recording of Mozart's Requiem.

I could see panic spreading through the technical crew.

I had spent the better part of the afternoon relaxing in the Chateau bar drinking martinis, courtesy of the Canadian taxpayer, and I was feeling pretty relaxed. I loafed up to the mic, cleared my throat and said, "So... what do Maureen McTeer and Margaret Trudeau have in common?"

The audience laughed, as they all knew the punchline, but there were high pitched castrati screams from the tech crew who had just received word in their head sets that the satellite link had been re-established, and we were going live, coast to coast, in a few seconds.

I was tackled and thrown to the stage by some panicked CBC staff.

I got up, brushed myself off, and we were introduced on air, and we did our show while various members of the CBC crew reeled about clutching their chests and calling for brandy.

It had been a close call.

We played well enough, and there were no further incidents, but as we came off stage some large and senior and terrified CBC staff member grabbed me and threatened to have us banned from the airwaves forever. Stan never mentioned the incident, or gave me hell over it. He was used to my verbal indiscretions by now, and in any case it hadn't gone out over the airwaves. No harm, no foul.

We packed up, and stored our gear in the security tent, and I headed back to the Chateau bar. Being on the radio was thirsty work.

There were thousands of people milling about. Various diplomats and grandees were standing about being interviewed by TV crews, and there were Ottawa city police and RCMP officers in full dress, and large bulky men in dark suits and Ray Bans who talked into their sleeves, keeping a close watch on things.

A few hours before, as I was going to the gig, I had noticed a large leather briefcase under a side table by the wall next to the bank of elevators. It was still there.

Huh.

I wondered who might have left it there. It was a nice case.

But the more I looked at it the less I liked it.

It was not so very long ago that the FLQ had been active, kidnapping diplomats and blowing up mailboxes. This was the big National Holiday. The place was jammed. It was the perfect time to make some sort of statement.

I went over to a Mountie.

"Excuse me, but I just noticed that the briefcase under the table over there hasn't been moved in over 4 hours."

Give the boy credit. He didn't hesitate or ask questions, or demand to see my ID. That came later. He got on his radio, and the lobby and the bar and the whole damned hotel was empty and cordoned off within minutes. Specialists were called in, sand bags were put up, and the bomb unit found the case to contain only paper documents, along with a cheese and olive loaf sandwich which was by now long past its best before date. The owner was located and order was restored.

Stan happened along just as I was finishing my interview with a couple of guys in uniform.

"That was you that caused all that? The sirens and the cops and the army coming in?"

"The army? I didn't know the army was called. Wow."

"Yes, the Army. Hundreds of men in uniform, with machine guns and tanks and helicopters."

"Fantastic. I never knew."

"But that was you?"

"Well, yeah."

"Jesus. Let's get out of here. I can't leave you alone for a damned minute."

"Fine by me. My work here is done."

I think it was around that time that we heard that Smales Pace on Clarence Street in London was in trouble and in danger of closing down.

It's tough in any market to keep a place going, what with the vagaries

480

of public taste, rents that always go up, and the tendency of artists who achieve a bit of success and habitually fill the place to move up and out of the club circuit, leaving the organizers scrambling to find the next big thing, only to have them leave a few years later. It's an endless and largely thankless task.

I was on stage with Archie Fisher a few years ago, and he said, "You play a club twice in your career, usually. Once on the way up, and once on the way down."

He paused, smiled at the audience and said, "Nice to see you all again." There had been for a few years, an extraordinary flowering of the scene surrounding Smales Pace, with people like Bruce Cockburn and Tom Rush and Murray MacLaughlan still coming through, but by the early 70's they had moved on. And although there were many great acts moving into the vacuum left by the stars, they were largely local to Ontario, and if you missed them this time you knew they would be back and you could catch them later. If you lived in London they might even be your neighbour and you'd had to call the cops more than once to move them off your lawn after a night on the tiles. Familiarity breeds contempt and all that. It could be tough to keep bums in the seats, no matter how good they might be.

In any case, the club was in serious trouble, and many of the people who had made up the scene were drifting away, and the Smale brothers had lost focus and energy, not to mention enough money to have bought themselves a small island in the Seychelles. A year or so later it went up on the market and closed for good.

Stan persuaded Annie and Carl Grindstaff to open a new version of the club at a different location, but with a nod to the old joint it was to be called "Change of Pace."

It was just around the corner from the bus terminal, which was handy. Performers could take the Greyhound into London, and find the place pretty easily after a short walk of only a few blocks.

That was the theory anyway.

Unfortunately, both the York hotel and a liquor store were located in between the bus station and the club. As a result, many performers' sense of direction suffered, and their relationship with the Space/ Time continuum fell apart completely.

The Grindstaffs were from Ann Arbor, Michigan originally. Carl was a Sociology professor at Western and one of the few men evolved enough to be a fierce and articulate champion of women's' rights back in those days.

They had quite literally been childhood sweethearts. Carl told me once that as a young boy, he had seen the sweet and angelic 12 year old

Annie, and had told a friend, "I'm going to marry that girl someday."
And he did, and after they finished their educations in Michigan and at
the University of Massachusetts they moved to London and began to
raise a family. All three kids were smart and beautiful and polite, and
Annie remains to this day, sweet and angelic. It just wasn't fair.
Annie kept the house, and raised their three kids and managed to stay
blissfully unaware that nearly every travelling male singer song writer
within a 1000 mile radius had a hopeless crush on her. Good luck pal,
with Carl in the room. It is difficult to describe just how extraordinarily
beautiful she and Carl are, not just physically, but in terms of their
kindness, and their gentleness, and the unconditional love they radiate
to anyone who is lucky enough to know them.
They are endlessly generous and sweet, and, as the years pass, seem
only to become more beautiful.
Luckily for us they seemed to have a huge gullible streak as well, and
some cash to spare, and the club opened on the second floor at 355A
Talbot Street in London.
I think the place did well for a season or two. Certainly we were filling
the place. We were drawing well enough that we could book a weekend
and expect to sell out every night. And there were lots of other acts who
did well enough that the place was keeping afloat. But there was always
Monday and Tuesday, and Wednesday was a bitch, and the heat had
to stay on and the rent kept coming due, and there now seemed to be
a restless and needy mob of up and coming musicians who wanted a
gig, and maybe even deserved a gig, but couldn't pull enough audience
within that tiny market to make it work. And it was hard to say no. In
terms of filling the room every night seemed like there were just too
many pigs for the teats.
And acts that should have filled the joint based solely on the strength of
their writing and their stage craft alone were now having to struggle.
Doug McArthur was helping out around the club, as well as playing
there, and he worked on some numbers. He discovered the very odd
fact that by far the most popular acts at the club, and most likely to
consistently fill the place were all male, blond, and over 6 feet tall.
Very odd, and it meant that a shorter, somewhat darker haired act like
Doug himself, who was a wonderful songwriter and really funny on
stage, or a David Essig who had massive, terrifying instrumental skills
and seemed to be drawing from some deep scary well of darkness in
his songs, might have to work a bit harder to fill the place, as opposed
to a guy like David Bradstreet. Bradstreet too, had great skills and
wonderful songs but was also so handsome it hurt your teeth just to
look at him.
Whatever it was the club was soon in trouble. Carl had some money

he was willing to use to keep the place afloat, and after some soul searching the club got a liquor license, but it was a mug's game. After a few years and some extraordinary nights, the cupboard was bare, and around 1982 or thereabouts, it had to be closed down.

By this time, Annie and Carl were living in a lovely old yellow brick Southwestern Ontario farm house a half hour outside of town. It had a large living room with a fireplace and a pool table. And a couple of times a month, after Carl had finished humiliating some folk singer/ would be pool shark in straight sets of snooker, the table would be moved back and chairs brought in, and the old Klipsch sound system from the club on Talbot would be fired up. Maybe 80 people would come in for the evening with wine and beer and brownies. It was the first house concert series I have ever heard of, and it was beyond lovely. The shows were warm and intimate, and thankfully, there had to have been less stress for the Grindstaffs, at least financially.

Annie and Carl have since moved to Hawaii for most of the year, and one of my great joys is to imagine the two of them sitting on a balcony somewhere, with their feet up surrounded by dear friends, and sipping a glass of wine as the sun goes down.

Some people deserve everything good that comes along.

CHAPTER 57

Ann Arbor / Pete Seeger

I made the initial approach, I think.
We had got word of a great little club in Ann Arbor which might hire us.
We still had no agent at the time, so the three of us had divided the
continent into three territories, each of us having responsibility for a
different area. David had New England. Stan had Canada, and I had
the Midwest.
The club was called The Ark, and while they had no money to pay up
front, they gave us a weekend gig when I took a deep breath and made
the call.
Stan and David and I drove down on the Friday.
The original Ark was in a creaky Victorian mansion on Hill Street, near
the university campus.
An attractive young couple named Dave and Linda Siglin ran the place.
They lived in the apartment upstairs from the concert room with their
beautiful daughter Anya, who was a child of maybe 6 or so when we
first met.
Dave and Linda are a hell of a pair.
Dave is tall and lanky and quiet. If you were making a western movie
and looking for the guy to play the part of a taciturn but funny cowpoke
who can pull out a violin while sitting around the campfire and break
your heart, Dave would be your guy. He is a wonderful player on both
guitar and violin, but who rarely lets it out.
Linda is short, with long yellow/ blonde hair and with a great hoarse
caw of a laugh. She is vulgar, and opinionated and wildly funny and
like Dave, extraordinarily kind and generous. Individually they were
great company, with a really skewed and off-kilter view of the world.
Together, they had an act they could have made a fortune with if
Vaudeville hadn't died.
We took to them right away.
The concert room in those early days had been two small rooms
originally. The sliding pocket doors had been pulled back to make one
bigger room and there was a small stage along the wall of the larger of

the two sections. There were some chairs I guess, but in my memory the audience sat on cushions on the floor. This made for an awkward debut that first night when Stan's unhealthy diet got the better of his GI tract and he inadvertently off-gassed while on stage. David and I were glaring daggers at each other. He took a deep breath, and came over to my side of the stage with his face averted and whispered, "You filthy pig."

"It wasn't me." I was looking for a place to retch.

It was then we realised Stan was looking embarrassed and sweaty, and that a toxic and unseen Plague was decimating our audience. People were fainting in the front row. Some were bravely staying and pulling the collars of their turtle-neck sweaters up to their eyes, and others were frantically scrambling to leave the room as the deadly contagion spread. Meanwhile, the curtains had burst into flames and the wallpaper was falling in huge strips onto the floor. We finished the song we were playing and took a break.

"WHAT THE HELL WAS THAT?" yelled Linda as we went back to the dressing room. She was staggering and laughing and waving her hand in front of her face. "DAVE, GET ON THE PHONE...YOU GOTTA CALL A FUCKIN' EXORCIST." Stan had gone upstairs to commune with Nature.

"I think Stan had an accident."

"WELL I HOPE IT WAS A FUCKIN' ACCIDENT...YOU DON'T WANT HIM DOING THAT ON PURPOSE! JESUS CHRIST...THAT WASN'T A FART...THAT WAS LIKE ONE OF THE PLAGUES OF EGYPT."

Linda never whispered.

We loved her.

We loved the club.

Over the years, after the show we habitually sat up with them all night drinking beer, telling jokes, and catching up on the gossip about our fellow travelers. Their daughter Anya would sit up with us, and she grew from a lovely child into a beautiful and funny teenager who had the inate grace and good manners to treat us as if equals, and never talk down to us.

Ann Arbor was a great town to hang out in. Lots of little bookstores, and a pretty good guitar shop, and a couple of great diners serving the kind of greasy carb-laden all day breakfast that sends you back to bed for a nap around 2 PM.

Lots of attractive students hanging around the campus, and David and I had fun signing ever more unlikely names from the Goon Show to the Equal Rights' Amendment petitions we were presented with.

Nice to think that Neddy Seagoon and The Famous Eccles might have

had something to do with enshrining a woman's right to vote in the
U.S. Constitution.

We were there one weekend, playing the Friday and Saturday, and we
decided to stay over for the Sunday, as Pete Seeger was doing a benefit
for the Ark at the State Street Theater.

I was assigned the job of taking phone messages while Dave and Linda
were busy with all the other stuff that had to be taken care of on the
day of a big show. I figured I could handle this. I had used a pencil and
paper before.

The phone rang.

"Hello, this is the Ark. Can I help you?"

"Yes, is Pete Seeger there?"

"No. Pete's not here. Can I take a message?"

"It's Ralph Nader calling and I ..."

I looked at the receiver and snorted.

"Pffft. Ralph Nader? Yeah right pal."

BAM.

And I hung up.

Maybe a minute later the phone rang again.

"Hello, this is the Ark. Can I help you?"

"Uh...yes...This is Ralph Nader calling. I'm looking for Pete Seeger."

"Ralph Nader, huh?"

"Yes, I would like to..."

"Yeah. And I'm the Queen of England."

BAM.

I hung up again. Stan came into the kitchen and got a beer out of the
fridge. He cracked it open and leaned against the counter and took a
pull. "Sounds busy. Who's calling?"

"Some asshole pretending to be Ralph Nader. Like we haven't got
better things to do."

The phone rang again.

"Hello this is Ralph Nader. Um...is there anyone else there I can talk
to?"

I'd had enough of pranksters by now.

"Listen asshole, this is a busy place. We don't have time for this
kind of shit. Now fuck off and find someone else to annoy."

BAM.

Stan shook his head and said, "Some people." He pushed himself away
from the counter and walked out of the room back to his book and
cigarette.

The phone stopped ringing after that.

Finally. Some peace.

About five minutes later the back door opened, and Pete Seeger loped in with his banjo case over his shoulder, followed by Dave Siglin. He came over shook my hand and said, "Hi, I'm Pete. Has Ralph Nader called yet?"

Pete and Dave were great about it.

For myself, I was haunted for years by the incident, until the 2000 election when Nader's Quixotic run for the Presidency bled enough votes away from Al Gore to let Dick Cheney's half-witted sock monkey at least appear to win. After that I didn't feel so bad.

Stan went to Pete's show that night.

I didn't attend. I was still feeling embarrassed over my faux pas. God only knew who I might inadvertently insult if I went in.

I hung around in the parking lot behind the theater while the concert went on. I could hear what sounded like a massive choir coming through the wall. After about 3 hours, Stan came out of the stage door. He had the same look on his face that Charlton Heston wore as Moses in the Ten Commandments, coming down from the mountain after being lectured by the burning bush. It was a life changing event for him, and our shows began to evolve from a mere performance by three guys to more of a participatory event, with us and the audience as partners. He began to take the time to line out the choruses of songs and even to teach the odd harmony from stage.

Pete's mastery of stage craft and his absolute sense of commitment to everything he did was a huge influence.

He, like Utah Phillips and Malvina Reynolds and others, had the dedication and humility which allowed them to see what they were doing as part of a continuum, or as Utah put it, "a river of song." The performer was no longer necessarily the most important part of the show, but rather the facilitator who brought people together as a community. It was diametrically opposed to the model we had grown up with, where the performer was the focus and the audience was a passive witness.

I don't know if Stan ever expressed the idea in those words per se, and we didn't talk about it that much, but there began a subtle change in how we approached the art of performance around then, not to mention other elements of our behaviour.

The life lesson was re-enforced maybe a year later, at the Philly festival. It was Sunday morning and Stan and I had opened the doors of the van so we could sit in the shade and relative cool beneath the trees near the main stage. The festival takes place in a densely wooded swamp, and it had rained overnight.

The sun had come up and then it clouded over had rained again.

Then more sun, and some pop-up thunderstorms with torrential rain, and then the clouds parted and the heat began in earnest.

Steam was rising from the filthy muck in front of the Main Stage, and we could see hundreds of people lining up for food at the top of the hill, or maybe to just get a breath of fresh air.

In front of the workshop stages, people were searching through the deep mud for coolers and lawn chairs and missing kids. Stan was drinking a coffee and smoking a Rothman's. I was having a morning bracer.

Down in the woods towards the Dulcimer Grove we could see a tall angular figure wearing a bright yellow rain slicker. He was carrying a green plastic garbage bag in one hand, and a stick with a sharpened nail in the other.

"Who's that?"

"I dunno...hard to see in this glare."

Stan squinted and leaned forward, shading his eyes.

"Holy shit. It's Pete Seeger."

"What's he doing?"

Stan shook his head and breathed out.

"He's picking up garbage."

"In this heat? You're kidding me."

"Yup."

"Holy shit. He's crazy."

We watched for a couple of minutes.

Pete was slowly advancing through the mud and the kudzu vines, stabbing at crap with his sharpened stick and putting it in the bag. This was the guy who travelled with Woody Guthrie. This was the guy who had sung with Leadbelly. This was the guy who, at enormous personal risk, stood up for Paul Robeson. This was the guy who stood up to McCarthy and his thugs, and had walked beside Martin Luther King Jr., and who had written songs which had become part of our DNA. He had made an enormous lasting impact on the environmental movement with the Clearwater sloop, and his campaign to clean up the Hudson River. If he had done only one of those things, his would have been an epic and heroic life. But he had done all that and more. And now, here he was, humbly picking up other peoples' trash, because he had a spare moment and he was Pete, and it was the right thing to do.

We watched for another couple of minutes, and then Stan flicked his cigarette butt away, stood up and ground it out, and then turned around and began to burrow in the back of the van.

He pulled out a couple of green plastic bags, handed one to me and said, "C'mon. Let's go. It's guys like him that make the rest of us look bad."

CHAPTER 58

Peter Bellamy

"Oh for God's sake, look at the size of the portions they serve in this country. It's no bloody wonder I go back home from these tours looking like a fat chick."

We were sitting with Peter Bellamy, and dinner had just been served.

I don't recall which club it was, but it was the late 70's and we were in Chicago, and Peter was playing a gig in a few hours, so it had to be either The Earl of Old Town, or Somebody Else's Troubles, both legendary music venues and watering holes.

Stan and I never got to play either joint, but we did manage to destroy a few brain cells at both places over the years.

We used to arrive in the small hours after our own show at some other venue, and maybe Fred Holstein would be sitting on the stage with a battered 30's Martin, and singing whatever song came into his head, or whatever request had been shouted out from the crowd. He wasn't known as a writer so much, but he was a great singer and a brilliant stream of consciousness performer.

Or, on another night you might be watching in wonder as Steve Goodman stood up to the mike and gave a master class on how to change all your strings on stage, and keep the audience on the ropes with laughter for half an hour. Jethro Burns might wander in later to sit in for a while.

I don't recall which of the two clubs it happened in, but there was one warm summer night where Stan and I were watching Fred play, and the door burst open and a mob of lunatics crashed into the place, and began leaping from table to table, knocking over drinks and breaking bottles as they ran. The leader leapt onto the bar and ran the length of it, then vaulted off and continued back through the room to the door where he vanished into the night, followed by the tail of the human comet.

Fred picked up the song he'd been playing before the interruption, and carried on.

"Fuckin' Belushi," someone said, near us.

So once again, we had a night off, and we were both thrilled that we were going to hear Peter.

489

We'd run into him a few years before at Mariposa.
He had been a member of "The Young Tradition" back in the late 60's, a
trio with Heather and Royston Wood, who after the band broke up later
formed a duo called "No Relation."
Royston wrote a clever song called "The Woodbridge Dog Disaster,"
which later became part of our repertoire.
Individually they were all great. As a trio they had been brilliant.
Thrilling powerful voices, wonderful harmonies, and great material
from many sources.
They looked interesting too, dressing rather more flamboyantly than the
average folk singer on this side of the water.
Peter had gone to art school, and was particularly given to wild colours,
and extravagant head gear. Stan and I were sitting in the shade one
afternoon on Toronto Island and Peter swept by with his long blond
hair, wearing bright scarlet bell bottom pants, with a wide white belt
with a buckle the size of a Roman shield, matching white high heeled
shoes, a scarlet shirt with a paisley neckerchief, and a hat that would
have caused the debutantes at Ascot to swoon and faint with jealousy.
I said, "Oooh...Swinging Carnaby Street."
    "Cuts quite the figure doesn't he?" Stan said.
    "Yup. Do you suppose he's ...um...one of Nature's Bachelors?"
Stan shook his head. "Gay? Nah. He's just English."
    "Hmmn. Whatever. He looks like he just mugged Carol Channing
for her clothes."
And now we were having dinner with Peter.
    "Look at this bloody muck. There's half a fucking chicken here, and
enough chips to feed a family of 5."
Peter picked at his plate a bit, then threw a napkin over the remains and
shoved it away.
    "No more for me. I've got to sing."
He pushed back from the table.
Stan and I were done as well, but we had wolfed down everything we'd
been presented with and I knew Stan was thinking about an order of
ribs.
God knows I was.
It was Chicago.
You had to have ribs.
Maybe later. There was a place called Big John's off Diversey Avenue.
No evening was complete in Chicago unless you wound up at a late
night rib joint, where you would leave with a half, or in Stan's case,
a full rack, with spicy sauce and creamy coleslaw on the side, and a
couple of slices of Wonder Bread on top to soak up the juices.
You'd wake up the next morning with your pillow case stuck to your

face and beard like a bloody field dressing, and have to stagger into the
bathroom to soak it off with warm water under the shower.
Yeah. Ribs later. And maybe a couple of hot links.
The waitress came over to clear off our table and Stan ordered a round
of Jameson's for the three of us. Peter was eyeing the young woman as
she walked away.
She was thin and wiry. She could have been moonlighting here from
her regular job as an exercise rider at Arlington Racetrack.
Peter crossed his legs, leaned back and ran his hand through his long
blond hair.

"I don't know, it must be the latent homosexual in me. "
"Excuse me?"
"The smaller the arse on a woman, the better I like it. That one there
would just about do. Cor. Look at her. Just skin and bones."
"Yeah, but the shoulders on her. She'd kill you."
"Probably, but that arse. I love it."
"Ah yes, the Tradesman's entrance. So, you went to Public school,
did you?"
Peter smiled, and the waitress came back with the booze.
"Cheers mate," and he tossed it back in one swallow. He shook his
head and winced, and hit the table with his fist.
"Bloody Hell. That's the stuff," and he got up to prepare for his
show.
Peter's voice was an acquired taste, high and strident, and with a
pronounced vibrato.
Or, as Stan put it, paraphrasing P.G. Wodehouse, "He sounds like a
sheep on a distant hillside, nursing a secret sorrow."
But God, what a performer.
That night at the club he came out and sang for nearly 3 hours. He had a
concertina which he used a bit for basic accompaniment, but mostly he
just stood with his eyes closed, head thrown back, and a hand over his
ear. He kept trying to leave, but we kept calling him back.
His songs ranged from terrifying and tragic murder ballads involving
incest and betrayal, to bawdy and obscene sea chanteys, to funny West
Country gems from the Copper Family collection, obscure American
cowboy ballads, songs by the Rolling Stones, Sacred Harp songs,
Vaudeville tunes, and God only knows what else.
He was trying to enlarge the definition of what people called folk music,
and you never knew what he might come out with.
He threw himself completely into it, and by the time he was done, or
thought he was done, he was soaked to the knees with sweat, and his
skin was pale and nearly transparent.
He had to do three encores.

He left the stage once more, and the applause was so insistent and prolonged he finally did come back, but this time carrying a borrowed guitar and a glass slide.

"Coals to Newcastle, this next bit, I'm afraid, but I've got to be able to go home and say I did it."

And then launched into another half hour of Blind Willie McTell and Elmore James songs.

A day or two later we were sharing a bill with him at a festival out on the end of Navy Pier.

Stan and I sat once again through his whole show. He was riveting, and in later years I was to shamelessly rip off his style of singing when I did the high nanny goat harmony in "Northwest Passage."

Peter went on to release a couple of records of Rudyard Kipling poems which he had set to music.

Kipling had long since fallen out of favour for his execrable racist politics, "The White Man's Burden," and all the rest of that horrible Imperialist swill. But he really could write, and his Barrack Room Ballads lent themselves perfectly to being paired with tunes.

Stan and I had been brought up on Kipling, having discovered him in our grandfather's library in Canso. Stan's favourite book as a young boy was 'Stalky and Co.,' and we loved Peter's take on the poems. He paired the poems with traditional tunes at first, and then began writing tunes of his own. It was brilliant stuff.

Peter's masterpiece was a folk opera called "The Transports."

It was an extraordinary song cycle about the whole social system in Britain that made it possible for someone to be banished to Australia for life, simply for stealing bread to feed one's family.

As a piece of writing, and as a performance, and just taken as a whole, it was an astonishing work. A massive accomplishment, which I don't think has ever been touched in folk music. Peter had brought in the cream of the British traditional folk world to perform it, and as I recall, no modern instruments were used. The arrangements were all done using cello, violin, oboes and flageolets. Peter only appeared a few times as a singer/narrator who moved the story along. All the rest of the singing was performed by people like Nic Jones, Cyril Tawney, June Tabor and the Watersons.

It was simply breathtaking, and Stan lived with that recording in his headphones in the van for the next couple of years. And being the competitive sort that he was he began tossing around his own ideas for a similar kind of extended work. He and I talked about it from time to time. I suggested at one point he could take Archie Fisher's song, "The Witch of the Westmereland," and expand on the story, writing a prequel to it, and have the 'the Witch' be the finale.

"It would be a chance for you to brush up on your French Horn."

"What?"

"I'm hearing French Horn when we go to record it."

"Huh."

He thought about that for a while.

He ran with the concept for a bit and in fact wrote what was to be the first song in the cycle, about a young boy going off to a war with high hopes of winning his spurs and losing his virginity. The song was never recorded or written down, but there is a picture, for the very little it is worth, of him playing his long necked tenor mandolin backstage at a festival somewhere, and at that moment he was debuting the song for me. I am out of the picture, but I was there, and I do recall the tune and bits of the lyrics.

I kept in touch with Peter in later years.

He remained the wild and funny man he had been back in the day, but he was having doubts about whether he and the music he was doing were relevant anymore.

Songs written from the point of view of a man press-ganged into serving on board a ship of the line during Nelson's time might not play with a younger audience. That was his worry anyway. Had he lived to see a whole generation of young men and women lied to, and suckered into fighting the wrong war in the wrong country at the behest of a band of cutthroats and their Texas-bred, half-witted hand puppet, Peter might have seen that his songs were as eternal as the evil they described.

He was not getting as much work as he needed, or deserved, given the kind of talent he was.

He was still obsessed with his weight, and I saw him grow thinner as the years went by.

Archie Fisher and I ran into him in North Carolina one weekend at a festival, and Peter was scarily thin, and now the colour of beef jerky.

He was on a tanning kick.

He told me he wanted to be the brownest and thinnest man in the British Empire, and with Gandhi having been dead for many years, he felt he had a shot. In any event the only solid food to pass his lips those days were the diet pills he was washing down with beer. It was a bad combination, speed and alcohol, and he was becoming difficult and erratic over the week or so Archie and I were with him.

He wasn't sleeping at all, and he'd put bright streaks of blue dye in his hair, and had taken to wearing deliberately torn T shirts and jeans in an effort to look more "punk," and thereby more current presumably. One night in a bar after the festival ended he made the mistake of walking up to an enormous ex-NAVY SEAL and, after telling the man he was dressed inappropriately, he reached up and ripped a huge hole in the guy's shirt. The SEAL, having no idea who this lunatic was, tied Peter into a granny knot and punted him into the parking lot.

The last time I saw him was at the Mariposa Festival in Barrie, Ontario. The CBC was there to broadcast the concert live coast to coast, but Peter was on just before the broadcast started. It was a shame, as he got up and did one of the best and most electrifying sets I have ever seen anyone do.
Just one thin high strung man with a concertina in front of a few thousand people.
And when he came off stage he was trembling, utterly spent. You could see the blood pulsing in the veins on his now very white arms.
Gail and I gave him a ride back to the hotel and he had a bite of food and recovered a bit.
We sat out on the hotel balcony to watch the sun set over the lake, and share a few drinks.
He was quiet now, just sipping a glass of scotch, and telling funny stories as the light dimmed.
Presently a cab pulled into the hotel parking lot, and two elderly African American men got out.
One of them was Blind John Davis.
Peter was beside himself. He revered the blues, particularly Chicago blues, and here was an absolute legend right in front of him.
The other elderly man was Blind John's bass player, who had been tasked with getting Blind John safely back to his room from the festival site.
Unfortunately the man was a wreck, completely, helplessly drunk.
He could barely stand, and was no fit companion for a frail blind man in his 80's. It was awful to watch. The drunk was thrashing around the lot with Blind John holding on to his arm and desperately trying to feel his way around with his white cane.
They both kept falling down, and there was no one nearby to help.
Peter, perhaps hoping to defuse the situation, leaned over the railing and spoke to the drunk.
  "I say...hello down there."
The drunk stopped and began searching for the voice.
  "WHO THAT?"
  "Hello, my good man."
The old man spun around, glaring angrily.
  "WHO THE FUCK SAID THAT?"
  "Up here. Excuse me." Peter waved. "Hello. We're up here."

I said, "Oh Jesus, we have to get down there and help. The guy's a mess. He's going to drag Blind John into traffic."
Peter called out again. "Hello. Look up. Please, we're up here."
The drunk began pulling Blind John violently around as he craned his neck trying to find where this mysterious voice was coming from. We gasped as Mr. Davis fell down. His cane rolled away under a car.
"WHO THE FUCK IS TALKING?"
Jesus, this was awful.
Once again Peter called out in his most respectful and soothing and plummy tones.

"My good man, I was wondering if you and Mr. Davis might like to come up here and relax with us and perhaps partake of some of this cheap and rather disappointing whisky."
The drunk had left Blind John to fend for himself, and Peter's hero was now on his hands and knees, feeling around for his cane.
The drunk staggered around the car, and still furiously looking around for the source of this voice, he shook his clenched fist and yelled,

"DON'T YOU DARE TALK NO FRENCH TO BLIND JOHN DAVIS."
He paused and took a deep breath.
"HE BE BLIND!"
It might have been a year or two later that we got word that Peter was gone.
Work had dried up almost completely for him.
He was a gentle and fragile soul, an extraordinary artist, and one of the very few people I have known whom I would call "genius."
But he had no gift for promoting himself.
Depressed and drinking too much, and still worried that he had wasted his time and energy on a dated and moribund style of music, he took his own life, reportedly on a small dock on a lake within sight of his own home.

CHAPTER 59

Bermuda

Another day, another early flight. Another liquid breakfast.

I was just finishing my third drink of the morning when the "fasten seat belts" sign lit up, and the flight attendant came down the aisle to shake the other passengers awake. The wing outside my window tipped down suddenly, sickeningly, and I could see the island below as we came in for the final approach.

Wide pinkish beaches, thousands of little multi-coloured houses came gradually closer, then suddenly sped past, and we were there.

I had never been anywhere tropical before.

The flight attendant opened the cabin door, and light and air from the outside world flooded into the plane.

The air was warm and salt, and sweet with flowers, with an overlay of two stroke engine smoke.

Magic

We had a gig, an actual gig in Bermuda.

No money, but the Folk club paid all airfares, and put us up, and kept us drunk and diverted for the week leading up to the show.

Stan had done the gig solo the year before, and had come back with a great song, "The Flowers of Bermuda," and a lot of lurid stories of drunken debauchery.

So I was ready.

I liked debauchery.

I'd been practicing for this moment all my life.

Going through customs, we came up against some searching questions about the instruments.

"How much is that guitar worth, sir?"

I'd heard stories from friends about border shake downs, and knew what was coming.

The deal was that they were worried about people bringing valuable instruments onto the island, where decent guitars were in short supply, and then selling them and leaving without having given Her Majesty's evil minions at Inland Revenue their rightful due.

"This guitar?"

"Yes sir."

"Oh that. That's just my old Telecaster. I paid about 150 bucks for it. And the fiddle is just an old thing my Uncle found in London after the war. I think he paid 11 shillings for it. It's on loan."

"Right. Next."

Stan stepped up and proudly unsnapped the locks on his custom Mark Leaf cases and took out one of the guitars and held it out to the guard. He said, "These are the best guitars ever made. They're from the workshop of William Laskin. He works out of Toronto."

"How much is it worth, sir?"

I interrupted. "Stan?"

He glared at me. "I'm busy. In a minute."

He turned back to the Customs guy.

"Sorry. You were saying?"

"How much are they worth?"

"Stan." I was pulling at his sleeve, trying to get his attention.

He swung his arm and batted me away.

He held the guitar up to the light and flourished it like Excalibur.

"I wouldn't take 10,000 dollars for them."

"Right." The guard made a note on his clipboard.

Stan took out his 12 string, and held it up as well.

"Look at that workmanship. Look at those inlays. Look at ..."

The Customs officer interrupted.

"You'll need to leave a three thousand dollar deposit, in cash, with Customs, and when you leave the island, after we have ascertained they are the same instruments, you will receive a refund cheque in the post."

What?

Three thousand dollars?

Jesus.

We didn't have three thousand dollars.

Not on us.

Not back home.

Not anywhere, combined.

Frantic phone calls were made, and the Director of the Royal Bank who was also a folk club member, came down with a cheque which was left in the safe for the week we were there.

We were released, and were taken to our billet.

We were staying with two guys.

They, like all the people in the Club were ex-pat Brits.

One was named Rab. The name of the other escapes me.

I don't believe I ever heard him speak.

He mostly stood around in a Levi's jacket, with a can of Heineken held permanently in his left fist.

Every half hour or so he would exchange it for a fresh one.

Decent and friendly guys though, particularly to share digs with a trio of strangers bent on mayhem.

We were taken to the moped rental and set up with transport.

The mopeds were tiny noisy flatulent things, and they left a blue plume of stinking two stroke engine smoke as you putted along, and we all felt vaguely ridiculous.

Stan, in particular looked like an over-sized and uncomfortable circus bear on his.

He had a very large head, and the helmet perched on top like an overturned tea cup.

No matter, it was transport, and now we were free to zip around as we pleased.

We putted back to our billet and were given beers and a map of Bermuda so we could navigate our way around the island on our own.

And so off to the beach.

We parked our bikes, and peeled off our sweaty clothes and started for the water.

I looked at Stan and David and then myself, and decided I should start exercising more than just my drinking arm.

We looked as if we were staging a reverse re-enactment of the Dawn of Evolution, three pale and flabby slug-like creatures, moving tentatively back to the sea, life on land having proved to be too confusing and fast paced for us.

God. Look at us.

We were so white, so fish-like.

David at least, had the beginnings of a tan, but Stan and I looked as if alligators had caught us and wedged us both into underwater mangrove roots to ripen, and then forgotten about us.

Maybe just for the sake of the public we should cover up.

Wait a minute. The locals are mostly Brits who still lived on their traditional diet of beer and chips and beer, and who still mostly "paddled" in the tradition of their Island Race.

The only way to tell us from the locals was the absence of rolled up trousers and knotted hankies on our heads.

We spent a few hours thrashing clumsily in the surf.

It was glorious.

Stan was a relatively strong swimmer, but I had never learned.

Bermuda

My only experience with water was either Lake Ontario, or Chedabucto
Bay in Nova Scotia.
If one was foolish enough to venture into the water of the Lake, you
came out with streamers of used toilet paper clinging to you.
The water in Nova Scotia during the summer was cleaner, if a bit on the
brisk side.
Even the fishermen didn't know how to swim.
"If I fall out of the boat I don't want to prolong the agony," was how
one of them put it to me once.
But this was wonderful.
We laid down the foundation for a really good sunburn, and then
mounted up and we (or rather our bikes) farted our way through the
narrow streets, back to the house to shower and change for the evening.

The organizers took us on a pub crawl.
 It was a pleasant night, walking through the narrow streets, with bright
flowers trailing down the whitewashed walls, and music and laughter
spilling out through the doors of the clubs.
The sky was brilliant in the hour after sunset, turquoise in the west,
deepening to violet above us, and the first stars were appearing
overhead.
I imagined they looked different here, somehow.
They couldn't be.
 We weren't that far south, but it was all new and strange, and exotic.
I decided privately that I could see the Southern Cross whether it was
there or not.

Back at the house I had decided to try to blend in with the locals.
 "I'm wearing Tropical Kit, tonight," I said, as I dressed.
Stan and David both pounced with the exact same line from the Goon
Show.
 "Tropical Kit! God, how I loved that woman." they both said in
unison.
So there I was, white linen shirt, baggy white linen trousers, sandals, a
lot of long blond hair.
I paused in front of a mirror as we went into a crowded and raucous
bar.
Yes, I had picked some sun that day. I looked healthier, more alive. By
God, I was just lovely.

We hit a couple of small pubs, one of which, "The Robin Hood,"
featured a guy singing cover tunes in a corner.
He had a steady job playing there in the off season, after which he

499

would work two shows a night on a cruise ship during the winters in the waters off Florida.

He was making a fortune doing it, and bragged to us that in addition to amassing a huge retirement fund, he was getting all the frenzied and angry sex he could handle from bitter middle aged widows who were taking their first cruise after their husbands had worked themselves into early graves.

We left after a few beers and as we walked up the narrow street, David and I speculated as to what it might be like to actually make money playing music, not to mention get attention from the female of the species.

David said, "The guy has it made. Look at him. All the money in the world and he's wearing pussy like a hat."

I wasn't buying it. "Yeah, sounds great in theory, but you'd still have to sing "Bad, Bad, Leroy Brown," and "Rocky Mountain High" every goddamned night of your life. I'd rather be torn apart by wild dogs."

We went down the street into another dark bar.

There was a lot of loud dance music and wild laughter coming out.

"Careful who you talk to in here," said one our hosts. "This is a gay bar."

We had no problem with that. We went in and found a table near a window. It was there we were introduced to "Dark and Stormies," the local drink, a lethal mixture of over-proof Black Seal rum and a fiery locally brewed ginger beer.

They derived their name from the famous opening line of that bad novel, which someone had no doubt once used as an apology for the previous night's transgressions.

"Sorry pet, it was a dark and stormy night, and besides, I thought of you the whole time."

I tossed down a few. God, they were tasty after a long hot day at the beach.

Stan said, "Careful with those. They'll creep up on you."

Nonsense. I was a veteran.

I was feeling invigorated, alert, and ready for adventure.

I stood up from the table, partly because I was restless, and partly just to prove I could.

"There." I said to Stan. "See? I'm fine."

"Okay, suit yourself."

A few minutes later, I was standing at a pinball machine, realising just how badly damaged my motor reflexes now were.

The ball kept disappearing, and the room was swimming a bit.

I was obviously dehydrated from the day's adventures and it was affecting my reactions, and I hadn't eaten since the airline breakfast

either, and my blood sugar was likely low. I ordered another Dark and
Stormy from a passing waiter. That should help.

There was a trio of strikingly handsome young black men leaning
against a wall, holding tall multi-coloured drinks with paper parasols in
them.

They were beautifully dressed and artfully made up, and they looked
like a row of hot house flowers. One of them pushed away from the
wall, and came over to the side of my machine.

He watched me play for a while, and then caught my eye when I yet
again lost my ball.

"Hello."

I glanced at him.

"Hello yourself."

"My friends and I have been watching you for a while now."

"Really?"

"Yes, and we think you look just like Jesus Christ."

I pulled the lever back to launch a new ball.

"Jesus Christ, huh? I think you've got the wrong guy. We left Jesus
back at the Robin Hood Bar."

He looked up at me through his long eyelashes.

It was the same coy, come hither look that Princess Diana perfected
years later.

"Oh I don't know. You look like you'd be worth 30 pieces of silver to
me."

At that moment Stan and the rest of our mob arrived to rescue me.

"How we doing over here?"

I said, "I think this guy wants to betray me with a kiss."

We had a few more drinks with the young trio and then left for another
bar.

I decided to switch to beer for the rest of the night.

The Dark and Stormies were making me too attractive evidently.

It wasn't fair to the others.

The night turned into a long debauch.

Many drinks.

Many bars.

A lot of stupid laughter, and falling down.

My memories are dim, but I do recall that at one point we all had a
heated conversation on the dock. We were looking at a United States
Navy nuclear submarine, which was moored in Hamilton harbour, as
part of a goodwill tour, if that makes any sense at all.

It was a massive dark and brooding presence, sitting there next to the
quay.

What the hell was this obscene thing doing here, we wanted to know?

Bermuda was a part of the Empire. This was Sovereign territory, for God's sake. It belonged to...well...yes, the Sovereign. This was an outrage.
Bloody Yankee Imperialists.
We decided to put things right.
We resolved to storm over the gangplank, where we could no doubt easily subdue the crew and take control of the sub, and then maybe fire it up and point it out to sea, open a stop cock, and scuttle it. We had no clear plan as to how we'd get back to shore after we sent it to the bottom, but probably felt that Providence would provide. We had Right on our side, after all.
Halfway across the gang plank, floodlights came on, a klaxon sounded, and some naughty sailors swarmed topsides out of a hatch, and kicked our stupid drunken asses back to the shore.

Later that morning we went to the beach, and flopped out on the sand to recover.
We fell into an exhausted coma and woke some hours later with sunstroke, and spent the next two days wrapped in cold wet sheets in a darkened room, sick and sore and nauseous.
David's sunburn was a wonder of nature.
He was bright scarlet, and in the weeks following our trip he made a hobby of trying to peel his skin off in one huge piece, like a thin translucent wetsuit.

The fourth night we were there, Stan and I decided we were feeling well enough to go for a midnight ride down to the beach to watch the moon rise over the water.
We got about 2 blocks from our billet, and some clown came out of a side street and ran his Mo-ped into Stan's, knocking him unconscious.
We got him to the hospital, and the doctors said he'd had a concussion, and had to remain awake and under supervision for at least twelve hours, so his vital signs could be monitored.
They were particularly worried about his enlarged pupil, until I showed them his Medic-Alert bracelet which indicated it was from a child hood bullying incident and not from bleeding on the brain. I hoped I was right.
I sat up with him back at the billet, checking his pulse every half hour and quietly talking with him. We wondered how people took the pace here.
I said to Stan, "The cops told me the guy who hit you was the town drunk."
Stan turned his head carefully, and looked blearily at me.
His eyes were red, his face was blistered and peeling, and he had a

bad case of road rash on his cheek where he'd slid on the pavement for some yards.

"The town drunk? The town drunk? In fucking Bermuda? What do you have to do to become known as the town drunk in this place?"
I had no answer.
We were clearly out of our league.

The gig, oh yeah...the gig.
The gig was an anticlimax for everyone.
The show was held in the old Colonial Club, as I recall.
It was a tall white-washed building with shaded balconies. Three storeys maybe, surrounded by tall palm trees.
Inside it was cool and dark, and ceiling fans turned slowly above us.
Everywhere was polished teak and brass, and dark leather.
We were given seats in some rattan arm-chairs in the lobby, and an elderly black waiter in full evening dress complete with white gloves, brought us Carlsberg Elephant beers on a silver tray.
Christ, we were in a Rudyard Kipling novel, or a David Niven movie..."Raffles, The Master Thief."
This could have been anywhere in the old Empire. Poona India, Singapore, or Kabul.
I felt deeply uncomfortable as a young privileged white layabout being served by an aged black man, who by rights should have been at home with his feet up.
We didn't belong here.
We drank up and went in to do the show.
We looked like the trio of soldiers from that painting from the American Revolution.
Sweating and weak and dehydrated, (ironic, given our combined liquid intake,) and with large strips of burnt flesh hanging from us, we were barely walking wounded.
We managed to struggle through the show, but we were all sick and shaky, and it was not what the club had shelled out for.
They were nice enough about it though.
Maybe they were used to only seeing what was left of folksingers after a week of self-destructive bingeing, road accidents, and attempted piracy.

Backstage, after the gig, we had another minor medical crisis, when David found that the weight of the strap of his bass guitar resting on his shoulder in the damp heat had fused his cotton Oxford cloth shirt into his burnt and swollen flesh.
It was a long and delicate and painful operation to get him freed, and he was difficult to hold down.

CHAPTER 60

Birth of a Nathan

Sometime in the fall of '78 Stan announced that he and Diane were expecting a baby.

For as long as I could remember it seemed to me that Stan had wanted to be a dad.

He had been peripherally involved with the care and raising of Diane's kids from her second marriage when he moved in with her the first time, some years before. As soon as he moved in with her the second time following their hiatus, he began to get serious. And for a guy who had been pretty fancy free for most of his life, he fell into it pretty quickly, although there were a few stumbling blocks.

During the time I was living in my grotty lair in their basement I was treated every morning to his ritual with Kate, the youngest. She was maybe 18 months old or thereabouts, and still in diapers. Stan would stumble down the stairs into the basement carrying her under his arm, and stand her up in the sink next to the washing machine. He'd step back, light a smoke, suck hard on it to get it going well, and to wreathe himself in protective smoke like a war-time naval destroyer, and then turn on the hose. He'd carefully adjust the water temperature and then gingerly undo the pins holding the diaper on. And then, holding her up by the shoulder, and squinting against the smoke from his cigarette, he'd wash the shitty diaper off her. The aroma from the night's accumulated toxins would rise up to his nose, and he'd take out his cigarette, and turn and barf into the other sink. The little girl would be having a great time, laughing and dancing in the warm stream. Stan would dry her off with a towel, slap on some lotion, shake on some powder, then wrap her up in a fresh cloth. Get the pins on, turn and puke once more, rinse out the sink, and then carry her up for breakfast and wait for the day care to arrive.

"Thank you," I'd call out. "When is the next performance?"

I could hear Stan's voice as he climbed back up the stairs. "I don't know how she does it. She's producing Agent Orange in her pants every night."

504

He'd carried pictures of Diane's three kids in his wallet right from the beginning, and while showing the photos off he always referred to them as "My kids." But I guess he felt the biological imperative, and now he and Diane were expecting one of their own the following summer. He jumped into the whole Lamaze thing too, learning how to be a coach and partner for the birthing process.

We had booked only local shows for the weeks around the due date, so Stan could race home at a moments' notice. He came to me and David Eadie at one point and asked that we do some rehearsal, just the two of us, so we could fill in as a duo in case the balloon went up. As it turned out, it all went fairly smoothly, and according to schedule, and I was awakened around 3 or so one morning by the phone. It was Stan, and he really needn't have called. He was only 5 miles to the west and I could have just stuck my head out the window and heard him.

"Hello?"

"IT'S INCREDIBLE. I'VE NEVER SEEN ANYTHING LIKE IT IT'S UNBELIEVABLE IT'S A FUCKING MIRACLE IT JUST CAME OUT AND HOLY SHIT IT'S A WHOLE NEW HUMAN BEING AND DIANE'S DOING GREAT AND HE LOOKS JUST LIKE ME AND YOU'VE GOT TO COME SEE HIM BUT NOT RIGHT NOW 'CAUSE SHE NEEDS TO SLEEP AND HE'S NURSING ALREADY AND..."

for about 15 minutes until he had to pause for breath. I had put the receiver down and was listening from a safe distance across the room.

"So it's a boy?"

"HUH?"

"It's a boy?"

"Yeah. It's a boy. He looks like me."

His voice was back to normal now. I went over and picked up the phone.

"And he looks like you. Poor little bastard."

"Shut up. It's great. It's the most incredible thing I've ever seen. She did the whole breathing thing and kept calm, and finally just bore down and pushed and pushed and then this big red..."

"Yeah, that's wonderful." I hurriedly put the phone receiver under my armpit. I didn't need the gory details.

I went down to the hospital later that day. Diane was looking happy and exhausted. The baby was across the room in a bassinet. I took a look. He looked much like all babies do. Stick a Havana in his mouth and jam a Homburg on his head and he'd do as a stand in for Churchill. He was a big bonny baby though, as my mother said when she saw him a while later.

I made some appropriately positive comments.

"Well look at that. Only one head."

The kid was deeply asleep, twitching his arms and legs.

"He must be dreaming about chasing a rabbit."

Stan was not in the room. He had gone into full "I love Lucy" mode and had bought a huge box of cheap, dry-as-tinder cigars in the hospital gift shop, each a foot long with a blue ribbon that read, "IT'S A BOY," and was busy handing them out to strangers in the hallways and down in the lobby, and in the parking lot, and out on the street and beyond, all the way back to Dundas.

"Well done. He looks great." I said to Diane. "I brought you something to read while you're here."

I'd brought her a book which I had just finished, called, "Hitler, My Part in His Downfall," by Spike Milligan, who wrote and performed on the Goon Shows.

It was the funniest book I had ever read, and in retrospect, I don't know if I could have done a crueler thing to a woman who had just expelled a new human the size of a Christmas turkey from her body, and was now carrying many stitches. I just wasn't thinking.

Stan bounced into the room, gave me a hug, and then shoved a what looked like a dog turd wrapped in plastic into my gob.

"Here. Everyone gets a cigar."

"Bleah." I took the nasty thing out of my mouth. "Thanks very much. Have you given any thought to a name?"

"He's going to be called Nathan Prescott Warren Rogers."

"Jesus. Better get a lawyer. He'll sue you when he gets old enough."

"Very funny. We like it."

And so it was. "Nathan," after Dad, and "Prescott" and "Warren" after Dad's younger brother, and Mum's brother in law, both of whom Stan admired.

Stan could not have been prouder. He took the kid everywhere. When he was only a few months old, I saw him walking down King Street in Hamilton with Nathan on his shoulders. Stan was holding onto the kid's legs and Nathan was holding onto either side of Stan's head, no doubt enjoying the view and the smoke from Stan's lit cigarette. We never thought about second hand smoke in those days.

I caught up to them at the corner of King and James, and walked up behind them and said, "Nice looking kid. Shame about the ugly wart on his ass."

"You're a riot, Alice." Stan said in Ralph Cramden's voice. He never turned around. He was looking north up James Street.

"Where the hell has the Hamilton Farmers' market gone now?"

"Behind the Mall. Go North on James to Cannon, and cut left. You'll see it."

"Thanks. See you later."

It was then that I could see Nathan going red in the face and bearing down. There was a faint gurgling sound like a mudslide.

"Um, you might want to get him off your shoulders."

"Shit."

"Exactly."

Stan reached up, grabbed the kid and swung him down, and then he did what all parents do. He held him up and cautiously sniffed at him.

"Jesus." He coughed and retched and then put Nathan under his arm like a bundle of firewood. "Gotta go."

And he walked off back to the van where he most likely had the diaper bag and all the requisite supplies. I didn't envy him. That was one big kid, and a hearty trencherman.

Mum and Diane inevitably had a few confrontations about child rearing after Nathan came along. Why Mum felt she needed to stick her oar in I don't know. Diane was far more the expert. After all she'd now had precisely twice as many kids as Mum.

In any case, there arose a terrible war between the two of them regarding various elements of infant care, particularly toilet training. As Mum so proudly told everyone, us, her neighbours, her sisters and cousins and nieces, grocery store checkout clerks, and startled random strangers on the street, and of course Diane, she had toilet trained Stan and me when we were only a couple of months old. We'd be fed, and then she would hold us over the bucket in the trailer and wait for us to open the bomb bay doors. After the payload had been delivered she would wipe us up and wrap us in swaddling clothes, and put us in the buggy for a few hours to air out in the parking lot. I guess it made a certain amount of sense. It was a tiny trailer, and Stan and I were processing a lot of food. Laundry was done by hand, in a tub, with water being hauled in a bucket from a communal tap and heated on the propane stove. She was just above the stage of having to take everything, the clothes and diapers and the two of us down to the river to beat against a rock. The fewer nappies to deal with, the better. However times had changed, and Diane preferred to toilet train Nathan like a sane person.

CHAPTER 61

Night Run From Vancouver

We were on the final leg of a month long run in the West.
The previous night we'd played in Victoria at a little club on the
waterfront. I can't recall the name but it was a pig of a load in. We'd had
to park the van down the street and carry all the gear along the
sidewalk, past the hippies and drifters and panhandlers, and then down
a long narrow alley, then up two flights of outside stairs, then through
the dining room, knocking over tables and chairs, and then finally into
the concert room, where we had to heave the whole mess up onto a
high stage. By the time we had set up and done sound check we were
all pissed off and knackered.
The show went okay though, and next day we caught the ferry to
Vancouver.
We were playing the East End Cultural Center, which was a wonderful
old church which had been converted into a performance space. It had a
high ceiling with dark wooden beams, and great acoustics. This was
more like it.
We sound checked and then went back to the dressing room to change
and relax.
Stan left the room for a few minutes and then came back and poked his
head around the door. He was smiling, and his eyes were very bright.
 "You're gonna love this."
 "What?"
He held out his hand. He was holding three cold Lowenbraus.
 "Wow, great. Thanks."
 "No, they're not all for you. It's where they came from. They have a
vending machine on the landing that dispenses these."
What?
I had to see this.
We ran down stairs and there it was. An old style water filled soft drink
dispenser just like the one from the corner store when we were kids.
You plug in your change and then carefully thread the bottle along the
slots and finally pull it free from the cold water it was suspended in.

Somebody with a quirky sense of humour had put a lot of thought into the comfort and care of the people who worked here.

I already had half a beer in my hand, but I had to plug in more quarters just for the pleasure of reliving my childhood. Wow. I almost wished it was an Orange Crush instead of imported beer. The machine still smelled faintly of pop, and childhood summers.

"Can we get one of these for the van?"

"Yeah, I thought about that already. We don't have room, and if we had to make a quick stop we'd be wearing it."

The show went well. We'd sold it out.

We were due to play Calgary the next night, so we couldn't stay in town. We packed up and said our goodbyes, and Stan started threading our way out of town to find the bridge to the highway up the Fraser Canyon. We were still pretty wound up from the show, and by the time we got to Cache Creek and the big turn to the East, we were all ravenous.

We stopped at a truck stop diner on the right and went in to grab a bite. The menu was printed and hung over the grill counter, and all the burgers were named after trucks. There was the "Kenworth," 3 quarter pound beef patties with cheese and bacon, and not just bacon, but peameal bacon too, for God's sake. There was "The Freightliner", which was 2 half pound patties, each the size of a dinner plate, with cheese, onions, tomatoes, more cheese, bacon, a slice of ham, and two fried eggs. Oh, and a side of fries. There were other even more terrifying offerings. There was one called the "Peterbilt," which, if I remember correctly consisted of 3 half pound patties, layered with slices of cheese, bacon, peameal bacon, 2 fried eggs, a small pork chop and topped with ham and a slice of Spanish onion. Oh, and don't forget the dill pickle.

By this time we were all nearly fainting with hunger. Stan got the Freightliner, with the side of fries. And another order of fries to go.

"Make it a large."

The guy at the grill with the stained apron and the spatula turned around and looked at Stan, then at the waitress taking our orders. She looked back at him and shrugged her shoulders.

"Anything else?"

I forget what David and I ordered, but in the end we three came away with about 40 pounds of death by grease.

Stan got back behind the wheel, put it in gear and drove slowly across the parking lot.

Before he launched us onto the highway again he stopped, put it into park, and carefully peeled back the waxed paper on his burger.

"Jesus." There was a reverent tone in his voice. "Would you look at this thing?"

He turned on the overhead light and held it up for us to see.
I said, "Wait."
I had collected a couple of handfuls of paper napkins before leaving and handed him a bunch. He carefully put the burger down and began tucking the napkins into his shirt front and spreading them over his lap.
"There."
I said, "Wait a sec." I pulled out the Rand McNally Road Atlas and opened it up and spread it over his lap. There was bound to be spillage and I didn't want him searching the floor of the van for scraps of precious burger while driving along a dark mountain road.
"Thanks," he said.
He took up the burger again, and opened his mouth as wide as he could and jammed about a quarter acre of meat into it.
"GGRROWLMMMPH."
"Good?"
"MMMMPH."
He chewed for a while, swallowed, and then let out a yell.
"AAAAAAAAAAAAAUUUUGH! I LOVE IT."
He put the van back in gear and pulled out onto the road.
It was tricky to drive with one hand while eating a burger the size of a hub cap with the other, particularly when the Fraser River is a thousand feet below you on the left, and the guard rails have disappeared, having been punched out by errant 18 wheelers on their way to the Abyss. In the end he had to use both hands to control the burger and his elbows for the steering wheel. And every once in while I had to reach out and grab the wheel to keep us from drifting over the center line into the next lane and vaulting into space.
We all shared the large order of fries. They had come in a large brown paper grocery bag. We kept the leftovers with us for a couple of days. They were cold and covered in congealed grease by that time, but we had developed a bond of sorts with them and it was a hard moment when we finally said goodbye and dropped the last few next to a dumpster in Regina. The magpies came down from the trees and had a look, but they had evidently retained some standards and flew off. The van smelled of decades-old deep fryer oil and malt vinegar for weeks.

It took us all the better part of an hour to finish the meal.
David wiped his mouth, his face and hands and shirt front, and then his pants and shoes, and then curled up on the Cadillac seat behind us and lit a smoke. I cracked open the first thermos. We'd filled both of them back at the truck stop and Stan had poured out a bit of coffee from each out onto the tarmac, and then topped them up with a good measure of Bailey's Irish Cream. We had full bellies, a clear road and money in our

pockets. For once we were happy boys.

It was about 8 more hours to Calgary, and if nothing went wrong we should be able to get there in time for a quick nap before the show.

The stars were extraordinary. No light pollution from the towns here. Just blackness overhead, the blacker blackness of the mountains and trees, and the Milky Way brighter than we'd ever seen it. We drove in wonder and silence except for the sound of quiet belching and the sucking of teeth for maybe an hour.

Stan swore suddenly and jammed on the brakes. I braced against the dashboard, and David catapulted off the seat onto the floor.

There was a herd of elk, maybe 30 or so, bedded down on the warm pavement in front of us.

They weren't afraid or even visibly startled. They just lay there, calmly chewing their cuds and looking into the head lights.

"What are we going to do?"

Stan leaned on the horn.

Nothing.

He rolled down the window and yelled at them.

"Move it will you? C'mon, get out of here. "

He banged his hand on the side of the door. "Outta the way you stupid bastards."

Nothing.

He edged forward slowly, and leaned on the horn again. We didn't want to hurt them, but we had some miles to make.

They didn't stir.

I opened the door and got out.

"What are you doing?"

I found a large branch in the ditch and walked out in front of the van, waving it.

"Shoo, c'mon. Move it. Let's go."

I poked gently at the closest elk and it gave a groan and grudgingly lurched to its feet, looking around and making munching noises with its lips like an old man waking from a nap. The others heaved themselves up as well, and in a minute or two the whole herd was on its feet. I kept waving the branch and moved them off to the left so we could pass.

I got back in.

Stan said, "Keep the branch. There's bound to be more."

Sure enough, every 10 or so miles we would be coming around a bend in the dark and there would be another group. Stan would slam on the brakes, I'd grab the dashboard, David would hit the floor, and I would get out with my branch.

We had been seeing reports in the news about some guy who had decided to show his commitment and love for Jesus by building a large cross out of barn beams. He was then going to carry it across Canada from the West coast to the East, wearing only a thin loin cloth and a homemade crown of thorns.

Stan had showed us the article a few weeks before as we were finishing breakfast in a Husky diner.

David gave it a glance, shrugged, and tossed it aside.

"Everyone needs a hobby."

The only concession the guy was making in terms of not being strictly authentic to the story of the Passion was a small wheel on the bottom of the vertical beam. And this was not for his comfort, but more to keep the cross from being worn down as he dragged it. I suppose otherwise it would be whittled down to a nub and gone by the time he reached Medicine Hat.

We were just coming out of the mountains and seeing the sky lighten in the East that morning when we spotted the guy.

Stan took his cigarette out of his mouth and said, "Holy shit. It's really him."

And it was. Not "Him," but "him."

He was standing next to a large road sign which read, "Calgary 100 miles."

There was a car as well, parked on the verge, and he was bending down towards the driver's side, talking and pointing at the sign.

We blew by, and Stan beeped the horn.

The guy with the cross waved briefly as we passed.

God he was skinny. And nearly naked. The temperature had dropped overnight and there was frost on the grass. How was he surviving? What did he do for money? Where did he keep his wallet? Traditionally there are no pockets in a loin cloth. Did he leave the cross outside chained to a bike stand when he ate lunch at a diner, or did he drag it in?

"I wish we had time to stop and talk to him."

Stan merely grunted. He was tired, having done all the driving that night. He tended not to   trust David or me on dodgy roads.

Then he said, "Holy shit."

"What?"

"Calgary." Stan was smiling.

"What?"

"Calgary."

"Yeah, Calgary. So what about it?"

"Maybe he just found out he got bad directions. He wanted Calvary. And now he just saw the sign for Calgary. He's way off track."

The guy never finished his quest.
A woman in Winnipeg, as we later heard the story, found out about him
and decided that he was her true love match. She built her own cross,
ran up a sack cloth bikini on the sewing machine, grabbed the crown of
thorns she no doubt had hanging on a coat hook, and had run out the
door to meet him.
The press got hold of the story of course, and as the weeks went by
there was a media watch as the two star crossed lovers drew ever closer
to each other.
I seem to recall a long distance camera view of them meeting on the
windy TransCanada near Mortlach, Saskatchewan. They approached
each other, stopped and had a brief consultation, as the cameras for
once kept a discreet and respectful distance. They talked for a few
minutes, and then the two of them began walking east.
I don't think they made it to the other coast.
Perhaps they simply got to Winnipeg and set up housekeeping.
I liked to imagine them, each having met their true match, living out
their lives in a quiet suburb of the city. He could lug his cross to the
office every morning, and she could be the home maker, dragging her
cross around the house as she vacuumed, and fondly looking out the
kitchen window at the kids with their little crosses, playing on the
swing set in the back yard.

CHAPTER 62

The Vancouver Folk Festival

Another rainy weekend, and another long drunken confused flight with a plane full of scruffy folkies, all having a rare taste of the high life, at least as we imagined it.

Mitch Podolak had started the Vancouver festival, deciding I guess, that one major festival and a new record company weren't enough on his plate.
In typical Mitch fashion, everything had to be done on a grand scale.
He chartered flights, whole planes to get us out there, which may have been a money saver, but what it actually it resulted in was plane loads of ragged musicians arriving at the airport with their worn out guitar cases, tatty string bags, and knap sacks full of bird seed, blitzed out of their tiny minds with high altitude carousing, only to land and then mill about the baggage area, helpless and confused until the Festival volunteers got them herded into the waiting vans.

We were staying at the Chateau Granville, at that time a new and very glitzy hotel in the heart of Vancouver. Granville Street was only then beginning its long descent into becoming the filthy trash strewn combat zone that it is today.
At that time you could still safely walk the street, and there were many young women on the corner across from the hotel, taking advantage of that very freedom.
We spent a few instructive hours lounging on the balcony with drinks, watching the hookers down below at their work.
Not that they actually were servicing the customers in plain sight, we were just seeing the courting ritual. The girls would stroll over to the car, lean in, make the pitch, and then get in and drive away with the John. It seemed to take on average about 20 minutes from the first contact, to being dropped off back at the corner to do it all over again while the previous customer drove his Volvo sedan with the kiddie seat back to the family in Surrey.

The three of us were leaning on the balcony watching the scene below, and David said, "I wonder what that works out to in terms of an hourly wage?"

Stan said, "Thinking about a career change?"

"Nah. I can't even chew Freshen-up Gum." (That being a brand of gum on the market in those days, which featured a vile liquid center, and had as its slogan, "The Gum that Goes Squirt.")

Tam Kearney and a few other members of the Friends of Fiddler's Green burst into the room.

"Come look at this hippie van."

They were all falling about laughing.

We got pulled across the hallway, and looking down, we could see a huge old 4 wheel drive Chev Suburban painted up in wild colours. It was sporting a large plexi-glass dome like a B-17 gun turret on the top. Tam was in hysterics.

"Look at it. It must be Valdy's."

Neither Stan nor I said anything.

We actually thought it was sort of neat.

There was something about its rugged, "I don't give a shit, I'm a hippie, take it or leave it," attitude.

Particularly the cool gun turret. I knew immediately that Stan wanted one for the old blue van.

When we got home he was going to commence a furtive search through the junkyards and flea markets for just such a thing.

At least that was legal, which was more than could be said for the recoilless rifle he was always fantasizing about getting whenever we hit Toronto during rush hour.

We daren't say anything though, in the face of Tam's scorn.

He was still cackling and holding onto the rail and wiping his eyes.

"Fuckin' Valdy must be here."

I said, "You know, it might not necessarily be Valdy's. It's probably some other wild man from the woods. I don't see even Valdy turning up in that."

The door opened and David Woodhead came in. He was playing the festival with another group.

"Hey, did you guys see Valdy's cool truck?"

We left for the festival site.

There we ran into a family who had been in pretty regular correspondence with our Mum, ordering multiple copies of the albums as gifts for friends and family.

"Be nice to them," Mum had told us. "Be sure to make a fuss over them. They're really good customers."

They seemed pleasant enough, and their young teenage daughter was working as a volunteer at the festival, this despite having a full length cast on her leg.

I hung about with them for a bit and then excused myself to catch the first part of the evening show.

We were due on later.

Mitch had a strictly acoustic, no electric instrument policy at the festival. For a guy who was pretty visionary in some ways, he could be a complete reactionary in others.

He didn't like our stage look. Three guys, three mics, and a lot of leaping and running about.

"What about one mic? Just the three of you crowded around one mic? You know, like the Weavers? That always looked so cool," he said one time, looking up at us through a tangle of matted hair.

He hated that we had an electric bass, and there had been a tense standoff the previous year at the Winnipeg festival, when he was insisting that we needn't mic the bass amp.

"It's loud enough." he said. This for a show in front of about 10,000 people.

But this night we were treated to the truly ludicrous end result of the no electric policy.

He'd booked Geoff Muldaur and Amos Garrett.

Amos is arguably one of the top 10 living electric guitarists, whose solo on Maria Muldaur's "Midnight at the Oasis," was a touch stone for anyone who loved the instrument.

Not this gig.

Amos was forced to plunk along on a borrowed acoustic during their set.

We were incensed.

Ah well. It was Mitch's festival, after all, and he was paying us a decent wage, not to mention all the usual perks of one of his festivals.

Mitch told us one time that he had seen the Saturday night performer's buffet at the Philly Festival. Cold baked beans and wieners, and stale white bread. And Kool-Aid. He said it reminded him of Jonestown. He vowed to show them how it really could be done.

The backstage buffets at the Winnipeg festival were over the top.

Dozens of whole roast turkeys, all minus the crispy skin, which the cooks were under orders to save for Mitch. There were steak and kidney pies, huge salads, baked salmon, barbecued ribs, Shepherd's pie and baked lasagna.

Vancouver was no different, except here the emphasis was on seafood. Endless platters of salmon, pacific prawn and mussels, along with piles of lobsters and clams.

Typically, Stan made a beast of himself about three hours before our main stage show, but he must have got a few bad prawns, or a couple of dozen clams that had gone past their best before date, or 3 or 4 iffy lobsters, or several pounds of doubtful salmon. Maybe it was the quart or so of pickled herring in sour cream. Something he ate didn't agree with him.

The end result was that two hours before show time, he turned the colour of the sky in a Turner painting, and began to explode from both ends.

As his brother, it fell to me to stand in attendance, in case he really went into a decline, but there was little I could do except keep a safe distance, and marvel at the human body's versatility as he kept reversing his position in the cubicle in the men's' room.

He was a human Catherine Wheel.

I found Mitch and alerted him that something was wrong.

"Stan's got a bad case of the flying axe handles. You'd better come take a look."

Mitch came into the bathroom with me.

I said, "He needs a doctor. Actually, he needs to get to a hospital."

I was standing with Mitch, watching the bottoms of Stan's shoes sticking out from the toilet booth.

The poor bastard was making a continuous lowing sound in there.

Mitch looked on moodily, and lit up a smoke.

"Keep an eye on him, I gotta figure out my evening line-up if he dies," and then bent double coughing and laughing.

He straightened up, wiped his mouth, looked at me and said,

"Seriously. Keep an eye on him. Call me if he gets worse."

About a half hour before show time we were standing in a circle around Stan, at what we hoped was a safe distance, watching warily for signs that the pole-vault vomiting was going to re-erupt.

He was calm enough, but still sweating buckets, and swaying on his feet like a boxer, or an exhausted horse, his eyes closed.

He had been losing fluid at a terrifying rate, and had not been able to keep anything down for more than a minute at a time. He had to be seriously dehydrated.

"We need to reschedule." I said.

Everyone standing there agreed, except Stan, who spoke actual words for the first time in some hours.

"No. I'm not missing a show."

"We'll do it tomorrow, when you're feeling better."

"No. We're going on."

Mitch spoke up. "Look Baldy, I don't want you dying on my fucking stage. I'll never live it down. We'll reschedule."

Stan belched and shook his head.

Jesus, he looked awful. He didn't smell so great either. We all took a couple of steps back.

"No, I'm doing it."

There was no arguing with him.

I got out his guitars, tuned them, and put the six string around his shoulders.

He was still swaying back and forth, blowing and gulping and hiccupping. His eyes wouldn't focus.

And so we went on and played.

We did the show. We did a good show by all accounts.

Came off stage, Stan slipped his guitar off his shoulders, handed it off to David, and went back to the bathrooms where he spent another lively and creative hour.

We loaded him into a van and took him back to the hotel, and I got him to his bed with a wastebasket by his pillow.

I made sure he was okay and then went downstairs to find where the party room was. In the lobby I ran into the young daughter of the nice couple.

"Hey there. I guess you're coming to the orgy?"

She blushed and lowered her eyes.

"No, I have to go home. Mom and Dad don't let me stay out late. I'm only 16. I'm too young."

"Oh. Okay. Oh well. Well, see you around the festival."

I left her and went to the party for a few hours, then packed it in for the night. It had been a long and stressful day.

Next morning I went in to check on Stan. He was sitting on the side of the bed, smoking a cigarette, holding his head up with one hand.

"How are you doing?"

"I missed the show."

"What?"

"I missed the show."

"What are you talking about?"

"Last night. I missed the damned show."

"No you didn't."

"First time in my life that I ever cancelled."

"No you didn't. We played the gig."

"Friday night main stage, and I..." He stopped and looked up at me.
"What?"
It took a while to convince him, but in the end he accepted that we had
in fact not missed the show, but he never had the dimmest memory of
playing it.

A few hours later we were standing in line backstage waiting for
breakfast, when a young woman in a black leather jacket came up
to us, and with no introduction, began describing what a wonderful
motorcycle ride she'd had that morning.
"It was magic. The sun was just coming up, and air was so sweet and
quiet, and I saw a deer. I stopped and she never ran away. We just
looked into each other's eyes. Incredible."
It was my first meeting with Ferron.
There was a huge buzz about her, partly because she was an out and
proud lesbian, which was a rarity in those days, but also because she
was an extraordinary artist. We didn't really look at her seriously
back then, mostly because we were assholes, and intimidated by the
sexual politics swirling around her, but also because we were naturally
suspicious and dismissive of anyone who might be a perceived threat to
Stan's primacy as an up and coming sensation.
Women performers back then had a really tough time of it.
Ferron and Connie Kaldor, and Heather Bishop, and Tret Fure and
Chris Williamson and every other female artist, regardless of sexuality
or talent, tended to get jammed into the "Women's Music" ghetto by
festival promoters who seemed to see them as a separate species.
Mitch was particularly egregious in some of his festival programming.
I don't recall any of the female performers getting a coveted late night
spot on the Main Stage, at least in the early years, and when it came to
workshops, they were all lumped in together for what was called the
"Women's Workshop," which was often their only day time exposure.
Even as stupid and unevolved as we were back then, we instinctively
knew it was wrong.
"Maybe we could do a "Men's Workshop." Stan said. We were
watching Connie Kaldor tear apart a side stage and flatten an audience
with her performance one day.
"Yeah. We could just there in front of a TV and drink beer and
scratch and fart."
"Works for me. Let's go tell Mitch."

I was doing a fiddle workshop with Rufus Guinchard that weekend.
Rufus was tiny, about the size of a jockey.
A wee dapper man from Newfoundland, who after a lifetime in the

woods working as a logger, retired at age 65, and then hit the road as a musician.

He had a unique style of playing. He opened his shirt and tucked the fiddle under his right armpit, and held the bow down by his right leg. He always wore a little silk neckerchief held on by a gold ring. He was, after all, in show biz.

He was kind and funny and utterly charming, and I spent a lot of time in his company over the years. He had great stories about life in the woods, which I could relate to as our Grandfather had worked at the same job.

During the years he had worked at the logging camps he'd found he only needed about 4 hours sleep per night, and was restless. He didn't want to turn on a light or otherwise risk disturbing his roommates so he would, as he told me, "just open a window and put in a chew of tobacco, and I sit there and chew and spit out the window until the sun is up."

Sitting in a chair, his shoes would barely touch the ground.

It was a lovely image to me, this bright eyed and funny little man sitting on a chair swinging his feet like a child, quietly spitting tobacco juice out into the night, waiting for it to be time to get up and go to work. Everyone loved him.

He had a travelling fan club of ex-pat Newfies, all of whom would turn up in T shirts that read "Rufus is Number First."

This morning in Vancouver none of his fan club was there. The crowd was mostly made up of a large contingent of women with a scattering of men and kids. The workshop was going along pretty much according to plan except that I had no business being there.

I can't play a fiddle tune to save my life.

I never could, and my presence there was an insult really, to Rufus and the other masters of the genre.

Luckily I was hosting it and rather than play I took it as my role to introduce the other players and ask questions about influences, to keep things moving, and make sure everyone got equal time.

So as the morning wore on, it got hotter, and presently a young guy in the audience stood up and removed his shirt. This was a cue for one of the women to stand up and start a speech to the crowd about just how unfair it was that this guy could go topless and they being women, could not. It was another example of male dominance, and the sexualization of womens' bodies without their consent, and it had to be stopped, and so on.

I'm not making fun here. This, in the context of the time particularly, was new and really important stuff. My younger women friends have no idea sometimes just how hard it was for the women's movement back in those days. They are able to take a lot of stuff for granted now that back then had to be fought for every damned day, and then the day after, and the day after that, because men aren't smart and have to be re-taught the same lesson over and over. Not that it's changed that much all these years later.

So today, at our little fiddle workshop we were suddenly once again on the crest of a cultural wave, and the woman in mid-harangue suddenly grabbed her top, pulled it over her head, and tossed it into the trees. That was the cue for the rest of the crowd to rise up and tear off their shirts. The air was full of brightly coloured damp cotton whirling towards the sky, and hundreds of bare breasted women were now waving their arms, and jumping up and down.

Poor Rufus was perched like a bird on the chair next to me, sweating and gaping at the scene. A large group of the celebrants started a mass unison boobie wobble, a horizontal version of "The Wave."

Ignoring the political aspect of the situation, and looking at it from a purely scientific point of view it was a tremendous demonstration of Newton's 2nd law. Rufus was now wiping his forehead with his neckerchief, and muttering, "Oh Jaysus Jaysus Jaysus. What are they goin' to do? I never seen nothing like this. Jaysus. Nothing like this." He turned to me and said, "What if they rush the stage?"

I opened my flask and offered him a drink, which he declined, and said "It's okay Rufus, I don't think they want violence. They just want to make a point. I think we're safe."

Things calmed down after a while, but the workshop was effectively over, and the remainder of the time was spent watching the demonstrators pick up and sort their clothing.

I looked at my watch. 1 o'clock, and already it had been a great day. God, I loved being in show business.

Things really came to a head later that night.

Robin Williamson, formerly of the Incredible String Band was on stage, and the lyrics of one of his songs contained the word "tits."

It wasn't meant to offend or be salacious.

Well, okay, it was a Scottish love song, so it probably was all that and more, but it was an old ballad and Robin is a sweet gentle guy, and probably thought as we did, that age had pretty much dulled the teeth and drawn the claws from the song.

There was no intent to offend.

But, there was that word, "tits" hanging out there suddenly in the night air, and the crowd erupted into a seething mass of feminist indignation. They were shouting him down, chanting, booing, and milling about the bottom of the stage.

Robin couldn't be heard over the tumult. He stood for a time and tried to reason with them, but they weren't having any. They wanted him gone.

He left the stage finally and handed his guitar to someone and collapsed sobbing on a road case with his head down between his legs.

"It's just a word. I meant no harm. It's just a fucking word."

Popular opinion was clearly not with him. The storm in front of the stage was increasing. Various other performers, all of them unfortunately male, went out to try to explain why they shouldn't be upset. Finally wiser heads prevailed, and one of the female performers, I forget whom, was sent out to restore order.

Jim Post saw that Robin was deeply hurt, and poured the better part of a quart of scotch down Robin's throat. Within minutes he was legless, and we had to carry him from the stage and set him down under a tree where he continued to rend his garments and moan.

His harp was retrieved from the stage, and that and his guitar was packed into a van. We loaded Robin in as well, along with a trio of gently solicitous women who were trying to comfort him.

He was by now shit-faced, wiping his nose, and mumbling to himself. "It was just a fucking word... Just a fucking...ah Jesus."

He turned to the three young hand maidens who were ranged alongside him in the back seat and said, "I feel terrible. At least one of you has to stay with me tonight. I can't be left alone."

There were soft murmurs from the women who were holding him and petting him and fondling his hair. "We won't leave you. You'll be alright. We'll take care of you."

I looked over at Stan. This could be problematic.

He and Robin were sharing digs back at the hotel.

We managed to get Robin loaded upstairs to the room. It was like trying to help a jellyfish climb a ladder. He immediately collapsed onto the bed, rolled over onto his side, and had another crying jag.

"WHY? OH GOD, WHY? IT'S JUST A FUCKING WORD."

Jesus, he was drunk. Frankly, I was a little disappointed. He was Scotsman for Chrissake. How could only one bottle of whisky have that kind of effect? Stan was watching, clearly pissed off, as the place was by now full of young women who were re-arranging furniture and turning off lights and lighting candles, fluffing pillows, and hanging brightly coloured gypsy scarves around the room.

"Let's get a drink." I said, and pulled Stan out the door and down the hall. We took the elevator down to the lobby and headed out along Granville Street, shouldering our way through the clusters of hookers.

"Hey handsome. Got 50 bucks?"

We ignored them. They had to be talking to someone else. We were neither handsome, nor were we likely to have 50 dollars.

We found a reasonably quiet bar, and put down a few beers, and watched the zoo outside on the street. Odd that the war zone that was Granville Street would be a haven of quiet and rest compared to a folk festival. We were shaken by the near riot. It could have been us up there. We ourselves were notoriously mouthy and stupid on stage. Not to mention having that sense of entitlement and privilege that only white men can display.

Stan and I both privately considered ourselves staunch feminists, which would have made anyone actually living with those issues fall over laughing, but we were in sympathy with all of this stuff. We were just smart enough to recognise it as a human rights issue, and yet stupid and stubborn enough that we were capable of singing or saying something equally offensive, and be unrepentant about it, thinking that our feminist credentials should somehow be self-evident, just because we had good intentions, and after all, for crying out loud, it was just a joke, sweetie, and don't get your knickers in a twist.

We had done a benefit concert in Toronto earlier that year, for the wives of the striking miners in Sudbury. At one point, we were getting set to play "Oh No Not I," a traditional song that had as its message the dangers of unprotected sex, particularly unprotected sex with Newfoundlanders.

Stan introduced the song as being an archaic, insensitive and sexist relic of the days of male dominance.

A woman in the crowd yelled, "Don't play it then," and the rest of the audience took up the cry.

We stood there for a minute or so, and Stan tried to reason with the little ladies, telling them it was okay, because that sort of thing was all in the past. Jesus, I thought. Why not pat them on the head while you're at it son?

Finally, he turned to David and me and said, "Turn it up," and we both cranked our amplifier settings from "merely annoying" to "intolerable." We ground out the song, the whole time being shouted at and pelted with crushed coffee cups and balled up chip bags. We left quickly after the song was over, and the stage was covered in trash.

Tam Kearney was standing in the wings watching, and as we went by he said, "Nice job, ye big idjit. Even I'm not THAT stupit."

Back on Granville Street we drank up and decided to go back to the hotel. The after concert volunteer party was due to start, which meant free booze, but we were also curious about how Robin was doing.

We walked down the hallway, and could hear harp music playing. The door was open, and we looked in. Robin was lying on the bed, his long

blond hair carefully brushed out across the pillow
He was under the covers, and there was a young girl on either side of
him, above the covers, one stroking his forehead, the other just gazing
at him in adoration.
Someone was playing the harp at the bottom of the bed, and a woman
in a long green velvet dress was sitting with a book and repeatedly
clearing her throat. It turned out she was reading Welsh poetry.
The room was full of candles and incense smoke. It looked like some
pre-Raphaelite painting of la Mort d'Arthur.
Stan turned to me and surprisingly, was smiling. We began to walk back
down the hall to the elevator and he said, "I think he'll live. Can I kip in
your room tonight?"

Later that evening I once again I ran into the young daughter of the
couple. She was hobbling bravely along on her cast, in the hotel lobby
on some sort of festival errand. I said Hi, and asked her again, out of
politeness, if she was coming to the after show bash.
"No, I'm too young. Mom and Dad want me home early."
Okay. I'd done my duty for the day. I'd been friendly.
I went off to the party.

The next day was much the same, except that when I went back to the
hotel the young girl was asleep in an armchair in the middle of the
lobby. She had a large page of foolscap pinned to her chest. With a black
Magic Marker she had written, "GARNET PLEASE WAKE ME."
Stan smiled an evil smile.
    "Package for you. Careful how you unwrap it."
Jesus. Probably only a thousand people had walked by and seen this
sign. My reputation was ruined.
Stan turned and headed for the elevators. "Good luck."
I carefully ripped the sign off her shirt and crushed it into a ball, then I
tapped her on the shoulder.
She woke, and stretched her arms out and arched her back.
    "Hi there." She smiled and batted her eyes.
    "Uh, yeah, Hi. You wanted me to wake you?"
    "Yeah. I can come to to the party tonight. Mom and Dad said it was
okay."
    "Well that's great."
Made no difference to me. I had only been trying to be polite as
instructed. It wasn't like I wanted to hang out with an underage girl, no
matter how many records her parents had bought.
She needed to go to the bathroom.
    "Can I use the john in your room?"

Yeah, sure, whatever. Probably the leg cast made things awkward for
her.
I took her up to the suite that David and I were sharing.
"The bog is in there."
"Thanks."
I was outside leaning against the railing, drinking a beer and watching
the young girls in hot pants and thigh high boots work the corner
below. It was a busy night. There were a couple of girls in grey knee
high wool stockings and Catholic school uniforms with white blouses. I
couldn't decide if they were catering to a particular kink, or maybe they
were just earning some extra lunch money on the way home, but they
had been kept very busy all weekend.
If someone turned up in a nun's habit and stiletto heels there was going
to be a riot.
She came back.
"Can I use your phone?"
"The phone? Yeah. Sure."
I could hear her talking.
"Hi Mom. It's me. Yeah. I think I'll be staying here tonight. Yeah. Uh
huh. Okay. I will. Thanks. Goodnight."
She came over and said, "I just talked to my Mom. I can stay out all
night."
Well good for you I thought.
I was just finishing my beer and getting ready to head down stairs and
ditch this inconvenient urchin when she moved in closer. She held out
her left arm.
"Know what this is?"
"What, what is?"
"This." She pulled at a small braided multi-coloured string around
her wrist.
"No. What?"
"It's a virginity bracelet."
"A what?"
"A virginity bracelet."
She took a step towards me.
"And I want to lose it."
She was getting closer.
"Tonight."
Huh?
"Right now."
I swear to God, Your Honour, I never saw it coming.
About 140 pounds of desperate and sweaty underage lust hit me in
the mid-section and I was pushed back against the rail, nearly over

balancing into the street below.

She was in a bad way, tearing at my shirt, crying and trying to grapple me to the floor.

I managed to lug her over to the sofa and throw her onto it and then back away.

If there is a more awkward creature to wrestle than a frantically struggling, barely pubescent girl in a leg cast, parts of whose sweaty anatomy are a certain prison sentence to even touch, however inadvertently, I don't want to know about it. I was scared to death.

I was wishing I had a set of tongs. Or oven mitts. Or maybe a can of Mace.

"WHAT THE HELL DO YOU THINK YOU'RE DOING?"

She was weeping and snuffling and wiping her nose.

"I want to lose my virginity. With you."

"Yeah, well, that's just great, I'm really honoured, but it's not gonna happen. Come on, get up." I grabbed her arm. "You have to leave."

Even if I had been attracted to a short tear-stained Lolita in a festival T shirt and gym shorts, it was suicide. Christ, she'd want me to autograph her leg cast afterwards.

I could see the headlines, and the picture of me on the front page, head bowed, being led into a police station in leg irons. "JUST DOING WHAT MUM TOLD ME CLAIMS ACCUSED CHILD MOLESTER." Christ.

"C'mon, get going. You're outta here."

She was hysterical now.

"No, please, let me stay."

I let her go and grabbed my jacket.

"Fine. Stay if you want."

She threw herself face down on the couch and started wailing.

I opened the door and ran down the hall. I pressed the elevator buttons, but after a few seconds I panicked. I didn't want her to catch up to me. I sprinted to the fire door and ran 12 floors down to the lobby. Except our rooms were on the 10th floor and I was now in the underground parking. I swore and ran back up 2 flights and burst into the party room. I needed to be seen by as many people as possible for an alibi, in case this twisted little nut case raised the alarm with some lurid fairy tale.

Stan was near the door with a beer in his hand and talking to someone. He turned and gave me a nasty leer.

"So, how was it? I didn't expect to see you so..."

"Fuck off. I need to talk to you." I grabbed him, and took him aside. "This is serious."

"What's wrong?"

"You know those lovely people Mum told us we were supposed to be nice to? Yeah? Well, I guess I was supposed to be extra nice to the daughter. Apparently they decided that it would be just the thing for the big tough sensitive folk singer to deflower their little darling."

"What?"

"The bastards set me up like a fucking human sacrifice."

"Bloody Hell."

"She's upstairs in the room. She attacked me. I had to run for my life."

I told him the whole story about the goddamned piece of string and the treacherous late night phone call home to Mommy.

"You see? They were in on it. The mother had a hand in this."

"Jesus. That's sick."

"Yeah, no shit. They're probably out on the sidewalk right now with the grandmother and the rest of the family, waiting for her to display the blood stained bed linen."

About 3 o'clock that morning I sent him into the room ahead of me to check it for varmints.

I handed him the fire extinguisher I'd pulled from the wall in the corridor.

"Make sure you look under the beds."

"You're clear."

We caught a few hours' sleep, and then took the shuttle to the airport.

I was desperate to get out of here before she appeared. I hadn't done a thing and still I felt like some kind of filthy pervert.

I looked around. There were lots of young women wearing volunteer T shirts, but no sign of the girl.

So far, so good.

As Stan and David and I walked out to the plane on the runway, I was hit in the lower back by a small freight train.

"I LOVE YOU! I LOVE YOU! OH PLEASE DON'T LEAVE, I LOVE YOU."

Oh God. Not now. I was so close.

Chopper McKinnon was walking by.

"Parting is such sweet sorrow, eh, Garnet?"

"You prick."

I was trying to push her off me. The front of my shirt was covered in tears and snot.

Finally, Stan peeled her away from me and sent her off.

He wiped his hands on his pants, and took me by the arm and marched me onto the plane.

I had stuffed my violin into the overhead and was just getting settled in my seat, when, Oh shit, there she was again, weeping and waving frantically to me from the tarmac. She was yelling something, but mercifully the jet engines were cranking up and I couldn't hear her. Richard Flohil came down the aisle.

"I say, Garnet, that young woman out there seems to have formed an attachment to you. A deep emotional bond as it were."

"Fuck off you Pommy bastard."

We took off and I was able to breathe again.

I ordered a drink as soon as I was able, closed my eyes, and tried to get my heart back to a normal rate.

After about a half hour Eadie came up the aisle and leaned into my seat. He had a familiar nasty smile.

"What do you want?"

"You know, the great thing about dating really young girls is their stories are shorter."

"Go fuck yourself."

I was going to have some things to say to my dear old Mum when I got back.

We had a session at the CBC in Toronto the next day.

Stan had been hired to write a new theme song for CBC's public affairs show, "Marketplace."

The session went fine.

It wasn't a great song, as songs went, and I don't recall it was ever used, but it was a session pay cheque for me and David, and mail box money for Stan.

About a week later, a large package arrived at my address.

It was from Vancouver.

Uh oh.

I opened it and there were only souvenir T shirts inside. Thank God.

No. Wait. There was a letter.

Oh Jesus.

"Dear Garnet. You certainly know how to make a girl feel loved. I can still feel your strong body against mine." And more. Much, much more.

I hadn't said a lot about the incident to the person I was with at the time. I was after all blameless. Stupid, but blameless, and anyway, least said, soonest mended.

I handed the letter to her and got up.

"What's this?"

"Read it."

"What are you doing?"

"I'm going to pack. I wouldn't believe me either, if I were you."

CHAPTER 63

Silly Wizard

It was at one of the Vancouver festivals that we met the guys from Silly Wizard.

They were a great band.

They played a wild and elegant brand of Scottish music; slow sweet ballads, original songs, as well as brilliantly arranged jigs and reels done at light speed. The two brothers, Phil and Johnny Cunningham on accordion and fiddle were telepathic. They had that sure and unerring sense of timing that only siblings have, and they were hugely popular right from their first tour.

They were also funny and friendly, and holy shit, could they drink. Most of us out on the circuit in those days could put it away. Some like myself, were poster boys for stupid abuse, but this was the first time we'd encountered true immortals.

They and the Tannahill Weavers, another extraordinary Scottish band, who were made even more dangerous by the inclusion of a piper, could put away incredible quantities of booze with little discernible effect, except their accents got more pronounced as the evening wore on, and by night's end one longed for sub-titles.

They could only understand each other, and then, with some difficulty. Arguments inevitably broke out and we were helpless to intervene, having no idea what they were saying.

Fights ensued, and furniture got broken and they had to be separated. Luckily the Tannihills were small and could mostly be managed.

Still, there were times when the appearance of a Scottish band on the festival bill was like seeing a distant Viking sail on the horizon.

You take in the laundry and hide the cattle.

No point in hiding the women, they are already out in the yard, waving their panties.

Stan and I were watching Johnny and Phil one night, playing an afterhours session at the festival volunteer party.

They had got in a huge supply of bottled beer, and had been working their way through it pretty steadily, and they were now surrounded by a ring of their slain.

The booze was having no effect save to make them play ever faster, with more impossible embellishments, and long passages of 128th note flurries and triplets in perfect unison.

It was jaw dropping.

Presently, Phil stopped and put down his accordion.

He said, "I have to piss," and tried to get up.

His legs wouldn't answer.

"What the...?"

He tried again and fell back.

"Ma fuckin' legs won't work. Fuck."

He sat there looking confused.

Stan and I decided to help. We picked him up by the arms and got him to his feet.

"There you go."

"I can't walk."

Phil was looking down at his treacherous extremities.

"Fucking hell."

So we dragged him out of the room and down the hall, his feet trailing behind, and got him into the bog. We propped him up in front of the urinal and Stan said, "You're on your own mate, I'm not holding it for you."

Phil pitched forward and managed to hold himself out from the wall by his forehead.

There was some fumbling with his garments, and we politely averted our gaze and he gave forth.

"Ahhhhh fuckin' hell...That's great."

We waited.

And we waited.

And then we waited some more.

Stan smoked most of a cigarette.

Outside the walls of the hotel, the gentle rhythm of the seasons was progressing. Flowers were blooming and dying. Birds were gathering for their annual migrations. The earth was tipping back away from the sun. It was the circle of Life.

Finally Phil was done peeing.

He restored his state of dress, and we dragged him over to the sink so he could rinse his hands, and then hauled him back down to the party room.

His legs were still lifeless, not even part of him.

We placed him in his chair, gave him back his accordion, and he went right back into another impossible and blindingly fast tune.

Stan shook his head and turned to me.

"I have a new hero."

I looked in on the two of them a few hours later, and they were still at it. It was too much for me and I went back up to my room and fell into bed.

Next morning we all reconvened, somewhat worse for wear, at a workshop stage.

It was 11 am.

A bad hour for the walking wounded to be up and about.

Stan and David and I were doing a workshop with Betsy Rose and Cathy Winter, two leading lights of what was called in those days "Women's Music," or sometimes, "Womyn's Music," depending on how the vote to spell it had gone at the meeting that week.

We were joined by the tattered remnants of Silly Wizard.

We, the men, were all were suffering from self-inflicted sucking head wounds, and were moving very carefully trying not to jar our brains.

I pulled a bottle of brandy out of my shoulder bag, poured a good measure into a Styrofoam cup, and handed the bottle over to Stan.

"Breakfast?"

He tossed out the remains of his cold coffee and poured in a couple of ounces.

"Thanks." And he handed the bottle over to David.

David, who was behind us sitting on his amp, simply upended the bottle into his mouth and gulped some down.

He gave an exaggerated belch that startled a couple of crows out of the tree overhead, wiped his mouth and handed the bottle back.

He lit a smoke and took a deep drag, and then, pulling the hood of his yellow rain jacket up, hunched over and closed his eyes. It wasn't enough. He reached into his pocket and pulled out his mirror shaded Ray Bans. He now looked like the guy in the wanted poster for the Unabomber.

I looked over at the lads from Silly Wizard, and one of them had brought along a bottle as well.

We were all feeling pretty seedy, and our mood was not helped by the realisation that our presence at the workshop was surplus to needs.

The audience was clearly, overwhelmingly there to see Betsy and Cathy, who, while friendly enough, were clearly repelled by a gaggle of hung over unshaved degenerates smoking, coughing uncontrollably, and passing large bottles of Courvoisier to and fro in clear view of young children.

Betsy and Cathy were up first, and they launched into what could only be described as a rant against the music world.

Silly Wizard

How it was controlled by men, who wouldn't give women a fair shake.
How women's music was strong.
Women's voices would be heard.
Women would take control of their own music, their own lives, their
own destinies, and the chauvinistic corporate bastards who were
holding women down would in the end be beaten, and the world
would be a better place for it.
It was like a revival meeting.
The audience was eating it up, and with each declaration more and
more of them were getting to their feet and cheering and chanting
"SISTERHOOD! SISTERHOOD!"

It was then that Betsy and Cathy launched into their song.
It was about how the music business was controlled by men who
wouldn't give women a fair shake, how women's music was strong,
women's voices would be heard, and they would take control of their
own lives, their own destinies and so on.
We had no argument with the general thesis.
We agreed completely.
We knew the business was controlled by swine.
Our Mum, who ran our record company, could give you chapter and
verse about how foul and evil and dishonest the corporate world was.
We were on their side.
But at the moment we all looked like exhibit A as to just how vile and
disgusting men could be.
Our brief and tentative evolutionary journey down from the trees
had been an obvious failure, so we hung our heads, and tried to make
ourselves smaller, and waited for the song to be over.
Finally it was finished, and was followed by a storm of applause.
Close to a thousand women were standing up and clapping and
whistling and chanting, and they wouldn't let up. For a time it looked
as if we might actually get away without having to play and expose
ourselves to cruel public scrutiny.
After a while though, it did begin to die down, and Stan looked at me
and David and we began to adjust our mics in order to play.
The last few cheers were just starting to fade and people were resuming
their seats when Johnny Cunningham leaned over to me, and not
realising my mike was hot...very hot, as it turned out, said in a very
loud and hoarse stage whisper, "Well, doesn't THAT just make you
want to cut your cock off?"

We beat the retreat to the safety of the backstage area after that little
disaster, and were having coffee in the shade.

We were watching the freighters glide slowly by out in the bay. We'd washed down some aspirins with more brandy, and we were now waiting for them to kick in and do their work.

I was sitting with Chopper McKinnon.

At that time he was the owner of the Toronto Folklore Centre.

He was an extraordinarily generous and kind man, and a true and loyal friend.

He had sold me my first ever good guitar, or more accurately, had sold it to my Dad, who then handed it over to me.

The coffee and brandy and pain-killers were helping restore our ragged constitutions, and I had just been telling him about the events of the last hour, when the co-host of CBC's "Touch The Earth" swept into the pavilion.

His name was Doug-something or other.

I've lost his last name, and he probably wouldn't thank me for printing it anyway.

I never could figure out why he was the co-host of Canada's only coast to coast network folk music show. He hated folk music and made no secret of his loathing and disdain for the scruffy rabble who perpetrated it. He was contemptuous of anyone he considered beneath him socially, (which was pretty much everyone), and was truly a mean-mouthed and nasty drunk.

We were ashamed and resentful that we had to tolerate him, as to do otherwise was to risk being banished from the airwaves.

At the time I had decided he was there simply because he possessed one of those big old time authoritative "radio voices."

Max Ferguson, years before on his "Rawhide" show, had created a radio announcer character named "Marvin Mellobell," whom Max used to parody and make fun of the vain, self-important and empty-headed radio hosts of the day.

Marvin could have been modelled on Doug.

But if his word meant anything, he was hell on the "ladies" as he called them, and he was a great dresser, and this morning he had out done himself.

He was a vision.

He was wearing tight pants, which may or may not have been velvet, tucked into knee high riding boots, and a large and shiny and no doubt very expensive leather cape that came down to about mid-thigh. The whole ensemble was topped off with a kicky matching wide brimmed leather hat.

Wow. Some cruel son of a bitch of a salesman had lied to him.

He was holding a briefcase in his right hand. He paused at the entrance to the big tent, to make sure we all could get the full impact of his

beauty. Probably in his mind's eye, he was back-lit, romantic theme music was playing, and a gentle breeze was ruffling his hair.
He strode manfully over to the table next to us, threw down his brief case, snapped it open, and began pulling out papers.
Oh sweet Jesus, even the briefcase matched.

Chopper called out, "Oh look everybody! It's the Accountant of Monte Cristo!"
Our hero froze.
He stood for a moment, staring into the briefcase.
Then he shoved the papers back in, smacked down the lid, and whirled around.
He flounced out of the tent, the cape streaming out behind him, and he was followed by a chorus of falsetto voices yelling, "My Hero!" and "Save me! Oh save me!," and a lone Scottish voice who called out, "Hey Mister, can I pet your horse?"
There never was a swordsman like D'Artagnon.

After the laughter died down, Stan turned to Chopper and said, "Remind me later, I need to buy you many drinks."
Chopper smiled, took a sip of his coffee, swallowed, and waved his hand modestly.

"Ah, it was nothing."

The Toronto Folklore Center was a wonderful store, and a great place to hang out. It was down the street from a Catholic girls' school, and every day about 3 PM as school let out, the store would fill up with guitar players who found an excuse to more closely inspect an instrument and maybe try it out right next to the front windows.
There was no doorbell to announce customers. Someone had taken an Ovation guitar, tuned it to an open chord, and then nailed to the ceiling over the door, using 7 inch long eaves trough nails. On the top of the door they had then nailed a giant souvenir advertising flat pick from Guild guitars. When the door opened the pick would strum a chord. It saved the repair guys a lot of awkward explanations when some poor guy came in needing to have his Ovation repaired.
The day my Dad bought me my first guitar he and I walked into the Center together.
Chopper was behind the counter wearing a Colleen Peterson T shirt. Sadly, Colleen has long since left this world, but back in the day she was a sweet voiced country singer and writer, and the object of much desire among the riff-raff who hung out at the store, being tall and blonde, with custom cowboy boots and Cheryl Tiegs hair. Moreover, she was really talented. Besides being a great singer, she could really play.

Dad was looking at the shirt. It wasn't made for someone with
Chopper's generous figure, and the tolerances of the cotton polyester
blend were being sorely tried.
"You're ruining that girl for other men." Dad said.
Chopper looked down at himself, then back up at Dad and smiled.
Here was a kindred spirit.
He took us upstairs and showed us his secret stash of "seconds" from
Jean Claude Larrivee's shop. He had saved one out for me, and at
500 dollars, had priced it well below half its normal value. It was a
great guitar, and it served me well through all the years on the road
with Stan, despite everything the airlines could throw at it. It has
had the neck broken in 3 places, having tumbled end over end down
the baggage chute. Lucky for me, it happened in Victoria BC where
Larrivee's shop was then located. I took it in that day. Jean simply
epoxied it back together. I still have it. It looks like it was built out of
matchsticks by some guy in prison.
Chopper was the best kind of company. Quiet, endlessly funny without
being manic or loud or show-offy. The kind of guy you might want to
take on a cross country drive, just for the pleasure of being able to listen
to him tell stories, and to share his bottle of Glenyarborough Single
Malt. Stan and I began inviting him along on shorter road trips through
southern Ontario. We had always planned to take him out on a cross
country run, but it wasn't to be.
In later years he moved from Toronto to Ottawa, and started a long
running radio show called "Canadian Spaces" at Carleton University.
His lifestyle caught up with him and he had a major heart attack about
25 years ago. He had a quintuple by-pass, and cut back on his cigarettes,
but not the booze or the reefer, and it was a steady and sad run
downhill for him. He passed a couple of years ago, and left a massive
hole in the scene in Ottawa, and in the hearts of all of us who loved him.

CHAPTER 64

My Big Mouth

It had been pissing rain for about a week, a cold steady downpour
sweeping in from the Arctic, over the Rockies, and onto the plains.
In the face of all this some brave souls had erected tents, and a stage,
and had put down power cables, and brought in port-a-potties and
generators. Miles of snow fence had been put up, and immediately
began to sag and fall over into the soft mud.
Small groups of people, bulky with sweaters and wrapped in bright
plastic against the storm began to slowly move into the rain-soaked
field.
They spread tarpaulins, set up lawn chairs, and carefully positioned
their drink coolers. The clouds were racing low against the sky, and
across the field past the snow fence, the wind had torn a tent from its
moorings and it was now tumbling across the prairie, being chased by
the EMS crew.
It was summer festival season in Alberta.
The water was a problem. There was still a large inland sea in front of
the stage. Behind the stage, the ground was quickly being churned into
a thick sloppy knee deep goo.
Bright yellow bales of straw had been broken out and scattered around,
and the volunteers were now huddling in small shivering groups,
talking quietly, stamping their feet, and drinking weak coffee out of
Styrofoam cups. Most of them were wearing clear plastic disposable
ponchos with hoods, and it looked like an advertisement for reservoir
tipped condoms.
Showtime.
We were due to go on first. Not the best spot on the bill, but at least we
could play before nightfall, when the temperature plunged, and the real
danger was frostbite, or a sudden blizzard as had happened in Canmore
a couple of weeks previous.
There was still an issue with our stage.
A large canopy had been strung up over the platform to keep the sound
system dry during the deluge, and now there were now about 2000

536

gallons of rainwater being stored in the canvas over our heads, and Stan refused to play under it.

"We'll be fricasseed if that tarp bursts," he said. "There's about 10,000 volts that are going to shoot through us if we get wet up there. We're not gonna do it."
The festival coordinator and the stage manager tried to reason with Stan, but he was adamant.

"I'm not going to allow you to risk the lives of my band. You better figure something out."
Someone got the idea of siphoning the water out. Great. That should work. A garden hose was found, and one end was flung up top into the water over the stage. The other end was spooled out about 30 feet away. A big stage hand bent down, and put his lips around the end of the hose, and tried to start the siphon.
No go. Another pushed him aside and said, "Let me try."
Still no luck. We were all waiting. The festival director was looking worriedly at the sky, and then pointedly at his watch.
Someone yelled, "Come on, let's get this moving," and the audience began gang-clapping with impatience.
Another stage hand was giving it a shot. Still no luck.
Damn. The sun was starting to head for the horizon, and the temperature was dropping.
A slender young guy walked over.

"Let me try," he said.
And he had it going almost immediately. Water was spilling out of the end of the hose, and the show was saved.
He smiled and waved off the applause from the crew. I walked over to the edge of the stage, and called down to him.

"Was that you?'

"Excuse me?"

"Was that you that got the siphon going?"

"Yeah."

"Can I see you after the show?"
It got a bigger laugh than it deserved from the crew. He smiled politely, and walked away, and we did our set.

Next morning I was standing in front of the motel, sipping a coffee, and enjoying the sunshine.
A front had come through that night and cleared away the clouds. It was going to be a warm and pleasant day.
David was still asleep after our prolonged jam session the night before, and I was thinking about setting fire to his bed to get him moving. The shuttle to the festival site was leaving soon, and we had a workshop to do.

Across the parking lot I saw Stan come out of the motel office. He was holding a Styrofoam cup of coffee. He saw me, and drifted over, smiling to himself.

"Morning."

I nodded and gestured with my coffee cup. "Morning. Lovely day for a change."

"Yeah. Finally. We could use a break."

He cleared his throat. "So...how did it go last night?"

"Sorry?"

"With that guy?"

"What guy?"

"You remember that guy at the park with the siphon?"

"Oh yeah, and the super powers. What about him?"

"He was looking for you."

"Looking for me?"

"Yeah, he came up to me after the show and wanted to know your room number."

"Eadie and I were doing some playing. Was he..."

And then it hit me. "No. Aw no. Aw God no, Jesus, please. Don't tell me..."

Stan took a sip of his coffee. He was rocking back and forth on his heels and toes, and his eyes were very bright.

"Uh huh."

"Aw No, please, not..."

I dropped the coffee cup and sat down on the window sill. This was awful.

I looked up at him. "So he's really...?"

"Yup."

"And I said..."

"Oh yeah."

He was loving this, the bastard.

"Aw, Christ. What did you tell him?"

"I just told him you and Dave have something going. I didn't know if it was permanent, but for right now neither of you were seeing anyone else."

"Oh thank God. I don't what I would have...Hey... Wait a minute." And then I thought, Who cares?

"Okay, then. Thanks. I owe you one. David isn't gonna be real thrilled about it though."

Stan pulled the screen door of the room open.

"Let's find out, shall we?"

CHAPTER 65

Northwest Passage

We had been touring the West for about three years or so, two of them successfully, thanks to Anne and Mansel Davies at the Calgary Folk Club, and some support from the local CBC affiliates. Despite the massive distances we had to drive, and all the other logistical nightmares involved with touring the West, we were starting to come home with actual money in our pockets.

It was the beginning of the oil boom in Alberta, and the province was being flooded with Maritimers who had left home to find work in the oil fields. Some of them had come out with the idea of staying for a year or two, and then going back home with a fortune and retiring. It didn't work that way.

The oil patch was paying big money, wages far above anything the Maritimes might offer outside of organized crime or being in government, but the local prices accordingly skyrocketed. You couldn't save enough of what you'd made to go back home and retire. It was a boom town economy, and after a few years out there you might find yourself with a hundred and fifty thousand dollar mortgage on a house that might have cost you 20 grand back home, groceries costing two or three times what you were used to, and a couple of kids starting school, and some friends you'd made along the way, and now the idea of going back to Miramichi, or Bonavista or Mabou was just a dream. You might fly back and see the folks at Christmas, but that was it. So there were a lot of displaced and lonely people out there between Medicine Hat and Grande Prairie.

It was in Alberta, and not Nova Scotia where Stan first came to be seen as a Maritime song writer, and not just another guy "from away." It was ironic because he was more determined than ever to get away from the sound which had defined him in many peoples' minds since we'd recorded "Fogarty's Cove." It wasn't until after Stan died that Nova Scotia claimed him as a native son.

Songs began arriving, based partly on his seeing the great diaspora that was flooding into the West, and also from a sense of the sheer size of the country we were having to navigate. It was 45 hours of driving time to get from home to Calgary, no matter which route you took, either through the US Midwest, or the dangerous and terrifying drive over the Lakehead.

Given we were touring the West at least two or three times a year, for a month at a time, plus the shorter runs out for summer festivals, we three spent a lot of time just staring out the windshield.

Staring out of the windshield, watching the road, watching the low rolling fields as they crept by, and watching the sky because the weather could change in minutes, and there was a very real chance that at some point you would find yourself in a snow-filled ravine, with no chance of help arriving, looking speculatively at the bass player and wondering how much of a fight he might put up when it came time to butcher and cook him.

And the day had started out so well, too.

In 1980 we had spent the better part of the month of August on a bus tour of Alberta in the company of Sylvia Tyson, and Stringband and others.

The morning after it ended we flew out of Edmonton to play the Faro Folk Festival again.

We'd been there the year before, and knew what was waiting for us. Even so, we were going back.

We came down hard when we landed in Fort St John on the flight to Whitehorse, and I can't remember whether we had to wait for another plane or for the front wheel to be fixed after the pilot had bent it when we pancaked and skidded out to the far end of the runway.

We were delayed anyway.

Stan and David and I spent a few hours outside the little terminal watching a squadron of former US Navy WWII Grumman Avengers as they flew in and out of the strip, working as water bombers on a forest fire. The noise was astonishing.

"Can you imagine a flight of 30 or so of those bastards coming in to bomb a Jap destroyer at Midway?" Stan said. "Christ, what a sound."

"Yeah, not much chance of a sneak attack."

A couple of them were still wearing their US Navy markings. It was an odd feeling to watch them touch and go, like watching an old film.

After a while our plane was ready and we got on and continued to Whitehorse.

The Yukon, we decided, was where you went to live if you were unable to stay out of jail anywhere else.

It was the fag end of summer and it still never got dark. It plays hell with your brain chemistry and your body clock. Within 24 sleepless hours you are well on your way to being as nuts as the inhabitants. I didn't know it at the time, and it was only in retrospect that I realised that I was then in the first stages of a massive clinical depression that would take the better part of two years to diagnose, and the rest of my life so far, to treat.

In any event, I was beginning to have terrible anxiety attacks, where suddenly my heart was racing, and I was pouring sweat, and unable to see or breathe. They might last an hour or so until the adrenalin left my system, or they could last all day. Of course, not knowing what was going on, I began to self-medicate even more than usual.

We were in the Yukon for about a week, and I don't recall that I ever slept while I was there.

The next morning we left Whitehorse for Faro.

It was about an hour and a half by twin prop Comanche, and 8 hours or so by gravel road.

Stan decided to fly up.

I chose the van and had the pleasure of sitting next to Odetta for the rest of the day, as she smoked and shared my bottle, and told stories about her life on the road as a black woman in the early 60's. I had no words. Her voice had been in my life since I could remember. My parents loved her music, and they were thrilled when Odetta took them into her circle of friends.

I had watched her one night at the Winnipeg Folk Festival. She walked out on stage in front of maybe 10,000 people, and with the very first chord she played on her guitar a string broke. Anybody else would have fainted. She put the guitar aside and stepped back up to the mic and said, "The human body was the original instrument," and she gave a little hip shake. She then sang acapella for the next half hour and the audience was utterly silent, rapt, watching her. Later that weekend I was watching The Tannihill Weavers playing their main stage concert, and Odetta was at the side of the stage, bopping and swinging to the music. Stan trotted over, grabbed her hand and swung her out into the dance area. I have mentioned before that Stan was a surprisingly graceful dancer for a man built like a Clydesdale. That night he danced her breathless until she had to beg him to stop. She was hanging onto him, gasping and laughing helplessly. She finally caught her breath and said, "You are a bad, bad man."

Her voice was a miracle.

I had a whole day next to that voice, hearing her talk about her life. It was wonderful and moving and hypnotic. She had started out training to be an opera singer. After a couple of years though, she left that world and along with other singers like Harry Belafonte and Josh White dove into the folk revival. She became deeply involved in the Civil Rights movement, and she had marched with Dr. King and had sung on the podium the day he gave his "I Have a Dream," speech at the Lincoln Memorial. She was elegant, and funny and passionate about everything going on around her. In later years when I was starting out again in the wake of Stan's death, she helped me get a work visa, and took me under her wing. I would see her standing at the side of the stage as I did my concert, and when I was done she would grab my arm and march me away sit and me on a chair, and give me a run down as to what worked, what didn't, and what was absolutely awful, while I mopped away the flop sweat with the clean towel she had provided. She was endlessly generous and supportive.

We stopped midway on the drive at a little Quonset hut next to a gravel airstrip which Valdy had christened "Cinnamon Bun Strip," after the massive pastries they made there. They were the size of a hub cap, warm and sticky and filled with pecans, and enough sugar to send you into a diabetic coma.

Inside the hut were rows of picnic tables, with maybe a dozen or so guys in plaid shirts and hunting vests bent over their plates, chowing down the breakfast special of eggs and bacon and ham and sausage and steak and homefries and pancakes and baked beans and toast as fast as they could. Gotta keep your energy up in the far North. There was a 45 gallon oil drum in the corner which had been converted to a woodstove, and it was keeping the place at sauna temperatures. The fried egg sandwich I had ordered had just arrived. It was about a foot across, hanging over the sides of the plate, and 4 or 5 inches thick, with maybe 6 scrambled eggs with ham and cheese and onions folded into it. Stan was going to hate hearing he'd missed this place.

At that moment the door swung open and Odetta stepped into the room.

She wasn't a tall woman, but in my memory she looked about 6 feet, standing there in the door. Purple floor length robes with gold and green sequins, and a fortune in gold around her neck and on her fingers. She wore a red sequined turban, and beneath that a small circlet around her head, with a single tear-shaped pearl in the middle. I couldn't imagine anyone had seen anything like her in that part of the world. I waited for the reaction.

Nothing. No one gave her so much as a glance. They had REAL eccentrics up there. A legend of music and a hero in the fight for human rights who dressed like Little Richard was small potatoes.

We arrived in Faro, and got checked into the one hotel in town. It had started out as a two storey building, but as the weight of the thing slowly melted the permafrost underneath they began adding more levels. It was now 4 storeys, I think, and it was settling into the ground at different rates depending on where you were. As a result, the hallways and floors rippled and undulated like a roller coaster or a carnival fun house, and doors no longer closed. Windows were cracking from the pressure, and the whole thing looked like it was going to break in half at any moment.

The locals called it the "Tiltin' Hilton."

I roomed with Stan that first night.

There was a loud and raucous party in the parking lot outside our room. After all, it was still daylight. Why would you go to bed?

So we got no sleep. We spent the night flipping through the channels on the TV. There were a lot of shows we weren't familiar with. In one, a lovely young woman was having trouble with her washing machine, and luckily enough there was a handsome neighbour with a moustache who offered to fix it for her. As they stood in the kitchen chatting about the problem, a saxophone began playing somewhere, and they quickly decided to take their friendship to a new and exciting level.

"Jesus. What the Hell is this?"

"Oh man. That's the kitchen table. PEOPLE EAT THEIR CHEERIOS THERE, YOU ANIMALS."

"Ah Jeez...That's just rude."

Stan changed the channel and in a strange coincidence, found a station playing "Midway," a heroic and atrocious piece of tripe starring Charlton Heston, in "Surroundsound" about the battle between US Naval forces and the Japanese in the aftermath of Pearl Harbour. This was better. Explosions and archival footage of aerial battles with real people dying as their planes cartwheeled flaming into the sea.

"I wonder if any of the Grumman Avengers in this piece of shit ended up in Fort St John?"

"Dunno. How many can be left?"

A few hours later we were still flipping through channels.

There was another happy couple, this time in a Jacuzzi. They were toasting each other with champagne, and kissing. All at once the woman decided to see how long she could hold her head under water. Ah no. Not again.

"Uh, Miss. You can't breathe through that thing. It's not a snorkel."

Stan changed the channel again.

A John Wayne movie. Fuck him, the racist warmonger.

Stan turned to me. "You know that son of a bitch never served in World War II? He stayed home and pretended to be a hero in front of the cameras."

"Yeah, and then spent years lecturing at colleges and telling kids they were cowards for not going to Viet Nam. I know."

"Crappy actor too."

Neither of us had slept for maybe 36 hours, and psychosis was setting in. The whole situation was unreal. We were exhausted, and couldn't think straight, and our bodies and brains were begging us to shut down, but we simply couldn't. Stan changed the channel again, and landed on a low budget commercial for a used car dealership. A guy in an ugly plaid suit was waving at a lot full of worn out beaters and relics from the last decade, and in a thick Southern accent was screaming, "SO, Y'ALL COME ON DOWN TO CRAZY EDDIE'S AND YOU'LL GET THE BEST DEAL YOU EVER DREAMED OF IN A QUALITY USED VEH-HICLE. WE'RE JUST OUTSIDE ATLANTA GEORGIA ON ROUTE 1. BE SURE TO COME ON DOWN. REMEMBER NOW, CRAZY EDDIE'S. OUR PRICES ARE INSANE!!!!!!"

Stan dropped the remote, stood up, and staggered over to the window. He wrestled with it for a second or two, there was a loud splintering sound, and then he shoved it open.

He leaned out and yelled at the people who were still milling about in the parking lot.

"WHERE THE HELL ARE WE?"

We had never run into satellite TV before.

The festival organizers held a barbecue for the performers. I expect it was hard to attract performers this far north to keep the mine workers amused, and lashing out a few bucks on a feast of Arctic Char and moose stew for the performers, plus what we were being paid was cheaper than paying the miners actual wages and benefits. There was a perpetual battle up there between the company and the workers who were struggling to keep their union intact. Mitch Podolak, who was an advisor to the Artistic Director here was under orders to keep Utah Phillips well away from the mine site. You didn't want no Wobbly talking to your serfs and peons and giving them crazy ideas about their right to a living wage. Mitch, being the subversive Commie Pinko he was didn't care, and he smuggled Utah into the mine to talk to the workers and sing a few songs.

On the drive over to the feast we overheard a conversation between the driver and his buddy.

"Winter's coming."

"Yup."

"Figured out who you're gonna cabin up with this year?"

"I was thinking Cheryl."

"Cheryl? Yeah, she's good. I cabined up with her last winter. Good cook and she knows lots of tricks in the sack."

"Yup, that's what I heard."

"Well good for you. I haven't decided yet."

Turned out "Cabining up" was just something people did up there to get through the winter. A couple of friends would discuss things and one would move in with the other over the winter months. It saved fuel, having to heat only one shack, and there were evidently other benefits as well.

It seemed friendly enough, but I couldn't see the practice spreading. Maybe the two guys were just yanking our chains, and it was a riff they worked on outsiders, the same way Stan would discuss getting rid of an inconvenient body while on a flight, when we thought the little old lady behind us was listening in.

The concerts took place in a school gymnasium, if I remember right. Outside, crowds of people milled about in the parking lot, smoking reefers and drinking beer. Some were walking around with open bottles of whisky while the RCMP just stood there and pointedly looked the other way. I was surprised at the level of benign indifference the cops were showing. I shouldn't have been.

The year before we had arrived in Whitehorse about a week after some guy had come into town driving a WWII vintage Sherman tank he had found abandoned in the muskeg miles from anywhere. The Americans had come through during the war and had built a supply road to Alaska. This was the Canol Road.

Fearing Japanese air raids, they had not built it straight, but with a sharp zig zag turn every hundred yards or so. It prevented potential strafing attacks, but from the air looked like a giant zipper. At the end of the war the US army had simply packed up and buggered off, leaving millions of dollars' worth of trucks and jeeps and armoured carriers and tanks... tanks... for Chrissake, to rot in the woods. This one guy had found one, some twenty miles from town, overgrown with aspens and birches and had spent the better part of a year secretly restoring it to working order. The rubber had all rotted out, so he couldn't get the hydraulics to work, but when he finally pressed the starter button the damned thing coughed into life.

As the story was told to us, he drove it into town, and pretty much tore the place to pieces. He had found he could operate the turret by cranking the handle, and people were praying no shells had been left behind. The cops couldn't do a thing. They just waited until he ran out of gas, and then pulled him out and beat 5 kinds of shit out of him and then carted him off to the slammer. He was a hero up there, even to those whose cars he had flattened. They were still picking up the mess when we arrived.

So given what the locals were capable of doing I guess the cops had learned to choose their battles. An open bottle of booze, or a lit reefer was no big deal compared to some looney with advanced cabin fever and the ability to mount his own personal armoured division.

It was an odd festival.

People stood in front of the stage in the gym and actually listened politely, but outside the listening room all bets were off in terms of civilised behaviour.

I was heading for my bed later in the evening, after having watched our friends in Barde play a typically wild and over the top show. They had driven the crowd into a seething sweating frenzy, as usual, and later as I left the hall I could hear shouting and chanting on the other side of the parking lot outside. I walked over to take a look, and there was a couple who had been dancing with each other in front of the stage while the lads were playing. They were now having sex under a massive old Dodge Power Wagon. Maybe 1948 vintage. As they raced for the finish line, the crowd was clapping and cheering and urging them on. I wondered if it was some sort of competition and another couple would take each other over the jumps after they were done. Maybe the crowd was judging them, and awarding points on technique and style and of course, the all-important dismount. I looked around, but didn't see anyone holding up score cards. I went back to the hotel to try again for sleep.

No luck.

The rest of the weekend is pretty much a blur. No sleep, too much booze, and the goddamned sun never set. We were turning into the walking dead.

I do remember playing our Sunday night concert, which went well enough, but afterwards the gloves came off in terms of stupid and depraved behaviour. Stan and Mitch Podolak began shaking and popping the corks on bottles of the cheap Spanish Champagne the festival had ordered, and they were hosing down everyone in the room. The floors were awash, and in retrospect it was embarrassing and ugly. Some poor underpaid cleaning person was going to have to wash the floors and walls after we left, and a bunch of self-righteous folkies and a Trotskyite Man of The People like Mitch might have kept that in mind. I had tried my best to stave off some of the waste and damage by drinking as much of the champagne as I could before it hit the floor and got lost, but I was only one person.

So I headed back to the hotel, but now it seemed a long way away. I was mortally tired and nearly paralytic, and walking the last hundred feet and climbing the stairs to the room seemed like a lot of trouble. I took a long look at the space under the PowerWagon which was still parked at the side of the lot. It looked comfortable enough. Maybe a short nap here before I went on. There were deep marks in the dirt where the woman from the other night had dug in her boot heels for leverage, and there was a large patch of dirty oil, most likely from the truck.

I decided to keep going. I still had standards.

I was just closing my eyes and feeling blessed sleep finally creeping up on me when David burst into the room we were now sharing.

David didn't drink to excess very often, maybe one night out of the year, and tonight looked like the night.

He leapt onto my bed, then onto the dresser, and from there onto his own bed, and began jumping like a 5 year old kid, trying to touch the ceiling with his head, wearing a flowered plastic shower cap he had found somewhere.

I rolled over and pulled the pillow over my head.

"Go to sleep, for God's sake."

There was a crash, and I opened my eyes. He had knocked the bedside lamp onto the floor and broken the shade.

He set it back on the table and began to perform and narrate a play, making shadow puppets with his hands on the wall next to him. He was manic like the rest of us. The only thing that was going to slow him down was a dart gun.

It might have been two hours later when Stan's fist hit the door.

I still hadn't slept. I was in my bed, staring at the ceiling, vibrating like a tuning fork.

"C'mon. Get up. Wakey-wakey, the both of you. Hands off cocks, on with socks. We need to be at the airport in an hour."

I dragged myself into the shower and sluiced off the champagne. My clothes were going to have to be burned.

We got to the airstrip outside of town. It had been built by grading off the top of a mountain and putting down gravel. There was one runway, and you took off simply by racing pell-mell towards the abyss at the end and dropping off the edge. If you were lucky you had enough airspeed to continue to gather lift, and not plummet like a set of car keys into the valley a mile below.

The pilot was from Texas. A long lean and taciturn guy straight out of Central casting, when the call had gone out for someone to play the part of the Marlboro smoking, cowboy hat wearing bush pilot. I buckled myself into the seat next to his, and tried to will my stomach to behave. I hated flying anyway, but small planes were more subject to the vagaries of weather and violent updrafts. This was not going to be fun. Stan was in the next plane. I could see him waving at me and then the lens of his little camera appeared in the window. David was sitting in the seat behind me looking pale and interesting.

"I saw a herd of caribou in the valley this morning as I came in." said the pilot.

"Oh yeah? That's nice." I didn't give a shit about caribou or moose or elk or even the whales and the poor manatees at this point. I was really ill.

"They're just over the end of the runway."

"Uh huh. Great."

"Wanna see 'em?" ·

Jesus. Yeah sure, whatever. Did they have barf bags on small planes? I started looking around my seat.

"You wanna see?" he repeated.

"Yeah, Caribou. Good. Let's have a look."

Anything to take my mind off myself.

Tex pushed the throttle forward, and the engines roared. He released the brakes and my head snapped back as we shot forward. We were racing down the runway, and then all at once the mountain fell out from under us. The plane didn't rise, it dropped over the edge and we began heading for the distant river at the bottom of the valley.

"Those caribou were just over here."

"Where?"

And the pilot dropped the right wing and we rolled violently over and plunged into a steep dive. I heard screaming from the back, and glass breaking and my face was pressed up against the Perspex window. Just below me, as the trees flashed by at a couple of hundred miles an hour, a herd of terrified caribou was running like the clappers with their eyes rolled back in their heads in panic.

I don't know how long we dove, but eventually the pilot pulled back on the control column and the added G force pinned us to our seats as we climbed back.

"WHAT THE HELL WAS THAT?" someone yelled.

"Ah, I was just showing my buddy up here the herd of caribou."

"What caribou?"

"Back there."

"Where?"

And he rolled into another dive and chased the poor creatures another half mile farther down the mountain. Once again, people were shitting themselves and screaming and yelling and crying for help.

He pulled up before hitting the river, and began following it through the valley, the trees flashing by on the left and right only a hundred or so feet away from us.

There was still a lot of weeping and sobbing coming from the back of the cabin.

The girlfriend of one of the performers very kindly passed a stolen hotel pillow up to me. "Would you like a Kleenex?" she said.

I removed the pillow case and pulled it over my head.

"No, I'm fine."

Someone handed me a bottle of spiced sherry. I lifted up the pillow case and took a drink. Jesus, it was awful. The worst thing I had ever tasted. Even worse than the wine we had once mixed with Luden's Cherry Cough Drops as a joke one night in Toronto.

I turned around and passed it back to David. He took a swig, winced, then swallowed and shook his head.

"I didn't know you were so religious."

"I'm not."

"Sure sounded like it back there."

He handed the bottle back. I took a pull on it and said, "Yeah, and who knew you were a soprano?"

It took us the whole 2 hour flight to finish it.

We landed in Whitehorse, and David got off the plane wearing an unused barf bag on his head like a Savoy Chef's hat.

Stan came over across the tarmac. He was smiling.

"That was fantastic. What a great day. Did you guys see the caribou?"

We had a gig that night in the Kopper King Tavern in Whitehorse. We managed to stagger through the show. We were thankful for a change that no one was listening. The evening was remarkable only for the fact that some guy got up on the pool table and mooned us. Nothing else.

Next morning we caught the milk run to Edmonton, via Fort St John and every other little fly speck of a town with an air strip big enough for the twin prop commuter plane we were on. In my memory there was a woman on the plane heading south to see her daughter, and she was sitting across the aisle from me with a live goose in a shopping bag. That can't be right. I must have been hallucinating by this time.

Upon landing in Edmonton, we found that we could catch the late night Red Eye directly to Toronto. So we did, and we got in around 5 a.m. I caught the limo to Hamilton, and when I got to the bus terminal on John Street, I told a cabbie to take me to 123 Bold Street, where I had a tiny apartment.

"123?"

"Yeah."

"123 Bold Street?"

"Yeah, take me there please. I really need to sleep."

"That place burned down last week."

As it turned out it was 125, next door which had had the fire, so I was able to finally collapse and pass out in my own bed.

I don't know when I woke up but the room was dark. I picked up the phone and waited for the front desk clerk to answer. Nothing, just an annoying beeping. I realised after a couple more tries that I was actually home.

I had moved to Bold Street the previous April having finally exited a
sad and dreary domestic situation of some duration. It had only lasted
as long as it had because I was never around. Stan and David and I
could be on the road for 6 or 7 weeks at a time back then. And upon
returning it wasn't uncommon for Stan to drop me off at the shared
apartment at 2 or 3 in the morning, and I would look at the front door,
then turn around and walk down the street to sleep at the YMCA. It
was cheap enough, and even with having to avoid the Greco-Roman
wrestling matches in the shower room, quieter and more restful.
The relationship had been dead for some time.
In truth, it had been just one of those things people drift into when
they're young, thinking when the time comes it'll be easy enough to
move on, with no hard feelings.
As time went by however, it became harder and more awkward for me
to extricate myself.
I tried the old trick of being such a distant and sullen asshole that I
would get thrown out, but the other party had a higher threshold for
bullshit than I had thought.
 I just didn't have the nerve or the honesty to have The Talk and make
the exit.
In the end, I secretly rented a small apartment on Bold Street, and spent
a couple of days painting and tidying, and then one day when the other
person was at work I called my Mum. She brought her pickup truck
down so I could move my few bits and pieces, a bookcase, a chair, and a
table and my bed into the new place.
To complete my sin, I left no forwarding address.
Men are swine.
So I was solo.
Life had expanded for me. I was close to being truly happy for the first
time in perhaps my whole life.
I had my own place which only cost me a hundred and thirty bucks a
month. My total bills amounted to almost nothing.
I had silence finally, blessed, wonderful silence.
I had a window to stare out of while I noodled on the guitar. At least for
a while.
The window looked out on a narrow alley between me and the other
building. There was a very sociable young woman living across the way
who had a penchant for sex on the kitchen counter. I had to buy some
blinds. She had a lot of friends.
I had a small stove to cook on. I began some culinary studies. I was in
search of the perfect fried egg sandwich. Over a period of weeks I keep
fine tuning the recipe until I hit upon the ultimate creation. It was a
spicy Italian sausage split in half and fried well done, then chopped and

mixed with 3 eggs, fried onions and roasted sweet red peppers, then topped with cheese, and served with mayonnaise between two slices of toasted rye bread. The pinnacle of the experiment was when I topped it with Bleu cheese and sweet caramelized onions. I had tried melted Limburger, but the smell set off the smoke detectors, and a delegation of neighbours and the apartment manager turned up outside my door with torches and pitchforks. I had to dial it down.

I was making enough money that I was able to keep an extra bottle of booze in the cupboard, ostensibly for guests, but people stopped visiting after the Limburger incident, so it was a win-win.

And I had my own easy chair in front of my own little black and white TV where I could settle in every day at 5 PM, and eat my perfect beautiful sandwich and drink a delicious cold beer, and watch two back to back episodes of Barney Miller.

Bliss.

Stan had been a bit grumpy with me for a while. It wasn't like him to hold a grudge and stay angry. Usually he would get mad and the storm would come and then it would be over, and the sun would come back out. But he was being short with me for a period of some weeks, and I couldn't figure it out.

We were driving into Toronto one day to rehearse with David, and I turned to him.

"Is there something bugging you?"

"What do you mean?"

"You seem pissed off at me. What's going on?"

He looked embarrassed.

"I'm sorry. It's nothing you've done to me. I guess I'm just a bit jealous."

"About what?"

"Well, you're doing what I always wanted to do, but never got to."

"What's that?"

"You're living alone."

"Really?"

"Yeah, I either lived at home, or went off to school and roomed with someone, and then I moved in with the Curry brothers, and then there was Brampton, and now I'm with Diane, and that's great, but I never had a time where I was just on my own. I've always lived with someone else, and I'm feeling like I missed out on something by not living alone for a while. I really would have liked that."

Huh.

"Well, I don't know what to say."

"It's alright, I'm happy enough, it's just, you know."

"Yeah. I know."

I did know. I was blissfully, perfectly happy.
Life couldn't get better.
And then, in September, after I got back from the Yukon I fell in love for
the first and only time in my life.

When we got back from the Western trip, we began to discuss the idea
of a new record.
It was to be called "Northwest Passage."
Stan and Mum had discussed the budget, which as always was going to
be tight, and we called Springfield Sound once more to book a week for
tracking.

For the most part, the songs we were going to be recording had been
in the band repertoire for a year or so. They'd been road tested and we
had a good idea as to where we wanted to take them in the studio. We
wanted to keep the core sound of the trio, and expand it just slightly
with some people we actually knew, and who understood what we as
a band were trying to do. David and I were both more seasoned and
confident with the recording process now, and felt more able to defend
our ideas as to how the songs should sound when the red light came on.
We called in a couple of the guys from Sylvia Tyson's band, Danny
Greenspoon on guitar, Frank Barth on lap steel and pedal steel, and
Claude Desjardins on drums. They'd heard most of the songs during
the Alberta tour, and knew what we wanted in terms of fleshing out the
core sound. We still needed a keyboard player, and Chris Crilly from
Barde got the call. Chris mostly played fiddle on stage, but he was a
beautiful and inspired pianist as well, and a good friend. We were all
glad to have him in on the project.
Tracking started in late October, and the sessions went pretty smoothly.
"The Field Behind the Plow" had been born early one morning as we
drove west along the Yellowhead Highway, en route to Edmonton. Stan
and I were cruising along drinking bad coffee, watching for wildlife on
the road, and half listening to the CB radio.
Far across the fields we could see a couple of very bright lights. They
weren't mercury vapour yard lights from a farm. They were moving
jerkily across the blackness.
    "What the hell is that?"
    "Dunno."
    "Is there a road over there?"
    "No idea."
It was a bit spooky. A couple of days of driving through mostly deserted
and featureless terrain, and you begin thinking UFOs. A large part of
Canada's total supply of "fuck all" was stored out here. Anything could

happen.

We kept on watching. Our path was converging with whatever the thing was, and after a while we could see big clouds of dust being whipped up and swirling around the lights. It got closer and we realised it was a combine. Some lone guy in one of those giant 2 storey high, 100 foot wide Massey Harris monsters, most likely drinking coffee, like us, and like us, bored out of his mind and waiting for the dawn.

"Wonder if he is on the CB?" Stan said.

"Maybe."

Stan turned the volume up a bit and picked up the mic and began running through the channels and calling out to the farmer.

"Break break. Hello, that farmer in the combine south of the Yellowhead. I'm flashing my high beams. Can you see me? Come back." And so on.

No response, and after a while he hung it up.

"Jesus. Makes for a long day's work."

"He's probably got kids. Maybe they do shifts."

"Yeah. Hope so."

It sure as hell looked lonely out there. One guy, by himself, in the middle of absolutely nowhere, guiding a half million dollars of heavily mortgaged iron across thousands of acres in the dust and dark, waiting for the sunrise, and listening to the radio for the latest report on how far the price of wheat had fallen so far today on the Tokyo markets.

We'd read a story around that time of a farmer who had tipped his tractor over some miles from home, and as he lay trapped under the machine he realised that help was not going to arrive in time to do him any good. He was terribly injured. Having no cell phones in those days, and being unable to reach the CB microphone, he did the only thing he could do, which was to scrawl a farewell message to his wife and family on the fender of the tractor using his finger and his own blood. His will read in its entirety, "Everything to Emily."

I remember Stan folding the paper after reading the article, and tossing onto the table next to us in the diner where we'd just finished breakfast. He shook his head and sighed. "What a life."

It wasn't too long after that the song came along.

"Night Guard" as Stan told the story, came from a conversation with someone who had told him about a resurgence in cattle rustling. It was getting modernised and becoming more high-tech. Good song, but Stan and I had had a brief discussion about the lyrics. I usually kept well away from making any suggestions about his writing. After all, he was brilliant. He didn't need me sticking my oar in. However, I felt that the chorus needed a bit of surgery.

"You know that line "to get this spread and a decent herd?""

"Yeah? What about it?"

"It sounds like you're singing "decent turd.""

"No it doesn't."

"Yeah, it does. Can't you simply rearrange it to "get this herd and a decent spread?""

"No." Stan was adamant. "I'm really careful with my enunciation. It's fine the way it is."

Okay. It was his song. I wasn't about to argue any further with someone as good as he was, and I sure as hell don't take any suggestions about my own songs all these years later.

I dropped it, except David and I of course made up a parody involving the use of the word "turd" and the final verse, where the line is, "It may be just the worst thing he could do, but he squeezes off a few," we of course, changed it to "Squeezes OUT a few."

The payoff came one night at the Groaning Board when Stan unthinkingly sang the parody.

David looked over at me and our legs buckled. I could see Stan's eyes as he realised his mistake and by the time we finished the song none of us were able to stand.

The recording of the song went well enough. It was done with Stan and the whole band playing together, live off the floor.

I think we got it on the 3rd take or so. I used my Telecaster on it, playing the same part I had worked up for our live performances. Danny Greenspoon was standing next to me, with his Stratocaster, smiling his usual toothy smile, and playing little "boom chuck" fills and keeping well out of the way.

When it came time to do the guitar solo, I had no illusions that what I had worked up for the live show was going to cut it, but Danny is a monster player. We all expected he was going to get the call. Instead, Paul in later weeks brought in a guy named Pepe Francis, who was a seasoned and much sought after studio player for the high pressure fast paced civil service gigs that Paul was used to producing at the CBC.

Pepe was a nice guy, and completely professional, but in the end he laid down a twanging and generic part that made the song sound like it was trying to be like every other piece of tripe on the A.M country radio.

"Working Joe" was a snap to record.

We played it much the same way as we had been playing it on stage for the past year or so.

David had worked up a funny Bing Crosby "Buh buh buh boo" bass part, and I overdubbed the violin later that afternoon.

Stan dedicated the song to our father, and I could hear echoes in the song of things our bricklayer Dad had told us over the years about the value of hard work and the importance of sticking to a task and finishing it, whatever it was.

"Best feeling in the world, quitting a job." he said. "Pack up your tools, and tell the foreman to go shove it up his ass. Nothing like it." It was bravado, of course, coming from him. He'd never quit a job in his whole terrified and miserable work life. No matter how cold or wet or grim, no matter how badly he was being paid, or how insulting the foreman was, he always stuck it out.

It was hard enough to come home and tell Mum he'd been laid off, and have to watch her as she rinsed and wrung out the dish cloth and hung it by the stove, and then come out of the kitchen, to sink down in her chair and say, "Oh my God. What are we going to do now?" Quitting just wasn't on the menu.

When he'd said that it had been to comfort his two spoiled and lazy sons after we had bailed on some crappy low paying unskilled job we had been unable or unwilling to handle.

"You Can't Stay Here" had been around for a while. Stan claimed the story and scenario was made up out of whole cloth, he having never been bothered, ("Thank goodness" as he said in the album notes,) by the problem of persistent groupies.

The lyric reminded me somewhat of a conversation I'd had with my Dad when I was young. He'd been trying to impress on me the value of chastity.

"Just remember," he said, "An hour's pleasure isn't worth a lifetime of shame."

"How do you make it last an hour?"

I was still experimenting with tape delays on my instruments, and the guitar part I came up with for the recording involved a second tape machine to delay the original signal, and the use of the volume control on the guitar to remove the attack on the note. It was a spooky and atmospheric sound, and for a first attempt it went okay.

"The Idiot" had an obvious genesis. As we began to tour the West more and more we were seeing just how huge the exodus of Maritimers had been to the new oil fields.

It was hard to believe there was anyone left back east of Montreal.

The song had a great and jaunty little tune, which Stan claimed had been influenced by Morris dancing. In turn, the tune got picked up over the years by Morris Dancers and occasionally we would be invaded at our shows by groups of bell jingling, hankie waving, sash wearing idiots in white, leaping and frolicking about in front of the stage.

By far the worst iteration I have seen of that phenomenon was a
few summers ago, at a small regional folk festival near our home,
where Gail and I were confronted by a group of Morris Dancers who
had turned up, wearing not the traditional uniform of white shirts
and trousers, with satin sashes, but instead were dressed as clowns,
complete with rubber fright wigs and scary Bozo the Clown make up.
They were leaping about to Stan's song, waving long wooden staves. It
hit a solid 10 out of 10 of the creepometer.

"What do you guys call yourselves?" I asked. "The John Wayne
Gacy Dancers?"
They simply glared at us and moved on.
I have yet to meet a Morris Dancer with a sense of humour.
Or a sense of rhythm, for that matter.
The recording of the song was fun. Chris Crilly and I had worked out
an arrangement for twin fiddles. We set up the mics across from each
other, maybe 10 feet apart, and rolled tape. During the playing he was
dancing and smiling and urging me along, and I began laughing, and
he began laughing, and in the end we nearly fell apart and lost the take.
I was sorry when it was over. We spontaneously decided to add a little
instrumental reprise after the song finished. David went out and laid
down a penny whistle track and that was that.
"Lies" was beautiful. Simply a perfect song. A companion piece to "The
Field Behind the Plow."
It was the sort of thing Stan could write with such perfect detail, and
such a tender and loving understanding of the ways of the human
heart, that time and time again I was able to forgive whatever horrible
thing he had said during the fight we had just had out in some rain
drenched parking lot, behind whatever club we were playing on any
given night. There was one night, in particular, when we arrived at
Godfrey Daniels' in Bethlehem, and it was a race to see if David and
I could quit and storm off with our gear before Stan got the chance to
fire us and commence pitching our belongings into the alley behind the
club. It happened all too often.

"It's my name on the poster you know. It's me that sells the show.
You two can always be replaced."

"Fine. Do the Goddamned show yourself. See how far you get. I'm
sick of this shit."
And so on. More hurtful words and insults. More accusations and long
held grudges coming to the surface.
The three of us decided for form's sake and for the good of the club and
the volunteers who were anxiously watching the whole thing play out,
to do the show, but that would be that. Fuck it. We were all fed up.
We went in, brushed past the friendly greetings of the staff, and set up.

The show was going pretty raggedly, as one might expect. None of us were able to concentrate.

Early in the second set Stan began playing "Lies."

How could such a stubborn, pig headed insensitive bastard write something that beautiful?

How could I stay mad at him?

How was I going to fix this and take back all the horrible things I'd shouted at him as we careened up the Bethlehem Pike from Philly?

How was I going to forget what he'd said as he savagely pulled the van around to get back to Route 22 West after he'd missed the turn off to 378? (Which, of course, had been the reason for the fight. Just frustration and road fatigue, and once more getting lost at that tricky junction where 309 and 378 meet south of town, and having to drive miles out of the way. Back in those days, Godfrey's seemed to exist in an alternate universe, one which we could never find.)

I looked over at David, and he too was having trouble keeping it together. As the fiddle player I could stop every few seconds and surreptitiously wipe my eyes. David was holding down the bottom end and couldn't spare a hand.

Those words, and Stan's perfect ability to paint the picture of the early morning school bus. I could see it starting up and heading down the dusty high plains prairie road, and the woman watching out the window. I could hear the silence of the now empty house.

I could see her taking the Easter dress out of the closet and running her hands down the seams.

I could smell the coffee.

And I could see the work-worn hand as she poured out a cup, and yes, dripped "Carnation from the can."

The detail. It was exact and wonderful.

I couldn't stand it.

We got through the show and patched things up until the next time.

"Canol Road" had come out of our first trip to the Yukon, and had been partly inspired by the story of the lunatic with the restored Sherman tank, although the song made no mention of the incident.

Once again we were going live off the floor with the whole band, and once again Paul brought in Pepe Francis to lay down a clichéd and to our ears, intrusive track, when who we had really wanted to play the part had been Danny.

"Free in the Harbour" went okay as well.

I had been playing violin on the song, live, but when it came time to record it was decided to have Frank lay down a couple of pedal steel parts . It made better sense, and my only regret was that we were not able to add the Hammond B3 organ part I was imagining for it.

"California" was several years old. A relic of the days at Campbell's Coffeehouse in Hamilton, when Stan and I were just starting out and connecting with the scene there. Steve and Leah Hayes had moved to Hamilton from Los Angeles while Steve was getting his medical degree at McMaster and the two of them had been a huge part of the local music scene there. Good friends too. Their stay in Hamilton was coming to an end, and Stan and everyone else was terribly sad to see them go. The song was also partly inspired by a tune Rick Taylor had written, which Stan loved if only for the title; "California, Please Don't Sink 'til I Get There."
We'd had no intention of recording it. It was an older song that hadn't been in the band repertoire for some years, but our Mum's older sister, our Aunt Nancy, had loved it and asked that we do it for her.
And that was that, except we still didn't have the title song.
I've read nonsense about how "Northwest Passage" was written on the spot, at the last moment by Stan as we were all standing about waiting. Stan himself told it that way. It made a good tale. The truth of the matter was he was working on it over a period of over a year, beginning with the first Western tour we did with David Eadie. We were coming out of the woods west of Kenora, on the Ontario/Manitoba border one morning, having driven all night over the Lakehead. The sun was coming up behind us and casting long shadows on the endless stretch of grassland now in front of us. It wasn't just wheat fields out there. There was every kind of native grass and wild flower before us, with the morning mist rising off it. It was so utterly lovely that Stan pulled over and lit a smoke and just sat there, looking at it. We were all silent. The vastness of the sky, and the sense of space was something we had never seen before. And for once, three of the mouthiest guys on the planet had no words. The angle of the sun grew, and so did the intensity of the colours as the flowers opened to the light.
After a bit, Stan put out his cigarette, and put the van back in gear. Looked in the side mirror, and then carefully pulled back out onto the Trans Canada. We drove along, still silent, just looking at the scene outside until after maybe half an hour David spoke up from the back.
"This must be the place where Kelsey came out of the woods on his first trip west and wrote in his journal about "the sea of flowers."
Stan filed that line away, and the song took shape over a period of months, and I heard brief bits of it from time to time. Stan would be singing it softly to himself as he took his turn behind the wheel on some late night drive when he thought we were asleep.
The melody and the form of the song were not like anything he had

written before. It had that extraordinary riveting chorus which started the song, but it was not a chantey form. My own personal feeling is that it carried at least a little DNA from Joni Mitchell's song, "Shadows and Light," from her "Hissing of Summer Lawns "record.

We'd had a copy of it in the house back in Brampton, and the album, and that song in particular had a strong effect on us. Like her music or not, and I for one don't really care for it, it was a remarkable piece of work, like nothing else we'd ever heard, and it had played on an endless loop during our time in that house.

In any case, Stan came upstairs with the lyrics finally written out that last morning, and spent a few minutes working out what key it felt best to sing it in. The tape rolled, and what is on the album might well be the first or second run through. Unfortunately, in his usual last minute haste to scribble down the words, Stan made a mistake and had it as "Kelso," the name of the beach where the Owen Sound Festival is held, as opposed to the correct "Kelsey." None of us caught it, and none of us cared when we were made aware of the mistake. Stan sang it with the wrong name as long as he lived. I expect everyone else will as well.

David and I spent some time working out our harmonies, me taking the easier high tenor part, and him having to work out the more difficult lower section, and then Chris Crilly came out and added of all things, a part a full octave below Stan's. How his testicles didn't explode, I'll never know.

We listened through, and I decided I wanted to add second high part, to get a little closer to Peter Bellamy's high, nanny goat style of singing. In retrospect I wish I had left it as it was. Still, the recording of that tune didn't take us much more than an hour or so, from first listen to final product, and at the time it sounded pretty good coming out of the big speakers in the studio.

People can make of the song what they will.

It is very personal for me, and when I hear it I am back again in that smelly smoke-filled van, with two other tired and lonely and frightened young men, with too many miles before us. Too many miles, and too many shows, and too little sleep before we got to turn the nose of the van around and head back east to hearth and home.

CHAPTER 66

A Prairie Home Companion

We had a weekend in Minneapolis, a live taping of a local Public
Television variety show, and a live Saturday afternoon radio show on
Minnesota NPR.

The radio show was called "A Prairie Home Companion," which of
course became a huge long running hit, and a cash cow for Public
Radio. We played it just before it went national.

Everyone by now is familiar with Garrison Keillor, and his persona as
"The World's Tallest Radio Comedian."

He was certainly tall. And he was on the radio. He would stand in
front of the mic with a sheaf of notes, and in between musical interludes
mumble like a man talking in his sleep. During the long pauses while he
shuffled through the pages, he would suck air in past his teeth, and then
exhale through his nose. It sounded like someone on life support with a
tiny harmonica lodged in his throat.

"Christ, "said Stan, standing at the side of the stage, "That is one
hell of a nose whistle."

"It was a quiet week in Lake Wobegone..."

"eeeeeeee..."

Long deep breath.

"Pastor Inqvist took a group of ladies..."

Long pause to suck in air. Then, "ffweeeeeeeee..."

"From the Lutheran Church..."

Deep breath. Then out.

"eeeeeeeeeee."

"On a bus trip down to St Cloud,"

"haaaaaaaannnnnnh."

And so on.

It was hypnotic.

I didn't realize he had made a cult of his shyness. I made the error of
walking up to him during rehearsal and asking him a question relating
to our performance and he simply froze, and stood staring at his notes.

Maybe he hadn't heard me. I stepped closer and repeated the question.
Nothing. He just stood there. There was a long and uncomfortable
pause, and then a staff member hurried up and led me away.
"He doesn't like it when you talk to him."
Stan and David and I went on and did our spot. I think we probably did
three songs in total, although I don't recall which ones. I do remember
that as we left the stage the audience jumped up in a prolonged
standing ovation. Keillor went out and tried to restore order, but it kept
on. We had to run out and take a bow and wave.
We were feeling pretty chuffed by the end of the show. It was exposure
to a larger audience, and we'd done a good job. Stan went over to
Garrison to shake hands and thank him, and either the shyness kicked
in again, or something else was at work. He gave Stan the briefest of
glances and then turned and walked away.
   "That was weird."
   "Jesus, yeah. What did we do?"
I could understand him being offended by me lurching up to him and
breathing whisky fumes in his face, but Stan was sober and friendly and
we had done a good set for the show.
   "What's his problem?"
We were told later by a staff member who witnessed the scene that, "He
doesn't like it when people do really well in front of him."
   "That's crazy. I don't believe it."
She shrugged, and walked away.
Whatever the problem was we were never invited back. The show took
off and has become a long running staple of NPR programming. And by
saying "the show," I mean pretty much that very same show we did on
that very day. For nearly forty years the jokes have stayed the same, the
format has never changed, and the same cast of characters appear every
week.
Most strangely to me, it has spawned imitators, and now in Canada,
one can turn on the CBC and listen to a guy with an aw shucks, Jimmy
Stewart delivery tell the same folksy tale every week about some guy
screwing up the Christmas turkey.

"A Prairie Home Companion" was giving us accommodation for the
weekend, which meant we were being put up with a sweet and friendly
hippie couple who lived in a big wood-framed Craftsman home on a
quiet shaded street on the West side of the river.
I am ashamed to say I don't recall their names, but they were relaxed
and generous and made us welcome. On the front porch, over the door
there was a hand painted wooden sign with the words "Sailor's Rest."
We came in and were shown our rooms, and by the time we got settled

dinner was ready. Spaghetti, garlic bread, and a big salad. Lots of wine. Perfect. When dinner was over I got up and began collecting the used dishes in order to wash them.

"Oh, don't bother, "said our host."We have a dish washer."

Wow. A dishwasher. Rich hippies.

"You sure? I'm happy to help."

"No, we're good." And he stuck his fingers in his mouth and whistled. Two big Golden Retrievers came rocketing into the room and the guy spread the plates out on the floor like he was dealing out poker hands. The dogs went to work, and within seconds everything was licked bare.

Right.

Stan disappeared upstairs for a while. Maybe 2 hours. I figured he was either having a nap or obsessively brushing his teeth, as I had done after watching the dogs. He came back down after a while, with his guitar and a sheaf of papers and sat down at the table.

"What's all this then?"

"You're always telling me to write something more oblique, less literal."

"Um, well, yeah, I guess so."

He spread the pages out, balanced his cigarette on the side of the ashtray, and began playing "Sailor's Rest."

Telling him he should write something more "oblique" hadn't been a criticism. It goes without saying that he was a wonderful writer, and it was not for me or anyone else to tell him what to do. It was just with his songs, you always knew what was going on, and where you were, and there was no room for interpretation of the lyrics. He was a brilliant story teller, but I liked the idea of allowing the listener to bring their own story to the song. Sometimes I wished for a little more ambiguity. In any case, as he played and sang, and the story unfolded, I was once again dumbfounded at the depth of my brother's gift, and his perfect eye for detail.

Our grandfather, Stan's namesake, had just been installed in the Veterans' wing of Camp Hill Hospital in Halifax, and was now simply marking time. He'd been a hard man, tough and stoic, who had served in two World Wars, and had run a wild gang of lumber jacks all over the Maritimes in between, and had fallen in love, and sired and raised a family, and taught them the value of hard work and honesty and everything else that counts. And now, here he was, sitting in a chair in a noisy hospital ward, where the slightest sound echoed and hurt the ears, waiting for the end, lost in the clothes that were now too big for him.

All of that, a whole lifetime lived, and the slow humiliating decline, and the confusion of finding himself in this strange and unfamiliar place was all contained for me in those five words that Stan sang: "This deck is too steady."

He finished the song. He picked up his smoke, took a final drag, and ground it into the ashtray.

He blew a lungful of smoke up to the ceiling.

"Well?"

In a lifetime of never being able to shut up, I had nothing I could say. I stammered and waved my hands. "It's uh... I dunno."

My voice wasn't working very well.

I hesitated, and then like an idiot, blurted out, "I wonder how it will fit into the show."

Which was stupid. It didn't matter whether it fit into the show. And it wasn't what he wanted to hear at that moment. But as beautiful and heartbreaking as it was, it was so unlike anything else we were doing at the time, I couldn't see us performing it in the show as we were then presenting it. His face clouded over and he gathered up the pages and stood up.

"Win some, lose some, I guess."

He was hurt. I'm sure he knew just how good it was. And having followed my suggestion, I'm sure he was expecting a more positive reaction. It was just that for once, I was stumped for words.

I went up to his room a while later, and stood in the doorway and listened while he played it again.

"It's a great song. I'm sorry I said the wrong thing."

He shrugged. "It's okay." But it wasn't, and even though he wasn't a guy to hold a grudge he was a little stand-offish for a day or two.

The song never entered the band repertoire, and that weekend at the house in St. Paul was the only time he played it in front of me. Even so, it left such a mark that years later I was able to call up all the words and the tune and even that odd passing A chord with the G bass in the bridge, after just those two hearings.

There is one recording of him doing it, as an encore in Halifax, but someone had made the tactical error of leaving a bottle of Talisker in the dressing room, and he decided to change the arrangement and the whole spirit of the song. It was now more up-tempo, with almost a reggae back beat.

CHAPTER 67

Winter Tour 1980

We had a two or three week tour of New England in December of 1980. It was pretty well laid out, with a minimum of the deadly and expensive off nights, and the band decided we could afford to do a favour for a friend.

We brought Doug McArthur along as a paid opening act. We were fans of his writing and his off kilter humour, both off stage and on, and we wanted to introduce him to our audience.

"I don't care about the money part of it boys, as long as I manage to come home with a few coins in my pockets, that's great." Doug was happy and grateful for the break.

But we had held a band meeting and decided he was going to get paid the same as us. A quarter of the take after expenses. It still didn't add up to much money, but it was far more than he was expecting.

We set off and drove across the Peace Bridge into Buffalo and then on to I-90 east towards Rochester. It wasn't the usual sort of drive that day. The band was better behaved because we had a guest in the van. Still, after a few hours, we settled back into our usual silence broken only by David's repeated requests that we stop and get something to eat.

Finally, somewhere south of Syracuse heading towards Binghamton, Stan relented and we dove off I-81 and found a chrome diner near the exit.

McArthur was in good spirits, no doubt imagining us all sitting around a Formica table and drinking coffee and swapping jokes and road stories for a couple of hours before continuing on. What happened of course, was that Stan parked the van, and the three of us silently picked up our paperback books and filed into the restaurant. We paused briefly, and then we divided up and each went to our own separate tables and began reading while we waited for the waitress to bring coffee and the menus. Doug stood there for a moment, and then walked over to the counter and sat down by himself. He wasn't used to band behaviour. Even after only a few hours on the road, if we didn't get a break from each other's' company there was going to be a murder.

We were playing that weekend in Oneonta New York, where Angela Page was running a college coffeehouse called "the Sidetrack Cafe," if I remember right. It might have been a remnant of the old college circuit we had heard stories about, or it might have been her own pet project. But it was a two night gig, and it paid fairly well, and we were being put up in rooms on campus.

For reasons I will never understand, the rooms were upstairs from the club, in the Women's Quarters. This was just foolish. The idea of putting notoriously horny and depraved musicians in with innocent and gullible co-eds was just asking for trouble.

It led to some awkward moments. I was stumbling along the corridor one morning, dressed in my ratty house coat, trying to figure out where the smell of coffee was coming from, and a couple of dewy eyed bunnies were shimmering along the hallway, dressed only in bath towels, their hair damp and curling at the ends from their morning shower. We saw each other at the same moment, and we all as one squealed in horror and ran away in panic.

The gig itself was in the basement of the Student Center, and we were playing only two sets a night, with Doug as the opener. The audience was mostly made up of cute co-eds in fluffy cashmere sweaters, and tight stretch après ski pants. They listened politely, and while we didn't make any converts, they didn't yell abuse or throw their own feces at us, as other audiences had done over the years.

We were relaxing after the show one night, Stan at one table, in earnest conversation with Angela's partner Jack Hardy, and David and I each at our own tables with a gaggle of sweet young things standing around us, asking us searching questions like, "Is it really LONELY on the road?" and "I like to write poetry. Do you like to read poetry?" and batting their eyes. If either of us had been the least bit predatory it could have been trouble. McArthur might have been up for the sport, but being in his thirties he was rather long in the tooth for these little angels, and to paraphrase Leonard Cohen, he'd had to "go home with his hard-on."

The girls finally disappeared into the night, and Eadie loafed over to my table with his hands in his pockets. He took the cigarette out of his mouth, smiled, and said, "My five were prettier than your five."

"Doesn't look like either of us won."

I got up, and we went over to where Stan was sitting with Jack.

Jack Hardy, sadly, now deceased, was a legend in the Greenwich Village scene, known for having started the Fast Folk club and magazine back in the 80's. John Gorka and Bill Morrissey and David Massengill, along with Rod McDonald and Suzanne Vega were all part of that fertile little scene.

Jack was really serious about writing. He was serious about what he called "the Craft," a term Stan and I never understood or particularly liked.

And he looked fantastic. He wore a long tweed cape, and high leather boots. He had a foot long Meerschaum pipe carved in the shape of a human skull. He didn't smoke it but he always had it with him, either clenched in his teeth, or as a prop to wave in the air when he wanted to make some point about "The White Goddess," who was evidently the Muse, or some other mythical Irish creature. We never could figure out precisely what he was trying to say. Jack's promo picture was perfect too. Himself standing on a bridge, silhouetted against the Manhattan skyline, looking very stern and windswept and Yeats-like, with yes, a portable Smith Corona held against his chest. If he hadn't been a really good songwriter and a smart and funny and ironic guy, we might have had to beat him up, just on general principles.

Stan was too busy writing, and we as a band were too busy performing an endless series of low paying and often humiliating gigs to have time to romanticize the whole concept of being "Bards."

We closed the Main Point in Bryn Mawr Pa.

We didn't know we were closing it. We found that out later.

The Main Point was an old and storied club, a relic from the older days, and it was a bit of a coup to be there.

We arrived and did sound check and then went downstairs to the dressing rooms. If you have ever seen a CD collection of Bruce Springsteen out takes and rarities, you'll have seen a picture of that room. He is lounging on a sofa, looking young bearded and handsome, and suitably world weary. Bruce and nearly everyone else had played that room over the years, and the posters pinned to the walls were impressive.

Jackson Browne with Bruce Springsteen opening.

Jackson Browne with Bonnie Raitt.

Joan Baez.

Ian and Sylvia.

John Denver.

Gordon Lightfoot.

 Bob Dylan. (That was an old one.)

Tom Waits.

Warren Zevon.

Laura Nyro.

Bruce Springsteen and the E Street Band.

"Christ, look at all this." Stan was peering at the collection.

A lot of the posters were signed.

"James Taylor and Joni Mitchell. What a history."

Wow. We were in the big leagues.

I went upstairs to find a bar and buy some off sale beer. Outside, there was a line of people around the block, waiting to get in the club. I ran back downstairs.

"Boys, we're rich. They're lined up forever out there."

Stan got up and took the stairs three at a time to have a quick look. He opened the door a crack and looked out.

"Wow. This is great. I think we sold the place out."

Turned out we had sold it out and the second show following.

This was unprecedented.

We went out on stage and for the next couple of hours tore the place to pieces.

When we were finally done we were all soaked and shaking and exhausted. It was then we got the news. The woman who owned the place had taken all the door receipts from the till and had disappeared into the night. The club was in receivership and she was getting what she could out of the wreckage.

We'd made exactly nothing.

There was a tense and heated conversation outside next to the dumpster about what we were going to do, but when all was said and done we were screwed. A couple of volunteers were with us and brought us up to speed on the situation. The owner was also suffering from dementia evidently, and there was no future in trying to chase her down. Not even she knew where she was.

"Well, shit."

Stan threw his cigarette butt on the ground and opened the door to go back in and get his guitars.

"Let's load up, boys and get the hell out of here."

Downstairs, in the dressing room, I was looking at the ancient pinball machine. It was a beautiful and gaudy antique, full of bells and chimes and glowing with a warm 50's era light. I had played it a few times that night and it was in perfect condition. A classic of the genre.

Stan came over.

"C'mon, let's get moving. I want a cheese steak and about 300 beers."

"How much do you think this thing weighs?"

"I dunno." He took hold and tested it. "Couple hundred pounds maybe. Why?"

"I dunno. I just feel like we should come out of this with something. I like pinball. This is a great machine. Do you think we could get it up the stairs and into the van?"

"You mean steal it?"

"The bailiffs are probably on their way here right this minute to put

the chains on the doors. If we don't save it, it'll wind up on a landfill."
He looked at it for a bit and did some calculating.

"We can get it up the stairs no problem, but we've got no tools to take the legs off and get it into the van, and you don't want to lay something like that on its side. You'd just ruin it."

"Shit."

"I know. Let's go."
As I packed up my stuff I looked at the posters.
Huh.
Gail was a big Bruce Springsteen fan. Maybe I'll take a couple of souvenirs home. I began carefully pulling them off the wall and stacking them.
David came in, and then Stan, and within a few minutes we had stripped the walls bare, leaving only John Denver behind.
There was probably a fortune in memorabilia there, and I might have one day been on the Antiques Roadshow coyly pretending to faint in surprise as the expert gave me the numbers for 20 some years of autographed posters from the creme de la creme of 60's and 70's singer songwriters.
But no. A couple days later Stan and David made the mistake of opening the side windows at the same time to ditch their cigarette butts, and the resulting cross draft blew the whole collection out onto the New Jersey Turnpike. Fitting, I suppose.

We played the Sounding Board in Hartford. We were worried how McArthur might be received there, as the club tended to focus on traditional or traditional sounding music only. Doug didn't sing traditional sounding songs. And his humour was an acquired taste for many people. We liked his humour, but his promo picture was of himself, eyes crossed, in Emmet Kelly clown make-up, holding a beat up National Duolian like a weapon, and screaming at the camera, with the caption, "Doug McArthur. HIRE ME OR I'LL KILL YOU."
He might be outside the average folkie's comfort zone.
He did fine though, and we moved on to the Folkway in Peterborough New Hampshire.
We had 3 or 4 nights there, all sold out well in advance. We were home. We settled into our routine there, sleeping late, and coming down mid-morning for breakfast. Stan always ordered coffee, orange juice and two toasted bagels, "with too much cream cheese."
Later we might go for a walk around the little town and do some Christmas shopping.
One morning I was sitting at my table finishing breakfast and one of the wait staff sat down across from me.

"I have a favour to ask of you."
I put down my book.
"Okay."
"Don't say okay until you hear what it is."
Turned out her friend, one of the other staff members, had seriously injured her back and was going to be laid up at home for some weeks, maybe the whole winter. She was not only missing work, but she was missing our shows, and could we possibly go out to where she lived and play a few tunes?
I went over to David's table, grabbed him up and then took him over to Stan's table where he was sitting with Doug.
"I have a proposition for you."
Stan said, "Shoot."
I told the boys about the situation and Stan picked up his book and his smokes and lighter and stood up.
"Let's go."
An hour later, we were driving through the woods, trying to find the house using the rather sketchy directions we had been given. We found the place, and to the poor woman's embarrassment began loading the guitars and amps and other gear into the house around her bed which was in the living room. It must have been a little awkward for her, but she was gracious and inclined to forgive the intrusion.
We played for an hour or so, then drove back to the club, had dinner, and then did the show.
Later that night, I called Gail once more to say goodnight and tell her I loved her for the umpteenth time, and she answered the phone in tears. John Lennon had been shot that night, and the word had just come that he was dead.
I went into the room where the other guys were and gave them the news.
Jesus.
We were shocked, as was everyone around the planet, but we had no TV, no radio, and the whole world seemed very far away from where we were in the deep woods.
Next day we all went out for a walk to look for a newspaper, but with no success. It was surreal. I was getting all my news from Gail over the phone. I think we had a go at trying to play "You've Got To Hide Your Love Away," that night during the show, but it fell flat. Everyone was gutted. There were no words.
The tour finished a few days later and we drove home.

I was full of conflicting emotions that December.
I was excited and happy that Gail and I were having our first Christmas

together, and finally I could throw myself into the spirit of things. I felt like a kid again. I met her family on Christmas Eve, and they all were warm and welcoming and sweet to me, and I don't recall any hard words being said about the drunken hippie wastrel Gail had brought home. I was in love.

But David was leaving the band.

Between his own poor health and the stress of living on the road with me and Stan, he was gradually falling apart. And the long war of words between him and Stan, both on stage and off, was escalating. They'd had a meeting away from me and had agreed that the best course was for David to stay on for a few more shows in the New Year, and then go before it descended into the inevitable mutually assured destruction. David was very fast, as middle weights tend to be, with a very hard and mean right hand, (as I well knew,) but Stan was huge, and when provoked had a terrifying and relentless psychotic strength, and chances were David was going to end up tied to a tree in the woods, with a hand lettered warning sign hung around his neck.

It was for the best.

Still...It was difficult.

Our last gig with David was going to be in Ann Arbor, at the Ark Folk Festival. It felt like it might be a good place to wrap it up.

The road life was getting to him. It was getting to all of us, but David was really suffering. None of us ever really slept in those days. At best we mostly napped or simply passed out. The exhaustion and the bad food, the weird hours, the constant uncomfortable bone-rattling travel, the inter-band squabbles, and the air of constant fear and apprehension as to when the next disaster might hit us was grinding us all down. I can't speak for David, but I suspect the rootlessness of the whole existence was wearing thin. Stan was a new father, and had a home-life when he came off the road. I was in love for the first time in my life, and the band was now mostly peripheral to what I cared for most. For David, to spend mad and chaotic weeks on the road and then come back to a more or less solitary life, it must have been very hard. And neither Stan nor I had it in us to be particularly supportive.

To be in a band is to be locked in an unnatural relationship, where everyone's personal needs are subsumed by the more urgent needs of getting to the show and doing the job. It doesn't matter if you're sick or drunk or depressed and haven't had any sleep for the last three nights. Everything, from the moment the day starts, points towards 8 PM and the start of the show. Every other need goes out the window.

Personal relationships may begin well, and in fact many bands form simply out of friendship and camaraderie and a shared lifestyle. But a few months on the road, and all that that entails will test the closest of friends.

David and I were about as close as two men could be without actually exchanging jewelry before he joined the band, but after only a few months of road stress and living in such close quarters we were no longer talking the way we used to.

We were scarcely talking at all, actually. Long held grievances, and petty annoyances, and even whether someone cut their toast straight across or on the diagonal in a restaurant could cause a sudden, and to outsiders, completely inexplicable outburst, and within seconds the whole band would be outside in the parking lot, circling each other, yelling threats and brandishing butter knives.

The really awkward part came when the fight was over, and everyone had quit or been fired, and the parking lot was littered with guitars and luggage and books and bedding. Words had been said which couldn't be taken back or forgotten, and you were now faced with the logistics of what to do next. How was the fired party going to get home?

"Fuck him...he can find his own way back if he's so fucking smart," was how Stan put it one morning as we drove off leaving David at the side of the highway, sitting on his bass amp, just north of the Chesapeake Bay Bridge/Tunnel.

The sad part was it had started out a beautiful and peaceful morning, and the fight had nothing to do with anything David had done. It was just stress, and the fact that all four tires on the van had suddenly self-destructed as we drove south through the cool shade of the Georgia pines.

We were on our way to play the Old Dominion Folk Festival in Norfolk. We'd had a decent gig the night before in Philly, with a full house at the Cherry Tree, and Jim's Cheese steaks afterwards. We'd even managed to get some sleep for a change. This morning we'd found a good breakfast at a diner in Delaware, and we were now rolling along drinking coffee and listening to a Goon Show on the tape deck.

The van began bucking and lurching wildly, as if we were driving over a ploughed field, and Stan pulled over and we all got out. The tires were all at least twice their proper size, rubbing against the inner wheel wells, and the sidewalls had burst and split. The van looked like it had been drawn by Robert Crumb.

I trotted over to a gas station and borrowed a tire gauge and we discovered that the tires had been inflated to well over a hundred pounds per square inch. And it was Stan who had done it the week previous on the New York Thruway. We all remembered the incident where he kept adding air and looking puzzled at the gauge on the air hose nozzle. It still showed dangerously low, so Stan kept adding more air. Obviously the gauge had been malfunctioning, and as a result for the past week we had been driving around the Northeast at high speeds with four small yield nuclear devices under our asses. We were lucky to be alive.

We managed to get the van into the gas station, and they had four tires to sell us. We got them installed and carried on. Disaster avoided. We'd been incredibly lucky.

But the whole incident left Stan feeling foolish and guilty, and an innocuous remark of David's caused him to blow up.

"I guess that's why our gas mileage has been so good the last few days," he said.

Stan pulled over, slammed the van to a halt and began throwing David's belongings into the ditch. David began picking them up and tossing them back in but Stan was bigger and faster and eventually all of David's wordly goods were scattered in the ditch and beyond.

I had been standing well out of the line of fire, wringing my hands and saying helpful things like, "Uh, now guys..."

Stan slammed the sliding door shut and walked around and opened the driver's door. He put one foot in, grabbed the wheel, glared at me and said, "Are you coming, or do you want to stay here? You got two seconds. Make up your mind."

We peeled off, spraying gravel in our wake, and in the rear view mirror I could see David hop up onto his amplifier and light a smoke. Maybe an hour later, after much pleading and begging on my part, Stan relented and turned around just before we got to the Bay/Bridge Tunnel toll booth, which would have been the point of no return.

We found David where we'd left him, on top of the amp, legs crossed, smoking a Camel, and reading his book. Sullen and reluctant apologies were made, and the gear was picked up and re-loaded into the van, except for the small stuff that was lost forever, having been hurled into trees and onto roof tops, or in the case of David's Water Pik, a fenced yard where it had been immediately torn to pieces and eaten by a Rottweiler.

"Fuck it. "Stan said, climbing back into the van. "I'll buy you a new one when we get to town and see a drug store."

We made it to the festival and in my memory had a pretty decent time, playing and visiting with old friends like Robin and Linda Williams, and Vin Garbut. However, David revealed to me just recently that Stan fired and rehired him at least twice more that weekend and I was never aware of it.

It's no life for a sane person.

Crises come and crises go.

And so the band continues on to the next show. It is depressing and exhausting and you never know when the next storm will come. Maybe tomorrow, or maybe a week from now, or maybe at the next meal break.

"YOU'RE EATING THAT JUST TO ANNOY ME!" I shouted at David one morning when he ordered breakfast.

He smacked the table top with the flat of his hand, making the cutlery jump and causing the water glasses to tip and spill. He yelled back, "WHAT THE HELL IS WRONG WITH YOU?"

I grabbed my plate and flounced across the room to another table.

"NOBODY EATS FISH AND CHIPS FOR BREAKFAST!" I yelled.

"THEY DO IF THEY DIDN'T GET ANY FUCKING DINNER THE NIGHT BEFORE!"

"WHAT'S THAT GOT TO DO WITH ANYTHING? IT'S 10 O'CLOCK IN THE MORNING! YOU SHOULD BE EATING BREAKFAST!"

"MAYBE TRY MINDING YOUR OWN BUSINESS FOR A CHANGE."

The other diners were staring at us, and the waitress was hovering nearby with the coffee pot in her hand, no doubt wondering if she was going to have to call the cops.

Stan was across the room, pointedly reading his book and pretending he didn't know us.

As we got busier and busier, the pressure mounted, and David's health grew frailer, and personal issues and resentments came out more frequently. Unfortunately, they often came out on stage. David was always very quick with a joke. Stan was less so, and in the final months of the trio there grew an uncomfortable running dialogue between the two of them, as David would stick the needle in and Stan would awkwardly try to respond. It was hard to watch.

So we drove down to Ann Arbor to be part of the Ark's big indoor fund-raising festival, which also served as a showcase for up and coming acts. I was in a state of denial about my feelings surrounding David's departure. Not wanting to be overwhelmed on stage with the realization that this was our last show together, and that the shape of our friendship would now change, he being an outsider to the band, I withdrew and spent the evening backstage with Eugene O'Donnell and Dave Siglin.

I had brought my viola along. I lent Dave Siglin my fiddle, and the two of us followed along behind Eugene's beautiful and expressive playing for a couple of hours until it was time for the trio's last set together.

It went fine. We were a bit distracted I suppose, but we got through, and the three of us awkwardly shook hands backstage after it was over, carefully avoiding any eye contact.

"It's a good place to end," David said. He went back to Toronto, and

Winter Tour 1980

I don't think we saw each other again until we played a couple of songs together at Stan's memorial concert at the Bathurst Street Theatre, two and a half years later.

574

CHAPTER 68

Klag

Stan called one afternoon.

"Good news."

"What's that?"

"I just hired a new bass player."

I looked at the phone receiver.

"You did what?"

"I just signed up a new bass player."

Jesus.

I had thought we'd agreed to do this together. Replacing David was going to take some doing.

We had been working as a duo for a month now. For bigger and better paying shows we knew we could rope in Allie Bennett if we needed him. Allie was the consummate sideman, and we had borrowed him from John Allen Cameron a number of times over the years. He was quiet and clean and completely professional. He was content to simply sit and play his parts every night, in perfect time and in perfect tune. He was without any known vices and there was a complete absence of drama in all the times he sat in with us.

I found it unsettling.

Stan and I were talking about him one afternoon in the van outside of Halifax.

"Allie's a good guy."

"Yup. Great guy."

"Maybe too good?"

"What do you mean?"

"I dunno, he's just a little scary, you know, sober, on time, always cheerful. I just worry."

Stan said, "It's okay. I think John Allan has a picture of him somewhere in bed with a goat."

Allie was great, but we were a band, and I felt we needed a little more presence from the guy on the left of the stage, even at the price of absolute professionalism. And besides, Allie had a full time gig with John Allan. Stan couldn't lure him away even when he offered, to my outrage, to pay him twice what John Allan was giving him.

"You never offered to double MY salary." I snarled at him later. Stan looked sheepish. "Sorry, I lost my head and got into a bidding war with him."

"No shit. Jesus."

It would have been pointless anyway. There was no extra money to throw at anyone.

So Stan put up some ads in a few of the guitar stores in Toronto, looking for a "bass player for a nationally known folk act," as if that wasn't a contradiction in terms.

The guy he hired after the first meeting and without my prior knowledge, was a darkness on the face of the earth, without form or void.

He is still alive, and I still hear of him from time to time, and as he is still dining out to some extent on his association with us, I will change his name if only to save him some embarrassment.

Let's call him "Klag."

He was a big fellow, maybe 6'3" or so, and on the chubby side, clean cut and pretty well groomed.

He could play the songs okay, and he had good equipment and was perfectly presentable, but something was wrong. He had no idea as to what we were trying to do musically, having spent the previous few years toiling in the bars with a rock and roll/pop/ show band fronted by a couple of Italian brothers.

Stan had given him the albums to learn the tunes, and he turned up at the first rehearsal knowing how to play the notes, pretty much, but there just didn't seem to be much soul or originality there. It was like listening to someone speaking English phonetically, not knowing what the words meant. He had no background in the scene we had come from. He brought in his own guitar one afternoon and played for us his version of "Rocky Raccoon," saying, "This is a show- stopper. You guys have to put this into the show. It always gets them singing along."

There was an uncomfortable silence as he stood between us singing, and Stan and I looked away, and I wondered just how long this guy was going to last.

"Klag, that's just not the kind of thing we do. We only play our own stuff."

He shrugged and said, "Suit yourself. But," he repeated, "It's a real show-stopper."

In the couple of months he was with us I got the impression that he wasn't so much a musician, but more a modestly talented and personable guy who had found playing guitar a means of tricking gullible and drunken women into his bed, and for that reason it was sometimes difficult to keep his mind on the task at hand.

During his tenure with the Italian pop band, they had played clubs and bars all over Canada, leaving behind them, if Klag was to be believed, a swooning legion of grateful and sexually sated women. He was looking forward to getting back on the road again and renewing some of his old acquaintances.

"Back in the saddle again," as he put it. He talked of little else between running down the songs in our repertoire. "So...are women in the folk scene easy?"

Easy. Jesus.

I began tormenting him with lurid fictions about the sex starved hordes waiting for him once we got on the road and free from the strictures of civilized behaviour.

"There may be more body and leg hair than you're used to, but if you can't get laid in a folk band, you're simply not trying."

Somewhere David Eadie's head was exploding. He and I had lived as monks during his time with the band, our sole entertainment on off nights being spent sitting in cheap motel rooms, flossing our teeth and searching for old Bing Crosby/Bob Hope "On the Road" movies.

To his credit, Klag was cheerful and kind, and not a bad house guest according to Stan. He got along well with Stan and Diane's kids and took them to Baskin Robbins most nights after dinner. And he had impeccable hygiene. At least that was what Stan hoped. Klag was spending a lot of time in the shower.

But he was obsessed with getting back out there and unleashing his charm on "the babes," as he called them.

"He's a nice enough guy. He's just pecker-happy," was Doug McArthur's verdict upon meeting him.

Our first gig with Klag was in London Ontario, opening for Martin Mull at Alumni Hall.

We loaded the van and Klag heaved in a large cooler and placed it between the two front seats. I took a look inside. Christ. It was full of Heineken.

"Gotta have beer for the trip."

Well, okay. Maybe I had mis-judged this guy.

We left Stan's home in Dundas, and 45 minutes later, about the time we got to Ingersoll, Klag had drunk maybe 6 beers in quick succession and had then put his head down for a little nap.

"I didn't think he was that much of a drinker."

Stan said, "No. Me neither. This is the first time I've seen him put it away like that."

This could be trouble. We already had one alcoholic on duty in the band. I didn't need a competitor.

Presently the van was filled some unseen and paralysing miasma. Stan and I glared at each other briefly and then we both turned around and looked at Klag. The bastard. We frantically rolled the windows down and drove with our heads hanging outside, coughing and gasping for breath. "Jesus Christ." My eyes were streaming. "What the hell was that?"

I reached back and opened the sliding door and the wind rushed in at about 60 miles an hour.

Klag woke and sat up. There was a stinking poisonous tornado in the van. Gum wrappers and empty coffee cups, and old newspapers, and the ashes from every cigarette Stan had smoked for the last two years were whirling around our heads in a deadly sulphurous cloud. He took a deep and appreciative sniff.

"Whoa. That was a good one."

He leaned to his left and raised his leg. There was a sound like a mud-filled trombone.

"Aahh...that's great." And with his hand wafted the bouquet up to his nostrils.

I took my sleeve away from my face. "YOU FUCKING PIG," I shouted.

"STOP THAT. RIGHT FUCKING NOW!" yelled Stan.

"What?"

"This van is a no farting zone. If you need to do that, just say the word and I'll pull over. But otherwise keep it to yourself."

Stan was leaning out the window, retching and spitting. "Ah God. I've got it on my fucking tongue. Jesus."

Stan pulled the van over to the side of the 401. He got out and walked around to the off side and grabbed the handle of the sliding door. He looked in at Klag.

"I mean it. Don't ever do that again." He violently slammed the door shut. He walked back around, got in, opened a beer, took a swig and rinsed it around his mouth and then spat it out the window. He lit a cigarette and then pulled the van back on to the highway.

"Jeez guys. It was just a fart." Klag was hurt and embarrassed.

It was revealed in the weeks to come that he was a connoisseur, an aficionado of his own personal body chemistry. He positively reveled in the stink, and would review his noxious discharges the way a wine expert might speak about the delicate nuances of a Pre-war Chateau LaFitte Rothschild Bordeaux. He would be standing in a dressing room somewhere, as he did that first night, and get a dreamy and distracted look on his face. "AAAhh...that's better. Garnet, come over here and check this one out."

I found him repellent and disgusting, and his cause was not helped one bit that first night when he saw a photo of Gail in my violin case. It was from her modelling days, and it was a study in tousled blonde hair and bottomless green eyes and a lower lip like a ripe plum, the mere sight of which made me weak in the knees.

"WHOOAA!!! Who's that?" he said, and grabbing the photo, commenced rubbing it against his groin with his eyes rolled back in his head. I grabbed him by the lapels and pushed him back into the lockers, where he bashed his head, and carefully taking the now forever sullied photo from him said, "Don't you ever touch that again." I shook him and pulled my fist back. "Ever. Or I'll fucking drill you."

I found Stan down the hall where he was smoking a cigarette and restringing his guitar. I said, "This guy isn't going to work out. He's an animal."

Stan shrugged and said, "I know he's a bit rough. Give him a chance. He might shape into something we can use."

Our first gig with him went okay.

Martin Mull was friendly and kind, and offered us a drink from the bottle of Glenlivet he had on his dressing room table. Stan and I told him how we had seen him a few years previous at Le Coq D'or on Yonge Street.

During our set, as we thumped and shuffled our way through "The White Collar Holler," I looked over and he was watching us. He caught my eye and raised his glass. Nice guy.

The most important thing to happen during that period of time, and in fact my whole life was that Gail and I were married a few weeks later. I had moved across the street from her in April of 1980, and had become very aware of her as I watched her walk to work in the mornings. She was like no one I had ever seen before, and I wanted more than anything to say hello to her, but never had the nerve. She herself said "hi" one night as she walked by while I was playing guitar on the front step of my little slum, but I was so gob-smacked and overwhelmed I wasn't able to open my mouth before she gave me up as a bad bet and moved on. We finally met through mutual acquaintances in September, and within a week or so, even before we had so much as coffee together, I was thinking marriage. She was probably thinking about getting and filling out change of address cards.

In any case, it all moved very quickly and within a month of our being a couple I had carried across the street my entire worldly goods, a bed, a chair, a small table, a black and white TV, my guitars and fiddle, and most importantly, my proudest possessions, some 60 pairs of perfectly matched socks.

After the New Year we decided to set a date to get married and it was a mad scramble to get ready in time, as it was only a couple weeks away. My parents were the first to hear about the change in my life. They were visiting one afternoon and as I served them their coffee I said, "Could you guys stand to hear some good news?"
Mum stiffened and sat up a bit straighter.
"What?"
"Gail and I are getting married in a couple of weeks."
Mum set down her cup, took out her tobacco and papers and began very carefully rolling a smoke. She was paying particular attention to the process, and after licking the paper and rolling it up, and picking off the ends and lighting it, and finally picking a bit of tobacco off her lower lip, she looked up and took a breath to speak.
I cut her off. "Don't say it Mum."
"Say what?"
"You were about ask us if there was any particular reason, like you did with Stan and that nurse years ago."
She avoided looking at me and lied, "No. I wasn't. But now that you mention it..."
Not a great start.
Stan was the next to get the news a day or two later.
He and Klag were over at our apartment for a rehearsal and I asked him if he was doing anything the following Friday.
"No, why?"
"Gail and I are getting married, and we were wondering..." and that was as far I as could get. He put down his guitar and came over and picked me up in a hug that cracked a couple of the ribs on my left side. He was my best man, and the service was to be very small and very simple. Just Gail, me and Stan, along with Gail's sister Margie as witnesses.
We had found a very patient and tolerant Baptist minister who agreed to perform the ceremony in spite of us being neither parishioners nor believers.
At one point during our first meeting, Gail asked if he could possibly refrain from putting "too much of the God stuff" in the service.
He took it pretty well. He merely threw his pen onto the desk and said, "It's His House. I have to at least say His Name. It's only polite."
In the end he agreed to only mention him in passing, and the day arrived.
It was pissing rain, and Stan and I had arrived at the church early to have a final chat with the minister and wait for Gail.
I stood in the doorway, in a state of increasing fear as my bride-to-be was now some 20 minutes late. It wasn't outside the realm of possibility

that she had changed her mind, and was now on the west side of town, taking the exit ramp to Highway 403 in a long skidding acceleration. Stan was at my shoulder to get a sip from my flask, and said, "I've just had a talk with the Man Upstairs, and he said everything is going to be okay."

"You mean the minister? Did she call?"

"No, I just went into the chapel and had a little chat with the Big Guy. You're gonna be fine."

I had no such confidence. Where the Hell was she?

She drove by at that moment. She had merely been lost, (5 blocks from home, I ask you...really...) and aside from nearly giving me a heart attack, everything else went well.

Gail's sister Margie was there along with Stan, who in keeping with his own personal beliefs kept muttering High Anglican incantations and gibberish and crossing himself every few seconds as the minister performed the ceremony.

"Sorry about all the praying and breast beating," he said to the minister as we walked in to sign the papers.

"It's okay. It was good to have at least one other member of the fan club present."

We opened some cheap Spanish bubbly, and had a drink in the minister's office, and then set out for Gail's sister's house to tell her parents they were batting 1000 in terms of eloping offspring. On the way we realised we hadn't filled Gail's Audi in a couple of days and so went into Canadian Tire for 3 quarts of oil and topped it up. From there to the Tim Horton's drive-through. Later we went to my parents' house for a small celebration, for lack of a more modest word. It was a very Canadian wedding.

As we were preparing to leave a few hours later I went out to start Gail's car, and inadvertently left the choke wide open for about half an hour as we said our goodbyes. There was a nasty BANG under the hood, and it turned out that my second last act as a new husband that night was to have blown up the number 2 cylinder on my beloved's car.

Meanwhile, Klag didn't shape up.

It was a shame. He was friendly and gregarious and always up to play. And aside from his foul bodily emissions and his terminal priapism he was well behaved and polite. But halfway through his first tour with us, we began to get hate mail from our audience. The poor bugger probably thought he was doing a great job for us by leaping about and licking his lips, and looking deep into womens' eyes as he spasmodically dry humped his bass. The women in our audience simply found it offensive, and one letter after our show at the Rebecca

Cohn Theatre suggested that Klag might be happier if we were to "give him an extra-long cable for his bass so he could remain in the dressing room and mug in front of the mirror." The intensity of the reaction from our normally patient and forgiving audience was frightening.

I was visiting my parents and Mum was shuffling through the hate mail and looking worried. "Just who IS this guy? I have never seen anything like this. I don't know how to respond to these people."

"I don't know. I'm not happy either. Stan wants to give him a chance to shape up."

I wondered how the next tour might go. We were headed for the west. We were doing a couple of weeks in Alberta, which by now was our most fertile ground. A couple of years of constant touring there with the help of Anne and Mansel Davies had given us a string of pretty profitable gigs which we could pick up two or three times a year. Annie was an expert at ferreting out little shows in out of the way places where we could make good money on off nights. In the meantime we had the run of their house on days off and it had become a second home for us. We always had a welcome there, and we loved them both. We didn't want to screw up our friendship.

As we drove out Klag kept up a running monologue about what he was going to do and to whom as soon as we lighted in Calgary. He had something I had never seen before in real life, a thing I had only read about in the pages of Playboy. He had an actual little black book. In it he had the names, numbers and attributes of a couple of dozen women who had fallen under his spell over the years, and he had carefully arranged them in order of preference according to their looks, their flexibility and athleticism, and their willingness to endure whatever sick perversion he might want to visit upon them.

"Some of them have had kids, and they don't look so great, but hey, all cats are grey when the lights go out."

Lovely.

By the time we got to Calgary we nearly had to keep him in a cage. He kept pawing at the stained and dog-eared little black book and favouring us with tales of past glory.

"Don't bother booking a hotel room for me. I got any number of places I can stay when we get there. Did I tell you about this one here?" And he launched into a disgusting and detailed reminiscence about some poor degraded denizen of Calgary's demi-monde. We got to town and Stan and I checked into our shared room and watched as Klag got on the phone. He started at the top of the list.

"Hello? Is this Susan? Uh yeah, Hi, It's Klag, You know? From last year with the Scumbaggi Brothers Band? I'm back in town and I was wondering if we could...Hello? Hello?"

And, "Hello? Is this Mary? Klag here. We had some fun together a couple of years ago when I was in town with the...Hello? Hello?"
And so on.

He worked his way through the top three into the also-rans, and further down the list, finally arriving at the primordial ooze which had once constituted his love life, and couldn't find a single taker for his offer to resume diplomatic relations. Stan was on his bed, pretending to read. I could see that newspaper shaking as he held it in front of his face. I had to leave. I was losing it.

I came back an hour or so later and the black book was now on the side table and he was in the motel office paying for a room.

"So. Did you change your mind?" I asked when he came back for his suitcase.

"I'll score someone tomorrow night at the gig."
But at the gig he struck out. And again the next night. And the next gig after that.

Maybe a week later we were on our way to Drumheller to play a show in the maximum security prison there. It was another off day gig Annie had found for us, with good money and probably less chance of personal danger than a lot of the places we had played in the old days. At least here there were armed guards.

"This could be your lucky day, Klag." Stan said as we drove through the checkpoint. "You're bound to score here."

I said, "Dear Penthouse letters. I never thought I'd be writing this, but today in the shower room, as I was bending over to pick up my shiv..."
Klag said nothing. He was sitting on the Cadillac seat with his arms folded and staring out the window, looking pretty sulky and dejected. We'd had a conversation on the way about a friend of mine who had recently come out of the closet. I had mentioned how proud I was of him, and that it made no difference to me as long as he was happy.
Klag spoke up and said, "I don't care if he's a homo. I just don't want him coming on to me. If he came on to me I'd lose all respect for him."
Stan was taking a sip of coffee. He wiped his mouth and cleared his throat and said, "It's okay Klag. If he made a move on you I'd lose all respect for him too."

The gig was odd and tense. We played in one end of the weight room for an audience of tattooed gym rats and their skinny boyfriends, most of whom were dressed like high school cheerleaders.

"See anyone you like out there?"
Klag glared at me and turned away.
Our sound guy came up during the interval to see if things were okay for us. He looked maybe 16 and was in prison after having killed his parents with a shot gun and then settling down and watching television

for a couple of days. A neighbour had dropped by and called the police after having noticed the smell from the bodies in the kitchen.

"Everything okay for you guys on stage?"
His eyes were as wide and innocent looking as a child's.
We all took a quick step back.

"Yup. Oh yeah. Perfect. Just great. Couldn't be better."

The tour wore on and to be fair, it was no picnic for him. He'd obviously had no idea of what he was getting into, and aside from having to live with not satisfying the insistent demands of Little Hitler, he also had to live with Stan and me in the difficult and tense atmosphere of the road.
We confused him. He walked in one night backstage where we were washing handfuls of mega- vitamins down with Bourbon straight from the bottle while we ironed our shirts for the night's show. "You guys." He shook his head. "You're both degenerates."

"Degenerates? I'm using spray starch for fucksake. We are the only band with our own ironing board. This..." I held up the steam iron. "This is not the act of a degenerate. This is fucking pathetic."
The end came for Klag as I had dinner with Anne and Mansel one night at their home. Stan was off visiting other friends, and Klag was seeing a relative who lived in town.
Over coffee they said, "We have something we need to say to you. You know we love you guys. Not just the music, but we love you personally. We've come to think of you as family, and you have to know you will always be welcome in our home."
Uh Oh. This was not sounding good.

"But we have decided that if you continue to work with Klag we cannot, in good conscience, represent you anymore. We love you and we wish you the best, but we have to move on if he stays with the band."
I was stunned.
I was speechless.
I was elated.
This was it. We couldn't possibly keep him on now. I called Gail that night and gave her the glad tidings.
I had a chat with Stan the next morning as we sat out on Anne and Mansel's back step drinking coffee, and he was thunderstruck.

"Well, that's that. He's out of here."
As I had talked to Anne and Mansel the night before they had told me just how widely the poor sap was disliked. He had managed to annoy and offend pretty much everyone we cared about and loved in Alberta. Getting rid of him was one thing. Making amends was another.

"Maybe we could have a public execution."

"I think that's against the rules."

"Stage a suicide?"

"Huh. I like that."

It was at that precise moment that a neighbour's Yellow Lab came trotting by with the hind leg of an elk it had found somewhere and dug up to bring home as a gift to its owners. Stan watched as the proud and happy creature went by and disappeared into the woods.

"Well, we can't bury him out here. That's for sure."

The last gig was in Lethbridge. Klag had yet to score and he was in the last stages of testosterone poisoning. He was drinking more, and spending increased time in the shower in the mornings. I made sure I got in there before him, or, failing that, wore my boat shoes.

We got to Lethbridge and picked up a suite of rooms at The Travelodge at the edge of town. We went over to the venue, the Germanic Hall, and did sound check.

The first set went fine, pretty much, and I was heading toward the restrooms at the end of the hall during the break. As I went along a woman walked very quickly past me with a set expression on her face. I could see Klag lurking by the washrooms looking furtive and vaguely guilty. Something was wrong.

We didn't find out what until later. According to the reporter who was there to review our show, Klag had made a drunken, and vulgar and to her, threatening move. I'm sure he meant no harm. It was almost certainly just some stupid and clumsily worded come on. But he was a big guy, and he had frightened and offended her. That was bad enough, but purely from a mercenary point of view, it was disastrous as she was the wife of the Mayor. Our career and our reputations were circling the plug hole.

I told Stan after the show and he was livid. He was ready to simply drop him at the side of the highway and let him fend for himself.

"We're ruined. I'm gonna drive a fucking stake through his heart. How the Hell are we going to live this down?"

"I dunno. But we should take him back to Ontario. We can fire him there."

To tell the truth I would have been happy to drop him off the railway bridge on the west side of town, but I wanted to have a couple of days to savour giving him the news.

We were sitting in the bar downstairs. Ordinarily we would have been drinking in our rooms, as it was cheaper, but we both needed some time away from Klag and Mr. Happy. Klag was taking yet another shower.

"He's very clean, isn't he?" I said, quoting from "A Hard Days' Night."

"Yeah, real clean, and I can't stand the thought of touching the soap after he's done with it."
I knew what he meant.
We finished our beers and went back to the room to find that Klag had drunk himself into a drooling stupour. He had found a soft core porn movie on the TV. "Emanuelle III" or something. The tender story of a young girl and her love for a rugby team. He was standing in front of the TV, his back to us, and having just showered was vigorously wrestling with something in his Jockey shorts.
Stan said, "I can't stand it," and went into his room and slammed the door.
No wonder Klag drank so much beer, I thought. He'd die from dehydration otherwise.
We drove home. Klag slept most of the way, from exhaustion and disappointment I think. Around Thunder Bay he once again picked up the little black book, and began leafing through it, this time in the "Ontario" section, presumably.
"There's this sick chick in Windsor I'm gonna see as soon as I get back. Did I ever tell you about the time when I...?"
Well, at least he was feeling better and looking towards the future. Somewhere north of Toronto, Klag woke from a nap, raised his leg and made a loud and prolonged sound like a New Year's rattle. Stan and I just rolled the windows down and pulled the necks of our T shirts over our faces. No point in chiding the poor lad at this stage.
"Oops. Sorry guys."
He looked around, sniffed appreciatively, rolled over and went back to sleep.
Maybe an hour later we pulled into the driveway of Klag's apartment. He stretched, farted, and sat up and said, "Hey Stan, can I borrow the van next weekend. I want to drive down to London."
Stan said, "Klag, just how awake are you?"
We pulled into a gas station parking lot and Stan gave him the news.
"Well, this is a surprise, " Klag said in a hurt tone.
Poor bastard. He still had no clue.
We drove him to his apartment and dropped him off.
Stan paid him for the last few weeks and we left him there on the sidewalk with his gear piled around him.
And so it was over.
To his immense credit, once Klag got the news about just why he was leaving he called Stan and carefully wrote down the names and addresses of all the people he had offended during the 2 weeks out west, and reportedly wrote very gracious and apologetic letters, saying he hoped his behaviour didn't reflect on us, and that Stan and I would

be able to continue to play within that world. His hand must have dropped off from writer's cramp by the time he was done, but it was a class act, and well done, Klag.

CHAPTER 69

The Gathering Of The Clans

John Allan Cameron called Stan and offered us a string of shows
through the Maritimes with him and some other folks beginning in June
of 1981. It was a warm up tour for The Gathering of the Clans to be held
in Edinburgh. He had always been a tireless and generous supporter
and wanted Stan and me in on what was to be a pretty lucrative
Government funded boondoggle. This, in spite of the fact that Stan and
I had nothing Scottish about us at all, unless one drew blood from my
arm. That alone was enough to qualify us I suppose.

Years later, when I finally put down the bottle, I got a letter from the
Glenlivet distillery, asking, "Was it something we said?" And Talisker
released a special run of 12 year old single malt with my picture on the
side label which read, "Have you seen this man?"

We were still without a bass player then, but once again Allie Bennett
agreed to sit in. That was fine. He was quiet and sober and absolutely
dependable. All the things I wasn't. Nice to have him aboard.

Gail and I, having wed the previous February, decided to take the week
following the tour as our delayed honeymoon. There was no budget for
me to go to Scotland, naturally, but I would have the use of the van after
Stan left. I would also have the use of Gail, so actually I came out the
winner.

We arrived in Cape Breton and commenced rehearsals with the rest
of the musicians. Someone decided that we must all dress the same
for the stage show. So we had to turn up for fittings, and in the end
we were all kitted out in matching dark blue jeans, 100% polyester
tattersall shirts with pearl snap buttons, black boots and belts, and black
leather vests, all topped off with a kicky little neck scarf with a gold
coloured ring to hold it on. We looked like the North Sydney production
of "Seven Brides For Seven Brothers."

I rebelled at the neckerchiefs.

"I'm not going to wear this on stage. Someone might be out there
with a camera. I could be blackmailed for life."

I also had a prolonged fight with the costume designer over the fit of my jeans. They were too loose and bunched up for my refined taste. "Tighter. I need them tighter." These looked like the jeans my mother made me wear when I was a teenager. Every year, two pairs of heavy blue "Husky Fit" denim jeans with the red plaid flannel lining from Sears would arrive by mail order.

"You'll grow into them." Mum said. Yeah right. I looked like a sack of shit tied in the middle.

Over the week that we were in rehearsal, the costume guy brought in ever tighter jeans and I kept rejecting them until he finally gave up and brought me what I wanted.

"Here," he said, throwing them at my head and flouncing out of the room. "As if anyone really cares to see what religion you are."

We kept on with rehearsals, and in the end the stage show followed much the same pattern as had John Allan's old TV show. Some high spirited fiddling, some high spirited step dancing, and a bit of carefully rehearsed high spirited banter between Stan and John Allan. Then, Stan and Allie and I would play a few songs, and then some more step dancing and fiddling. After the intermission there would be more of the same, and John Allan would have changed into full Highland drag, with the kilt and sporran, and we would finish the show with Stan and me playing "The Mary Ellen Carter," and John Allan step dancing like a maniac, after which we'd all sing "Rise and Follow Charlie." John Allan was one of the sweetest and dearest men I ever met, but the show was boring me to death. Of course, when we actually took it out on the road, it sold out everywhere we went, and left people begging for more. So much for my artistic and commercial sensibilities.

The show we did at the DeCoste Center in Pictou was notable for one thing. I learned many years later that it was the very first live music that the young Dave Gunning was to see, his mum having taken him along to the show that night. Inevitably, it ruined his life, and he too decided to become a musician. He's grown up well though, and has become a great singer and song writer himself, as well as an active and devoted campaigner for his community and a better environment.

The tour continued on to Truro and by now Diane had arrived to be with Stan for the last few shows before he flew off to Scotland. Gail was due to fly down the day after it ended.

We were having lunch in some inevitably Scottish themed restaurant called "The Tartan, "and as Stan was getting into the van after our meal, he was seized with a terrible crushing pain in his chest and back and arm.

Oh shit, I thought. This is the Big One. And he's had it coming.

He'd always been heavy, right from early childhood, and a pack a day

or more smoker from the time he was 16. He had taken a fitness test
a few years before and was told that at age 29 he had the body of a 50
year old man. It had scared him, as well it should. I've had the body
of a 50 year old man myself, some 10 years ago, and it is no picnic. He
had cut back on the smokes, and booze and bacon fat and began going
to the YMCA. He resolved that within 6 months he was going to lose 30
pounds and be able to bench press his own weight. And he had done it.
But after he hit his target, he had fallen back on his old evil ways. And
there was no point in nagging him.

He was now sitting at the wheel, sweating and gasping and rubbing his
chest, and smoking, yes, smoking a cigarette, the great big idiot.

"I'm sure it's nothing. Just indigestion."

Right.

Diane wasn't having any. She got him to a doctor, and it turned out to
be a back spasm, and a shot of muscle relaxant and a couple of whiskies
and he was right as rain. Lucky for him. Less lucky for those of us who
loved him and wanted him to clean up his act and had planned to use
this incident as an excuse to heap coals on his head.

The tour finished in Halifax, at the Rebecca Cohn, and during the day I
had gone into an antique store on Barrington Street, and bought him a
lovely engraved silver pocket flask for the flight over to Scotland. I filled
it with single malt and handed it to him the next night as the airport
shuttle was leaving from the Lord Nelson. Diane was standing in the
rain outside the van, wiping her eyes, and as I ducked my head in the
door I could see Stan was crying too. Ah shit.

"Here." I said, handing him the whisky. "Coals to Newcastle. Travel
safe. Send me a card."

We gave each other an awkward hug, and then I slammed the door and
we waved them off.

I found the post card he had sent a few weeks later when I got back
home. It had a picture of some highland cattle on the front. On the back
he had written, "The one on the right looks just like the girl we had to
chase out of Dave McIsaac's room this morning. The shows are a mess.
Seeing Archie tonight. Love S."

After Stan died, I would discover some new recording or singer and of
course feel deep regret that he had never got the chance to hear them.
I felt exactly that when I first heard Nic Jones' extraordinary album,
"Penguin Eggs." And a few months later I found Dick Gaughan's
"Handful of Earth." In the midst of my joy and wonder in hearing that
music I was saddened that these were just two more artists Stan would
never hear or meet. A few years ago, though, I was talking with Archie
Fisher during a long drive on one of our tours, and he told me about
taking Stan and John Allan to a small folk club on the Borders where

Archie was living, and they heard Nic Jones play. In the course of the evening they were joined by Dick Gaughan and the night proceeded to unravel. I was glad to hear it. I'm sorry I missed it but I'm grateful it happened.

Stan said the tour was a disaster. The venues in Scotland weren't equipped for even the modest technical needs of the show. They had found themselves having to run around Edinburgh and scrounge bits of sound system and other gear, and the stages were too small for step-dancing. It was a mess, and in any sane person's eyes, a waste of taxpayer dollars. And in any case, who needed a Cape Bretoner and a Canadian doing a tribute to Scottish music in the middle of Edinburgh? But Stan got to spend some time with Archie on Archie's home turf, and he loved it.

Back home, I had picked Gail up at the airport the day after Stan left, and we drove up to Halfway Cove for our honeymoon. It was June, and Gail had brought the appropriate June honeymoon/ holiday by the sea wardrobe. She had a swim suit, and some shorts and light cotton shirts, a pair of sandals, and not much else. She didn't reckon on June in Nova Scotia. I might have warned her. I had once been caught in a mid-June blizzard while hitch-hiking at the summit of Mount Thom near New Glasgow. We arrived at Halfway Cove, and she got her first look at what our family had always thought of as paradise. A tiny damp falling -down shack, with no running water, no plumbing, and no heat except for the clanky old wood stove in the corner of the kitchen next to the door to the main bedroom. It began to rain, the roof began to leak, and it didn't stop for the entire ten days we were there. The day after she arrived we drove into Canso so she could meet my Grandmother, and to borrow some long pants and a few flannel shirts, and a couple of sweaters and a down vest and a red plaid hunting jacket with its matching Elmer Fudd hat, and some thick wool socks, and a pair of heavy lace up rubber boots with the crampons still attached. She put on the lot, and I realised that I was going to have my work cut out for me later that night when we got back to the little shack.

"Try to see it as a challenge." Gail said, as she zipped the down vest up to her chin.

My Grandmother was living with her younger sister, Elsie Hart, in one of the old Commercial Cable Company houses in Hazel Hill, just across the road from the Cable building itself, and a few hundred feet from where she had lived before the war with our grandfather.

I took my little flower in to meet them, and after getting everyone introduced and settled, I went into the kitchen to make some tea. Gail told me later that there was a long and awkward silence while I was in the next room rattling the kettle, dropping spoons and looking for cups and plates. She has a very soft speaking voice, and was having trouble making herself heard as both Grandma and Elsie were quite deaf. After a bit she gave up and just sat there smiling sweetly at them as they fumbled with their knitting.

Where the hell was I with that damned tea?

And then my grandmother looked carefully around, leaned forward, and tapped Gail on the knee and in a loud whisper confided, "I had a good BM this morning."

There was another government sponsored overseas junket which Stan did without me as well.

The CBC and the BBC got together, and it was decided that it might be a good thing to travel over to Britain with Kate and Anna McGarrigle, and have them and Stan record with the BBC Orchestra, on one of the Channel Islands. I couldn't make sense of it. Even given that two government funded public broadcasters were organizing it, this was waste and mismanagement on a truly heroic scale. Surely it would have been cheaper to not transport 30 or 40 musicians and support staff to an island, and put them up, and pay them to rehearse with juicy per diems, and instead do it on in London. Apparently not. In any case, the budget with which they could have restaged the Normandy landings didn't have enough to bring me along, so I only heard how badly it all went second hand from Stan.

They set up and began to rehearse, and according to Stan that mostly meant sitting around and waiting for Kate and Anna to arrive. They were both wonderful singers and writers, and their albums made us swoon, and Kate is much missed, but they were not even remotely organized as professional musicians.

Stan told me he spent most of his time in a small hotel room in Guernsey, eating sardines with cheese and crackers and listening to BBC 2 and trying to track down whoever might have information about his royalties from Mary O'Hara's Number One recording of "45 Years."

In the end he had to actually turn up at the offices of her manager, Jo Lustig, and make threatening noises but it was all for naught. I don't think he ever saw a penny out of it.

The BBC recording was a complete frost as well. I heard a bit of it years later, and it was uncanny to hear some Welsh operatic tenor singing my part from "Northwest Passage" as the BBC orchestra sawed away behind them. But there was nothing they could use of the McGarrigles, and without them it was decided to not broadcast the recordings.

CHAPTER 70

Jim Morison

Stan called me on the phone one morning.

"Hey, how's it going?"

"Good. Fine." He cleared his throat. "You got anything going on today?"

"No, what's up?"

"Can you come out to Dundas today, and bring your stuff?"

"Yeah, I guess. What's going on? Do you have something new you want to run over?"

There was a pause, and I could hear him take a breath.

"Well, I hired a new bass player."

What?

I looked at the phone receiver. I couldn't believe he was doing this to me again, after the whole Klag debacle.

"You did what? For fuck sake, I thought we had an agreement. You weren't going to take on anyone without me being in on the decision. Jesus Christ."

I was furious.

"So what kind of half-witted farting numbskull are you trying to foist on me this time?"

Stan said, "Calm down. You've actually met him. He seems like a good guy, he knows the material already, and besides, I told him we were just going to let him try out. Nothing's firm yet."

"So who is he?"

"Jim Morison."

"Who?"

"Jim Morison."

"Not THE Jim Morrison, obviously."

"No, Morison with only one "r.""

"Never heard of him."

It turned out I had in fact met the guy a few years before, one afternoon during the disaster in Jasper. I had been napping in my hotel room when I heard voices next door. I wandered over to investigate, and it was there I first met Bill Bourne and this new Jim Morison guy, although I couldn't put a face to his name.

"So what are we doing?"

"I thought we would rehearse him and have him do the Ottawa gig with us next week and see how he shapes up."

"If he shapes up."

"Yeah, if he shapes up. But he says he already knows all the songs. He's heard us before and it shouldn't take long to whip him into shape."

Right.

I gathered my gear and went over to Stan and Diane's little condo in Dundas.

I was steaming mad. He had committed us to at least spending a week or so rehearsing this clown, and trotting him out in front of our audience to see if he could fit into the act, and once again, he had made the move without consulting me or giving me the slightest heads up.

I arrived and loaded my stuff into the house.

"So where is he?"

"He's downstairs getting dressed."

I looked at my watch. Holy shit. It was well past noon.

Stan said, "He was out late last night visiting family in town. He'll be up soon."

I got a coffee and presently I heard slow and heavy steps coming up the stairs from the basement accompanied by laboured breathing and a deep hacking cough.

I got a brief glimpse of our newest band member as he stumbled into the little bathroom at the top of the stairs.

Christ, he was huge.

Maybe 6 foot 6, and big with it.

His face was obscured by a mess of unruly blond curls, and as he stumbled into the bog he gave a feeble and uncertain wave to the room. Just that brief glimpse of him looked like an outtake from some grainy backwoods film of Big Foot fleeing into the forests of the Pacific Northwest.

The door closed, and there commenced a prolonged urination, the duration and volume of which I now associate with micturating brood mares, interspersed with staccato post stern blasts. It went on for a while, and then there was a period of more coughing and hacking and nose blowing and finally prolonged violent retching.

I heard the toilet flush.

"Well, isn't he just lovely? Did he make it here under his own steam last night, or did they carry him in on a shutter?"

Stan said, "Yeah, he's a little under the weather."

"He's a mess. Great first impression."

Jim came out after a while, and he wasn't pretty. Sallow blotchy complexion, bags under his eyes, and a bad case of morning after sweats and trembles.

There were some awkward introductions, and Jim collapsed into a chair and put his head in his hands.

Stan had made him a coffee, and before Jim could even get a sip of it, I cruelly said, "Okay, I have other things to do today. Let's get going on this rehearsal."

He was game. I had to give him that.

He immediately got up and got out his bass and amp and plugged in, but not without a lot of deep sighing and heavy breathing. He could barely open his eyes.

We tuned up and began running a song.

It was a complete train wreck.

Aside from his sad and degraded condition, the fact of the matter was he had obviously never heard any of the songs before, regardless of what he might have claimed. We pressed on for an hour or so, during which time Jim had to go back into the bathroom to heave some more. He was painfully hungover. He had yet to say more than a dozen words, and his motor skills were impaired to the point where his whole being was focused on just breathing and trying not to blow lunch out his nose. He had no brain cells to spare for other work.

After a couple of very bad hours, I'd had enough.

I packed up my stuff and said, "I'm off for home. I'll call you later."

And I left without waiting for Jim to return from the bathroom where he had gone for another spew.

Stan called later that night.

"Look, I know today didn't go so great."

"No shit."

"But give the guy a chance. He was visiting his brother last night and overindulged a bit. He's had some coffee and supper now, and he's going to be fine."

"So I have to come out and put up with this crap again tomorrow?"

"Just give him a chance. It's not like you've never been hung over."

"I don't get hangovers."

It's hard to get a hangover if you stay drunk.

"But he lied. He said he knew the songs. He hasn't a clue."

Stan cleared his throat. "Well, that might have been my fault. What he actually said was that he had seen us play at a festival and liked what we did. He never said he knew the tunes. That was me, I guess."

Great.

"He's serious though. He came all the way out here from Alberta just to audition for us."

Wonderful. So he was desperate too.

So next day I went back out and we picked up where we had left off, and this time it went much more smoothly. Jim had recovered from his alcohol poisoning. He had stopped sweating and shaking, and was now able to speak in complete sentences. And it turned out he really could play. He was now learning the songs quickly, and was adding great parts. He had good equipment, a nicely worn old Fender bass, and he was pulling great tone from it.

Unlike most bass players he didn't keep his right hand near the bridge. Jim plucked the strings well up the body near the neck of the guitar, and he was using a strange brand of strings made from copper. It was a lovely and warm and melodic sound, and it fit beautifully with Stan's guitar. He could also sing really well. He picked up the harmonies after just a few passes. And I was to find out later that once he learned a part, it was in the bank forever. He never missed a note, no matter how tired, or drunk or strung out he might have been.

He turned to be a funny and sweet natured guy too, a large island of calm in the midst of all the yelling and swearing and drama that Stan and I lived out on a hourly basis.

Jimmy had spent a decade or so on the road, playing with various bands in a string of terrifying rural bars in BC and Alberta. Some of his war stories made our own histories sound like a Jane Austen novel.

He talked about one incident where he was awakened in the wee small hours by a Keystone Kops style chase going through his third floor hotel room. He and his partner had been playing a week long gig at a typical rural Alberta cowboy bar, in a little fly blown shithole town where they counted the tumbleweeds as part of the population. Three sets a night for the drunken shit kickers yelling requests for "Rocky Top," or "Fox on the Run." There were a handful of semi pro hookers working the place. The management put up with it as long as they were more or less discreet and stuck to giving furtive ten dollar hand jobs and hummers to the cowboys and rig pigs out in the parking lot. No jerking off the customers under the table. We're trying to run a classy joint here.

Anyway, as Jim told the story, or as I remember the telling, he was wakened around 4 one morning by his door being kicked open and some young cowboy being pursued by one of the scrubbers who was waving a knife. She in turn was being chased by the manager, and bringing up the rear of the parade were a couple of young Mounties who had obviously graduated so low in their class as to be sent to this distant rural pig wallow to tighten up their act. The whole bunch of them leapt over Jim's bed like a pack of fox hounds in full pursuit, and disappeared out the open window to clatter down the iron fire escape. Jim was just getting back to sleep when the terrified cowpoke burst back into the room, this time through the window, followed once again by the girl, the manager, and the rozzers. They crashed through the now broken door and disappeared down the hall.

He had another story about driving south on the Glacier Parkway from Jasper during an ice storm, towing a large and heavy trailer full of amps and guitars and a full sound system. The tires on his station wagon had seen better days, and the electrical connection between the car and the trailer's braking system was tenuous at best. Jim looked out the driver's side mirror at one point, and saw the trailer slowly passing the car, sliding sideways on the glare ice. It had become unhooked from the ball hitch and was now only held on by the safety chains. He had no choice but to speed up and try to get ahead of it, but it was a long incline, maybe a couple of miles, and there was a sharp turn at the bottom with a guard rail. Beyond the guard rail was a drop of about a thousand feet. If he couldn't get the rig stopped in time he was likely to blast through the guard rail and hurtle out into the void, startling some innocent grizzly out for a bite of salmon in the river half a mile below. Speeding up and racing a couple of tons of loose pig iron on wheels seemed counter intuitive. The car and the trailer did a series of slow and graceful 360 degree turns as they slid down the hill, and eventually Jim was able to ever so carefully bring the whole mess over to the right and get on the gravel verge, where there was a little more traction. He was able to continue the trip that way and managed to make the next gig. He said, "If I ever write my memoirs I'm gonna call it, "Highlights of the Lowlife."

We took him up to Ottawa for the regular week long gig we had there with the two Lebanese drug lords. They had a band house for us, and we were able to rehearse more material during the days while waiting for show time.

Jimmy was still on probation.

Just on general principles I was disinclined to trust anyone Stan brought into our midst.

Between the managers and agents he had unilaterally decided to give all our money to over the years, and the great farting wasteland that was "Klag," his track record was abysmal.

Jim was playing well, though, and had shown an unexpected gift for the odd well-timed joke during the show.

And if nothing else he filled out the other side of the stage pretty well.

He was a big guy, and his presence balanced things better visually.

Stan was now in fact the shortest person in the band. We were halfway through the week run, and Stan and I were on stage tuning up for the last set of the night while Jim was sitting at a table visiting with some old friends from out of town.

Jim had brought along a very rare and expensive item. It was a Korg digital tuner. We had never seen one before. They cost a ton. Maybe 300 bucks, and I was grudgingly impressed with the level of commitment it showed.

Up to now, Stan tuned to my flute, or relied on whatever battle scarred old piano that might be on the stage. He also kept a tuning fork in his case but in places like this you couldn't hear it.

Stan was plugging his 12 string into the Korg and watching the LED read out in wonder. What a great machine. He loved the 12 string, but as he said, "For every year you own one, you spend 6 months tuning the damned thing."

He leaned over to speak to me.

"I like this guy. He's serious. I mean, look at this tuner. He's a lifer. He seems like a steady guy. If you're okay with it, I'd like to give him the job."

Okay. Fine by me. We could always fire his ass later.

"When do you want to tell him?"

Stan said, "Let's wait until we get back to the band house. It'll be nice to give him the good news in front of his friends."

So we went back after the show, and as Jim was opening beers for his friends, Stan stood up, cleared his throat, and said, "Uh, look Jim. We need to talk. We know you've been working really hard this past week, and we want you to know we really appreciate all the effort."

Jim went very still and then hung his head. He knew what was coming. This sounded like the preamble to being let go.

"Anyway, Garnet and I have been talking it over and..."

Jim interrupted at this point, and still looking down at the floor, waved his hand and said, "Yeah, yeah, I know. It's okay. I appreciate you guys giving me a shot."

Stan continued. "So we just feel, if you...you know... want the gig, it's yours."

Jim's head snapped up.

"What?"

I spoke. "Welcome to hell, you poor bastard."

Jim's friends applauded and Jim began a clumsy circus bear dance around the room. He smacked his head into the ceiling fan, over balanced, tripped over the coffee table, broke it, and then fell into the couch. It pitched over backwards, hitting a floor lamp, and plunged the room into darkness.

As Stan was searching for the wall switch we heard Jim's voice.

"Thanks guys."
It was a nice moment, and the start of a sweet and fruitful relationship.

CHAPTER 71

Jim Fleming

It was Jim Post who introduced us to Jim Fleming back in 1980.
We had been on the road in Alberta for the better part of a month with
Post, among others, as part of a pointless debauch on wheels called
"The Travelling Drunken Rabble Goodtime Let's See Just How Much
Taxpayer Money We Can Waste Folk Festival," or something.
It was the centennial of Alberta's joining Canada. There was a lot of
public money being thrown around as part of the celebration, and Mitch
Podolak, bless him, managed to get some thrown our way.
The premise was simple enough. Jam about forty or so full grown folk
musicians with all their luggage and gear, onto a cramped and un-air-
conditioned school bus built for 30 tiny preschoolers, and send them
off into the bleak dusty plains of Alberta to play a different windblown
rural crossroads town every night, and see if how many of them die of
boredom or cirrhosis of the liver.
The tour started in Edson, Alberta, and ended in up a few weeks later
in Edmonton. In between, we crisscrossed the province and hit every
fly speck on the map. There was nothing for us to do during the day
except sit and stare out at the dun coloured plains and wonder what
the next town's liquor store might have if it was open. There had been
rotating liquor strikes that summer and supplies were low, and choices
were dwindling. At times I had been reduced to drinking off-brand
rye whisky which tasted like chemotherapy, and a couple of even more
desperate souls had even been seen furtively and shamefully clutching
bottles of Advocaat and cherry brandy.
The morning after that first show in Edson, there was some sort of cock
up with luggage and when we arrived at the next town Stan's suitcase
was missing. For reasons which were never clear to me, he decided that
Jim Post was responsible. I was throwing my own gear into the room I
was sharing with David Eadie, and I could hear a lot of shouting from
Stan, and I went to investigate. It was a rare treat to not be the object of
Stan's wrath, and I wanted to observe from a safe distance. Jim Post
was watching Stan and listening attentively, saying nothing. Stan was

in a frenzy. He was stomping around in front of the motel, swearing and waving his arms, kicking dried clods of mud across the gravel, and overturning small cars. When he finally wound down and paused for breath, Post said quietly, "I know you're mad now, and you don't like me, but I promise you, I'll fix this, and by the time this is all over, you're gonna love me."
Huh?
Stan stopped in his tracks. It was such a strange and confusing response. He clenched his fists a few times and his mouth worked a bit, but in the end he spun on his heel and simply stomped away. Post turned to me and said, "So I borrowed the sound crew's van, you want to go for a ride?" We drove back to Edson and collected Stan's suitcase, and over the weeks following, Stan and Post became good friends. They were an odd pair. Stan was a new dad, and now pretty conservative in his lifestyle. He saw this tour simply as exposure, and a chance to get some money in the bank, without having to worry personally about the day to day logistics of getting the trio from town to town. But after a few days he was bored to death, chain smoking and sitting with his knees under his chin in a clanking and fetid death trap of a bus all day, listening to the guys in Sylvia Tyson's band bicker as they conducted their 24 hour poker game. He missed home, he missed his family, and oddly, he found he missed having to sort out the logistics of getting the band around. There was just nothing to do. After a few days all three of us were nearly brain dead, and just wanted to get this job over with. Post on the other hand, even as he approached middle age was still checking out the sideshows on the cosmic midway. He'd had a varied and interesting life so far. He'd had a hit song back in the 60's called "Reach out in the Darkness," as part of a duo called "Friend and Lover," and he'd been a child preacher back in Texas, "Little Jimmy David," doing faith healing and working the audience into a seething frenzy until they fell down and spoke in tongues. He told me, "It wasn't until I grew up and got to be with a woman that I realised all those ladies whose hands I was holding while they were passing out were having orgasms."
Of all the people I knew back then, he was the only one who had not left more serious drugs behind. He still was using mescaline and mushrooms, and it was a struggle sometimes to get him down from trees or to keep his clothes on. The bus stopped one afternoon at the badlands near Drumheller, and a couple of busloads of Japanese tourists with their inevitable cameras were treated to the sight of Post leaping from crag to crag, bollocks naked, with his pecker flapping in the sun. During the tour, Post told us about his agent, a guy named Jim Fleming, who worked out of Ann Arbor, Michigan. According to Post, Jim

Fleming was hard working and kind. He was good humoured and responsible. Above all, he was inexpensive and honest. Yeah, right. First of all, as much as we liked him, we were disinclined to take anything that Post said at face value. And secondly, Fleming was an agent. Enough said. But we agreed to meet with him anyway after the tour was over, and see just what sort of lizard he might be. Being in Ann Arbor, at least, he was within driving distance and we could kill him quickly and get back across the border if we signed with him and things went as they usually did.

My memory is that we first met Jim Fleming at his little office in Ann Arbor, just around the corner from the State Street Theatre. My, he was a handsome devil. Dark haired, medium height, neatly dressed, with a moustache, and warm eyes, and an easy sleepy smile. He still had a hint of southern accent from his Kentucky boyhood, and he was quiet and funny, and he had the effortless good manners that only generations of breeding and exceptional innate kindness will bestow. I mistrusted him on sight.

We talked back and forth for a bit, and then Stan and I went out for a coffee, and to discuss it.

It was rare for me to be in on any decisions and I wanted to make the most of it.

Stan said, "Well, what do you think?"

"He's a fucking disaster."

"What?"

"Do you know how many women are in this town? Look at him. This guy is a fucking dream boat. He's wearing pussy like a hat. He's not gonna have any time for us."

"Jesus, calm down. He seems like a good guy, and this time we're not going to be handing him the keys to the kingdom the way we did with Ronald."

"We? What means we, white man? It was you that made that deal with Ronald. 25 fucking per cent and all expenses. Jesus."

"Alright, I know. I want to give him a shot though. Post says he's a good guy."

Right. So now we were taking career advice from a guy who started each day by chewing through the restraining straps.

We went back and talked some more with Jim, and he outlined some plans for what he saw as our future. One of the interesting things, from my point of view, was that he wasn't a fan of us in particular, or of folk music in general.

"I mostly listen to jazz. Big Band stuff. Folk music doesn't really do it for me."

"What the hell do you want with us then?"

602

"You guys are good. You work hard. I'm a good salesman. I think I can sell you."

Huh.

Well there was honesty for a start.

We talked some more and Stan began to lay down some laws.

"You get 10 per cent of the gross. "

"No. I need 15."

"12."

"No. Look, this is not a negotiation. I simply need 15 and I'll pay my own expenses."

Well okay then.

Stan moved in closer to Jim, to intimidate him no doubt. He poked the table with his finger.

"And the most important thing of all that you have to understand, is that we don't work for you. You work for us."

Jim shook his head. "No."

Stan sat back.

"What?"

"No, I don't work for you. We work together. It's a partnership. If you don't understand that we can't do business."

This was new.

I don't recall anything being signed. We shook hands, and Stan and I drove back home.

Within a couple of days, Jim booked us a string of shows in the Midwest which filled the giant and disastrous hole we had in our upcoming schedule in the next year. The only folk club show we played on that tour was the Blue Whale coffeehouse in Green Bay, Wisconsin. The rest of the gigs were at small community colleges, where every night we played to a handful of bored students and curious strangers, in nice soft seat theatres, and getting paid lovely, lovely Arts Council money. That first tour was a bear. We were getting up around 6 every morning, and two of us would load the van while the third would grab 6 large take out coffees with extra powdered creamer and sugar, along with 6 toasted fried egg sandwiches, and then we'd take off. I don't think we saw a main highway during the whole trip. Just awful narrow secondary roads, with slow moving farm equipment whose drivers were prone to come up to the stop sign on your right, look carefully both ways, and then pull slowly out in front of you at the very last moment. You'd frantically wrench the wheel to the left and the van would tip up on two wheels as you hurtled around 20 tonnes of combine. You'd get the van settled back down and keep on without a pause, gripping the wheel, and hoping your heart would someday slow down. And as early as we left each day, we would just barely make the venues in time for the gig.

We got to Mankato Minnesota one night, with about 30 minutes to spare before show time. The van roared into the parking lot of the little Christian college we were playing, and Stan put it into his patented controlled drift and slid up to within 6 feet of the stage door, scattering gravel against the side of the building. We loaded into the hall at a run, and did a quick mic check and then went back to the van to change.

Jim cracked open some beers, handed them around, and we clinked the cans in a toast. "Made the gig." he said. At that moment a soft looking young man in Khakis and a shirt with an alligator on the pocket came around the corner of the van and said, "I'll have to confiscate those beers."

"Huh?"

"This is a Christian campus. There is no alcohol allowed. Please hand over those beers."

"Who the fuck are you, Sonny, the hall monitor?" said Stan.

"I'm with student security and I'm here to enforce the rules."

Stan said, "Shouldn't you be banging out the blackboard erasers for Teacher?"

"I bet that's all he's gonna be banging."

The kid ignored me and continued. "There is a strict no drinking policy on this campus."

I said, "That's fine, but we have a strict no sobriety policy in the van."

Stan drained the last of his beer and crushed the can in his fist. He stood up on his toes and threw it into the garbage bin by the stage door.

"Look at that. A three pointer."

We had maybe 7 minutes before we were due on stage. Stan took out his tweed jacket and shouldered into it.

The kid stomped off.

I cupped my hands around my mouth. "Hey Junior...5 bucks to see your boobs."

The kid flinched and walked a bit faster. It was a cruel thing to say, but he did have a pretty impressive set of man breasts. God knows how he made it out of the shower.

Jim said, "He's probably going for back up. We better hide the beer."

So we hid the beer. By which I mean we drank the entire case, and threw the empties into the dumpster. We were standing outside the stage door a couple of minutes later with our instruments, when Junior came marching up with a couple of pudgy uniformed campus rent-a-cops.

One of them waded in and put his hand on the butt of his nightstick, and said, "We have a report of beer on these premises."

Stan took the cigarette out of his mouth and leaned into the cop's face.

He belched out a noxious cloud of smoke and semi digested bratwurst with an overlay of Wisconsin string cheese and beer fumes, and said, "Beer? What beer? There's no beer around here officer."
The cop reeled back and turned away coughing, and we then went into the hall to play to the handful of people who had wandered in. The first part of the first set was fine. But at the half hour mark the beer took hold and the rest of the evening was a bit wobbly.
The rest of the tour was much the same.
Long days behind the wheel, with a pointless and surreal gig in front of people who had never heard of us, followed by a race to the hotel to fall into a coma. But we did make the shows, and most importantly, Jim Fleming had made us some money during that run, and for once we were coming back feeling if not flush, then at least not completely broke.
Jim recalled how the three of us, Stan, Jim Morison, and I walked into his office, and in his words said, "I thought there had been an eclipse. The whole office just went black." We looked terrible, and he thought we were coming in to beat him to death. Stan merely dropped the envelope of cash on Jim's desk and said, "Nice job."
About a month later we were driving through Detroit on a cold dark night, and saw Jim as he got out of his car on the way to some concert downtown at Cobo Hall. He was by himself, and we hatched a plan. We had a large envelope of cash to give him, commission money for another string of well-paying shows we had just finished.
Stan said, "I'm going to pull up right next to him. You guys jump out and grab him and throw him into the van. We'll kidnap him."
The next thing Fleming knew was a clapped out and salt stained blue van pulled up, and two clapped out and salt stained men in parkas jumped out. A hand was put over his mouth, and he was bundled into the back. The door was slammed shut.
Credit to Jim. He didn't scream and cry or beg for mercy, or pee his pants, the way I would have. He was, after all, a trained negotiator. There had to be some way of talking himself out of this situation. He just lay there quietly as Stan pulled over about a block later, and parked and turned on the overhead light. Jim realised it was us, and not a mob of outraged husbands come to teach him a lesson. Stan handed Jim a wad of cash, and we opened the door and shoved him back out into the windy night.
"Thanks Jim. Goodnight."
And we drove off.

As good a job as he was doing for us, I was still reluctant to trust him, even after a few months. The change came when he accompanied us to an Arts Council showcase in Sackville, New Brunswick. The four of us flew out from Toronto on the Thursday to play showcases all weekend, and to dry hump the legs of anyone who looked as if they might have public money to waste on a trio of degenerates.

It was a terrible flight. There was a bunch of loud and aggressively drunk assholes in the back of the plane. They were making the flight attendants' lives hellish, yelling for more drinks,   playing grab-arse as they went by, and refusing to sit down when the seatbelt light came on as we flew into a series of thunderstorms. They were all singing some smutty song as the plane lurched to the right and the flight attendant fell across me and Stan.

Stan said, "We can take care of those assholes for you, Miss. Just say the word."

She apologized and pushed herself back onto her feet.

She brushed her hair from her face and looked back at the mob.

"No, we can handle them. It's the Flying Fathers Hockey team. They always get a bit frisky on a road trip."

The what? The Flying Fathers?

"Those guys? They're priests aren't they?" I said to Stan.

"Assholes." Stan shook his head. "I'd like to go back and sort them out."

"Yeah, but they're priests. You can't deck a priest."

"I don't care. I'm Anglican. I got no problem hitting a Catholic."

The flight continued. I could see lightning flashes in the clouds far below us, and the massive up drafts from the storm were tossing us about like a cork. The men of the cloth kept up a continuous din of yelling and singing and off colour remarks in the back. I think perhaps the flight crew kept serving them in hopes they might simply pass out, but no luck.

We had to make three attempts to land due to the bad weather. If the third didn't work we were going to have to divert to Newfoundland. On the third try we emerged from the dense cloud into a cold horizontal pissing rain, came down too hard and too fast, and skidded past the terminal before coming to a halt a quarter mile down the runway at Moncton airport.

There was no ramp directly into the terminal. The flight attendant opened the door into a wind driven deluge, and we carefully made our way down the steps and ran into the terminal, soaked to the skin. In the terminal we pushed past the drunken rabble of priests who were now riding the baggage carousel, grabbed our gear and caught a cab to Sackville.

The cab driver was about 120 years old, and was wearing a uniform and a chauffeur's cap. He drove an ancient Lincoln limousine, and he refused to let us help with loading the bags into the trunk. "You have to do it just so, " he said, "or the load shifts and you can have an accident." He'd probably learned his lesson after his last job with Amelia Earhardt. He didn't want to make that mistake again. Half an hour later we got underway, and the cab pulled out onto the foggy highway and accelerated, if that is the correct word, to about 30 miles per hour. 30 was definitely the outer edge of the envelope. He backed it down to 20 or so whenever we came to a curve in the road, or had a hill to climb. It had been a long and tiring day.

We all wanted several drinks and our beds. Jim Fleming spoke up from the back of the car.

"Is there any chance you can go faster?"
The driver's response was to lift his foot off the gas pedal and back it down to 20.
We were now a menace to navigation.
Stan spoke up.
"This is dangerous. Someone is going to drive right up our asses in this fog."
Now we were down to 15.
Jesus.
Stan kept peering over his shoulder in the back seat, keeping a watch out for any 18 wheeler that might come hurtling out of the night and turn us into an oily smear on the road.
Half an hour went by.
Jim Fleming leaned forward with a wad of cash in his hand. "I'll give you a hundred dollars to take this thing up to the speed limit." No answer. The driver hunched his shoulders and peered through the cracked and smeary glass.
It took us about 2 hours to make what should have been a half hour drive.
When we got to the tiny motel on the east side of Sackville, Fleming was horrified to find he was rooming with me.

"I don't share rooms. Never."
"Well, sir, we are full up. Everyone is in town for the conference this weekend. It's all we've got."
"Is there anything in that town we flew into? Moncton?" He walked over to the door and looked out into the parking lot. "Is that cab driver still around?"
Jesus, what was the problem here?
"It's okay, Jim, I know it's your first time. I'll be gentle with you."
The lady behind the counter smiled to herself, and gave him the key and we walked over to our little love nest.
"Shall I carry you across the threshold?"

"Oh shut up. I just don't like sharing rooms, that's all. I'll need some privacy in the morning."

"What?"

"I'll need you to leave the motel room tomorrow when I use the bathroom."

Okay Princess, whatever. I wondered what he'd been eating.

We got into the room, chose our beds, and settled in for the night.

I opened a bottle of bad red wine and offered him a swig.

"No thanks."

Fair enough. I turned on the TV.

There was only one channel still broadcasting at that hour and it was some panel discussion in French on economics. I think so anyway. It might have been a discussion on how to artificially inseminate a goat. There were a lot of hand gestures.

Jim turned it off and lay back on his narrow single bed.

"God, I hate this."

I was propped up in the dark, nursing the wine.

"Hate what?"

"Sharing a room. I've never shared a room before."

"If you want I can take a walk while you inflate your Japanese love doll."

"Fuck off."

Next morning I sat on a chair on the sidewalk outside the room, and played guitar and sang some songs while Jim performed an ornate and lengthy toilette. I wondered if he had a truss or some other secret appliance that required privacy to put on and adjust.

Stan came out of the room he'd been sharing with Jimmy and saw me.

"How's it going over there?"

"I dunno. He's still in the bathroom."

I raised my voice.

"I think I might have been a little rough on him last night. He was walking a bit sore when he got out of bed."

An old man who was just finishing packing his car stood and glared at me. Then he got in and started the car and burned rubber as he drove out of the parking lot.

Damned Sodomites.

After about an hour and a half, Fleming came outside. He was a vision of loveliness. He smelled divine. He looked like a shining and well-oiled Midwestern god.

I stood up and threw my arms wide.

"But you're beautiful darling...Come, give me a kiss. Let me take you away from all this."

He put his head down and started walking towards town. "Shut up. I need some breakfast."

"Okay."

I followed along. He was moving at a pretty fast clip towards town. This was good. I was starving and we might still be able to catch breakfast at the Marshlands Inn, a lovely B and B where Gail and I had spent a night during our honeymoon.

"Did that French whore put up much of a fight when you took her perfume away?"

He shook his head and walked faster.

We did a couple of showcase concerts that day, and then Jim Morison and Stan and I pressed the flesh for a couple of hours. I got tired of it after a while, and left and walked back to downtown Sackville. There was an antique store in what had been a bank building at the corner of the two major streets. I went in and began to look around. After a few minutes, I could smell the rich and now familiar scent of pomade from the mysterious and exotic East, and I realised that our so-called agent was not back at the conference furthering our careers, but rather wandering around this store picking up old books and examining odd bits of pottery. The bastard. This is not what we were paying him for. I'll kill him. I'll do worse than that. I'll tell Stan, and Stan will kill him. A minute or two later I lost track of him. Where the hell was he now? And then he was at my side. I was just about to make some cutting remark, when he leaned in and spoke very softly, "I'm wondering, shouldn't you and I be holding hands or something?"

I don't want to embarrass Jim more than I have already, but since that day he has become one of my dearest, most precious friends. It was Jim Fleming who changed our fortunes, and showed us that all the work, the stupid drives and sleeping on floors, and bad food, and the humiliating gigs for no pay, and everything else we had endured for so many years was in fact, going to pay off. The last couple of years of Stan's life we both knew that we'd made it. We were getting offered more work than we could possibly accept. We were actually having to juggle our schedules and turn down paying gigs, simply because we were too busy, and we were now booked far into the future.

Stan and I talked about it many times, and we were now both hopeful and confident about what was to come. We trusted Jim, and grew to love him. Stan took to using Jim's house in Ann Arbor as a refuge where he could think and relax and repair his nerves after a road trip, away from the increasing pressures and confusion of life at home. And given what happened later, the knowledge that Stan had in effect seen the Promised Land before he died was a huge comfort for us. I'll never be able to express the love and gratitude I have for Jim Fleming and his friendship.

CHAPTER 72

Fast Forward

It was after Jim Morison arrived in the band and Jim Fleming took over the booking that it felt like someone had hit the fast forward on the tape. We were now getting so busy that we were hardly ever home. We were all feeling the strain. Jim had pulled up stakes and brought his partner Lillian and her kids out from Alberta and got them settled in a school in Brantford.

Lil had to deal with being in a completely new town where she knew no one. It was a big adjustment for all of them.

Stan was trying, without any luck, to balance work and home time.

He was anxious to capitalize on the work that was coming in, and the higher profile we suddenly had, and he was also desperate to be around to see all the milestones his new son was going through. He missed a lot, and it hurt.

Diane was frustrated with her increased work load, and the problems of raising 4 kids in a tiny three bedroom condo, while holding down a difficult full time job. The condo was cramped, and I think she and Stan were making plans to sell and move. In the meantime there were renovations to be made, and the basement was going to see major changes with the addition of at least one new bedroom, which of course Stan was going to build. He was getting no rest.

I was now fully in the throes of a major clinical depression. It had been coming on for years, with no one able to diagnose my problem, and with my increased self-medicating my moods and behaviour were getting more and more erratic. I couldn't sleep or keep food down, and the anxiety attacks were so common now I was in a perpetual state of barely managed terror.

It was ironic, as for the first time in my life I was in love, and felt loved, but mental illness has its own agenda. I was beginning to be a liability to everyone around me.

Finally, there was one morning where we were to drive into Toronto to re-record "The Bluenose" so it could be played at the Canadian pavilion at Disneyworld in Florida. Chris Crilly from Barde had flown in the night before, to play piano for the session, and we had picked him up at the airport. I was delegated to go in and get him while Stan and Jim waited in the parking lot. I hadn't eaten or slept in what seemed like nearly a week, and while I was waiting for Chris to arrive I made a side trip into a bar, and grabbed a quick drink and wolfed down a sandwich. Chris appeared, and we picked up his bag and went out to the van, and we hit the 401 and began to drive home. I had to get Stan to pull over, and there were some awkward and dangerous moments while I stood next to the guard rail and puked into the ditch, as 18 wheelers roared by only inches away. I was at the end of my tether, and the next morning when Stan and the boys arrived to take me to the studio I was in no shape to go. I looked like the character from the painting, "The Scream." They went off without me, and did the session with Chris having to recreate the echo-plex violin part I had played on the original recording, as well as play piano. I spent that day in the Emergency Psychiatric Unit of St. Joseph's Hospital in Hamilton, where I was finally diagnosed correctly with clinical depression and given some proper medications and hope for a more normal life. But it took years to come out of it, and in many ways it never really leaves a person who has had it.

But with the medication, and for the first few weeks daily monitoring by the doctors and by backing away from the booze, I was now able to work and function better, at least, most of the time.

My doctor had strongly recommended that I stay off the road and check into the hospital, but I was determined to keep working, and with Gail's help get better without a stay in the bug house. He said later he had wanted to over-rule us, but had relented when he had seen the depth of the bond we had.

Stan and Jim and I were touring so much that there were times when we would have a few hours' stop over at Toronto airport, and the wives would meet us there, and Gail and I would go off for a dinner and maybe catch a precious hour or so together in a nearby hotel.

I know we played in Regina twice within a 6 month period, and during a visit to my parents' house, my Mum handed me a letter from a disgruntled fan. He had been to both shows, and not only did we play the same songs, but we played them in exactly the same order with all the same lame jokes in between as well. He was furious, and felt cheated. I could hardly blame him, and I wrote back to apologize, saying we were all just over worked and some nights we did occasionally phone it in. I showed the letter to Stan, and he flinched and shook his head, but said nothing. There was no excuse.

Jim Fleming had us doing more Arts Council Showcases all over the country. We did one in Edmonton, and another in Vancouver. Jim flew out to represent us and after our showcase we all decided to go out to dinner. We piled into Jim's rental car and set off. Jim was driving, and it seemed to be taking a long time to get out of the parking lot. I was sitting in the back seat with Jim Morison. Stan was in the front and I couldn't see past him. Fleming kept turning this way and that, and muttering to himself.

"That's not it. Maybe over here."
He'd stop and back up and turn around.
We were trying to be patient, but after maybe 20 minutes of this, it occurred to Stan that perhaps Jim had a problem other than being born with no of sense of direction.

"Jim?"
"Yeah?" He was peering out the windshield and cranking the wheel towards what looked like an exit lane.
"Have you been drinking?"
"No. Jesus. I lost a friend to a drunk driver. I would never drive drunk."
"Have you been...um...smoking?"
"You mean like weed?"
"Yeah. Are you stoned?"
There was a silence. After all Jim was now in charge of our careers, and was supposed to be the smooth and highly organized face we presented to the world. Getting hopelessly wrecked at a conference might not be seen as the most professional behaviour.
After a bit he spoke. "Maybe a little bit."
A pause. He stopped the car and sat for a moment. He put his head against the steering wheel, sighed heavily, and said, "Boys, I'm sorry. I'm fucked up." The three of us burst out laughing.
We gave up on dinner and spent the next hour or so careening wildly around the parking lot on two wheels, laughing like idiots, and trying to get the rental airborne.

"Nothing handles speed bumps like a rental car." Stan said.
When we weren't flying back and forth across the country, we were driving our tired asses through some flat wasteland like Indiana, or Ohio to get to a gig we had never heard of in a town we had never been in, and then loading up and driving all night to the next one.
We played the Canal Street Tavern in Dayton. It was a run down, pissy-smelling tap room on 1st Street, crouching between abandoned warehouses, next to wind-blown rubble-strewn lots where factories had once stood. It was run by Mick Montgomery, a soft spoken guy with shoulder length hair, and dreams of establishing an arts scene in the midst of this post-Apocalyptic Hellscape.

Jim Fleming had asked us to do the gig as a favour to Mick, as if having us there was somehow going to raise the profile of a new club. We couldn't see how that was going to happen. We had never been here before and figured it was going to be another poorly attended dreary show in an even drearier slum of a town. Dayton was having a hard time of it, economically. As we came into town, the only businesses we could see that were open were pawn shops, porn theatres, and discount electronics stores.

I have never been able to figure out the relationship between those three.

Having travelled over most of the USA the last 40 or so years, I have noticed that porn theatres, pawn shops and Radio Shack stores are always clustered together on the same street, often on the same block. Maybe it just has something to do with obsessive male loners who need something to do with their hands.

We checked into a rough-looking hotel under the highway overpass. It gave a discount for musicians playing at the club, but even so it was 45 bucks, and we were three to a room. We had time to grab a shower and a meal, as Mick liked to start shows around 9 30, which was late by folk club standards. We drove towards the club, looking for somewhere to eat. It wasn't looking too good. Everything was closed. I looked at my watch, and wondered if we could find something a couple exits down the highway. Just then Stan pulled over and parked.

"What are you doing?"

"White Castle."

"Huh?"

He pointed.

"There's a White Castle. I've always wanted to try one."

We had played up in Green Bay Wisconsin a couple months back, and the guy who ran the club, Tom Slothower, had talked enthusiastically about having White Castle burger eating contests when he was in school. They called them "sliders," and it wasn't uncommon for someone to wolf down 30 or 40 of the disgusting little things in the race for gastronomic supremacy.

According to Tom, if a contestant barfed during the contest, he wasn't necessarily disqualified. They just carefully estimated what he had lost and docked it from his total, and he would continue on.

And now Stan wanted to be part of the dream.

He dove into the place and came back out a few minutes later with a large paper bag.

He climbed in and opened it up. The van was now filled with the smell of sweet yeasty bread, and warm canned dog food.

"Want one?"

I held up my hand. "No. I'm good."

I couldn't face it. Not then, and not now. Not ever.

He gobbled down the whole mess of them, maybe 10 or 12 altogether.

"They don't toast the bun," he said. "They steam it. Makes it easier to go down."

"Not to mention coming back up."

"Well, there's that too."

We got to the club. It was a smallish narrow room with a large stage facing the bar. Beside the bar were several rows of beat-to-shit wooden theatre seats set up as bleachers. Given the nature of the other entertainment establishments in the neighbourhood, I wasn't going to touch those seats for anything. God only knew were they had been.

We did a sound check, and I ate a couple of slices of dried out bar pizza, which had been probably spinning around under the infra-red lamp for a week.

Jim made do with a couple of hot dogs from the roller grill behind the bar, and a plate of microwaved nacho chips, with canned refried beans on the side.

Amazingly, none of us had any lasting ill effects from our meals, although the smoke detector in our room went off around 4 that morning. Probably just coincidence.

The show went really well. We had a good audience, who, amazingly, were familiar with the songs from having heard them on the college radio at WNKU across the river from Cinncinnati.

Mick was a good guy, although none of us could figure out what he was saying as he counted out the cash in his tiny office after the show. He would launch into some long meandering story with no point or plot or ending, and then drift off into another topic entirely. We were looking back and forth at each other trying to see if the other guy was following, but we were all equally confused. After some time he mentioned just in passing that he had spent the 2 years between 1966 and 1968 living in a second floor apartment at the precise corner of Haight and Ashbury streets in San Francisco.

Ah. Now everything became clear.

The next day we drove north out of town to the Air Museum, and spent a few hours climbing in and out of antique fighter jets, and space modules and training vehicles, and if my memory doesn't play false, the Enola Gay, which had been originally based in Dayton and was back home as part of a good will tour, if that makes any sense at all.

There was probably a reason for all those little signs saying "DANGER! DO NOT TOUCH" next to the large red buttons in the cockpits, but we never found out what it was. We, of course punched them repeatedly, but nothing ever happened.

The only real crisis we had was when Stan got stuck trying to crawl into one of the Apollo Space modules. The hatch just wasn't built for a guy his size, and Jim and I had to drag him out by the legs.
We finished the museum tour and got in the van, and drove all night to another gig in another town.

CHAPTER 73

At Last I'm Ready For Christmas

Stan and Jim Morison and I were on what had become our annual pre-Christmas tour of New England. We loved it. We could look forward to nearly a week of sold out shows at the Folkway in Peterborough, New Hampshire. And as well there would be a three night run at Passim in Cambridge, again, always sold out. In between we could either pick up a few smaller shows in Upstate New York, or simply crash at Rick and Lorraine Lee's home in Natick, and spend the evenings playing music with them.

We could also get our Christmas shopping done.

It was a working holiday.

But this year, in the middle of that tour we had also picked up a pretty juicy gig playing a couple of songs for a CBC TV Christmas special at the National Arts Centre in Ottawa, with the National Ballet, and the National Arts Centre orchestra. The show was going to be taped live in front of an audience for later broadcast, and Patrick Watson, a highly respected and revered veteran broadcaster was going to be the host. We of course had "First Christmas" to play, but it was unrelievedly bleak, and we needed something lighter to bring to our part of the show.

Of course, Stan left the actual writing of the song to the last minute.

I saw him a couple of times, sitting by himself in Rick and Lorraine's front room, with the guitar and some paper trying to finish it, but as usual, by the time we were on our way to the gig, we still had no idea of what we were going to play.

We caught a plane from Logan to Ottawa and caught a cab to the Chateau Laurier.

It was there that I found Gail had come up on the bus, a trip of some 7 hours in the snow and ice over bad roads, to surprise me, despite having a terrible cold. Diane had taken her to the Greyhound station in Hamilton and very kindly brought along a gift basket with a thermos of hot lemon tea, and lozenges and paper tissues. It was a nice gesture, the effect being somewhat lessened by her saying, "You'll probably get to his room and find him fucking some girl," and then laughing wildly as she drove off.

In any case, I was thrilled to see my sweetheart.

I was still worried about the show. We as yet had not heard the new song, and at rehearsal that night Stan had to tell the director that after we played "First Christmas," there would be a 4 minute segment where we would be doing another as yet un-named song.

Next morning Stan called a rehearsal in his room and we heard the song for the first time. It was a funny piece starting out with the wife having bought half price wrapping paper on Boxing Day last season, but losing it track of it a year later when it was needed. The tune was close to that of "The Idiot," and in the same key. Jim and I had a fairly easy job learning our parts, but Stan had to keep track of the tune, the new lyrics, and a fairly complex guitar arrangement. He was in a bad way. By dress rehearsal he still hadn't been able to get through it without screwing one of the three elements up.

We had a snack backstage and kept running the tune. He managed to get all the way through twice and felt he now had it fixed in his memory. We'd be okay for the show.

The show opened with Patrick Watson sitting in a wing back chair in front of a cozy fake fireplace, wearing a velvet smoking jacket. Patrick had greeted us warmly before the show, and said some nice things about the music.

Lovely man.

We were standing backstage watching the opening of the show and I suddenly had the sensation that I was standing in the middle of a herd of goats.

I looked around and saw I was surrounded by the dancers from the Ballet.

They were all young and fit and extraordinarily beautiful, but I had not known about the superstition about never washing or cleaning their costumes. My eyes were watering.

Ballet is lovely, the epitome of grace, and poetry and athleticism. But you really need to see it from a distance. Otherwise, over the music you will hear the thumping of feet landing on the hardwood, and the grunt of effort as the dancers are lifted and flung about the stage, not to mention the overwhelming pong. I was crushed. Another illusion gone.

Patrick Watson gave us a nice intro from his chair at the side of the stage.

We opened with the new tune. Partway through the first verse Stan drew a blank, stumbled on the words and we ground to a halt.

There was a smattering of applause, and Stan turned to Patrick and said, "Sorry. It's a brand new song. Can we try again?" So Patrick re-did his intro, the audience applauded, and we went into it again.

This time we managed the first verse, and the chorus, and the audience began clapping along.

As I watched Stan's face over the scroll of my fiddle, I could see he was coming up dry again.

I knew that haunted, deer in the headlights look.

We came to a halt again, and again he apologized.

This was awful. At least for Stan. I was enjoying the thought of the fun I was going to have chewing him out for being a slack and dilatory songwriter after the show.

Once again, Patrick introduced us, and I think I might have said to the audience, "Once more, please. Just for us."

This time we were able to finish the song, and got our due applause.

We went on to play "First Christmas," and after the nightmare of the previous song, it was a dawdle.

We took our bows and ran off stage.

We were packing up our instruments in the dressing room, and I turned to Stan and cleared my throat. Now was my chance to tell him off.

He froze me with his look. "I know what you are going to say, and don't bother. Don't even fucking open your mouth. Okay?"

He slammed the lid down on his guitar case, snapped the locks and began going through his jacket pockets looking for his cigarettes and lighter.

I gave him the lecture anyway. "Maybe next goddamned time you'll be a bit better prepared, for Chrissake, so as not to embarrass yourself in front of a national audience, and for the sake of the poor bastards who have to play with you."

But this was only after he had grabbed up his case, had walked out of the dressing room and pushed through the outer door to the street, and was safely out of earshot three blocks away.

Next morning, we took a cab to the Greyhound station. We put my sweetheart, who was by now near death from the flu, on a stinking smoke filled bus back to Hamilton, and then went out to the airport where we caught a flight back to Boston. Lorraine Lee picked us up and took us back to the house in Natick, and the next day we resumed the tour.

CHAPTER 74

The Iron Horse

We were going back to play in Northampton, Massachusetts that week.
We'd been there before, but the debut had not been a smooth one.
It was the previous summer, and we'd been doing three nights,
Thursday to Saturday, at the Folkway, in Peterborough, and then
picking up some odd stuff on weekdays for extra dough, then going
back to the Folkway for three more nights. Jim Fleming kept finding all
sorts of little money-making gigs for us in unexpected out of the way
places. We were thrilled with him.
Stan came down one morning while we were having breakfast in the
Folkway dining room, and told us that we had just been offered a show
for the coming Sunday in an 80 seat club down in Northampton, an
hour and a half south of Peterborough.
The place was called the Iron Horse, and it was a straight door deal, but
what the hell, it filled an empty night. We might sell a few albums.
Later that day, he caught up with Jim and me and said, "That show at
the Iron Horse just sold out. They want to try the Monday as well."
Sounded great. He came back a while later with the news that the
Monday sold out too.
Selling out two shows within hours? We had never done anything like
that before.
Before the weekend was over we had picked up two more nights at the
Iron Horse for the following weekend, and they looked like selling out
in advance as well.
What was going on here?
We arrived at the Iron Horse that Sunday, and walked in.
Nice looking place, a long narrow room with a tiny stage to the left of
the door, and some booths along the walls to either side.
There were tables and chairs in front of the stage.
It looked good, and smelled good, and felt friendly.
The owner, Jordi Herold, came out of the basement, and introduced
himself.
A pleasant looking guy with a mullet hair-do, and a David Letterman

smile; he seemed a bit stand-offish. He told me years later that he was annoyed that we had sold out his club for four nights, and he had never heard of us until Jim Fleming had phoned and pitched the shows.
He felt like he'd missed something, and as a professional, it offended his sense of self.
Jordi left us to set up, and we did our sound check.
Our habit in those days was for me to stand out in front of the stage and help the sound person get Stan's guitar sounding right, then we would balance Jim's bass against it.
Following that I would get back up, and Stan would make sure the fiddle and my guitars sounded okay in the room.
Finally, we would all do an acapella number, to balance the voices in the monitors, and we'd be done. Given a reasonably competent sound person it never took more than 5 or 10 minutes.
We were finishing up with the last part of the sound check, singing the chorus to "Northwest Passage", when I noticed Jordi standing at the top of the stairs with his mouth open.
He said to me years later that he had been sitting at his desk downstairs, and when we started singing he found himself racing to the top of the stairs to see.
"I'd never heard anything like that before."

We finished with the sound check and went back to the bar.
They had an assortment of imported beer that had probably never been seen outside of Jim's dreams. They had stuff we'd only heard about, strange beers from South America, and Scotland and Holland.
Jim was looking pretty verklempt.
He wiped his eyes and cleared his throat.
"You know, you dream about stuff like this. You know it exists somewhere, but you never think you'll actually see it."
We ordered 3 Whitbread's Pale Ales.
Stan said to the bartender, "We're playing here tonight, can we run a tab and settle up later?"
No problem.
We went back to a booth, put our feet up and relaxed.
This was great. 4 sold out shows in a nice club, with a good beer selection, in a pretty cool looking town. We clinked glasses and had a drink.
Jim and Stan were looking at the menu. Jim was no doubt planning his campaign on the beer selection, and Stan was pleased to see a breakfast item which consisted of eggs, home fries, Swiss cheese, and Kielbasa, with onions and peppers, all mixed together and baked in an earthenware dish. The immediate future looked very promising.

I finished my beer, and went out for a walk around the square.
There was a big stone city hall building up at the end of the block, and a
great looking Main drag, with lots of cute boutiques and specialty stores
facing the street. They had managed to preserve most of the old facades
of the buildings. A rare thing then, and even rarer now.
There are a number of Ivy League women's colleges in Northampton,
and the streets and coffee bars were filled with clusters of intense young
girls in wool skirts and turtleneck sweaters, all busy writing in their
journals, or reading "The Bell Jar," or just sitting quietly and holding
hands before going back to their dorm rooms at Radclyffe Hall, and
watching the Jodie Foster film festival on cable.
It begged the question, how did three big meaty guys like us sell out a
bunch of shows in this town?
I found a great bookstore on the street leading out to the highway. It
was everything a bookstore should be. Crowded messy shelves all the
way to the ceiling, and a faint odor of mold and crumbling paper. The
owner was a quiet and pleasant looney in a cardigan, who walked
about murmuring endearments to the orange tabby cat on his shoulder.
I found a complete set of the collected works of Mark Twain, printed
in 1905, before Twain had died, and I got all 40 volumes for 30 bucks.
There was also a wonderful leather bound collection of Dickens there.
Some 40 volumes, and when I went back to the Iron Horse to get the
van to carry away my purchase, Stan decided to come along and he
bought the lot. The Dickens set travelled with us for the next 6 months,
and I believe Stan might have actually worked his way through the
complete collection.

The show that night was intense.
The place was jammed, and we went on feeling pretty confident and
snotty.
The heat in the room was suffocating, and we were working our way
through the Whitbread's pretty steadily. None of us could get drunk, we
were all sweating so much.
At the end of the night we were in the dressing room downstairs,
feeling tired and happy, and Jordi came in to settle accounts.
He was looking pretty glum for a guy who had just jammed a hundred
thirsty people into a room that held 80, with every prospect of doing it
all over again the next night, and twice again next week.
He tossed the envelope of cash onto the sofa next to Stan and began to
read off the list of expenses we'd run up.
There was the sound guy's fee, and a percentage for the ticket agency,
and our meals, and some other stuff. That was all okay.
But apparently we had managed to drink over two dozen Whitbread's

Pale Ales between the three of us, and Jordi stopped reading at that point, looked at Stan and said, "That bar tab of yours represents my profit margin. I made exactly nothing off this show tonight."
And with that he turned and left the room.
Stan grabbed the pay packet and jumped off the sofa.

"Now wait just a goddamned minute. We never expected anyone to pay for our beer. We were running a tab all day. We pay for our own drinks."
Jordi was taking the stairs two at a time and waving him off.
He got to the top of the stairs, and turned and said, "Drinks for the performers are always on the house at the Iron Horse."
Well for a start we didn't know that, and secondly, it made no sense; we had seen on the calendar that he had some Scottish bands coming in later in the month.
He was courting financial suicide.

"We pay for our own drinks."

"No."
Jordi was adamant.

"We expect to provide hospitality for all the performers who play here. I just never expected to see all my profits drunk up in one night."
Stan lost his temper at that point.
He pulled out his wallet, and counted out some cash and threw it on the table in front of Jordi.

"We pay our own way in this band. Don't you dare call us free-loaders."
Jordi ignored the money and walked away.
"Don't you fucking walk away from me when I'm talking to you."
Jim and I began loading out the guitars.
We had planned on leaving the amps there overnight, but it now looked a bit doubtful as to whether we were going to play here again the next evening. We grabbed the amps and threw them in the van as well.
The argument heated up, and at one point Stan picked up the pay packet and threw it as hard as he could at Jordi. His aim was off, and Jordi picked the envelope up and threw it back at Stan. Jim and I kept slinking past them with the gear, while Stan and Jordi took it in turns to throw the pay envelope back and forth at each other's head, while yelling insults and abuse.
They were on the sidewalk as I slammed the back doors shut and jumped into the van. Stan threw the envelope once more at Jordi, who caught it and drilled it back at him. It hit the side of the van and landed at Stan's feet. It was getting a bit tired looking.

Stan yelled, "We're never coming back here again!"

"Fine! I'll call your agent first thing tomorrow."

Stan hooked his toe under the envelope and kicked it towards the police station across the street. He then jumped in the van, fired it up and jammed it into gear. The tires chirped as he hit the gas. As we drove up Center Street, Jordi came running alongside the van, and tossed the envelope into the driver's window, where it landed on the dash and burst open. 20 dollar bills were everywhere now. Stan stopped the van, frantically gathered up the money, stuffed it back into the envelope, and got out and ran back down the street, but it was too late.
Jordi had bolted back to the club, locked the door, turned out the lights and had disappeared into the basement.
Bastard.
He had won.

It got sorted, at least partially, the next day over the phone between Jim Fleming and Jordi, and we went back to the club and continued our run.
We established that we were paying for our own drinks.
Relations were still a bit strained between Stan and Jordi though, and the latter kept mostly out of sight. Jordi was later to become a good friend, and a major supporter of the band.
Within a year of our first show at the club he managed to put us in the Opera house in Northampton. The club couldn't hold us anymore.

Years later, Jordi told me how after that first disastrous weekend he wrote a letter to Stan, saying,
"Look, we're both professionals.
We both care intensely about our work.
Why can't we get along?"
Stan came back with a brief reply:
"Dear Jordi, if you and I were standing in a room with 200 other people, and someone stuck their head in the door, and yelled "Hey Pig head!" you and I would be the only people to turn around."

CHAPTER 75

Speeding

We had a short Mid-western tour in front of us.
The first show was at the Coffeehouse Extempore in Minneapolis.
Great joint.
It was upstairs from the street, in the student quarter on the West Bank
of town.
We loved the neighbourhood. It was Bob Dylan's old stomping
grounds, and it still retained the down-at-heel Boho student vibe. There
were lots of dusty little book stores and head shops to explore during
the day, and a handful of really great neighbourhood bars that stayed
open late, although for some reason after a certain hour they were
compelled by law to serve a very weak pissy tasting beer. Perhaps
it was a nod to keeping the really paralytic drunks off the road. You
couldn't drink it fast enough to get really hammered. God knows, we
tried.
There was a wonderful greasy little joint called the 400 Club, just kitty
corner across the street from the Extemp. It had a long dimly lit bar
down one side, and a pool table and a strange wide window sill next to
the bar which served as a stage for bands to play.
We were thunderstruck one night, to walk in after a gig, and find
Spider John Koerner up there ripping into a Leadbelly song with an old
Epiphone 12 string. He had a harmonica in a holder around his neck,
and was shaking the room with a right foot which evidently weighed in
around 500 pounds.
Spider John. Wow.
I had discovered a record some years before called, "Running Jumping
Standing Still," by Koerner Ray and Glover. It was an odd little item;
blues, and ragtime and jump music and hollers, all balled up into a
glorious exuberant and chaotic mess. It sounded as if someone was
playing the piano while riding it down a flight of stairs.
I brought a tape of it into the van one day, and after hearing the first
tune, "The Red Palace," Stan said, "That is some of the weirdest shit I
have ever heard."

"No kidding."

He reached out and hit the replay button on the deck and for the next half hour or so we never got past that first track.

And now here was Spider John, in the flesh, blasting away.

We were too overwhelmed to approach him, but we had a great night. The room was full of happy people, mostly students, drinking beer and playing pool and kicking it loose after a long week of sweating over the books. We mostly stood to one side of the room, drinking our watery beer and watching Spider John as he thumped out a great version of "Froggy Went a 'Courtin'."

The Extemp was a pretty nice gig, barring the second floor load in. The only real issue was the presence of a couple of volunteers who were apt to sidle up behind you when you weren't looking and begin giving you a deep tissue massage, as a prelude, I suppose, to something more meaningful later. We found it creepy. You daren't sit down for long. You had to keep moving or sit with your back to the wall.

There was one particularly sad and obnoxious creature who was under age, under dressed, and underfoot. Under the influence most of the time, as well.

Around 3 o'clock on a given afternoon she would turn up at the club, visibly addled, wearing a sun dress that had been stitched together out of scraps of muslin, and announce that she was going up to the roof to sunbathe naked.

"And don't you dare sneak up and try to see me. I'll be completely in the nude. You hear me? Naked."

We were sitting with a couple of the local wastrels, drinking coffee and enjoying the perfect sunny spring day which we could see through the dusty fly specked window.

"There's an invitation if I ever heard one, "someone said.

I shuddered at the thought.

Stan assumed a pirate's voice. "She's a Fire Ship, boys. Best give her a wide berth."

She was a determined thing.

You would be wakened by the phone ringing in your motel room around 7 a.m.

"Hello?"

A breathy voice..."Hello."

"Who is this?"

"It's (name withheld)"

"What time is it?"

"Nearly noon."

I squinted at my watch. "No it isn't. It's still the middle of the night."

"I was wondering if you'd like to go out for breakfast?"

"What? How did you find me?"
We made a point of never telling anyone where we staying for this very reason.

"Oh, I just called every motel in town until I found you."
I hung up.
She accosted me one night after our show, and handed me an album which had been recorded live at the club.

"Who's this?'
She moved in closer and breathed Juicy Fruit Gum and Peppermint Schnapps into my face. "He's the best songwriter in the world." I looked at the cover, which featured a staged black and white shot of a couple kissing in a doorway.
It was called "One Night."
Right. I decided anything she liked had to be swill. And I had never heard of this guy. And besides I was working with a pretty good songwriter. I had no interest in some local usurper. Fuck him. After she staggered off I folded Greg Brown's record up, snapped it in half and savagely stuffed it into a trash bin. I only got to hear Greg and become friends with him a couple years later. Stan missed him completely.

So, a weekend at the Extemp. We set out from home to drive to the Twin Cities. It was about 16 hours if you didn't dawdle.
Around St Joseph Michigan Stan noticed a red light briefly wink on and then off on the dashboard.

"Shit."

"What?"

"One of the idiot lights just came on."

"Which one?"

"I dunno. It was on for just a second."
He pulled over to the side of the road. There it was again. The alternator. Dammit. This wasn't like an oil light where you could just put a piece of tape over it and keep going. We were going to be dead at the side of the road within minutes if we didn't attend to this.
Stan drove up to the next exit and pulled into a gas station and made some calls. There was a shop that would get us up and running, but not before 1 PM the next day. This was going to be tough, but we had no choice. We pulled into the Red Roof Inn near the exit, got a couple of rooms, unloaded the van, and then had it towed over to the shop.
It was still early evening, and I went for a walk around the wasteland of cheap motels and convenience stores and theme restaurants that surrounded us. I was hungry, and there was a pizza place on the far side of the garbage-strewn lot. It was called Chuck-E-Cheese. Maybe I could get a slice to go.

I walked inside, took a quick look around and then ran out, found a phone booth and called Stan at the motel.

"You guys gotta come over here and see this."

"What?" Stan was tired and anxious about the van and making the gig.

"Come see this."

"What is it?"

"Just come over here. Bring Jimmy. I can't even begin to describe it."

A few minutes later he and Jim walked up and I took them in the door. There was a stage to our left with a band of large animatronic Disney-style animals, playing guitar and fiddle and banjo and wash tub bass. They were dressed like hillbillies, and they were scarily alive, and disturbingly familiar. The wash tub bassist was the tallest of the bunch and was wearing jeans, a plaid shirt and a leather vest, precisely what Jim wore on stage. The fiddling robot, a hound dog, I believe, was thin and cross eyed with a bad case of the shakes. The lead singer was a massively fat bear with a guitar, a deep booming voice, and an annoying line of in between song patter. As we watched, the robot bear was just announcing that they were going to take a short break but they would be back in "two twitches of a lamb's tail." It was deeply wrong and completely surreal, and as the curtain closed on the scene Jim said, "Holy shit. I'm really glad I don't do drugs anymore."

The bear with the guitar had shaken Stan too.

"Let's get outa here. I've seen enough."

We left and walked back to the Red Roof Inn.

Stan had been mostly silent during the walk, but as we came up to our rooms he muttered to himself, "I gotta lose some weight."

We got the van back around noon the next day, and Stan burned rubber all the way up the entry ramp to I-94. We had done the math and it didn't look like we could even remotely make the gig in time. Not in a universe where Einstein's rules applied anyway.

Still, we had to make the try.

Miraculously we made it through Chicago in under the usual 2 or 3 hours. They were just then beginning the now 30 odd years of construction on the Dan Ryan Expressway, and we breezed through.

We hit Rockford and changed drivers. Jim took the wheel. He cranked it up to about 85 and Stan and I set up positions to keep a sharp eye out for state troopers. I was in the front. Stan was in the back seat craning his neck to see out behind us.

"We need a turret on the top, like a B-17. It'd be a help to keep an eye out for cops."

Stan often fantasized about modifications for the van.

"A turret. That would be good. Like that camper we saw in Vancouver years ago. Wind resistance might be an issue though."

"Yeah, but what about a set of JATO bottles?" Stan said.

"What's that?"

"Jet Assisted Takeoff. They use them for Hercules aircraft on short runways in the Congo. If we had a set of those we'd be there by now." Jim pulled the wheel sharply to the right, and we slid past an 18 wheeler who was in the passing lane where he had no business being. Jim had flashed the high beams at him as we approached but the trucker didn't move. After we were past Jimmy smoothly pulled it back to the left, and then to the right again, as we slalomed through a cluster of trucks and four wheelers who were poking along being a menace to shipping.

"Well done Jim." Stan said.

Jim was a lovely driver. A veteran. Give him a pack of smokes, a full tank and a six pack, and he was good to go, gliding like an eel through any sort of traffic and weather.

Stan continued.

"I'd like a flare gun too."

"A flare gun?"

"Yup. One of those big brass World War Two Navy flare guns with the lanyard. A guy like that trucker back there, he doesn't want to pull over out of the way, you just blow by and fire a flare into the cab. Let him deal with that rocketing around inside for a while."

"Dunno if that's legal."

"Probably not."

"Shame."

We were silent for a while, just watching as Jim floated us through the herd into open space where he could really air it out. We were near Tomah Wisconsin now. There was always a chance that a deer might leap out even during the day. We had to stay sharp.

"I've been thinking," Stan said.

"About what?"

"Those robots last night."

"Jesus, that was creepy."

"I know, but what about when we are older? They'll have the technology improved in a few years. We could just send out crews with animatronic versions of ourselves. Nobody would ever know, and we would have more time at home."

Jim said, "Yeah. I like it. Robo-Stan."

Stan said, "Ah Shit. Where the hell did he come from?"

"What?"

"There's a cop coming up behind us. Goddammit."

Over the years we had developed a careful and mostly effective ritual for dealing with cops when being pulled over for speeding.

First, if you pass a parked cruiser with the radar gun out, wave in a friendly manner to signal that you know he's there and yes, you know you are breaking the law, but you are an expert driver and this is a special case requiring more speed than usual and we are after all, professionals, and there must be a good reason for all this haste.

When that failed, and the lights came on we'd put on the turn signal and pull over immediately in the first safe place.

Put it in park, turn on the four way flashers.

Roll down the driver's window, turn off the motor and place the keys on the roof of the vehicle. If it is dark, turn on all the interior lights so the cop doesn't have to worry about walking up alone to where some loon in the back seat might be training a large calibre hand gun on his forehead. Have the driver's license, insurance and ownership in hand as the cop comes up to window to show that again, you are a veteran, and we should be able to settle this quickly and in a friendly manner, and get on with our respective days.

Almost invariably the cop would relax and let you off with a warning, or at least knock 20 or 30 MPH off what you were doing.

Jim pulled over and we went through the usual ritual, except this time the young cop wasn't buying it, and we were made to slowly and sedately follow the cruiser over to the State Troopers' Headquarters to pay the fine. 280 bucks. In cash. It took a precious half hour.

Even worse, the cop said, "I could have just given you the ticket, and sent you on your way, but you're from out of State, and I don't believe you would have paid the fine. And I wanted to teach you a lesson that speeding is bad."

Asshole. He was probably a born again Christian, who home schooled his kids and made them sit in the dark in their "shame closet " every night after prayers, before their bedtime spanking with the special Jesus paddle.

We agreed to split the ticket three ways as a cost of doing business, and when we left the station house Stan once more took the wheel and floored it out of the parking lot, spraying gravel all over the parked cruisers. He raced down the side road and took the entry ramp onto I-94 in a controlled drift. He gunned it up to 85 again and we carried on. Our ritual hadn't worked this time. Luck of the draw.

Years later, I was doing an interview with Vicky Gaberau on CBC Radio

in Vancouver.
She asked me how did I travel, and how far was I from home on this
month long tour.

"Oh, It's about 60 hours of driving from here to home."

"Oh my God. What a haul."

"Yeah, it's tough, but I break it up into 4 days and it's okay."

"What do you drive?"

"A Stealth Volvo."

"A what?"

"Stealth Volvo. The thing is, a Volvo Wagon is the most boring car
on the planet, and I can pretty much breeze by traffic cops well over
the speed limit, and they simply don't believe a Volvo can go that fast.
It's like it's invisible. And anyway, if they do pull me over, I can usually
charm my way out of the ticket."

"You charm your way out? This is you talking, remember."

"Thanks very much, but yes. I charm my way out."

"How do you do that?"

And I described the whole procedure of stopping immediately, turning
off the motor and throwing the keys on the roof, and all the rest of it.
"They're just so grateful when you cooperate and don't present a threat
they almost always let you off."

Maybe a week later, I was in Nelson BC, enjoying a slow start to what
I thought was a day off. I opened my day-planner just as I was taking
my first sip of a latte, and realised that I had screwed up and did in fact
have a show that night in Cranbrook, and it was some hours away, and
I was going to lose an hour in the time change between West Coast and
Mountain Time.

I leapt up and ran out the door, as mothers in yoga pants covered their
kids' ears to save them from learning new words. I sprinted to the car,
fired it up, and blasted out of town.

I was maybe 3 miles out when the RCMP cruiser came over the hill
towards me and immediately put his circus lights on. Damn it.

I pulled over and began the ritual.

Flashers on, window rolled down, car turned off, and the keys tossed
on the roof.

I was waiting with my documents out when the cop walked up.

I couldn't see his face, but began a friendly and calm explanation as to
why I was speeding.

"Sorry about all this officer, but I just realised I have to be in
Cranbrook in a few hours and the car is really heavily loaded and with
only 4 cylinders I really have to get up speed to not be a danger to other
drivers, and so I was ..."

He interrupted me.

"Garnet Rogers eh?"
He was presumably looking at my license. I couldn't see his face from
where I was. I had been in effect talking to his heavy black leather belt,
with the massive gun in the black leather holster, the black leather hand
cuff case, the pepper spray, and the black leather baton holder, along
with some other nasty hardware I didn't recognize. It all looked pretty
phallic and disturbing though, and as I remember it now, it was less
like a conversation and more like trying to order from the drive through
window at a 50 Shades of Grey theme restaurant.
"Yes, uh, yeah. That's my name."
Again the disembodied voice.
"So this must be the Stealth Volvo."
Oh Shit.
"Wait here. This will take a few minutes."
He walked away.
Dammit. I had been nabbed by the only cop who listened to the CBC.
He came back a couple minutes later with my documents and a ticket
for 200 bucks. He handed them to me and said, "You can pay by cash or
credit card when you get to Cranbrook."
He then leaned down and I saw him for the first time. He was a young
guy, with a handsome lean face, strong manly jaw, sinister mirrored
Ray Bans, and a smile like a moray eel.

"I don't think you're gonna charm your way out of this one."

Oh Hell, where was I?
Yes, the Extemp.
As we came into the Twin Cities we could see dark clouds racing in
from the West.
One of those killer fronts was coming down from the north, the kind
that would occasionally arrive in the Mid-West after a couple of warm
days, with lightning and high winds and hailstones that would pummel
and crush cars into pock-marked flattened wrecks, and leave in its wake
ripped up trees and over turned trailers in a kind of random End of
Days Feng Shui.
Within minutes the storm closed in on us and it was like driving
through a car wash. We got to the Extemp, and I jumped out of the van
and ran up the front stairs to let Steve Alarik who ran the place, know
we were alive. Stan drove the van around back into the alley.
I opened the door off the stage which led to the fire escape, and a
torrent of rain and wind blew into the room, soaking the audience who
had been sitting in the dark for some time wondering no doubt, just
where the hell we were. I looked down. Stan and Jim were outside on

the iron stairs, struggling to drag the guitars and amps up through the deluge. There were huge lightning strikes snapping everywhere around us as they clambered up. Christ, if lightning hit the iron railing they'd be fried. The scene looked like an out take from Frankenstein. Within minutes we were loaded in, and we ran into the back room to towel off, side-stepping the offers of a "soothing backrub," or maybe a relaxing prostate massage, and then ran out onto the stage.
Made the gig with maybe a minute to spare.

CHAPTER 76

Dad's Western Tour

A couple of weeks later we were going out west to Alberta and
Saskatchewan yet again. It was a tightly booked tour this time, with
only a couple of days off here and there. We were playing a lot of
tertiary markets where the presenters had no access to a sound system,
and so we were forced to carry our own.

Even if they did have a system, we had learned over the years that
it might not be anything we could use. Too often, some small town
might get a government grant and a new multiple use community hall
would be commissioned. And a useless and over-priced architect would
be hired at great cost, and after the place was finished the committee
would meet and the need for a sound system would be discussed.

Inevitably, someone would ask, "So what kind of budget do you have?"
A number would be quoted.

"What an incredible coincidence. My brother in law in Edmonton has a
music store, and he could get you something pretty good for just about
that much money. "

And sometime later the community would be presented with a truck
load of broken down and badly maintained rental crap that had been
destined for the dump, and which would then be improperly installed
in the special sensory deprivation tank that the architect had designated
as a sound booth. The booth would be located on another floor and
behind a thick plate of bullet proof glass. The sound engineer was
expected to mix the band through a couple of tiny metal clad speakers
that would have made Paul Robeson sound like an angry bee in a tin
can.

There was one place we played which had in the sound booth entire
walls of wonderful and impressive black boxes with glowing meters
and winking red lights, and a massive 24 channel state of the art mixing
desk. The problem was the desk was built in England for English
voltages, and so was useless. It set up a massive buzz from the ground
loop and we couldn't be heard over it. And all the magic black boxes,
the graphic equalizers and compressors were plugged in but not

connected to anything. They were only keeping the room warm.
And the poor presenters couldn't have been more proud. Stan took one
look at the set up and said, "All architects should shot to death with a
ball of their own shit."

So we rented a system. It took every bit of hard earned expertise and
spacial visualization that we had for Stan and me to figure out where
everything was going to be stored in the van. In the end there wasn't an
inch to spare, and Stan had a couple of extra leaf springs installed in the
back suspension, and kept a careful watch on the level of the tires. The
poor old van wasn't liking it, and had taken to handling like a willful
drunken pig.
Our Dad had just recently taken early retirement. After 30 odd years of
working as a brick layer his knees were shot. He had a bit of a disability
pension, and some meagre savings. He was grateful to not have to stand
in a trench all day, or climb around on a scaffold in high winds without
a safety line, but he was restless, and when he wasn't prowling the
back roads in his pickup truck looking for wood to cut and split to heat
the house, he was back home driving Mum nuts by criticizing her TV
viewing and pointedly rewashing the dishes after she was done.
There were some other more long standing issues between them. Mum
liked to strive for at least the illusion of gentility, having grown up poor
and pretty much staying that way all her life. Dad, on the other hand
had little use for many of the conventions. At an early age for example,
he discovered that he had a particular talent for controlling and then
releasing his wind. It was a gift, but he'd worked on it, and practiced
and perfected what the fates had given him. He had an enormous post
stern vocabulary. Long trombone-like notes, short staccato bursts, and
his habitual morning fanfare, which when performed sounded like a
firefight between the Allies and the Germans in the narrow cobblestone
streets of Normandy during the race to liberate Paris. And he never
seemed to run out. He was able to punctuate his conversation with
them. It would have been funny if it hadn't been so disgusting. No,
hell, it was funny.
In later years when "the Clapper" came out on the market, that device
which allowed one to turn lights on and off with a simple sharp clap of
the hands, Mum ordered a couple and had them installed. She called
me later that night, angry and outraged that Dad was turning the lights
in the living room and kitchen on and off just by lifting his leg and
bearing down.
I could hear him in the background as she complained. Behind her it
sounded as if they were under a mortar attack, and I could visualize
the lights going off and on, and him with a smile on his face, waving a

newspaper back and forth.

"He's doing this deliberately. He just wants to ruin this whole experience for me," Mum yelled.

I couldn't help her. I was on my knees sick from laughing.

Anyway, when we invited him out on the road for the tour they both jumped at it.

Dad could revisit his old haunts, and Mum would get some much needed peace and quiet and send the curtains out to be dry cleaned. We were going to be visiting a lot of the towns where Dad had been stationed during the war, when he was training as a radio operator and gunner.

"Has Calgary changed much?" he asked.

Stan said, "Since you were there Pop? Yeah, I expect it has." Calgary had changed enormously just in the few short years we had been going there. When we first arrived it was a just a medium sized town, barely a city, surrounded by some hills, with the Rockies gleaming white off to the West.

Oil money had turned it into a mess of steel towers downtown, and an ugly sprawling disaster zone of housing developments that covered the hills as far as you could see under the cloud of partially burned petro-chemicals that now hung over the valley. The mountains were now visible only on days when a cold front came in and scoured the air clean. What seemed like a million cars were now in a permanent holding pattern on the network of highways that surrounded the city.

"Yeah. It's bigger now."

"Huh. Is the old Palliser Hotel still there?"

"The Palliser? Yup."

"I spent a weekend at the Palliser back during the war. There was a girl with me. Goddamned room was so big I could never catch her. I kept getting lost."

I'd had my own experience with the Palliser. It was downtown, near the train station, and was one of the great old CP hotels. The rooms were in fact enormous, about the same floor space as a tennis court. David Eadie and I a couple of years before had shared digs there over a festival weekend. Out of boredom and alcoholic high spirits we had devised a vicious game called "Kill Frisbee" where you were not allowed to let your feet touch the floor. You could only make your way around the room by hopping from table to chair to sofa. David, being faster and lighter and more athletic was winning until the house detective came and ruined our fun. Just as well. I was covered in welts.

We taught Dad how to do sound. He was a natural. We had seen him in action a couple of years before at a show we were doing in Northern

Ontario. We had been having a terrible time with the house engineer, and Stan's guitar had either been inaudible or was generating waves of feedback. I watched nervously as Dad left his seat and went over to the board. I was worried that he might hurt the guy physically or simply reduce him to a pile of smoking cinders with a well-timed sarcastic comment. He pushed the sound tech aside and bent over to look at the board. Within seconds everything smoothed out, and we were able to hear, and it felt like we were playing music again. The house engineer threw up his hands, put on his jacket, and left for the evening.
During the break, Stan asked, "How the hell did you do that?"
Dad shrugged and said, "Everything was labelled. I just turned stuff up or down until it sounded good to me."
What a concept.

I think we played Winnipeg first, and then on to Regina and after that, Saskatoon. We stopped for lunch one day in some dusty fly blown town where the only place open was the one inevitable Chinese joint. There was a Chinese restaurant in every town, no matter how small, in Western Canada. The menu never varied. Deep fried chicken balls in fluorescent orange sauce, pork fried rice, Won Ton soup, and a hot beef sandwich with gravy and a side of fries. The gravy did double duty as sauce for the Egg Foo Young.
The family lived as outcasts from the rest of the town in the apartment above the cafe. The kids went to school, learned English, got straight A's on their homework which they worked on as they waited on tables, and served as interpreters for their folks in the evenings.
Stan and Dad and Jim and I walked in and sat down. We were the only customers. The owner came over with the menus and we all ordered beer. The beers came, we ordered our meals by simply pointing at the lurid colour photos on the menu, and then we sat looking out the dusty window and played "Count the tumble weeds."
The owner kept coming out of the kitchen and looking at us and smiling nervously. We smiled back to reassure him. We probably didn't look all that comforting. Four guys, all well over 6 feet tall, and all of us, including Dad, with leather jackets and earrings, looking tired and rumpled.
The food arrived and it was tolerable. Not good, not bad. With luck it would do its job and fill the gap in our guts, and not leave us all frantically unbuttoning our pants and squatting in a dusty bottle-strewn ditch an hour up the Yellowhead.
The owner seemed like a nice guy. He kept re-filling our water glasses, and quickly brought us another round of beer when we asked. We were all sitting back and wondering how bad the coffee might be here, and

Dad was speculating about whether raisin pie might be on the menu,
when the man came over with a small pad of paper and a pencil.
He held them out to Stan, and said something we couldn't catch.
Stan looked at the pad. It wasn't the bill. It was blank. He looked at the
owner and raised his eyebrows.
The little man bowed and bobbed his head and made a scribbling
motion with the pencil and the palm of his hand.
After a lot of broken English and miming, we realised he was asking for
our autographs.
Autographs?
Wow. A fan. In this town. Of all places.
Stan signed his name and then passed it over to Jim. Jim signed and
then passed to me, and I scribbled my name. I passed it over to Dad,
who refused at first, but then shrugged and signed the paper as well.
The owner of the cafe looked closely at the signatures and frowned. He
looked at Stan and shook his head.
What now?
It was then a young Chinese girl, the man's daughter, came in the door.
Her dad spoke to her, and she put down her school books and came
over. After a brief whispered conversation in Mandarin she came over
to our table.
  "I'm sorry. My father wanted your autograph but now he doesn't
know you."
  "Who did he think we were?"
  "Professional Wrestlers."

About 14 days later we were on the homeward leg of the tour. It had
gone reasonably well. We had been frantically busy. The distances
between the shows were fairly humane for a normal vehicle, but with
the van loaded down as it was we'd had to leave an extra couple of
hours of travel time every day, and as a result we were all short on
sleep.
Dad was having fun. While we were playing he mostly sat behind the
mixing board and pretended to move the controls. During the break
he'd stand by the record table in his fringed suede jacket and cowboy
hat, and charm the older (and some of the younger) ladies. The days
he spent in the back, looking out the side window of the van, peering
up at the mountains, sipping a cup of coffee laced with dark rum, and
reminiscing about failed trysts with young women in whatever town
we might be travelling through. He had seemingly been stationed
everywhere during the war, and never once got lucky.
We were outside of Golden BC, when we all saw a tiny white creature
at the side of the road. It was very small and not moving the right way.

Stan pulled over and got out to look.

Ah shit. It was a little white kitten. It was malnourished, and had a badly injured leg. We were miles from anywhere. The poor thing had obviously been left there by some heartless bastard who, rather than take responsibility for it simply dumped it out of the car, so it could frolic in the woods and live on rabbits.

There was nothing we could do.

Stan took the little creature back into the woods by himself, and Dad and Jim and I sat in the van and waited. After maybe half an hour he came back, and wiped the dirt off his hands with a rag from under the seat. He fired up the van, put it in gear and pulled back out on the road. We all knew he had given it a quick and humane end, and then had most likely searched until he found some small and appropriate resting place and buried it, using his bare hands and a stick. I wouldn't have been surprised to hear he had planted a small tree and placed a ring of stones around the grave.

In any event, we were all four of us snuffling and wiping our eyes for the next few hours.

Late that night we were loading our gear into our motel rooms after the show, and I looked over at Stan and said, "Goodnight. Thanks for taking care of the kitten."

He shook his head. "I'd give a lot for just 5 minutes with whoever did that."

We finished up in Winnipeg again.

Stan had a booking to do Al Simmons' kids' show on the local TV station. Jim and I were relieved for once that we weren't included. We unloaded his bag and guitar in the parking lot of the Comfort Inn on the Pembina Highway, south of the city. We were going to carry on home by road, and Stan would fly back a few days later.

"Make sure you get rid of that filthy pornographic guitar strap before you sing to the wee kiddies."

"Shit. You're right. I always forget it's there."

And he did forget it, too. Too often. I watched him once at the Owen Sound Festival, as he sang "Abiyoyo the Giant" to a cluster of kids in the Children's' Area. He was crouched on a tiny stool to make himself appear to grow into a giant when he stood up at the end of the song. There was a little girl behind him, listening and leaning forward, looking intently at the depictions of people performing anal sex and fellatio. That he didn't wind up on a sex offender registry somewhere as a result was just a matter of luck.

We left Stan and drove across the border at Pembina. We caught

Highway 2 East at Grand Forks, and made our way to Duluth where
we racked up for the night. I have always loved Duluth, and the great
heroic sweep of the harbour as you come over the high hill overlooking
the town. Everything is laid out before you. The rows of giant grain
elevators and the girdered bridges, the clusters of ships waiting, and
the vast cold iron grey lake stretching off into the east. We came down
the hill, crossed over to Superior Wisconsin, and carried on until we
came to a series of old rail cars on a siding under a wooden trestle on
the right. There was a diner there, and one of the great ones. We went
in, and I bought Dad a breakfast of eggs and toast and fiery homemade
sausage patties with home fries. He ate the lot, shaking his head and
pounding the Formica counter, and gasping and sweating. Before we
left I ordered him a sausage sandwich for the road.

"What are you doing?"

"Never mind." I said, handing him the bag. "You'll thank me later.
The place is gone now, as is my Dad, but he talked about that breakfast
for the rest of his life.

CHAPTER 77

By Any Other Name

I don't recall the exact time of year, but it was likely in 1982, and we had
been out on the road for a couple of weeks. Stan had been pretty quiet
during the daily drives over that time, and I could tell something was
bothering him. For months now I had been hearing him on the phone
through the thin walls of whatever cheap motel we were in, and there
had been a lot of shouting. I didn't ask what was going on, and I didn't
want to know. I would knock on the door of his room when it was time
to leave for the gig, and he would emerge looking sad and defeated and
distant.
 It was none of my business. Couples go through stuff. It's part of the
deal. Still, something seriously wasn't right, and he was looking more
tired and tense than usual. The worst of it from my own selfish point of
view, was the phone calls that began to come nightly at whatever venue
we were playing.
A club volunteer or a staff member would come back stage and tell Stan
there was an urgent phone call for him from his wife. He'd jump up and
race out the door. Sometime later, he'd come back looking beaten down
and shaky and soaked with sweat. There had been no accident with the
kids, no emergency requiring his immediate attention, it was just
another negotiation about whatever was going on, and the only time to
discuss it seemed to be just before a show. This of course was in the
days before cell phones, and the only place we could reliably be found
was at the venue. Still, on those nights I soon learned to move my mic
stand a foot or so closer to Stan so I could feed him the lyrics I knew he
was going to be missing.
And we always did a bad show.
It had been happening for months, and for purely those selfish reasons I
hated it.
We came home, and went our separate ways until the next trip.
It was a few days later when we met again. Stan picked me up before
driving to Brantford to grab Jim. I could see a marked change in him.
He seemed easier, more relaxed, and the strain had gone from his face.

He was bright and upbeat as we loaded my stuff into the back of the van, he turned to me and asked, "Did you ever get that light over the back door fixed?"

I hadn't. There was a burned out light bulb over the back door of the apartment Gail and I lived in, and having no ladder, I was unable to replace it. It was a worry, as the door was under the fire escape, and a prowler could easily lurk there in the dark when Gail came back from work in the evenings.

"No, I can't reach it."

"Go get a bulb. I'll boost you up to it."

"We'd never reach it, it's nearly 20 feet, and besides there's no way you can lift me."

"Get the damned bulb."

Gail brought a fresh bulb out and handed it to me, and Stan made a stirrup out of his fingers and bent down.

"Step up."

I put my foot in his hands and with one astonishing move he simply lifted me over his head like a caber. I still couldn't reach it, and then he stood on his toes and I stood on mine, and I was just able to replace it.

"All done. Thanks."

He let me down and dusted off his hands.

"There."

Christ, he was strong.

We finished loading the van, and he kept up a running series of jokes before giving Gail a crushing hug goodbye.

This was better. I hadn't seen him this happy in what seemed like years. As we drove up the 403, Stan began talking about the sudden and wonderful and extraordinary change in his home life. He had been expecting, he said, to be told to pack up his stuff and leave the previous week after the tour. Actually, he was half -expecting to find his few possessions piled in the front yard. Things had been rough over the last few months, and as much love as there might be between him and Diane it had looked for a while as if a hiatus might be the best way to handle it until it got resolved. He had been depressed and deeply afraid. Trial separations almost never work. He knew that Diane loved him. He loved her and the kids, and the idea of having their little family unit threatened and broken was terrible. He'd felt like a failure.

Wow. I hadn't known it was so tough.

I felt bad that as his brother he had not confided in me, or asked for my support, but that is what happens in bands. You spend so much time together that no matter how close you are, you stop communicating. I had kept a similar cone of silence during my own crises over the years. And now everything had changed, and seemingly overnight. Diane had been as sweet and loving and welcoming as it was possible for a person to be when he had furtively poked his head in the door after that last tour. And he simply couldn't believe how lucky he was. Love had come back into his life. Sweet, overwhelming and unconditional love.

Well this was good news.

According to him Diane had gone to some weekend-long seminar run by a guy from the States, whose name escapes me, where the attendees were forced to remain in the room for hours, forbidden to leave even for a bathroom break as the speaker tore down their illusions about their lives, and made them see the error of their ways, and the bad habits they had picked up in their dealings with the world.

This sounded less good to me. It sounded like a cult, like brainwashing. And the more he told me the less I cared for it, particularly when he revealed that he was going to pay a small fortune to attend the same seminar in New York City in a few weeks so he could see the magic first hand.

It was none of my business though, and anyway, this wasn't the first Road to Damascus moment he had ever experienced.

He had undergone a serious and lasting conversion to Christianity when he was 20 or 21, being confirmed and baptized into the High Anglican Church. I didn't get that one either at the time, and I still don't, but I am a godless heathen, and an unrepentant sinner.

Still, I was trying to be glad for the two of them. Everyone, (with a few exceptions,) deserves to be happy, and I was glad things had suddenly improved so much.

My feelings towards whatever batshit cult this might be didn't enter into it. And as long as Stan was content and feeling loved, all was well with the world, provided he didn't become a Mormon, or start voting Tory or something.

We arrived at Jim's and he got his gear loaded into the van.

We drove out to Highway 2, and began heading west across country towards Woodstock to get to the 401. Once again, Stan told us just how wonderful life had become and how happy he was with the change in his fortunes.

"That's great Stan, I'm really happy for you," Jim said from the back seat.

Stan pulled out a large Tupperware dish and opened it. He pulled something out with his left hand and then passed it over to me.

"Here. Try these."

"What is it?"

"Ribs. Take one."

I looked inside the tub. Apparently he'd mugged Fred Flintstone for his lunch. It was filled with massive meaty ribs, and they smelled

wonderful.
I took one out of the pile and then handed the dish back to Jim. I bit in.
"Wow, these are good. Unbelievable. I haven't had anything like this since Big John's in Chicago."
Within seconds we were all covered in spicy and delicious red/ brown sauce. Stan pulled out a box of Kleenex and handed it over to me, but it was too late. We all looked as if we had just come out of a knife fight. My shirt was a ruin. Screw it. It was worth it.
"These are fantastic. Thanks."
"You're welcome." There was a pause. "Yup," he said, "Ariel makes damned fine ribs."
"Who?"
There was another pause.
"Ariel."
"Who's that? One of Diane's friends?"
Another longer pause. He cleared his throat.
"No. Diane made them. But she has decided she wants to be called "Ariel" from now on."
"Ariel?"
"Yes. Ariel."
"Like the sprite from Midsummer Night's Dream? That Ariel?"
"I don't know and it doesn't matter. She has never liked the name Diane, and now she wants to be known as Ariel. It's part of this change in her life."
I could see Jim in the back seat. He had paused in his eating, and was now looking carefully and intently out the window, holding a large and succulent rib in his fist. His chest was shaking and he would not meet my eye. He was going to lose it.
"Ariel."
Stan was looking embarrassed.
"Yes, Ariel. She wants to be called Ariel from now on. Is that so hard for you to understand?"
"No, but..." I stopped and we sat in silence for a minute or two, but being an asshole, I couldn't help myself.
"Presumably "Galadriel" was taken..."
Stan blew up.

"LOOK PAL, I'VE BEEN HAVING A REALLY FUCKING TOUGH TIME OF IT OVER THE LAST FEW MONTHS, WHAT WITH YOU AND YOUR HEALTH AND WORK AND ONE THING AND ANOTHER, AND UP UNTIL LAST WEEK I THOUGHT MY MARRIAGE WAS OVER, AND NOW I FIND OUT IT ISN'T, AND THE WOMAN I LOVE HAS DECIDED TO CHANGE, YES, CHANGE HER

GODDAMNED NAME AFTER ALL THESE YEARS! AND I WOULD
REALLY, REALLY LIKE IT IF FOR ONCE YOU COULD STOP BEING
SUCH A SMART ASS AND JUST COOPERATE FOR MY SAKE, AND
STOP TRYING TO MAKE HER LOOK FOOLISH! IS THAT TOO
MUCH TO ASK?"

Well, no. Not when he put it like that.
Ariel, though. Jesus.
  "Okay. I'm sorry. I'll do my best."
  "Thank you."
  "So how is she going to deal with the transition? Do we have to start
right now? Is there going to be an announcement in the mail? It's going
to be confusing."
  "Her women friends are calling her Ariel already, and it's okay if
you want to refer to her as "Diane/Ariel" until you get used to it."
Fair enough.
I should have handled it better. It was her choice, and in the years since
then a number of my male friends have transitioned to life as women,
and I haven't had any problem with that. A simple name change should
have been a dawdle, but no one ever accused me of being smart.
  "Well, I guess I can do that."
  "Thank you."
I turned around to Jim and held out the Tupperware dish. He was still
only barely holding himself together and would not look at me.
  "More ribs Kal-El?"

CHAPTER 78

Madison Wisconsin

We were on our way that morning to the Midwest, where among other things we had a gig in Madison Wisconsin with Gamble Rogers, and Sally Rogers.

No idea who came up with the idea, but a fairly large hall had been rented on the University of Wisconsin campus and I think it was billed as "The Importance of Being Rogers."

Gamble was a wonderful performer, like a combination of revival preacher, and gun- slinger, only with terrifying guitar skills. He was a tall and gaunt fair haired-man in cowboy boots and a pearl buttoned shirt, who would stop in mid song, and fly off into wonderful rhetorical firework displays, stalking the stage with a hand-held mic, and coming off from his performance shaky and spent and pouring sweat.

Sally, we had known since the old days at the Ten Pound Fiddle in East Lansing.

She's a wonderful singer, and a great performer, and back then was singing mostly traditional songs collected from the British Isles and Appalachia. She was a good friend, and we were delighted to have her and Gamble on the show.

It all went pretty well, and we closed the night with our set, during which we were invaded by a large team of Morris Dancers, as we played "The Idiot."

It was a fun night, but it was the last time I was ever to see Gamble. He died a couple of years later, typically, as he was trying rescue someone from drowning near his home in Florida. He was endlessly kind and generous, and it was no surprise he drowned trying to save the life of someone he didn't know.

He suffered from arthritis in his hands, and mentioned in the dressing room that he had to practice for hours before a show to get his fingers loose and his hands warm.

While he was on stage I sneaked a Butane hand warmer into his guitar case. Having him sit around and play the way he could for hours was just making the rest of us look bad.

The show was recorded for NPR, and we were all quite pleased by the end of things, and Jimmy and I celebrated perhaps a little too much. I was still just getting my depression under control, and should not have been drinking at all.

I paid for it around 5 o'clock the next morning, when I woke up with a massive panic attack, brought on by the alcohol leaving my body.

Stan and I were sharing a room at a place called the Edgewood Motel, in Monona, with Jim getting the single.

I can't remember why. Perhaps it had to do with Jim's snoring, which after a night on the tiles was so loud and reverberant that he would wake up in the morning with his bed and all the rest of the furniture having vibrated to the other side of the room.

Anyway, I woke with my heart pounding and my head spinning, short of breath and half fainting with terror.

I got dressed as quietly as I could so as not to wake Stan who was passed out in the next bed, and went for a brisk walk in the pre-dawn dark along Monona Lake.

Did about 4 miles in a freezing cold wind, and got back to the motel, feeling somewhat better.

As I tried to creep back into the room, the wind blew a gust, and there was a loud crash as the aluminum storm door flew back and hit the wall.

Stan sat up in bed, looking angry and scared and confused.

"What the Hell is going on?"

"Sorry. Ah shit. I was having a walk, and the wind caught the…"

"What time is it for God's sake?"

He peered at his watch and then fell back onto his pillow.

"Aw, Jesus Christ. You know, I'm getting pretty goddamned sick of you and your habits, and the hours you keep. You're getting more and more erratic, and you have no respect for anyone around you, and no concern at all that other people might need to get," his voice rose, "A LITTLE FUCKING SLEEP!"

He sat up again, and threw aside the covers, stood up and staggered over to the desk where his cigarettes were.

He shook one out, and lit it, and violently threw the lighter onto the desk where it skittered and bounced against the wall and disappeared forever.

I was still having trouble getting my breathing under control in the aftermath of my panic attack and the brisk walk. I sat down on my bed and put my head in my hands.

Stan came over and stood in front of me, maybe 2 feet away.

"I know you're still having some problems with this depression thing, but I'm trying to keep this whole fucking show together, and trying to write, and…"

I looked up and lost track of what he was saying right about then. Sometime during the night his testicles had made a brave bid for freedom, and now were hanging out the side of his jockey shorts, and they were right at face level.

Every time he took a step, they jiggled obscenely, and I quickly lowered my head to avoid having to watch.

"You know, you're becoming a huge fucking liability to this whole operation, and I've had all these other fucking pressures at home, and I'm not getting any rest anywhere, and the least you can do for me is maybe, JUST MAYBE try to keep your shit together. Even just a little bit."

Try as I might not to look, I could visualise his wedding tackle flapping like a couple of apples in the wind, and I could feel the helpless laughter boiling up as the storm raged over my head.

As he continued to yell and pace the room I put my head ever lower, but my shoulders were starting to shake with suppressed laughter.

He stomped over to the desk and lifted it up over his head to look for his lighter, but it was gone forever. He had evidently thrown it hard enough to send it into another dimension. Somewhere, in an alternate universe, another version of Stan was just finding a battered blue Bic. But it was gone from our world.

"Shit." He put down the desk and turned around.

"Now my fucking lighter is gone, and I haven't had any time with my kids in weeks, and…" He paused, apparently noticing me. "Garnet? What's going on?"

I had my eyes closed and my head between my knees now, and was rocking back and forth and shaking with the effort of trying not to laugh.

His voice got softer.

"Garnet? You all right? Are you crying? Ah Jesus. Were you having a panic attack? Look, I'm sorry… Ah shit…I didn't know."

He put a hand on my shoulder. Oh Christ. His nuts had to be only inches away from my face now, and at that point I yelled and fell over onto the bed and rolled onto my side in hysterics.

I was sweating and shaking and I couldn't get my breath.

He must have thought I was having a seizure.

"Garnet! Are you all right? Come on. Garnet? Talk to me…" He was squeezing my shoulder.

I fell off the bed. He and his bollocks followed.

"Look, I'm sorry I yelled at you. It's just that the door…"

I was sobbing and thrashing helplessly in the narrow space between the bed and the wall. He had his hand on me again, and was now stroking and patting my shoulder in an attempt to soothe me.

"Garnet, come on. Look at me. I'm really sorry." He gave me a shake. "I'll try to be more understanding next time."
His voice got softer still.

"Come on." He grabbed my shoulder more firmly and pulled me up into a sitting position to face him. "Look at me...I'm really ..."
I opened my eyes. Oh Jesus, they were still there, right in front of me. I exploded.

"YOUR NUTS...I'M SORRY...YOUR NUTS ARE OUT AND I'M SORRY I WOKE YOU, BUT YOUR FUCKING NUTS ARE ...OH JESUS CHRIST! and I rolled over and fell back onto the floor, hysterical.
He looked down and said, "Oh for God's sake," and quickly adjusted himself.
He went into the bathroom, and by the time he came out I had made him a cup of coffee to take back to bed, and had set his cigarettes on the table with a book of motel matches on top, and then left the room so he could smoke and read and more properly start his day.

CHAPTER 79

Home In Halifax

A week or two later we were playing the Rebecca Cohn Auditorium again. We had grown our audience in Halifax to the point where we could return every 6 or 8 months, as opposed to waiting out a full year the way we had been doing.

For us, those sold out shows were evidence that we were making real headway, and that eventually we would be able to leave behind the dire shit holes we were still facing in parts of the country in those days, just to bring home a pay cheque. Things were definitely looking up generally, but there were still a lot of nights where we'd get on stage and have to grit our teeth, knowing it was just for that thin envelope of cash at the end of the night.

The Cohn shows were also a chance to reconnect with family down there, and we were happy to be able to rent a large suite at the Lord Nelson, overlooking the Public Gardens, and after the show treat various aunts and uncles and cousins to a bit of return hospitality.

I'm not sure whose idea it was to have the CBC record the show for network broadcast, but as Paul Mills had once again been parachuted in to play with us, it might have been him working behind the scenes. Having him play would be a means for Stan to thank him for the extra dollars we were getting, not to mention the added network exposure, but Jim and I weren't happy about it. After these years, Paul still wasn't able or willing to rehearse, in spite of Stan and I having several serious fights about what the band had always considered to be an intrusion, no matter who was playing bass at the time.

"So why do we never see Paul when we're playing some crappy little bar? Tell me that. Why only the good gigs? And why won't he rehearse?"

We might have added, "And why are we paying him a full band share of the gig money? " but we knew why. Stan was loyal, and having Paul on the gig was payback.

Over the years Stan would repeatedly promise that Paul would rehearse, but with the exception of the live album, it never happened.

At least not enough for him to understand or pay any attention to the nuances we'd worked so hard to put in the music. So for me and Jim, it was another lost opportunity, and now instead of the band being able to play a nice relaxed show in a beautiful room, with good sound for a change, Paul would stand between me and Stan and drown him out as he played 18 notes to the dozen on every song. I would spend much of the evening standing back from my mic, bored rigid, waiting in vain for an opening.

The real blow came when we arrived at the Hall.

We had been trying to change the public impression that had grown since the release of the first record that we were a mostly Maritime act. Three albums and a couple of dozen great songs later that perception refused to go away. Tunes like "Barrett's Privateers" and "Fogarty's Cove" had entered the set lists of countless ersazt Irish bar bands, and those songs were still first in the hearts of those who liked to swill back beer, and clap along on the front beat. And we still felt compelled to include the songs in our own shows.

It is heresy to say it, but by now we were thoroughly tired of having to sing "Barrett's" every damned night. It had been written as a joke, a one-off years before, and during our years in the student bars was useful to get the attention of the drunks who were otherwise ignoring us. But enough was enough. We wanted to move on.

"I feel like I stepped in dog shit," Stan said, one night as we left the stage. "I'm never gonna be able to scrape that song off my foot."
We dealt with the boredom by singing parodies of it and laughing amongst ourselves when the audience didn't notice.

"Goddamn them all, I was told we'd cruise the streets for American boys," slid right past them, along with our personal favourite, written by our Aunt June and her daughter Kim.

"Oh antelope poop is a sickening sight...etc...
Be it hard and flat or so loose it sprays, to make takes an antelope two whole days..."

There were other, more obscene versions, involving cabin boys and apple barrels.
Anything to get through.

So when we went into the hall to set up and saw the nets and the ships' timbers and the dories and lobster pots littering the stage, Stan and I were furious.

"WHAT THE HELL IS ALL THIS?"
It was appalling. Every stupid cliché that defined the Maritimes for brainless tourists was piled on the stage. I'm not sure there weren't a couple of stuffed seagulls somewhere in the mess.
Stan was standing in the middle of it, looking around.

"Who did this?"

We heard a voice.

"What do you think boys? Isn't it great?"

"Who's that?" said Stan, shading his eyes from the stage lights and looking out into the auditorium.

It was the local producer for CBC whose idea it was to fill the stage with storm wrack and tourist trash. He had met us at the airport a few hours before, along with a piper, but had never mentioned he was perpetrating this nonsense.

Stan shook his head, and turned and gestured at the junk behind him.

"Get this shit off the stage. Right now. I'm not having it."

"Oh no, we can't do that. The crew is on a break, and besides, we got nowhere to stash it back stage. It's all from the CBC. We'd have to load it into the truck."

"Then do it. I'm not playing a show with all this crap."

Well, of course it was no go. The Cohn was an IATSE house, and the CBC was controlled by the same union as well, and getting the junk off the stage in time for the show would have eaten into sacred break time. We would have had shop stewards and union reps pouting and stamping their little feet, yelling "Grievance," and driving the budget into the red.

And of course it got worse, didn't it?

The producer, of his own accord, and with no prior warning or consultation with us, had decided to turn our concert into a Maritme Comedy/ Variety Show. He had hired a trio of so-called comedians who dressed up in yellow oilskins and Sou'Westers and rubber boots, and did tired schtick about lobsters and leaky boats in a Music Hall Nova Scotian accent.

We hated their act.

We hated the whole idea.

We hated that our one really good gig was being hijacked. But there was no arguing. Contracts had been signed and the show would go on.

Worst of all, the producer seemed to feel he was doing us a favour. He simply didn't understand, and we were helpless in the face of the same bloated bureaucracy that had hired him and the rest of these talentless civil service hacks in the first place.

And the final straw was that the clowns in the rain gear were not an opening act. The CBC guy wanted us all on stage together as they did their schtick and intersperse their act with our own songs, so it looked like we were endorsing the whole stupid shabby mess.

Stan was sitting in the dressing room with his head in his hands. The concert was ruined.

We got dressed, and he hurriedly planned out what songs we were going to play during the "Variety" portion of the evening. The producer had told us we could "maybe go out and play a few tunes, " after it was all over, (as if it was his damned decision,) presumably so the audience wouldn't feel completely swindled and burn the box office down and lynch the ticket seller.

The doors opened, and the audience came in and we all went out on stage. There was some laughter as Stan pointedly looked around at the mess and shrugged and shook his head.

We sat and tried our best to look pleasant as the guys in the rubber suits did their tired act, and by 9:30, around the time we should have been halfway through our second set, it was done.

We told the audience that the show wasn't over, but we were coming back in a few minutes, so please stick around.

We went back stage, re-grouped, and had a quick drink or two, and then the lights dimmed again.

Jimmy and I walked out first as we always did at the bigger shows where Stan wanted to make an entrance. Jimmy and I plugged in, and I re-adjusted my microphone, and said, "Now we can have some fun."

Stan and Paul came out and we played another hour and a half or so, sending the union deep into costly overtime, and no doubt giving the bean counters heart attacks. We didn't give a shit. It was nearly midnight by the time we were done.

Back in the recording truck, things were going as per usual. The recording engineer, who had the IQ of a potted fern, kept turning off my mic whenever he noticed I wasn't playing, in an effort I suppose, to cut down on sound leakage between the mics. Of course when I came back in there would only be a faint ghost of what I was playing before he hurriedly reached out and turned me up again. As a result, the original CBC release of the show was a disaster.

It didn't help that our nerves were still on edge from the unwelcome surprise we'd been met with. There were a couple of places where I had to desperately vamp for time as we waited for Paul to re-tune his guitar. For all his much vaunted reputation as a player, he only seemed to be comfortable in the key of G. So whenever we played in D, for example, he was forced to jam his capo up on the 7th fret so he could use familiar chord shapes, and as a result had to nearly rebuild his whole instrument to re-tune. It took ages.

I ended up doing some improvised schtick involving cows dressed as Shriners, and some other drunken foolishness. I was embarrassed later to learn that it was kept and included on the release.

The show was later edited and re-released, but I have never been able to listen to it.

CHAPTER 80

Calgary Folk Festival 1982

The CBC had launched a national weekly folk show, based out of
Calgary, called "Simply Folk."

Stan got signed up to write and record a regular report from the road,
as we made our way around the country playing the string of summer
festivals we'd been booked into. I suppose these days it might be more
in the nature of a "blog," just impressions and comments about other
performers, and short interviews, and bits of behind the scene colour.
For Stan it was a chance to stretch a bit and try a different kind of
writing. I think he liked doing the voice overs as well. We had grown
up on CBC radio, and we both knew the magic that came from good
writing, and a narrator with warm and intimate voice who knew how
to set a scene.

We were at the Calgary festival, on Prince's Island, downtown, in the
middle of the Bow River. Calgary still hadn't exploded to where it is
today, and the site had a lot of quiet charm. You could sit under the
giant willows and listen to music while guys with hip waders and split
cane rods stalked salmon out in the river with the office towers rising in
the distance.

The hotel we were being put up in was on the edge of Chinatown, and
it was a pleasant walk of a dozen or so blocks to the site entrance. You
could have a quiet dinner, and then stroll down through the shade of
the buildings past the flocks of brightly dressed underage hookers who
congregated on the corners, and catch the evening show. Afterwards,
there was a massive piss-up and jam session at "The Unicorn Pub,"
which was one of a chain of faked-up Olde Oirish tourist traps owned
and run by the Irish Rovers.

I had a room to myself for some reason. Jim Morison was commuting
back and forth from Calgary to Red Deer every night so he could visit
his folks.

Stan was rooming with Tom Paxton.

God knows why, but the organizers had jammed them in together.

Tom was a legend, and a bona fide star. If anyone deserved a private room with some peace and quiet it would be him. Maybe Tom had actually requested it. Over the years he has worked a lot with co-writers, and he might have felt he and Stan would catch lightning in a bottle if they got put in an enclosed space. Maybe it was just a cruel practical joke on the part of the organizers, as Stan and Tom were polar opposites in life-styles,

Tom had quit drinking some years before, and now kept regular hours, even at festivals. Stan liked to drink and carouse and sing late into the night.

Tom is also a tennis fanatic, and was going to bed early during the festival so he could get up at 4 a.m. to catch the live broadcast from Wimbledon. He would just be getting comfortable with his cup of tea in front of the TV, and Stan would burst through the door and begin destroying the room, overturning tables and breaking small chairs as he struggled to peel his sweaty clothes off before passing out and making noises like a sea lion in rut.

We had first met Tom back in '77 at Mariposa on Toronto Island. He had been friendly and tremendously encouraging to Stan, and although we only ran into him occasionally over the years there was a bond between them, and a great deal of mutual respect.

Maybe they had both asked to share a room. It was a bad mistake from Tom's point of view. Stan was in full festival mode, and burning the candle at both ends.

Unlike me, Stan was not a regular daily drinker. At home he might have a couple beers of an evening, or a shot or two of rum, but he was nowhere near me in terms of his consumption. Few people were. Even on the road, he rarely took more than a couple of drinks either before or after the show. For me it had been a daily task just to get enough down my throat to manage the panic attacks.

Beyond a couple of years when I was fooling around with pot, which I quit using in '76, I never had any interest in drugs. I was too scared. I couldn't even really handle the mild ditch weed everyone smoked back in the day. It left me confused and paranoid and stupid, and I didn't need external stimulants to achieve that.

But Stan told me that he had decided when he was young to try everything out there, just to see what it was like. During his days in London he was a daily, sometimes hourly pot smoker, and continued after he and Diane/Ariel were together, but after Nathan was born, he began backing away from it. He took a lot of LSD for part of one summer during the Cedar Lake days, but he dialed it down after careering down a long hill on a stolen bicycle in Guelph one morning, and hurtling into the Speed River, where he spent some time thrashing helplessly about in the shallows, laughing hysterically and yelling, "ACID!" at the top of his voice. The gendarmes arrived and had pulled him out, helped him wring out his clothes and sent him home.

He'd been around cocaine a bit during the days in London, and liked it a lot, but as it was expensive it didn't become a habit until the last few months of his life when he suddenly developed a taste for more. It might have turned into a real issue had he lived. We were to have a couple of arguments about it during the rehearsals for the last studio album. Quite rightly, he said I was in no position to criticise anyone's habits.

He told me he'd tried heroin when he was very young as well. Twice. Twice was enough.

He said, "With smack, you feel like you've never been sick or tired a day in your life. Nothing can hurt you. You haven't a care in the world. You're warm, and happy and peaceful, and you love everybody. And I never want to be in the same room with that shit ever again. I don't trust myself."

I never tried heroin, but that weekend I discovered in a very small way exactly what he meant.

We had gone to the evening show on the island and had come back to the hotel to clean up and head out to the party. I was not drinking right then, as I had finally been prescribed a couple medications for my depression and the accompanying anxiety, and I didn't want to mess up my recovery. I was walking towards the club, when I was suddenly seized with a terrible panic attack. Tunnel vision, pouring sweat, inability to get a breath, racing heart, body tremors, the whole works. Unless you've had one you can't imagine. Someone once described it as the feeling when you are balancing on two legs of a tall stool, and then overbalance, and begin to wildly flail your arms and desperately grab for a safe hold onto something. "That is what a panic attack is like. Except it is ALL THE TIME." It's all that and more.

I turned, and ran the 12 or so blocks back to my hotel room where I had a couple of Valiums in my shaving kit. A legally obtained and carefully controlled supply of Valium.

I got to my room, washed one down with water, and then curled up on the bed, weeping and shaking for an hour or so in the fetal position to wait it out. After a while I felt better, although still weak and pretty wobbly. I didn't want to be alone, so I walked the half hour or so back to the Unicorn where Stan was in full flight, singing some chorus song with Margaret Christl and others, and holding a pint in his hand, with a dozen or so empties on the table in front of him. I sat down next to someone and a volunteer came by and handed me a beer. I looked at it. I knew full well it wasn't the best thing to do, but I was thirsty after a couple hours of the sweating terrors.

So I took a careful sip, and nursed it along, listening to the singing and watching the other folk in the room chatting and having fun. Presently I was aware of a beautiful and extraordinary warmth spreading through me. I couldn't remember ever feeling so good. So happy. So in love with the world and every person in it. Holy shit.

I looked my glass. This was just one beer. And .5 mg of Valium as well. Someone set another beer in front of me, and I looked carefully at it. Hmm. I felt confident, and strong and able to handle anything. One more couldn't hurt.

And then some other part of my brain was speaking to me. The smart part. The very small, almost impossible to locate smart part that I almost never listened to.

"Okay, asshole... Just this once, I am going to allow this. You can have ONE more beer. But that is it. And it is the last time. And you and I are going to have a very serious talk tomorrow morning."

I woke the next day after a lovely and restful sleep, and knew I could never do that again. Alcohol was one thing. If I was going to be addicted to that, at least I had easy access to it. But Valium was strictly controlled, and needed a doctor's prescription. Getting my hands on what would surely be an ever increasing supply was going to eventually take every waking hour, and probably all of my income. And I didn't want to end up on a corner in a mini skirt and uncomfortable heels like the young girls a few blocks away.

I ran into Paxton later that night as I was working out an electric guitar part for a new song Stan had written. It was a lovely and dreamy piece called "Lockkeeper", partly inspired by a story from "The Wind in the Willows," which was a favourite of ours growing up. I still have Stan's copy somewhere. It was a gift from his first serious girlfriend and is inscribed, "To my own big bunny." There's an image for you.

I was in the dressing room trailer with my Telecaster and amplifier, learning how to play volume swells by using my left hand to tap the note on the fret board with the volume off, and with my right hand using the volume control to bring the sound up. It removes the "attack" of the note, the plucking sound. With a little delay and reverb it is a beautiful and spooky effect, very violin-like. I had stolen it from listening to John Martyn records, and I have employed it ever since. Tom was sitting across from me, listening.

"How are you doing that?"

"Sorry, I know it sounds kind of weird when you don't have the context. Probably sounds weird anyway."

"No, I like it."

So I gave him the Tele and he slung the thing around his neck, and I
wished at the time I'd had a camera. I showed him the basic technique,
and he spent a few minutes with it, but it takes a different kind of
coordination, and he soon passed it back to me.
He stood up. "I'd keep at it. It sounds good."
And he left.
Nice guy.

Speaking of which, Paxton went well out of his way for me a few years
later, when I was touring Alberta with him and Connie Kaldor. We were
playing big rooms all over the province and the distances were such
that they were flying to the shows. I was driving. I had given up on air
travel after Stan's death, and the days behind the wheel followed by
a high pressure show were killing me. That, coupled with the return
of my depression and the anxiety attacks had me in a bad way. I was
getting no sleep, and was unable to eat. I was without my medication
and had gone back to drinking to try to control the panic.
Tom could see I was struggling, and one morning he hunted me down
at the hotel where I was staying in Calgary and offered to take me to an
AA meeting.
  "No, Tom, thanks anyway. I'm fine." I lied.
  "I know you're not fine Garnet. You're trying to white knuckle it,
and I can tell you it never works. You need help. There's an AA meeting
in every town, and I'll sponsor you and take you to meetings for the rest
of the tour."
  "No thanks, really. I'm good."
  "Okay." I could hear the disbelief in his voice. "Let me know if you
change your mind."
It was a kind and generous thing to do, and I paid him back by shocking
and annoying him that night. We were playing in Red Deer, and in spite
of my condition, I went out and managed to do a pretty decent show.
Tom was in the wings, watching and being supportive, and as I walked
off the stage he looked out and saw I was getting a standing ovation.
  "Looks like you blew me off the stage."
I clapped him on the shoulder and said, "Hell Tom, for an extra 5 bucks
I would have blown you ON the stage."
He's been a bit leery of me ever since.

But once again, I digress.

I left the trailer a bit later and found Stan backstage to the right of the
big speaker towers, and talking quietly into a small microphone. He
was reading from some scribbled notes.

"This is the time I love best. It's a clear night, and you can still see a few stars above the city through the tangled branches of the ancient willows. The crowd is out there waiting in the darkness, and in a few minutes I am going to be up on that stage. On my left I will have Big Jim, from Innisfail Alberta, playing bass, and on the other side my brother Garnet, my strong right arm, on fiddle and guitar."
There was more to come, but he noticed me and switched off the machine.

"You ready to go?"

"Yeah, we should get back stage. I think I've figured out that part for "Lockkeeper." That weird guitar thing? I played it for Paxton and he liked it."

"Great." He wound up the mic cable and shoved everything into his shoulder bag. He turned and picked up a Styrofoam cup and tossed back whatever was in it, then crumpled it and threw it into a garbage bin. He wiped his mouth and suppressed a belch.
I was downwind. Ah. Single malt. Lovely, even second hand.

He said, "Let's get after it."

The next day I ran into Stan as he carried a large blackboard and tripod across the compound.

"What's all this in aid of?"

"Song writing workshop. I'm going to try and come up with something on the spot in front of the audience."
Right. I had forgotten about this.
The plan was for Stan to get in front of a small group of people in a tent, and have them toss out ideas for a song, and then they would discuss where the story was going to go next, and who the characters were, until the song was done. It was an interesting alternative to the way workshops had developed over the years.
These days, most performers, particularly the young ones, see the workshop merely as a way of plugging their latest record, and there is almost no interaction between them and the other performers on stage. In recent years I have learned to bring something to read. But once upon a time, performers would get together on a workshop stage and try to interact with each other a bit. Maybe play along if they knew the song, or if it wasn't too complex. It felt important to get the audience involved and maybe even singing along.
I have fond memories of sitting on various stages over the years, with Steve Goodman, and Martin, Bogan and the Armstrongs, and watching the sparks fly. The workshop would develop into a party, and Louie the fiddler player would be out in the audience, playing and dancing and rubbing up against girls young enough to be his granddaughters, who

in turn were dancing and laughing and rubbing right back. The whole thing would end up a sweaty ecstatic and tangled mess. Louie would be at the side of the stage at the end, giving out little trinkets and necklaces he'd made himself, along with the number and location of his hotel room, the hound. He was in his 60's back then. They must have had to keep him in a cage back when he was young.
That was folk music back in my day, you young whippersnappers.

And dammit, I digress again.
Stan had pitched the idea of this solo workshop, and the festival bit at it. He set up the blackboard in small tent in front of some folding chairs, and a dozen or so people sat and threw out suggestions. I didn't stay for the whole thing, but within a few minutes he had scribbled a list of ideas and potential plot lines using pieces of different coloured chalk. I don't think he had ever worked in such a formal way before, laying out the arc of a story the way a novelist might do before beginning a project. And it was working without a net in a big way. I was impressed that he was willing to try something so out of his usual comfort zone, where to fail was to fail in public.
I also remember wondering if he was going to share writing credit with the audience should he come up with something worth saving. It could be awkward.
I decided I needed a coffee or two and drifted away. When I came back at the end of the hour, he had the bare bones of "The Last Watch on the Midland."

CHAPTER 81

I Leave The Band

"You can always quit, you know."
The sad part is I don't even remember what the fight was initially about.
I do remember Stan and me standing nose to nose, and yelling at each
other back stage before a show. I expect as usual, it had to do with some
minor detail, a disagreement that sane people would have bumped up
against, and had a reasoned discussion, and then come to some sort of
equitable solution. Sane people might have, but this was us.
We had been getting busier and more exhausted by the week. There was
another album in the near future, but as we were on the road almost
constantly, and Stan's time at home was busier than ever, we had only a
couple of new songs. He had no time for reflection or reading, and
given that much of what he was writing was to have some sort of
historical basis, he was falling behind.
The planned album was going to be a big budget affair.
Our company, Fogarty's Cove Music and the CBC under the aegis of
Paul Mills were going to partner together and combine funds, and a
truly enormous recording tentatively called "the Great Lakes Project"
was on the schedule for the very near future.
Paul this time was going to have the money to bring in an orchestra and
an arranger, and as many outside musicians as it took to erase any trace
of the core sound of the band. This was not just my opinion or take on
it. He was quite upfront about it in meetings with us months before the
recording started. He even said as much in a press statement after the
whole sorry and embarrassing mess was released.
Stan and I had had many heated discussions about Paul's approach
over the years, but the situation was becoming particularly difficult as
this project was getting closer.
     "It's the band, you and me and Jim who go out every goddamned
night and sell the records. Why is he so intent on getting rid of us when
we get into the studio?"
Stan was in a bad place. He hadn't been happy with Paul's work for
some time, partly for his own reasons, and also because I wouldn't shut

up about it. I had been bitching about Paul's presence at live shows for years, and the antipathy between us in the studio as regards how the albums were produced and rearranged had been a constant sore point ever since the first recording.

"This is going to be the last project with Paul. I promise."

"Right. Sure."

"No, I want to try something else next time. Maybe have a shot at producing one ourselves."

That sounded better.

"I'd like that."

"But I owe him. He's my friend and he has been there for me all these years, and he's been there for you too."

"No, he's been there for you. I've just been excess baggage to him. He's been trying to get rid of me right from the beginning."

"Yeah, well, Okay. For me. But it's not like you haven't benefitted."

Fair enough. The huge amount of CBC work that Paul had brought Stan's way and the resulting exposure particularly back in the early days, had kept us from utter starvation. I had to give him that. But he'd always hired the trio only grudgingly, and when all was said and done I simply didn't want to work with him again, either live or in the studio.

At least now it was out there that Paul's days as producer were numbered. Stan had said it, and I was going to do my best to hold him to it.

In the meantime, this huge and expensive and as yet unwritten project was on our immediate horizon and the stress was terrible.

Stan had also received a commission to write a half dozen or so songs for the opening of the new Frank Slide Memorial Centre in the Crowsnest Pass in Alberta. They wanted a series of recordings which would be played as visitors wandered through the exhibits.

There was also a rumour of another recording project in the future, most likely at the behest of Mitch Podolak. It was to be a full album's worth of songs written about the Winnipeg General Strike, and the history of Labour struggles in Manitoba.

And then on top of all that, we got an approach from a fellow in Pennsylvania who wanted us to record a bare bones, all-acoustic album of traditional songs, and was willing to put up the funds. Stan didn't have it in him to refuse. More pressure and now even less time. The only good thing about the idea of doing a traditional album was that we would be producing it ourselves, and in doing so could pick up a few studio moves. It would be handy when we went in to do the next band album without Paul.

With all of this on our plates, it didn't help that my own health was still at best, fragile. I had finally found a doctor who'd been able to correctly diagnose my clinical depression, but that was only after a couple of years of hell for me and for everyone around me. I was only now beginning the long process of backing away from the abyss, and our schedule was such that my wheels could fly off at any moment. Whatever it was, and whenever it was, Stan and I had had a disagreement about some small thing, and instead of it being discussed and resolved, he had fallen back on his old standby, which he had used for years whenever things got thick.

"You can be replaced you know. It's my name on the poster, and fiddlers are a dime a dozen. If you don't like it, you can always quit." That stopped the discussion as it always did, resolving nothing, and I shut up, and we did the gig. But afterwards, the more I thought about it, the more sense it made for me to leave.

I had been on the road almost nonstop for 8 or so years, and dead broke for most of that time. I was beyond tired, and dangerously ill. And I now had someone at home whom I missed all the time, and I wanted desperately to be with her. I needed sleep and decent food, and regular hours, and if I was going to continue to work with the band I needed to feel that what I was doing had some sort of value, and that I was being respected and acknowledged for my work. I had lost track of the times I'd been fired or had been threatened with being fired before or after a show somewhere in North America. Simply being told that I could take it or leave it every time I disagreed with Stan was intolerable. We were coming up on a break from the road. The time was right.

I got home and discussed it with Gail, and I'm sure she quailed at the thought of having to support the two of us. But she supported my decision, and I called Stan and told him the news.

It was a very brief conversation.

"I'm coming over."

He arrived where Gail and I were living about half an hour later.

It was a fairly tense meeting.

"What's all this?"

He had sat down and lit up a smoke.

"I'm tired. I am tired of the shit we're having to go through on the road. I'm tired of fighting with you, and I'm tired of you simply telling me that I can always quit, whenever we have a disagreement. If that is what all these years of work and loyalty are worth then fuck it. That's what I'm going to do. I'm quitting."

He was perched like a circus elephant on the tiny footstool by my favourite chair next to the fireplace. He wasn't saying anything, so I continued.

"Every time we disagree about something you tell me fiddlers are a

dime a dozen, and I can always be replaced. Well, fine. I'm sure you're right. I never made any pretensions about being a good fiddler. But let's see you find a fiddler who also plays guitar. Let's see you find one who plays flute and electric guitar as well. How about a fiddler who can sing harmony and lead vocals, and tell jokes on stage? And good luck finding a fiddler who is willing to drive around the fucking planet in that stinking van and put up with your bullying and daily bullshit. Let's see you find that one magic guy. I think you're gonna need a bigger payroll."
He finished his smoke, stubbed it out on the hearth, and began to light another.
"Don't do that."
"What?"
"I'm sick of having to breathe in your smoke all the time. I don't want you smoking in here anymore."
Boy, I was getting feisty.
He put the cigarette back in the pack, and put the pack in his breast pocket.
He still wasn't saying anything.
I had the bit in my teeth by now, and with nothing left to lose I said, "And I am sick and tired of you never standing up for me around Paul. I have had your back all these years, through every shitty little gig we have ever done, and the whole time he has shown zero respect for me, and has done his best to undermine me in the studio. And you have never stood up for me or Jim, or David, when he was playing with us. And I'm fed up with it."
Stan cleared his throat. "He's my friend. I'm trying to be loyal to..."
"Yeah, and I'M supposed to be your fucking friend too, as well as your brother. Where's your loyalty to me? Where's your loyalty to the band? I've had enough. I want out."
And that was that. To my astonishment and relief he didn't say anything or break my neck.
He just stood up and left the apartment.

There was no more discussion about it, just complete radio silence, except after that a week or   two he dropped over without calling beforehand. We were polite enough with each other, and I poured him a coffee, and he lit a Rothman's and sat down in my chair.
I looked at him, and he said, "Oh, sorry," and got up to put the cigarette out in the fireplace.
"It's okay. Never mind."
I got up and went into the kitchen, and pulled an ashtray out from under the sink and brought it back into the living room.

He put it on the arm of the chair, took a drag, and began talking in an offhand way about what was going on in his life. Big things were happening. Jim Fleming had been booking shows like crazy. The Fall was looking really busy. The annual gig in Bermuda was coming up in the Spring. He had a run in the Maritimes, including two nights at the Rebecca Cohn. There was a tour of Newfoundland after that, playing the big halls we'd done years before with Ryan's Fancy. Now he was headlining. There was a big tour coming up in late May of next year on the West coast, all the way down to Los Angeles and from there to a festival in Texas. Then, back to New England. All kinds of well paying, cushy gigs. The years of grim and dismal low rent gigs and fighting for life in the bars looked like finally paying off.

He took a drag of his smoke, and exhaled and put his feet up. He waved his cigarette about.

"I can guarantee you, I will be playing a solo show at the National Arts Centre within the year."

I was sitting on the couch across the room, with my knees pulled up against my chest and sipping a coffee. A body language expert might have had a field day in that room.

I shrugged and said, "That all sounds great. Have you found a new fiddler?"

"No, but I'm getting lots of calls."

"Are you holding auditions? Anyone I know?"

"We're playing some big rooms in New England in the spring too. Not just the usual round of clubs. Payne Hall at Harvard. The Academy of Music in Northampton."

"Great. Really. I'm happy for you. Have you talked to Fleming about me leaving?"

"No."

"Better get on it. He's your agent. He deserves to know. I can make the call if you like."

"No. I'll do it."

We had made no mention of me hanging on until he did find a replacement. I had decided that I was leaving immediately in lieu of whatever pathetic severance there might be.

We talked a bit more about other things, and then Gail came home from her job at the television station, and it was time for me to make dinner. He left.

Maybe a week or so later, Gail and I were visiting Mum and Dad in Woodburn.

Most uncharacteristically, Mum was saying nothing. I don't know whether she was scared and upset about this huge schism between her sons, and didn't know what to say, or if she was simply suffering from an unprecedented case of diplomacy.

In any case, nothing about the fight or my leaving the band was said until we were getting ready to go.

Mum went to the buffet in the dining room and pulled out a manila envelope.

"Here." She said. "Stan was here the other day. He left this for you."

"What is it?"

"Open it."

I pulled the flap back and inside there were a few sheets of paper, with Stan's handwriting.

The gist of the message was that in return for me paying him the sum of 1 (one) dollar, he was signing over to me 49% of his writing and publishing, for all his songs, both current and future, in recognition of my hard work and loyalty.

I handed it back to Mum.

"I don't want it. It's too little, too late. And if he's going to hand out shit like this it should be you and Dad getting it. God knows he owes you."

Mum said, "Please. Just take it."

She never cried about anything, but her hand was shaking badly and she was looking at the floor.

Shit.

I was still furious.

"I'm not coming back to the band. Not for this."

"He knows that."

Fine. I guess I should let him make the gesture. I didn't want to spend the rest of my life not talking to him.

I felt in my pocket.

"I don't have a dollar."

Mum said, "I'll lend you one."

"Fine. But this doesn't change a thing."

"I know."

I'm not sure how much time passed, a couple of weeks anyway, and I have no memory of when or where we met, but Stan and I had a meeting, and I agreed to come back to the band after we both laid down some ground rules. No more tantrums. No more firings. No more walking out. At least not without some sort of calm and reasonable discussion, preferably with a third party like Jim Fleming present to mediate.

Nothing more was ever said about the publishing.

CHAPTER 82

The Great Lakes Project

So I was back and nothing else had changed.

Between the frenzy that was now our life on the road, and the frenzy that was his all too brief time at home, Stan was still getting no opportunity to write. In past years he had always been able to keep something going on the back burner, some tune, or a fragment of a verse which he would toss around in his head, sometimes for months. The long hours behind the wheel were perfect for quiet reflection, when he could turn a phrase over and over and look at it and think about where it might fit with another. But now we were now spending much more time in airports and taxis as we were flying to shows, and it was not a sane or calm or reflective way to travel.

He'd had periods of time before where no new songs were arriving, and he had mostly didn't worry about it. We always had other people's songs to work up, however briefly, to change the show, and the whole vast canon of traditional music was there for the taking as well. He knew something would come along eventually.

When the drought broke it was usually signaled by him waking up with a tune in his head. If he was lucky he might be able to spend a moment or two with the guitar nailing down the chord changes, so as to be able to work on it during the day's drive. But more often he just seemed to be able to mull it over and let the words and tune unfold. He referred to the process as "the record player inside my head." But it had been a while since he'd heard from it or had the time to pursue whatever he was hearing.

Meanwhile, we were still facing what Stan was calling "The Great Lakes Project," and we needed new songs.

Paul wanted more than anything else to get Stan into the studio and surround him with a much bigger sound. He'd been granted a massive budget compared to what he'd had to work with in the past, and he envisioned hiring a full orchestra with an arranger, and getting in the sidemen he was used to working with over the years at the CBC. The trio wasn't going to factor into it at all anymore. Maybe he felt this

666

would make some difference in our lack of commercial airplay, although a brief glance at what was current and hot on the radio in those days would have put that to rest. A fat prematurely bald folksinger with more than a passing resemblance to Burl Ives was not going to compete with Bruce Springsteen or bands like The Police, no matter how many faceless sidemen got hired, or how many syrupy string tracks you buried him in. In any case, the results speak for themselves. The album had a few good songs, but the production was a disaster.

Stan needed the space to write. He wangled an Arts Council grant and was able to rent a small basement office on Locke Street in Hamilton. He moved in with a desk, a swivel chair and a coffee pot, and commenced keeping regular writing hours. He would arrive in the morning, brew up a pot, and get out the guitar. Down the hall he could hear his neighbours arriving for work, and aside from the woman one door down whom he suspected was running a rub and tug parlor, it was quiet.

I don't know how many songs came out of that office. It wasn't his usual way of working. He was reading a lot of history and travelling around the province, looking for stories.

He made a day trip to Welland to watch the big boats glide by on the canal between Lake Erie and Lake Ontario. It was likely to get more of a sense of atmosphere during the time he was working on "Lock Keeper." In any event, it was a pleasant day trip under the guise of working.

He also went to Port Dover on the shore of Lake Erie, as part of his research for "Tiny Fish for Japan," and was able to cadge a trip out on the water on board a turtleback fishing boat. They're called turtlebacks because they have no open deck space at all. The entire boat is enclosed topside to provide shelter against the cold wind and spray. Stan was a pretty good sailor, and he'd never got sick during any of the dozens of rough ferry crossings we'd made over the years in the Maritimes. But Lake Erie is really shallow, and the waves are nasty and choppy. The salami sandwich which Diane/Ariel had so kindly packed for his lunch, and which Stan had wolfed down before setting out was launched like a navy depth charge off the side of the boat a couple of miles off shore, and Stan came back looking pretty green and shaky.

Stan and Jim and I held a rehearsal at the apartment Gail and I shared on Bold Street one afternoon.

Stan had a new song he wanted to run by us. He tuned the guitar to open G, and capoed up to A, and began. It was "White Squall." As the story about the young kid unfolded I could feel my eyes stinging. I felt there was a little bit of me in there, with the line about "the pictures of the girl he'd wed in spring."

Gail and I were still very new to each other then, and still deep in the throes of first love, and Stan had had to put up with a lot of moody silences and sighing and tears from me on the road, as I wanted nothing more than to be home with her. I was unable to think about anything else, and couldn't stop talking about her.

He never said anything about it but I always felt the song was a little nod to me, and a gift, part of that secret code our family used. That he killed the kid off in the song was probably just wishful thinking on his part.

He ran it by us twice, and then Jim and I began the process of sorting out what we were going to play. I decided to use my new 12 string, and by the end of the afternoon we had an arrangement, and the song had come together nicely.

There was another day when he and Jim came over. Stan had just finished "The Last Watch on the Midland," the piece he had begun at the songwriting workshop at the Calgary Festival. He had Dad and Mansel Davies from Calgary in tow, and I know the story of a man facing a bleak and shabby future after a lifetime of hard and honourable work resonated pretty deeply with our Dad. Having blown his knees out at age 50 and being faced with living on a tiny disability pension was not what he had likely envisioned for himself as a young man. He'd felt largely pushed aside and humiliated.

He and Mum had both recently begun getting paid a small salary for their work for the record company, and Stan and I both foresaw a day when it would be an actual living wage, but to Dad, it might have felt a bit like charity.

In any case when the song was over, Dad got up and walked out to the kitchen. Mansel, being a kind and sensitive man, followed and poured Dad a shot of Glenlivet and they had a quiet drink and a chat while the trio began running through the song.

With only a handful of the songs written, sessions began at Grant Avenue Studios in Hamilton. Bob and Dan Lanois had long since moved out of their mom's basement, and had set up in a two storey brick house just around the corner from where I had worked as a waiter that one terrible summer years before. It was a comfortable place to work, with a nice mixture of new equipment along with the older stuff that the lads had searched out because they had great ears, and they were smart.

Things were difficult and confused for the three of us, starting a project

with no clear idea of where it might be going, and only a few songs
written and road tested. The situation was made worse by the size of
the budget looming over us. The amount of money on the line wasn't
having any kind of freeing effect. It just meant that so much more was
at stake, and we now had an office full of bean counters back at the CBC
looking for results. What finished it off for me was that Paul was now
completely in charge, and had brought with him an engineer from the
CBC who had at best, only average engineering abilities, and zero social
skills.

The act of recording requires a great deal of trust and support between
the various parties. My own experience over the last 30 odd years
has been that the producer spends more time acting as a midwife for
the people doing the playing. If the musician is uncomfortable, or
feeling anxious or not hearing well, it is the job of the producer and
the engineer to fix that and try to draw out the best performance they
can. Paul and David Dobbs the engineer, made no secret of their lack of
respect for both me and Jim now that they were firmly in control. And
it made working with them even more of a trial.

Jim Morison had almost no experience in the studio and was sick with
nerves. And given the songs we were trying to lay down were very new
he was having a bad time of it. And he was getting no support at all,
either from Paul, or our civil service engineer.

No encouraging comments like, "That was great, but maybe try the last
half again," or any of the other kindly lies and helpful bullshit one uses
in those circumstances when a player is having issues with the part,
or is simply intimidated by the tense atmosphere and the dreaded red
"RECORDING" light.

Just utter silence after a failed take, and then a terse "Try it again," over
the intercom.

Jim was sweating bullets. While the rest of us would break for lunch
at the restaurant around the corner, Jim would sit and eat his brown
bagged sandwiches and rehearse the songs. After I realised that was
how he was spending his time, I took to hanging back and running the
tunes with him on my guitar during the break.

I was in the control room one afternoon, sitting against the back wall,
watching as Jim was trying to put down a part, and after he had nailed
it Paul turned to Dobbs, shrugged, and said, "Well, I guess it'll do, but
he's no Tom Szczesniak," Tom Szczesniak, being the current go-to bass
player at CBC sessions.

That was it for me. We loved Jim. He was a great player, with great
ideas, and he was a wonderful friend, and a sweet and funny guy on
the road. He never gave less than a hundred per cent for us, and we
felt lucky and blessed to have him on the left side of the stage. Whether

he was up to Paul's CBC standards didn't matter. We were a band. We were THE band. Paul and Dobbs were just outsiders, and I had no illusions that they weren't making exactly the same mean spirited comments about me when I was out there.

I walked out onto the floor where Jim was sitting hunched over his bass, collecting himself, and patted him on the shoulder, and ruffled his hair. "That was great, Buford. Good work. Take a break."

Now it was my turn. I was trying to put down a flute track, and was having a pretty hard time of it. The part itself wasn't an issue. I'd written it , and I knew could play it, but I was nervous and frazzled and pissed off, and that is the last thing one needs in the studio, particularly trying to play flute. The muscles in the face and around the mouth get tense and your embouchure goes to hell. It becomes impossible to play in tune. I'd screw up a take and look to the control room and see the two of them smoking and conferring and no doubt bemoaning how someone else could have done a better job. Well, no argument there.

I stepped away from the mic and put the flute down.

"I need a break."

Then I went upstairs.

Stan was sitting with a cigarette in one hand and a cold congealed coffee in the other, looking at a dozen or so pages covered in scribble. His guitar was in the corner. He was trying to finish yet another song. He looked up at me. His face looked tired and haggard.

"What's up?"

I sat down and said very quietly, "Okay. I know we are in a tough place here. You're under a lot of pressure, and you and I haven't been doing so well with each other lately. And I'm sorry. But I need to say this right now. Here is the deal. I will play any gig anywhere you want for whatever money, or no money, as long as you need me, but I am never going to work with Paul again. I'm done with him. I'm willing to see this project through, but I don't want him in the studio while I'm working. And if you want to do another record with him, hire someone else to play in my place. It's what he's wanted all along anyway. I've had it. Okay?"

Stan nodded. "I know." He rubbed his face. "I'm fed up too. I promised you, this is the last project with Paul. We'll get a little seasoning with this traditional record, and learn a few moves, and when the time comes we'll do the next one ourselves."

"Yeah, you said that before. But have you talked about this with him yet?"

"No, but I will. I made a promise. I'm just waiting for the right moment. He's not going to be happy."

"Okay. But I'm gonna hold you to it."
He nodded and waved me away, and pulled the pages he was working on back towards him.
I got up and went back downstairs. I could hear a flute. What the Hell was this?
I opened the door to the studio floor, and Dobbs was standing in front of the microphone with the head phones on, playing my damned flute to the track.
I walked over and very carefully took it away from him and began disassembling it and wiping his filthy spit off it.
"You never touch someone else's flute. Never."
"I was just trying to..."
I leaned into his face.
"I don't give a fuck what you were trying to do. Don't ever touch anything of mine ever again."
I don't know how I managed not to hit him.
I packed it up along with my violin and guitars and amp, and had the secretary upstairs call me a cab and I went home.

In the end it was me who got to drop the big one on Paul. We were in Toronto, at CBC Studio 4S. We had taken a meal break, and somehow or other Paul and I were eating, just the two of us, at the same table at an outdoor cafe on Yonge Street. I wouldn't have sought out his company alone, but Stan had failed to join us. I suspected he had gone off with Claude Desjardins, the drummer, and was getting tightened up. Claude liked his cocaine, and unlike most coke users was fairly generous about sharing it. Stan was developing a serious taste for it.
During the meal with Paul I let slip that this was the last time out for him, and we were going to find someone else to work with on the next project, whenever that happened.
I looked him right in the eyes and I lied.
"It's nothing personal."
He was understandably very upset.
"Well I certainly take it personally. I take it very, very personally. I brought you guys this far. I'm part of the team."
No. He wasn't part of the team. And he never was. We were the team. He was Stan's friend, and Stan was endlessly loyal to his friends, but for the band Paul was an intrusion; a stubborn and to our ears, merely competent impediment to our own plans, with only a limited number of ideas as to how to further enhance the music we had worked so hard to develop. Moreover, his continued unwanted presence at live shows was driving a wedge into the act.
Dan Lanois had not yet struck gold with U2 or Bob Dylan, or any of

the other heavy weights he would later work with, but he had proved himself capable of doing wonderful work and we liked him as a friend as well. He had a relaxed and experimental attitude to the recording process and it occurred to me more than once that it was ironic that while we were struggling with Paul in the studio that Dan had built, Dan himself was sitting upstairs twiddling his thumbs.

There were many other really good producers out there who'd actually had to make it in the real world on the strength of their talent. And I wanted to try working with at least one of them.

So I was enjoying our little talk.

"Well, I'm sorry but we're moving on. We're going to finish this project, however long it takes, and then have a shot at doing this traditional album ourselves. After that we're going to look at someone we can collaborate with, or maybe even just continue on our own."

He was not happy. He started in at me again about how key he had been to our success, but I didn't care and had stopped listening.

He got up and threw a few bills on the table and left the restaurant.

I felt great. It was a sunny day, and a huge weight had been lifted from my shoulders.

Moreover, Paul had just paid for lunch. I caught the waiter's eye and ordered another beer.

I know there were discussions between Paul and Stan, and I have no doubt at all that Paul has a much different memory of the project and the time around it than I do. And I am doubly sure he has no memory at all of being told he was on the way out.

But he was. Stan had promised me that we were finished working with Paul, and I meant to hold him to the promise when the time came.

In the meantime, fate had managed to find a way to tighten the screws down on us even further.

A guy named Tor Jonassen from Philadelphia had approached Stan a few months previous   with the idea of doing an album of traditional songs for his little family-run boutique label.

If we were willing to go into the studio, just the three of us, and lay down some simple bare bones arrangements of mostly Maritime tunes, he would put up the money.

The timing was completely wrong. We were already stretched too thin, and besides, doing another record of traditional Maritime-themed stuff was potentially going to put us back in that pigeon hole again, and I hated the idea. But Stan didn't have it in him to say no.

So, in spite of once again having nothing ready we began going into Grant Avenue during what was supposed to have been our days off, and putting down whatever Stan had dug up, dusted off, and hammered into shape the night before. We recorded a couple of our Uncle Lee Bushell's songs, mostly as a a nod to him, and a thank you for the gift of the homemade guitar all those years ago. And Stan set one our Grandfather's poems to a traditional acapella tune. It wasn't a great poem by anybody's standards, and Stan was forced to perform some clumsy surgery on the tune to make it fit the words.

It was for the most part a pretty weak collection of material, and if we'd had our wits about us we'd have pushed the project into the future when we might have had more time and been better able to prepare. But once you get on a roll it becomes difficult to say no to anyone or anything, and other parts of your life are going to suffer, and inevitably the wheels are going to come off.

It's easy enough to say with hindsight, but I have felt that had the ultimate disaster not happened, and Stan had lived, we still would have had a major crisis on our hands within maybe 6 months to a year. The amount of touring we were doing and the resulting strain on Stan's home life in particular, and my still fragile health, and the massive writing projects on the horizon, and the lame and repetitive shows we were now doing, and the unfocussed substandard records we were making all would have combined to bring us to a complete halt, and there would have been an inevitable shake up and reassessment in our world.

For me, the one high point of the "For the Family" project was how good Stan's voice was suddenly sounding. We were working with an engineer named Greg Roberts, who had been dropped in on us one day to fill in for Dobbs who'd had to leave us one afternoon to go back to the CBC in Toronto to work his magic on someone else's recording. We'd been having another typically tense day. The band was sitting in the control room glaring at each other, and nothing was getting done. Dobbs left, and Greg came in and was introduced, and he sat down at the mixing desk.

I don't know how he did it, but within minutes the whole atmosphere of the room changed. People were smiling again, and shoulders were coming back down, and the afternoon suddenly got way more productive.

So when it came time to record "For the Family," we knew he was the guy we wanted. Back then he'd been mostly working with local Hamilton bands like Teenage Head, and The Forgotten Rebels, along with a trans-gender punk band from the States called Jayne County and the Electric Chairs, whose guitar player, Eliot Michael, in later years became one of my dearest friends. Not exactly in the same wheel house

artistically, as us, but Greg was quiet and helpful, with a great attitude
and wonderful ears, and was patient and willing to try anything, even
if it wasn't how they did it by the Book, back at the Corp.
We began to enjoy the work.

"Why can't Paul make my voice sound like that?"
Stan and I were listening to a quick mix of a song on the way home one
day. At my request he had taken a shot at recording "Cape St Mary,"
a song from Newfoundland, which had been a childhood favourite of
mine from listening to records by Omar Blondahl.
Stan had taken my 12 string, and laid down a breath-taking
performance at the very bottom of his vocal range. And whether it was
the fact that it was a bare bones recording of just him with my violin off
in the distance, or the wonderful old Neumann microphone Dan Lanois
had rescued from somewhere, or Greg's calm and supportive presence
in the room, it was an extraordinary moment, and I was reminded again
that in the midst of all the trouble and nonsense going on in our lives
right then, my brother had a supreme gift, and it was a blessing to be in
its presence.
We had a rehearsal at Jim's house in Brantford one morning, and Stan
had brought in a poem called "Three Fishers," by Charles Kingsley,
along with a scrap of a tune he'd either picked up somewhere or had
cobbled together on the spot. He had envisioned the song as an acapella
tune, but I borrowed his guitar, changed the tune around and found
some chords, and it seemed to work better as a band piece. When we
came to record it I once again went out onto the studio floor to record
a space echo violin to the song and it seemed to fit, in spite of Tor's
insistence that this be a straight folk album, with no tricks.
It only took a couple of takes, and I felt it was okay.
Greg hit the talk back and said, "That's great."
I said, "Let me take a listen," and went back into the control room.
Stan was sitting next to Greg, with a smoke in his hand.
"Was that okay?"
"Yeah," he said. "Tor's not gonna like it, but I do. It stays."
He went back upstairs, and once again began shuffling papers, trying to
finish yet another song for the Great Lakes Project.
I spent the rest of the afternoon layering up a dozen or so violin and
viola tracks for a song called "The Scarborough Settler's Lament." It
took a couple of hours to lay down, and in the end it was a real job to
try to sort out all the tracks and mix them into a cohesive section, as I'd
never before had the time and freedom to try such a thing. But Greg
did a great job of untangling it.
Oddly, Paul approached me a few days later at the CBC and said, "Stan

played me the tracks you did for that string section the other day."

"Yeah?" I didn't care about Paul's opinion at this point, good or bad.

"I think I should stay out of the studio when you're working from now on. You seem to do better without me."

Well, at least we agreed on something, and it was nice of him to say it.

We booked a couple more days to finish "For the Family," to do the final mixes.

We left town then, for a week or so of shows, and then we had to come back and continue work on the Great Lakes Project.

The songs Stan had been coming up with over the months we'd been trying to knit the whole mess together were uneven, ranging from the beautiful and moving "Last Watch, "and "White Squall," to substandard filler like "The Nancy," which had been inspired by Steeleye Span, and "Half of a Heart," which once again had him turning to his Joni Mitchell-inspired bag of lite jazz tricks.

He'd heard a story about a fellow somewhere around the Great Lakes who had discovered an old schooner which had been built in the Smith and Rhuland yards in Lunenburg back before the War, and which was in effect a sister ship to the Bluenose. The guy was trying to restore it single-handedly, and while the story might have had some appeal, the song Stan wrote about it, "Man with Blue Dolphin," sounded forced, and wasn't anywhere near his present standard of writing, and never got played in public more than once or twice.

"Flying "was another one. We managed to put together a bed track for it, but it didn't feel like a keeper, and it was put aside to be looked at later. It was only after Stan's death that it was taken any further. Paul brought in a studio guitarist to add some electric lead, and the background vocals were done by a woman from BC named Holly Arntzen, whom I think Paul had dreams of producing, and David Dobbs, who now seemed to feel his skills extended to being a singer as well as a lack lustre engineer and would-be flautist.

"MacDonnell on the Heights" had come from Stan's reading and research. He'd begun speculating about the now forgotten second in Command to General Sir Isaac Brock who had led an attack on Queenston Heights near Niagara Falls during the War of 1812, and was now apparently buried next to the General, like a pet spaniel.

Once again, the song felt forced, and would have been dropped as a bad bet had we not been under so much pressure to deliver the record. Stan didn't have the time or leisure to beat it into shape, or write something better. It went into the band repertoire for a couple of shows at the most, and then we gave up on it.

There were a couple of other songs which got tracked and then rejected

after sober second thought. There was "The Puddler's Tale," which was
also a lift from the style of Steeleye Span, and "Your Laker's Back in
Town," a bit of Country and Western boiler plate.
The whole project was becoming a desperate and scattered mess.

We had a couple more days to work on the recording before we left
for an extended tour that was going to take us from one end of the
continent to the other. Stan picked me up, and we drove into Toronto for
an evening session at Studio 4S. On the way, he played a tape of a new
song he wanted me to add a flute track to.

He said, "I've got Grit coming in to lay down a small pipes track for
this. Key of F."

"Fine."

He punched the tape into the dashboard and hit play.

Stan and Ariel had a neighbour in the little condo complex, who was
divorced and raising a couple of kids on her own. A good person, by all
accounts, and she had managed to save enough to take her daughters
back home to England to visit the folks. She and the girls were watching
the Horse Guards trot by near Buckingham Palace one morning, when
an IRA bomb was triggered, killing and injuring several of the guards
and their mounts, and blowing the woman's legs off at the knees.
Stan was devastated.

"Cowards. Worthless fucking cowards. The whole lot of them."

He felt very strongly that England had no business messing about in
Ireland, and that they should just get the hell out and let them sort their
own issues. But he had only hate and contempt for the kind of mind
that could see wiring up a baby carriage full of gelignite and nails,
and leaving it to explode in a crowded street as some sort of political
statement.

He was beside himself with rage for weeks.

"Hang them. Hang every last one of the sick murderous sons of
bitches. If I could, I'd sign up and volunteer to do it for them."

There was also a neighbour whom Stan had been complaining about
for some months, a loud and aggressive drunk who'd come over
from Ireland and moved into the little condo complex with his wife.
He'd come home from a night in the bars and smack her around until
either she or the neighbours called the cops. Stan had had to intervene
on a couple of occasions, and in between times the two of them had
exchanged words out in the parking lot. The asshole hinted that he had
"friends," powerful and dangerous friends, who, if he so much as said a
word would be happy to drop by and give Stan a short sharp lesson in
the fine old IRA tradition.

As Stan told the story, he had met with a couple of the other men on the street, and they had tossed around some plans to grab the guy up one night when he was too drunk to put up a fight and they would take him out to the countryside and maybe give him a taste of the same medicine. I don't know how much of that was true, or whether it was Stan just making a good story of it. And I have no memory of how the problem was resolved, or if it was resolved at all. But the song I was now hearing had the ring of truth, and I was left speechless once again at the extraordinary power of what Stan could do. The song was "House of Orange," and for a guy who always maintained that politics had no place on our stage, it was a hell of a manifesto.

"Wow."

"What do you think?"

I was having a little trouble with my voice, and I had literally broken into a cold sweat.

"Wow. I don't know what else to say. Just, fucking wow."

We got to the studio, and I laid down a basic flute track for the solo, which would combine nicely with Grit's small pipes. I don't recall if he was there to lay down his part at the time, or whether it was done while we were away.

That night was the last time we would be in the studio together, and the final time I would ever work with Paul, barring the session a few weeks after Stan's death when Paul called me in to Studio 4S.

"I need you to approve the mixes."

"What happens if I don't approve them?"

"We have to go with them anyway. We're thousands of dollars over budget."

Right.

CHAPTER 83

Last Tour / The East Coast

We were hitting the road with the hope that some time away from the stress and confusion of the studio might re-invigorate Stan's songwriting. We needed better material than what we were currently working with.

We played the Extemp in Minneapolis, and it was there we debuted "The House of Orange." We finished the first set with it, and while I was standing in the hallway with a beer a smallish guy came up and pushed into me.

"Hey you."

"Hello?"

"That last feckin' song. I want a feckin' word wit' you."

"Excuse me?"

He stuck his finger into my chest. "My brother is a freedom fighter in the IRA, and the feckin' English locked him away in H Block."

H Block, back in the day was the special part of the British prison system where they kept anyone they deemed a terrorist and a threat to the common good. God knows where they keep freedom fighters these days. There seem to be a lot of them about.

"H Block, huh?"

"Yer feckin' right."

"And a freedom fighter to boot. Wow. Tell you what," I pointed out Stan. "Why don't you go over and tell all that to the big bald guy? He's the one who wrote the song. I'm sure he'd love to hear from you."

"Right."

The guy left me and I could see him as he pushed between Stan and the woman he was talking to, and began poking his finger into Stan's chest, trying to back him into a corner. I was called away at the moment, and never found out what Stan did with the body.

We came back and did a show in Toronto, which was presented by our old buddy Harry Stinson, at a theatre near Bloor Street. Our parents were there, and Sylvia Tyson dropped by to say hello and sat with them for the show. It was about a 300 seat room, as I recall, and we had sold it out. We had agreed to a smallish guarantee versus a bigger payday after a certain number of tickets sold. It was a decent chunk of money for us, or would have been had Harry been ready to settle up on the night. But he claimed he didn't have the final figures, so we agreed to settle the back end of the deal later as we had to leave town the next day. I'm sure Harry has kept that money safe somewhere.

There was a quick trip to Bermuda, and this time we were able to bring our wives. Gail and I were billeted with a good looking young guy who I assumed was a doctor. Women kept coming to his little house and removing their clothing, staying for a bit, thanking him and then leaving.

For a change, we actually did a decent show at the end of our stay. There had been no drunken binges, no attacks on foreign submarines, no trips to the hospital. It was a quiet and sedate and peaceful little holiday.

We played some shows in Northern Ontario. We took our Dad along, as we had a run in Nova Scotia right after and he wanted to visit his brother Prescott in the Annapolis Valley.

We did a show at the Y'arc in Yarmouth, and then drove up to Halifax where we had two nights at the Rebecca Cohn. The first night was a gift from Eric Perth. There was some sort of professional association having their convention in town, and they had wanted an evening of entertainment laid on. Eric sold them on us for a flat fee, and then the next night would be ours for our regular audience.

We arrived, set up and did sound check, and then went back to the dressing rooms to get ready. About two hours before show time a lady from the front of the house came in and said to Stan, "You're wanted on the phone. It's your wife. She says it's an emergency."

Stan went pale and ran out of the room. Something might be wrong with one of the kids. Jim and I sat and waited. A half hour went by.

"Think we should go check on him?" Jim said.

I said, "There's nothing we can do," but we were beginning to really worry.

I got up to look for Dad, and found him with Eric Perth just behind the curtain, as Eric was giving some last minute instruction to the tech crew. We began chatting to pass the time, and it came up that Dad had boxed a bit in the Air Force during the war, and had tried to pass on a bit of what he had learned to Stan and me as kids, to help cope with the bullying. Eric bonded with Dad over that. He had been heavy weight champion of the Danish Navy back in the day.

That was no surprise to us. He was a hard, hard man. Enormously kind,

but under no circumstances would a sane person mess with him.
He turned to me.

"Let's see what you know."

He put his fists up and began a quick side to side shuffle, with his head tucked down between his shoulders.

"Come on, Eric, I just had a couple of lessons in the basement, and I would never call myself a..."

Just then, he moved in and did a quick left-right-left feint at my midsection and face, not intending to hit, just being playful.

I clumsily brought up my guard, and back-pedaled a couple of steps. I tripped over a cable, and then went windmilling into a full set of drums back by the wall. The crash sounded like a car wreck on the highway and when I came to rest there was a terrible pain in my right elbow, and my arm was hanging useless.

At first I thought I'd broken the elbow, which is pretty much the kiss of death for a fiddle player, not to mention a dedicated drinker. But it turned out I had simply smashed down on the sensitive ulnar nerve, and the arm was only paralysed. Eric and Dad had pulled me out of the wreckage and stood me up.

I couldn't move my arm at all, and I was terrified. How the hell was I going to do a show? Eric was sick with remorse. He ran and found a bag of ice and sat me down on a chair and began fussing over me, and apologizing over and over.

"It's okay Eric, you didn't mean to do it."

But I was worried. The feeling was slow to come back.

After maybe 10 minutes I was able to move my fingers and close them into a fist. But I still couldn't lift the arm properly, and show time was getting ever closer.

Stan came back to the dressing room, and he looked awful.

There had been no emergency. The kids were fine. Everybody was okay. But Stan was sweating and shaking, and I could see he'd been crying.

I picked up the bottle of Glenlivet with my left hand and pulled the cork out with my teeth. I spat the cork out and poured a couple of shots.

He looked at me and said, "What's wrong with you? What's with the pirate routine?"

"I'm okay. Eric and I were fooling around a bit and I fell down. My arm's just a bit sore."

Stan took the drink and sank about half of it. Then he put the glass down and got up and went into the washroom to blow his nose and wipe his eyes.

I followed him and stood in the doorway while he dried his face.

"What's going on with you?"

He waved me away. "I'm alright. I'm fine." But he wasn't, he was a mess, shaky and distracted and in no condition to go out in front of 1200 people.

A stage hand came in.
"Showtime."
We had to go.
Most of the people out in the audience had not seen us before. We were just the entertainment for their little conference, so we only got a lukewarm reception when we went out. And when we finished the first song it wasn't the wild and rapturous response we were used to, and as a result all our timing went to shit.
Halfway into the second song I looked at Stan's eyes and knew he was coming up dry with the lyric. I quickly moved my mic stand in closer to his, as I had learned to do over these past few months, and fed him the next line, and that was what I had to do for the rest of the night.
My right arm slowly came back to life, but for the first half hour or so I had to hold the bow stationary and awkwardly move the fiddle back and forth.
It was a shambles.
We staggered through the gig and left the stage to polite applause.
Stan was sitting and rocking in the chair in the dressing room, and crying with his head in his hands. Eric was patting him on the shoulder and saying, "It's okay. You did fine. No one out there noticed."
   "But I noticed. I fucking noticed. It's the Cohn. I fucked up on stage at the Cohn."
There was nothing we could say to help him.
We were fine the next night. There was no last minute phone call, my arm was working again, and the hall was filled with people who were happy to see us. It was a great night, and for once it was just the trio, and no guitar playing interloper had been dropped in.
I think the next day we drove up to Canso for a quick visit to see Aunt June and Uncle Sam, and then continued on to Glace Bay. We might have played the Savoy Theatre there. We may have just visited with Dad's eldest brother, Emerson. I simply don't remember.
I do remember leaving Dad near the exit to the ferry terminal. We were going to Newfoundland for our first headlining tour of the big Arts Centres, and he was going to go back to the Annapolis Valley to continue his visit with his brother.
There was an odd moment as we parted.
As I have mentioned, we had never been a touchy-feely family. Stan and I had always hugged each other, and lately had even taken to kissing each other hello and goodbye on the cheek, but for our Dad, the biggest display of affection he could muster was a crushing handshake with

the eyes carefully averted. This time however, he moved in past Stan's outstretched hand and gave him a hug. I could see Stan's face over Dad's shoulder. He looked stunned.

Dad said, "I'm proud of you."

This was unprecedented.

Dad released him and they stepped back. Stan was still standing there, gob smacked, unable to speak. Dad quickly got into the car he'd borrowed from his brother and drove off.

We loaded into the van and got under way. Nothing was said for some time.

We were just passing the drive in restaurant near the turn off for the ferry, the famous "Lik-A-Chik," and I turned to point it out to Stan.

"Hey, look..." I stopped. Stan was crying. Just quietly crying and driving.

We drove onto the ferry and got settled in for the night.

"Isle Aux Morts."

"The Island of the Dead."

That is the sign that greeted us as the ferry pushed into the quay the next morning around 6.

Stan guided the van out of the ship and onto the ramp.

He nodded at the sign.

"Hell of a welcome."

It was cold and grey and foggy, and there were still huge piles of filthy snow at the side of the road. None of us had slept during the trip over. We had a show that night in Stevensville, and we checked into the motel and collapsed into our beds.

The tour was being funded by the Canada Council, which meant we were actually making a fee regardless of whether anyone turned up. And a good thing too, as it happened.

We woke up from our naps, had a meal, and then went over to the hall. The story we'd heard was that it had once been part of the Newfoundland exhibit at EXPO 67 in Montreal. The building had been cut to pieces after the exposition and then shipped back home and repurposed as a concert hall, seating maybe three or four hundred people. The other half of it was in the next town where we were playing the following night.

We were standing at the side of the stage getting our bearings, and wondering where the staff was.

Stan said, "Did you hear the one about the two Newfoundlanders talking about EXPO 67?"

"No. What?"

"Guy gets back from Montreal, and his buddy asks him what was the very best thing about being there."

"Yeah?"

"Yeah, and the guy thinks about it and then says, "I think the very best thing about EXPO was that you could get laid for 10 cents." And his friend says, "Really? Did you? "

"No, but my sister did."

"Make sure you tell that one tonight during the show."

There was no stage crew as yet, so we found some mics and stands and set up ourselves.

The sound system was a nightmare. The mixing desk had only three working channels, and we needed a minimum of six. Stan spent a hour or so with a screwdriver and a borrowed soldering gun, rewiring the thing, but in the end we still had only 5 to work with, and one kept cutting out.

The sound guy turned up finally, looked at what Stan had done and shrugged and said, "Looks like you got it all sorted," and walked out. It didn't matter anyway.

The doors opened and 5 people came in and sat down in the middle of the room, maybe 20 rows back, five people. That was it. Didn't matter. They got the show, as best as we could manage, given how difficult it is to strike a spark in a near vacuum.

We packed up and went back to the hotel. There were no restaurants open, and the bar was just closing for the night, so we had a couple of quick beers and a few handfuls of peanuts and went to bed.

The next day was much the same.

We drove to Cornerbrook and played to maybe 10 lonely souls.

At the end of the show they all crept furtively out of the room, past our merchandise table and out into the rainy night.

And so on.

We did maybe 5 shows that week, working our way towards St John's which was the final gig.

We were picking up a few more audience members every night, and the second last show we had nearly 30 people to play to in a room that would have held four or five hundred.

It was depressing and humiliating, but given what we'd had to contend with in years past, we couldn't really complain. We were getting paid, and sleeping in decent rooms, and so far we hadn't had to take anyone outside for a stern talk before wiring a concrete block to their feet.

We got into St John's and checked into the old hotel on Signal Hill. I looked out to the harbour and could see it was blocked by a massive iceberg. There was a flotilla of ships outside the harbour, presumably waiting to get in. Stan came into my room with a beer for me, and we stood and looked out at the scene.

"I wonder if they just have to wait for it to move along."

"I dunno. I would think they'd only be able to wait so long. Those ships have schedules. Maybe they get tug boats in to move it. Maybe they bring in a gun boat and start blasting it to bits."

"Oh man. I'd give a lot to see that."

"No kidding."

We decided we wanted a closer look, and grabbed up Jim and drove the van over to Marconi's Tower across from Cape Spear. Astonishingly, the iceberg had drifted along during the few minutes it had taken us to get there and was now nearly vanished in the fog that was coming in. What a great place. Everything here, the sea, the cliffs, the weather, was on a grand and epic scale.

We spent a few minutes on the high rocks looking eastward, but there was nothing to see. It was the just the feeling of being as Far East as one could be before hitting Europe.

Stan was standing next to the tower with his hands jammed into the pockets of his denim coat with a cigarette held between his teeth. It was cold, and he was stamping his feet and moving from one foot to the other.

"Someday, boys. Someday."

We went over to the Arts and Culture Centre, and loaded in.

By now we had zero expectations about the show. We figured we'd play to another handful of people who knew nothing about us, but who had won or been given tickets to the show, and only stuck it out because they were too embarrassed on our behalf to leave.

But tonight we had around 200 people. Maybe a quarter of a house. A disaster anywhere else, but after the last week it was like a party. Some of them had remembered us from years before with Ryan's Fancy, and had come anyway. Some had heard us on the CBC. Whatever the reason, we finally had a lively and friendly group of people to play for. At one point I ran back to the dressing room and got my camera and took a picture from the stage.

We had given up setting up a merchandise table after the first couple of shows, having sold only a couple of LPs, but tonight people actually asked about albums so I ran out to the van and brought in the boxes.

We sat on the edge of the stage and began selling and signing. We were all feeling pretty good. We'd finally connected, and the folks here were extraordinarily friendly.

At one point, I slashed open my thumb, trying to get the cellophane off a record and try as I might, I couldn't get the bleeding stopped. There are maybe 40 or 50 signed Stan Rogers LPs out there that look like they came from a crime scene.

A couple of years ago, I was cleaning out my parents' house after they had passed, and found a letter among the thousands Mum had saved, from a lady who had been there that night, and in her memory it had been Stan whose blood had stained the album cover. It now held pride of place on their living room wall, framed as a holy relic. This is how religions get started I guess.

Next day, we set out early from St John's. We had an 8 or 9 hour run to catch the ferry on the other side of the island, and the roads and the weather weren't great.
We grabbed a quick breakfast, loaded up the van and set out. Stan insisted on doing all the driving. He was eager to get back to the mainland, and there was no way we were going to miss the ferry. He held it steady about 15 miles per hour over the speed limit all the way, except of course, for the towns we had to go through. Jim and I kept careful watch for cops and moose. We were maybe 60 miles away from Port aux Basques and it looked like we were going to make in time. We had 2 hours in hand. Still, Stan kept his foot on the gas. But he was starting to relax a bit now.
"Looks like we're going to make it boys. I'll be glad to get on that boat and get a bite to eat."
We hadn't stopped since breakfast except for fuel, and we were all ravenous.
"Garnet, check the liquor cabinet. Do we still have the makings for gin and tonic?"
I crawled back and looked inside the cupboard behind his seat.
The limes looked a little withered but they'd do. We had no ice, but we were enured to hardship at this point.
"Yup. You want one?"
"Yeah. Heavy on the gin."
I made a round for all of us, and we clinked glasses.
Stan said, "Well, we didn't set any records, but we survived. Next time will be better."
We all took a drink. Stan and Jimmy lit up smokes and I kicked off my shoes and put my feet up on the dashboard.
We were going home.
Stan kept our speed steady and I watched the side of the road ahead for any sign of movement. Hitting a moose at this speed would mean death for all of us.
I finished my drink. "How about another?"
Stan said, "Sure. Same as before."
I set them up, and once again we clinked glasses. And then Jim and Stan simultaneously yelled, "Holy Shit. The cops!"

We all drained our glasses, except for Stan, who passed his over to me and said, "Get rid of that." I gulped it down, and chewed the lime wedges and swallowed them, getting rid of all the evidence. Stan hit the signal and pulled over to the side of the road.

He threw a handful of mints into his mouth and crunched down on them, then he lit another smoke, and drew on it deeply.

I could see the RCMP cruiser with its lights flashing behind us. There were two cops in the car, and the driver was on the radio, no doubt calling in our plate number.

Stan unbuckled his seat belt and opened the door.

"I'm going to try and head them off and not let them see into the van. You guys hide the booze."

Jim and I were already frantically jamming the half dozen or so bottles from the cabinet into our luggage, but the air inside the van smelled of gin and limes and tonic water and cigarette smoke. The cops would know there were only two possibilities. We'd either been drinking or we had kidnapped Noel Coward. We were doomed if they came close and got a whiff.

Stan opened the door and stood up beside the van. He straightened his collar and began walking back to the cruiser. That is never a good idea. The last thing a nervous cop wants to see on a routine traffic stop is a six foot four behemoth walking briskly towards them. In the side mirror I could see the cop from the passenger side of the cruiser getting out. When he saw Stan he stopped and pulled his billy club out, whirled it around a few times on the leather strap, and began to slap it against his leg.

Shit.

Stan disappeared out of my line of sight, and I crawled across the engine cowling to get a better view out the open window. The cop who'd been driving was younger than the guy with the billy club. I could see his face as Stan walked towards him. It suddenly lit up with recognition.

"STAN ROGERS?" He stopped, turned to his partner and pointed at Stan. "MY JEEZ, IT'S STAN ROGERS."

Huh?

Stan stopped, and the young cop came over and put out his hand.

"Jesus Christ, Stan, you gave us a hell of a fright coming out of the van like that. But holy shit, it's really you. The wife and I saw your show the other night. Great stuff, buddy. Just great stuff. I bought your record after the show too. What a thrill, what an honour to meet you."

He turned to his partner.

"This is the feller I was telling you about. Jesus Christ, he can sing some. You missed a hell of a show."

His partner was still not a happy man. He kept swinging the billy club back and forth and frowning.

"I don't give a shit about how he sings. He was well over the limit, and we need to search the van."

"Search the van? Christ no. This is Stan Rogers. No need to search this feller. I can vouch for him. I have to tell ya Stan, I love that record I bought the other night. I wanted to buy more, but I was short of cash. Do you have any more I could buy now?"

I couldn't see Stan's face. He had his back to me, but I saw him wave off the cop's offer to pay and then he turned around and came back to the van and began pulling records out of the boxes. He had a funny little smile. If he couldn't pull this off we would be looking at certain jail time, or at least a massive fine. He had to be careful and not overplay his hand.

He took the albums back to the two cops, and handed them over, once again waving off the younger guy's offer of cash.

"WOW. Really? Jeez Stan, this is great. Look, could you sign these for the wife? She thought you were great too."

So Stan signed the albums, even the ones which the other cop grudgingly accepted, and the young guy shook hands with Stan again.

"Now Stan, I know you're in a hurry and want to catch the ferry, but you're only half an hour away, and there's lots of time, so you just back her down, and be safe, and we'll see you next time through. Okay? Off you go now."

Stan came back and got behind the wheel. He ground out his smoke, and dropped it out the no draft window. Put the van in gear, and waited for a chance to pull onto the road. I could still see the two cops in the rear view on my side. The older cop still wasn't happy, and he was yelling at the younger guy. The younger cop was still smiling and shaking his head, and waving off the criticism. They got back into the cruiser and pulled a quick U turn and drove off. Stan pulled out and took it up to legal speed.

Nothing was said. A miracle had just occurred and none of us wanted to break the spell.

After maybe 20 minutes Stan said, "I wouldn't mind another short one if you guys didn't drink all the evidence."

"Okay. Coming up."

"Not all the tonic this time, Jeeves."

We made the ferry with an hour to spare.

We went home for a brief rest and then we had a week's run in New England.

We'd been booked into Payne Hall on the Harvard campus, having grown past the point where we could comfortably fit into Passim. We hated leaving that wonderful room, particularly as we loved Bob and Rae Anne, but the only alternative would have been to book a week's run there. We didn't have time.

When we arrived we discovered we had an opening act.

His name was Bill Morrissey. We'd heard his name, but knew nothing of his music or what sort of person he might be. We were at the stage where any opener was seen as either an amateurish intrusion, or, if they were any good at all, a dangerous interloper to be stomped and overwhelmed and humiliated. Stan in particular had a real competitive streak, and Bill was being touted as this year's version of "The Next Big Thing."

Huh. We'd see about that.

We watched him warily as he and his bass player, Grieg, shambled in, set down their cases, and walked over to shake hands and say thanks for letting them be on the bill.

Seemed like decent guys. We decided we were going to try to be friendly. We brought a case of beer in from the van and opened a few and had a drink. There followed a certain amount of standing around and some cautious joke telling, and Stan politely admired Bill's Epiphone Texan guitar. "I used one of those on the first record."

We were to sound check first, being the headliners, and for some reason Stan departed from the usual routine and began playing "The Sultans of Swing."

Jimmy and I picked up on it and we played the whole song. I could see Bill smiling and leaning over to whisper into Grieg's ear just before I tried that damned impossible final solo.

Then it was their turn.

Stan was sitting back by the sound desk, working on the set list for the show.

Bill and Grieg began playing "Small Town on the River."

I saw Stan stop writing and he went very still.

I sat down next to him, and waited for the end of the song. It was one of those rare songs, (and Bill was to write more than his share,) that stopped time. When it was over we both gave a deep exhale. I realised we'd both been holding our breath for about two minutes.

"Wow."

He played another song. They made some small adjustments to the monitors and sound check was over.

Stan was now savagely stroking out large sections of the set list. This guy was trouble, and we would need the big guns. His name was after all, on the poster. We couldn't simply thump him on the head and throw him into a dumpster.

Sound check was over, and we opened some more beers and went outside to watch the sun go down over what Bob Dylan had once called "The green pastures of Harvard University."
It was a sweet evening. A perfect day in May.
The audience came in and the show started.
Bill and Grieg simply killed.
We all watched from the wings. We never bothered much with listening to openers back then, but this was one of those new comet in the night sky moments, and here was a guy who was fully formed and in complete control of his deal.

While our act by then was a carefully scripted series of rehearsed and tired jokes, interspersed with Stan's wonderful songs, Bill's show was a series of verbal riffs and one liners and songs all interwoven and effortlessly tossed out like a trout fly. He always hit his spot and he always got a perfect float.
His timing was wonderful.
He paused, and affected to be confused and distracted for a moment.
   "I'm sorry, " he said, "I'd really like to sing this next song, but I ...uh...I mean, you've never lived until you've heard Stan Rogers sing "The Sultans Of Swing." I mean, I feel like I want to join the Marines or something."
Bill and Stan got on great that night, and I know they would have become friends but Stan was gone less than a month later.
And Bill is gone now too, and mourned by those who loved him and watched helplessly as depression and addiction took him away.
We all watched from a distance, because that is how it is with an addict.
Russell Brand wrote a concise and to the point article about addiction in the wake of Amy Winehouse's death a few years ago, the same week that Bill passed. He said, and I am paraphrasing, that with an addict there is always a third entity in the room with you, and that entity is the disease. And the addict is never quite present with you. They are always looking past you, searching for the object of their desire, or rather, need.
Being with Bill was like that, mostly in later years. There was always a veil or a filter through which everything had to fight to be heard.
From my own long battles with depression and alcohol, I know of the shame which accompanies any addiction. You are ashamed of your weakness and feel that everyone, your friends, your family, and your co-workers can see it. And you are right.
They can see, and because they love you they put up with it, and if they are wise, they know it is your battle to fight, and in the end, because it is such a selfish disease, they are little more than collateral damage.

No one can fix the deeper problem which causes one to drink or shoot
up except the addict.
And stopping is only the beginning of sobriety. The real work comes
later.

I put down the bottle in the Fall of 1988. I had come to the end of my
rope, and had my moment of clarity in the parking lot of a cheap motel
in Brandon Manitoba. I was up to a bottle and a half of spirits a day and
I still needed more. Something had to give.
I had heard that it takes 72 hours more or less, to de-tox, so I went
into the office, handed the owner my car keys and wallet, told him I
needed the room for three days, and if he saw me leave the room any
time before that to call the cops. I spent three days sweating it out,
hallucinating, tearing at the bugs under my skin, and climbing the
walls. I came out looking pretty pale and interesting, and drove home.
I never went back to it, and I never went to any sort of rehab or 12 step
programme.
The very little I knew of AA and the "Higher Power" stuff put me off.
I knew nothing about the AA prayer, or what the 12 Steps were, or who
Bill W., the founder of AA was. I knew nothing of his story. I decided I
was going to work through it myself, with Gail's help and support.
I was on stage about a month later, in Northampton Mass., and was of
course talking about my adventures.
A woman came up to me after the show and said, "So, you're trying to
get sober?"
   "Yeah. I'm doing my best."
   "Are you a Friend of Bill's?"
I didn't know that phrase was code for being in the Programme.
I said, "Yes, I AM a friend of Bill's, and I'm really worried about him.
He's still hitting the vodka pretty hard."

The last time I saw Bill was in Kansas City or St. Louis. I'd been touring
in the area with Lucy Kaplansky, and had heard he was fresh out of
rehab and doing shows again, and I wanted to say hello and give him
my support.
I was taken back stage and there he was, re-stringing his guitar. He
didn't say hello or anything. He just looked up and said, "They take a
picture of you when you arrive at rehab and give it to you when you
check out, so you can see just what a mess you were. Sort of a memento
and a warning. My picture makes Nick Nolte's mug shot look like a
Prom photo."
And then he laughed and stood up and shook my hand with his dry

thin grip.

This was a Bill I'd never met. Fresh and bright and clear-eyed, and so damned quick. Way beyond the whip sharp mind I'd thought I'd known.

He had a bunch of new songs, and he gave me a cd of the demo. We agreed to keep in touch but never did. The disease took hold once more, and he went into deep cover. No one could reach him, and he passed a couple of years later. He was gone and I had no good words to say to any of us who loved him, and would mourn him, and will remember him in their own way.

What I do remember are the songs and the way his face looked as he left the stage that night at Payne Hall. He'd sung a very funny bit called "Morrissey Falls in Love at First Sight," having introduced it as "an old Library of Congress song."

Stan and Jimmy and I were standing at the side of the stage, applauding and laughing as he walked into the wings.

"Great song," said Stan, touching him on the shoulder.

Bill ducked his head and smiled. "Thanks. Sometimes all you have to do is write them down."

CHAPTER 84

On To Texas

After the New England run we came home for a week or so to get ready
to fly out for a tour of the West. We were mostly going to be playing on
the coast, between Vancouver and Los Angeles, finishing up with a 3
day stint at the Kerrville festival in Texas.

With the exception of a couple of shows, I have only the vaguest
memory of where we played or in what order. I know we played
Vancouver and Victoria and Portland and Seattle, as well as San
Francisco, and maybe Tacoma, and I'm sure there were others, but
there was no geographic order to the shows. I recall flying over Crater
Lake and Mount St. Helens four times in as many days on the way to
whatever gig we were doing that night.

We were spending hours in airports, waiting to be loaded into a
cramped and smelly metal tube for an hour or so, to finally be extruded
like dog droppings onto a rain swept runway in some new and
confusing town. We'd line up with the other members of the damned,
and negotiate for a rental car that stank of cigar smoke and industrial
solvent, load it up, and then Stan would begin the process of getting us
to the hotel, while Jim or I navigated from the passenger seat.

We hated it. We all felt dislocated and we missed the van. At least the
van had familiarity in the midst of a world with no other known and
comforting landmarks. With the rental cars we felt like hermit crabs
being forced to try on a succession of unfamiliar and ill-fitting shells.
Every day followed the same dreary ritual. Waking in some new hotel,
setting out to fight morning rush hour to the airport, the interminable
line ups, and saying goodbye, potentially forever, to the instruments
as they tumbled end over end down the baggage conveyer belt. A
cramped and terrifying flight, as the plane bucketed through a series
of thunderstorms, and then another town, and another cigar-scented
rent-a-pig. Another hotel, and then the gig. Somewhere in there would
be a couple of bad meals. And above all, there was a complete lack of
a sense of place. It wasn't until years later when I was driving through
Seattle, having only flown into it before, that I realised it was in fact a

port city, and everything there centered on the sea.

As the tour wore on we began to notice that there were little ways to game the system.

We would be standing in line, looking at the information boards and realise that if we exchanged tickets we could catch an earlier flight, or a more direct flight, and gain an hour or so of precious rest at the other end. There was a chance we could grab a nap or a meal that hadn't been made two years previous, frozen, and then micro-waved and served in cling film.

And so it began, sometimes changing tickets two or three times a day in different airports in an effort to get ahead.

I'm not being dramatic or clever after the fact when I say that at one point I was looking at the new ticket in my hand and thinking we were taking a lot of risks here. I was worried that Fate was going to intervene, and we were going to lose a guitar, or crap out in some other terrible and spectacular way.

The Vancouver show was a disaster.

After a couple of years of playing the East End Cultural Center, and filling it, the best Gary Kristal was apparently able to do for us was to book us into a little brew pub on Granville Island, just under the bridge. There was no stage, just an area set up between the washroom doors and a couple of crappy speakers tethered to the ceiling 40 feet above our heads as a sound system. One microphone, and no monitors. And no audience. We might have been able to pull off a show of some kind if people had known about the gig and had shown up, but someone dropped the ball on promotion as well.

We played to a bare handful of disinterested yuppies and lawyers who never stopped yelling at each other at the tables in front of us, while the wait staff walked by, in front of us or behind us with trays, calling out drink orders.

We had to plug Stan's guitar into my amplifier to be able to hear it above the din.

At one point Stan noticed Gary sitting off to the side. He had wandered in to see how we were doing.

Stan stopped his song intro. It was pointless anyway, as no one was listening.

"What's going on here Gary?"

Gary merely raised his eyebrow.

"This won't do, Gary." Stan gestured at the room. "It's not good enough."

Gary just sat there with his massive belly spilling down between his splayed legs. He shrugged and yawned and looked away.

No point in pursuing it further. He clearly didn't give a shit.
It was a bad end to a day that hadn't started out great anyway. We'd got
into town fairly early, and had checked into the Holiday Inn downtown.
It was a sunny day in Vancouver for a change, and I decided to have a
dip in the outdoor pool and get some sun on what was left of my body.
I got to the room and changed into my shorts and grabbed a towel and
went down to poolside. A few hours later I came back to the room and
went into the bathroom for the first time since arriving. I lifted the lid
on the toilet and discovered the previous occupant had had a series of
apocalyptic events and had either neglected to flush properly, or had
simply tired of trying to chop the mess into manageable pieces and send
it on its journey to the Straits of Juan de Fuca. I shrieked and leapt back
in horror, and then, carefully balancing on one foot, pushed the lever
down with the other.
Well, of course the whole damned mess didn't go down, did it? No, as
the water poured in, the great Kraken rose from the depths and made
its escape and slithered over the edge of the bowl and began to spread
across the floor. There was no end to it, and it was following me into
the hallway. I jumped onto the bed and phoned the front desk and told
them as calmly and circumspectly as I could about the problem, making
sure they understood that it wasn't my doing. I was the victim in this.
  "Don't worry, sir. We'll take care of it."
Well, that was a relief.
Some 20 minutes later I was still waiting. I was sitting on the window
sill 12 stories up, with my head out the open window, trying to breathe.
There was a knock at the door. I tip-toed along the baseboard at the
edge of the room and opened it. A guy in soiled coveralls handed me a
plunger and then turned and walked away. That was it.
Half an hour later, after much yelling and pouting and stamping of feet
in the lobby and then in the manager's office, I was given a new room.
Next day we went to Victoria. We were playing at some event called the
Inner Harbour Festival.
Upon arriving at the airport I opened my guitar case and found my
Larrivee in several pieces. The headstock was broken off, there was
a break at the seventh fret, and the whole neck joint itself had been
wrenched out of the dovetail. The pimply faced Hitler youth behind the
counter at the Air Canada desk merely shrugged and told me I needed a
better case.
Ah. So it was my fault. Never mind then.
Stan decided to intervene. He carefully turned his gold and turquoise
pinky ring around so it wouldn't flatten out when he began pounding
the desk, and summoned up his Voice Of Doom, which he reserved
especially for Satan's pissy and officious minions who typically

worked behind airline ticket booths and car rental counters.

"Better case? A BETTER CASE?"

I could see people in the terminal look around nervously and cross themselves as the lights dimmed and small blue flames flickered in the corners of the room.

He bent down and pulled the wreckage of my guitar out of the case and handed it to me. He then shut the case and snapped the locks, and proceeded to leap up and down on the thing.

"SEE? NOTHING. IT'S ONLY THE TRAINED CHIMPS YOU HAVE BACK IN THE BAGGAGE AREA WHO CAN DO THIS KIND OF DAMAGE. A NORMAL HUMAN BEING..."

At this point a couple of RCMP officers came over, attracted by the noise.

One of them was speaking in a low voice into his radio, and the other was twirling a pair of handcuffs around the index finger of his left hand, and holding onto the handle of his billy club with the other, and no doubt wondering whether his can of Mace was fully charged.

"Something wrong here sir?"

I tugged on Stan's arm. I needed to get him out before he threatened to rip the kid's lungs out or worse. It was likely some kind of federal offense to dismember an airline employee.

"Let's go." I said. "There's nothing we can do here."

I was distraught. This was my first good guitar, and the one Dad had bought for me years before.

We took the rental car over to our hotel and I called Jean Larrivee at his shop in Victoria, and told him my story.

"If I leave it with you, is there some way you could maybe build another neck for me and send it back in a few months?"

He said, "How long are you in town for?"

"Just today."

"Bring it over. I'll set you up."

Two hours later I was leaving Jean's shop with the guitar back in playing condition. Jean had simply epoxied it back together and it has held perfectly ever since. He waved off my offer to pay and sent me out the door. Great guy.

We drove over to the harbour where some of the festival volunteers were waiting for us. They helped us load our gear into a motor launch, and we had a very pleasant ride over to the floating stage in front of the Provincial Parliament buildings.

The town looked lovely from the water. It was getting towards dusk, and the lights were coming on and reflecting everywhere. There were antique ships all around us, some steam powered, and every one of them gleaming with polished brass and copper and teak and mahogany, and many of them with hundreds of fairy lights strung all through their rigging. It looked like a Van Gogh painting.

Stan was perched up on the bow of the launch with a cigarette, enjoying the breeze and the view.

"Cute town." he said.

We were playing on a stage about 30 feet wide, with the speaker enclosures floating beside us. We were maybe a hundred feet or so off shore. The audience was sitting on the grass and only just visible in the dark. We played okay, in spite of the occasional nitwit speed boat operator cutting in between us and the crowd, leaving a rooster tail of spray behind, and a wake that rocked the stage. Aside from that, my main memory is the sound of our voices echoing back to us from the buildings behind the crowd, and having some after show drinks on board an old motor launch, where Stan sat next to a small boy who was on board, and sang a cleaned up version of Barrett's Privateers. Beyond that, nothing.

We had a couple of days off and took a series of ferries over to Galliano Island, where our cousin Lorna was living with her then partner Cam. Cam played in the first violin section of the Vancouver Symphony.

We had met him the year before at the Vancouver Folk Festival. He and Lorna had dropped by the student detention center where we and the other performers were housed. We were having a jam session that night with Eric Bogle, whom we had finally met after years of admiring his songs. He had brought his guitar player John Munro along, and it had been a lovely and quiet and very sweet session. Lorna had a strong contralto voice, and there had been a great deal of wonderful harmony singing. Cam had his violin with him but was not playing. At one point he turned to me and said, "How do you know what notes to play?"

"Huh?"

"Do you know all these songs?"

"Well I know Stan's tunes. Eric's not so much."

"So how do you know which notes to play?"

I didn't know what to say. Cam was in a whole other universe of violin, one that I could not even begin to imagine.

"I don't know. I just kind of know where the chords are going to go. It's not really very complicated music."

He shook his head. "I just don't know what to play without the notes in front of me."

"That's okay. I can't play the Kreutzer Sonata."

It was at that point the door crashed open, and Dave Van Ronk and Aly Bain charged into the room at a dead run. They both hit the wall in front of them, and bounced back. Dave sank to his knees and then fell over.

Aly ricocheted off the wall, windmilled backwards several paces, and landed on my violin which was sitting beside me on the sofa in its case. There was a loud and nasty snap and a crunch. My heart stopped.
I pushed him over to try to pull it out from under his drunken ass, but he might have misinterpreted my intentions. He smacked me in the face with his right elbow, pushed my hand away, and then reached under himself and pulled the fiddle out. He held it up. The bridge was gone, and the strings were hanging loose. It looked awful.
I reached out. "Give me that."
He looked at it briefly, shrugged, and then passed it over to me.
"I wouldn't grow flowers in that fucking thing."
I carefully turned it over and inspected it. Miraculously, apart from the broken bridge, which I could replace myself with a couple of hours of work, there was no major damage. But I was furious. It was the fiddle my Uncle Prescott had bought for a few shillings in London years before and had lent to me. It wasn't mine, and it was beyond precious. I took it and the case over to a table and then turned around, trying to decide what I was going to do to him first. Several possibilities presented themselves. For a start I was going to break both his arms. It would at least slow down his drinking, and he'd have to hire someone to pick his nose for him.
Stan was at my side, and he leaned in and grabbed my arm.
"I know you're angry. But he's really drunk. You can't beat up a drunk. You might really hurt him."
"That's the whole point of beating someone up."
"But you might kill him."
"So?"
"Get a grip. Wait until he's sober. When he sobers up, you can hit him all you want."
Where did this new rule come from?
We had never waited before.
"I want to hit him now."
"Come on. Don't make it worse. Besides, if you beat the snot out of him now, he'll wake up tomorrow and won't remember why. He'll probably just think he's fallen down the stairs."
I wasn't used to Stan being the voice of reason in situations like this. If he'd been the injured party here, Aly would be nothing more than a damp stain on the wall.
"Okay. I'll let it go for now. But as soon as he sobers up I'm drilling the little fucker."
And all these years later Aly Bain has remained safe and unharmed, as I have yet to run into him when he wasn't shit faced. I doubt he would remember the incident anyway.

I sat down and looked over where Van Ronk was now standing upright, having dragged himself hand over hand up the wall. He had found our last unopened bottle of Glenlivet. Before any of us could move he expertly peeled off the foil, pulled the cork, and then upended the thing into his throat. It was gone in seconds. Holy shit. He was the Linda Lovelace of drinking.
Eric stood up.
"JESUS CHRIST YOU GREEDY PRICK. WHAT THE FUCK DO YOU THINK YOU'RE DOING?"
Hospitality was one thing, but you don't break into a man's room and drink his last drop without asking.
Van Ronk wiped his mouth and belched, dropped the empty bottle onto the carpet, and then staggered over to a chair in the middle of the room and fell into it. He was already paralytic. God only knew what was going to happen when a full bottle of single malt entered his blood stream.
He looked around and seemed to notice us for the first time.
"I wanna sing..." he belched..."a song..." He paused and belched again, "that my grandmother used to sing for me..." He hiccupped... "when I was a boy."
I think Stan actually made a move to offer Van Ronk his guitar to play, but Dave began to sing unaccompanied. It was some tuneless Appalachian dirge, involving a bag of gold and a horse, and incest and murder by the banks of some river, and he got through maybe 20 or so verses before his eyes rolled back in their sockets, and he passed out.
His head fell back, and he turned into a great snoring and farting beast. Bogle was from Glasgow, and was now living in Australia. He'd had a lifetime's worth of experience with this sort of thing. He said, "Christ, get him out of here before he shits himself."
Good idea.
Aly Bain had passed out as well, and was also making ugly noises from both ends. Time to go before we were faced with a toxic spill. We pulled Van Ronk off the chair and he pitched over onto the floor. He was completely limp. From there Jim and I dragged his body out into the corridor. It was hard work. Van Ronk was over 6 feet tall and big with it. Stan wouldn't let me near Aly, but grabbed him by the feet and dragged him roughly off the couch where his head made a loud and satisfying thwop on the thinly carpeted concrete floor. It sounded like a coconut hitting the roof of a parking garage.
Wow. That was going to hurt in the morning.
Stan looked over at me, raised his eyebrows and smiled. Once again, it was the little gestures in our family that said, "I love you."   He hauled Aly out the door into the hallway, and threw him down in a sodden

stinking pile next to where Van Ronk was still snoring.

"We can't leave them here. Someone might come along and trip over them."

"Yeah. You're right."

We slapped them more or less awake, stood them up, and sent them on their way.

So now, a year later, in a quieter situation, we were happy to see Lorna. She had been in our lives a lot when we were all much younger, and she was as close to being an older sister as either of us would ever have. She was funny and smart, and we both loved her dearly.

We arrived at the little house she shared with Cam, and after getting unpacked set about making dinner. It was strange to be in an actual home and eating real food after a couple of weeks of nothing but hotels and rental cars, and sitting in planes eating chicken that had been bred and raised in an underground bunker, and prepared by robots in some factory in Nebraska.

We finished dinner and broke out some more wine.

I was still cautiously trying out my Larrivee, making sure the repair was holding. It seemed okay and I spent most of the evening trying to figure out a Joe Pass arrangement of "Somewhere Over the Rainbow," of all things, while Lorna and Stan went off to talk and catch up on their lives.

I think the next gig might have been in San Francisco, at a club called Plowshares.

It was a big airy room on the second floor of an old warehouse down by the waterfront. There were tall windows facing the water, and we had a decent time and a good turnout, but that is pretty much all I recall about the actual show.

What I mostly remember was yet another ghastly faux pas I perpetrated on a kindly and unsuspecting stranger. We had arrived in town the day before the gig and I had been taken to my billet. A woman whose name I think, was Nancy, had a lovely apartment in the second floor of a large Victorian house overlooking the Bay. The place was beautifully furnished in period antiques and there was a full sized grand piano by the large window. She was friendly enough, but I don't think she was all that impressed with me. Weeks of bad food, and breathing second hand air during the flights, and no sleep, and three different kinds of anti-depressant medications, each with their own special set of side effects had made me look as if I had just fought my way out of Bedlam, having first strangled the staff, and was now living in a cardboard box under the Oakland Freeway. As soon as I arrived I asked to use her phone so I could make a collect call home to Gail and tell her I loved her and missed her for the hundredth time that day.

My host was on her way out the door to a dinner date, and had just enough time to show me my room and point out the phone.

I picked it up and began dialing.

"There's beer in the fridge. Help yourself." She waved and was out the door.

Gail and I talked for a while and then said goodbye. I would call her later to say goodnight.

I turned on the TV and opened the bottle of wine I had in my bag, and got quietly drunk to pass the hours. After a while it was time to call home again, and in the middle of the call my host came in with her date. From the looks of it I had been on the long distance line ever since she had left, 4 or 5 hours earlier. And there was a large empty wine bottle in front of me. The TV was on, and for all she knew I had been ordering Ginzu Knives off the K-Tel channel, which I would later use to fillet her in her sleep, having charged them to the credit card which I had found after going through her bedside table in search of drugs. I quickly said goodnight to Gail and made to get up from the sofa and be polite to her friend. I stuck my hand out to shake, and said, "Just so you know, I reversed the charges on the calls I was making." And with that I over- balanced and sat down heavily on what looked very much like an original Philadelphia chair, likely worth thousands. It splintered and broke and I was suddenly laying on my back in the middle of a pile of priceless kindling.

There was a long silence. I was staring at the ceiling, trying to figure out what the rules for this sort of situation might be. This was awful, but I couldn't help myself. I said, "Well, how do you like me so far?"

I'm not sure where we played after San Francisco. Tacoma, maybe. And Portland, but I have no memory of the order. I have a dim memory of Stan yelling at me in a rain soaked alley in Seattle, after I had left the rental car unattended, unlocked, and worst of all, with the keys still in the ignition. He and Jim had trudged off through a teeming cloudburst to look for the venue address, and after some time had passed I had run a hundred feet up the alley to have a much- needed pee behind a dumpster. They came back to find the car running with no one guarding it. I'd broken a big rule of the road. But I have no memory of the show, or how it went.

I do know the last stop on the west coast part of the tour was Los Angeles.

We had a two night run at McCabe's Guitar shop.

We were staying with our old friends Steve and Leah Hayes. I had not seen them since the days of Campbell's Coffeehouse back in Hamilton, when Steve was studying to be a doctor when he wasn't playing piano and guitar and backing up whoever came through to play the club. He had finished medical school, and had become a psychiatrist and moved to L.A. where a shrink could have an endless supply of low hanging fruit.

They hadn't changed in the years since I had last seen them. Still beautiful. Still crazy. Still wildly funny.

We had invited Steve along to play the shows with us. In spite of his doctor's schedule he had kept up with his playing and hadn't lost a step. He had obviously listened to the records Stan had sent him, but more than that, he still had that rare sense of what to play and when to play, and when to sit out. And he was a great singer. We had a quick rehearsal at their house but soon realised it was going to be fine, and we left for the gig.

McCabe's back then was mostly a music store with a stage and a sound system at one end of the show room. There were a hundred or so guitars hanging on the walls and it made a nice effect when they would begin to sympathetically vibrate along with whatever music was playing. It was like a faint and ghostly reverb.

We loaded in and set up, and began the usual ritual with the sound check.

Tonight was different only because we had to fit Steve's guitar and piano into the mix, but it didn't take very long.

I was just beginning to sound check the violin when I was seized with another terrible panic attack, maybe the third one of the day. It was the usual thing, tunnel vision, racing heart, the inability to get a breath, and the utter conviction that I was about to fall to pieces and die on the spot. All the hits.

I was trembling so badly that I couldn't play. There was some verbal miscue between me and Stan. He barked at me and I snapped at him, and then said, "It's fine. I gotta go." And I left the stage and ran upstairs to the dressing room. He followed me a minute or so later and began tearing into me. His nerves were shot too, and I hadn't been behaving very well, and he was tired and worried and fed up. And besides all my problems and personal drama, he was having his own issues to deal with. The nightly pre-show phone calls from home had not stopped. He was in a bad way, and he was now letting me have it.

I don't recall precisely what was said, but he was going into some detail once again, about just what a pain in the ass I was being, particularly over the last few weeks, how much I needed to get my shit together, and how completely sick and tired of it all he was. I'd heard it all before, and sat there with my head in my hands and waited. I was desperately trying to keep from losing control and wondering if I was about to black out. It felt very much like when I was a child just before I would have a grande mal seizure. I hadn't had one in many years, but this could be one coming now. I was really frightened.

All at once, two massive streams of bright blood exploded out of my nose, as if from a pair of garden hoses. I leapt up in a panic to try to get to the sink and stop the bleeding but tripped and fell before I got there. Blood was everywhere. The room looked like a killing floor.

Jesus. What the hell was happening to me?

Stan grabbed a towel and got it over my face, and then with his thumb and forefinger began squeezing hard on my nose.

"We need ice over here. Jim! Get some ice."

To complete the drama, I then burst into uncontrollable sobs. I couldn't stand up and sank to my knees by the wash basin. Stan kept the towel on me and Jim arrived with the ice.

Luckily, we were able to get the bleeding stopped before one of them had to remove his belt and put a tourniquet around my neck. I realised that my blood pressure must have been through the roof. I was lucky. I could have stroked out had my nose not turned into a grenade.

I was exhausted and limp, and in no real shape to do anything but lay on a fainting couch having my temples bathed in rosewater, with a lavender scented handkerchief pressed under my nose, while servants fanned me and brought me mint juleps. Certainly a high pressure gig was out of the question.

Steve came in and checked me over. He put his head against my chest and listened. He held my face up to the ceiling light and looked at my pupils. They were both the same size. He took hold of my wrist and counted while looking at his watch, and then said, "I think you'll be fine. Just take it easy for a while." I had given him the list of the drugs I was taking and he told me that extreme highs and lows in blood pressure were among the side effects. Every band needs a doctor and psychiatrist to travel with them on the road.

I think we started the show a bit late, maybe 15 minutes, and I was pretty subdued on stage. I was still feeling frail and shaky, but we got through it and the sold out house seemed to think it was fine.

Next day, I was up early and went out to the front porch at Steve and Leah's. I had a coffee and my guitar and I put my feet up and began trying to remember how to play an old instrumental of Steve's from years before called "Riley's Blues," named for his old tabby cat when they lived on Robinson Street in Hamilton. I wanted to surprise him with it when he came home from tending the looney and afflicted of LA.

An hour or so later I was just about getting the hang of it when Stan came out with a coffee. He sat down and lit a smoke. He didn't say anything, just sat for a while and listened.

It was a tough piece, although of course Steve had made it look effortless back in the day. Open "D" tuning, and there was a difficult series of bends in the second part. I got through it without a mistake twice, and decided to take a rest. I put the guitar down and drank back the last of my cold coffee.

Stan took the smoke out of his mouth.

"Sounds good."

"I dunno. I'm working on it. Got a ways to go."

"You gonna play it for Steve?"

"Yeah. I thought it might give him a laugh."

There was a long pause. He finished his Rothmans, stamped it out, kicked the butt into the bushes in front of the porch, and drained the last of his coffee.

He put the cup down and cleared his throat.

"Listen. About last night."

I shook my head and waved him off.

"It's okay. I had it coming. I know I haven't been firing on all cylinders lately. This tour is kicking my ass."

"Yeah, well, me too. But I shouldn't have yelled at you."

"No. Really. It's okay. You didn't know. I have those attacks all the time. Not as bad as last night. That was awful. I've never bled like that before. But pretty much every day I have at least one, and they can last for hours, and they really take it out of you. The pills are helping, but I need to be getting more rest."

"You could try laying off the booze for a bit too. That can't be helping."

"I know. You're right. I'm just trying to manage the anxiety until I get home and get some rest. My doctor says I really shouldn't be out here at all."

"You want to go home now? You can if you want."

"Yeah. I do. But we only have a couple more days out here and I think I can make it through the rest of the run."

"Okay. I just wanted to say I'm sorry again. I'll try to be more understanding from now on."

"Really. It's okay. You've been fine."

"So we're good?"

"Yeah. We're good."

He stood and picked up the empty coffee cups.

"I need another coffee. Want me to build you one too?"

"Sure. Thanks."

And then he bent down and gave me an awkward one armed hug. It wasn't a hug so much, as a half Nelson, and it nearly snapped my neck.

In fact, there was a loud "clunk" just below my skull, and I felt a sharp pain. Stan heard it too, and he released me and jumped back. "Jesus. Sorry. You all right?"

I slid off the chair and gasped, "I can't feel my legs."

Stan looked stricken. He yelled, "NOOO!" and bent towards me, and I burst out laughing.

He straightened up.

"You prick."

He dislocated my right knee with a kick, and then picked the cups up from where he'd dropped them and went back into the house.

The show that night was much better. I'd got some rest, and we'd had a nice meal with Steve and Leah and the kids.

We went over to the club and set up. Once again, we had a sellout, and the show was being recorded by Howard and Roz Larmon. They ran what became a nationally syndicated folk radio show, and had been huge supporters of us from the get go. Sweet people, and kind. Both of them.

We had just finished sound check and had gone back upstairs to relax. Stan was re-stringing his guitar. Jim was also putting new strings on his bass, in honour of the radio show.

Jim changed his strings as much as once a week, far more than any bass player we'd ever heard of. Jack Zaza, an old CBC studio sweat, who'd been the partial cause of Jim Ogilvie leaving us years before, had had a 1952 Fender Precision bass with the original strings still on it. He could tune it without hearing it, simply by lining up the grooves on the bottoms of the strings with the frets underneath.

But Jim Morison liked the sound of new strings, particularly the bright red copper ones he was getting some sort of bulk deal on. They did sound wonderful, like the bottom end of a grand piano.

I was drinking a coffee and for the umpteenth time checking the neck on my Larrivee to see if it was still among the living.

The door to the dressing room opened slowly, and Noel and Maggie Harrison poked their heads into the room.

"OH MY GOD. WHERE THE HELL DID YOU GUYS SPRING FROM?"

Stan and I leapt up and ran over to them to lift them up and crush them in our arms. It had been years, and we had lost touch with them completely. It was wonderful to see them.

They were in town visiting Rex, and had seen that we were playing a show.

Maggie needed a night out. She'd had a bad day. Rex was on perhaps his sixth wife at that point in his life, and she wasn't inclined to get along with anyone from Rex's circle, particularly the kids, so the atmosphere in the house was tense.

To get Maggie out of the line of fire, Rex had given her a large-ish sum of money and sent her and her sister off to cruise the stores on Rodeo Drive.

They looked fine by any standards that I might use, clean hair, tailored jeans and good cheek bones, but not even in the ball park with what the snobby shop assistants in Hollywood required from a customer.

Still, Maggie and her sister carried on unintimidated, slowly walking around the store, chatting brightly and looking at various items and inwardly blanching at the price tags.

No snippy shop girl working on commission was going to run them out of the damned place.

It was then that Maggie happened to look down and discovered she had a pair of underpants around her right ankle where they had fallen out of her pant leg. She had been walking around the store and most of Beverly Hills perhaps, with it trailing behind her.

We tried to reassure her that we'd all been there, but she needed a drink. Maybe several drinks.

I ran downstairs and asked a staff member where the closest beer or liquor store might be.

There was one only 4 blocks away, just beyond an overpass. She took me outside and pointed it out.

"Thanks." And I set off on foot.

I was maybe 2 blocks along the way when a police car pulled up and two cops got out and jumped me. I knew better than to resist, and allowed them to hustle me over to the cruiser where they bent me over and pulled my arms behind my back. I felt the cuffs snap closed and then they stood me up, turned me around, and asked for my ID.

"It's in my wallet in my back pocket."

One of them took out my wallet and began going through it.

"What did I do, Officers?"

The guy was still closely inspecting my papers. He didn't look at me.

"Where are you from?"

"Canada. I'm a Canadian citizen."

"Canada? What are you doing here?"

"I'm a musician. I'm playing a show tonight at McCabe's just over there. I have a work permit."

"So where were you going?"

"Just over there to get a case of beer."

"Where's your car?"

"My car? Why would I drive a car a couple of blocks?"

"No one walks anywhere in this town."

"Even a couple of blocks? For a few beers?"

"Nope. That's why we stopped you. You didn't look right."

Well, Christ. I never looked right. It was no reason to arrest me.

They turned me around and unlocked the cuffs and let me go. I had noticed that in movies everyone rubs their wrists when the cuffs are taken off, and now here I was doing just that.

"Can I go now?"

"Yup." He handed me my wallet. "Be careful."

Of what? Overzealous cops? Jesus, what a place.

I continued over to the store and bought a case of Lowenbrau. I was walking back to the club and just as I got to the overpass another cop car swooped in and skidded to a stop in front of me, blocking my path. I put down the case of beer and put my hands over my head. I could see the cop behind the wheel talking on the radio. I guess his colleagues who had just shaken me down gave them the all clear, and they peeled away and left me in a cloud of dust and dirt and pigeon shit.

I picked up the beer and continued walking.

I got to the club and took the beer upstairs. Stan looked at his watch.

"What the hell took you so long?"

We did a good show. The three of us were feeling pretty high, and Steve played beautifully. We had old and dear friends in the room, and a full house besides, and after months of stress and seemingly endless travel we had one more gig before going home.

We went back to Steve and Leah's and showered and packed our gear. We had an early flight to Texas. Early enough that by the time we got squared away it didn't make a lot of sense to actually try to go to sleep. Still, I caught an hour or so before we crept out of the house in the pre-dawn dark.

We got to LAX and ditched the rent-a-pig, and got in line for the daily ordeal.

We arrived in San Antonio around noon, Texas time.

There was a van waiting to pick us up, and some volunteers helped us load the gear. We got in and began driving north to Kerrville. I had never been to Texas before. Stan and Jim had been through the year previous, on a short run to the West which I had missed for health reasons. At the time I was just beginning the first round of medications. My doctor allowed me to travel as far as Ann Arbor and Chicago to play a couple of shows and see how I managed, but that was it. We had decided a 3 week long run and being thrown right back into life on the road was too much too soon. So Stan and Jimmy had dropped me off at

O'Hare and I flew home. They had taken what was left of the old Route 66 to the coast, and had passed through Oklahoma and Texas. Stan later showed me a blurry black and white picture of a flat featureless plain with a single tumble weed crossing the road in the distance.

"What's this?"

He said, "That is the single most interesting thing we saw in Texas."

So what I was seeing now was a surprise and a wonder and a delight. As we left San Antonio we began to drive through a series of lovely little valleys. There were beautiful clear streams and low hills, and everywhere there were carpets of wildflowers with clouds of butterflies of every size and colour hovering over them. I had never seen anything like it. Small herds of deer were grazing quietly in the fields. They would pause and look at us as we went by then go back to eating. I felt like I'd been dropped into a Disney cartoon, or a Watchtower magazine illustration.

I said, "I wonder what kind of deer that was. Didn't look like a whitetail. Too small. Anybody know?"

There was no answer from any of the volunteers. Stan and Jim merely shrugged.

A small and awkward tank-like creature crossed the road ahead of us and the driver slowed down so as not to hit it. Christ. It was an armadillo. I'd never seen one. It was a small thing, and for the locals the equivalent of seeing a squirrel or a house cat, but I was thrilled. I was sitting in the front passenger seat, and I rolled the window down and stuck the upper half of my body out to have a better view as it trundled into the weeds in the ditch. "Holy shit, Stan. An armadillo. Wow." Everything was new and beautiful. I had never seen flowers in such profusion. I found out later that Lady Bird Johnson had been responsible for the replanting and regeneration of the native wild flowers in this part of the world. Good for her. It's a hell of a legacy. After weeks of spending my time in airports and planes and rental cars and stale smelling hermetically sealed hotel rooms this was complete sensory overload. Or maybe my meds were finally kicking in. There were literally flocks of hummingbirds zipping around the fields, winking like bright emeralds in the sunlight. When I was a kid, the sight of a hummingbird was so rare I had privately decided, using a child's logic, that there was only one hummingbird on the planet, and only I could see it. And now here were thousands of them.

"Stan, Jim, look at this. I can't believe it."

Stan and Jim were dutifully looking at whatever I was pointing out, but not saying much. Jim had got into the Drambuie the night before, it being his favourite accompaniment to cold Lowenbrau, and he was feeling a little rocky. Stan had mentioned merely that it had been weeks since he'd slept, as opposed to just passing out from exhaustion. He was slumped in his seat with a cigarette, likely dreaming of a decent cup of coffee, one that didn't come in a Styrofoam cup.

We passed a rabbit. It wasn't the rabbit I was used to seeing. It was a jack rabbit, rangy and skinny, with the huge hindquarters and extra-long ears. It looked very much like the Albrecht Durer woodcut I'd cut out from a magazine as a kid, and had pinned to the door of my room.

"Holy shit." I craned my neck around to get a better view.

Someone in the back said, "Ooo, Look everyone. Thumper."

Just behind me I heard Stan sigh, and say quietly, "You boys will have to excuse my brother. He's just out on a day pass. It's all kinda new to him."

We got to the hotel where we were staying. It was lovely as well, but I managed not to go into a swoon over it. We got checked into our rooms and I called home and gave Gail a full report on the wonders of the place. It really was a revelation to me and made more so by my preconceptions about what I was expecting to find here.

I finished my call and slid open the screen door that led out to the patio by the pool.

Stan was already there, in a chaise lounge, smoking a cigarette and drinking a beer.

"Where'd you get that?"

"Bar in the room."

I went back in and lo and behold, there was a small fridge with cans of Lone Star in it, and a note saying "Welcome to Kerrville." Well, that was nice. I pulled one out and then went back to the pool and pulled up a lounge chair next to him.

I pulled the tab off mine, we clinked cans together and took a drink.

"Hell of a place."

"Yup. This isn't anything like what I was expecting."

"Me neither."

There were hummingbird feeders everywhere, even given the huge number of flowering bushes around us. The air was full of the tiny birds, darting in and out of the branches, and making the feeders swing to and fro.

"Jesus. Listen to them. I never realised they were so damned loud."

Stan said, "Yeah. I've only ever seen them through a window. They sound like a squadron of tiny chainsaws."

The plan was that we were going to play a show later that night, and then tomorrow do a special "Celebration of Canada" concert around midday, with Connie Kaldor and Al Simmons.

Then we were invited to hang about for a few more days as guests of the festival and be taken on a series of tours of the area, to see some more of the countryside and the wildlife. Rod Kennedy, the festival director, wanted to show us all a good time.

There was talk of how wonderful the after show jam sessions around the campfires were.

Stan said he was looking forward to a bit of rest and relaxation before going home.

It sounded good enough to me, but the idea of hanging around out on the road, and being away from Gail without working didn't feel right, no matter how lovely it might be here.

I wondered if there might be a way to change my air ticket once more on this trip.

Stan finished his beer and got up. "I'm gonna have a nap. I'll see you later." He crushed the can in his fist, dropped it into a waste bin, and walked away.

Sounded good to me. I finished my beer as well, and went back to my room and pulled the shades.

That evening a van came and once more we loaded up and drove out to the site.

The area around the festival was just as lovely as what I had seen earlier, but I managed to keep my mouth shut. I was wondering just what sort of mindless shit kickers we were going to be playing for that night. It was pretty here and all, but this WAS Texas. We were probably in for some good ol' rootin' tootin' tail twistin' whoop 'em up fun. I hoped there was going to be some sort of security to manage the drunken cowboys we were going to have to deal with during the show. We pulled into the site and drove backstage. I got out of the van, expecting to hear some sort of mindless twanging drivel thumping out from the speakers. What I heard instead was an acoustic guitar and a cello, and a sweet and high and lovely male tenor. It was vaguely reminiscent of Jesse Winchester, and voices didn't get much better than that.

Who the hell was this?

I took my gear over to the check in table, dropped it, and then ran around to the front of the stage. It was my first sight of Lyle Lovett in the wild.

Stan and Jim came over and the three of us stood and watched the whole show. It was extraordinary. How could this guy be from Texas, as someone assured us he was?

Something was very wrong here. There were no banjos on stage. No overloud Telecasters. No whining pedal steel. No songs about pickup trucks and Jesus. This wasn't country music. Just a tall quiet man with a sweet and husky voice, playing guitar with a guy on cello behind him. He finished his set and we rushed over to say hello and congratulate him.

He listened patiently and politely while we raved at him, looking at us with that lop sided smile and those quizzical, unreadable eyes.

He shook hands, bowed, and then backed carefully away, keeping an eye on us in case we followed.

Connie Kaldor was up soon, and we wanted to catch her show. We went over to the refreshment booth and got paper cups of beer. They were the size of waste baskets, made of flimsy waxed cardboard that got even softer as your hand warmed the wax on the outside. There was nothing for it but to drink them down as quickly as possible.

Jesus. It was impossible that beer could be that cold and still remain liquid. As the paper cups began to collapse, we guzzled the entire contents down in one long gulp to avoid spilling it, and then all of us fell down from the crippling brain freeze that ensued.

Stan and Jim were on their knees, holding their hands over their eyes and moaning softly.

My tongue wasn't working properly either.

I couldn't speak. I couldn't think. I was effectively dead from the neck up.

After a while though, we were able to get back up and order another round.

This time to be safe, we had them double up the cups so we could sip it at a more reasonable rate.

We went back stage and sat on a picnic table to listen to Connie.

We hadn't seen her since a terrible gig we had done together at Gerde's Folk City in New York the previous December.

We had come from Philly that day, after a show the night before at the Cherry Tree. During the break at the Cherry Tree a fellow came up to me and handed me a piece of paper.

"I hope you won't be offended by this."

"What is it?"

"I wrote a parody of "Northwest Passage." It's about my marriage to a Jewish American Princess."

I looked at the page. "NorthEAST Passage." Okay. I began reading the lyrics. They were full of local references to caterers and jewelers, head-aches and withholding sex on the wedding night, and a chorus which went, "Ah for just one time I would take a Northeast Passage, to find a Jewish Princess reaching for my wallet thin"...and so on.

"Can I show this to Stan?"

"Uh, sure. I hope he doesn't kill me."

"No, he'll love it."
I took it backstage and showed Stan, and of course we had to perform
the parody back to back with the original in the next set. It got a huge
reaction, and the next night at Gerde's where we were sharing a bill
with Connie, we decided to sing it again.
The show had been going well enough, but then we sang the parody,
and all hell broke loose. The woman who managed the place decided
we were anti-Semetic, and we'd had to cut the show short and flee for
our lives without saying a proper goodbye to Connie.
So here in Texas we saw her briefly before she went on, hugged and
caught up a bit on the news, and then settled in to listen. She did a great
set, funny and touching and typically full of life. There was always one
moment in her shows, and it was never the same moment, when she
would have me in tears. Tonight, it was her song, "One of these Days."
The chorus went:
"One of these days
You just might surprise me, make my heart stop
Just for a while
One of these days, when I'm coming home so tired
could you make my heart leap
at the sight of your smile."

I decided that was that. I was going to cut short the proposed post-
festival holiday and get the hell home if at all possible.
I could see Connie's back through the stair railing as she sat at the
piano. She was wearing a white blouse and a tight red skirt, and leaning
forward, tossing her blonde hair about, and really digging into the
keyboard.
"Hell of a song. " I said.
Stan tipped up his beer cup and took a swig. "Yup." He smiled. "Hell of
an ass too."
"Pig. She's your friend."
"Just because she's a friend doesn't mean I can't appreciate how
well her clothes fit."

And then it was our turn.
We got on stage and set up, and then waited as someone from the
Canadian Embassy came on to present Stan and Connie and Al
Simmons with some sort of award. Jim and I weren't involved, and
mostly kept to the side of the stage, and chatted and finished our beers.
Rod Kennedy made a rather lengthy and (I thought) overly generous
introduction, and with that we were off.
Our last show was a disaster from start to finish.

The sound was appalling. Waves of feedback kept washing over us, and none of us could hear the other. It must have been a hell of an anticlimax after such a buildup.

Nothing worked. The whole set was a train wreck. I looked out front and what audience was left was mostly laying on their backs looking at the stars, or asleep.

Ah well.

We finished to polite applause and skulked off the stage.

Sometime later, I mentioned to someone backstage that I was thinking about changing my ticket home, and was there any way to do that? Not long after a woman whose name, I think, was Paisley came up to me and introduced herself as the travel coordinator. Did I really want to go home?

"Well, yeah, I do, kinda. I really appreciate Rod's generosity in wanting to keep us around for a while, but we've been out a long time and I'd like to get back to my wife."

"I can understand. How long have you been on the road?"

"Since 1974."

"Haha. No, how long has this tour been?"

"We've been out pretty much nonstop since last summer. I've been pretty sick and we all need a break."

"Okay. I'll see what I can do. Is it just you, or do all of you want to go home?"

"Just me, I think."

"Okay. I'll catch up with you tomorrow."

Next day we had to do a very strange and uncomfortable workshop on the main stage. I reckon Rod wanted to impress upon Texans that Canadians had been wrongly overlooked as artists and entertainers. He'd organized a 2 hour long event where Stan and Jim and I would sit on stage with Connie and Al, and Rod would act as host and ask us questions about what we did and where we came from, and what our influences had been. Al arrived wearing massive red and white-striped pants that came up to his armpits, a swallow tailed coat with feathered wings strapped to his arms, and a crash helmet with a large plastic propeller that spun when he wound it up with a key. Explaining where he came from and what his influences were was going to take some doing.

Al was nominally a children's performer, but there was also a deep streak of surreal humour mixed into his act. He had a tiny harmonica, maybe an inch long, with which he would play "Scotland the Brave," using the air from a blown up balloon to work the drone. He had a

Sousaphone which would give off clouds of soap bubbles when he played it. His on-stage box of props was full of PVC plastic pipes and strange spring-loaded devices that looked as if they had been looted from a Martian OB-GYN clinic.

I turned to him at one point and said, "Someday, I'd really like to be around as you take this shit through Customs and explain what it's all for."

"Yeah," he said. "Sometimes I'm in an office in a back room, doing half my show for them, trying to prove I'm harmless."

"Good luck with that."

And all the time as he performed these gags he never cracked a smile. His face was perfectly calm and serene, but if you looked behind the wire rimmed glasses his eyes were those of a zealot just before he pressed the big button on the suicide belt. Offstage he is a sweet and kind and utterly gracious man, but for anyone like myself, who at the time had only a tenuous grip on reality, his act could be a bit unsettling. If Terry Gilliam ever made a movie about life in the Wild West, Al would be cast as the handsome but troubled and mysterious hero who rides into town on a inflated rubber sea horse and cleans out the bad guys with a pair of squirt guns.

For the Texans it must have been something to watch. Rod was terribly in earnest, and kept asking us all searching questions about our lives and our homes, and other important stuff, but we were all embarrassed with being taken so seriously, and kept fooling around and making bad jokes in an effort to divert attention from ourselves.

We played "The Idiot," after having talked about the great movement from the Maritimes to the Canadian West, and the similarities between Texas and Alberta. As we played, Al jumped up and began running through the crowd and flapping his wings, leaping over the startled audience, who were scrambling away in panic from the foreign looney with the clown shoes and the whirling propeller hat.

We finished the workshop, and that was the end of our official duties. It was a beautiful day, sunny and warm and dry. I walked around the festival site for a while. It was larger than I had previously thought, and there were trails leading away from the concert field, back through the trees to where folks were camped. This was where the famous campfire sessions happened, I guessed.

I caught a ride back to the hotel and called Gail again, and told her I was working on getting an earlier flight home.

"It's really lovely here. There are all kinds of things I've never seen before, and the guy wants to keep us around for a bit, and take us out to ride a long horn or something. It's kinda tempting, but I think I'm

gonna pass, if I can swing it. I want to come home."
I went back to the site later in the evening and I was sitting out in the field, watching a band up on the stage.
It was a beautiful night. Cool and clear, and a light dew was falling on the grass and sweetening the air. The sky overhead was deepening into violet, and the first stars were beginning to appear. This was a hell of a place. I still hated John Wayne, and the Alamo, and all the loud- mouthed gun-toting brag and bluster that was the face that Texas showed to the world. But this place was different. The people here were quiet, and polite and kind. I decided I might need to re-assess my pet prejudices. Maybe it wouldn't be a bad thing if I stayed on with Stan and Jim for a couple more days.

I looked over to the left side of the crowd and the festival travel coordinator was walking over to me. She sat down and handed me a folder with a computer printout inside.
"I managed to catch the travel agent at home just as he was sitting down to dinner. He has a home computer and he was able to fix you up. You're leaving here early tomorrow morning. You'll fly out from San Antonio and change planes in Dallas. You'll be home by early afternoon."
"Wow, this is great. Thank you."
"Glad to help. I hope you enjoyed yourself here."
"Absolutely. People here are great. I'm looking forward to getting home though."
"Great. Travel safe."
She patted me on the shoulder and walked away.
I caught a ride back to the hotel to call Gail and pick up the mess from the laundry bomb which had gone off in my room. If I was going to leave by 8 a.m. I needed to get my head down.
I knocked on Stan's door but there was no answer.
I tried Jim's room too, but there was no response there as well.
No problem. I'd catch up with them later.

The wakeup call came at 6:00. I grabbed a shower, got dressed and did a final check of my luggage and instrument cases. Checked my wallet.
I was low on funds and didn't have enough to get home. I was going to have to wake Stan.
I went next door and knocked. No answer. I knocked again, harder this time.
Inside I heard some grunting and then a session of prolonged coughing. There was a thump, presumably as Stan's feet hit the floor. The door opened a crack, and Stan looked out over the safety chain. It didn't need

more than a glance to see he was brutally hung over. His eyes were swollen, and he was in obvious pain.

He cleared his throat. "What's up?"

"I'm going home. I managed to get my ticket changed, and my flight leaves in a couple of hours. I need some cash for travel."

"Okay. Just a second."

He closed the door slightly, slid the chain off and let me in. He staggered into the bathroom for a pee, then came out and sat down on the side of the bed and lit a smoke, and then rubbed his head and coughed for a while. He looked up.

"How much do you need?"

"I dunno. A couple of hundred bucks will tide me over until you get back and we can do a final divvy."

"Okay."

He heaved himself to his feet and walked unsteadily over to his suit bag. He dug around and fished out a brown envelope. He put the cigarette in his mouth, and then, squinting against the smoke counted out some twenties. He replaced the envelope, came over and handed them to me.

"That okay?"

I flipped through the wad. "That's loads. Thanks."

He sat back down on his bed, rubbed his eyes and yawned.

"Catch any of the show last night?"

"Yeah, a bit."

"I didn't see you. Where were you?"

"Oh, I was sitting about halfway back on the right. Were you there?"

"Yeah, but I was on the left side. I came back early when I found out I could go home today."

"Yeah. Good idea."

"You look like you're hurting."

"Yeah. I had a few beers while I was watching the show."

"Only a few?"

He shrugged. "Okay, a lot of beers. Then I went back to the campfire area and hung out for a while and played a bit. There was some wine going around. And later there was a guy with some single malt. I was just heading for the shuttle when someone offered me some tequila, and that might not have been my best move."

"No shit. It wasn't mescal was it?"

"No, just tequila."

I looked at my watch.

"I gotta catch the airport shuttle."

"Okay. Be safe."

I stood up. "What about you? Are you gonna stay here or go home?"

He stubbed out his smoke and got up and went to the bathroom and pulled a bottle of Aspirin out of his shaving kit. He shook out a handful and swallowed them down with water he caught from the tap in his cupped hands. He splashed some water on his face while he was at it, then dried himself with a hand towel and came back out and sat down again.

"What did you say?"

"You staying here, or going home?"

"I'm gonna stay here for a few days, hang out a bit and look around...do some thinking. I've got some decisions to make. I need some rest, and I'm not getting any back in Dundas."

"Okay."

I looked at my watch again. "Listen, I gotta go."

"Yup."

He got off the bed and picked up his cigarettes and lighter again. He pulled one out, and holding it in his right hand, came over and gave me a hug and a whiskery kiss on the cheek. I kissed him back and said, "Love you. See you later."

He let me go, thumped me on the shoulder and said, "Love you. Be safe."

As I pulled the door shut, I could see him lighting his cigarette and turning back towards his bed.

I closed the door, gave it a tug to make sure it was locked, and then gathered up my suitcase and instruments and walked down the hall.

CHAPTER 85

Night Drive

Saskatchewan. East of the Battlefords.
About 6 PM.

It is autumn on the Northern Prairies, and I am standing on the
Westbound side of the Yellowhead Highway, watching the great flocks
of migrating birds as they come down from the Arctic where they have
spent their summer on the tundra, fighting for territory, courting and
mating, building their nests, and raising their young. The air is full of
their high and ecstatic cries as they wheel and spin above the river and
the distant stubble fields, looking for a place to light and rest and feed
before the next leg of their long journey south.

It is still early evening, but there is at best only an hour or so of daylight
left, and I have to decide whether to rack up in the town an hour west
of where I am, or press on for three more hours to the Alberta border.
There are more options for food and motels the further west I go, but it
has been a long day's drive already, and my eyes are tired, and I don't
want to risk running into whatever wild life is lurking out on the road
after dark. There are creatures out there, large and small, with a devil
may care attitude towards large fast-moving metal objects, and I'd
rather not meet them.

It's a choice between giving in to the addictive rhythm of the drive, and
the habits of a lifetime that urge me to press on, versus an older and
somewhat wiser man's need to listen to common sense, and rest more
often on a journey like this. And the patient and faithful and beloved
person who waits for me back home, the one whose steadying hand
rests always on my shoulder and my heart, would rather I listen to
the better angels of her nature, if not my own, and not risk a few more
hours in the falling darkness. She knows the light is tricky this time of
day, and my eyes are not what they used to be.

But if I stop sooner, it adds to tomorrow's drive, and the frantic Meth-
head on the all-news radio is yapping that the weather may change
in the next 24 hours, and depending on how much early snow comes
piling out of the mountains life as we know it on this planet could be

wiped out, and it might be difficult making the first show on this tour.
Maybe I should press on.

Besides, the motels in the next town along will likely be full of rowdy
young oil patch workers, full of beer and flush with unaccustomed
cash. The parking lot will be jammed with their giant tricked-out 4
wheel drive pick-up trucks with the portable welding units in the back,
and a gas barbecue will be outside the door of every room. And there
will be the constant parade of taxis, honking their horns and racing
their motors as they drop off and then later pick up the hookers who
follow the oil workers. There tend to be noisy confrontations outside
the rooms when one party or the other is left unsatisfied with the
transaction. Even if I manage to get a bed, I'm unlikely to get much
sleep.

And I know the best meal I'll be able to get is at the "All-you-can-stand-
to-eat" Chinese buffet, and at this hour the pickings will be slim, not to
mention like myself, old and tired and grey.

What to do?

Meanwhile, I am standing next to the van, breathing in the scented air
as the dew falls on the dry earth and sweetens the deepening twilight.
There are late season crickets in the long grass in the ditch, slowly
ratcheting up the silence, and I can hear a distant 18 wheeler out to the
east, its tires humming and thumping against the pavement as it grinds
its way up the long hill. Sound travels better in the moist air of evening.
The driver is having to change gears every quarter mile or so.

And out here every other sense is magnified as well. I can see
everything, both near and far, in clear and precise detail. The river
below me has a dull leaden gleam as it cuts through the shadows
between the deep hills. A kingfisher plummets out of the air and
disappears into the water briefly, and then reappears and flies into a
cottonwood tree. And far to the west the sun is dipping between the
clouds and the horizon and shining through ribbons of rain as they
move over the patchwork fields. I can see farmers' combines out there,
like Matchbox toys in the distance, kicking up clouds of dust, trying to
get the last of the wheat in before the snow comes. To the south, other
fields are being plowed, and there are clouds of white gulls following
the machines as if they were fishing boats at sea. As the sun dips lower,
the breeze picks up, and the dark smell of the fresh earth comes to me,
and I throw back my head and take a deeper breath.

It was right about here, near as I can reckon, and almost exactly the same
time of year that we stopped one night, Stan and I, driving west from
home to begin a month long tour, literally a life time ago.

We had left about 40 hours previous, in the evening, as we usually did, after the bent and smoking wreckage from rush hour had been cleared away. We'd taken the Queen Elizabeth Way to the 427, and then up to the 401 to catch the 400 North towards Barrie.

Back then, before Toronto had metastasized, it was around Major MacKenzie Drive that you felt you had finally shaken the Big Smoke and were now on your way, free from the constraints of civilization. There were no noisy theme parks back then, no endless rows of cookie cutter houses, just farm fields opening up to the horizon.

Cross the Holland Marsh and stop for take-out coffee just south of Barrie.

And then get back into the van and settle down for the overnight drive. Stan would have the first shift. He'd take it as far as Sudbury, and we'd change over. Another round of take-out coffee and maybe fill the thermos for the wee small hours when everything was closed. He'd settle in on the Cadillac seat with a book and a cigarette and a shot of rum in his cup. Eventually he'd get sleepy, and the book would drop out of his hand. Some part of his brain though, would remain aware of what was going on and he was never quite unconscious. One time, I was driving between Fredericton and Edmundston New Brunswick, and I had thought he was completely chalked out behind me. I was still a new driver, with only a beginner's permit, and technically shouldn't have been behind the wheel without an observer in the next seat. As I climbed a long hill I looked carefully in the mirrors and pulled into the slow lane without putting the signal on.

He immediately sat up and said, "Don't ever do that again."

"Do what?"

"Change lanes without signaling."

"How did you know? I thought you were asleep."

"I was, but I felt the van change lanes and I never heard the signal. Don't do that."

"But I checked my mirrors. There was nothing there."

"You don't know that. You only know that you didn't see anyone. There might have been someone in your blind spot, and the only chance they'd have was if you'd signaled."

And all these years later, I can be driving through some barren and deserted wasteland like South Dakota, or Nebraska or (God help me,) Utah, and I will not have seen another car for half a day, and if I have to change lanes to avoid the wreckage from a burnt out and abandoned Winnebago, or the charred and twisted remains of a fallen satellite, I will not only check all my mirrors at least twice, but I will put on the signal, dammit.

So as the three of us headed west, one of us would drive, one would sleep, and the other would sit up and help watch for trouble. As you left Sudbury and headed into the deep woods past Espanola and Thessalon, the deer and moose would be a constant worry. You needed two pairs of eyes.

There were other issues as well. One morning around 5 or so, I was at the wheel and we came out of the forest to an unexpected line of US Customs booths. It was just west of Desbarats, and I had inadvertently taken the turn off to Michigan. Neither Eadie nor I had noticed the mistake at the time. We were deep into a debate about what constituted the perfect sandwich, the way other men might argue over Kant's Critique of Pure Reason or the perfect baseball dream-team line up. We were at an impasse over the use of sweet versus spicy Italian sausage, and although there was only one road, I had managed to get us lost.

Then up past Wawa, the secret hitch-hiker's graveyard. We'd heard any number of stories from friends who had been stranded there, sometimes for days and weeks on their way across Canada. Doug McArthur once told us how he had been there for a couple of days, with no one so much as slowing down to throw a beer bottle at him, when a guy in a battered truck picked him up, drove him three miles to the next exit to town, and then dropped him off.

He'd seen Doug that morning on the way to work, and now he was coming back. And although he was only going to the other side of town, he'd felt sorry for him and decided that a change of scenery might at least cheer him up a bit. Doug walked back to his original spot where the sight lines were better.

There was a story of how someone had been marooned there long enough to have taken a knife and carved a 500 yard long crie de couer on the wooden guard rail, about how they'd "been stuck for 3 goddamned days in this motherfucking shit hole of a dump and not one fucking person has given me a ride and now I've been here 4 goddamned days, and still no luck and now there's some asshole standing a mile in front of me and he's going to steal my ride and..." and so on.

He probably gave up, walked into town, settled down, and got elected Mayor.

Past Wawa, through Marathon and up along the top of the Lake. We always changed drivers before trying that part of the drive. You needed to be fresh.

There were still any number of moose and deer that might wander into your path, but now you also had to worry about the weather, which could turn on you in a moment. Rain and snow, sudden ice storms, and hailstones the size of steam irons might engulf the van and pummel it flat almost any time of the year.

And on your right was a wall of jagged rocks waiting to kill you if your attention happened to wander and your right front wheel dropped onto the soft shoulder. On the left, a dizzying drop into the water below, or worse, you could meet an 18 wheeler coming around the corner, lit up like a small town, with the trailer swinging out into your lane, and a Benzedrine-crazed driver who hadn't slept since the Nixon administration.

The truckers were terrifying. Back then, there were virtually no regulations around the issue of how much sleep you had to have per trip, and as the saying went, "If the wheels weren't turning, you weren't earning." So they tended to push their luck and it always ran out somewhere. There was one place where we were the first on the scene after a flatbed hauling steel reinforcing rod hit a concrete abutment and came to an abrupt halt. There was nothing to stop the load from flying forward and continuing another forty feet or so through the cab and the windshield. All that was left of the driver was a bunch of blood soaked flannel rags hanging at the ends of the rods.

That gets your attention.

We came to a backup one morning. Cars and trucks and Winnebagos had been stopped and waiting for hours in a narrow canyon leading down a long hill, where there was a sheer cliff in front of you as the road curved sharply to the right. Some cowboy hadn't made it and had run himself into the wall at a high rate of speed and it was taking longer than normal to pull the wreckage aside and rinse his remains off the rocks, as he had been hauling dynamite. They had to be careful so as not to set off the load. We sat there for an hour or so, waiting and listening to the morbid chatter on the CB radio, when there was a huge flash of light past the trees, and then the van was rocked by a shock wave and a massive boom. I seem to recall it was a controlled blast and no one else was killed, but it took the better part of the day before we got under way again.

You could never relax, never for a moment take your eyes off the road. We were slowly making our way over the top of the Lakehead about 3 in the morning, one trip, under a clear and starlit sky, and a sudden gust of wind brought a wall of wet snow down over us, and within minutes the road was hub-deep in slippery muck which was now freezing as the temperature dropped. I was behind the wheel, anxiously trying to steer into the deep ruts a trucker had left. The snow kept falling, the visibility was down to maybe a hundred feet, and the wheels began slipping, and I was terrified.

Stan was in the passenger seat, and ordinarily we might have stopped and changed over to the more experienced driver, but there was no safe place to pull over on this dark and narrow road. I kept going, and Stan had his hands braced against the dashboard and I could hear his right foot banging the floorboards, as he kept pumping the imaginary brake.

"Slow down," he kept saying.

"I'm trying, but I can't use the brakes. I'm afraid of going into a spin. It's slicker than a snotty marble. I'm going to gear down to second."

That helped our stability a little on the downhill, but the rear of the van was still fish-tailing wildly in the frozen slush when we had to climb. Stan said, "We should have put chains on the tires."

David Eadie was in the Cadillac seat having a nap, and it must have penetrated his subconscious, because he sat up and said, "Why? Are they trying to get away?" and then lay back down. He'd never opened his eyes and didn't remember saying it when daybreak came.

We kept on past Thunder Bay, and into the woods towards Kenora, through darkened towns that weren't towns at all, just a crossroads and a sign, with some boarded up store fronts, and a blinking yellow light swinging in the night wind.

Kenora, like all towns in the North had its own mascot statue. Sudbury had the giant Nickel. Wawa had a huge and angry-looking Canada Goose with outspread wings which could startle the living hell out of you at 4 in the morning if you'd forgotten about it. There were any number of smaller towns, each with their own bit of folk art. They were usually carved out of stumps by some obsessive local codger who had a chain saw, a sense of grievance and too much time on his hands. Others were made of chicken wire and plaster. There was one somewhere along the route, of a Yeti or Bigfoot made from plaster and wire and leftover remnants of shag rug, and was dyed a bright orange. That was a hell of a thing to see at 3 in the morning after a couple days with no sleep. Kenora had a giant muskie, or a pike or something.

We drove by. David gave it the once over and said, "I think Ontario is a Cree word for "Land of the Giant Ugly Statue."

Kenora was a major stop for us before we hit the prairies.

We'd pull over for coffee once again, and maybe a bottle of something at the liquor store in the middle of town. Stan and I ducked in one day, and looked over the selections. I had chosen my usual quart of Teacher's, but Stan wanted a change. Nothing else appealed to him though, and in the end he gave up and pulled a bottle of Appleton's Rum off the shelf.

"I guess I'll stick with Old Facefull."

Back in the van, and over to the chip wagon on the left side of
the highway for a shopping bag full of French fries. Then up the
road another mile where we could get a couple of toasted western
sandwiches each to go, (on whole wheat of course, as we were trying to
eat healthier,) and we were set for the next leg.

It was later that morning that Stan gave me my first "official" driving
lesson. I had been behind the wheel before, but usually only for fun and
excitement, when we'd buy a bottle of cheap sherry and ferry the old
Datsun over to Wolfe Island near Kingston, where I'd spend the day
learning the intricacies of The Bootlegger's Reverse, the Capriole, and
the flashy and difficult Immelmann Turn.
Today was different. This was an official lesson. The band needed
another responsible driver.
We were a couple hours east of Winnipeg when he pulled over to the
side of the Trans Canada, and put it in park.
"What's up?"
He got out and walked around to the passenger side where I was
sitting.
"You are. You're going to drive for a while. Come on. Change over."
I got into the driver's seat, adjusted the mirrors a bit as I'd seen people
do, and took a deep breath.
"Now what?"
He said, "Look in your side mirror and see if anyone's coming.
Okay. Now the inside rear view. Now look over your left shoulder.
Good. Is it clear?"
"Yup."
"Good. Now check it again."
"Okay."
"Alright. Put your signal on, and take it up to about 30 and then
pull out onto the pavement, and accelerate up to 60. You don't need to
floor it, but do it smartly, and as quickly as you safely can."
So I did, and we were now cruising along in the right hand lane.
Stan said, "Okay. You need to check your mirrors on both sides every
30 seconds or so. More if you're in heavy traffic. Check left, check right.
And now in the middle. Good. Keep doing that. Good. You're doing
great. Now get within 10 car lengths of that school bus, and keep station
on him."
I sped up slightly and tucked in behind at the right distance.
"Great. Now keep it there. Keep checking your mirrors."
It was right about then that a bee came in through the no draft, and
began rocketing around the inside of the van. I gave a yell, and Stan and
David began furiously swatting at the poor creature with a rolled up

newspaper and one of David's boat shoes, all the while squealing like debutantes. The van meanwhile was swerving wildly back and forth and taking the width of the road on two wheels.

After a couple of minutes the bee decided its work here was done, and it flew back out the window, and order was restored, but when I looked for the bus I'd been following the highway was empty. I looked in the mirrors and everyone behind us had pulled over and parked until our crisis was over, or whatever drugs the driver was on had worn off.

We felt the presence of those who had gone before us, everywhere along that route.

The place names were full of romance, and spoke of incidents from a history we would never know. "Lost Knife River," "Mad Woman Lake," and "I Got Sick Of His Constant Whining So I Throttled Him In His Sleep Falls."

The past was always with us, particularly in Saskatchewan. You'd be driving through the low hills near the river, watching the fluff from the cotton wood trees drift along the surface of the water, and there might be a small plaque to show that men had met briefly on this lonely spot and only some of them left alive.

You could easily imagine being a frightened young kid in a red serge coat and a pill box hat, sweating in the heat, straining to hear over the dry whirr of the grasshoppers and the pounding of your own heart, knuckles white on your rifle, and watching the horizon where you just knew Riel and the lads were about to arrive. Except while you were watching the horizon over there, the boys had come up on your flank over here, and your horses were now off making new friends, and large caliber soft-nosed bullets were snapping past your head, blowing the cottonwoods into deadly splinters, and you might just have to file a strongly worded complaint with upper management about workplace conditions if there's much more of this.

Many of the south Saskatchewan towns are gone now, dried up and blown to dust after the CN rail lines got moved or closed. But back in the day, there would be a collection of houses and commercial buildings, a grocery store, and a gas station with a restaurant attached, all in the shelter of the faded red CO-OP grain elevator by the tracks.

We'd pull over for a pit stop and walk through the door.

It was like a bad western movie where the piano music stops, and everyone turns around to glare at the intruders.

There'd be a couple of tables of farmers, who having done their morning chores would now be sitting around in their faded feed caps, and drinking what the restaurant fondly referred to as coffee, and

724

working their tired jokes on the lone waitress. We'd walk in and the place would go silent. We'd grab a table and wait for the server to bring menus. Usually one or all of us would have brought in our shaving kits and there would be time to have a quick wash and brush up in the men's room. It was disheartening to look in the mirror under the cruel fluorescent light, and see what just a couple of days of bad food and poor sleep and constant gnawing anxiety had done. Bags under the eyes, blotchy skin, and ragged patchy stubble. You'd get out the razor and shaving cream, and discover there was no hot water. You'd shave anyway, brush the teeth, and then take down the mirror from over the sink and try to see if you'd developed bed sores from sitting in the van too long, after which you'd let someone else have a turn.
As you walked by the farmers' table conversation would have resumed, and you'd overhear one of them say something like, "Yeah Earl, I know. They look like Faggots to me too, but they're too big to fuck with. Best leave 'em alone."
David once came back from his turn in the loo with a haunted look.
"What's your problem? Not the old trouble again?"
He sat down and began stirring non-dairy creamer and sugar into his cup of brown swill.
He shook his head. "Jesus. I just looked in the mirror. I look like I was drawn by Ralph Steadman."

We'd look at what the locals were eating and order whatever looked safe. A hot beef sandwich may not be what you wanted, and in fact for me it rarely was, but out here it was something you hoped not even this place could screw up.
We'd have our meal, pay the bill, and Stan would go out to gas up and check the oil and lighten the weight of the van by carefully scraping off the crusted layer of grasshopper corpses that had accumulated on the grill during the last leg of the drive, and which were now slowly roasting and giving off a sick making smell. They were disgusting creatures, each about the size of a small canning lobster, and they sometimes arrived on the plains in such Biblical numbers that they would pile up on the road and the footing would get slippery, and you could hear them crunching and squishing under the tires. We had learned that a species of wasp had evolved which would swarm over any parked vehicle and helpfully carry away and consume the dead bodies. We sometimes might linger over pie and coffee a while longer to let them finish the job.
The last thing would be to order 3 more large cups of coffee to go, and a half dozen of the butter tarts that were under the glass by the cash register.

The butter tarts were about 5 inches across, and weighed maybe half a pound or so. They were made of soft doughy pastry, which likely had as its first ingredient beef tallow, or industrial lubricant, and were filled with a gooey brown mixture of caramelized sugar and what we hoped were raisins, all tightly sealed with Saran Wrap.

I always imagined them being baked by some local farm wife, a sweet faced woman named Muriel, with a home perm, a flowered apron and big soft upper arms dusted with flour. She would whip up a batch in her bright and spotless kitchen, wrap them up, and get them ready for delivery, and her husband, a skinny and taciturn farmer named Dean, would drive them over to the cafe in his old Studebaker pick up. More likely they had been mass produced in China, flash frozen, brought across the water, and shipped out from the warehouse in Portland Oregon.

They had enough sugar to launch a missile, and a half hour or so after eating one you were stricken with the shakes and sweats and a bad case of burning cramps in the lower G.I tract. Not the best thing to eat when there were no bathrooms for the next couple of hours, and with not so much as a scrap of sheltering bush to crouch behind.

The coffee was less like coffee, and more like lukewarm feed lot run off that had been strained to remove the solids. We kept a jar of instant Nescafe in the van liquor cabinet. We'd stir in a spoonful to give it some needed oomph, then break out the Bailey's Irish Cream, "Coffee Improver," as Stan called it, and we were ready to go.

Back out on the road.

It was usually after a meal break where there might be a bit of conversation between the three of us, but nothing of any real importance ever got discussed. Most likely it was along the lines of what David said one afternoon as he took his turn behind the wheel. There had been a period of silence while we tried to digest lunch. I was already having the sweats and cramps. It felt and sounded like the downstairs neighbours were moving furniture around the apartment, and the hardwood floors were taking a beating. I had begun scanning the horizon in hopes of seeing a field of round bales.

And then David spoke.

"Man, that kid back at the last gas station really did a great job on the windshield."

That by itself was worth a couple of hours of discussion, and fond remembrances of windshields past.

We were very nearly brain dead after a couple of days.

We didn't play much music during the drives.

We had a few old Rolling Stones compilations, and those first 3 Dire Straits records to keep the blood moving during the small hours. We were listening to "Tunnel of Love," one night, cranked as loud as possible, coming over the top of the Lake, and as that last long guitar solo faded away, Stan said, "I always feel like he should be standing on a mountain top, with a cape flapping behind him when he's playing that." And then he hit the rewind button.

But mostly the van was silent as we ground along the highway.

The fact was there were almost always disagreements and negotiations about what we could or couldn't listen to in the van. Stan began bringing in Steeleye Span tapes, and after a couple of plays we asked that he wear the headphones and leave us in peace. Likewise, I had to pick my moments to play the Haydn string quartets I loved. Stan liked the Beethoven symphonies I brought in, but I soon stopped playing them as he had an annoying habit of pretending to conduct with a Bic pen as he drove along, and he always brought the horns in too soon in the second movement of the 5th.

That Paul Brady/Andy Irvine record got a lot of play, as did the first Barde record. We loved them.

We liked JJ Cale a lot. John Martyn was on nearly every day; "Solid Air," usually around sundown. It just felt right, like a soundtrack for the movie we were all watching outside the glass. We played a lot of Fred Neil too, and John Hurt.

We listened to our friends. David Essig, and Willie Bennett, along with Doug McArthur's second record, "Sisteron."

The Red Clay Ramblers' "Merchants Lunch" never left heavy rotation in the van.

We all loved the first couple of McGarrigle records. The songs were wonderful, and the harmonies were gorgeous. Siblings singing together make a wonderful sound.

And Stan's personal fallback position for late night driving was Joni Mitchell's "Blue" along with "Court and Spark."

But there were whole genres of music Stan missed, either because we never turned on the radio except to get the weather report, or he didn't want to have something playing while he was working on a song in his head.

I got into the van one day, a few weeks after the disaster with Klag, and Stan slipped a tape into the dashboard player and cranked the volume.

"Listen to this. Klag left it in the van. I don't know who it is, but it's amazing."

It was a compilation tape of the Eagles, and the song was "Heartache Tonight."

I reached out and turned it down. "You gotta be joking."

"What do you mean?" he said. "It's great." He cranked the volume back up. "Listen to the slide guitar."

"You're telling me this is the first time you've ever heard this shit?"

"It's not shit. Here." He pushed the fast forward button. "Listen to this."

And so help me, it was "Hotel California," and after that damned song had been everywhere on the radio 24 hours a day, for what seemed like forever, and the rest of the entire world was sick of it, Stan was discovering it for the first time.

During the years that David Eadie travelled with us, we mostly listened to those strange and surreal BBC Goon show tapes, to the point where we could perform the scripts ourselves. The world outside the van was so bleak and forbidding and relentlessly dull, that we took refuge in the bizarre world that Spike Milligan had created, where one man might attempt to drink all the water in Loch Lomond in order to retrieve a buried treasure, or be tricked into stealing Napoleon's piano from the Louvre, and rowing it across the English Channel to earn a couple of pounds. Somehow these plays about hapless idiots on a pointless quest made a kind of sense and we took comfort in the madness of the scripts. But mostly we just had silence as we sat in our fetid tin prison and watched the world crawl by outside the window.

At least until the CB arrived.

The CB radio got installed mostly as a tool at first. With it Stan could find out what traffic conditions were like up ahead, where the cops were, and what the weather was going to be doing. And it was useful the odd occasion when we had filled the gas tank and had failed to note the time.

The van's gas gauge had broken long ago, along with the speedometer, and the only way we could deal with it was to fill the tank every 4 hours and check the clock. Then we'd take it up to what we felt was 60 MPH based on the noise from the tires. On the Trans Canada and the Yellowhead it was easier to estimate, as they were both jointed roads back then. The thump- thump- thump of the tires against the joints had a distinct and even rhythm, and after a while the sound was in our DNA. So 4 hours at 60MPH, and we were due for another fill up.

But if we were tired or distracted one might look at the time and wonder, "How long has it been since the last fill up? Are we almost out of gas?" And then the CB was handy as some friendly trucker could guide us in to a filling station that wasn't visible from the road.

What caused problems after a while was Stan's fascination with the whole world of trucker radio. He began listening to it almost exclusively and it drove the rest of us mad. The people on the radio were racists and homophobes, and violent misogynistic red necks who spent every waking moment spewing their hateful filth to anyone who couldn't get out of ear shot. It was like an early version of Facebook or Twitter, a collection of mindless idiots with nothing to say, but who nevertheless, WOULD NOT SHUT UP.

It was made worse by Stan's insisting on getting on the radio and engaging with them, using the same faux Southern drawl the rest of them affected.

"Why are we listening to this shit? These people are horrible. It's bad enough they're out there, but why do we have to listen in on their filth?"

Stan had no good answer. "I dunno. I just like listening."

"But you're not just listening. You're egging them on. You're getting on the radio and baiting them."

"Yeah, but it's fun."

"For you maybe. But to me it's pointless. It's like poking a mad dog through a fence. You're not going to persuade them of anything, and I hate having these people in the van with me."

After a while Stan would have finished his driving shift, and would hand over to either me or David or later, Jim Morison.

With David, we would wait until Stan fell asleep, and then carefully switch the accursed CB back on, and tune into the trucker's channel, and... pretend to be a gay couple.

We've come a little ways, in the intervening years, in terms of tolerance and acceptance of other peoples' sexuality and lifestyles. To be sure, we still have a long way to go, but we have in fact, made some real progress. But back then, the very idea that some disgusting homosexual pervert was spoiling and fouling the sacred CB radio waves with his Godless filth was enough to drive these stupid rednecks into a seething frenzy.

"GODDAMMIT YOU FAGGOT. WHAT THE HELL ARE YOU DOING ON THE RADIO? WHAT BUSINESS DOES A QUEER GOT WITH A WALKIE TALKIE ANYWAY? WHERE THE HELL ARE YOU, YOU FILTHY FAGGOTY SCUM? GODDAMMIT I AM GOING TO FIND YOU, YOU DISGUSTING LITTLE PIG. I'M GONNA FIND YOU AND DRIVE YOU OFF THE ROAD AND PULL YOU OUT OF THAT FAGGOT TRUCK OF YOURS AND... IT'S PROBABLY NOT EVEN A REAL TRUCK. YOU'RE PROBABLY DRIVING A FOURWHEELER YOU FILTHY PERVERT, OR SOME KIND OF QUEER FOREIGN JAPANESE FAGGOT TRUCK. I'M GONNA FIND YOU AND I'M GONNA DRIVE YOU OFF THE ROAD AND I'M GONNA PULL YOU OUTTA THE CAB AND I'M GONNA KICK YOUR FAGGOT ASS, SO

HELP ME JESUS."

"Really?"

"YOU'RE GODDAMNED RIGHT I AM. I'M GONNA STOMP YOUR FAGGOT ASS INTO THE GODDAMNED GROUND."

Long pause.

And then, in a breathy voice, "What are you going to be wearing?"

"WHAT?"

That's the way to handle these closet case assholes. Confront them with their deepest desires.
Stan would hear the ruckus and crawl down out of the sleeping compartment and grab the microphone away and go back to bed.

Always westward.
The distances we were driving were daunting. Theoretically we knew we were a long way from home, but at 6 in the morning, tired and hungry, and shaky from caffeine, after driving pretty much nonstop for 40 hours, and where not one single thing was familiar, the reality of it began to wear you down. You had not even begun the tour yet. This was just the drive to get to the place where the tour would begin, and then you had another 3 or 4 or 6 weeks of this to look forward to.
We were west of a tiny town called Findlater one morning, the sun rising behind us, and I was wondering if it might have been named for a Scots piper who'd won the Victoria Cross during the Battle of Dargai Heights in Pakistan in the late 1800's.
There was a farm near the highway, and the lights were on in the house, and smoke was rising from the chimney, and as we drove closer I could see in just those few seconds the man standing in the barnyard, and his wife as she walked towards him with two steaming cups of coffee.
A mother cat was winding in and out of the man's legs, her kittens following unsteadily behind, their little tails like exclamation marks.
The woman reached him and handed him the cup, stood on her toes, and kissed him on the cheek. And then we were past.
Stan was at the wheel, and I settled back into my seat and tried to not think about the month on the road that lay ahead.
I heard a sniff, and then another, and I looked over at Stan, and he was wiping his eyes, much the same as I was doing. We didn't say anything. There was nothing to say.

We were watching the sun set one evening. As we drove further west, the road began to rise visibly. We were always climbing now, and at one point we crested the top of a long hill, and all at once we were able to see forever. The sun was maybe a palm's breadth from dipping below the horizon. Hundreds of square miles of patchwork fields were spread out before us. They dwindled and disappeared into the shadows at the far edge of the earth. The eastern slopes of the smaller hills below us were in deep blue shadow, but we could see the cottonwoods along the river gleaming bright gold in the waning light. Everywhere we looked was gold. The light burnishing the stubble fields, was gold. The dust clouds behind the distant combines were gold, and the very air itself was a deep thick amber colour, like warm toffee.

We could see a couple of different weather systems as we craned our necks and looked around. On our right, to the north, there were dark swollen and bruised looking clouds, and the van was hit by a brief rattling gust of ice pellets, like a blast of buckshot. To the left, maybe 10 miles away, there was a thunderstorm. Lightning was flickering inside a tall dark anvil shaped cloud, and rain was coming down in a dark curtain.

But everywhere else in this vast landscape, gold, in every shade imaginable, like a Klimt painting.

There were other clouds moving slowly across the sky, and their shadows on the earth looked like they were from the hands of some giant divine being as it carried out its act of creation.

I decided if there was in fact a God, he was a rather busy and show-offy kind of guy.

Stan spoke.

"The Ancient of Days."

I turned to him. "Sorry?"

"The Ancient of Days. I keep thinking about that William Blake drawing. I keep expecting to see a giant bearded figure in a loin cloth come over the horizon."

"Jesus. Keep out of my head, man. I was just thinking that."

The wind has picked up now.

I get back into the van and close the door.

I start the motor and turn the heater on HIGH. I am sitting behind the wheel, shivering, and staring through the windshield glass and remembering that moment.

The sun has gone below the horizon now, and I haven't yet decided if I am going to pull in for the night at the next town or keep on for a while. I reckon I'll see how busy the town looks and play it by ear. I'll figure it out when I get there.

All those years ago, the night we watched that sunset, Stan and David
and I had many more miles to make. We had lost some time along
the way. We had stopped for a few hours in a motel the night before,
desperate to catch some rest, and more importantly, to shower and
change our clothes. The alternative would have been to buy a can of
Raid.
We got a couple of rooms. David and me in one, Stan in the other. We
were on a tight schedule and had to be up early the next morning.
We lugged our gear out of the van and piled it into the rooms. Stan
sat with us for a bit, and we had a couple of quick night caps to ease
the road jitters, and then he stood up. He reached into his pocket and
pulled out a fist full of quarters and proceeded to jam them into the
Magic Fingers machines on our beds.
    "Oh, you bastard."
    He smiled, and said, "Sleep tight." and went out the door, as the
beds began to rumble and vibrate.
Oddly enough, it was strangely restful, and I slept pretty well.
My alarm woke me in the pre-dawn dark, and I sat up. The beds
had migrated across the room during the night, and the door to the
bathroom was blocked. David and I managed to get showered and
packed and ready to go pretty quickly. I was just going to knock on
Stan's door when it opened. He was fully dressed and looked relatively
fresh.
    "Oh, you're up. Good. I was beginning to worry."
He said, "I've been up for half an hour." He smiled and held up a
couple of empty beer bottles.
    "I drank my alarm clock."

We had really needed the bed rest, but now we were a bit behind in our
schedule. And so we drove relentlessly all that day, once again stopping
every four hours to grab a coffee and a bite, fill the tank and check the
oil, and to change drivers.
It was now about 3 in the morning, and we were just coming up to
where I am currently parked. Stan was behind the wheel. I was riding
shotgun, and David was wrapped up in a sleeping bag on the Caddy
seat.
Stan hit the turn signal and slowed down.
    "I need to pee."
    "Good. Me too."
He pulled over and parked. He turned the van off and hit the 4 way
flashers.
I got out and stepped onto the gravel, and cautiously made my way
in the dark down the slope, away from the road, and well away

from where Stan was. We had been driving and drinking luke warm thermos coffee without a break for some hours and I didn't want to be downstream from him. I'd get washed into the river.
I finished my business and zipped up.
All around us were thousands of birds. All calling and yelping and greeting each other in the darkness. We had been watching them as we drove through the twilight some hours before. Vast flocks of them in the distance, looking like clouds of dark smoke against the sky, as they wheeled and circled above the fields and sloughs. Canada geese, snow geese, trumpeter swans, and Sandhill cranes, along with the last precious remnant of the whooping crane flock. Tens of thousands of them in long lines and ragged formations all dipping down and dropping out of the sky to gather in the fields around us. We heard a single loud honk of warning overhead, and the soft huff of wings as more and more of them came gliding in from behind us, flying just over our heads to land in the slough.
Way off in the distance there were brightly glowing lines of fire, crawling slowly across the fields, as the Hutterites burned off their stubble. The sharp smell of the smoke was like frankincense as it mixed with the scent of the Sweetgrass rising up from the damp earth.
There was no wind. It was quiet, save for the distant exultant cries of the birds in the darkened fields, and the ticking of metal as the engine cooled down.
To my left there was a bright flare of light as Stan lit a smoke. He pulled in a lungful and then breathed it out and coughed.
"Beautiful here."
"Lovely. Yeah."
"I wonder where they winter?"
"The birds? Dunno. There's a lot of them. They'll need some room."
"No kidding."
We stood for another minute or two, listening and breathing in the sweet spicy smell of the nighttime prairie.
Stan said, "Well, better get moving, we..."
He stopped, with a sudden intake of breath.
"Sorry?"
"Oh my God." He breathed out. "Look."
He was looking up.
The whole sky above us was lit up with the ghostly pale green curtains of the Northern Lights. They seemed brightest over our heads. They shifted and danced and changed shape as we watched. We'd both seen them before, but never like this. It was breath-taking, overwhelming, and we stood there in silence and wonder for maybe a half hour, our necks creaking as we watched.

I shivered and went back to the van to get the scotch bottle and
something warmer to wear.

I took a swig, and then handed the bottle to Stan as I shrugged into my
leather jacket.

He had a drink, and we stood there maybe another 15 minutes,
watching the miracle above us, while he lit and smoked another one
and I had a couple more sips.

All this time neither of us had said a word.

Presently, he dropped the cigarette butt on the gravel and ground it out
with his heel. He made a good job of it. He didn't want to take a chance
of starting a late season wildfire.

Time to go. We still had miles ahead of us.

We got back into the van. Stan fired it up, turned off the blinkers, hit the
turn signal, and pulled back onto the highway. The spell of the lights
was still on us, and neither of us spoke, not wanting to break it.

We continued on for maybe half an hour. Every once in a while he
would turn off the headlights, lean forward and crane his neck to try to
get another look, much the same way he always would if he saw a Red-
tailed hawk flying overhead or sitting on a fence post.

I was looking out the passenger side of the van. As we came over
another hill, I could see the lights of the Battlefords in the distance,
looking as if someone had kicked over a campfire and the embers had
scattered across the darkened hills.

Another 6 hours before we could stop.

Stan picked the pack of Rothmans off the dashboard, pulled back the
flap, shook one out and put it in his mouth. He dug the lighter out of
his denim jacket, lit the smoke, threw the pack back on the dash, and re-
pocketed the lighter. He leaned forward and pushed open the no draft
window.

He blew the smoke out into the night, settled back in his seat, and
finally spoke.

"Well, that's that."

"Sorry?"

"I said, that's that."

"That's what?"

"I've been thinking about it, and I've come to a decision."

"What are you talking about?"

"We have a couple of days off in Edmonton next week."

"Yeah? So?"

"There's a used parts place off Highway 2, south of town. I'm gonna
poke around a bit and see what I can find."

"I still don't know what you mean."

He put the cigarette back in his mouth, and the end of it glowed brightly and lit up his face as he took a deep drag. He pulled it out of his mouth and once again exhaled.

"I've made up my mind. Next week the van turns into a convertible."

Top: Mum circa 1946.

Right: Dad circa 1946.

Below: Christmas 1957 or so.
My Mickey Mouse guitar, and
Stan is proudly showing off his
new watch.

Top: Looking east to Canso from the Tickle.

Left: Christmas portrait 1958.

Below: Christmas dinner 1958.

Top: In our grand parents' front yard. Water Street.

Left: Stan circa 1956.

Below: Fishing trip with Dad circa 1959 or so.

Left: On his way to choir practice.

Above: Grade 13.

Below: Fishing off the wharf on Water Street, Canso.

Above: Trent University days.

Right: ...and your Momma dresses you funny. Around the time Stan moved to London.

Below: With Nigel Russell.

Top: Rehearsing at home.

Left: Early morning expedition for mushrooms.

Below: "It's Your Bag Day." Hamilton early 70's. Packing them in.

Top: St. John's airport. "It's okay, it'll all fit into the overhead."
Photo by David Woodhead.

Left: 1976 Band promo picture.
Photo by Carol Noel.

Below: Stan on Signal Hill,
St. John's NFLD.

Top: Stan loading the Burro.
Love the pants.

Left: Having just knocked out
Rick Scott from Pied Pumpkin,
Stan comes after the audience.
Photo by Richard Chapman.

Top: With David Alan Eadie at
Godfrey Daniels in Bethlehem.
Photo by Cindy Dinsmore.

Left: Mariposa circa 1977.
Photo by Richard Chapman.

Below: Mariposa circa 1977.
David didn't get the memo about
wearing pants.

Top: The Rocky Mountain
Folk Club, Calgary.

Left: Mariposa circa 1977.
Photo by Richard Chapman.

Below: Vancouver Folk Festival
with Silly Wizard. Just after the
"cut your cock off" incident.
Photo by Allison Green.

Top Left: Between sets on board the Gazella.

Top Right: On deck. The Gazella. Philadelphia.

Below: Vancouver. Photo by Allison Green

Top: Ottawa Folk Festival. I'm trying to remember the song.

Below: Edmonton Folk Festival. Photographer unknown.

Right: My sweetheart.

Below: Out of gas.

Top: Morden Manitoba, 1982.

Below: Sound check The Rebecca Cohn. Spring 1983

Top: Sound check. Rebecca Cohn
Auditorium. Halifax, 1983.

Left: Backstage at the Rebecca Cohn
with Jim Morison. Spring 1983.

Below: The romance of the road.
The view from Klank.

ABOUT THE AUTHOR

Garnet Rogers was born in Hamilton, Ontario in 1955.

Upon finishing High School, he began playing music full time with his older brother Stan. For nearly 10 years, they travelled across the North American continent, logging over a million miles together, and during that time recorded seven albums which changed the face of Canadian folk music, and became a template for the music of a hundred other acts around the world who followed in their wake.

After Stan's death in 1983, Garnet began a successful solo career, logging over two million miles across the continent, and playing as many as 200 shows a year. Having no wish to be part of "the music business," he founded, with the help of his parents, his own label, Snow Goose Songs, and has recorded sixteen albums, both solo, and with other noted artists such as Archie Fisher and Greg Brown and Karen Savoca.

He lives with Gail, his cherished wife of 35 years, on a farm outside of Brantford Ontario, where Gail breeds and raises thoroughbred horses for sport, and Garnet is sometimes trusted with operating the wheel barrow without supervision.

www.garnetrogers.com